BIODIVERSITY AND NATURE CONSERVATION LAW AND POLICY IN THE MIDDLE EAST AND NORTH AFRICA REGION

This book offers a comprehensive and authoritative account of the guiding principles and rules relating to biodiversity, nature conservation, and the protection of cultural heritage in the MENA region. The book introduces readers to the applicable legislation, institutions, and rules underpinning the design, approval, financing, and implementation of biodiversity and nature-based solutions across the MENA region. It also explores larger questions on legal and institutional frameworks that can help address broader issues of fragmentation, gender inequality, inadequate stakeholder engagement, lack of transparency, limited access to environmental information, and lack of comprehensive domestic legislation, all of which stifle the nexus and integrated implementation of biodiversity and nature conservation treaties and the equitable sharing of the benefits derived from biodiversity and nature in the region. Written in a user-friendly style, the book closes with recommendations and reflections on legal and regulatory innovations. This title is also available as open access on Cambridge Core.

Damilola S. Olawuyi is a Professor and UNESCO Chair on Environmental Law and Sustainable Development at Hamad Bin Khalifa University College of Law, Doha, Qatar. He is also the Director of the Institute for Oil, Gas, Energy, Environment and Sustainable Development at Afe Babalola University, Nigeria. Professor Olawuyi is an independent expert on the United Nations Working Group on Business and Human Rights and Chair of the Association of Environmental Law Lecturers in Middle East and North African Universities.

Riyad Fakhri is Professor of Law and Director of the Research Laboratory in Business Law at Hassan 1st University, Settat, Morocco. He is Vice-Chair of the Association of Environmental Law Lecturers in Middle East and North African Universities.

Biodiversity and Nature Conservation Law and Policy in the Middle East and North Africa Region

Edited by

DAMILOLA S. OLAWUYI
Hamad Bin Khalifa University, Doha, Qatar

RIYAD FAKHRI
Hassan 1st University in Settat, Morocco

CAMBRIDGE
UNIVERSITY PRESS

CAMBRIDGE
UNIVERSITY PRESS

Shaftesbury Road, Cambridge CB2 8EA, United Kingdom

One Liberty Plaza, 20th Floor, New York, NY 10006, USA

477 Williamstown Road, Port Melbourne, VIC 3207, Australia

314–321, 3rd Floor, Plot 3, Splendor Forum, Jasola District Centre, New Delhi – 110025, India

103 Penang Road, #05–06/07, Visioncrest Commercial, Singapore 238467

Cambridge University Press is part of Cambridge University Press & Assessment, a department of the University of Cambridge.

We share the University's mission to contribute to society through the pursuit of education, learning and research at the highest international levels of excellence.

www.cambridge.org
Information on this title: www.cambridge.org/9781009519670

DOI: 10.1017/9781009519663

First published 2025

A catalogue record for this publication is available from the British Library

Library of Congress Cataloging-in-Publication Data
NAMES: Olawuyi, Damilola S. (Damilola Sunday), 1983– editor. | Fakhri, Riyad, editor.
TITLE: Biodiversity and nature conservation law and policy in the Middle East and North Africa region / edited by Damilola S. Olawuyi, SAN, FCIArb, Hamad Bin Khalifa University, Doha, Qatar; Riyad Fakhri, Hassan 1st University in Settat, Morocco.
DESCRIPTION: Cambridge, United Kingdom ; New York, NY : Cambridge University Press, 2025. | Includes bibliographical references and index.
IDENTIFIERS: LCCN 2024046056 | ISBN 9781009519670 (hardback) | ISBN 9781009519663 (ebook)
SUBJECTS: LCSH: Biodiversity conservation – Law and legislation – Middle East. | Biodiversity conservation – Law and legislation – Africa, North. | Nature conservation – Law and legislation – Middle East. | Nature conservation – Law and legislation – Africa, North. | Environmental law – Middle East. | Environmental law – Africa, North.
CLASSIFICATION: LCC KMC706 .B56 2025 | DDC 346.5604/595–dc23/eng/20241008
LC record available at https://lccn.loc.gov/2024046056

ISBN 978-1-009-51967-0 Hardback

Contents

Figures

Tables

Contributors

Mohsen Abdollahi, Associate Professor of International and Environmental Law, Head of Human Rights and Environmental Law department, Shahid Beheshti University, Tehran, Iran.

Adenike Adebukola Akinsemolu, Vanguard Fellow, University of Birmingham, United Kingdom and Senior Fellow, Institute for Oil, Gas, Energy, Environment and Sustainable Development, Afe Babalola University, Ado Ekiti, Nigeria.

Emem Anwana, Associate Professor and researcher in Business Law, Department of Applied Law, Durban University of Technology, South Africa.

Elena I. Athwal, LL.M. (Harvard), Research Fellow, UNESCO Chair on Environmental Law and Sustainable Development, and SJD candidate at the Hamad Bin Khalifa University College of Law, Doha, Qatar.

Funmilola Ayotunde, Assistant Professor, University of Victoria, Canada.

Ghita Chehbouni, Ph.D. candidate at the University of Law and Economics of Marrakesh, Morocco.

Eghosa O. Ekhator, Associate Professor of Law, University of Derby, United Kingdom.

Riyad Fakhri, Professor of Law and Director of the Research Laboratory in Business Law at Hassan 1st University, Settat, Morocco.

Qaraman M. Hasan, Research Scholar, University of Houston Law Centre, United States of America.

Youness Lazrak Hassouni, Professor and Researcher in Business Law, Institute of Sport Sciences, Hassan 1st University, Settat, Morocco.

Robert Home, Emeritus Professor of Land Management, Anglia Ruskin University, United Kingdom.

Tasniem Ahmed Elyass Hussain, MBA candidate at the George Mason University, Incheon, South Korea. She holds a Juris Doctor degree from the Hamad Bin Khalifa University College of Law, Doha, Qatar.

Samira Idllalène, Cadi Ayyad University, Polydisciplinary Faculty, Law Department (Safi, Morocco), International Development Cooperation Research Laboratory, Faculty of Legal, Economic and Social Sciences, Marrakesh, Morocco.

Chidimma Ewelukwa-Ike, PhD student at the Faculty of Law, University of Victoria, Canada; and Lecturer at the Faculty of Law, Nnamdi, Azikiwe University, Awka, Nigeria.

Josephine Ilesanmi, BSc (Aberdeen), MSc (Aberdeen), PhD candidate, Durban University of Technology, South Africa and Research Fellow, Institute for Oil, Gas, Energy, Environment and Sustainable Development, Afe Babalola University, Ado Ekiti, Nigeria.

Irehobhude O. Iyioha, Associate Professor and inaugural holder of The UBC Professorship in Race and Access to Justice, Peter A. Allard School of Law, University of British Columbia, Canada; Associate, Department of Philosophy, Harvard University, Cambridge, USA; Full Professor, Adj., Dossetor Health Ethics Centre, Faculty of Medicine and Dentistry, University of Alberta, Canada; Visiting Professor, Executive Masters Program, Osgoode Hall Law School, York University, Canada.

Almas Lokhandwala Maniar, LL.M. (Harvard), Research Fellow, UNESCO Chair on Environmental Law and Sustainable Development, Doha, Qatar.

Rozhgar A. Mahmood, Lecturer in Law, University of Raparin, Iraq.

Hicham Masski, Research Director, National Institute for Fisheries Research, Casablanca, Morocco.

Damilola S. Olawuyi, SAN, FCIArb, Professor and UNESCO Chair on Environmental Law and Sustainable Development, Hamad Bin Khalifa University College of Law, Doha, Qatar. He is also Chancellor's Fellow and Director of the Institute for Oil, Gas, Energy, Environment and Sustainable Development, Afe Babalola University, Ado Ekiti, Nigeria.

Oluwatobi Mary Owojori, Postdoctoral Fellow at the Tshwane University of Technology, South Africa.

Aphrodite Smagadi, Legal Officer at the Law Division, United Nations Environment Programme, Nairobi, Kenya.

Devyani Tewari, Assistant Professor, OP Jindal University, Sonipat, Haryana, India.

Jackline Wanja Wanjiru, Legal Officer at the Law Division, United Nations Environment Programme, Nairobi, Kenya.

Editors

Damilola S. Olawuyi is a full professor and UNESCO Chair on Environmental Law and Sustainable Development at the Hamad Bin Khalifa University College of Law, Doha, Qatar. He is also the Chancellor's Fellow and Director of the Institute for Oil, Gas, Energy, Environment and Sustainable Development at the Afe Babalola University, Nigeria. Professor Olawuyi holds a doctorate in energy and environmental law from the University of Oxford, an LL.M. from Harvard University, and another LL.M. from the University of Calgary. He is an independent expert on the United Nations Working Group on Business and Human Rights, Vice Chair of the International Law Association, and Chair of the Association of Environmental Law Lecturers in Middle East and North African Universities (ASSELLMU). He was formerly an independent expert on the African Union's Working Group on extractive industries, environment, and human rights violations in Africa.

Professor Olawuyi has published more than 150 articles, books, and reports on energy, environment, and natural resources law, including *Environmental Law in Arab States* (2022), which received the 2023 American Society of International Law Certificate of Merit for High Technical Craftmanship and Utility to Practicing Lawyers. Professor Olawuyi is a regular media commentator on all aspects of natural resources, energy, and environmental law. Further information about his profile and publications can be found at www.damilolaolawuyi.com.

Riyad Fakhri is a full professor of law at Hassan 1st University in Settat, Morocco and Vice-Chair of ASSELLMU. He received his University Proficiency Certificate in March, 2007 and his State Doctorate in Business Law, First Class Honors, from the Law Faculty, University Ain Chems at Cairo, Egypt, 1996–2000. He served as the Vice-President (in charge of pedagogical and academic affairs) of Hassan 1st University in Settat, and from 2005 to 2012 as the Vice-Dean (in charge of pedagogical and academic affairs) of the Faculty of Law. Dr. Fakhri is a representative member of the administration of the joint committee of Hassan 1st University and has been the Founder and Director of Research Laboratory in Business Law since 2009. In addition, Dr. Fakhri has held posts as the President of the Pedagogical

Commission of the Council of Hassan 1st University of Settat since September 2012 and the Director of the Joint Research Center on the Belt and Road Initiative and Sino-Moroccan Relations since April 2018. Dr. Fakhri is the author and director of several national and international scientific publications, books, and articles in the field of business law in three languages: Arabic, French, and English. Furthermore, Dr. Fakhri is an active member of the board of several civil associations, is a supervisor of more than seventeen defended doctoral theses, and is currently supervising more than seven doctoral theses. Moreover, Dr. Fakhri is a member of the jury of defense of several doctoral theses at the national and international level (in Morocco and France), the Academic Director of the website www.droitetentreprise.com, and the Academic Director of the journal *Le droit et les affaires*.

Foreword

The triple planetary crisis – climate change, biodiversity loss, and pollution – is threatening the survival and well-being of millions of people across the world and future generations. In the Middle East and North Africa (MENA) region the crises are compounded by increasing environmental threats, such as water scarcity, rising temperatures, land degradation, the overexploitation of fauna and flora, habitat destruction, oil-related pollution, and weak resource management frameworks.

Among the environmental challenges faced by the region, biodiversity loss emerges as a critical concern. The region safeguards a diverse and valuable biological, natural, and cultural heritage, which is essential for the economic, social, and cultural well-being of its growing population. However, escalating environmental threats are exacerbating ongoing biodiversity loss both within the region and beyond. In this context, the recent international agreement adopted under the United Nations Convention on the Law of the Sea on the conservation and sustainable use of marine biological diversity of areas beyond national jurisdiction (the BBNJ Agreement) is a landmark agreement to prevent biodiversity loss. This follows the adoption of the Kunming-Montreal Global Biodiversity Framework (GBF) in December 2022 – a call for global action to protect nature through to 2030 and beyond. It is now imperative for countries to take the necessary actions to support the BBNJ Agreement's ratification and implementation and meet the GBF's twenty-three targets for 2030 and four goals for 2050.

In this era defined by unprecedented environmental challenges, it is essential to understand the legal and policy frameworks that underpin the region's conservation efforts. This book, *Biodiversity and Nature Conservation Law and Policy in the Middle East and North Africa Region*, sheds light on the latest legal landscapes that shape the future of our invaluable biological, natural, and cultural heritage. It is the culmination of a combined effort from legal academics and professionals to raise awareness, inform, and provide reflections on how MENA countries can advance strategies, policies, and legislation in a region rich in biological diversity.

This book, the second book project by the Association of Environmental Law Lecturers in Middle East and North African Universities, delves further into the dynamics of environmental law and policy in the MENA region, building on the foundation established in its previous work, *Climate Change Law and Policy in the Middle East and North Africa Region*. Recognizing the ongoing need to build capacity in the region to develop clear and comprehensive legal and institutional frameworks that coherently address existing and emerging environmental threats, this book seeks to support MENA countries by fostering an exchange of information and best practices, with a specific focus on biodiversity and nature conservation law and policy.

The United Nations Environment Programme is dedicated to continuing its support for MENA countries in enhancing their capacity to tackle environmental challenges, including from a legal and institutional perspective. This commitment is especially crucial as biodiversity concerns gain prominence on countries' agendas.

Patricia Kameri-Mbote, SC
Director, Law Division
United Nations Environment Programme

Preface and Acknowledgments

The Middle East and North Africa (MENA) region is rich in biological, natural, and cultural resources. The region's diverse natural ecosystem ranges from semi-arid savanna to mountain upland plateaus, riverine and coastal plains, sand deserts, coastal mangroves (*qurm*), seagrasses, dry river valleys (*wadis*), wetlands, swamp forests, coral reefs, and oases.[1] In addition to the vast array of flora and fauna, the MENA region is also known for its rich cultural heritage, being home to several United Nations Educational, Scientific and Cultural Organization (UNESCO)-designated world heritage sites.[2] The diversity and richness of natural and cultural resources across the MENA region has been pivotal in catalyzing significant economic, touristic, cultural, social, medicinal, and eco-entrepreneurial activity in many parts of the region.

However, several of the biodiversity resources in the region increasingly face major threats. Environmental stresses relating to the overexploitation of plant and animal species, destruction of wildlife habitats, oil-related pollution, climate change, and underdeveloped resource management frameworks, coupled with gaps in environmental awareness and education, contribute to progressive biodiversity loss across the region. These debates have assumed greater significance and urgency as the United Nations Sustainable Development Goals (SDGs) 12, 14, and 15 underscore the need for all countries to protect the environment and avoid the unsustainable use of biological resources.[3] The devastating impacts of the COVID-19 pandemic have also accentuated calls for a more balanced relationship with nature and all elements of the ecosystem in order to reduce the rising scale of pandemics and zoonotic diseases in areas where they did not exist before. As MENA countries implement COVID-19 economic recovery plans, understanding the scope and application of extant biodiversity law and policy across the region, the gaps that remain, and

1 Damilola Olawuyi, *Environmental Law in Arab States* (Oxford University Press 2022) 245–275.

2 Ibid., see also UNESCO, "Arab States" UNESCO World Heritage Centre https://whc.unesco.org/en/arabstates/ accessed January 13, 2023.

3 United Nations, *The 2030 Agenda for Sustainable Development: Transforming our World – The 2030 Agenda for Sustainable Development* [2015] A/RES/70/1 https://sdgs.un.org/partnerships accessed January 13, 2023.

innovative environmental law education approaches for addressing those gaps can help policymakers and stakeholders to plot a clearer path for systemic integration and reform.

Despite the rise in public awareness and policy formulation on biodiversity and nature conservation across the region, only a few MENA countries have developed clear and comprehensive legal and institutional frameworks that coherently address the emerging threats. Furthermore, biodiversity education is still at an alarming stage of infancy in the region. One key reason for the slow pace of the expansion of legal education on biodiversity, nature conservation, and the protection of cultural heritage in the region is the absence of an authoritative text that unpacks the nature and guiding principles of biodiversity law and policy in the region. For example, while there are several cutting-edge books on biodiversity law and policy in other world regions, the law, governance, cultural, and ethical dimensions of biodiversity and nature conservation in the MENA region have yet to receive a detailed, authoritative, and book-length exposition. This book fills a gap in this regard.

This book also introduces readers to the latest legislative developments on biodiversity, nature conservation, and the protection of cultural heritage in the MENA region. Through a mix of thematic and case study chapters, the book explores the applicable legislation and institutions as emerging innovative and bottom-up approaches to foster greater coherence in the implementation of biodiversity and nature conservation treaties across the region. The gaps that stifle the coherent implementation of biodiversity treaties, including issues of regulatory fragmentation, gender inequality, inadequate protection of land rights in biodiversity programs, insufficient stakeholder engagement, limited access to environmental information, and a lack of comprehensive domestic legislation, are unpacked across the book. The book also provides legal assessments and reflections on how MENA countries can advance existing national strategies and visions on access and benefit sharing, biodiversity financing, biodiversity entrepreneurship, biodiversity education, nature-based solutions, and restoration of natural ecosystems, among others, through clear and comprehensive legislation.

Overall, the book aims to enhance an understanding of the interrelationships between biodiversity, nature conservation, and the attainment of water, energy, and food security, as well as resilience to global disasters such as climate change and global pandemics. Second, it explores and appraises the laws, policies, and institutions that address biodiversity, nature conservation, and the protection of cultural heritage in the MENA region. Third, it aims to foster an understanding of the various legal, policy, and governance challenges that hinder a nexus and integrated implementation of biodiversity and nature conservation treaties at national and municipal levels in the MENA region. Finally, the book analyzes how decision-making and information sharing on biodiversity and nature conservation can be enhanced across diverse institutions and stakeholders, and how this can be simplified and integrated in practical terms, including through environmental education.

In examining these issues, this book takes an international and comparative approach that benefits immensely from the cutting-edge research and professional and teaching experience of the editors and contributors from across the region and beyond. Furthermore, the book is prepared in a user-friendly style to enhance its utility among its primary audience, namely students, corporations, environment departments and ministries, law firms, courts, and arbitrators, notably international and regional committees and tribunals before whom arguments over biodiversity, access and benefit sharing, and resource management often come for resolution. The book analyzes the key roles that international institutions such as the United Nations Environment Program (UNEP), International Renewable Energy Agency, Global Environment Facility, World Trade Organization; regional institutions such as the League of Arab Nations, Gulf Cooperation Council, Asian Development Bank, African Development Bank; and national institutions such as ministries and departments, play in biodiversity, nature conservation, and the protection of cultural heritage in the MENA region.

It remains for us to register our profound gratitude to many helping hands, without whom the publication of this book would not have been possible. This book is the second book project of the Association of Environmental Law Lecturers in Middle East and North African Universities (ASSELLMU), a professional network of leading environmental law academics in the MENA region, which was established in 2018. The book was conceived at the 4th ASSELLMU Conference held at the University of Jordan, February 27–28, 2023. Special thanks to the President of the University of Jordan, Dr. Nathir Obeidat, as well as Dr. Omar Khataibeh, Dr. Ghufran Hilal, and everyone at the University of Jordan for their exceptional contributions to the success of that conference. Thanks are also due to Dean Susan L. Karamanian of the College of Law, Hamad Bin Khalifa University (HBKU) for her exceptional and steadfast support for ASSELLMU's events and activities. We must especially acknowledge UNEP and SADER Legal Publishing for their timely research funding and support without which this book, as well as all other ASSELLMU initiatives and programs, would not have been possible. We are deeply grateful to Professor Patricia Mbote and Aphrodite Smagadi at UNEP for their support and contributions to the success of this book. We also appreciate the UNESCO Chair on Environmental Law and Sustainable Development at HBKU; the Research Laboratory on Business Law of Hassan 1st University, Settat, Morocco; the Jordanian Society for Climate and Sustainable Development; the Institute for Oil, Gas, Energy, Environment and Sustainable Development at Afe Babalola University, Ado Ekiti, Nigeria; and the Rule of Law Programme Middle East and North Africa, Konrad-Adenauer-Stiftung, for their technical cooperation and partnership for the conference and the eventual publication of this book.

Special thanks are due to the editorial staff of Cambridge University Press, especially Toby Ginsberg, for the smooth and professional review process which guided this book through to its timely completion. Our profound appreciation also goes to

Elena Athwal (Harvard Law School) and Tasniem Ahmed Elyass Hussain (HBKU College of Law) for providing remarkable and thoughtful research assistance. They assisted greatly in collating chapters at submission, review, and editing stages. We specially acknowledge the dedication and collegiality of all the contributing authors, whose substantial research and commitment to leading-edge scholarship in this field have been pivotal to the production of this book.

Finally, the editors are grateful to their family for their love, support, and inspiration. Thanks are also due to our exceptional students whose class contributions and ideas greatly shaped the conceptualization and development of this book.

This book has endeavored to state the position of the law as of March 2024, although authors have been able to take into account subsequent developments in a few instances.

Damilola S. Olawuyi, SAN, FCIArb, Doha, Qatar
Riyad Fakhri, Settat, Morocco

Abbreviations

AAOIFI	Accounting and Auditing Organization for Islamic Financial Institutions
ABS	Access and Benefit-Sharing
ACCOBAMS	Agreement on the Conservation of Cetaceans of the Black Sea, Mediterranean Sea and contiguous Atlantic area
AEWA	Agreement on the Conservation of African-Eurasian Migratory Waterbirds
AFED	Arab Forum for Environment and Development
ALESCO	Arab League Educational, Cultural and Scientific Organization
AR3T	Avoid, Reduce, Restore and Regenerate, Transform
ASSELLMU	Association of Environmental Law Lecturers in Middle East and North African Universities
CBD	Convention on Biological Diversity
CITES	Convention on International Trade in Endangered Species of Wild Fauna and Flora
CMS	Convention on the Conservation of Migratory Species of Wild Animals
CNR	Chah Nimeh Reservoir
COP	Conference of the Parties
DSI	digital sequence information
EIA	environmental impact assessment
ESD	Education for Sustainable Development
ESG	environmental, social, and governance
FAO	Food and Agriculture Organization
GAP	Güneydoğu Anadolu Projesi
GBF	Global Biodiversity Framework
GBO5	Fifth Global Biodiversity Outlook
GCC	Gulf Cooperation Council
HRBA	human rights-based approach
IB	Islamic banking

ICJ	International Court of Justice
IEL	International Environmental Law
IFI	Islamic financial institution
ILCs	indigenous and local communities
IMF	International Monetary Fund
IPBES	Intergovernmental Science-Policy Platform on Biodiversity and Ecosystem Service
IsDB	Islamic Development Bank
ISIS	Islamic State of Iraq and Syria
IUCN	International Union for Conservation of Nature
KBA	key biodiversity area
LAS	League of Arab States
MAT	mutually agreed terms
MCC	Millennium Challenge Corporation
MD	ministerial decision
MEA	multilateral environmental agreements
MENA	Middle East and North Africa
MPA	marine protected area
MPA-F	fishing-oriented MPA
MSP	multistakeholder participation
NBS	nature-based solutions
NBSAP	National Biodiversity Strategy and Action Plan
NB-SMEE	nature-based small and medium eco-enterprise
NDC	nationally determined contributions
NGO	nongovernmental organization
OECD	Organisation for Economic Co-operation and Development
OIC	Organization of Islamic Cooperation
OUV	Outstanding Universal Value
PDAP	Master Plan for Protected Areas
PES	Payment for Ecosystem Services
PIC	prior informed consent
PRTRs	Protocol on Pollutant Release and Transfer Registers
SDGs	Sustainable Development Goals
SIBE	Sites of Biological and Ecological Interest
SLE	substantive legal effectiveness
SMEs	small and medium-sized enterprises
SP	state party
SPAMI	Specially Protected Areas of Mediterranean Importance
SRI	sustainable and responsible investments
SWF	sovereign wealth fund
TTT	Train-the-Trainers
TWP	Tropical Water Project

UAE	United Arab Emirates
UNCCD	United Nations Convention to Combat Desertification
UNDP	United Nations Development Programme
UNDRIP	United Nations Declaration on the Rights of Indigenous Peoples
UNEA	United Nations Environment Assembly
UNECE	United Nations Economic Commission for Europe
UNEP	United Nations Environment Programme
UNESCO	United Nations Educational, Scientific and Cultural Organization
UNFCCC	United Nations Framework Convention on Climate Change
UNGA	United Nations General Assembly
WH	World Heritage
WHC	World Heritage Convention
WHO	World Health Organization

PART I

Introductory Context and Principles

1

Nature and Sources of Biodiversity and Nature Conservation Law and Policy in the MENA Region

Damilola S. Olawuyi

1.1 INTRODUCTION

This book examines the laws, policies, and institutions on biodiversity, nature conservation, and the protection of cultural heritage in the Middle East and North Africa (MENA) region.[1] It analyzes the interrelationships between biodiversity, nature conservation, and the preservation of cultural heritage, as well as lessons learned from emerging nexus and integrated approaches to the implementation of multilateral environmental treaties in these fields at regional and domestic levels.

Halting the rapid loss of biodiversity is one of the triple planetary emergencies facing our present generation, the other two being climate change and pollution.[2] Biodiversity "refers to the different forms of plants, animals, and biological forms of life that make up the ecosystem."[3] The 1992 United Nations Earth Summit defined biological diversity as "the variability among living organisms from all sources."[4] All of the elements of the ecosystem are interlinked and depend on each other to survive. For example, without bees, food crops may not grow, which may lead to food scarcity, hunger, and a total collapse of the global food industry.[5] Similarly,

[1] Twenty countries are typically included as part of the MENA region: Algeria, Bahrain, Djibouti, Egypt, Iran, Iraq, Israel, Jordan, Kuwait, Lebanon, Libya, Morocco, Oman, Palestine, Qatar, Saudi Arabia, Syria, Tunisia, United Arab Emirates, and Yemen. Some classifications also include Malta, Sudan, Turkey, and Israel as part of the MENA region. See for example, The World Bank, "Middle East and North Africa" www.worldbank.org/en/region/mena accessed January 25, 2024.

[2] J. Richardson et al., "Earth beyond Six of Nine Planetary Boundaries" (2023) 9 *Science Advances* 37; see also W. Steffen et al., "Planetary Boundaries: Guiding Human Development on a Changing Planet" (2015) 347 *Science* 736.

[3] Damilola Olawuyi, *Environmental Law in Arab States* (Oxford University Press 2022) 245–275. See also Edward O. Wilson, *The Diversity of Life* (Harvard University Press 1992) 1–15.

[4] Rio Declaration on Environment and Development (adopted June 14, 1992) UN Doc A/CONF151/26 (vol I), 31 ILM 874 (1992). See also Article 2 of the CBD, which defines biodiversity as the "variability among living organisms from all sources and within species."

[5] Damilola Olawuyi and Elena Athwal, "Halting Biodiversity Loss and Protecting Nature: The Important Role of International Environmental Law" (*Daily Trust*, May 7, 2023) https://dailytrust.com/halting-biodiversity-loss-and-protecting-nature-the-important-role-of-international-environmental-law/ accessed January 12, 2024. See also IPBES, "Assessment Report on Pollinators, Pollination

without plants, humans and other life-forms may lack access to the essential sources of nutrition, medicines, and clean air needed to sustain life on earth.[6] In addition to the intrinsic and ecosystem value of these biological resources in providing pivotal support for the subsistence and survival of current and future generations, such resources also have enormous religious, cultural, recreational, and economic value, especially for diversifying revenue sources through a prosperous ecotourism industry.[7] The need to preserve and protect the various biological and cultural resources that sustain the ecosystem has therefore remained one of the most fundamental priorities of international environmental law.[8] Goal 15 of the United Nations Sustainable Development Goals (SDGs) expressly calls on countries to ensure "the conservation, restoration and sustainable use of terrestrial and inland freshwater ecosystems and their services, in particular forests, wetland, mountains and dryland in line with obligations under international agreements" by 2020.[9] The 2030 Agenda envisages, among other things, "a world in which humanity lives in harmony with nature and wildlife, and other living species are protected."[10]

Yet environmental stresses from the destruction of wildlife habitats, overexploitation of plant and animal species, poaching, use of toxic pesticides, illicit trade in plants and animal resources, and climate change impacts, coupled with gaps in environmental awareness and education, have for many years contributed to rapid biodiversity loss across the world, including in the MENA region.[11] Recent studies indicate that society's activities have pushed biodiversity loss beyond the planetary boundaries needed to sustain life on earth.[12] One alarming study found that earth's wild mammals comprise less than 10 percent of the total biomass of humans and less

and Food Production" (2016). See also, United Nations Environment Assembly Resolution 3/4 on Environment and Health, which notes that human, animal, and plant health and the environment are interconnected.

6 W. G. Fernando, "Plants: An International Scientific Open Access Journal to Publish All Facets of Plants, Their Functions and Interactions with the Environment and Other Living Organisms" (2012) 6 *Plants* 1, 1–5.

7 For example, Saudi Arabia's Vision 2030 identifies ecotourism – such as viewing wildlife and visiting important natural and cultural sites – as a tool for economic diversification. See also Oman's Vision 2040 and the United Arab Emirates' National Ecotourism Project, which emphasizes the preservation of natural and cultural heritage as tools for tourism and other ecosystems services. Qatar has also announced its priority to develop ecotourism destinations. See "MoECC, Qatar Tourism to Develop Ecotourism Destinations" (*Qatar Peninsula*, November 19, 2023). See also Anthon Garcia, "Growth of Ecotourism in the Middle East" (September 20, 2023) https://economymiddleeast.com/news/growth-of-ecotourism-in-the-middle-east/ accessed January 12, 2024.

8 See Chapter 2.

9 United Nations General Assembly (UNGA), "Transforming Our World: The 2030 Agenda for Sustainable Development," Resolution adopted by the General Assembly on September 25, 2015, UN Doc A/ RES/70/l.

10 Ibid. See also UNEP, Biodiversity and Health Resolution adopted by the United Nations Environment Assembly on March 2, 2022, UNEP/ EA.5/Res.6.

11 Olawuyi (n 3) 245–275, see also UNEP, *Environmental Outlook of the Arab Region: Environment for Development and Human Well-being* (UNEP 2010) 287–290.

12 Richardson et al. (n 2).

than 4 percent of that of domesticated animals.[13] These studies highlight how biodiversity loss and land degradation are taking place at an unprecedented rate, and the urgent need for legal responses to enhance biodiversity and nature conservation. The devastating impacts of the COVID-19 pandemic have also accentuated calls for a more balanced relationship with nature and all elements of the ecosystem in order to reduce the rising scale of pandemics and zoonotic diseases – that is, infectious diseases that are transferred from animals to humans – in areas where they did not exist before.[14] Furthermore, the rapid loss of biodiversity has also been highlighted as a threat to the realization of several human rights, including the right to life, right to food, and right to health.[15]

Halting the threat of biodiversity loss is a particularly urgent imperative for the MENA region, arguably more so than any other region in the world. The MENA region is often categorized as a biodiversity hotspot, meaning that it contains "at least 1,500 species of vascular plants found nowhere else on Earth, and has lost at least 70 percent of its primary native vegetation."[16] The region is home to more than 5,000 recorded species of plants, more than 10,000 species of animals, and 5 of the world's 34 internationally recognized biodiversity hotspots.[17] Key habitats such as the marshes and wetlands of the Jordan Valley provide critical stopover points for around 500 million migratory birds each year. Furthermore, countries in the Gulf Cooperation Council (GCC) and the Mashreq host diverse landscapes such as mountains, inland and coastal plains, sand deserts, and wetlands that are home to over 5,500 endemic plant species.[18] Similarly, the MENA region is home to rare animal species, such as the Queen of Sheba's gazelle, Arabian oryx, Arabian tahr, Arabian wolf, Asiatic jackal, Arabian camel (dromedary), Arabian leopard, striped hyena, and birds such as the Arabian bustard and honey buzzard.[19]

However, due to the impacts of climate change and rapid urbanization, the rise in construction activities, poaching, unsustainable agricultural practices, conflicts,

[13] L. Greenspoon et al., "The Global Biomass of Wild Mammals" (2023) 7 *Proceedings of the National Academy of Sciences of the United States of America*. See also R. J. Scholes and R. Biggs, "A Biodiversity Intactness Index" (2005) 434 *Nature* 45–49.

[14] IPBES, *Workshop Report on Biodiversity and Pandemics of the Intergovernmental Platform on Biodiversity and Ecosystem Services* (IPBES Secretariat 2020) 2–5.

[15] See UNEP, "Environmental Rule of Law: Tracking Progress and Charting Future Directions" (UNEP 2023) 104–105. See also Council of the European Union, "Council Conclusions on EU Climate Diplomacy: Accelerating the Implementation of the Glasgow Outcomes" (February 21, 2022).

[16] Critical Ecosystems Partnership Fund, "Biodiversity Hotspots Defined" www.cepf.net/our-work/biodiversity-hotspots/hotspots-defined accessed January 12, 2024.

[17] Ibid.

[18] Iyad Abumoghli and Adele Goncalves, "Environmental Challenges in the MENA Region" (UNEP) https://wedocs.unep.org/bitstream/handle/20.500.11822/31645/EC_MENA.pdf?sequence=1&isAllowed=y accessed January 25, 2024.

[19] For a list of rare flora species in the MENA region, see Appendix I of the Convention on the Conservation of Wildlife and their Natural Habitats in Countries of the Gulf Cooperation Council (adopted December 30, 2001, entered into force April 2003).

and political instability, and a lack of comprehensive conservation laws and practices, among other factors, the MENA region has lost more than 95 percent of its natural habitats, resulting in accelerated loss of nature and biodiversity across the region.[20] In Morocco, for example, studies show that more than 1,700 plant species are endangered or threatened with extinction, while more than 600 animal species face the risk of extinction.[21] Similarly, critical habitats such as mangroves, seagrass beds, and coral reefs in the Arabian Gulf are endangered, while several endemic species in the region are assessed as threatened with extinction in the International Union for the Conservation of Nature (IUCN) Red List.[22] Estimates indicate that 17 percent of the endemic mammals in the region could become extinct before 2050 due to climate change and other factors.[23] Similarly, the increasing destruction of cultural sites and theft of cultural artifacts by militant and terrorist groups raise key concerns across the region.[24] Given the high potential for scarcities and exacerbated resource-driven conflict in biodiversity hotspots, MENA countries face an urgent task to halt biodiversity loss.[25]

Despite the grim reality of the rapid loss of biological and cultural resources across the MENA region, the clear and comprehensive legal frameworks needed to halt and address the loss have not been forthcoming in many parts of the region. The absence of quality, accessible, and reliable statistics and indicators on the status, trends, and programs carried out to advance the conservation of biological and cultural heritage remains a key hindrance to monitoring progress.[26] For example, only a few MENA countries actively update the status of biodiversity programs through the Convention on Biological Diversity (CBD) clearing-house mechanisms. Similarly, biodiversity education is still at an alarming stage of infancy across

[20] Rajaa El Kassab, "Biodiversity in the Arab Region" www.greenpeace.org/static/planet4-mena-stateless/2022/08/9dd732cb-biodiversity-in-the-arab-region-rajaakassab.pdf. See also Abumoghli and Goncalves (n 18).

[21] El Kassab (n 20) 3–4.

[22] Earth's Endangered Creatures, "Endangered Mammals of the Middle East" www.earthsendangered.com/continent.asp?gr=&view=&ID=8&nogroupall= accessed January 25, 2024. See also Sana Hussain, "Qatar's Iconic Arabian Oryx at Risk from Plastic Pollution" (*Doha News*, March 4, 2021) www.dohanews.co/qatars-iconic-arabian-oryx-at-risk-from-plastic-pollution/ accessed January 25, 2024.

[23] In Yemen, for example, seven of the mammal species in the country face the risk of extinction, including the Queen of Sheba's gazelle, Arabian oryx, Arabian tiger, and the Asiatic cheetah. El Kassab (n 20) 3–4. See also Alaaeldin Soultan, Martin Wikelski, and Kamran Safi, "Risk of Biodiversity Collapse under Climate Change in the Afro-Arabian Region" (2019) 9 *Scientific Reports* 955.

[24] Andreas Dittmann and Hussein Almohamad, "Devastation of Cultural Heritage and Memory in Syria and Iraq: Component of a Multi-level Provocation Strategy?" (2015) 5 *International Journal of Humanities and Social Science* 11, 30; A. Al-Azm, "The Threat to Cultural Heritage in Times of Conflict and Its Dynamic Relationship with Gulf Society" in M. M. Rahman and A. Al-Azm (eds), *Social Change in the Gulf Region* (Springer 2023) 271–286.

[25] UNEP (n 15) 153–154.

[26] Ibrahaim Abdel Gelil, "The Sustainable Development Initiative in the Arab Region: Third Progress Report" (Council of Arab Ministers Responsible for the Environment 2011) noting the "general lack of coherent environmental information and information systems in the region."

the region. Currently, only very few universities in the MENA region have dedicated law courses that advance knowledge and capacity on biodiversity law and policy. According to the findings of recent regional conferences on environmental law, one key reason for this slow pace of environmental legal education is the absence of an authoritative text that unpacks the nature and guiding principles of biodiversity and nature conservation law and policy in the region.[27] While there are many journal articles and book chapters that survey and analyze various aspects of biodiversity law and policy in the MENA region, a clear, comprehensive, and book-length exposition of the normative underpinnings, value, and best practices on biodiversity and nature law and governance in the region has yet to emerge. This book fills this gap by providing an analytical examination of best practices in the design, application, implementation, and enforcement of biodiversity and nature conservation law and policy in the MENA region.

The book introduces readers to the latest legislative developments on biodiversity, nature conservation, and the protection of cultural heritage in the MENA region, including the applicable legislation and institutions, as well as lessons learned from emerging innovative and bottom-up approaches to their implementation across the world. It also explores larger questions on legal and institutional frameworks that can help address broader issues of fragmentation, gender-based exclusions and inequality, inadequate stakeholder engagement, lack of transparency, limited access to environmental information, and lack of comprehensive domestic legislation, and how they stifle the nexus and integrated implementation of biodiversity and nature conservation treaties and the equitable sharing of the benefits derived from biodiversity and nature in the region.

This chapter provides a conceptual overview of the nature and scope of biodiversity and nature conservation law and policy in the MENA region. Section 1.2 provides an overview of the different sources of law that underpin biodiversity and nature conservation law and policy in the region. It discusses the character, status, and force of the different sources, including the interrelationships between them. Section 1.3 outlines the overall aim and structure of the book.

1.2 SOURCES OF BIODIVERSITY AND NATURE CONSERVATION LAW AND POLICY IN THE MENA REGION

Conservation is "the protection and preservation of plants, animals, and other biological and cultural resources for the benefit of current and future generations."[28] Therefore, biodiversity and nature conservation law is that branch of environmental

[27] Salam Al-Zahran, "Conference on Law on Biodiversity, Nature Conservation, and Cultural Heritage Protection in the Middle East and North African Region" (March 2, 2023) www.kas.de/en/web/rspno/veranstaltungsberichte/detail/-/content/conference-on-law-on-biodiversity-nature-conservation-and-cultural-heritage-protection-in-the-middle accessed January 12, 2024.

[28] Olawuyi (n 3) 248–249.

law that provides the general legal framework for the protection of plants, animals, and other biological and cultural resources that make up the ecosystem from overexploitation and abuse.[29] While biological diversity focuses mainly on natural heritage and species such as plants, animals, and humans in the ecosystem, cultural diversity refers to the wide range of "generational values, shared beliefs, customs, practices, objects, and artistic expressions" that are relevant to the overall smooth functioning of our world.[30] Due to their vital roles, and their interdependencies, addressing the common and multiscale threats to the conservation of biological diversity, cultural diversity, and conservation of all aspects of the ecosystem, through a nexus and integrated approach, has become an important aspect of international law for the last several decades.[31] Since the Stockholm Conference in 1972, we have seen the adoption of a wide range of multilateral treaties relating to biodiversity, nature conservation, and the preservation of cultural heritage.[32] Biodiversity and nature conservation law is therefore an amalgam of a wide range of interrelated legal regimes relating to environmental protection, trade, investment, land use, human rights, biosafety, and energy, among others.[33]

Since the adoption of the CBD in 1992, the discipline of biodiversity and nature conservation law and policy has developed incrementally worldwide.[34] Initially, it emerged as a tool to curb the overexploitation and degradation of biodiversity. Laws focused on conserving specific threatened species, though a general approach was still rare. The continued loss of key species created urgency for targeted protection. In the second phase, there was acknowledgment that conserving biodiversity and species requires preserving natural habitats and cultural heritage.[35] Laws shifted to integrate species and habitat conservation efforts. Currently in the third phase, the nexus and integrated management of biological and cultural resources to advance sustainable development has become a major concept in law, embedded

[29] See Elisa Morgera and Jona Razzaque (eds), *Biodiversity and Nature Protection Law* (Edward Elgar 2017) 1–10; Daniel M. Bodansky, "International Law and the Protection of Biological Diversity" (1995) 28 *Vanderbilt Journal of Transnational Law* 623; William J. Snape, *Biodiversity, and the Law* (Island Press 1996) 1–10.

[30] See The UNESCO Universal Declaration of Cultural Diversity (adopted November 2001), which highlights the importance of culture and cultural diversity to present and future generations.

[31] Olawuyi (n 3). See also, M. G. Bastos Lima and U. Palme, "The Bioeconomy–Biodiversity Nexus: Enhancing or Undermining Nature's Contributions to People?" (2022) 2 *Conservation*, 7–25.

[32] Olawuyi (n 3).

[33] See Guillaume Futhazar, Sandrine Maljean-Dubois, and Jona Razzaque, "Introduction: Setting the Scene" in Guillaume Futhazar et al. (eds), *Biodiversity Litigation* (Oxford University Press 2020) 8–10. See also Morgera and Razzaque (n 29).

[34] Désirée McGraw, "The Story of the Biodiversity Convention: From Negotiation to Implementation" in Philippe Leprestre (ed), *Governing Global Biodiversity: The Evolution and Implementation of the Convention on Biological Diversity* (Ashgate 2004) 7–10.

[35] See Aphrodite Smagadi, "Analysis of the Objectives of the Convention on Biological Diversity: Their Interrelation and Implementation Guidance for Access and Benefit Sharing" (2006) 31 *Columbia Journal of Environmental Law* 243, 253.

in many regional and global instruments.[36] The need for such harmonized efforts has assumed greater significance and urgency with the adoption of the UN SDGs. SDGs 12, 14, and 15 emphasize the need to protect various aspects of biological diversity. SDG 11.4 specifically highlights the need to protect the world's cultural and natural heritage; SDG 17 also underscores the need for enhanced partnerships – globally, regionally, nationally, and locally – as a required step for attaining all of the SDGs, including those on biodiversity and nature conservation. SDG 17.14 specifically encourages all stakeholders to enhance cooperation and policy coherence for sustainable development.[37] The important roles of nature and nature-based solutions as tools for economic diversification (bioeconomy), climate action, and integrated health management have also become important. For example, recent studies, including reports of the Intergovernmental Science-Policy Platform on Biodiversity and Ecosystem Service (IPBES),[38] have underlined the urgent need for a nexus approach to ecosystems governance as a framework for the coherent, holistic, and integrated implementation of biodiversity and nature conservation treaties to address fragmentations and to advance all of the associated SDGs.[39]

Biodiversity law has therefore progressed from urgent species-specific protections to a more holistic view linking conservation to habitats, cultural heritage, bioeconomy, and broader sustainable development priorities.[40] Generally, there are three key sources of biodiversity and nature conservation law and policy in the MENA region: international law, domestic legislation, and judicial decisions and scholarly publications.

1.2.1 *International Law on Biodiversity and Nature Conservation*

International law governs relations between sovereign nations. International biodiversity and nature conservation law is therefore a field of international law that regulates the behavior of states and international organizations with respect to the protection and conservation of plants, animals, and other biological and cultural resources. As recognized in Article 38 of the Statute of the International Court of Justice, the major sources of international law, and by extension international

36 J. Maradza et al., "Perspectives on the Applicability of Nexus Thinking to Private Protected Areas: A Case Study of Mokolodi Nature Reserve, Botswana" in J. Saarinen, B. Lubbe, and N. N. Moswete (eds), *Southern African Perspectives on Sustainable Tourism Management* (Springer 2022). See also Damilola Olawuyi, "Sustainable Development and the Water–Energy–Food Nexus: Legal Challenges and Emerging Solutions" (2020) 103 *Journal of Environmental Science and Policy* 1.

37 See also SDG 15 on biological diversity and SDGs 4.7, 8.3, and 8.9. UNGA (n 9).

38 United Nations IPBES, "Scoping Report for a Thematic Assessment of the Interlinkages among Biodiversity, Water, Food and Health" (March 21, 2021) IPBES/8/3 https://ipbes.net/sites/default/files/2021-05/IPBES_8_3_nexus%20assessment_en.pdf accessed January 25, 2024.

39 Maradza et al. (n 36).

40 See Secretariat of the Convention on Biological Diversity, "Global Biodiversity Outlook 3" (CBD 2010) www.cbd.int/gbo3/?pub=6667&section=6711 accessed December 15, 2023; also Bastos Lima (n 31).

biodiversity and nature conservation law, are international conventions and treaties, international customs, general principles of law, and the judicial decisions and teachings of highly qualified publicists.[41]

As early as the 1900s, multilateral agreements that recognized how unregulated trade in plant and animal species may impact the environment and its resources began to emerge: for example, the Convention for the Preservation of Animals, Birds, and Fish in Africa, signed in London on May 19, 1900 (1900 London Convention), the first formal agreement on trade-related environmental issues.[42] Although the 1900 London Convention never entered into force, due to lack of ratification, it started an important conversation on how the unregulated trade in African elephants and game species may lead to their extinction.[43] As discussed in Chapter 2, this impetus led to the adoption of a number of legally binding instruments on biodiversity and nature conservation.[44] The most important of these instruments is the CBD which in Article 1 sets out the three objectives as: the conservation of biological diversity, sustainable use, and access and benefit-sharing.[45] Each of these objectives are discussed across the book.[46]

As indicated in Table 1.1, several MENA countries have adopted and ratified the CBD and other key multilateral treaties on biodiversity and nature conservation. The rise in international awareness and instruments on this subject has also resulted in the development of regional treaties aimed at enhancing the conservation of the region's rich natural and cultural heritage.

1.2.2 *Regional Instruments*

As indicated in Table 1.1, several treaties have been adopted at the regional and subregional levels which aim to protect and preserve flora, fauna, and cultural heritage from all sources of pollution and degradation.

41 United Nations, Statute of the International Court of Justice, April 18, 1946, 33 UNTS 993. See Olawuyi (n 3) 269.

42 International Union for Conservation of Nature and Natural Resources (IUCN), *An Introduction to the African Convention on the Conservation of Nature and Natural Resources* (IUCN 2004) 3–4.

43 Ibid.

44 Biodiversity and nature conservation treaties include: the Convention on Biological Diversity (adopted June 5, 1992) 1760 UNTS 79, 31 ILM 818; Convention on International Trade in Endangered Species of Wild Fauna and Flora (CITES) (adopted March 3, 1973, entered into force July 1, 1975) 993 UNTS 243; Convention on the Conservation of Migratory Species of Wild Animals (June 23, 1979) 1651 UNTS 331; Convention on Wetlands of International Importance especially as Waterfowl Habitat (adopted February 2, 1971, entered into force December 21, 1975) 996 UNTS 245 (Ramsar Convention); the United Nations Convention to Combat Desertification (adopted June 17, 1994, entered into force December 26, 1996); International Treaty on Plant Genetic Resources for Food and Agriculture (entered into force June 29, 2004) 2400 UNTS 303; Convention Concerning the Protection of the World Cultural and Natural Heritage (adopted November 23, 1972, entered into force December 17, 1975) 1037 UNTS 151 (World Heritage Convention).

45 Arts. 6–8, 10–13 of the CBD, ibid. See also Futhazar et al. (n 33) 17–18.

46 See Chapters 2, 3, and 9.

TABLE 1.1 *International conservation agreements ratified and acceded to by MENA states*

Treaty	MENA states (ratification/accession)
International	
Convention on Biological Diversity	Algeria, Bahrain, Djibouti, Egypt, Iraq, Jordan, Kuwait, Lebanon, Libya, Mauritania, Morocco, Oman, Qatar, Palestine, Saudi Arabia, Somalia, Sudan, Syria, Tunisia, United Arab Emirates, Yemen
Convention on Wetlands	Algeria, Bahrain, Djibouti, Egypt, Iraq, Jordan, Kuwait, Lebanon, Libya, Mauritania, Morocco, Oman, Sudan, Syria, Tunisia, United Arab Emirates, Yemen
Convention on the Conservation of Migratory Species of Wild Animals	Algeria, Djibouti, Egypt, Iraq, Jordan, Lebanon, Libya, Mauritania, Morocco, Saudi Arabia, Somalia, Syria, Tunisia, United Arab Emirates, Yemen
Convention on International Trade in Endangered Species of Wild Fauna and Flora	Algeria, Bahrain, Djibouti, Egypt, Iraq, Jordan, Kuwait, Lebanon, Libya, Mauritania, Morocco, Oman, Qatar, Saudi Arabia, Somalia, Sudan, Syria, Tunisia, United Arab Emirates, Yemen
The UNESCO Convention for the Protection of the World Cultural and Natural Heritage	Algeria, Bahrain, Djibouti, Egypt, Iraq, Jordan, Kuwait, Lebanon, Libya, Mauritania, Morocco, Oman, Qatar, Palestine, Saudi Arabia, Somalia, Sudan, Syria, Tunisia, United Arab Emirates, Yemen
Regional and subregional	
Kuwait Regional Convention on Protection of Marine Environment and Protocols	Bahrain, Iran, Iraq, Qatar, Kuwait, Oman, United Arab Emirates, Saudi Arabia
Regional Convention for the Conservation of the Red Sea and Gulf of Aden Environment	Djibouti, Egypt, Jordan, Saudi Arabia, Somalia, Sudan, Yemen
African Convention on the Conservation of Nature and Natural Resources of 1968 (and revised in 2017)	Algeria, Djibouti, Egypt, Sudan, Tunisia. Signatories only: Libya, Mauritania, Somalia
Convention on the Conservation of Wildlife and their Natural Habitats in GCC Countries	Kuwait, Saudi Arabia, Bahrain, Qatar, United Arab Emirates, Oman

Source: Compiled by author. Prepared using information from the United Nations Treaty Collection website, https://treaties.un.org, accessed January 12, 2024.

The regional instruments are discussed extensively in Chapter 2 and they include the Kuwait Regional Convention on Protection of Marine Environment and Protocols (Kuwait Convention) and its protocols; the Regional Convention for the Conservation of the Red Sea and Gulf of Aden Environment (Jeddah Convention); the Convention on the Conservation of Wildlife and their Natural Habitats in

GCC Countries (GCC Wildlife Convention); and the African Convention on the Conservation of Nature and Natural Resources of 1968 (and revised in 2017) (African Convention).

In addition to these binding international and regional biodiversity and nature conservation law instruments, a number of nonbinding declarations and strategy plans have emerged at the regional level that provide foundations for the development and application of biodiversity and nature conservation law and policy in the MENA region. These include:

1. The 1991 Arab Declaration on Environment and Development and Future Prospects: which contains a commitment by all Arab countries in the MENA region to work together to preserve the biological diversity of the region and guarantee the conservation of land, marine, and freshwater resources.[47] It also encourages states to develop policies, legislation, and education initiatives aimed at the preservation and conservation of natural heritage from harmful environmental effects and calls on countries to introduce environmental subjects into syllabi and curricula at all levels of education.[48]
2. The 2001 Arab Declaration to the World Summit on Sustainable Development: which enshrines the commitment of Arab countries in the MENA region to work together to preserve the ecosystems and biodiversity of the region. It also recognizes the need for states to maintain the unique cultural and religious heritage of the region and to utilize it to achieve sustainable development.[49]
3. The Strategic Plans of the Arab League Educational, Cultural and Scientific Organization (ALESCO). ALECSO is a specialized institution of the League of Arab States,[50] established to promote, preserve, protect, and conserve tangible and intangible Arab cultural heritage, and to foster coordination among Arab states in the fields of education, science, and cultural heritage.[51] ALESCO provides training to heritage conservation specialists across the region and promotes the restitution of stolen or missing cultural heritage items.[52]

Although these soft law instruments are aspirational and not legally binding, they have prompted the development of a wide range of domestic laws and policies designed to enhance the conservation of nature and cultural heritage in MENA countries.

47 Arab Declaration on Environment and Development and Future Prospects (September, 10 1991) UN Doc. E/ESCWA/ENVHS/1992/1, para 2.

48 Arab Declaration on Environment and Development and Future Prospects (n 115), para IX.

49 Arab Declaration to the World Summit on Sustainable Development (2002), preamble and para 1(6) www.hlrn.org/img/documents/Arab_Declaration_Sustainable_Dev.pdf accessed January 25, 2024.

50 ALESCO was established pursuant to Article 3 of the Arab Cultural Unity Charter of 1964.

51 See ALESCO, "About Us" www.alecso.org/nsite/en/component/content/article/814-who-are-we-v2?catid=63&Itemid=220 accessed January 12, 2024.

52 Olawuyi (n 3) 269.

1.2.3 *Domestic Legislation*

The aim of conservation laws across the MENA region is to ensure the conservation of flora, fauna, and natural habitats, and to halt the illicit trade and trafficking in wildlife and other biological and cultural specimens. Several of the key international and regional conventions on conservation of nature and cultural heritage adopted by MENA countries have been reflected in domestic legislation on environment and conservation.

Although the nature and scope of domestic legislation relating to biodiversity and nature conservation law varies from one MENA country to another, biodiversity and nature conservation law and policies at domestic levels can be divided into three main categories.

1.2.3.1 The Constitution

The primary source of law across the MENA region is the constitution as it sets the basic principles and norms that define other legislation enacted by the legislature or the Shura Council. The constitution is the supreme law, and it has binding force on all authorities and persons in a country.[53] The constitutions of several MENA countries expressly codify provisions on environmental protection and sustainable development.[54] For example, Article 33 of the Permanent Constitution for the State of Qatar declares: "The State shall conserve the environment and its natural balance for the comprehensive and sustainable use of its resources for all generations."[55] Similarly, Article 9(h) of Bahrain's Constitution of 2002 provides that "the State shall take the necessary measures for the protection of the environment and the conversation of wildlife."[56] These constitutional provisions directly incorporate the protection of all aspects of the environment and conservation, from degradation to pollution, and provide strong foundational basis for subsequent policy and legislative action to address biodiversity and nature conservation.

Additionally, given that Islam is the dominant religion in the MENA region, Shari'ah law is constitutionally recognized as the principal source of law in essentially all the countries of the region.[57] For example, Article 1 of Qatar's 2005 Constitution clearly states that Qatar is "an independent sovereign Arab State. Its religion is

53 D. Olawuyi, *Principles of Nigerian Environmental Law* (Afe Babalola University Press 2015) 108–113.

54 See D. Olawuyi, "Human Rights and the Environment in Middle East and North African (MENA) Region: Trends, Limitations and Opportunities" in J. May and E. Daly (eds), *Encyclopedia of Human Rights and the Environment, Indivisibility, Dignity and Legality* (Edward Elgar 2018).

55 *The Permanent Constitution of the State of Qatar* (n 43), article 33.

56 *Constitution of the Kingdom of Bahrain* (2002), article 9(h) [Bahrain Constitution].

57 K. S. Vikør, "Sharī'ah" in E. El-Din Shahin (ed), *The Oxford Encyclopedia of Islam and Politics* (Oxford University Press 2014).

Islam, and the Sharia law shall be the principal source of its legislation."[58] The Constitution of Kuwait states: "The religion of the State is Islam, and the Islamic Shari'a shall be a main source of legislation."[59] Article 7 of the Constitution of the United Arab Emirates states that "Islam is the official religion of the United Arab Emirates (UAE). The Islamic Shari'a is a main source of legislation in the UAE."[60]

Consequently, the four sources of Shari'ah law – the noble *Quran*; the *Sunnah* or teachings of the Prophet Muhammad (peace and blessings be upon him); *Ijma* or teachings of consensus of various scholars of Islam; and *Qiyas* or analogical reasoning both deductive and inductive – all provide pivotal foundations for the development and practice of environmental law and policy, as well as biodiversity and nature conservation across the region.[61] Islamic environmental philosophy emphasizes the obligations of human beings to safeguard and conserve nature and its resources. The concept of *khilafah* and *amānah* (custodianship and trust) derived from the Quran[62] and Sunnah emphasize the role of humans as stewards or trustees of the earth, making it a fundamental duty to protect and preserve nature.[63] Islamic law also includes many universal guiding principles pertaining to protecting the environment, including the protection of animals and plants, the conservation and sustainable management of land, water, and air, and the protection of the balance of nature and biodiversity.[64]

1.2.3.2 Primary Legislation

Key environmental legislation across the region contain general provisions on biodiversity and nature conservation.[65] For example, in Qatar, Article 9 of Law No. 30 on Environmental Protection tasks the competent national authorities to issue regulations and decisions relating to the conservation of wildlife and endangered species, and to prohibit the catching of rare wildlife species. Articles 16–19 of Law No. 4 of 1983 on the Exploitation and Conservation of Living Aquatic Resources in Qatar elaborate on the conservation of aquatic resources and the sustainability standards for fishing and harvesting of living aquatic resources.[66] Law No. 4 of 2002 regulating hunting of wildlife animals, birds, and reptiles prohibits and criminalizes the

58 *The Permanent Constitution of the State of Qatar* (n 43), article 1.

59 *Constitution of the State of Kuwait 1962, as Amended to 2012*, article 2 [Kuwait Constitution].

60 *United Arab Emirates "Constitution of 1971 with Amendments through 2009*, article 7 [UAE Constitution].

61 Olawuyi (n 3).

62 Quran, Surah Al-Baqarah: 30; Surah Sad: 26; Surah Al An'am: 165.

63 See also, Quran, Surah As Shams: 7–8.

64 S. Sikandar Shah Haneef, "Principles of Environmental Law in Islam" (2002) 17 *Arab Law Quarterly* 3, 241–254.

65 Olawuyi (n 3), 33–54.

66 See also Yemen's Law No. 2 of 2006, regulating fishing, exploitation, and the protection of aquatic organisms (amended by Law No 3 of 2011).

indiscriminate hunting of wild animals, birds, reptiles, and marine turtles. Article 4 of Qatar's Law No. 19 of 2004 Conservation of Wildlife and their Natural Habitats specifically outlaws any "acts, transactions, activities or procedures that would dilapidate, destroy, distort or deteriorate the wildlife environment, or affect the richness of the natural reserves." Prohibited acts include hunting or killing, injuring, or polluting land or sea animals, as well as the dilapidation, transfer, or destruction of natural habitats for flora and fauna. It also prohibits the "construction of buildings or erection establishments, roads, driving vehicles, or the exercise of any agricultural, industrial, pastoral or other activity at the natural reserve." Additionally, to address the illicit trade in wildlife fauna and flora species, Article 3 of Qatar's Law No. 5 of 2006 on the Regulation of Trade in Endangered Wildlife Fauna and Flora and their Products expressly prohibits the trade, transit, and shipment of endangered species listed in the appendices to the law.[67] Similar legislation that prohibits trade in wildlife species and indiscriminate hunting can be found in other MENA countries, some of which are extensively discussed in Part II.[68]

1.2.3.3 Secondary Legislation

The third main source of domestic biodiversity and nature conservation law and policies flows from the second, comprising a range of detailed regulations, by-laws, national visions and plans, ministerial decisions, and guidelines that are used to flesh out much of the detail of the primary legislation. Ministries or departments overseeing environmental regulation often issue regulations, rules, notices, permits, and guidelines under their enabling statutes. These provide specifics on implementing national strategies, visions, and policies that businesses must comply with. As state legal instruments authorized by legislation, they significantly shape policy and practice. Noncompliance can mean losing business opportunities or penalties, depending on enforcement powers granted.[69]

In addition to binding legal provisions, several MENA countries have also put in place declarations, action plans, directives, and national visions that address various

[67] Article 4 of Qatar's Law No. 5 of 2006 on the Regulation of Trade in Endangered Wildlife Fauna and Flora and their Products; Jordan's Law No. 6 of 2017 on Environmental Protection, which at Article 12 prohibits activities that result in the degradation of plant and animal species inside and outside their natural habitat, while Article 20 prescribes fines and sanctions for marine pollution; see also Jordan's Regulation No. (Z/2) of 2010 Concerning the Instructions on the International Trade of Endangered Wildlife Flora and Fauna.

[68] See Chapters 5–14. See also Bahrain's Legislative Decree No. 2 of 1995 on the Protection of the Wildlife in Bahrain; Egypt's Law No. 102 of 1983 on Natural Protected Areas; Jordan's Act No. 113 on the Protection of Birds and Wildlife, and on Regulating their Hunting; Jordan's Protected Areas and National Parks Bylaw No. 29 for the year 2005; Kuwait's Resolution No. 93 of 2003 Regulating Sale and Trade in Endangered Wildlife Species; and Morocco's Dahir No. 1-11-84 portant promulgation de la loi n° 29-05 relative rela tive à la protection des espèces de faune et de flore sauvages et au contrôle de leur commerce, among others.

[69] Olawuyi (n 3) 12.

aspects of the sustainable management and conservation of biological and cultural resources.[70] Several MENA countries have also released national biodiversity and conservation master plans that set out targets and approaches for accelerating the conservation of biodiversity and natural heritage as part of their implementation of international treaty provisions, such as the CBD, Convention on International Trade in Endangered Species, and the World Heritage Convention.[71] For example, Qatar's National Vision 2030 rests on four key pillars, the fourth of which is to "manage the environment such that there is harmony between economic growth, social development and environmental protection."[72] Biodiversity and nature conservation is considered vital, especially in the face of its fast-paced development and industrialization and in light of challenges such as increasing groundwater salinity, degrading soil quality, air pollution, climate change, rising sea levels, and biodiversity and species under threat.[73]

1.2.3.4 Judicial Decisions and Scholarly Publications

In the MENA region, the development of biodiversity and conservation laws is influenced not just by primary sources such as constitutions, statutes, and treaties but also by secondary sources such as the judicial decisions of courts and tribunals, as well as the scholarly works of highly qualified jurists.[74] However, contrary to the *stare decisis* rule applied in the common law system, case law does not constitute a binding source of law in civil law countries,[75] and the decisions of courts, such as the Court of Cassation and Court of Appeal, can be consulted persuasively to guide the court but do not normally bind either themselves or lower courts.[76]

The geometric rise of biodiversity litigation in many parts of the world emphasize the potential legal liability and risks that governments and business enterprises may face for failing to integrate biodiversity and nature conservation in development

70 For example, State of Qatar, Planning and Statistics Authority, "Qatar's National Development Strategy 2024–2030 (QNDS)" www.psa.gov.qa/en/nds1/pages/default.aspx accessed January 25, 2024. See also Tunisia's Five-Year Development Plan 2016–2020 for the Agricultural, Marine Fisheries, and Natural Resources Sectors.

71 See Egyptian Biodiversity Strategy and Action Plan 2015–2030; Morocco's Stratégie et Plan d'Actions National pour la Diversité Biologique du Maroc (SPANB) 2016–2020; Oman's National Biodiversity Strategy and Action Plan; Biodiversity Strategy of the United Arab Emirates 2014–2021; and the National Strategy for Conservation of Biodiversity in the Kingdom of Saudi Arabia, among others.

72 State of Qatar, *General Secretariat for Development Planning, "Qatar National Vision 2030"* (General Secretariat for Development Planning 2008).

73 State of Qatar, *Ministry of Environment and Climate Change, "Qatar National Biodiversity Strategy and Action Plan 2015–2025"* (MoECC 2014).

74 Olawuyi (n 3) 12.

75 D. Olawuyi, "Energy Poverty in the Middle East and North African (MENA) Region: Divergent Tales and Future Prospects" in I. Del Guayo, L. Godden, D. N. Zillman, M. F. Montoya, and J. J. Gonzalez (eds), *Energy Law and Energy Justice* (Oxford University Press 2020).

76 For example, Article 7 of Qatar's Law 10/2003 of the Judiciary Act.

planning processes.[77] As biodiversity and nature conservation laws develop across the region, biodiversity litigation is expected to rise in scale and volume. While international decisions are not binding on MENA courts, they provide persuasive and instructive guidance for resolving such disputes. Furthermore, courts may also consult the commentaries and opinions of highly qualified jurists and scholars, such as law professors, attorneys, and judges, especially in shaping the development of new, emerging, and developing areas of law, such as biodiversity and nature conservation law. These include the reports of international bodies, such as the International Law Commission, the Academic Advisory Group constituted by the International Bar Association's Section on Energy, Environment, Natural Resources and Infrastructure Law, the academy of environmental law of the IUCN, the International Law Association, and the Association of Environmental Law Lecturers in Middle East and North African Universities, among others, which offer authoritative analyses of a wide variety of issues pertaining to biodiversity and nature conservation.[78]

Similarly, a number of nonbinding biodiversity-related documents have been released by eminent scholars and clerics. For example, though not legally binding, the *Islamic Declaration on Climate Change of 2015* calls on Muslims worldwide to tackle "the root causes of climate change, environmental degradation and the loss of biodiversity." It called upon Muslims to work to preserve the environment using Islamic principles such as *khalifa* (caretaker), which sees human beings as vicegerents of God on earth, responsible for all beings and the environment, and entrusted with nature to benefit society while safeguarding it from overconsumption, highlighting the importance of respecting the environment, and considering the impact of our economic activities on the environment.[79] These nonbinding declarations provide faith-based frameworks and guidance on how governments,

77 See for example, *Friends of Nature, Shan Shui Conservation Centre, and Wild China Film v China Hydropower Engineering Consulting Group in China* (2020) in which the Chinese Kunming Intermediate People's Court ordered the suspension of work on the construction of hydropower on the Jiasa River to protect this last major habitat of the endangered green peafowl, which is the only native peafowl in China. See Li Yunqi, "Green Peafowl's Last Habitat vs. 3.7-Billion-Yuan Dam" https://news.cgtn.com/news/2020-03-21/Green-peafowl-s-last-habitat-vs-3-7-billion-yuan-dam-P2bT7sSi5i/index.html accessed January 25, 2024. See also African Commission on Human and Peoples' Rights, 276/ 03 Centre for Minority Rights Development (Kenya) and Minority Rights Group International on behalf of *Endorois Welfare Council v Kenya*, paras 162 and 291 (May 2009); IACtHR, *Yakye Axa Indigenous Community v Paraguay*, Judgment of June 17, 2005, Series C No 125; IACtHR, *Mayagna (Sumo) Awas Tingni Community v Nicaragua*, Judgment of August 31, 2001, Series C No 79; *Maya Indigenous Community of the Toledo District v Belize*, Case 12.053; IACtHR, Report No 40/04, OEA/SerL/V/II.122, doc 5 rev 1 (2004) 727; IACtHR, *Saramaka People v Suriname*, Judgment of November 28, 2007 (Preliminary Objections, Merits, Reparations, and Costs), Series C No 172; IACtHR, *Kichwa Indigenous People of Sarayaku v Ecuador*, 2012, Series C No 245 [186]. For in-depth discussion of biodiversity litigation, see Futhazar et al. (n 33).

78 Olawuyi (n 3) 13.

79 Islamic Declaration on Global Climate Change (2015) www.ifees.org.uk/wp-content/uploads/2020/01/climate_declarationmmwb.pdf accessed January 12, 2024.

national authorities, investors, and other stakeholders across the MENA region can contribute to global biodiversity and nature conservation efforts.

These sources provide a legal foundation for mainstreaming biodiversity and nature conservation into all aspects of development and investment planning across the MENA region. While the codification of specific biodiversity legislation remains in progress in many countries of the region, a wide range of environmental legislation and regulations, including constitutional principles on environmental protection and sustainable development, outlaw practices, including hunting, poaching, and illicit trade, that may deplete or degrade natural and cultural heritage and resources. Furthermore, as discussed in Chapter 4, all MENA countries have designated or established focal ministries, departments, or committees that oversee biodiversity and nature conservation programs, including forest management. The chapters in this book review and evaluate how the plethora of policies, instruments, and scientific studies are shaping responses to biodiversity loss across the region.

1.3 AIM, SCOPE, AND STRUCTURE OF THE BOOK

As discussed, the nexus approach to biodiversity and nature conservation emphasizes the need for multistakeholder and multisectoral partnerships in the design and implementation of biodiversity and nature conservation treaties. It seeks to promote hybrid, interconnected, and integrated biodiversity programs among a wide range of institution and sectors, including water, energy, food, health, climate change, and human rights.[80] While the need for a nexus strategy for mainstreaming biodiversity and nature conservation into national development is becoming increasingly recognized in the literature, the multidimensional and intersectional nature of implementing a nexus approach to biodiversity and nature conservation in practice in the MENA region has yet to receive a detailed, book-length exposition. This book fills a gap in this regard.

The chapters unpack a wide range of legal and regulatory innovations that can help unlock a nexus and integrated approach to the design, application, and implementation of biodiversity, conservation, and nature-based solutions across the region to achieve a coherent and comprehensive response to global sustainability challenges. With case studies from across the region, this book provides in-depth analysis and exposition of the latest legislative developments on biodiversity, nature conservation, and the protection of cultural heritage in the MENA region, including the applicable legislation and institutions, as well as lessons learned from emerging innovative and bottom-up approaches to their implementation across the world and the challenges that remain.

[80] At the recent COP15 conference in Montreal, Canada, the conference welcomed the nexus assessment of the interlinkages among diversity, water, food, and health by IPBES. See CBD/COP/15/L.11, para 4. www.cbd.int/doc/c/99c0/97dd/710d06f04fdb9a90c61af454/cop-15-l-11-en.pdf accessed January 12, 2024. See also Olawuyi (n 36) and Bastos Lima (n 31).

While this book offers a scan of the sources and underpinning principles of biodiversity law and policy law and policy in the region, it is clearly acknowledged that the substantive chapters cannot unpack and analyze every applicable piece of legislation and instrument in all MENA countries. The book aims to enhance understanding of the interconnections between biodiversity, nature conservation, and attaining water, energy, and food security and resilience to disasters such as climate change and pandemics. It examines the laws, policies, and institutions on biodiversity, conservation, and cultural heritage protection in MENA. The goal is to foster an understanding of the unique legal, policy, and governance challenges faced in the region in seeking to achieve the SDGs and other international instruments and documents relating to biodiversity and conservation.

1.3.1 *Structure*

Part I introduces the interrelationships between biodiversity, nature conservation, and the attainment of water, energy, and food security, as well as resilience to global disasters such as climate change and global pandemics. It explains key concepts and underlying themes such as "biodiversity" and "nature conservation" and the wide range of multilateral environmental agreements (MEAs) in place at the international level to advance biodiversity and nature conservation.

Part II consists of a series of case studies that examine emerging approaches and challenges to the nexus and integrated implementation of biodiversity and nature conservation treaties in different sectors and countries in the MENA region. The case studies identify the various legal, policy, and governance challenges that hinder the nexus and integrated implementation of biodiversity and nature conservation treaties at national and municipal levels across the region. Concerns of fragmentation, gender inequality, inadequate stakeholder engagement, financing gaps, inadequate support for biodiversity entrepreneurship, limited access to environmental information, and lack of comprehensive legislation on biodiversity and access to benefit-sharing are unpacked.

The case studies demonstrate how inappropriately designed and implemented laws and policies on biodiversity and nature conservation could result in land rights violations in biodiversity and nature-based programs, social exclusions, and incoherent implementation. Part II also identifies positive and high-leverage laws, policies, and strategies that advance nexus thinking, the contexts in which they are being implemented, barriers to their effective implementation, and innovative legal approaches to advance such strategies.

Part III offers reflections on the case studies and addresses how lessons from diverse jurisdictions may inform thoughts on how to effectively design, apply, and implement sustainable and rights-based frameworks to enhance integrated decision-making and information sharing on biodiversity and nature conservation. The need to integrate biodiversity and nature conservation in environmental impact assessments and human rights due diligence processes for development activities and construction projects are specifically highlighted.[81] The role of higher education institutions in promoting environmental law education and capacity development on biodiversity through enquiry-based learning methods is also discussed.[82]

All eighteen chapters provide a worldwide audience of scholars, business leaders, policymakers, and administrators with an authoritative and invaluable guidebook and toolkit to access, understand, and appreciate the legal, fiscal, and institutional frameworks applicable to the effective design, application, and implementation of biodiversity and nature conservation programs and policies in the MENA region. It also offers as an invaluable guide to ongoing efforts by the United Nations to define and conceptualize the biodiversity–climate–water–food–energy–health nexus.[83]

1.4 CONCLUSION

There is a growing recognition and awareness across the MENA region regarding the need to protect and conserve the region's abundant biological and cultural resources, so that present and future generations can enjoy access to these resources. In addition to their environmental and ecosystems value, MENA countries have significant potential to unlock social and economic activities such as tourism and biodiversity entrepreneurship, as well as increased trade, tax, fees, and payment for ecosystem services (PES) and nature-based innovation, all of which can accelerate economic diversification.[84]

Addressing the widescale adverse impacts of the loss of biodiversity on lives and livelihoods in the MENA region is therefore an urgent sustainable development priority. To achieve this objective, there is a need for clear and coherent laws and policies that mainstream biodiversity and nature conservation into all aspects of national planning. Practical challenges to the nexus and integrated implementation of biodiversity and nature conservation must be carefully unpacked and addressed. A comprehensive analysis and study of the structural and nonstructural challenges that arise in the design, application, and implementation of biodiversity and nature conservation law and policy across the region can help us to plot a comprehensive path for achieving policy coherence and reform.

The systemic and multijurisdictional survey of the unique and underlying features of biodiversity and nature conservation regulation in diverse jurisdictions offered by this book can simplify the task of advancing nature-based solutions to complex sustainability challenges in the region, as well as the integration of ecosystems approaches into key sectors and industries in MENA countries, including financing, entrepreneurship, and healthcare.

81 See Chapter 15.
82 See Chapter 17.
83 CBD (n 80). See also UNEP (n 8).
84 Organisation for Economic Co-operation and Development, "Biodiversity, Natural Capital and the Economy" (2021) www.oecd.org/environment/resources/Executive-Summary-ENV-Policy-Paper-no-26-Biodiversity-Natural-Capital-and-the-Economy.pdf accessed January 12, 2024. See also L. Croitoru, & H. Daly-Hassen, "Using Payments for Environmental Services to Improve Conservation in a Tunisian Watershed" (2010) https://lib.icimod.org/record/14626, accessed January 12, 2024.

2

The International Legal Framework on Biodiversity and Nature Conservation

Aphrodite Smagadi and Jackline Wanja Wanjiru

2.1 INTRODUCTION

This chapter examines the international legal framework on biodiversity, reflects on the scope of its implementation in the Middle East and North Africa (MENA) region, and highlights the way forward for enhancing coherent, holistic, and integrated implementation of biodiversity treaties in the region.

Nature and its contributions are essential to human survival due to their wide-ranging economic, social, and cultural benefits. The value of nature-derived ecosystem services is estimated at US$125–140 trillion per year.[1] These vital services include anything from provision of food, water, medicines, genetic resources, and energy, to the regulation of environmental processes such as climate change and ocean acidification and pollination, to the creation of livelihood opportunities and the facilitation of recreational, cultural, and spiritual well-being.[2] Yet the variety of nature, collectively known as "biodiversity," faces multiple threats that continue to intensify.[3] It is no wonder that in 2023, biodiversity and ecosystem loss ranked fourth as the most severe global risk for the coming decade.[4]

The authors acknowledge the research support of Tiffany Collard and Adjoa Saaba Eshun, interns at the UNEP Law Division. The views expressed in this chapter do not necessarily reflect the views of the organization.

1 Organization for Economic Co-operation and Development, "Biodiversity: Finance and the Economic and Business Case for Action" (May 2019) www.oecd.org/environment/resources/biodiversity/Executive-Summary-and-Synthesis-Biodiversity-Finance-and-the-Economic-and-Business-Case-for-Action.pdf accessed January 12, 2023, 4. See also M. Grooten and R. E. A. Almond (eds), *Living Planet Report – 2018: Aiming Higher* (WWF 2018) 6.

2 K. A. Brauman, L. A. Garibaldi, and S. Polasky et al., "Chapter 2.3. Status and Trends – Nature's Contributions to People (NCP)" in S. Díaz, J. Settele, E. S. Brondízio et al. (eds), *Global Assessment Report of the Intergovernmental Science-Policy Platform on Biodiversity and Ecosystem* (IPBES 2019) 313.

3 S. Díaz, J. Settele, E. S. Brondízio et al. (eds), *Global Assessment Report of the Intergovernmental Science-Policy Platform on Biodiversity and Ecosystem* (IPBES 2019) 5.

4 World Economic Forum (WEF), *The Global Risks Report 2023*, 18th edition (WEF 2023) 6.

Biodiversity loss is one of the three contributors to the triple planetary crisis, along with climate change and pollution.[5] Human activity is a driver of this loss and it has the potential to cause permanent damage to about 75 percent and 66 percent of land- and marine-based environments, respectively.[6] Already, a record number of one million animal and plant species are threatened by extinction,[7] with wildlife populations having declined by an average of 69 percent since 1970.[8] Every year that biodiversity loss persists, the global gross domestic product drops by US$2.7 trillion.[9] Unfortunately, this loss and degradation disproportionately affects marginalized populations.[10] Of additional concern is the linkage between the degradation and the emergence of zoonotic diseases, such as the COVID-19 pandemic that wholly disrupted the world.[11]

Certainly, a rich and healthy biodiversity is integral to the attainment of the 2030 Agenda for Sustainable Development. While all Sustainable Development Goals (SDGs) are connected to biodiversity, Goal 15 especially calls for the protection, restoration, and promotion of sustainable use of terrestrial ecosystems and the halting of biodiversity loss.[12] This goal is complemented by Goal 14 on marine ecosystems. The progress is falling behind expectations.[13] The 2022 SDG report notes that the risk of species extinction continues to rise, yet biodiversity was largely neglected in COVID-19 recovery spending.[14]

[5] United Nations, *The Sustainable Development Goals Report 2022* (UN 2022) 50; UN Framework Convention on Climate Change (UNFCCC), "What Is the Triple Planetary Crisis" (UNFCCC.int, April 13, 2022) https://unfccc.int/blog/what-is-the-triple-planetary-crisis accessed January 12, 2023.

[6] Olivia Lai, "UN Reports Animal Species Extinction Rates Are Record High and 'Accelerating'" (Earth.org, July 28, 2021) https://earth.org/un-reports-animal-species-extinction-rates-are-record-high-and-accelerating/ accessed January 12, 2023; S. Díaz, J. Settele, E. S. Brondízio et al. (eds), *Global Assessment Report of the Intergovernmental Science-Policy Platform on Biodiversity and Ecosystem* (IPBES 2019) 15.

[7] S. Díaz, J. Settele, E. S. Brondízio et al. (eds), *Global Assessment Report of the Intergovernmental Science-Policy Platform on Biodiversity and Ecosystem* (IPBES 2019) 16.

[8] R. E. A. Almond, M. Grooten, D. Juffe Bignoli et al. (eds), *Living Planet Report 2022 – Building a Nature-Positive Society* (WWF 2022) 4. The period of the study in relation to a decline of wildlife population was from 1970 to 2018.

[9] J. Justin Andrew, R. Giovanni, U. Baldos et al., "The Economic Case for Nature" (June 2021) https://openknowledge.worldbank.org/handle/10986/35882 accessed January 12, 2023, 6.

[10] IUCN, "Post-2020 Global Biodiversity Framework Emphasizes 'All-Hands-on-Deck' approach" (Crossroads blog, September 5, 2021) www.iucn.org/crossroads-blog/202109/post-2020-global-biodiversity-framework-emphasises-all-hands-deck-approach accessed January 12, 2023.

[11] In 2016, the United Nations Environment Programme (UNEP) forewarned of a heightened increase in zoonotic diseases, such as Corona viruses, due to human-created ecological disturbances that enable pathogenic spill overs from wildlife to livestock and human beings. UNEP, *UNEP Frontiers 2016 Report: Emerging Issues of Environmental Concern* (UNEP 2016) 18; also see Secretariat of the Convention on Biological Diversity, *Global Biodiversity Outlook* 5 (Secretariat of the Convention on Biological Diversity 2020) 176.

[12] UN General Assembly (UNGA), "Transforming Our World: The 2030 Agenda for Sustainable Development" (October 21, 2015) UN Doc A/RES/70/1, 14.

[13] UN (n 5).

[14] UN (n 5) 56.

The MENA region is not exempt from the global trends in biodiversity loss. This region boasts a wealth of terrestrial and marine habitats that include mangrove stands, productive wetlands, and endangered species such as dugongs.[15] While MENA countries have adopted numerous and varied measures to protect nature and safeguard biodiversity, more needs to be done to advance the kind of implementation required to fulfill the biodiversity-related SDGs.[16] The Fifth Global Biodiversity Outlook (GBO5) underscores the urgency for measures to slow down and end biodiversity loss for the benefit of, among other things, climate action, long-term food security, and health.[17] As Mrema, the immediate former executive secretary for the Secretariat to the Convention on Biological Diversity (CBD) rightly notes, "nature is the backbone for maintaining and restoring balance within planetary boundaries."[18]

The effective implementation of biodiversity-related international treaties is a powerful approach to responding to the biodiversity crisis. Worryingly, weak implementation and enforcement is a global trend that is exacerbating environmental threats, despite prolific growth in environmental laws and agencies worldwide over the last four decades.[19]

This chapter therefore examines current progress made in implementing biodiversity and nature conservation treaties in the MENA region. The chapter is divided into five sections. After this introduction, Section 2.2 outlines the key international law instruments on biodiversity and nature conservation. Section 2.3 evaluates the MENA countries' approach to implementation of the CBD. Section 2.4 proffers recommendations on how to advance a more coherent, holistic, and integrated implementation of biodiversity and nature conservation treaties in the MENA region, based on the Global Biodiversity Framework (GBF), and Section 2.5 conclusion.

2.2 INTERNATIONAL AND REGIONAL FRAMEWORK ON BIODIVERSITY AND NATURE CONSERVATION

Humankind, particularly indigenous communities, have conserved nature and biodiversity for eons, equipped by a diversity of ancient traditions and knowledge. With the advent of the agricultural and industrial revolutions in the eighteenth and nineteenth centuries, however, a concerning rise in the destruction of nature occurred. Early legal attempts to address this phenomenon were observed in the twentieth century at both national and international levels, through the enactment of frameworks such as the colonial 1933 Convention relative to the Preservation of Fauna and Flora

[15] UNEP, *Global Environment Outlook GEO-6, Regional Assessment for West Asia* (UNEP 2016) 57.

[16] UN (n 5) 54–57. The report refers to "Northern Africa and West Asia," which is geographically inclusive of part of the MENA region.

[17] Secretariat of the Convention on Biological Diversity, *Global Biodiversity Outlook 5* (Secretariat of the Convention on Biological Diversity 2020) 14.

[18] IUCN (n 10).

[19] UNEP, *Environmental Rule of Law: First Global Report* (UNEP 2019).

in their Natural State.[20] Since then international environmental law has exponentially grown, albeit in an unstructured and ad hoc manner, into a distinctive complex legal system. That an international legal framework to protect biodiversity and conserve nature is needed is not in question, given the transboundary dimensions of biodiversity loss and the migratory nature of some species. The development of this framework, however, suffers a disordered trajectory attributable to the several phases of its development. As aptly put by one commentator in the 1990s: "Internationally, biodiversity law possesses [other] obstacles. Not only must it deal with the interdisciplinary challenges of biodiversity itself, but it is also stuck with the inherently diffuse and sometimes chaotic character of international law generally."[21]

Modern international biodiversity law was largely influenced by the birth of international environmental governance institutions such as the United Nations Environment Programme (UNEP),[22] in the 1970s, building on earlier frameworks such as the Food and Agriculture Organization, United Nations Educational, Scientific and Cultural Organization (UNESCO), and the International Union for Conservation of Nature (IUCN). International biodiversity law is further informed by soft law instruments, mostly emanating from famed conferences, such as the Stockholm Declaration and Action Plan for the Human Environment (1972), the World Charter for Nature (1982), Our Common Future (Brundtland Report) (1987), the Rio Declaration on Environment and Development and Agenda 21 (1992),[23] and the 2030 Agenda for Sustainable Development (2015). Early on, the international legal framework on biodiversity took a sectoral approach by focusing on the protection of specific species, for example wildlife or migratory birds. Over the years, this has shifted to a general focus on conservation as well as their natural habitats, underpinned by the concept of sustainable development.[24]

As discussed in Chapter 1, when talking about the origin, scope, and sources of international biodiversity law, reference must be made to Article 38 of the International Court of Justice, which sets out the sources of international law.[25] These are primarily *international conventions*, whether general or particular, *international custom*, as evidence of a general practice accepted as law, *general principles*

20 Convention relative to the Preservation of Fauna and Flora in their Natural State (adopted November 8, 1933, entered into force January 14, 1936).

21 William J. Snape, III, "Biodiversity and the Law: An Introduction" (1994) 8 *Tulane Environmental Law Journal* 5.

22 Definition provided in Law and National Biodiversity Strategies and Action Plans' (UNEP 2018).

23 UN Conference on Environment & Development, "Agenda 21" (June 1992) 149. Chapter 15 of the agenda is wholly dedicated to biological diversity. The agenda calls on states to ratify the CBD and to develop corresponding national strategies.

24 See for instance discussions in: UN, "Plan of Implementation of the World Summit on Sustainable Development" (2002) www.un.org/esa/sustdev/documents/WSSD_POI_PD/English/WSSD_PlanImpl.pdf accessed January 17, 2023, para 44; UNGA, "The Future We Want" (September 11, 2012) UN Doc A/RES/66/288, paras 197–204.

25 United Nations, Statute of the International Court of Justice www.un.org/en/about-us/un-charter/statute-of-the-international-court-of-justice accessed January 17, 2024.

of law, and the *judicial decisions and teachings of the most highly qualified publicists* of the various nations as subsidiary means for the determination of rules of law. The modern international biodiversity law, like other bodies of international law, derives from these sources.[26]

2.2.1 *Key International Multilateral Environmental Agreements on Biodiversity and Nature Conservation*

There is a multiplicity of international biodiversity and nature conservation treaties. By becoming parties to these agreements, states agree to be bound by the legal obligations therein and are expected to do so in good faith based on the Vienna Convention on the Law of Treaties (1969).[27] Biodiversity multilateral environmental agreements (MEAs) stipulate the definite rules and mechanisms to protect and conserve biodiversity and some of the key MEAs are explored in more detail in Section 2.2.1.1, with a focus on the MENA region.

2.2.1.1 Convention on International Trade in Endangered Species of Wild Fauna and Flora

The 1973 Convention on International Trade in Endangered Species of Wild Fauna and Flora (CITES) entered into force in 1975.[28] It regulates international trade in endangered and threatened specimens of wild animals and plants in their natural habitats, currently protecting more than 40,900 species of animals and plants from overexploitation. CITES classifies species into three appendices based on their conservation status. Appendix I includes species that are at the highest risk of extinction. Commercial trade of these species is prohibited. Appendix II includes species that are not currently endangered but could become so without trade restrictions. Trade of these species is allowed but only with a permit from the exporting country and only if the specimens were legally obtained and the trade will not harm the species or its environment. Appendix III includes species for which a country has asked for help from other CITES parties in regulating international trade. Trade of these species is regulated through CITES export permits and certificates of origin. MENA parties to CITES are Algeria, Bahrain, Djibouti, Egypt, Iran, Iraq, Israel, Jordan, Kuwait, Lebanon, Libya, Morocco, Oman, Pakistan, Qatar, Saudi Arabia, Syria, Tunisia, Turkey, United Arab Emirates, and Yemen.[29]

26 North Sea Continental Shelf Cases (*FRG v Denmark*; *FRG v Netherlands*).

27 Vienna Convention on the Law of Treaties (adopted May 23, 1969, entered into force January 27, 1980) 1155 UNTS 331 (Vienna Convention) Art 26.

28 Convention on International Trade in Endangered Species of Wild Fauna and Flora (signed March 3, 1973, entered into force July 1, 1975) (Washington Convention).

29 CITES, "List of Contracting Parties" https://cites.org/eng/disc/parties/chronolo.php accessed November 8, 2023.

2.2.1.2 Convention on the Conservation of Migratory Species of Wild Animals

Also known as the Bonn Convention, the 1979 Convention on the Conservation of Migratory Species of Wild Animals (CMS) aims to conserve, and to ensure the sustainable use of, migratory animals and their habitats.[30] It entered into force in 1983, and covers a wide range of migratory animals and their habitats, which can include wetlands, forests, grasslands, marine areas, and migration routes. Appendix I of the CMS lists migratory species that are in danger of extinction throughout all or a significant portion of their range. Appendix II lists migratory species that have an unfavorable conservation status or would benefit from international cooperation to conserve them. Numerous MENA countries are party to the CMS, namely: Algeria, Bahrain, Djibouti, Egypt, Iran, Iraq, Israel, Jordan, Lebanon, Libya, Morocco, Saudi Arabia, Syria, Tunisia, United Arab Emirates, and Yemen.[31]

2.2.1.3 Convention on Wetlands of International Importance Especially as Waterfowl Habitat

The 1971 Convention on Wetlands of International Importance Especially as Waterfowl Habitat (Ramsar Convention) took effect in 1975 and aims at safeguarding, preserving, and responsibly overseeing wetlands.[32] It fosters collaboration at both national and international levels to ensure the sustainable utilization of wetlands. It has a broad definition of wetlands, including all "lakes, rivers, aquifers, swamps, marshes, wet grasslands, peatlands, oases, estuaries, deltas, tidal flats, mangroves, other coastal areas, coral reefs, and human-made sites such as fishponds, rice paddies, reservoirs, and salt pans." The Strategic Plan is the central document directing the Ramsar Convention's implementation. Among the contracting parties are Algeria, Bahrain, Djibouti, Egypt, Iran, Iraq, Israel, Jordan, Kuwait, Lebanon, Libya, Morocco, Oman, Syria, Tunisia, Turkey, United Arab Emirates, and Yemen.[33]

30 Convention on the Conservation of Migratory Species of Wild animals (adopted June 23, 1979, entered into force November 1, 1983) (Bonn Convention).

31 "Parties and Range States" (Convention on Migratory Species) www.cms.int/en/parties-range-states accessed November 8, 2023.

32 Convention on Wetlands of International Importance especially as Waterfowl Habitat (adopted February 2, 1971, entered into force December 21, 1975) 996 UNTS 245 (Ramsar Convention).

33 "List of the Contracting Parties and date of entry into force of the Convention" (Convention on Wetlands) www.ramsar.org/document/list-contracting-parties-and-date-entry-force-convention-each accessed November 8, 2023.

2.2.1.4 United Nations Convention to Combat Desertification in those Countries Experiencing Serious Drought and/or Desertification, Particularly in Africa

The 1994 United Nations Convention to Combat Desertification (UNCCD) took effect in December 1996.[34] Its objectives, as highlighted in Article 2, are to combat desertification and mitigate the effects of drought, through effective action at all levels, supported by international cooperation and partnership arrangements. This is reinforced by Article 4, which sets out general obligations for contracting parties, requiring them to, among other things, adopt an integrated approach addressing the physical, biological, and socio-economic aspects of desertification and drought, increase strategies for poverty eradication in combating desertification and mitigating drought, and promote cooperation among affected countries, at subregional, regional, and international levels and within relevant intergovernmental organizations. Algeria, Bahrain, Djibouti, Egypt, Iran, Iraq, Israel, Jordan, Kuwait, Lebanon, Libya, Morocco, Oman, Pakistan, Qatar, Saudi Arabia, Syria, Tunisia, Turkey, United Arab Emirates and Yemen are parties.[35]

2.2.1.5 Convention Concerning the Protection of the World Cultural and Natural Heritage

Adopted in 1972 and effected in 1975, the Convention Concerning the Protection of the World Cultural and Natural Heritage calls on parties to do all they can to ensure the "identification, protection, conservation, presentation and transmission to future generations" of the cultural and natural heritage that is recognized under the convention.[36] Regarding heritage, the convention requires them to, among other things, take appropriate legal, scientific, technical, administrative, and financial measures necessary for the identification, protection, conservation, presentation, and rehabilitation of this heritage. Notably, the convention establishes the World Heritage Fund to support countries in its implementation. It is administered under UNESCO and enjoys near universal membership with 195 parties, including Algeria, Bahrain, Djibouti, Egypt, Iran, Jordan, Kuwait, Lebanon, Libya Morocco, Qatar, Tunisia, Turkey, United Arab Emirates, and Yemen.[37]

[34] The UNCCD in those countries experiencing serious drought and/or desertification, particularly in Africa (adopted June 17, 1994, entered into force December 26, 1996) 1954 UNTS 3.

[35] "Depository" (United Nations Treaty Collection) https://treaties.un.org/Pages/ViewDetails.aspx?src=IND&mtdsg_no=XXVII-10&chapter=27&clang=_en accessed November 8, 2023.

[36] Convention Concerning the Protection of the World Cultural and Natural Heritage (adopted November 16, 1972, entered into force December 17, 1975) Article 4.

[37] "States Parties" (UNESCO World Heritage Convention) https://whc.unesco.org/en/statesparties/ accessed November 8, 2023.

2.2.1.6 Convention on Biological Diversity

In 1992, at the United Nations Conference on Environment and Development in Rio de Janeiro, states adopted the CBD.[38] The CBD entered into force in 1993 and has since remained the principal framework international law instrument on biodiversity, counting 196 parties, including: Algeria, Bahrain, Djibouti, Egypt, Iran, Iraq, Israel, Jordan, Kuwait, Lebanon, Libya, Morocco, Oman, Palestine, Qatar, Saudi Arabia, Palestine, Syria, Tunisia, Turkey, United Arab Emirates, and Yemen.[39] The CBD begins by recognizing the value, importance, and benefits of biological diversity and expressing the need to protect it. Its preamble encompasses several international and environmental law principles including sovereignty over resources, sustainable development, intergenerational equity, prevention, and the precautionary principles. The preamble also underscores the declining nature of biological diversity and the role of human intervention as an accelerating factor.

Grounded in the preambular context, Article 1 sets outs key objectives as: conservation of biological diversity and the sustainable use of its components; and fair and equitable sharing of the benefits arising out of the utilization of genetic resources. This article embodies the equal importance that the CBD places on its two core themes, that is, conservation and benefits sharing. The CBD is further supplemented by the 2000 Cartagena Protocol,[40] and by the Nagoya Protocol on Access to Genetic Resources and the Fair and Equitable Sharing of Benefits.[41]

2.2.2 *Key Regional MEAs on Biodiversity and Nature Conservation*

2.2.2.1 Convention for the Protection of the Marine Environment and the Coastal Region of the Mediterranean

The 1976 Convention for the Protection of the Marine Environment and the Coastal Region of the Mediterranean (Barcelona Convention) entered into force in 1978.[42] Its objectives include combating pollution, protecting marine ecosystems,

[38] Convention on Biological Diversity (adopted June 5, 1992, entered into force December 29, 1993) 1760 UNTS 79 (CBD).

[39] "List of Parties" (Convention on Biological Diversity) www.cbd.int/information/parties.shtml accessed November 8, 2023.

[40] Cartagena Protocol on Biosafety to the CBD (adopted January 29, 2000) 2226 UNTS 208 (Cartagena Protocol).

[41] Convention on Biological Diversity, "About the Nagoya Protocol" (CBD.int) www.cbd.int/abs/about/ accessed January 15, 2023. See also https://treaties.un.org/Pages/ViewDetails.aspx?src=TREATY&mtdsg_no=XXVII-8-b&chapter=27&clang=_en accessed January 17, 2024.

[42] Convention for the Protection of the Marine Environment and the Coastal Region of the Mediterranean (adopted February 16, 1976, entered into force April 15, 1978) (Barcelona Convention).

and ensuring that their natural marine and coastal resources are sustainably managed.[43] Article 10 requires contracting parties to *take all appropriate measures* to protect biological diversity, rare or fragile ecosystems, and, among other things, endangered species and their habitats. Together with its seven protocols, the Barcelona Convention is heralded as the main regional legally binding MEA in the Mediterranean.[44] While the entire framework is relevant, one protocol explicitly addresses biodiversity: the Protocol Concerning Specially Protected Areas and Biological Diversity in the Mediterranean, adopted in 1995 and effected in 1999. The protocol creates obligations for parties to, among other things, establish specially protected areas, protect, preserve, and manage threatened and endangered species, cooperate, compile biological diversity inventories, and adopt relevant strategies, plans, and programs. Algeria, Egypt, Israel, Lebanon, Libya, Morocco, Syria, Tunisia, and Turkey are parties, both to the Barcelona Convention and to this protocol.[45]

2.2.2.2 Agreement on the Conservation of Cetaceans of the Black Sea, Mediterranean Sea Contiguous Atlantic Area

The 1996 Agreement on the Conservation of Cetaceans of the Black Sea, Mediterranean Sea Contiguous Atlantic Area (ACCOBAMS) entered into force in 2001, with an aim to protect cetaceans in the Black Sea, Mediterranean Sea, and the nearby Atlantic area west of the Straits of Gibraltar.[46] Though, in 2010, the parties agreed to expand the geographic area to include the exclusive economic zones of Spain and Portugal. ACCOBAMS promotes the conservation and sustainable management of marine mammals and their habitats by, among other things, developing and improving the current knowledge on these animals. £It sets out conservation, research, and management measures to be adhered to by parties, in relation to the adoption and enforcement of national legislation; assessment and management of human-cetacean interactions; habitat protection; research and monitoring; capacity building, collection, and dissemination of information, training, and education;

43 Article 1 of the Convention outlines its geographical scope as "the maritime waters of the Mediterranean Sea proper, including its gulfs and seas, bounded to the West by the meridian passing through Cape Spartel lighthouse, at the entrance of the Straits of Gibraltar, and to the East by the southern limits of the Straits of the Dardanelles between Mehmetcik and Kumkale lighthouses."

44 "Barcelona Convention and its Protocols" (Mediterranean Action Plan – Barcelona Convention) www.unep.org/unepmap/who-we-are/barcelona-convention-and-protocols accessed November 8, 2023.

45 "Contracting Parties" (Mediterranean Action Plan – Barcelona Convention) www.unep.org/unepmap/who-we-are/contracting-parties accessed November 8, 2023.

46 Article 1 sets out the geographic scope of the agreement as, "by all the maritime waters of the Black Sea and the Mediterranean and their gulfs and seas, and the internal waters connected to or interconnecting these maritime waters, and of the Atlantic area contiguous to the Mediterranean Sea west of the Straits of Gibraltar."

and responses to emergency situations.[47] The MENA contracting parties are Algeria, Egypt, Lebanon, Libya, Morocco, Syria, Tunisia, and Turkey, while Israel is a signatory.[48]

2.2.2.3 Agreement on the Conservation of African-Eurasian Migratory Waterbirds

The 1995 Agreement on the Conservation of African-Eurasian Migratory Waterbirds (AEWA) entered into force in 1999,[49] under the Convention on Migratory Species (CMS), with the goal of protecting migratory waterbirds and their wetlands environment within Africa, Europe, the Middle East, Central Asia, Greenland, and the Canadian Archipelago, as they migrate across their habitats. It covers the conservation of 255 species of birds dependent on wetlands during some part of their yearly life cycle. They include a diverse array of birds, including divers, grebes, pelicans, cormorants, herons, storks, rails, ibises, spoonbills, flamingos, ducks, swans, geese, cranes, waders, gulls, terns, tropic birds, auks, frigate birds, and even the South African penguin. AEWA has in place an Action Plan that specifies various measures that parties must take to ensure the conservation of migratory waterbirds. The following MENA countries are party to AEWA: Algeria, Djibouti, Egypt, Israel, Jordan, Lebanon, Libya, Morocco, Saudi Arabia, Syria, and Tunisia.[50]

2.2.2.4 Regional Convention for the Conservation of the Red Sea and the Gulf of Aden Environment

The 1982 Regional Convention for the Conservation of the Red Sea and the Gulf of Aden Environment (Jeddah Convention) entered into force in 1985. There are seven parties to the Jeddah Convention, including Djibouti, Egypt, Jordan, Saudi Arabia, and Yemen. It addresses environmental issues and the sustainable use of natural resources in the region, including pollution, overfishing, and habitat destruction. The geographical coverage is of the entire sea area, taking into account integrated ecosystems of the Red Sea, Gulf of Aqaba, Gulf of Suez, Suez Canal to its end on the Mediterranean, and Gulf of Aden, as bounded by rhumb lines (lines on the surface of the earth that cross all successive meridians at a constant angle).

47 Article II (3) and Annex 2 of the Agreement.

48 "Introduction" (ACCOBAMS) https://accobams.org/about/introduction/ accessed November 8, 2023.

49 Agreement on the Conservation of African-Eurasian Migratory Waterbirds (adopted June 19, 1995, entry into force November 1, 1999) (AEWA).

50 Parties and Range States (AEWA) www.unep-aewa.org/en/parties-range-states accessed November 8, 2023.

2.2.2.5 Kuwait Regional Convention on Protection of Marine Environment Convention

The 1978 Kuwait Regional Convention on Protection of Marine Environment Convention (Kuwait Convention), which took effect in 1979,[51] aims to prevent, abate, and combat pollution of the marine environment and calls for parties to take all appropriate measures to prevent, abate, and combat pollution of the marine environment; to cooperate in taking necessary measures to deal with pollution emergencies, in scientific and technical research relating to marine pollution; and to establish appropriate roles and procedures for the determination of civil liability and compensation for damage related to the subject matter of the convention. Although focused on matters of pollution, the Kuwait Convention aims to protect, by extension, biodiversity in the marine environment. The Kuwait Convention is complemented by four Protocols: the 1989 Protocol concerning Marine Pollution resulting from Exploration and Exploitation of the Continental Shelf (in force since 1990); the 1998 Protocol on the Control of Marine Transboundary Movements and Disposal of Hazardous Wastes and Other Wastes (in force since 2005); the 1978 Protocol Concerning Regional Co-operation in Combating Pollution by Oil and other Harmful Substances in Cases of Emergency (in force since 1979); and the 1990 Protocol for the Protection of the Marine Environment against Pollution from Land-Based Sources (in force since 1993). The parties to the Kuwait Convention are Bahrain, Iran, Iraq, Kuwait, Oman, Qatar, Saudi Arabia, and United Arab Emirates. Most of the Kuwait Convention parties are also parties to the protocols.[52]

2.2.2.6 Gulf Cooperation Council Wildlife Convention

The 2001 Convention on the Conservation of Wildlife and their Natural Habitats in Gulf Cooperation Council (GCC) Countries (GCC Wildlife Convention) entered into force in 2003 and aims at conserving ecosystems and wildlife, especially the species threatened with extinction through legislation, habitat protection and management, environmental impact assessment studies, environmental education, research cooperation, and training, among other things. The GCC Wildlife Convention also provides for the establishment of the Permanent Committee for Conservation of Wildlife and its Natural Habitats in the Gulf Co-operation Council of States formed by representatives from the GCC states, as an implementing body with the responsibility to establish requirements of

51 Kuwait Regional Convention for Co-operation on the Protection of the Marine Environment from Pollution (adopted April 24, 1978, entry into force June 30, 1979) (Kuwait Regional Convention).

52 Ibid.

wildlife conservation and evaluation of the effectiveness of the approved measures, monitoring, and research and data collection.[53]

2.2.2.7 African Convention on the Conservation of Nature and Natural Resources

The 1968/2017 African Convention on the Conservation of Nature and Natural Resources (African Convention) entered in force in 1969. It aims to encourage the conservation, utilization, and development of soil, water, flora, and fauna for the present and future welfare of mankind, from an economic, nutritional, scientific, educational, cultural, and aesthetic point of view. The Organization of the African Union discharges the secretariat functions.[54]

2.3 IMPLEMENTATION OF BIODIVERSITY AND NATURE CONSERVATION TREATIES IN THE MENA REGION

MEAs share common structures and implementation mechanisms, whether institutional, capacity building, monitoring and review, or compliance mechanisms. Effective implementation, however, differs according to various variables, many of which depend on the capacity to implement the treaty obligations at the national level, and others referring to the clarity/severity of the treaty provisions and the treaty regime's capacity to promote implementation, such as resources available for technical assistance, implementation, reporting, and/or compliance mechanisms. As the global umbrella treaty on biodiversity, the following sections highlight implementation successes and challenges under the CBD, within MENA.

2.3.1 *Implementation under the CBD*

Through decision X/2, at the tenth CBD Conference of the Parties (COP), parties adopted the 2011–2020 Strategic Plan for Biodiversity, including the Aichi Biodiversity Targets (Strategic Plan).[55] The Strategic Plan was not only pertinent for the CBD but for other biodiversity-related conventions, the UN system, and biodiversity stakeholders at large.[56] It set out a collective vision of "Living in Harmony with Nature," where, "[b]y 2050, biodiversity is valued, conserved, restored and wisely used, maintaining ecosystem services, sustaining a healthy planet and

[53] Convention on the Conservation of Wildlife and their Natural Habitats in the Countries of the Gulf Cooperation Council (adopted December 30, 2001, entry into force April 2003).

[54] African Convention on the Conservation of Nature and Natural Resources (adopted September 15, 1968, entered into force June 16, 1969).

[55] Conference of the parties to the Convention on Biological Diversity (10th meeting) "The Strategic Plan for Biodiversity 2011–2020 and the Aichi Biodiversity Targets" (October 29, 2010) UNEP/CBD/COP/DEC/X/2.

[56] Ibid.

delivering benefits essential for all people."[57] The Strategic Plan had five strategic goals, accompanied by twenty Aichi Biodiversity Targets.[58]

In the same decision X/2, CBD parties agreed to translate this overarching international framework into National Biodiversity Strategies and Action Plans (NBSAPs), within two years, and to report on the plan's implementation.[59] NBSAPs are the primary instruments for the plan's implementation at the national level. The parties also set out general implementation guidance such as fostering inclusive participation at all levels, developing national and regional targets, mainstreaming gender considerations, updating NBSAPs and using them to integrate biodiversity targets into national development policies, and reporting on the plan's implementation progress.[60] The parties even agreed on indicators[61] and actions[62] for implementation. Additionally, the CBD itself provides mechanisms to support parties in effective implementation, including financial mechanisms (notably the Global Environment Facility), a clearing-house mechanism and partnerships.[63]

However, despite the Strategic Plan's ambition and the implementation mechanisms, none of its targets were achieved by 2020. The GBO5 estimates, with varying levels of confidence, that only six targets were partially achieved. The report suggests that there had been gaps in the ambition and commitment of countries to address nature loss over the past decade. It also indicates that the national biodiversity plans had generally been poorly aligned to, and are insufficient to meet, the Aichi Targets.[64] Together with the parties' national reports, NBSAPs are great sources of information on respective parties' national targets and their progress on the Strategic Plan.[65]

2.3.1.1 National Biodiversity Strategies and Action Plans

Article 6 (a) of the CBD requires parties to "[d]evelop national strategies, plans or programmes for the conservation and sustainable use of biological diversity." Target 17 of the Strategic Plan stipulates that, "[b]y 2015, each Party has developed, adopted

57 Ibid., Annex para 11.

58 Ibid., Annex para 13.

59 Convention on Biological Diversity, "National Biodiversity Strategies and Action Plans (NBSAPs)" (CBD.int) www.cbd.int/nbsap/ accessed January 15, 2023.

60 Convention on Biological Diversity, "Implementation of Strategic Plan for Biodiversity 2011–2020, including the Aichi Biodiversity Targets" (CBD.int) www.cbd.int/sp/implementation/ accessed January 16, 2023.

61 Convention on Biological Diversity, "Strategic Plan Indicators" (CBD.int) www.cbd.int/sp/indicators/ accessed January 16, 2023.

62 Convention on Biological Diversity, "Actions to Enhance Implementation of the Strategic Plan for Biodiversity 2011–2020" (CBD.int) www.cbd.int/sp/actions.shtml accessed January 16, 2023.

63 Convention on Biological Diversity, "Mechanisms for Implementation" (CBD.int) www.cbd.int/mechanisms/ accessed January 16, 2023.

64 Secretariat of the Convention on Biological Diversity (n 17) 10; see also IUCN, "Post-2020 Global Biodiversity Framework" (IUCN.org, November 2022) www.iucn.org/resources/issues-brief/post-2020-global-biodiversity-framework accessed January 16, 2023.

65 Secretariat of the Convention on Biological Diversity (n 17) 35–37.

as a policy instrument, and has commenced implementing an effective, participatory and updated national biodiversity strategy and action plan."[66] This is one of the few Aichi targets that was partially achieved by 2020. NBSAPs are integral to national biodiversity planning in that they provide a roadmap on how parties will fulfill the CBD's objectives and the corresponding steps to be taken.[67]

Overall, 99 percent of CBD parties have developed at least one NBSAP,[68] including a majority of the MENA countries. About fourteen of the MENA parties revised or updated their NBSAPs following the inception of the 2011–2020 Strategic Plan.[69] However, of the fourteen, only the United Arab Emirates and Jordan had prepared or updated their NBSAP by the December 2015 cut-off date. Morocco, Tunisia, and Turkey have submitted three versions of their NBSAPs so far.[70] Israel, Oman, Syrian Arabic Republic, and Saudi Arabia all submitted their last NBSAP prior to the Strategic Plan in 2010, 2004, 2006, and 2008, respectively.[71] From the CBD's repository, Libya and Palestine do not appear to have submitted any pre- or post-2011 NBSAPs, at the time of writing this chapter (Table 2.1).[72]

Notably, the number of parties that have adopted their NBSAPs as policy instruments is limited.[73] While the development of the NBSAPs reflects positive efforts toward achieving the objectives of the CBD, the delay between adoption of the Strategic Plan and the NBSAPs may have slowed down actions to achieve Aichi targets.[74]

It is a challenge to provide a neat analysis of the NBSAPs given that parties adopt different national targets and apply national indicators in an uneven way that may not correspond to the global targets.[75] Nonetheless, it is worth noting that, unlike the first generation of NBSAPs, several of the revised/updated NBSAPs were developed through a consultative process. This is shown, for instance, in the Bahrain 2016–2021 NBSAP, where the NBSAP project team engaged national stakeholders from the public and private sectors, academia, research institutions, civil society, and

66 Conference of the parties to the Convention on Biological Diversity (10th meeting) (n 55) Annex para 13.

67 Convention on Biological Diversity, "Latest NBSAPs" (CBD.int) www.cbd.int/nbsap/ accessed January 16, 2023.

68 Convention on Biological Diversity, "What Is an NBSAP?" (CBD.int) www.cbd.int/nbsap/introduction.shtml accessed January 16, 2023.

69 Convention on Biological Diversity, "Strategic Plan for Biodiversity 2011–2020, including Aichi Biodiversity Targets" (CBD.int) www.cbd.int/sp/ accessed January 15, 2023 (according to the record at this date).

70 Turkey's 2018–2028 NBSAP is an addendum to its 2007–2017 NBSAP, which remains in place.

71 This is based on the information provided on the CBD website at the time of writing the chapter. Convention on Biological Diversity, "National Reports and NBSAPs" (CBD.int) www.cbd.int/reports/search/?country=bh accessed January 16, 2023.

72 Ibid.

73 Secretariat of the Convention on Biological Diversity (n 17) 16.

74 Ibid., 110.

75 Ibid., 32.

TABLE 2.1 *MENA countries that have submitted post-2011 NBSAPs*

Item no.	Country	NBSAP	Date of submission/ publication (2011–2022)
1	Algeria	Version 2 (2016–2030)	November 23, 2016
2	Bahrain	Version 2 (2016–2021)	July 14, 2016
3	Djibouti	Version 2 (2014–2017)	May 21, 2017
4	Egypt	Version 2 (2015–2030)	April 25, 2016
5	Iran	Version 2 (2016–2030)	November 24, 2016
6	Iraq	Initial (2015–2020)	February 3, 2016
7	Jordan	Version 2 (2015–2020)	March 17, 2015
8	Kuwait	Version 2 (2011–2020)	January 9, 2019
9	Lebanon	Version 2 (2016–2030)	June 3, 2016
10	Morocco	Version 3 (2016–2020)	July 13, 2016
11	Qatar	Version 2 (2015–2025)	April 20, 2016
12	Tunisia	Version 3 (2018–2030)	December 22, 2017
13	United Arab Emirates	Version 1 (2014–2020)	October 28, 2014
14	Yemen	Version 2 (2015–2025)	November 6, 2017
15	Turkey	Version 3 (2018–2028)	April 16, 2019

Source: Secretariat of the Convention on Biological Diversity, *Global Biodiversity Outlook 5* (Secretariat of the Convention on Biological Diversity 2020) 32.

media, through consultative workshops, focus group discussions, and one-on-one sessions.[76] Other countries that took a similar approach include Egypt (2015–2030 NBSAP), which set up a National Biodiversity Committee of stakeholders, supported by national and international consultants, and informed by stakeholder consultations.[77] In Djibouti, the NBSAP was developed in consideration of Vision Djibouti 2035, which recommends that populations should be consulted and participate in policy processes.[78] For Iraq, stakeholders were consulted, including the State Ministry for Women's Affairs, Ministry of Oil, Ministry of Planning, provincial councils, media and communications agencies, private sector, celebrities, indigenous and local communities, and religious leaders.[79] Looking ahead, the Jordan 2015–2020 NBSAP prioritizes a national consultation process for the review of the next iteration of the NBSAP.[80]

[76] Kingdom of Bahrain, "The National Biodiversity Strategy and Action Plan 2016 2021" (February 2016) www.cbd.int/doc/world/bh/bh-nbsap-v2-en.pdf accessed January 16, 2023, 2.

[77] Arab Republic of Egypt, "Egyptian Biodiversity Strategy and Action Plan 2015–2030" (January 2016) www.cbd.int/doc/world/eg/eg-nbsap-v2-en.pdf accessed January 16, 2023, 7 and 56.

[78] Republic of Djibouti, "Stratégie et programme d'action nationaux pour la biodiversité" (March 2017) www.cbd.int/doc/world/dj/dj-nbsap-v2-fr.pdf accessed January 16, 2023, 12.

[79] Republic of Iraq, "Iraq's National Biodiversity Strategy and Action Plan 2015–2020" (April 2015) www.cbd.int/doc/world/iq/iq-nbsap-01-en.pdf accessed January 16, 2023, 42.

[80] Jordan, "The National Biodiversity Strategy and Action Plan 2015–2020" (March 2017) www.cbd.int/doc/world/jo/jo-nbsap-v2-en.pdf accessed January 16, 2023, 60.

This consultative aspect is closely complemented by a whole-of-government approach adopted by about sixty-nine NBSAPs globally, including within the MENA region. For instance, in Algeria, about ten sectors, such as transportation, public works, education, and fisheries, have prepared biodiversity action plans.[81] The country's 2016–2030 NBSAP encourages the integration of biodiversity into sectoral action plans and local policies.[82]

The MENA parties have adopted diverse national goals and targets within their NBSAPs. Most of the goals are aligned to the goals under the global Strategic Plan. From a sample of the NBSAPs, one major area that has been prioritized by the countries is good governance and the mainstreaming of biodiversity into national and sectoral planning and the wider society.[83] Another emerging theme is that of prevention through goals to minimize anthropogenic pressures on biodiversity, conserve terrestrial aquatic and coastal ecosystems, and promote sustainable use of natural resources.[84] As such, several parties aim to establish or enhance protected areas, safeguard ecosystem services, and protect priority species and genetic resources.[85] Others, such as Jordan, Tunisia, Egypt, and Djibouti, recognize the linkages between protecting biodiversity and addressing climate change through goals on enhancing climate resilience and adaptation, among others.

[81] The Algerian NBSAP indicates that the action plans were undergoing approvals at the time of drafting the NBSAP.

[82] Algeria, "Stratégie et plan d'action nationaux pour la biodiversité 2016–2030" (November 2016 [date of submission]) www.cbd.int/doc/world/dz/dz-nbsap-v2-fr.pdf accessed January 16, 2023.

[83] Examples include Kingdom of Morocco, "Stratégie et Plan d'Actions National pour la Diversité Biologique du Maroc, 2016–2020" (July 2016 (date of submission)) www.cbd.int/doc/world/ma/ma-nbsap-v3-fr.pdf accessed January 16, 2023; Jordan, "The National Biodiversity Strategy and Action Plan 2015–2020" (March 2017 [date of submission]) www.cbd.int/doc/world/jo/jo-nbsap-v2-en.pdf accessed January 16, 2023; Kingdom of Bahrain, "The National Biodiversity Strategy and Action Plan 2016 2021" (February 2016) www.cbd.int/doc/world/bh/bh-nbsap-v2-en.pdf accessed January 16, 2023. (This list is not exhaustive and is based on a sample.)

[84] See for instance Jordan, "The National Biodiversity Strategy and Action Plan 2015–2020" (March 2017 [date of submission]) www.cbd.int/doc/world/jo/jo-nbsap-v2-en.pdf accessed January 16, 2023; Republic of Yemen, "National Biodiversity Strategy and Action Plan II 'Achieving a Resilient, Productive and Sustainable Socio-ecosystem by 2050'" (November 2017 [date of submission]) www.cbd.int/doc/world/ye/ye-nbsap-v2-en.pdf accessed January 16, 2023; Kingdom of Bahrain, "The National Biodiversity Strategy and Action Plan 2016 2021" (February 2016) www.cbd.int/doc/world/bh/bh-nbsap-v2-en.pdf accessed January 16, 2023; Tunisia Republic, "Actualisation de la stratégie nationale et du plan d'action nationaux sur la biodiversité" (November 2017) www.cbd.int/doc/world/tn/tn-nbsap-v3-fr.pdf accessed January 16, 2023; Islamic Republic of Iran, "Revised National Biodiversity Strategies and Action Plan (NBSAP2 2016–2030)" (November 2016 [date of submission]) www.cbd.int/doc/world/ir/ir-nbsap-v2-en.pdf accessed January 16, 2023. (This list is not exhaustive and is based on a sample.)

[85] For instance, see Jordan, "The National Biodiversity Strategy and Action Plan 2015–2020" (March 2017 [date of submission]) www.cbd.int/doc/world/jo/jo-nbsap-v2-en.pdf accessed January 16, 2023; Arab Republic of Egypt, "Egyptian Biodiversity Strategy and Action Plan 2015–2030" (January 2016) www.cbd.int/doc/world/eg/eg-nbsap-v2-en.pdf accessed January 16, 2023; Qatar, "Qatar National Biodiversity Strategy and Action Plan 2015–2015" (April 2020) www.cbd.int/doc/world/qa/qa-nbsap-v2-en.pdf accessed January 16, 2023. (This list is not exhaustive and is based on a sample.)

Moreover, the sampled MENA countries give prominence to enhanced awareness, knowledge, and understanding of biodiversity by different facets of society, including through capacity-building initiatives, communication outreach, bridging gaps between scientists, citizens, and decision-makers, and developing traditional knowledge.[86] Some countries, such as Tunisia, Yemen, and Morocco, have mainstreamed gender considerations into their NBSAPs, recognized women, rural communities, and indigenous peoples as guardians of nature, and encouraged their participation in national biodiversity planning. Lastly, several NBSAPs highlight enhancing monitoring and reporting of implementation as a strategic goal.

The broad strategic goals or prioritization areas are complemented by the national targets, and the envisaged implementation measures toward these targets are enumerated in the NBSAPs.[87] Such measures include resource mobilization strategies, establishment of stakeholder and governmental coordination committees, stakeholder engagement and partnership building, capacity-building initiatives, research studies, development of local and regional biodiversity plans, media and communication campaigns, and development of legislation. The common anticipated challenges included limited resources to implement the NBSAPs, lack of proper indicators to measure use of the NBSAPs as policy instruments,[88] and limited biodiversity expertise and scientific knowledge.

The progress of implementation of the NBSAPs is further explored in the latest, sixth round of national reports.

2.3.1.2 National Reports

Article 26 of the CBD calls for parties to report measures taken for implementation of the CBD and their effectiveness in meeting the CBD's objectives.[89] Many of the MENA parties to the CBD have adhered to Article 26 by submitting their latest round of reports, the sixth national reports. From the CBD repository, Bahrain,

86 See e.g. Republic of Iraq, "Iraq's National Biodiversity Strategy and Action Plan 2015–2020" (April 2015) www.cbd.int/doc/world/iq/iq-nbsap-01-en.pdf accessed January 16, 2023; Islamic Republic of Iran, "Revised National Biodiversity Strategies and Action Plan (NBSAP2 2016–2030)" (November 2016 [date of submission]) www.cbd.int/doc/world/ir/ir-nbsap-v2-en.pdf accessed January 16, 2023; Qatar, "Qatar National Biodiversity Strategy and Action Plan 2015–2015" (April 2020) www.cbd.int/doc/world/qa/qa-nbsap-v2-en.pdf accessed January 16, 2023; Tunisia Republic, "Actualisation de la stratégie nationale et du plan d'action nationaux sur la biodiversité" (November 2017) www.cbd.int/doc/world/tn/tn-nbsap-v3-fr.pdf accessed January 16, 2023; Kingdom of Bahrain, "The National Biodiversity Strategy and Action Plan 2016 2021" (February 2016) www.cbd.int/doc/world/bh/bh-nbsap-v2-en.pdf accessed January 16, 2023, etc.

87 For a quick search of the targets, see Convention on Biological Diversity, "Online Reporting Search" (CHM.CBD.int) chm.cbd.int/search/reporting-map?filter=nationalTarget accessed January 16, 2023.

88 Secretariat of the Convention on Biological Diversity (n 17).

89 Convention on Biological Diversity, "What Is an NBSAP?" (CBD.int) www.cbd.int/nbsap/introduction.shtml accessed January 16, 2023.

TABLE 2.2 *MENA countries that have submitted national reports for the sixth reporting cycle*

Item no.	Country	Sixth national report	Year of submission
1	Algeria	Report	2018
2	Bahrain	Not available	Not available
3	Djibouti	Report	2019
4	Egypt	Report	2019
5	Iran	Report	2020
6	Israel	Report	2020
7	Jordan	Report	2019
8	Kuwait	Report	2020
9	Lebanon	Report	2019
10	Libya	Not available	Not available
11	Morocco	Report	2018
12	Oman	Report	Not available
13	Qatar	Report	2019
14	Syria	Not available	Not available
15	Tunisia	Report	2019
16	United Arab Emirates	Report	2019
17	Yemen	Report	2019
18	Iraq	Report	2018
19	Saudi Arabia	Report	2019
20	Turkey	Not available	Not available
21	Palestine	Not available	Not available

Source: Authors.

Libya, Palestine, Turkey, and Syria had not submitted their sixth national reports by the time of writing this chapter (Table 2.2).[90]

A random sampling of four national reports (Iraq, Egypt, Yemen, and Jordan) suggests that there is a breadth of national targets and corresponding activities carried out in the region. The following subsections provide a summary of some of the key matters reported.[91]

LEGISLATIVE ASPECTS During the reporting period, the sampled MENA countries put in place legislative measures to implement the national biodiversity targets. For instance, Iraq changed its forestry laws, introduced legislation for the control and dispersal of nonnative species, and drafted a decree to establish protected areas.[92] The country also took steps to assess the effectiveness of existing laws and to

[90] Convention on Biological Diversity, "National Reports" (CBD.int) www.cbd.int/reports/ accessed January 16, 2023.

[91] Disclaimer: As the reports are from several years back, the situation may have changed.

[92] Iraq, sixth national report of Iraq to the Convention on Biological Diversity (December 2018) www.cbd.int/doc/nr/nr-06/iq-nr-06-en.pdf accessed January 19, 2023, 38 and 67–68.

determine legal gaps with the aim of developing relevant environmental standards.[93] Similarly, Egypt either amended or drafted new laws dealing with matters such as protected areas, fisheries, and waste management,[94] while Jordan developed a new environmental protection law, among others.[95] Some gaps were also identified, for example, the lack of a law on access to genetic resources and on traditional knowledge in Jordan and the absence of a regulatory framework on safe distribution and use of pesticides in Yemen.[96]

Nonetheless, the countries faced challenges regarding legislative processes. A recurring challenge was the delay occasioned by different arms of government involved in the process, particularly parliament, and the lack of prioritization of biodiversity legislation. Other specific obstacles included inadequate legal capacity and experience in drafting legislation for the conservation of threatened species or biodiversity-related pollution,[97] and limited awareness of the importance of forest biodiversity by communities among others.[98] The countries are also grappling with weak enforcement of the existing and newly enacted or amended laws.

INSTITUTIONAL ASPECTS Effective institutions are necessary for the implementation and enforcement of legislation and policies.[99] Four MENA countries have active ministries and regulatory authorities that advocated for biodiversity considerations. The countries also put in place various committees or working groups either at the governmental or sectoral levels. In Iraq, there was a committee of ministries to develop the laws on protected areas. In Egypt, a national committee was established to implement the Egypt Initiative, an initiative tasked with rolling out a coherent approach for addressing biodiversity loss, climate change, and land ecosystem degradation. The countries were also keen on improving the institutional landscape: For example, Jordan carried out a review of the roles and capacities organizations working on genetic resources. Further, there were initiatives established to encourage partnerships with nonstate actors within the conservation space.

The reports indicated poor coordination within different sectors of government and among relevant stakeholders. The response rate and engagement of

93 Iraq, sixth national report of Iraq to the Convention on Biological Diversity (December 2018) www.cbd.int/doc/nr/nr-06/iq-nr-06-en.pdf accessed January 19, 2023, 72.

94 Egypt, Sixth National Report (June 30, 2019) https://chm.cbd.int/database/record?documentID=246662 accessed January 19, 2023.

95 Jordan, Sixth National Report (April 9, 2019) https://chm.cbd.int/database/record?documentID=243506 accessed January 19, 2023, 6.

96 Yemen, Yemen Sixth National Report to Convention on Biological Diversity (CBD) (March 2019) accessed January 19, 2023, 20.

97 For example, see Iraq, sixth national report of Iraq to the Convention on Biological Diversity (December 2018) www.cbd.int/doc/nr/nr-06/iq-nr-06-en.pdf accessed January 19, 2023, 73.

98 Iraq, sixth national report of Iraq to the Convention on Biological Diversity (December 2018) www.cbd.int/doc/nr/nr-06/iq-nr-06-en.pdf accessed January 19, 2023, 68.

99 Damilola Olawuyi, *Environmental Law in Arab States* (Oxford University Press 2022) 55–83.

governmental entities was also a challenge in gathering important data and developing policies and laws, for instance. The lack of interest by decision-makers in policy coherence was another obstacle. Additionally, the security situation in some of the countries also adversely affected governmental operations.

TECHNICAL ASPECTS All the countries presented technical needs that slowed their biodiversity action. Largely, limited awareness and understanding of biodiversity across government, communities, and relevant stakeholders was a recurring theme. A selection of the identified areas of support includes fundraising and proposal writing, biodiversity awareness campaigns, capacity building for legal drafters, capacity building for youth, women, rural communities, indigenous peoples, and other vulnerable communities, development of knowledge-based platforms and means for recording traditional knowledge, and biodiversity needs assessments.

FINANCIAL ASPECTS All the reports indicated limited financial resources as a major impediment to implementation of their NBSAPs. Yemen reported insufficient government funding coupled with low level of Official Development Assistance from international sources and a lack of partnerships with the private sector, nongovernmental organizations, and local communities in the management of biodiversity resources.[100] In instances where finances were available, for example, for some targets in Jordan, late disbursement delayed the NBSAP's activities.[101] Overall, nearly all activities were contingent on financial support, which implied a delay in or lack of implementation if no such support was forthcoming.

Although the findings here are indicative based on four countries, they illustrate common challenges in the region relating to a lack of policy coordination, dependence on funding, and lack of awareness in appreciating the value of the measures required. Globally, countries have recently adopted the Kunming-Montreal GBF to address these and other implementation shortcomings. This framework is addressed in Section 2.4.

2.4 PROMOTING COHERENCE: REFLECTIONS ON THE WAY FORWARD

2.4.1 *Kunming-Montreal GBF*

Evidently, the Strategic Plan for Biodiversity 2011–2020, including the Aichi targets, did not achieve the level of success that was intended. There was a need for a successor framework that would bring about the required transformational change for reduction of biodiversity loss. During the 14th Conference of Parties (COP14) in

[100] Yemen, Sixth National Report to Convention on Biological Diversity (CBD) (March 2019) accessed January 19, 2023, 20.

[101] Jordan, Sixth National Report (April 9, 2019) https://chm.cbd.int/database/record?documentID=243506 accessed January 19, 2023, 74.

2018, the CBD parties agreed to develop a post-2020 GBF.[102] The GBF would be prepared through a comprehensive, consultative, and participatory process based on a set of agreed principles (participatory, inclusive, gender responsive, transformative, comprehensive, catalytic, visible, knowledge-based, transparent, efficient, results-oriented, iterative, and flexible).[103] Numerous opinions and suggestions were provided on the best way to craft a suitable and effective GBF, with a common desire being the need for the GBF to focus on implementation and to have an enhanced monitoring and review process.[104]

During COP15, CBD parties adopted a package of six decisions on the post-2020 GBF,[105] its monitoring framework, resource mobilization, digital sequence information, capacity building, and mechanisms for planning, monitoring, reporting, and review.[106] The GBF is now the overarching global strategy and roadmap toward the previous 2011–2020 Strategic Plan's vision of living in harmony with nature.[107] It builds on the achievements, gaps, and lessons learned from the Strategic Plan and is to be used as the plan for the implementation of the CBD and its protocols, its bodies, and its secretariat over the period 2022–2030.[108] The GBF embodies a whole-of-society and whole-of-government approach, with many subnational governments, cities, and local authorities having pledged their support through a declaration called "the Edinburgh Declaration."[109]

The GBF's four long-term goals on safeguarding and restoring all ecosystems, sustainably using and managing nature's resources, fair and equitable sharing of monetary and nonmonetary benefits from the utilization of genetic resources and digital sequence information on genetic resources, and equitable access to adequate means of implementation, including closing the annual biodiversity

[102] Conference of the parties to the Convention on Biological Diversity (14th meeting) "Comprehensive and Participatory Process for the Preparation of the Post-2020 Global Biodiversity Framework" (November 30, 2018) UN Doc CBD/COP/DEC/14/34.

[103] Convention on Biological Diversity, "Preparations for the Post-2020 Biodiversity Framework" (CBD.int) www.cbd.int/conferences/post2020 accessed on January 17, 2023; Preparation for the Post-2020 Global Biodiversity Framework, "Post-2020 Global Biodiversity Framework; discussion paper" (January 25, 2019) UN Doc CBD/POST2020/PREP/1/1, para 3.

[104] Convention on Biological Diversity, "Thematic Consultation on Transparent Implementation Monitoring Review and Reporting" (CBD.int) www.cbd.int/convention/mechanisms/thematic-consultation.shtml accessed January 17, 2023.

[105] Conference of the parties to the Convention on Biological Diversity (15th meeting, Part II) "Kunming-Montreal Global Biodiversity Framework" (December 19, 2022) CBD/COP/DEC/15/4.

[106] Ibid., para 2.

[107] Convention on Biological Diversity, "X/2. Strategic Plan for Biodiversity 2011–2020" (CBD.int) www.cbd.int/decision/cop/?id=12268 accessed January 17, 2023.

[108] Conference of the parties to the Convention on Biological Diversity (n 106) paras 3 and 8.

[109] Subnational governments, cities, and local authorities on the post-2020 global biodiversity framework, "Edinburg Declaration" (August 31, 2020); IUCN, "Post-2020 Global Biodiversity Framework Emphasizes 'All-Hands-on-Deck' Approach" (Crossroads blog, September 5, 2021) www.iucn.org/crossroads-blog/202109/post-2020-global-biodiversity-framework-emphasises-all-hands-deck-approach accessed January 12, 2023.

finance gap of US$700 billion, are to be achieved by 2050 in alignment with the 2050 vision for biodiversity.[110]

The four goals are to be fulfilled through the attainment of twenty-three targets by 2030.[111] The targets cover a variety of issues and appear to have more quantitative markers than the previous targets. One of the GBF's main highlights is the agreement to protect 30 percent of terrestrial, inland water, and coastal and marine ecosystems by 2030 as encapsulated in Targets 2 and 3, respectively. The 30 percent is up from the 17 percent of terrestrial and inland water and 10 percent of coastal and marine areas provided for in the 2011–2020 plan. While this seems like a promising start, some stakeholders have decried the lack of ambition and the vague wording of some of the provisions, which would likely contribute to ineffective implementation.[112]

Notably, the GBF's provisions on biodiversity-related pollution and climate change are more pronounced in scope, with specific measures to be taken such as working toward eliminating plastic pollution and adopting nature-based solutions, respectively. The framework is also relatively stronger and more active on the integration of gender considerations, having not only mainstreamed gender, for example, in Target 22 on inclusion and participation, but also dedicated a whole target, Target 23, to a demand of gender equality in its implementation.

Further, the obligations imposed on states in relation to businesses, particularly multinational corporations and financial institutions, are fairly elaborate, including requirements for measures to enable assessment and disclosure of biodiversity risks, to provide relevant consumer information, and to report on compliance.[113] Another notable target is Target 18, which unlike in the predecessor Strategic Plan,[114] quantifies the amount of harmful subsidies to be reduced by 2030 to US$500 billion per year. Other noteworthy matters covered by the targets include halting extinction of species, ensuring sustainable trade of wild species, minimizing biodiversity-related pollution risks, mitigating climate change, and building capacities for implementation.

Implementation of the GBF will benefit from support mechanisms and strategies existing under the CBD.[115] Adequate financial resources, effective capacity building, transfer of technologies, cooperation, and collaboration will provide an enabling environment for the framework's implementation.[116] As the CBD parties agreed at COP15, the framework's implementation would be mutually reinforced through implementation of the COP's decisions on the: monitoring framework for the GBF;

110 Conference of the parties to the Convention on Biological Diversity (n 106) Annex para 30.
111 Ibid., Annex para 31
112 See for instance India Stephenson, "BES Response to the New Post-2020 Global Biodiversity Framework" (British Ecological Society, December 19, 2022) www.britishecologicalsociety.org/bes-response-to-the-new-post-2020-global-biodiversity-framework/ January 16, 2023.
113 Conference of the parties to the Convention on Biological Diversity (n 106) Annex para 31, target 15.
114 Ibid., Annex para 13, target 3.
115 Ibid., Annex para 32.
116 Ibid., Annex para 33.

planning, monitoring, reporting, and review; resource mobilization; long-term strategic framework for capacity building and development to support nationally determined priorities for the implementation of the GBF; digital sequence information on genetic resources; and cooperation.[117] These decisions enjoy an equal status to that of the GBF.

In terms of tools for implementation, the post-2020 GBF takes cognizance of the importance of legislative action in achieving the targets. In at least two targets, 13 and 15, the GBF requires parties to put in place effective legal measures to respectively ensure the fair and equitable sharing of, among other things, benefits arising from utilization of genetic resources, and to encourage and enable businesses to take an active role in progressively reducing negative impacts on biodiversity and promote sustainable use of resources.

Notably, NBSAPs remain the main vehicle for the implementation of the post-2020 GBF and parties have been called upon to revise or update their NBSAPs accordingly.[118] To foster effective implementation of MEAs within MENA, there is a need for the coordinated and coherent implementation of the applicable biodiversity MEAs. This should be coupled with improved approaches for implementation, most of which are encompassed in the Kunming-Montreal post-2020 GBF. The following subsections include some areas for consideration.

2.4.1.1 Contribution and Rights of Indigenous Peoples and Local Communities

The GBO5 identifies a need to further integrate the role of indigenous peoples and local communities into biodiversity planning and implementation.[119] Indigenous peoples own, manage, or occupy at least a quarter of the world's land.[120] Together with local communities, they have a wealth of traditional knowledge and customary practices on conservation and sustainable use of natural resources. The framework's reference to these two groups is a result of deliberate efforts at the international level to ensure that their long-standing contribution to safeguarding biodiversity is recognized. Their consideration was a prevalent theme in stakeholders' submissions to the GBF development process.[121] In fact, one of the working groups, WG8J-11, focused on examining the role of collective actions of indigenous peoples and local communities to the GBF.[122]

117 Conference of the parties to the Convention on Biological Diversity (n 106) para 2 and Annex para 32.
118 Ibid., Annex para 34(a).
119 Secretariat of the Convention on Biological Diversity (n 17) 11.
120 P. Bates and P. Trakansuphakon, "Indigenous Peoples: Informed Custodians of Biodiversity" (UNESCO Courier 2021) https://en.unesco.org/courier/2021-3/indigenous-peoples-informed-custodians-biodiversity accessed January 17, 2023.
121 Preparation for the Post-2020 Global Biodiversity Framework, "Post-2020 Global Biodiversity Framework; Discussion Paper" (January 25, 2019) UN Doc CBD/POST2020/PREP/1/1, para 9(m).
122 Ibid., para 5(a).

The GBF cements the position of indigenous peoples and local communities as guardians of biodiversity and as partners in its conservation, restoration, and sustainable use.[123] The framework requires parties, including MENA parties, to ensure that the "rights, knowledge, including traditional knowledge, innovations, world views, values and practices of indigenous peoples and local communities are respected, documented, preserved with their free, prior informed consent."[124]

The concept of *prior informed consent* is a significant addition to the framework. It is associated with treaty norms such as under the UN Declaration on the Rights to of Indigenous Peoples,[125] and the Indigenous and Tribal Peoples Convention by the International Labour Organization (ILO),[126] and is also embodied in the CBD itself, which subjects access to genetic resources to prior informed consent,[127] as well as conventions such as the Basel[128] and Rotterdam[129] Conventions. The concept is also connected to the enjoyment of rights, primarily access to information and the right of public participation in environmental decision-making.

In other regions, namely Europe, the Biodiversity Strategy for 2030 calls for respect of the rights of, and the full and effective participation of, indigenous peoples and local communities.[130] The European Union has also called on its member states to ratify the ILO Convention on Indigenous and Tribal Peoples.

2.4.1.2 A Human Rights-Based Approach

The right to a clean, healthy, and sustainable environment is universally recognized through a 2022 UN General Assembly resolution that was supported by several MENA countries, led by Morocco.[131] About eighty-eight countries globally, including Algeria, Egypt, Morocco, Palestine, Iraq, Turkey, and Tunisia have already enshrined a

123 Conference of the parties to the Convention on Biological Diversity (n 106) Annex para 8.

124 Ibid., Annex para 8.

125 For a full definition see United Nations Declaration on the rights of indigenous people (adopted October 2, 2007) UNGA Res 61/295 (UNDRIP) art 19.

126 Convention (No. 169) concerning indigenous and tribal peoples in independent countries (adopted June 27, 1989) 1650 UNTS (Indigenous and Tribal Peoples Convention).

127 CBD, art 15 (5).

128 Basel Convention on the Control of Transboundary Movements of Hazardous Wastes and Their Disposal (adopted March 22, 1989) 1673 UNTS 57 (Basel Convention).

129 Stockholm Convention on Persistent Organic Pollutants (adopted May 22, 2001) 2256 UNTS 119 (Stockholm Convention).

130 European Commission, "Communication from the Commission to the European Parliament, the Council, the European Economic and Social Committee and the Committee of the Regions, EU Biodiversity Strategy for 2030, Bringing Nature Back into Our Lives" (May 20, 2020), 20 https://eur-lex.europa.eu/resource.html?uri=cellar:a3c806a6-9ab3-11ea-9d2d-01aa75ed71a1.0001.02/DOC_1&format=PDF accessed January 17, 2024, 20.

131 UNGA "The Human Right to a Clean, Healthy and Sustainable Environment" (July 26, 2022) UN Doc A/76/L.75 following the Human Rights Council (HRC) "The Human Right to a Clean, Healthy and Sustainable Environment" (October 18, 2021) UN Doc A/HRC/RES/48/13.

variation of this right into their constitutions.[132] The right is related to other substantive rights, such as the right to life, right to water, right to culture, and right to a private family life, as well as procedural rights, such as the rights of access to information, public participation, access to justice, and nondiscrimination,[133] most of which are captured under the Universal Declaration on Human Rights,[134] and treaties such as the International Covenant on Civil and Political Rights.[135] Overall, environmental rights contribute to environmental rule of law as they provide a framework for enforcing laws and providing redress, especially for vulnerable populations.

While there are differing views on what a human rights-based approach means for biodiversity, especially in regard to conservation, the Office of the United Nations High Commissioner for Human Rights (OHCHR) describes it as an approach that promotes respect, protection, promotion, and fulfillment of the full range of human rights and emphasizes the obligation of duty bearers to fulfill their human rights obligations.[136] The full implementation of MEAs such as the CBD is a prerequisite for the right to a clean, healthy, and sustainable environment.[137] Practically, biodiversity plans, policies, and processes should be anchored in a system of rights and corresponding obligations where all persons are empowered to claim their rights.[138]

MENA countries may integrate human rights in the update and implementation of their NBSAPs. OHCHR provides guidance on how to do this through a 2022 brief that provides a step-by-step human rights lens on NBSAPs development, content, and implementation processes.[139] The brief encourages a participatory, bottom-up, consensus building in the NBSAP development phase, mainstreaming of international and domestic human rights obligations into the NBSAP content,

[132] An additional 62 countries have enshrined environmental protection in their constitutions in some form – a total of 150 countries from all over the globe now have constitutional rights and/or provisions on the environment. This is the estimate according to UNEP, *Environmental Rule of Law: First Global Report* (UNEP 2019) 2. The number may have changed since then.

[133] Human Rights Council (HRC) "The Human Right to a Clean, Healthy and Sustainable Environment" (October 18, 2021) UN Doc A/HRC/RES/48/13, 1–2.

[134] Universal Declaration of Human Rights (adopted December 10, 1948) UNGA Res 217 A(III) (UDHR) Art 5.

[135] International Covenant on Civil and Political Rights (adopted December 16, 1966) 999 UNTS 171 (ICCPR).

[136] United Nations Office of the High Commissioner for Human Rights, "Integrating Human Rights in National Biodiversity Strategies and Action Plans" (March 2022) www.ohchr.org/sites/default/files/2022-03/Integrating-Human-Rights-in-NBSAP.docx accessed January 19, 2023, 8.

[137] UNGA, "The Human Right to a Clean, Healthy and Sustainable Environment" (July 26, 2022) UN Doc A/76/L.75, 3.

[138] United Nations Office of the High Commissioner for Human Rights draft, "Integrating Human Rights in National Biodiversity Strategies and Action Plans" (March 2022) www.ohchr.org/sites/default/files/2022-03/Integrating-Human-Rights-in-NBSAP.docx accessed January 19, 2023, 9.

[139] United Nations Office of the High Commissioner for Human Rights draft "Integrating Human Rights in National Biodiversity Strategies and Action Plans" (March 2022) www.ohchr.org/sites/default/files/2022-03/Integrating-Human-Rights-in-NBSAP.docx accessed January 19, 2023.

and safeguarding of human rights procedural and substantive elements in NBSAP implementation. Another area that MENA countries could explore is the emerging notion of nature rights where distinct biodiversity elements are assigned rights as though they were living beings.[140]

2.4.1.3 Consistency with International Agreements or Instruments

Article 22 of the CBD suggests consistency with other international conventions to the extent that such conventions do not cross purposes with the objectives of the CBD. The article further requires the parties to implement the CBD in line with the rights and obligations under the law of sea in regard to the marine environment.

Parties to the CBD hold value in promoting synergies between relevant conventions, particularly biodiversity-related conventions. Through a process known as the Bern process, UNEP fosters the engagement of other MEAs in the advancement of the GBF.[141] In the lead-up to the post-2020 GBF, and based on a request by CBD parties, a workshop was organized among the parties of biodiversity-related conventions to assess their contribution to the framework.[142] In fact, in the decision 15/13 on cooperation, the CBD COP invited the governing bodies of the other conventions to endorse the framework and support its operationalization. Among the numerous international and regional biodiversity-related conventions applicable in the MENA region, CITES is a good example of a convention that aims to synergize with the CBD. The CITES Strategic Vision 2008–2020 was mapped against the Aichi Targets in the 2011–2020 Strategic Plan for Biodiversity,[143] and now CITES COP19 has adopted a decision to strengthen cooperation, collaboration, and synergies at all relevant levels between CITES and the GBF.[144] Other MEAs have also taken similar steps: For example, the Ramsar Convention in COP

[140] IPBES, "Policy Instrument – Rights of Nature" www.ipbes.net/policy-support/tools-instruments/rights-nature-ron accessed November 8, 2023.

[141] The Bern III Conference took place from on January 23–25, 2024, with the objective to contribute to the efficient and effective implementation of GBF by identifying opportunities to drive and coordinate an inclusive collaborative approach towards implementation of the framework while respecting the respective mandates of biodiversity-related conventions and other relevant multilateral agreements and United Nations. www.unep.org/events/conference/bern-iii-conference-cooperation-among-biodiversity-related-conventions.

[142] Conference of the parties to the Convention on Biological Diversity (14th meeting) "Comprehensive and Participatory Process for the Preparation of the Post-2020 Global Biodiversity Framework" (November 30, 2018) UN Doc CBD/COP/DEC/14/34, para 12.

[143] CITES, "CITES Strategic Vision" (CITES.org) https://cites.org/eng/documents/Strategic_vision accessed January 19, 2023.

[144] CITES, "SG's Statement on Cooperation at CBD CoP15" (CITES.org) https://cites.org/eng/news/sg/sgs-statement-on-cooperation-at-cbd-cop15 accessed January 19, 2023.

Resolution XIV/26,[145] CMS COP Decision 13.4,[146] and the Decision 44 COM 7.2 of the World Heritage Committee.[147]

Paragraph 24 of the GBF envisages collaboration, cooperation, and synergies with other MEAs as well as international organizations and processes. Given the interlinkages between the triple planetary crises, it is important for MENA countries implementing the GBF to align to climate commitments and pollution- and waste-related processes. To provide an example of such alignment, two-thirds of nationally determined contributions under the Paris Agreement refer to nature-based solutions.[148]

Additionally, MENA parties should be conscious of relevant ongoing processes such as the development of a legally binding instrument on plastic pollution, including in the marine environment,[149] and the recent establishment of a treaty on high seas.[150]

2.4.1.4 Science–Policy Interface

Effective policies to combat biodiversity loss must be based on the best available knowledge.[151] This is why the GBF requires that it is implemented based on "transformative, innovative and transdisciplinary education, formal and informal, at all levels, including science–policy interface studies and lifelong learning processes, recognizing diverse world views, values and knowledge systems of indigenous peoples and local communities."[152] The aspect of a science–policy interface is particularly important and was focused on in the lead-up to the GBF through an Ad Hoc Technical Expert Working Group on digital sequence information on genetic

145 "Ramsar Convention" Resolution XIV.6 – Enhancing the Convention's visibility and synergies with other multilateral environmental agreements and other international institutions www.ramsar.org/sites/default/files/documents/library/xiv.6_synergies_e.pdf accessed November 8, 2023.

146 "Decisions 13.4 to 13.5 – Options for a Follow-up to the Strategic Plan for Migratory Species 2015–2023" (CMS) www.cms.int/en/page/decisions-134-135-options-follow-strategic-plan-migratory-species-2015-2023 accessed November 8, 2023.

147 "Decision 44 COM 7.2 – Conservation Issues" (UNESCO) https://whc.unesco.org/en/decisions/7678/ accessed November 8, 2023.

148 IUCN (n 10).

149 UNEP, "Intergovernmental Negotiating Committee (INC) on Plastic Pollution" (UNEP.org) www.unep.org/about-un-environment/inc-plastic-pollution accessed January 19, 2023.

150 UN, "Intergovernmental Conference on an International Legally Binding Instrument under the United Nations Convention on the Law of the Sea on the Conservation and Sustainable Use of Marine Biological Diversity of Areas beyond National Jurisdiction (General Assembly Resolution 72/249)" (UN.org) www.un.org/bbnj/ accessed January 23, 2023, also: www.unep.org/news-and-stories/story/marine-biodiversity-gets-lifeline-high-seas-treaty.

151 N. Wagner, S. Velander, L. Biber-Freudenberger et al., "Effectiveness Factors and Impacts on Policymaking of Science-Policy Interfaces in the Environmental Sustainability Context" (2023) 140 *Environmental Science & Policy* 56.

152 Conference of the parties to the Convention on Biological Diversity (n 106) Annex para 22.

resources.[153] A science–policy interface is beneficial as it's typically coupled with stakeholder consultations, diversity in experts and expertise, and the ability to break down complex issues for policymakers.[154] It is important for MENA countries to heed evidence-backed findings from credible institutions and traditional knowledge at a global and national level.

2.5 CONCLUSION

International law on biodiversity and nature conservation seeks to promote conservation and the sustainable use of biological resources as well as the equitable sharing of their benefits. It is a complex system, mostly weaved together by MEAs. UNEP recognizes this complexity and, as shown in Box 2.1, it has developed a wide range of initiatives aimed at supporting countries across the world and in the MENA region. UNEP's Law Division, particularly, supports the fields of environmental law, governance, and related policy issues, including those related to MEAs. It provides, in close collaboration with the MEA secretariats, technical legal assistance and capacity-building support to countries to develop/strengthen and implement environmental law, and to build capacity of various stakeholders and institutions with respect to the development and implementation of, compliance with, and enforcement of, environmental law, including commitments set out in MEAs.

BOX 2.1 UNEP's Activities Related to Biodiversity and Nature Conservation Law and Policy in the MENA Region[155]

1 ENVIRONMENTAL GOVERNANCE

UNEP promotes sound environmental governance, for example, by helping with the development of National Biodiversity Strategic Action Plans. Under UNEP's Fifth Montevideo Programme for the Development and Periodic Review of Environmental Law (Montevideo Environmental Law Programme), countries can make requests for technical legal support through the Law and Environment Assistance Programme. UNEP also provides law enforcement support through initiatives such as the Green Customs Initiative.

[153] Preparation for the Post-2020 Global Biodiversity Framework, "Post-2020 Global Biodiversity Framework; Discussion Paper" (January 25, 2019) UN Doc CBD/POST2020/PREP/1/1, para 5(b).
[154] Wagner et al. (n 151).
[155] The activities in the box are not exhaustive of all UNEP's activities related to protection of biodiversity.

2 ECOSYSTEMS SUPPORT AND COORDINATION WITH BIODIVERSITY-RELATED CONVENTIONS

UNEP hosts the CBD Secretariat that supports parties to implement the CBD's Program of Work and governing bodies' decisions.[156] The CBD's portfolio encompasses capacity building and knowledge management, monitoring, and review of implementation and policy and governance support, among other things. For instance, the secretariat, together with UNEP and other partners, has developed NBSAP training modules and tools such as the Data Reporting Tool for MEAs.[157] UNEP also works closely with and hosts the secretariats of the Bonn Convention and the CITES and the Intergovernmental Panel on Biodiversity and Ecosystem Services.[158] UNEP also administers the Regional Seas Programme for protection of marine and coastal biodiversity.

3 KNOWLEDGE PLATFORMS

UNEP hosts several comprehensive biodiversity knowledge hubs such as the UNEP's World Conservation Monitoring Centre. The center works with scientists and policymakers worldwide to place biodiversity at the heart of the environment and development decision-making to enable enlightened choices for people and the planet.[159] Another platform is the World Environment Situation Room, which collects, analyzes, and shares the world's best environmental science and research, as well as the mass of new data from satellites, drones, and citizen science. The platform includes critical tools to review progress toward the achievement of the SDGs. UNEP also supports knowledge platforms on ecosystems and biodiversity, such as the Great Apes Survival Partnership, Global Forest Watch, the Global Peatlands Initiative, and the Interfaith Rainforest Initiative.[160]

156 Convention on Biological Diversity, "Welcome to the CBD Secretariat" (CBD.int) www.cbd.int/secretariat/ accessed January 19, 2023.

157 CBD, art 7; Convention on Biological Diversity, "NBSAP Capacity Building Modules" (CBD.int) www.cbd.int/nbsap/training/ accessed January 17, 2023; Information Portal on Multilateral Environmental Agreements, "Welcome to DaRT" (dart.InforMEA.org) https://dart.informea.org/ accessed January 19, 2023.

158 UNEP, "UNEP and Biodiversity" (UNEP.org) www.unep.org/unep-and-biodiversity accessed January 19, 2023.

159 Ibid.

160 Ibid.

4 Legal Scholars' Network in the MENA Region

UNEP supports the establishment and strengthening of networks for environmental law scholars within MENA, primarily the Association of Environmental Law Lecturer in Middle East and North African Universities (ASSELLMU)[161] and the Association of Environmental Law Lecturers in African Universities. The support extends to the development of training-of-trainers programs, convening of scientific conferences, development of scientific publications, and drafting of training modules.

[161] Association of Environmental Law Lecturers in Middle East and North African Universities https://assellmu.org accessed January 19, 2023.

3

Water Scarcity and Biodiversity in the MENA Region

Almas Lokhandwala Maniar

3.1 INTRODUCTION

This chapter examines the opportunities and challenges for the integrated management of biodiversity in desert and water-scarce regions. It examines the effects of water scarcity – although ever-present but now exacerbated by climate change – on the rich biodiversity of various subregions of the Middle East and North Africa (MENA) region. It explores the need for a more integrated management of water and biodiversity in the MENA region and how the current international, regional, and national legal framework of biodiversity management can advance such an integrated governance approach, as well as the gaps in integrative governance in the MENA region and how those gaps can be better addressed.

The entire MENA region is rich in nature and biodiversity resources.[1] The Mediterranean Basin region of the MENA is replete with various ecosystems and biodiversity hotspots, with the highest rate of endemism globally at 20–30 percent.[2] Specifically, 43 percent of plants, 26 percent of mammals, 3 percent of birds, 48 percent of reptiles, 62 percent of amphibians, and 63 percent of freshwater fish are endemic to the Mediterranean hotspots.[3] The areas of greatest plant diversity in North Africa and the Levant are the High and Middle Atlas Mountains in North Africa, coastal strips of Morocco and Algeria, southern Turkey, Lebanon, and Cyrenaica in Libya.[4] Areas rich in reptile species are in southern Turkey, Lebanon, southwestern Syria, the Palestinian territories, northern Egypt, coastal portions of Morocco and Algeria, and the Atlas and Taurus Mountains.[5] In a similar fashion,

1 Damilola Olawuyi, *Environmental Law in Arab States* (Oxford University Press 2022) 245–274.

2 "Biological Diversity in the Mediterranean" (UNEP) www.uneorg/unepmap/resources/factsheets/biological-diversity accessed January 3, 2023.

3 Doga Dernegi, "Mediterranean Basin Biodiversity Hotspot" (*BirdLife International*, July 27, 2010) 8 www.cepf.net/sites/default/files/resources/Donor%20Council/DC_Draft_Mediterranean_EP_Rev_27_July.pdf#:~:text=The%20Mediterranean%20Basin%20biodiversity%20hotspot,northern%20Italy%20to%20Cape%20Verde accessed January 2, 2023.

4 Ibid., 8–9.

5 Ibid.

areas of high precipitation seem to have a high diversity of endemic freshwater fish, such as the mountains of Turkey and North Africa.[6] There are two major factors that have resulted in these high levels of biodiversity in the region. First, the location of North Africa and the Levant is at an intersection of the Eurasian and African landmasses, thereby bringing in rich diversity from both landmasses; and second, the region contains diverse topographical and altitudinal variations, resulting in varied climatic conditions.[7] Hence, the region is brimming with both endemic as well as nonendemic flora and fauna in need of protection.

However, when compared to other similar-sized regions of the world, the MENA region has very few freshwater resources.[8] The entire North African portion of the MENA region is a semi-arid desert, and so is the inhospitable Arabian Peninsula, with a UN agency confirming that the MENA region is "the most water-stressed region on Earth."[9] With the absence of long-flowing rivers and an extremely low level of precipitation, this region is quite hostile to the propagation of many life-forms and is popularly known as the "empty quarter." However, in terms of biodiversity, despite the scarcity of water, the MENA region is home to various endemic species of flora and fauna, as well as numerous concentrations of biodiversity hotspots.[10] The region consists of various biodiversity hotspots concentrated along the Red Sea coastline as well as the Arabian Sea coastline, especially the "Dhofar region of Oman, the wadis of the central Yemeni mountain ranges, south-west Saudi Arabia and the Socotra archipelago."[11]

Even through the MENA region is the most water-stressed region in the world, it has surprisingly diverse terrestrial, freshwater, and marine ecosystems and

[6] Ibid.

[7] Ibid.

[8] UNESCWA, *Water Supply and Sanitation in the Arab Region: Looking beyond 2015* (UNESCWA 2015) 6–7. By 2025, all the Arab states will be under the water poverty line, see the *Arab Strategy for Water Security in the Arab Region – Meeting the Future Challenges and Needs of Sustainable Development (2010–2030)* (UNESCWA 2014). See also International Center for Agricultural Research in the Dry Areas (ICARDA), "Middle East and North Africa (MENA) Is the Most Water-Stressed Region on Earth" www.icarda.org/media/news/middle-east-and-north-africa-mena-most-water-stressed-region-earth accessed January 23, 2024.

[9] See ICARDA (n 8).

[10] David Mallon, "Global Hotspots in the Arabian Peninsula" (2011) 54 *Zoology in the Middle East* 13; Friedhelm Krupp, Masaa Al-Jumaily, Michael Bariche, Maroof Khalaf, Masoumeh Malek, and Bruno Streit, "The Middle Eastern Biodiversity Network: Generating and Sharing Knowledge for Ecosystem Management and Conservation" (*ZooKeys*, December 28, 2009) www.tandfonline.com/doi/abs/10.1080/09397140.2011.10648896 accessed January 2, 2023; Doga Dernegi, "Mediterranean Basin Biodiversity Hotspot" (*BirdLife International*, July 27, 2010). www.cepf.net/sites/default/files/resources/Donor%20Council/DC_Draft_Mediterranean_EP_Rev_27_July.pdf#:~:text=The%20Mediterranean%20Basin%20biodiversity%20hotspot,northern%20Italy%20to%20Cape%20Verde accessed January 2, 2023.

[11] N. García, I. Harrison, N. Cox, and M. F. Tognelli (compilers), "The Status and Distribution of Freshwater Biodiversity in the Arabian Peninsula" (IUCN 2015), 91 https://portals.iucn.org/library/sites/library/files/documents/RL-53-003.pdf accessed January 23, 2024.

biodiversity hotspots, including "deserts, steppes, mountains, broadleaf and coniferous forest, wetlands, coral reefs and mangroves."[12] The already scarce water resources support very fragile ecosystems. When compounded with climate change-induced water shortages, these ecosystems are on the brink of collapse. Rampant industrialization and development, rapid population growth, inadequate protection policies, and climate change-related water shortages have put considerable pressure on the biodiversity.[13] The MENA region has long been projected to become the first region to essentially run out of water.[14] Other major factors contributing to the loss of terrestrial biodiversity are "habitat destruction for development, deforestation, hunting, overgrazing and degradation of rangelands."[15] These numerous factors work in tandem, bringing ecosystems to a brink of collapse, and thereby reducing biodiversity. The loss of biodiversity would result in a loss of "services rendered by ecosystems: protection against soil erosion, water purification, flood and drought mitigation, food supply, pollination, carbon storage, and cultural and recreational services."[16] Water scarcity and declining water resources are one of the major reasons for the decline in biodiversity of the region. Hence it is imperative to put a stop to the loss of habitats and biodiversity in the MENA region.

In order to tackle the rapid decline in biodiversity, various nations of the region have individually and collectively formulated certain national, regional, and international regulations. This chapter examines the integration of the regulations on biodiversity and water preservation at the national and regional levels. This approach reveals the extent to which the integrated governance of water and biodiversity has taken place in the region, as well as the gaps in the integration, and provides suggestions for addressing the said gaps.

This chapter proceeds in five sections, this introduction being the first. Section 3.2 examines the need for the integrated management of water and biodiversity resources to effectively address the cross-cutting impacts of climate change and other ecological pressures on biodiversity. It examines the meaning, nature, and elements of integrated water and biodiversity governance and the implications for the MENA

12 Kira Walker, "MENA's Biodiversity Shrinking under Pressure of Climate Change" (*Nature-Middle East*, December 13, 2022) www.natureasia.com/en/nmiddleeast/article/10.1038/nmiddleeast.2022.79 accessed January 3, 2023.

13 David Mallon, "Global Hotspots in the Arabian Peninsula" (2011) 54 *Zoology in the Middle East* 13; Friedhelm Krupp, Masaa Al-Jumaily, Michael Bariche, Maroof Khalaf, Masoumeh Malek, and Bruno Streit, "The Middle Eastern Bodiversity Network: Generating and Sharing Knowledge for Ecosystem Management and Conservation" (*ZooKeys*, December 28, 2009); Doga Dernegi, "Mediterranean Basin Biodiversity Hotspot" (*BirdLife International*, July 27, 2010).

14 Tony Allan, *The Middle East Water Question: Hydropolitics* (I. B. Tauris 2001); Jonatha Chenoweth et al., "Impact of Climate Change on the Water Resources of the Eastern Mediterranean and Middle East Region: Modeled 21st Century Changes and Implications" (2011) 47 *Water Resources Research* https://doi.org/10.1029/2010WR010269 accessed January 23, 2024.

15 Krupp et al. (n 13).

16 UNEP, "Biological Diversity in the Mediterranean" www.uneorg/unepmap/resources/factsheets/biological-diversity accessed January 3, 2023.

region. Section 3.3 evaluates the wide array of cross-subregional and cross-national initiatives that have been developed to advance the integrated management of biodiversity in the desert and water-scarce countries of the MENA region. It evaluates the gaps that hinder their effective and coherent implementation. Section 3.4 provides recommendations on how these gaps can be addressed. Section 3.5 is the concluding section.

3.2 INTEGRATED GOVERNANCE OF WATER AND BIODIVERSITY IN THE MENA REGION

The integrated governance of biodiversity and water preservation, particularly in the context of the MENA region, refers to a holistic, coordinated, and strategic approach to the policymaking, implementation, and management of both biodiversity conservation and water resource management. It means aligning objectives, strategies, and actions in both domains to ensure the sustainable use and protection of natural resources.

As demonstrated in this chapter, the integrated governance of water and biodiversity in the MENA region is essential due to the interdependence of the biodiversity and water resources, the shared challenges these resources face, and the significant benefits of a coordinated approach. The most significant reason for integration is that water scarcity directly affects biodiversity. As discussed earlier, the MENA region is one of the most water-scarce regions in the world. This has been compounded by the synergistic adverse effects of climate change (including changes in water resources) to species of fauna in regions of the world.[17] It would follow that synergistic solutions could help to adapt the land, flora, and fauna to the adverse effects of climate change. By addressing water and biodiversity issues in tandem through robust integrated governance, the region can bolster its resilience against climate change, desertification, and other environmental challenges.

Reduced water availability can lead to habitat degradation, loss of wetlands, and adverse impacts on freshwater ecosystems. Conversely, biodiverse ecosystems, such as wetlands, play a crucial role in water purification, groundwater recharge, and flood control.[18] The degradation of these ecosystems can lead to decreased water quality and quantity. Further, many major water resources in the MENA region,

[17] Matthew G. Betts, Javier G. Illán, Zhiqiang Yang, Susan M. Shirley, and Chris D. Thomas, "Synergistic Effects of Climate and Land-Cover Change on Long-Term Bird Population Trends of the Western USA: A Test of Modeled Predictions" (2019) 7 *Frontiers in Ecology and Evolution: Population, Community, and Ecosystem Dynamics* (May 29, 2019) https://doi.org/10.3389/fevo.2019.00186 accessed January 23, 2024.

[18] Wetlands International, "Collaboration for a Water-Wise World" (August 21, 2023) www.wetlands.org/blog/collaboration-for-a-water-wise-world/#:~:text=Wetlands%20are%20a%20vital%20nature,filtering%20pollutants%20like%20heavy%20metals accessed January 23, 2024.

such as the Nile, Tigris, and Euphrates rivers, are shared among multiple countries.[19] These shared resources require cooperative management to ensure equitable distribution and avoid potential conflicts.[20] Further, many species, including birds, migrate across national boundaries in the MENA region.[21] Protecting their habitats requires a coordinated approach across countries, as well as the proper integration of regulations that protect biodiversity and water resources.

Finally, integrated governance can lead to the pooling of resources, knowledge sharing, and the formulation of joint strategies, which can be more cost-effective than managing these resources separately.[22] This approach also allows for consideration of the entire ecosystem, enabling comprehensive solutions. This can prevent narrowly focused decisions that may benefit one aspect of the environment but harm another.

3.2.1 *Elements of Integrated Water and Biodiversity Governance*

As discussed, the integrated governance of biodiversity and water preservation in the MENA region is essential, given the unique environmental, social, and political challenges the area faces. To be effective, such governance must be built on certain core elements, and achieving these requires a mix of strategies.

Ensuring proper policy coherence is paramount. Policy coherence refers to the systematic promotion of mutually reinforcing policy actions across government departments and agencies to achieve agreed objectives.[23] In the context of integrated governance for biodiversity and water preservation in the MENA region, policy coherence implies that regulations, strategies, and actions related to these

19 National Geographic, "Fertile Crescent" https://education.nationalgeographic.org/resource/fertile-crescent/ accessed January 23, 2024.

20 Achref Chibani, "Water Politics in the Tigris-Euphrates Basin" (Arab Center, Washington, DC, May 30, 2023) https://arabcenterdc.org/resource/water-politics-in-the-tigris-euphrates-basin/ accessed January 24, 2024.

21 UNEP, Convention on the Conservation of Migratory Species of Wild Animals, "Fact Sheet" (September 2019) www.cms.int/sites/default/files/publication/abu_dhabi_fact_sheet_0.pdf accessed January 24, 2024; J. A. Lindsell, G. Serra, L. Peške et al., "Satellite Tracking Reveals the Migration Route and Wintering Area of the Middle East Population of Critically Endangered Northern Bald Ibis *Geronticus eremita*" (July 14, 2009) 43 *Oryx* 3, 329–335 www.cambridge.org/core/journals/oryx/article/satellite-tracking-reveals-the-migration-route-and-wintering-area-of-the-middle-east-population-of-critically-endangered-northern-bald-ibis-geronticus-eremita/097533C867806B80E8D093113AB6128 accessed January 24, 2024; Arabia Weather, "100 Million Migratory Birds Cross the Skies of Saudi Arabia Every Year" (May 14, 2023) www.arabiaweather.com/en/content/100-million-migratory-birds-cross-the-skies-of-saudi-arabia-every-year accessed January 24, 2024.

22 See Chapter 18. See also Olawuyi (n 1).

23 Mans Nilsson, Tony Zamparutti, Jan-Erik Petersen, and Björn Nykvist, "Understanding Policy Coherence: Analytical Framework and Examples of Sector–Environment Policy Interactions in the EU" (2012) 22 *Environmental Policy and Governance* 395 www.researchgate.net/publication/260357612_Understanding_Policy_Coherence_Analytical_Framework_and_Examples_of_Sector-Environment_Policy_Interactions_in_the_EU accessed January 24, 2024.

two domains complement, rather than contradict, each other. This policy coherence will allow for better coordination where the combined impact of separate policies is greater than the sum of their individual effects.[24] Further, without coherence, there is a risk of one policy undermining the objectives of another. The initial costs of the coordination required to ensure harmony between the ends and means of different environmental policies and projects would be trivial in comparison to the resources saved by avoiding redundant or conflicting projects and the value gained by preserving biodiversity. For instance, a water resource management strategy that focuses solely on maximizing extraction might endanger biodiversity in aquatic ecosystems.

Policy coherence can be best achieved through inter-agency collaboration, especially through fostering communication and collaboration between different government departments or agencies responsible for biodiversity and water management. Additionally, agencies can establish shared platforms or databases where data related to biodiversity and water resources are accessible to all relevant stakeholders. This ensures that policy decisions are made based on comprehensive, up-to-date information. Lastly, proper policy coherence may also require periodic reviews of policies to identify any potential overlaps, gaps, or conflicts. This can be complemented by impact assessments to evaluate the effectiveness of current policies.

While there are many elements of integrated governance, this chapter focuses on a more pivotal component – that of transboundary collaboration. Transboundary collaboration is of utmost importance in a region such as the MENA,[25] in terms of shared ecosystems, water bodies, and common environmental challenges which necessitate cooperative action.

Achieving integrated governance in the MENA region requires a holistic approach combined with immense political will. Given the pressing nature of the challenges facing biodiversity and water in the region, such efforts are not only beneficial but essential for the region's long-term sustainability and stability. Water scarcity and the loss of biodiversity have immediate and long-term destabilizing effects, with consequences that ripple across economic, social, and political spheres.

Water scarcity, exacerbated by climate change, can lead to reduced agricultural yields, impacting food security and leading to potential economic downturns.[26]

24 Asa Persson, "Environmental Policy Integration: An Introduction," Policy Integration for Sustainability Background Paper (Stockholm Environment Institute, June 2004) https://mediamanager.sei.org/documents/Publications/Policy-institutions/EPI.pdf accessed January 24, 2024; also: Nilsson et al. (n 23).

25 UNECE, *Convention on the Protection and Use of Transboundary Watercourses and International Lakes* (Helsinki 1992).

26 World Bank, "High and Dry: Climate Change, Water, and the Economy" (May 2, 2016) www.worldbank.org/en/topic/water/publication/high-and-dry-climate-change-water-and-the-economy accessed January 24, 2024.

Coupled with the loss of biodiversity, this diminishes the ecological resilience of various habitats, further compromising the livelihoods of many, especially those dependent on natural resources.[27] More directly, scarcity of clean water and increasing temperatures can result in health challenges, such as dehydration, heat stress, and associated fatalities.[28]

Further, experts are already raising alarms about the onset of a massive climate refugee crisis.[29] Many regions are becoming uninhabitable due to a combination of drought, famine, floods, and extreme heat.[30] The current global refugee situation, which is already destabilizing many climate-stressed regions and destination countries, offers just a glimpse of what may be to come.[31] Future environmental catastrophes could lead to an exponentially larger and more severe refugee crisis, putting even greater strains on global resources and geopolitical stability. Therefore, addressing the intertwined challenges of biodiversity loss and water scarcity is not just an environmental imperative but a crucial step in averting broader regional and global crises.

3.3 REGIONAL AND NATIONAL INITIATIVES IN THE MENA REGION FOR INTEGRATED GOVERNANCE OF REGULATIONS FOR THE PROTECTION OF BIODIVERSITY AND WATER RESOURCES

3.3.1 *The North African Mediterranean Region and the Levant*

3.3.1.1 Biodiversity

Egypt, as the most populous country in the Arab world,[32] has long grappled with challenges related to water scarcity and biodiversity conservation. Given its heavy

[27] Elsa E. Cleland, "Biodiversity and Ecosystem Stability" (2011) 3 *Nature Education Knowledge* 10, 14 www.nature.com/scitable/knowledge/library/biodiversity-and-ecosystem-stability-17059965/#:~:text=Diversity%2DStability%20Theory&text=Biologically%20diverse%20communities%20are%20also,adapt%20to%20a%20changing%20environment accessed January 24, 2024.

[28] UNICEF, "Water and the Global Climate Crisis: 10 Things You Should Know the World Needs to Get Water Smart. Everyone has a Role to Play, and We Cannot Afford to Wait" (March 2, 2023) www.unicef.org/stories/water-and-climate-change-10-things-you-should-know#:~:text=When%20disasters%20hit%2C%20they%20can,dangerous%20for%20people%20to%20drink accessed January 24, 2024.

[29] John Podesta, "The Climate Crisis, Migration and Refugees" (July 25, 2019) www.brookings.edu/articles/the-climate-crisis-migration-and-refugees/ accessed January 24, 2024.

[30] Ibid.; Yossi Mekelberg and Kate Fanning, "The Coming Climate Migration Crisis in the Middle East and North Africa" (New Lines Institute, December 8, 2021) https://newlinesinstitute.org/displacement-and-migration/climate-migration/the-coming-climate-migration-crisis-in-the-middle-east-and-north-africa/ accessed January 24, 2024.

[31] Ibid.

[32] CIA Factbook, "Egypt: Demographic Profile" www.cia.gov/the-world-factbook/countries/egypt/#:~:text=Egypt%20is%20the%20most%20populous,5%25%20of%20Egypt's%20land%20area accessed January 24, 2024.

reliance on the Nile River for fresh water and its rich biodiversity, particularly in areas such as the Red Sea and Sinai, Egypt has developed comprehensive strategies to address these issues. Egypt's strategies, such as the National Water Resources Plan (NWRP)[33] and the Biodiversity Strategy and Action Plan,[34] while distinct, both concern the protection of biodiversity and water resources. For instance, the Biodiversity Strategy may highlight the importance of freshwater ecosystems,[35] and the NWRP might emphasize the ecological importance of maintaining water quality for habitats.[36]

Tunisia has made efforts to align its environmental strategies with global standards, particularly in line with the Sustainable Development Goals.[37] Wetland conservation, such as the Tunisian government's preservation and desalination efforts in Ichkeul National Park, represents an area where water and biodiversity issues naturally intersect.[38] While there are specific initiatives addressing water and biodiversity issues, respectively, explicit integrated strategies that bridge both domains at the national policy level remain elusive.

Jordan's vulnerability to water scarcity has led it to be very proactive in its water governance. Similar to Tunisia, the Azraq Wetland Reserve is a notable example where water management and biodiversity conservation intersect.[39] The reserve, once a significant stopover for migratory birds,[40] had faced ecological challenges due to the overextraction of groundwater. Restoration efforts have aimed at reviving the wetland and, in the process, preserving its biodiversity. This example indicates some level of integrated strategy, although it may not be systematically applied at a national policy level.

Lebanon has faced myriad environmental and political challenges, which may have impacted its ability to systematically integrate water and biodiversity governance. The country has, however, made strides in designating and conserving its

33 Arab Republic of Egypt, "Water for the Future: National Water Resources Plan 2017" (Ministry of Water Resources and Irrigation, January 2005) https://faolex.fao.org/docs/pdf/egy147082.pdf accessed October 10, 2023.

34 Arab Republic of Egypt, "Egyptian Biodiversity Strategy and Action Plan (2015–2030)" (Ministry of Environment, January 2016) www.cbd.int/doc/world/eg/eg-nbsap-v2-en.pdf accessed October 10, 2023.

35 Ibid., 16, 18, 42, 43, 48, 49, 50, 51, 52.

36 Arab Republic of Egypt (n 33) 1–6.

37 Republic of Tunisia, "Voluntary National Review: Sustainable Development Goals Progress Report at the High Level Political Forum" (July 2019) https://digitallibrary.un.org/record/3866743?ln=en accessed October 5, 2023.

38 UNESCO World Heritage Convention, "Ichkeul National Park" https://whc.unesco.org/en/list/8 accessed October 5, 2023; UNESCO World Heritage Convention, "Ichkeul National Park: Tunisia" https://whc.unesco.org/en/soc/482 accessed October 5, 2023. We can see the progression of conservation efforts from 1985 to 2010.

39 European Commission, "Conservation: Azraq Wetland Reserve (Jordan)" (1978) https://econservation.jrc.ec.europa.eu/site/11856 accessed January 24, 2024.

40 UNESCO World Heritage Convention, "Azraq: Description" https://whc.unesco.org/en/tentativelists/5156/ accessed January 24, 2024.

Important Plant Areas[41] and Important Bird Areas,[42] some of which are wetlands, indicating a recognition of the intersection between water and biodiversity. However, broader integrated strategies at the national level may still be in the nascent stages or facing implementation challenges due to other pressing issues in the country.

While these countries have demonstrated an understanding of the importance of both water governance and biodiversity conservation, explicit and comprehensive national strategies that integrate both domains may still be in development in the North African and Levant subregions of the MENA. Integrating these domains requires a multifaceted approach, considering socio-political, economic, and ecological factors, which can be complex in rapidly changing environments.

3.3.2 *Arabian Peninsula*

Oman, in the Arabian Peninsula, has been at the forefront in its efforts to combat the loss of biodiversity as well protect its natural resources – especially water. Law 114/2001 on the Conservation of the Environment and Prevention of Pollution was enacted to oversee environmental and biodiversity conservation projects and initiatives in Oman.[43] Its role is instrumental in ensuring the protection and preservation of Oman's diverse ecosystems, flora, and fauna, in the context of protection of the environment of the state in general. Law 114/2001 also has provisions for the protection of water resources – both fresh water and salt water. This law is one of the examples of integration of biodiversity and water protection regulations. The law recognizes the need to protect water resources in order to protect biodiversity.

Saudi Arabia has taken significant steps to protect its unique biodiversity and vital water resources. Over the years, it has enacted a series of laws and regulations to safeguard its environmental heritage and ensure sustainable water management. Notably, the Saudi National Transformation Program 2020[44] and Vision 2030[45] emphasize the importance of environmental sustainability and water conservation, highlighting the nation's commitment to these issues. While both domains of biodiversity and water protection may be addressed in the broader context of environmental and sustainable development strategies, it is not clear to what extent there

41 Magda Bou Dagher-Kharrat, Hicham El Zein, and Germinal Rouhan, "Setting Conservation Priorities for Lebanese Flora – Identification of Important Plant Areas" (June 2018) 43 *Journal for Nature Conservation* 85–94 www.researchgate.net/publication/321224250_Setting_conservation_priorities_for_Lebanese_flora-Identification_of_important_plant_areas accessed January 24, 2024.

42 SPNL Homat al Hima, "Important Bird Areas – IBAs" (April 21, 2009) www.spnl.org/ibas-kbas/ accessed January 24, 2024.

43 The Sultanate of Oman, Royal Decree No 114/2001 issuing the Law on Conservation of Environment and Prevention of Pollution (November 14, 2001) www.fao.org/faolex/results/details/en/c/LEX-FAOC098254/ accessed January 24, 2024.

44 Kingdom of Saudi Arabia, "Vision 2030: National Transformation Program" www.vision2030.gov.sa/en/vision-2030/vrp/national-transformation-program/ accessed January 24, 2024.

45 Kingdom of Saudi Arabia, "Leadership Message: Saudi Vision 2030" www.vision2030.gov.sa/en/ accessed January 24, 2024.

is direct integration between specific laws on biodiversity and water protection. The nation's approach to sustainable development, environmental protection, and resource management is informed by its Vision 2030 strategy, which emphasizes environmental sustainability among its goals.

3.3.3 *Regional Frameworks for Integrated Water and Biodiversity Governance*

The integration of biodiversity protection and water conservation regulations within the MENA region is gaining increasing momentum in regional strategies and instruments. For example, the Arab Water Strategy is an example of subtle integration.[46] While the primary focus is on water management and addressing water scarcity, the strategy also underscores the need for sustainable management practices that do not harm ecosystems. By emphasizing sustainable use and ecosystem conservation, it implicitly promotes the protection of biodiversity.[47] Similarly, one of the most successful examples of integrated governance is the Mediterranean Wetlands Initiative (MedWet).[48] Wetlands are zones of high biodiversity, and their conservation not only ensures water storage and purification but also protects numerous species. MedWet's initiatives directly target the conservation of these ecosystems, acknowledging the dual importance of water management and biodiversity. MedWet has established a network of scientific and technical experts to share knowledge, data, and best practices on wetland conservation, biodiversity, and water management.[49] This network plays a critical role in bridging the gap between biodiversity conservation and water resource management. Further, MedWet's strategic frameworks emphasize the interconnectedness of water management and biodiversity conservation.[50] This integrated approach acknowledges that protecting biodiversity is instrumental in ensuring water quality and quantity in Mediterranean wetlands.

MedWet's collaborative approach, combined with its emphasis on integrating biodiversity and water resource management, has made it a flagship initiative in the

46 Technical Secretariat of the Arab Ministerial Water Council, "Arab Strategy for Water Security in the Region to Meet the Challenges and Future Needs for Sustainable Development (2010–2030)" (2012) www.susana.org/_resources/documents/default/3-3431-189-1539510564.pdf accessed January 24, 2024.

47 See also Tarek Abulhawa and Tricia Cummings, *Rapid Cultural Inventories of Wetlands in Arab States including Ramsar Sites and World Heritage Properties: Building Greater Understanding of Cultural Values and Practices as a Contribution to Conservation Success* (Wetland Link International 2020) https://wli.wwt.org.uk/wp-content/uploads/2020/12/2017-06-28_arab_states_report_web.pdf accessed January 24, 2024.

48 The Mediterranean Wetlands Initiative (MedWet), Wetlands for a sustainable Mediterranean region https://medwet.org/ accessed January 24, 2024.

49 The Mediterranean Wetlands Initiative (MedWet), Wetlands for a sustainable Mediterranean region, "The Scientific and Technical Network" https://medwet.org/the-scientific-and-technical-network/ accessed January 24, 2024.

50 The Mediterranean Wetlands Initiative (MedWet), Wetlands for a sustainable Mediterranean region, "The Strategic Plan (2026–2020)" https://medwet.org/observatory/strategic-plan/ accessed January 24, 2024.

Mediterranean region. The initiative recognizes that the health of wetland ecosystems, their biodiversity, and water resources are deeply interconnected and that an integrated approach is essential for the long-term sustainability of these vital habitats. Similarly, the Regional Organization for the Conservation of the Environment of the Red Sea and Gulf of Aden has adopted a comprehensive Regional Master Plan for marine protected areas (MPAs) in the Red Sea and Gulf of Aden aimed at protecting the rich and delicate wetlands of the Red Sea and Gulf of Aden.[51] Focusing on twelve MPAs across the MENA region, the Regional Master Plan "is a regionally agreed framework for the planning and management of each of the MPAs in the Regional Network that will facilitate the achievement of regional objectives for sustainable resource usage, conservation of biodiversity and for economic development."[52]

While these initiatives signify a move toward integrated governance, practical integration at the domestic level often varies. Challenges frequently arise in implementing policies cohesively across sectors. The mere existence of such initiatives does indicate a recognition of the intertwined nature of water resources and biodiversity, and it is a good indication of whether the nations recognize the importance of such integration.

3.4 ADDRESSING GAPS IN INTEGRATED MANAGEMENT OF BIODIVERSITY AND WATER RESOURCES

The MENA region has shown a growing awareness of the need for integrated governance of biodiversity and water preservation. Integrating biodiversity conservation and water resource management is essential for the region's sustainable development. However, the presence and robustness of such integrated governance varies significantly across the region – nationally as well as regionally. These gaps pose considerable challenges to achieving holistic and effective resource management. The most common reason for presence of such lacunae in integrated governance is the diverse political landscape of the region. The MENA region comprises countries with varying political systems, governance structures, and priorities. While

[51] The Red Sea and Gulf of Aden (RSGA) is recognized for the rich biological diversity of its coastal and marine environments and the associated social, economic, and tourism value. See Olawuyi (n 1) 71–72; the Regional Organization for the Conservation of the Environment of the Red Sea and Gulf of Aden (PERSGA), *The Red Sea and Gulf of Aden Regional Network of Marine Protected Areas: Regional Master Plan* (PERSGA 2002) https://iwlearn.net/resolveuid/a76ab1cb7a5b8d749bed4551ec6abce0 accessed January 12, 2024. See also G. Bawazir, *Marine Biodiversity of Aden Wetlands Protected Areas* (Aden Wetlands Conservation Project, Wings Over Wetlands 2009).

[52] The twelve MPAs are: Iles des Sept Frères and Ras Siyan (Djibouti); Ras Mohammed National Park; Giftun Islands and Straits of Gubal (Egypt); Aqaba coral reefs (Jordan); Straits of Tiran; Wajh Bank, Sharm Habban and Sharm Munaybirah; Farasan Islands (Saudi Arabia); Aibat and Saad ad-Din Islands, Saba Wanak (Somalia); Sanganeb Marine National Park; Mukkawar Island and Dungonab Bay (Sudan); Socotra Islands; Belhaf and Bir Ali area (Yemen). PERSGA (n 52).

some countries have made strides in environmental governance, progress has been slow in others due to challenges such as political instability, conflicts, or other pressing socio-economic issues.[53]

These countries also have varied economic realities on the ground. Historically, the economic emphasis in many MENA countries has been on oil and gas extraction. Although there is a growing recognition of the need to diversify economies and focus on sustainable development, the transition has been uneven across the region.[54] Uneven institutional capacities also play a significant role. While some countries, especially the wealthier Gulf states, have invested in building institutional capacity for environmental governance, others might lack the expertise, infrastructure, or resources to implement and oversee integrated regulations effectively.[55]

There is also an epidemic of policy silos in the MENA region. Institutions responsible for water resource management and biodiversity conservation operate in isolation in many countries of the region.[56] This siloed approach results in fragmented and sometimes conflicting policies and actions. Water policies rarely incorporate biodiversity considerations and vice versa.[57] Addressing the gaps in the integration of biodiversity and water protection regulations requires a multifaceted approach that combines technical, institutional, policy, and community-based strategies.

Most crucially, there is a need for policy integration.[58] The nations need to develop frameworks that weave together biodiversity conservation and water management, ensuring that both issues are addressed in every relevant policy and initiative. Policymakers need to encourage a systems-thinking approach that recognizes the interconnectedness of water systems, ecosystems, and human communities and develop policies that account for the entirety of the water–biodiversity–human nexus rather than piecemeal solutions.

The region as a whole must also create or strengthen central bodies responsible for overseeing both biodiversity and water resources to ensure a unified approach, while promoting inter-agency coordination and taskforces that bring together experts from various domains. In order to have integrated policies that are robust, effective, and actionable, there needs to be enhanced monitoring of the efforts as well as in-depth, on-the-ground research on the requirements and effects of the policies. This should be coupled with facilitated data sharing between institutions and the development integrated databases that are easily accessible to policymakers. It is imperative that in

53 Olawuyi (n 1).

54 Ibid.

55 Iyad Abumoghli and Adele Goncalves, "Environmental Challenges in the Mena Region" (UNEP) https://wedocs.unep.org/bitstream/handle/20.500.11822/31645/EC_MENA.pdf?sequence=1&isAllowed=y accessed January 24, 2024.

56 Damilola Olawuyi, "Sustainable Development and the Water–Energy–Food Nexus: Legal Challenges and Emerging Solutions" (2020) 103 *Journal of Environmental Science & Policy* 1.

57 Ibid.

58 Nilsson et al. (n 23) 395.

a politically fractured region, such as the MENA, there is a mode of legal enforcement regionally. This can be carried out by strengthening the legal framework to ensure compliance with integrated regulations and establishing penalties for non-compliance along with mechanisms for conflict resolution.

The MENA region stands at a critical juncture where the integration of biodiversity conservation and water resource management can no longer be an afterthought. Addressing the highlighted gaps is crucial for the region's sustainable future, ensuring that its unique ecosystems thrive alongside its growing human population.

3.5 CONCLUSION

The MENA region, characterized by its rich biodiversity and precarious water situation, stands at a unique crossroads in the realm of environmental governance. The intricate linkage between biodiversity and water is evident not just ecologically but socio-economically, playing a pivotal role in the sustenance and livelihoods of its diverse communities. It becomes vitally important, then, to ensure that the governance structures in place address these connections holistically.

While countries in the MENA region have made strides toward recognizing the intrinsic relationship between biodiversity and water, comprehensive integration in the legal and policy frameworks remains a challenge – both nationally and regionally. Fragmented legislation and sectoral approaches often lead to gaps, redundancies, and sometimes contradictions in management practices. To truly foster sustainable development and resilience in the face of changing climatic conditions and growing anthropogenic pressures, there is an urgent need for a more cohesive, integrated approach.

The MENA region's path toward the integrated governance of biodiversity and water preservation is a journey marked by both promise and obstacles. While recognition of the need for harmony between these vital aspects of resource management is growing, significant gaps persist at both the national and regional levels.

The region's diverse political landscape stands out as a key challenge to integrated governance efforts. The region's particular vulnerability to destabilization and the impending climate refugee crisis is also notable. The climate refugee crisis is predicted to dwarf the current refugee crisis. Further, variations in political systems, governance structures, and priorities among MENA countries have led to disparities in environmental governance progress. Political instability, conflicts, and pressing socio-economic issues further compound these challenges. Economic disparities also play a pivotal role, with a historical emphasis on oil and gas extraction overshadowing efforts to diversify economies and promote sustainability. Uneven institutional capacities further hinder progress, with wealthier Gulf states having more resources for environmental governance. The prevalence of policy silos, where water resource management and biodiversity conservation operate independently, leads to fragmented and sometimes conflicting policies and actions. This separation limits the effectiveness of integrated resource management.

To address these gaps effectively, a nexus and multifaceted approach is essential. Policy integration is paramount, requiring the development of frameworks that embed biodiversity conservation and water management in every relevant policy and initiative, adopting a systems-thinking perspective that recognizes their interconnectedness. Establishing or strengthening central bodies responsible for overseeing both biodiversity and water resources is crucial for a unified approach and improved inter-agency coordination. Effective monitoring and on-the-ground research, coupled with enhanced data sharing and accessible integrated databases, support evidence-based decision-making.

In a region marked by political fragmentation, regional legal enforcement mechanisms are imperative. Strengthening the legal framework, ensuring compliance with integrated regulations, and establishing penalties for noncompliance, along with conflict resolution mechanisms, can help create a unified approach to resource management. The MENA region stands at a critical juncture where addressing these gaps in the integration of biodiversity conservation and water resource management is not only necessary but also essential for its sustainable future. By confronting these challenges thoughtfully, the region can ensure that its unique ecosystems thrive alongside its growing human population, promoting resilience and prosperity for generations to come. It is crucially important to remember that true sustainability lies not just in the protection of individual components of our environment but in understanding and preserving the intricate web of relationships that bind them together.

4

The Role of National and Regional Institutions in Biodiversity and Forest Conservation

Riyad Fakhri and Youness Lazrak Hassouni

4.1 INTRODUCTION

This chapter examines the role of national and regional institutions in promoting the integrated regulation and administration of biodiversity and forest management in the Middle East and North Africa (MENA) region. Drawing lessons from Morocco, it evaluates current legal and institutional challenges to integrated management of forest and biodiversity.

We cannot discuss the environment and biodiversity without analyzing the forest domain. Any damage to the forest has serious repercussions on the wider ecosystem and biodiversity. The need to reverse the rapid loss of biodiversity and forest resources is, undoubtedly, one of the key environmental challenges in the Maghreb.[1] While there has been a rise in biodiversity legislation, a coherent implementation of forest conservation as part of biodiversity management remains largely absent or unevenly developed across the region.[2] For example, the ecological system in Morocco is characterized by biodiversity, and the forest is the most important reservoir for this diversity, which controls its balance.[3] The forest also plays an important role in reducing global warming and climate change. Forests constitute approximately 9.5 million hectares, which is about 13 percent of the total area of the Kingdom of Morocco.[4] The latter is characterized, thanks to its geographical location,[5] by a great eco-biological diversity and a variety of different natural environments.[6] Morocco ranks among the countries with the highest levels of diverse

1 See Damilola Olawuyi, *Environmental Law in Arab States* (Oxford University Press 2022) 1–15.

2 Ibid.

3 See Marijke van Kuijk, Francis E. Putz, and Roderick Jan Zagt, "Effects of Forest Certification on Biodiversity" (Tropenbos International 2009) 19 www.tropenbos.org/file.php/52/forest_certification_and_biodiversity.pdf accessed January 22, 2024.

4 Mohammed Ellatifi et al., "Wood Harvesting and Sustainable Forest Management in Morocco" www.fao.org/3/Y9351E/Y9351E36.htm accessed September 20, 2023.

5 Agence nationale des eaux et forêts (ANEF) www.eauxetforets.gov.ma/AccueilAR/SitePages/Forets-En-Chiffres.aspx accessed September 20, 2023.

6 At the level of land use and real estate status, the forest is owned by the government an area of about 9,619,090 hectares. Ellatifi (n 4).

terrestrial ecosystem, which are characterized by their habitat of more than 4,000 vascular plant species, nearly 550 species of vertebrate animals, and thousands of invertebrate organisms.[7] Forests are home to two-thirds of all flora and one-third of Morocco's animal species.[8] This makes them play a pivotal role in biodiversity. At the level of the Mediterranean basin, Moroccan biodiversity ranks second only to the Anatolian region (Turkey), with a total localization rate of 20 percent.[9] There is no doubt that the natural resources in Morocco are of high quality, and are considered an important resource for economic and social development, but they remain fragile in the face of a range of natural risks, perhaps the most important of which are climate change and human behavior. Therefore, the need to protect forests from overexploitation has been a key objective of environmental regulation in Morocco. Environmental law in Morocco mandates that the exploitation of forests must be in accordance with specific procedures and conditions.

Morocco organized the forest domain for the first time with the *1912 Circular of the Grand Vizier*.[10] After this circular, the Dahir of January 3, 1916, entitled *The Special Regulation for the Public Property* and in which the forest property was determined, was issued,[11] followed by the Dahir of October 10, 1917, on conservation and forest exploitation, which is the most important legal framework in this field.[12] Several other laws and decrees have also been issued directly and indirectly related to the forest field, including the Dahir of March 4, 1925, relating to the protection and identification of "Argan forests amongst others."[13]

Furthermore, international bodies and forums, such as the Group of Eight, Interpol, the European Union, the United Nations Environment Programme, and the United Nations Regional Crime and Justice Research Institute, have identified some acts as environmental crimes in nature regardless of the nature of the harm.[14] For example, according to the Convention on International Trade in Endangered Species of Wild Fauna and Flora, the illegal trade in endangered wild species; illegal, unreported, and unregulated fishing, contrary to controls imposed by various regional fisheries; and logging and the related trade in stolen timber, in contravention

[7] Convention on Biological Diversity, "Morocco – Main Details" www.cbd.int/countries/profile/?country=ma accessed September 26, 2023; see also Agence nationale des eaux et forêts (ANEF), "Biodiversité au Maroc" www.eauxetforets.gov.ma/Biodiversite/Biodiversit%C3%A9%20au%20Maroc/Pages/Biodiversit%C3%A9-au-Maroc.aspx accessed September 26, 2023.

[8] Ibid.

[9] Royaume du Maroc: Ministère de la transition énergétique et du développement durable, "Biodiversité" www.environnement.gov.ma/fr/biodiversite#:~:text=Le%20taux%20d'end%C3%A9misme%20global,l"%C3%A9chelle%20de%20la%20M%C3%A9diterran%C3%A9e, September 26, 2023.

[10] The first Official Bulletin of Morocco, February 1, 1913, 3.

[11] The Official Bulletin of Morocco, No 141, January 10, 1916, 28.

[12] The Official Bulletin of Morocco, No 235, October 29, 1917, 901. See Rachid Attahir, "The Legal Framework for the Penal Aspect in Forest Offenses" (2021) 4 *JEMED* 2.

[13] The Official Bulletin of Morocco, No 647, March 17, 1925, 526.

[14] See INTERPOL, "Our Response to Environmental Crime" www.interpol.int/en/Crimes/Environmental-crime/Our-response-to-environmental-crime accessed January 22, 2024.

of national laws, among others, are governed by several international and regional instruments, which aim to conserve flora and fauna from overexploitation.[15]

In the same vein, a recent study by the United Nations Environment Programme (UNEP) found that acts harmful to the environment constitute the fourth largest criminal domain in the world after drugs, counterfeiting, and trafficking in human beings.[16] The illegal exploitation of forests and illegal logging is also widely recognized as one of the five most prevalent areas of environmental crime globally.[17] These crimes are the most lucrative form of transnational criminal operations, with an estimated monetary value in 2016 between US$91 and US$259 billion annually.[18]

Although the protection of the forest in Morocco was initially motivated by the subsistence and livelihood it provides, especially for forest-dependent communities, its important role in achieving ecological balance, preserving biodiversity, and reducing global warming has become widely acknowledged from the 1970s onwards.[19] This recognition is reflected in several conferences held and international conventions about forest preservation and protection, including the 1992 Earth Summit, which ended with special attention on the sustainable management of forests.

So how effective is Morocco's legal and institutional framework protecting Morocco's forest and biodiversity? Moreover, how effective are the institutions, departments, and agencies specialized in the management of forest in Morocco, with procedures that are described as complex and strict, at least nominally, in protecting this national wealth at the level required nationally and internationally? To answer these questions, this chapter examines four fundamental themes raised by the legal and judicial protection of the forests. First, it examines the need for the integrated regulation of biodiversity and forest management given the interconnectedness of these two elements. Second, it evaluates integration gaps and challenges in laws relating to forest management and biodiversity in Morocco. Third, it evaluates institutional arrangements in forest management in Morocco, especially the role of the Water and Forestry Agency in activating the integrated management of

15 See Olawuyi (n 1) 1–15.

16 United Nations Environment Program, "The State of Knowledge of Crimes that Have Serious Impacts on the Environment" (UNEP 2018) https://wedocs.unep.org/bitstream/handle/20.500.11822/25713/knowledge_crime_envImpacts.pdf?sequence=1&isAllowed=y accessed January 22, 2024.

17 Environmental Investigation Agency Report, "Environmental Crime – A Threat to Our Future" (October 14, 2008), https://eia-international.org/report/environmental-crime-2/ accessed January 22, 2024.

18 See Christian Nellemann, Rune Henriksen, Arnold Kreilhuber, Davyth Stewart, Maria Kotsovou, Patricia Raxter, Elizabeth Mrema, and Sam Barrat (eds), "The Rise of Environmental Crime – A Growing Threat to Natural Resources Peace, Development and Security," A UNEP/INTERPOL Rapid Response Assessment (United Nations Environment Programme and RHIPTO Rapid Response – Norwegian Center for Global Analyses 2016) 7 https://23af4a98-6f9f-4a7d-b229-cbf91315456e.filesusr.com/ugd/655326_da17a489dedb467a957358b6cb8bba37.pdf accessed January 22, 2024.

19 Olawuyi (n 1).

forest and biodiversity in Morocco. Fourth, it offers recommendations on how to advance the integrated management of forest and biodiversity in Morocco and across the Maghreb region.

4.2 THE NEED FOR THE INTEGRATED MANAGEMENT OF FORESTS AND BIODIVERSITY

Forests play several roles: ecological, economic, and social. Hence there is a need for an ecosystem management approach that sustains the integrity of the forest space in a sustainable way.[20] The preservation of forests is not a new concept. It is intimately linked to the broader nature conservation movement that emerged in the 1860s. Its main objective is to conserve rare or endangered species through the establishment of reserves that allow free evolution. This is a single-functional management approach often realized in the creation of national parks and reserves. However, most natural resources exist outside these so-called protected areas.[21] In this regard, acting effectively for the protection of biodiversity in the forest environment requires an integrated or so-called multifunctional approach.[22] In this sense, the forest can be assigned several functions, with a main objective and other secondary ones. These functions can be compatible and allow the achievement of several objectives simultaneously.

Thus, the integrated or multifunctional management of the forest domain will guarantee the achievement of many objectives that are of general interest (environmental, social, and economic).[23] It will also guarantee the preservation and protection of the forest biodiversity simultaneously. This is achievable in a participatory approach, especially with the active involvement of forest neighbors. This approach is based on four tenets. The first one is the management of space, essential for integrated forest management to identify the entire forest domain and to grant it strong legal protection. Terrestrial management is an operation that will make possible the definition of the rules of access to resources, clarify property rights, and define participatory management methods with all stakeholders, including the local population.[24]

The second point concerns the multisectoral and multidisciplinary approach in the design of public policies during the implementation of these policies. An integrated approach to the management of forests and biodiversity makes it possible to reconcile local, national, and international constraints and to use economically viable procedures for all.

[20] See Chapter 5.

[21] See Janus Bodgan Falinski and Frédéric Mortier, "Biodiversity and Sustainable Forest Management in Europe," (1996) 48 *Revue forestière française* 89 https://hal.science/hal-03444336/document accessed January 22, 2024.

[22] See Philippe Lejeune, Hugues Claessens, Matthieu Alderweireld, and Jacques Rondeux, "Towards Integrated and Participatory Forest Management? The Example of the Municipality of Nassogne" (2007) *Forêt Wallonne* 86, 11 https://hdl.handle.net/2268/25233 accessed January 22, 2024.

[23] Ibid.

[24] Ibid.

The third point is the social and cultural aspect. No integrated management is possible without all actors being responsible and attentive to the effects of their activities on the forest. It is necessary to educate and raise awareness so that each actor can integrate the objectives of sustainable forest management into his or her actions, which implies the empowerment of the local population and the transfer of certain tasks to them.[25]

The fourth point relates to the forest economy. Any management of forest land must take account of the economic activities and ensure that the exploitation of resources does not call into question the viability of the forest and that it is not considered as agricultural land. This means that any economic activity must take on a sustainable dimension and not threaten the ecological role of the forest. An integrated management approach makes it possible to achieve the three conditions necessary for the conservation of the forest biodiversity: namely, enabling ecological systems to continue their biological evolution and to keep them in the best conditions of adaptability to changes in environmental conditions; maintaining the components of biological diversity to better know and understand them; and advancing the science and conservation of natural resources that can be useful to humans.[26] The implementation of these conditions necessitates the integration of sustainable forest management beyond the protected areas.[27]

4.2.1 *International Instruments Relevant to Forests and Biodiversity*

Although the international community is aware of the importance of the integrated management of forests and biodiversity, there is currently no specific international or regional instrument on integrated forest management.[28] The need for an international instrument for the protection of forests is felt more strongly for developing countries, since the forest resources in these countries require protection against climate, agriculture, livestock, industry, and energy.[29]

25 B. Dupuy, H.-F. Maître, and I. Amsallem, "Tropical Forest Ecosystem Management Techniques: State of the Art" (FAO Forestry Policy and Planning Division, Rome, July 1999) www.fao.org/3/X4130F/X4130f08.htm#TopOfPage accessed September 20, 2023.

26 See Falinski and Mortier (n 21).

27 See Georg Winkel, Jakob Derks, Agata Konczal, Andreas Rigling, Andreas Schuck, and Frank Krumm, "Advancing Biodiversity Conservation through Integrated Forest Management in Europe," assessment and actions needed policy brief resulting from the INFORMAR and Forest projects under the European Network Integrate. (December 2020) 182–189 www.researchgate.net/publication/348490373_Driving_factors_for_integrated_forest_management_in_Europe_-_findings_from_an_empirical_case_study_assessment accessed January 22, 2024.

28 See Barbara M. G. S Ruis, "No Forest Convention, but 10 Tree Treaties" (2001) 52 *Unasylva* 206, www.fao.org/3/y1237e/y1237e03.htm accessed January 22, 2024.

29 Koadima Lissiéni, "The International Protection of Forests," Master II research thesis in public international law, Université Ouaga II (March 2019) 10 www.pif-burkina.org/wp-content/uploads/2021/03/Memoire-KOADIMA-Lisieni.pdf accessed January 22, 2024.

There is no global consensus on the need for an international instrument specific to forests. The adoption of a convention on forests was on the agenda at the United Nations Conference on Environment and Development, better known as the Earth Summit, held in Rio de Janeiro, Brazil, June 3–14, 1992.[30] No binding instrument has seen the light, since it is impossible to compromise on the principle of the sovereignty of states over natural resources.[31]

The absence of an international convention specific to forests does not prevent the existence of many conventions having a direct impact on biodiversity and forests, and a distinction must be made between nonlegally binding instruments and general environmental conventions.

4.2.1.1 Nonbinding Instruments

Though not legally binding, the United Nations General Assembly Declaration of Principles of August 14, 1992, for a global consensus on the management, conservation, and sustainable development of all types of forests, is a source of inspiration for all actors involved in forest protection.[32] This declaration recognizes that forest protection is a cross-cutting issue touching on all environmental, economic, social, and environmental issues. National policies and programs must consider the relationship between the conservation, management, and sustainable development of forests and consider all aspects related to the production, consumption, and recycling of forest products.[33]

In addition to this declaration, there is the 2030 Agenda Sustainable Development Goals (SDGs), one of whose goals concerns the sustainable development of forests and the preservation of biodiversity.[34] SDG 15, which most directly addresses

30 United Nations, Rio Declaration on Environment and Development, UN Doc.A/CONF.151/26 (Vol. I), August 12, 1992, www.un.org/documents/ga/conf151/aconf15126-1annex1.htm (accessed December 12, 2023.

31 The International Tropical Timber Agreements are the only binding global agreements specific to forests. They are signed under the auspices of the UN. The first agreement was signed on November 18, 1983, in Geneva, and was replaced by a second agreement signed on January 26, 1994. It was adopted January 27, 2006, and entered into force on December 7, 2011. This agreement sets out the rules to prevail in the trade in timber from tropical forests to promote the sustainable management of tropical timber-producing forests. United Nations Conference on Trade and Development (UNCTAD), International Tropical Timber Agreement (adopted January 27, 2006, and entered into force December 7, 2011) TD/TIMBER.3/12 https://treaties.un.org/Pages/ViewDetails.aspx?src=TREATY&mtdsg_no=XIX-46&chapter=19&clang=_en accessed January 22, 2024.

32 United Nations Conference on Environment and Development, "Non-legally Binding Authoritative Statement of Principles for a Global Consensus on the Management, Conservation and Sustainable Development of All Types of Forests: Note by the Secretary-General of the Conference" (April 21, 1992) A/CONF.151/6 https://digitallibrary.un.org/record/144461?ln=en accessed January 22, 2024. Principles 5, 6 and 7 of the Declaration.

33 Ibid.

34 UN General Assembly (UNGA), "Transforming Our World: The 2030 Agenda for Sustainable Development" (October 21, 2015) A/RES/70/1 www.refworld.org/docid/57b6e3e44.html accessed January 22, 2024.

biological diversity, calls on countries to ensure "the conservation, restoration and sustainable use of terrestrial and inland freshwater ecosystems and their services, in particular forests, wetlands, mountains and drylands, in line with obligations under international agreements." It also encourages countries to "promote the implementation of sustainable management of all types of forests, halt deforestation, restore degraded forests and substantially increase afforestation and reforestation globally."[35]

Obviously, this will not be possible without the mobilization of significant resources from all sources and at all levels to finance sustainable forest management and to encourage developing countries to give priority to sustainable forest management, including forest conservation and reforestation.

4.2.1.2 General Environmental Conventions

The forest and its biodiversity are at the crossroads of all environmental protection instruments, so there is the climate regime based on the United Nations Framework Convention on Climate Change (UNFCCC), the biological diversity based on the Convention on Biological Diversity (CBD), and the protection of wetlands because of the Ramsar Convention.[36]

First, mention should be made of the content of the Convention concerning the Protection of the Natural and Cultural Heritage adopted on November 16, 1972 and ratified by Morocco on October 28, 1975.[37] The second article of this convention considers natural sites or strictly demarcated natural areas which have outstanding universal value from the point of view of science, conservation, or natural beauty to be part of World Heritage, and forests meet this definition. Thus, state parties must identify, protect, enhance, and transmit them to future generations.[38]

The Convention on Wetlands of International Importance, especially as Waterfowl Habitat, adopted on February 2, 1971 and known as the Ramsar Convention,[39] was ratified by Morocco on October 10, 1980.[40] As of 2020, the country had designated thirty-eight Ramsar sites, covering a total area of 316,086 hectares.[41] The first four wetlands of international importance were inscribed in 1980 and twelve new ones were inscribed in 2019.[42]

35 Ibid.
36 See Chapter 2.
37 Ibid.
38 Ibid., Article 4 of the convention.
39 See Chapters 1 and 2.
40 UN Treaty Collection, "Convention on Wetlands of International Importance Especially as Waterfowl Habitat" https://treaties.un.org/pages/showDetails.aspx?objid=0800000280104c20 accessed January 22, 2024.
41 Convention on Wetlands of International Importance Especially as Waterfowl Habitat, "Morocco" www.ramsar.org/country-profile/morocco accessed January 22, 2024.
42 UNESCO, "Ramsar convention on wetlands of international importance Especially as waterfowl habitat" (February 2, 1971, as amended by the Protocol of December 3, 1982 and the Amendments of May 28, 1987) Paris, July 13, 1994 https://rsis.ramsar.org/fr accessed January 22, 2024.

This convention indirectly concerns forests since some fall within their scope. This convention also concerns biodiversity, the forests being important reservoirs of fauna and flora. Thus, to be classified as a Ramsar area, it is necessary to support endangered species or species important for the conservation of biodiversity.[43]

In addition, the CBD does not contain forest-specific provisions.[44] However, it is a space for the protection of biological diversity. Morocco signed the CBD in 1992 and ratified it on August 21, 1995.[45] Indeed, forests are indispensable because of their role as habitats. State parties should adopt procedures to require environmental impact assessment of projects likely to harm biodiversity. In the same context, the role played by the United Nations Convention to Combat Desertification, signed on June 17, 1994, is particularly significant.[46] Since the destruction of forests is usually the cause of desertification, it is necessary to protect forests and to reforest.

Finally, international instruments for environmental protection cannot be discussed without emphasizing the link between climate and forests. In this sense, the UNFCCC was adopted to stabilize greenhouse gas concentrations in the atmosphere.[47] There is no need to demonstrate the relation between climate and forests. These are a means of combating climate change, just as forest degradation is a source of greenhouse gases. The Kyoto Protocol encourages states to promote sustainable forest management and reforestation.[48] Forest conservation and restoration can be an element of these nationally determined contributions in the Paris Agreement adopted at the Conference of the Parties (COP) 21, 2015, in Paris.[49]

Ultimately, despite the goodwill of the international community, expressed through the disputed instruments set out here, some of their stipulations show flexibility by using terminology such as "as far as possible."[50] This greatly influences the implementation of these stipulations and their incorporation into domestic law.

43 Ibid., Article 2.2 of the convention.

44 See Moïse Tsayem Demaze, "International Conventions on the Environment: Status of Ratifications and Commitments by Developed and Developing Countries" (2009) 3 *Geographic Information* 73, 84 www.cairn.info/revue-l-information-geographique-2009-3-page-84.htm accessed January 22, 2024.

45 Royaume du Maroc: Ministère de la transition énergétique et du développement durable, "La Convention sur la Diversité Biologique" http://environnement.gov.ma/fr/115-theme/biodiversite/3384-la-convention-sur-la-diversite-biologique#:~:text=Au%20cours%20de%20ce%20sommet%2C%20le%20Royaume%20du,y%20compris%20les%20%C3%A9cosyst%C3%A8mes%20et%20les%20esp%C3%A8ces%20vivantes accessed January 22, 2024.

46 See Chapter 2.

47 UNFCCC, Rio Conference on Environment and Development (adopted on May 9, 1992, entered into force on March 21, 1994). It consists of a preamble, twenty-six articles, and two annexes.

48 Kyoto Protocol to the United Nations Framework Convention on Climate Change (December 10, 1997) 2303 UNTS 162, Article 2.

49 Paris Agreement to the United Nations Framework Convention on Climate Change (December 12, 2015) TIAS No 16-1104 Decision 1/CP.21.

50 The Convention on Biological Diversity (June 5, 1992) 1760 UNTS 69, Article 8.

The doctrine adds that the CBD attaches great importance to commercial imperatives and the commitment of financial resources is also the Achilles' heel of environmental protection.[51]

4.3 THE SEARCH FOR INTEGRATION OF FOREST CONSERVATION AND BIODIVERSITY AT NATIONAL LEVELS: LESSONS FROM MOROCCO

Overlogging, overexploitation, and the unsustainable use of forest resources remain key causes of the decline in vegetation cover and the damage caused to forests in many parts of the MENA region. In Morocco, for example, the most important threat to forest conversation and biodiversity is the illegal logging of trees, which increases the pressure on the forest area, with legal felling estimated to be between 600,000 and 800,000 cubic meters per year.[52] Although the legal text attempts to control grazing,[53] the reality sometimes bears witness to the fact that there is still room for herding activity for neighboring residents. This is mainly due to social considerations, since most of the population of pastoralists are from vulnerable and poor social classes, and the public authorities face logistical difficulties due to the material and human resources necessary to monitor and punish violations. Public authorities face greater risks such as monitoring construction, logging, overshooting, construction, plowing, fires, and other hazards that pose a more serious threat to forest areas than grazing. In practice, the legal provisions governing the right to graze are sometimes not respected, whether in terms of the number or type of livestock, the times allowed for grazing in forests, or even the lack of control and custody of livestock.[54]

To address these concerns, the Moroccan legislature, through Law No. 113.13 on pastoral nomadism and the development and management of forest areas and pastures, has regulated pastoral areas and forest rangelands.[55] Article X expressly refers to the possibility of exploiting and using forest resources by populations enjoying exploitation or usufruct rights for grazing and pastoral activities.[56] The second paragraph of this article adds that forest areas can be opened, on an exceptional basis, for grazing in the event of climate disasters associated with drought or flooding and in

[51] Serge Maljean-Dubois, "Biodiversity, Biotechnology, Biosafety: International Law Disarticulated" (2000) 4 *Journal of Drug Issues* 950; see also: Lissiéni (n 26).

[52] Fourth Report on the Environmental Situation in Morocco, Ministry of Energy Transition and Sustainable Development-Sustainable Development Sector (2020) 107.

[53] Dahir No. 1.16.53 of April 27, 2016, implementing Law No. 113.13 on pastoral nomadism and the preparation and management of areas and rangelands forest (The Official Bulletin of Morocco, No 6466 of May 19, 2016) 3859.

[54] See Azgoudi Abdrahim, "The Forest Domain in Morocco, between the Constraints of Administrative Management and the Reality of Judicial Protection," (2020) Special Issue 19 *Moroccan Journal of Legal Systems and Politics* 240.

[55] Dahir No. 1.16.53 issued on April 27, 2016 (The Official Bulletin of Morocco, No 6466 of May 19, 2016) 3859.

[56] Ibid.

the event of any other disaster threatening the national herd. In this case, forest areas can be temporarily opened for grazing as a refuge to meet the needs of the herds.[57]

In this regard, the Water and Forest Department estimates that more than 80 percent of the forest area is exploited indiscriminately and all year round, a situation that negatively affects forest areas.[58] The Moroccan legal system evokes the social status of the population adjacent to the forests and balances this situation with the need to preserve forest wealth as one of the most important reservoirs of the ecosystem and biodiversity.

Despite the existence of various public policies put in place by the government to cope with the overexploitation of forest rangelands and ensure their renewal, social pressure and the lack of population involvement represent the impediments to reaching a solution to this phenomenon and result in the exploitation of forest pastures beyond their capacity.[59] In addition to the subsistence activities of the inhabitants living near the forest, there are many legal, institutional, and material obstacles that can prevent the implementation of an integrated policy for forest management and therefore ensure the protection of biodiversity in this area.

Morocco also recognizes the integrated management of forests and biodiversity through a new public policy called the Forest Strategy 2020–2030; the National Agency for Water and Forests is the authority in charge of the enforcement of this new strategy.[60] This strategy is based on four main pillars related to the creation of a new model with a participatory approach involving the population living nearby the forests, the management and development of forest spaces according to their qualifications, the development and modernization of forest professions, and the institutional and legislative reform of the sector.[61] The objective is to rectify the equivalent of thirty years of forest cover degradation by 2030, create more than 27,000 additional direct jobs, and achieve the goal of making the revenues of the valorization of production chains and ecotourism reach five billion dirhams as an annual trade value.[62]

57 Ibid.

58 See Abdrahim (n 54).

59 See Mohamed Ellatifi, "The Economy of Forests and Forest Products in Morocco: Assessment and Prospects," doctoral thesis in economic sciences (University of Montesquieu-Bordeau IV, Law, Social and Political Sciences, Economics and Management Sciences, June 5, 2012) 58.

60 Dahir No. 71-21-1 of July 14, 2021, implementing Law Nos 20-52 on the creation of the National Agency for Water and Forests (The Official Bulletin of Morocco, No 7006, July 22, 2021) 5639. The updated legal text of the agency is considered as the beginning of a review of the forest domain governance. This text grants broad and multiple powers to this agency, as the first paragraph of Article 3 of the law stipulates that the agency is responsible for implementing the strategic orientations of the government policy in the areas of protection, conservation, valorization, and sustainable development of national forest wealth and resources, as well as in the field of combating desertification, creating and managing protected areas, especially national parks, the management of hunting resources, fishing, and aquaculture in wild waters, as well as the preservation of wild flora and fauna and endangered species.

61 Fourth report on the environmental situation for the year 2020. See "Forests of Morocco 2020–2030: Programming of 600,000 ha of Forest Plantations by 2030" www.maroc.ma/en/news/forests-morocco-2020-2030-programming-600000-ha-forest-plantations-2030 accessed January 22, 2024.

62 Ibid.

It is an ambitious strategy based on the best international practices, yet the existence of an international convention or treaty specific to the protection of forests can greatly facilitate the implementation of this type of management.

4.3.1 *Institutions Charged to Protect Forests*

To fulfill all environmental protection requirements in general and integrated forest and biodiversity protection in particular, many laws have been enacted and several governmental institutions have been established. These institutions and bodies are established to ensure that economic actors and individuals adhere to environmental protection laws in general. Other bodies have a specialized role in dealing with biodiversity and forests. Institutions involved in this area can be classified into two categories: horizontal bodies (ministries, the Economic, Social and Environmental Council, and the police, judiciary, etc.), and sectoral bodies (the National Water and Forestry Agency, the High Water and Climate Council, the Environmental Police, etc.). Some of these bodies can also be classified as institutions making decisions while others have a consultative role only.

There are also several consultative bodies, including the National Council of the Environment and the Regional Councils for the Environment.[63] All these councils have a consultative role only. They track studies and propose legislative drafts and regulatory texts related to the environmental field.[64] They also raise awareness and sensitization of the importance of preserving the environment and its components. Furthermore, the Economic, Social and Environmental Council was established with the mandate to monitor the coherent implementation of environmental policies and legislation and to develop proposals that could contribute to sustainable development at all levels,[65] in addition to the High Water and Climate Council, which educates public authorities on the national policy relating to water resource management and weather and climate monitoring.[66] Besides consultative organs, the country has established the necessary reporting bodies with the capacity to take measures to protect the environment and punish environmental offenders. Among these bodies is the National Agency for Water and Forestry, which is primarily responsible for protecting forests, ensuring their development and managing various forest-related areas.

63 Decree No. 2.79.247 of May 12, 1980, on the reorganization and improvement of the institutions responsible for the protection of the environment (The Official Bulletin of Morocco, No 3527 of June 4, 1980) 719.

64 Decree No. 2-93-1011 of 18 Chaabane 1415 (January 20, 1995) on the reorganization of organizations responsible for the protection and improvement of the environment https://faolex.fao.org/docs/pdf/mor16650.pdf accessed January 22, 2024.

65 Royaume du Maroc, "Le Conseil Économique, Social et Environnemental" www.cese.ma accessed January 22, 2024.

66 Article 78 of Dahir No. 1.16.113, issued pursuant to Law No. 36.15 on water (The Official Bulletin of Morocco, No 6494 of August 25, 2016) 6305.

However, the main challenge remains how to create strong synergies between all the stakeholders dealing with environmental policy.[67] The duplication of institutions concerned with the environmental field intertwines the issue of environmental protection between many sets of programs and policies adopted by several government agencies. There is a wide range of institutions in charge of environmental study and planning (ministries, the Economic Social and Environmental Council, the Supreme Water and Climate Council, the National Environment Council, the National Water and Forestry Agency, etc.). This can also lead to overlaps between the competences of local authorities (regions, prefectures, provinces, and communities) and those of line ministries and certain public institutions. For example, the regulatory laws of local authorities provide a series of competences related to the environment, including the development and management of regional parks, while departments and ministries retain the same competences without specifying their limits or the coordination and cooperation between these bodies.

To ensure coordination and efficiency between all those institutions, the legal provision needs to be clarified.[68] This situation led to inflation in planning and programming, and thus to sectoral planning, which goes against the philosophy of integrated forest management. In the absence of coordination between the organs and institutions entrusted with these functions, there will be a problem with the effectiveness of the government's programs, a weakness that has been recognized by the government.[69]

4.3.2 *Issues Related to the Legal Framework*

Several legal provisions and instruments in Morocco may constrain or limit the integrated management of forests and biodiversity. Three major issues in this sense are discussed.

4.3.2.1 The Protection of the Forest Domain

The preservation of the forest domain against any encroachment is the cornerstone of any integrated management strategy. In Morocco, there is a practice which consists of separating plots of land from the forest and making them available to investors. This practice challenges any public forest protection policy.

67 Hadi Miqdad, *Environmental Law* (Imprimerie Najah ElJadida 2012). For more details, see the official website of the Ministry of Energy, Mines and the Environment, Department of the Environment www.environnement.gov.ma/fr/ accessed January 22, 2024.

68 On the importance of enacting clear and comprehensive climate change laws, see D. Olawuyi, "Energy Poverty in the Middle East and North African (MENA) Region: Divergent Tales and Future Prospects" in I. Del Guayo, L. Godden, D. Zillman, M. Montoya, and J. Gonzalez (eds), *Energy Law and Energy Justice* (Oxford University Press 2020) 254–272.

69 Morocco Climate Change Policy (March 2014) www.umi.ac.ma/wp-content/uploads/2020/11/ODD-13-A9-politique_du_changement_climatique_au_maroc.pdf accessed January 22, 2024.

The forest domain has a strict protective regime. It is not transferable and not acquired by prescription, nor can it be seized. However, this protection accepts one exception, which is provided for in the first paragraph of Chapter II of the *Dahir* of October 10, 1917, on the conservation and exploitation of forests, which states: "The property of the forest store cannot be sold, and its separation from the forest system can only be done for the benefit of the public interest."[70] There is a possibility of separating the forest from its system if there is a public interest.[71] Although the separation process is complex and requires the intervention of different parties and multiple procedures, it ends with the issuance of a decree published in the official bulletin, based on the opinion of the administrative committee established by the decree of June 6, 1959.[72] This decree subjects the separate piece of forest to the rules of the private property of the state, allowing it to be freely disposed of.

If the rule requires the separation of the forest domain from its system in the public interest, the reality sometimes testifies otherwise, as it will be down to the forest to assign its real estate to serve various projects. The parts separated from the forest may be allocated to tourism projects or the creation of industrial zones, dams, mines, quarries, etc. During the last fifty years, 7,000 hectares of forest domain have been allocated to such projects, without searching for alternatives.[73] Among the factors that allow these abuses is that the legislative and regulatory texts regulating the procedure for separating property from the forest system do not deal with the destiny of the property after the separation process. There is nothing to prevent the Directorate of State Property from changing this allocation from one specific project to another, as the condition of public benefit may be achieved during the initiation of the separation procedure. After the completion of the process, the allocation is changed to another project that does not necessarily achieve public benefit and can be related to commercial purposes.

This leads to the degradation of the forest and consequently its biodiversity. Without the preservation of the forest domain, all reforestation efforts will be ineffective. In addition, the forest may be the scene of more important economic or social activities. This fact poses a problem for environmental approval granted to economic activities within the forest area.

70 *Dahir sur la conservation et l'exploitation des forêts, modifié par Dahir du 17 avril 1959 et du 21 juillet 1960*. www.fao.org/faolex/results/details/en/c/LEX-FAOC002830 accessed January 22, 2024.

71 It relates to the following projects: dams, roads, motorways, railways, airports, ports, and their technical installations; hospitals and clinics of the health sector; educational institutions of the National Education Sector. According to the circular of the High Commissioner for Water, Forests, and the Fight against Desertification No 2088 of May 3, 2011.

72 Decree No 2-58-1371 of June 6, 1959, defining and establishing the committee in charge of expressing its opinion in the event of separation the forest from its system (The Official Bulletin of Morocco, No 2435 of June 16, 1959) 1953.

73 Kingdom of Morocco, Ministry of Energy Transition and Sustainable Development-Sustainable Development Sector, Third Report on the Environmental Situation in Morocco (2015), 110. www.environnement.gov.ma/PDFs/Rapport-reem.pdf accessed January 24, 2024.

4.3.2.2 Environmental Assessment

The second legal problem which largely influences the protection of forests in Morocco is the authorization granted to certain types of economic projects within the forest area. It is on this occasion that the role of Law No. 49.17 on Environmental Assessment is highlighted.[74] In fact, by expanding the field of environmental impact study and opening new areas for it, Law No. 49.17 was considered a qualitative leap in the policy of strengthening legal and institutional governance in the field of the environment.

The practice of studying the impact of economic projects on the environment has shown significant shortcomings and a series of abuses. These abuses are particularly related to the fact that the said studies are entrusted to technical study offices that are selected by the entrepreneur and paid out of his/her own pocket. A fact that raises doubts about the impartiality and objectivity of the study, especially in the face of the difficulty of conducting counter-experiences given their cost.

The obligation to conduct an environmental impact study before creating any economic activity in the forest is natural and necessary, since any activity of whatever nature may cause damage to the natural resources of the forest and thus affect the ecosystem. Despite the negative repercussions of these activities, they are licensed, and perhaps among the most controversial activities are quarries because of their serious effects on the ecological balance. A number of reports explicitly indicate that the exploitation of quarries within the forest property causes the destruction of existing shrubs and leads to an imbalance of the forest ecosystem.[75] Moreover, the bodies directly involved in the management of forest property are also aware of the negative impact of this type of project on the ecosystem and ecological balance of the forest, as explicitly indicated in the report on the environmental situation in Morocco, which was prepared by the Ministry of Energy Transition and Sustainable Development for the year 2020.[76] Motivated by its awareness of the negative impact of economic projects on the forest system, the Water and Forestry Department asked for an environmental impact study before the issuance of the law itself.[77]

74 Dahir No. 1.20.78 issued on August 8, 2020, implementing Law No 49.17 on Environmental Assessment (The Official Bulletin of Morocco, No 6908 of August 13, 2020) 4346, which replaced the 2003 Law No 12.03 on the study of the impact on the environment.

75 Report of Moroccan Court of Accounts for the year 2009, 80 https://tinyurl.com/32evxtz4 accessed January 24, 2024. See also Taha Mebtoul, "Morocco's Parliament Creates Commission to Explore Sand Quarries" (September 21, 2020) www.moroccoworldnews.com/2020/09/320288/moroccos-parliament-creates-commission-to-explore-sand-quarries accessed January 22, 2024.

76 The fourth report on the environmental situation for the year 2020, 93. 4ème Rapport sur l"État de l"Environnement du Maroc- version intégrale (mtedd.gov.ma) accessed January 24, 2024.

77 High Commissioner's Circular No. 31901 of September 5, 2007 (unpublished document).

This did not prevent these authorities from granting a license to establish a gravel quarry in a forest nature reserve, for example.[78] This issue raises an obvious question: How it is possible to license a quarry to extract gravel inside the forest while this activity has clear effects that should require in-depth studies to be carried out? In fact, the extraction process requires the use of explosive materials, the uprooting of young trees, and the spread of dust, all of which are easy to prove. This raises doubts about the objectivity of environmental impact studies carried out by companies involved in economic activity, which were mentioned earlier, and which call for legislative intervention since the new law maintained the same procedures specified in the previous text.[79]

4.3.2.3 The Fragmentation of the Legal Framework on Forest and Biodiversity

The third issue which can prevent the integrated management of forests in Morocco is that the legal framework related to environment and specifically to forests and biodiversity is fragmented and dates back to the beginning of the twentieth century. Indeed, there are at least eleven laws about forest and biodiversity, most of them issued in the first years of the twentieth century.

For example, we have the Dahir issued on January 3, 1916, establishing special regulations to determine private properties of the state (Amlak Makhzaniya); the Dahir dated October 10, 1917, regarding the preservation and exploitation of forests;[80] the Dahir dated March 4, 1925, relating to the protection and identification of argan tree forests;[81] the Dahir issued on August 15, 1928, specifying the conditions to make lands planted by the "Hulfa" part of private property;[82] the Dahir dated July 23, 1930, regarding the preservation and exploitation of the "Hulfa" plant;[83] the Dahir issued on September 20, 1976, regulating the population's contribution to the development of the forest economy;[84] the Dahir of April 11, 1922, regarding fishing and aquaculture in wild waters, as amended by the Decrees of January 23, 1957, June 16, 1961, August 17, 2011, and August 4, 2015;[85] Law No. 54.03, issued on June 15, 2006, amending and supplementing the Dahir, issued on July 21, 2023, relating to the control of hunting;[86] Law No. 22.07, regarding protected areas issued on July 16, 2010;[87]

78 Decision No. 177 issued by the Court of Cassation on March 29, 2012 in the administrative file No 775/4/2/2011 (published in the Real Estate Files Journal issued by the Court of Cassation "Water and Forests Issues," No 4, 2014) 139.
79 Abdrahim (n 42) 244.
80 The Official Bulletin of Morocco, No 235, October 29, 1917, 901.
81 Ibid., No 647, March 27, 1925, 526.
82 Ibid., No 830, September 18, 1928, 2610.
83 Ibid., No 927, August 1, 1930, 1698.
84 Ibid., No 3334, September 22, 1976, 2915.
85 Ibid., No 6388, August 20, 2015, 7123.
86 Ibid., No 5435, June 3, 2006, 1648.
87 Ibid., No 5861, August 2, 2010, 3904.

and Law No. 29.05, regarding the protection of species of wild plants and animals and the control of trade in them, issued on July 2, 2011.[88] All these laws have several implementing provisions (decrees and decisions).[89]

This multiplication and fragmentation of the legal framework about forest and biodiversity make the legal provision difficult to understand and enforce, and it can also lead to the absence of coherence between all the texts of laws. This situation is not specific to forest and biodiversity but it concerns all the environmental legal frameworks.

To this fragmentation one may add the multiplication of the implementing provisions. Those enforcement texts are one of the most important obstacles to the activation of legal texts related to the environment in general, as some laws require more than twenty enforcement texts, which limits their effectiveness. For example, the activation of Law No. 03.12, on environmental impact studies, required two decrees, two decisions, and a ministerial circular, which was changed in 2020 by Law No. 49.17 on environmental assessment, which raises the need to prepare new implementing provisions as well as to amend other legal texts referring to the contents of the old law. Moreover, there is a set of legal texts that were never implemented in the field since they were waiting for the publication of the implementing provisions (Law No. 08.01 on Quarries 2002, which did not come into force, and was replaced in 2015 by Law 27.13).[90]

4.3.3 *The Lack of Awareness, Scientific Research, and Human and Financial Resources*

In Morocco, there are many civil society associations and nongovernmental organization (NGOs) which are active in the field of environmental protection and are considered to be essential partners in preserving the environment's wealth. This role reflects their contribution to the development and monitoring of government programs at all levels. The National Strategy for Environment and Sustainable Development gives priority to civil society associations by strengthening their capacities.[91] A series of annual activities have been organized since 2014, with the objective of pushing NGOs toward professionalism and transparency in environmental work.[92] One successful example of civil society associations' role in environmental

[88] The Official Bulletin of Morocco, No 5962, July 21, 2011, 3474.

[89] A collection of texts is available at the following link: www.eauxetforets.gov.ma/AccueilAR/SitePages/Textes-Reglementaires.aspx accessed January 22, 2024.

[90] Dahir No. 1.15.66 was issued on June 9, 2015, implementing Act No. 27.13 on quarries. The Official Bulletin of Morocco, No 6374 of July 2, 2015, 6082.

[91] Kingdom of Morocco, "National Strategy for Environment and Sustainable Development" www.greenpolicyplatform.org/sites/default/files/downloads/policy-database/ENG-SNDD_RESUME%20EXECUTIF-V24-D%20(1).pdf accessed January 22, 2024.

[92] In this context, twelve training workshops are organized annually at the level of each of the kingdom's entities for some 360 collective frameworks on; *inter alia*, local action to combat climate change

protection is the Mohammed VI Foundation for Environmental Protection. The Mohammed VI Foundation works under a well-defined strategy aimed primarily at fostering environmental education and sustainable tourism.[93]

In the same context, a project called Mobilizing Civil Society to Support Dialogue in order to Adapt to Climate Change in Morocco launched in 2018 under the auspices of the World Wildlife Fund office in North Africa.[94] The project involves the active participation of sixteen associations representing various regions of the kingdom and aims to support, train, and strengthen their capacities. It aims to sensitize the authorities about the importance of integrating climate change adaptation and mitigation into public policies for development, particularly in the areas of water and forests.[95]

However, despite the importance of these initiatives, from what we know there is no association specializing in the protection of forests or biodiversity in Morocco, and even if this type of association existed, it would be difficult for it to have an impact given the lack of means available to environmental associations in general. Furthermore, Moroccan law does not allow civil society associations to present legal actions to defend the general interest and the right to live in a healthy environment,[96] which largely limits their actions.

The intervention of the public authorities alone will not achieve the expected objectives in terms of forest protection. Indeed, civil society, as an intermediary between the government and citizens, must be involved in all facets of public intervention in the protection of forests and biodiversity, especially through awareness-raising actions addressed to citizens living next to the forests and exploiting their resources.

The question of human, logistical, and financial resources is now acute given the multiplication of risks that the forest is facing, especially because of the effects of climate change and the recent wildfires. This testifies to the need for all the necessary tools and technical capacities to combat this increasingly devastating phenomenon, and scientific research can be used to face those challenges.

and societal action. For more information on the work to promote the role of environmental protection associations, please see the following associations: www.environnement.gov.ma/images/ONG-Partenariat/AR/Appui-au-financement-des-projets-associatifs-ar-link.pdf accessed September 19, 2022.

93 For more information about the Mohammed VI Foundation for Environmental Protection: https://fm6e.org/en/ accessed January 22, 2024.

94 www.afd.fr/fr/carte-des-projets/societe-civile-et-changement-climatique-au-maroc-et-en-tunisie accessed January 24, 2024; and https://jamaity.org/project/mobilisation-de-la-societe-civile-pour-la-resilience-aux-changements-climatiques/ accessed January 24, 2024.

95 See Article 22 of the Framework Law No 99.12 for associations.

96 For example, the Algerian legislator, which authorized the associations for the defense of the environment to sue and contest all acts and behaviors that constitute an attack against the environment (Article 36 of Law No 10.03 related to environmental protection and sustainable development in Algeria). In Morocco, only associations with the status of public interest have the right to resort to the judiciary.

This question of resources is even more important when one analyzes the ambitious projects undertaken by the Forests and Water Agency.

4.4 ADVANCING THE INTEGRATED MANAGEMENT OF FORESTS AND BIODIVERSITY: RECOMMENDATIONS

The elements covered in this chapter clearly illustrate the need to review some legal provisions concerning environmental law in general and especially those related to biodiversity and forests. In this section we suggest possible solutions to fill the gaps that may have an impact on the protection of the forest and its biodiversity.

4.4.1 *Improving Institutional Frameworks*

The success of integrated forest and biodiversity management depends on multisectoral government action, which requires the involvement of all relevant public actors. To advance integrated forest and biodiversity management, clear and comprehensive legal and policy frameworks are required to address concerns of regulatory overlap, lack of coordination, and inefficiency that have been identified in the implementation of climate change law and policies in North African countries.

There is a need to create mechanisms for coordination between the various institutions involved in protecting the forest. The best approach is to create an intergovernmental institution on environmental protection in general, because the forest and biodiversity protection cannot be limited to the direct protection of this area but depends on global action that concerns all aspects of the environment and climate change. It is certain that the existence of a positive synergy between the different components of the environment can have better results than any action that targets only one of these components (water, forest, air, plastics, etc.), especially when it comes to implementing public policies or programming.

This institution must involve representatives of all the various ministries and agencies that have relevant roles to ensure the integrate management of the forest. In this way there will be a sharing of experience, resources, and work toward improving their consistency and complementarity.

To succeed in this challenge, there is a need for legislative provisions that clarify the roles of the respective agencies to avoid role duplication and overlap. Improving the quality of legal texts governing these institutions would generate greater efficiency in their programs and actions.

Regarding forest biodiversity, the National Agency for Water and Forests can be the tool for the implementation of public policies concerning the forest, but without coordination and financial and human resources the work of the agency will be ineffective.

In Morocco, effective forest protection requires thinking about reviewing the legislative and regulatory provisions concerning environmental law or at least the organization and legislative techniques used by the country. Pending the general overhaul of environmental law, there are certain provisions concerning forest protection that must be reviewed immediately.

4.4.1.1 The Forest Domain

The Dahir of October 10, 1917, on the conservation and exploitation of forests, allows the government to separate part of the forest domain to devote it to a social or economic project.[97] The impact of this practice on the forest sector is certainly negative, as explained earlier. This is why it is imperative to put an end to it.

This situation necessitates legislative intervention that expressly prevents the separation of the forest from its system. In the face of climate change and the disasters that the forest suffers, chiefly fires, which have greatly affected the forest area, there is no justification for maintaining this separation rule. This is due to its repercussions on the area of the forest property in Morocco, and thus on the indicators of ecological balance and the country's ecosystem.[98] If it is hard to achieve, at least some provisions shall be stipulated to prevent the allocation of the separated property for a purpose other than the public benefit. This should be done while specifying a mechanism to monitor this process and issuing a decree by the head of government to retract the separation process in case it is proven that the rule of public benefit has been violated.

The government should not rely on the forest as a real estate container, as its tasks go beyond its pure real estate nature, and it is also represents a basic component of the ecosystem, an ecological balance reservoir, and a natural heritage shared by all members of society. It is a fragile component that should be preserved and developed rather than depleted and allocated to projects of whatever nature.

In general, the management of the forest domain must imperatively be part of a sustainable logic, therefore any economic project that does not guarantee the sustainability of the forest and its biodiversity must be abandoned. The provisions of Law No. 49.17 on environmental assessment must be unequivocally on the harmful repercussions of certain economic projects in the forestry areas and prohibit their implementation.

4.4.1.2 Improving Legal Frameworks in the Environment

The predominance of legal fragmentation illustrates the need to review the philosophy of legislation in the field of the environment through the establishment

[97] Dahir of October 10, 1917 (n 70).

[98] Khalil Rahmani, "Mechanisms of Formation and Protection of the Real Estate Balance of the Private Property of the Country," master's diploma in private law, Course of Contract and Real Estate Law, Faculty of Legal, Economic and Social Sciences, Mohammed I University Oujda, Morocco, Academic Year 2007–2008, 39.

of an "environment code" that would put an end to sporadic legislation related to different areas that do not have a global logic surrounding the environment in its general context.

Developing an environmental code would simplify a series of legal and administrative procedures related to environmental protection. The code would not be sufficient to accommodate all the texts related to the environment but it can include the most important of these texts, which have a direct impact on the protection of the environment in Morocco. The most important tasks of the environment code would be to simplify the process of preserving the environment and the process of implementing the legal text. It would allow for the streamlined teaching of environmental law and the identification of responsibilities and the creation of a special institution in charge of applying all the legal texts related to environment protection and the climate change adaptation and mitigation efforts; this institution should oversee the coordination between the different departments and all the stakeholders.

This environmental code should have two sections. The first section should concern the legislative provisions, whose first part should include common requirements (definitions, basic and general principles related to the environment, environmental impact study, public institutions, environmental protection associations, environmental protection programs, common requirements regarding violations and penalties, financial requirements, administrative procedures, and disputes).

The second part should be concerned with the physical environment (water, seawater, climate, air, forests, the land and what is below, grazing, quarries, and violations of the environment). The third part could contain natural spaces (coasts, coral reefs, nature reserves, protected natural sites, landscapes, hiking and access to nature, green belt, and blue belt). The fourth should concern the natural heritage (protection of natural assets, fishing, and hunting). The fifth and last part could focus on pollution and risk prevention (natural risk prevention, industrial risk prevention, audiovisual pollution, waste management and disposal).

The second section of this code should contain all the regulatory provisions that enable the content of the code to be applied procedurally. They would be decrees, decisions, and other texts that codify the organizational aspect of the process and that do not require a legislative framework and are mainly aimed at demonstrating the mode and methods of implementing the code provision (registration forms, model contracts, professional cards, documents for obtaining licenses, etc.).

An environmental code can be easily developed in Morocco because there are existing legal provisions on environmental protection in general, so the work will be limited to compiling and standardizing certain requirements, particularly regarding the implementing provisions. The environmental code can clearly identify the competencies and powers of all stakeholders in environmental management, as well as those responsible for coordination between all stakeholders. If the implementation of an environmental code is difficult, the alternative would be at least to develop a code for forests.

4.4.2 *Strengthen Awareness and Scientific Research*

Improving legal and institutional frameworks in the environment will be ineffective without simultaneously setting up practical mechanisms likely to guarantee its effective implementation. Citizens' awareness is an essential component of any public policy concerning environmental protection, and this awareness is particularly important regarding the protection of the forest or the implementation of integrated forest management, since part of the damage caused to the forest is due to the direct actions of citizens, as specified earlier.

For this purpose, involving citizens in the implementation of forest protection is not a choice but a necessity, and obviously it is on this occasion that the role of civil society can be decisive, especially for awareness-raising and education actions. This is why environmental associations working on forests must be involved in coordination with public authorities. These associations must be considered as partners and must be given all the necessary means to carry out their actions; it is unacceptable for this type of association not be recognized as a public utility.

In addition, the availability of an environmental code would simplify the teaching of environmental law, as the diversity and fragmentation defined by the current Moroccan legal system makes it difficult to understand all components. This explains the absence of environmental law from the curriculum, and the law cannot be activated without being introduced and educated to young people. This subject must be included in secondary courses or at least within the early years of university, whatever the specialty, because environmental protection is a common concern of all.

Furthermore, the National Forest Strategy 2020–2030 does not sufficiently elaborate on the important role of research in the preservation of biodiversity and the sustainable use of forest resources.[99] Certainly, the success of integrated forest and biodiversity management depends on continuous scientific research on modalities and tricks that can adapt to climate change.[100] In most cases, individual scientists work in isolation, which hampers the interdisciplinary approach essential for integrated forest management. In other words, governmental efforts should focus on investing in forest- and biodiversity-oriented scientific research. This should include supporting interdisciplinary and collaborative research through the establishment laboratories. This is of paramount importance, considering the evolving nature of forest biodiversity, which constantly changes. In this regard, it becomes compulsory to understand how these changes might affect the functioning and stability of ecosystems and develop strategies to address these changes.[101]

99 Kingdom of Morocco (n 91).

100 Winkel et al. (n 27).

101 D. Kraus and F. Krumm (eds), *Integrative Approaches as an Opportunity for the Conservation of Forest Biodiversity* (European Forest Institute 2013).

4.5 CONCLUSION

The status and importance of the forest in preserving the ecological balance and biodiversity for a country such as the Kingdom of Morocco, which is suffering from the consequences of climate change, especially the recent wave of fires, is incontrovertible. To strengthen the efforts made by the government and public institutions to protect the patriarchal space and to promote biodiversity, some measures must be taken; perhaps the most important is the reform of the legal framework for the forest, which is characterized by the dispersion and obsoleteness of most of its provisions. This reform must work on the compilation of legal texts into a code of the forest domain. It must also specify the adaptation of these legal texts to modern requirements, especially climate change.

Public authorities should also create awareness-raising programs on the importance of preserving the forest property and its ecosystems for the benefit of inhabitants living near to the forests as well as other citizens and visitors. The government must create alternative resources to the forest property for the benefit of neighboring populations and motivate them by considering them as partners in the preservation of the forest. This can be done by creating specific training for them to integrate the public policies related to forests and entrust them with some tasks, such as monitoring the forest environment against compensation. The real problem that needs to be worked on is to consider the neighboring populations as partners in the process of protecting the forest, and to achieve this, it is necessary to fight the poverty that drives them to use the forest as a livelihood resource. Given the current situation of the forests, the government must put an end to the procedure of separating the forest domain from its system. Real estate that has not been used or discarded, either totally or partially, must be recovered and returned to the forest property.

Finally, since the National Agency for Water and Forests is the institutional mechanism responsible for the implementation of public policies related to forestry, the state must provide this agency with all the human, financial, and logistical resources needed to ensure that it fully accomplishes its tasks. The legal provisions referred to in this chapter involve multiple and varied tasks but the implementation of these provisions will be possible only if the state allocates all the necessary means to do so.

PART II

Case Studies

5

Landscape Alterations in the MENA Region

Threats, Factors, and Priority Actions

Oluwatobi Mary Owojori and Emem Anwana

5.1 INTRODUCTION

This chapter examines the legal and institutional frameworks for promoting landscape and biodiversity conservation in the Middle East and North Africa (MENA) region. It examines the drivers of landscape alterations and biodiversity loss in the region, the legal barriers that hinder coherent responses to such problems, and how such barriers can be coherently addressed.

As one of the world's oldest regions, the MENA region has one of the most diverse landscapes. Mountains, oceans, and rivers form the foundation for a diverse mosaic of subregions with different types of soil, plant cover, and microclimates.[1] The long-term struggle against aridity has profoundly altered the social and technological means of interacting with the landscape, giving rise to several local activities. Long-standing environmental and cultural systems have been destroyed as a result of the recent rapid urbanization that has altered and changed the integration of culture and the physical landscape.[2] As the number of people on earth grows geometrically, increasing amounts of land are set aside for their requirements, including housing and food production.

Due to its long history of human habitation, the MENA region possesses one of the highest population densities, and for hundreds of years it has been continuously losing biodiversity as a result of land cover alteration resulting from land grading, forest removal, and excavation activities, among other things.[3] This practice, described as landscape alteration, results in the disturbance and invasion of natural habitat, including the flora and fauna. The MENA landscape is increasingly altered by natural and anthropogenic (human-induced) events, such as fires, storms, and/or human-driven construction, agricultural expansion, and urbanization, which have significant effects on biodiversity and ecosystem services.[4] Previous research

1 Sareh Moosavi, Jala Makhzoumi, and Margaret Grose, "Landscape Practice in the Middle East between Local and Global Aspirations" (2015) 41 *Landscape Research* 3, 265.

2 Ibid.

3 Damilola Olawuyi, *Environmental Law in Arab States* (Oxford University Press 2022) 1–25.

4 Ibid.

has shown that variations in land use conditions have a negative worldwide impact on local biodiversity.[5] Loss of biodiversity and the resulting reduction in ecosystem service delivery have substantial economic and social consequences that affect not only the ability to maintain the environment but also the ability to combat global poverty, hunger, and illness. As metropolitan regions and their human populations expand, effective landscape protection and biodiversity conservation become more crucial, not only to meet conservation goals but also because ecosystems supply services that humans and animals depend on. The MENA region's peace initiatives could be hampered by landscape conversion. A higher population competing for scarce natural resources such as water and arable land could complicate their distribution, leaving more people without access and resulting in greater hardship.[6]

A small number of studies have looked at the effects of landscape changes and conservation management strategies on trade-offs between biodiversity and ecosystem services.[7] Studies on landscape alterations from the MENA region, however, have received minimal investigation. Since previous studies have not conducted a meta-analysis or integrated review, despite the fact that they have provided insightful information about the trends of land use change or the operation of natural ecosystems, this chapter fills a significant gap in this regard. This chapter uses an integrated review to identify the factors influencing landscape changes in the MENA region.

The subsequent sections of this chapter follow a structured sequence, delving deeper into the subject matter. Section 5.2 examines the nature, scope, and drivers of landscape changes and biodiversity loss in the MENA region, shedding light on their intricate dynamics. In Section 5.3, the focus narrows down to a survey of legal and institutional barriers that hinder effective landscape alteration and biodiversity preservation efforts. Section 5.4 provides a set of strategic legal and institutional recommendations designed to overcome the identified barriers. Finally, Section 5.5 concludes by synthesizing insights from the preceding sections, offering a forward-looking perspective on how these recommendations could reshape landscape and biodiversity preservation in the MENA region.

5.2 NATURE, SCOPE, AND DRIVERS OF LANDSCAPE CHANGES AND BIODIVERSITY LOSS IN THE MENA REGION

This section discusses the factors associated with landscape changes and biodiversity conservation in the MENA region. The review identifies natural/spatial, policy/

[5] E. C. Ellis et al., "Used Planet: A Global History" (2013) 110 *Proceedings of the National Academy of Sciences* 20, 7978.

[6] Katharina Waha et al., "Climate Change Impacts in the Middle East and Northern Africa (MENA) Region and Their Implications for Vulnerable Population Groups" (2017) 17 *Regional Environmental Change* 6, 1623.

[7] L. Kirch et al., "World Risk Report Analysis and Prospects 2017" (2017) http://weltrisikobericht.de/wp-content/uploads/2017/11/WRR_2017_E2.pdf accessed January 27, 2024.

institutional, socio-economic, technological, and cultural factors as those influencing land alterations in the region.

5.2.1 *Natural/Spatial Factors*

Urban land use and land cover patterns can alter as a result of natural environmental occurrence or disasters such as climate change, flooding, erosion, and wildfires.[8] Extreme weather conditions brought on by climate change, such as heavy and erratic rainfall, flooding, and droughts, influence landscape alterations. This is a major threat for biodiversity and ecosystem functioning.[9] Major land alteration processes in the MENA region include overgrazing, wildfires, landslides, water and wind erosion, salinization, a reduction in soil fertility and organic matter, and salinization that impacts more than 40 percent of the region's land.[10] Only 2.9 percent of the land in the MENA countries is covered by forests and bushes, many of which have been destroyed by wildfires, used as fuel, overgrazed, turned into agriculture, or destroyed by urbanization.[11]

The various ecological components are greatly impacted by the local climatic conditions in the Arab region. The region's predominantly dry ecosystems are fragile by nature, which have significant effects. According to NASA, the current dry period in the MENA region is the worst it's been in 900 years.[12] Since 1998, the region has seen practically constant drought. These regions are predicted to have the highest population exposure to accelerated desertification, according to the Intergovernmental Panel on Climate Change assessment.[13]

Water scarcity and associated unsustainable practices constitute another factor responsible for increased land alterations and biodiversity loss. Prolonged water scarcity plays a prominent role in driving land alteration in the MENA countries.[14] The region grapples with chronic water shortages due to factors such as excessive groundwater extraction, inefficient irrigation methods, and shifting precipitation patterns

8 Damilola Olawuyi (ed), *Climate Change Law and Policy in the Middle East and North Africa Region* (Routledge 2021) 1–11.

9 Virginie Lepetz et al., "Biodiversity Monitoring: Some Proposals to Adequately Study Species' Responses to Climate Change" (2009) 18 *Biodiversity and Conservation* 12, 3185.

10 Razieh Namdar, Ezatollah Karami, and Marzieh Keshavarz, "Climate Change and Vulnerability: The Case of MENA Countries" (2021) 10 *ISPRS International Journal of Geo-Information* 11, 794.

11 Wilco Terink, Walter Willem Immerzeel, and Peter Droogers, "Climate Change Projections of Precipitation and Reference Evapotranspiration for the Middle East and Northern Africa until 2050" (2013) 33 *International Journal of Climatology* 14, 3055.

12 Benjamin I. Cook et al., "Spatiotemporal Drought Variability in the Mediterranean over the Last 900 Years" (2016) 121 *Journal of Geophysical Research: Atmospheres* 5, 2060.

13 Mehmet Ishak Yuce and Musa Esit, "Drought Monitoring in Ceyhan Basin, Turkey" (2021) 9 *Journal of Applied Water Engineering and Research* 4, 1.

14 Kira Walker, "MENA's Biodiversity Shrinking under Pressure of Climate Change" (Nature Middle East, December 2022) www.natureasia.com/en/nmiddleeast/article/10.1038/nmiddleeast.2022.79 accessed January 27, 2024.

influenced by climate change. These elements contribute to soil salinization and erosion, effectively transforming once fertile land into unproductive terrain.[15]

Sea level rise also puts low-lying coastal regions in Kuwait, Qatar, Libya, Tunisia, and the United Arab Emirates at risk of flooding, as well as the northern coast of Egypt, such as in Alexandria, Egypt's second-largest city after Cairo.[16] Yemen's 2008 flood cost the nation US$1.6 billion (6 percent of Yemen's gross domestic product),[17] and the Djibouti flood of 2004 harmed 100,000 people, claimed 230 lives, and caused extensive damage.[18] Additionally, according to vulnerability severity levels, the low-vulnerable category is predicted to experience floods much more frequently as a result of climate change, and due to inadequate citywide drainage systems, minimal structural protection, and informal urbanization of watershed areas, floods also frequently damage landcover in the MENA region.[19] The necessity for measures to maintain biodiversity and the unfavorable effects of climate change are consistent. Although the causes of these changes are undoubtedly complex, there is some indication that the worst effects could be mitigated if habitat degradation could be stopped, notably in semi-arid grasslands and the rainforests of equatorial regions.

According to the UN State Habitats of the World's Cities 2008–2009, by 2070 coastal cities such as Alexandria (Egypt), Algiers (Algeria), Casablanca (Morocco), Djibouti (Djibouti), and Tunis (Tunisia) might be badly impacted by increasing sea levels. A few member nations of the medium and highly vulnerable classes, including Saudi Arabia, have acquired foreign arable lands in Africa and elsewhere after realizing the unreliability of water resources in order to produce food grains and satisfy their rapidly expanding population's rising food demand, further altering the landscape.[20]

5.2.2 *Socio-economic Factors*

Population growth and rapid urbanization are intrinsic to economic diversification. As cities expand, they often encroach upon natural landscapes. The conversion of rural areas into urban centers, including the development of residential and commercial zones, can significantly alter land use and lead to increased infrastructure

[15] World Bank, *Sustainable Land Management and Restoration in the Middle East and North Africa Region: Issues, Challenges, and Recommendations* (World Bank 2019).

[16] R. Zaaboul, "Climate Change Impacts on the Agricultural Sector in the Arab Region" (2020) 176 *Desalination and Water Treatment* 436.

[17] World Bank, "Water in the Arab World: From Droughts to Flood, Building Resilience against Extremes" (March 21, 2014) www.worldbank.org/en/news/feature/2014/03/20/floods-and-droughts-in-mena accessed January 27, 2024.

[18] Ibid.

[19] Ibid.

[20] Brian Wright and Carlo Cafiero, "Grain Reserves and Food Security in the Middle East and North Africa" (2011) 3 *Food Security* S1, 61.

needs.[21] Approximately 60 percent of the one billion people who reside in the MENA region's cities are urban dwellers.[22] A significant population increase is predicted until the 2060s to 2070s, after which there will be a decline until the year 2100. More than 90 percent of the people in the MENA region are anticipated to live in cities by the end of the century as urbanization is predicted to continue.[23]

Over the past century, the MENA area has the greatest pace of population growth worldwide.

The MENA region's economically underdeveloped regions are where urbanization and population increases are occurring at the fastest rates. Fourteen out of twenty MENA countries' urban environments are under extreme pressure due to the rapid rate of urbanization. Furthermore, according to UN estimates, 430 million people will live in the MENA region by 2020, with 280 million of them predicted to reside in urban areas. Similarly, in seven of the low- and middle-income countries, over 90 percent of the population will live in cities by 2030, resulting in the loss of significant land areas to urbanization and other types of land closing.[24]

Furthermore, MENA countries, traditionally reliant on oil and gas revenues, have recognized the need to reduce their dependence on a single income source. Mega-projects play a pivotal role in this diversification strategy by catalyzing investments across various sectors, including tourism, hospitality, real estate, and transportation. These projects create new economic opportunities, stimulate job growth, and enhance global competitiveness, which are essential for long-term sustainability.[25] The MENA region has witnessed a significant surge in mega-projects and construction endeavors in recent years. These projects, ranging from massive infrastructure developments to sports stadiums for global events such as the FIFA World Cup, have been strategically employed by MENA countries to diversify their economies. However, this economic diversification through mega-projects often comes at the cost of extensive landscape alterations, which raise concerns about its impact on landscape and biodiversity.[26] The boom in mega-projects has led to extensive landscape alterations across the MENA region. Vast tracts of land are

[21] Damilola Olawuyi, "Construction and Town Planning" in D. S. Olawuyi (ed), *Environmental Law in Arab States* (Oxford University Press 2022) 138.

[22] "MENA Countries: Urbanization in 2021" (May 2023) www.statista.com/statistics/804824/urbanization-in-the-mena-countries/ accessed February 2, 2024; also Karim Elgendy and Natasha Abaza, "Urbanization in the MENA Region: A Benefit or a Curse?" (February 10, 2020) https://mena.fes.de/press/e/urbanization-in-the-mena-region-a-benefit-or-a-curse accessed January 27, 2024.

[23] George Zittis et al., "Business-as-Usual Will Lead to Super and Ultra-Extreme Heatwaves in the Middle East and North Africa" (2021) 4 *Climate and Atmospheric Science* 1.

[24] Hakan Tropp and Anders Jagerskog, *"Stockholm International Water Institute" Water Scarcity Challenges in the Middle East and North Africa (MENA)* (United Nations Development Programme 2006) https://hdr.undp.org/content/water-scarcity-challenges-middle-east-and-north-africa-mena accessed January 27, 2024.

[25] A. Rizzo, "Rapid Urban Development and National Master Planning in Arab Gulf Countries: Qatar as a Case Study" (2014) 39 *Cities* 50.

[26] Olawuyi (n 21).

repurposed to accommodate these projects, resulting in substantial changes to natural environments with profound environmental consequences.

Greater demand for an affluent consumer-oriented lifestyle, partly as a result of rising income levels in the region, is another factor. This frequently denotes luxurious residences near reliable, convenient transportation in masterplanned neighborhoods, which raises the demand for urban land and housing.[27] Economic downturns and the unemployment rate are additional factors impacting urban growth that may cause a loss of people in an urban core or deteriorating suburbs, which would result in urban degradation.[28] As a result, economic downturns can significantly influence how landscapes are altered, thereby impacting biodiversity.

In pursuit of agricultural diversification, some MENA countries have sought to expand their agricultural sectors. This expansion often involves converting natural landscapes, such as deserts or semi-arid regions, into arable land. Intensive irrigation and farming practices can lead to soil degradation and alterations in the natural topography.[29] Resettlement is another issue that has resulted in the vast alterations in landscape, such as the relocation of populations to new locations due to the movement of people from rural areas to cities, as well as from other countries.[30] This population increase has resulted in the conversion of grazing and woodland areas to agricultural land and thus it is claimed that economic growth and population render land use alterations almost inevitable. Urbanization in the MENA region has failed to deliver the expected benefits of economic, social, and environmental development. Instead, it has worsened the existing problems of resource scarcity, service provision, and inequality.[31]

5.2.3 *Environmental Factors*

The most significant environmental factor in the MENA region flows from habitat clearing and modification, with a significant amount of it being done for extractives and urban and infrastructure development projects. Deforestation for the lumber industry, oil and mineral extraction, construction of mega-projects such as airports and sporting infrastructure, and the cultivation of cash crops are a few examples of activities that have contributed to the increased habitat destruction in the MENA

27 Janina Kleemann et al., "Peri-Urban Land Use Pattern and Its Relation to Land Use Planning in Ghana, West Africa" (2017) 165 *Landscape and Urban Planning* 280.

28 Luca Salvati, "Urban Dispersion and Economic Crisis: Empirical Evidence from a Mediterranean Region" (2018) 62 *Journal of Environmental Planning and Management* 7, 1205.

29 Statista, "Organic and In-Conversion Agricultural Land Area in the Middle East and North Africa Region in 2018, by Country" (Statista 2019) www.statista.com/statistics/990370/middle-east-and-north-africa-organic-and-in-conversion-agricultural-land-area-by-country/ accessed January 27, 2024.

30 Anne Schneibel et al., "Assessment of Spatio-Temporal Changes of Smallholder Cultivation Patterns in the Angolan Miombo Belt Using Segmentation of Landsat Time Series" (2017) 195 *Remote Sensing of Environment* 118.

31 Elgendy and Abaza (n 22).

region.[32] In several MENA countries, land degradation worsens biodiversity and ecosystems, lowers productivity, exacerbates water scarcity, and causes a decline in arable land (just 5 percent of the region's total land area, except Israel and Turkey, is arable land). Presently, irrigation is required to make 40 percent of arable land fit for cultivation.[33] While overgrazing in Jordan is thought to have diminished the supporting capacity, the landscapes making up approximately 80 percent of the nation's total area are largely arid and semi-arid lands. Iraq is predicted to lose about 250 square kilometers of arable land annually due to continuous desertification processes. This tendency jeopardizes MENA regions' landscape and biodiversity security, which further jeopardizes their socio-economic stability.[34] The expansion of industrial activities often involves land clearing and the construction of factories, warehouses, and transportation infrastructure. These alterations fragment natural habitats and disrupt ecological corridors, making it difficult for wildlife to move freely. Fragmentation can lead to isolated populations, reducing genetic diversity and increasing the vulnerability of species to environmental changes and diseases.[35]

5.2.4 *Cultural Factors*

The practices, ways of life, and values that define a society make up the cultural components of the environment; socio-cultural variables include things such as language, norms and values, language use, and attitudes toward social duties.[36] These factors have an impact on how the landscape changes or how certain societal groups influence it. People frequently make major land use decisions under the impact of cultural, economic, and political factors.

Additionally, a cultural shift has taken place in the region, from the less intensely employed cultural anthropogenesis of hunter-gatherers and early farmers to the intensive, larger-scale agrarian and industrial societies. The global extent of intensive anthropogenic activities have been steadily expanding for the majority of the last 12,000 years. Significant sustenance was provided to previous and present cultures through wild animal and plant hunting and gathering, whether in defined areas or

[32] Shemsu Ahmed, "Traditional Beliefs and Institutions for the Conservation of Biodiversity in Ethiopia: A Review from a Conservation Perspective" (2022) 7 *International Journal of Natural Resource Ecology and Management* 1, 1.

[33] Organisation for Economic Co-operation and Development (OECD)/FAO, "OECD-FAO Agricultural Outlook 2018–2027," OCDE editions, Paris/FAO edns, Rome (July 3, 2018) www.oecd-ilibrary.org/agriculture-and-food/oecd-fao-agricultural-outlook-2018-2027_agr_outlook-2018-en accessed January 27, 2024.

[34] Ibid.

[35] Steven Brandt, Book Review of Marijke Van Der Veen (ed), *The Exploitation of Plant Resources in Ancient Africa* (Kluwer Academic/Plenum Publishers 1999), in (2002) 67 *American Antiquity* 4, 781.

[36] E. Engobo, "Social Responsibility in Practice in the Oil Producing Niger Delta: Assessing Corporations and Government's Actions" (2009) 11 *Journal of Sustainable Development in Africa* 2, 113.

opportunistically in regions used for other land uses.[37] Land alterations and degradation in the MENA region stems from the culture of conventional tillage, monocropping, and increased pressure from human populations. The culture of conservation agriculture to protect biodiversity is poorly developed in the MENA region.[38]

The adoption of plows and draft animals to facilitate larger-scale crop cultivation and surplus output in support of larger and more unequal nonagricultural populations in cities by agrarian societies is also a contributing factor.[39] On the one hand, cultural issues may also limit the growth of agriculture into protected areas such as forests.[40] Final land use decisions are often made by users influenced by cultural, economic, and political considerations. Such cultural factors include the utilization of natural environments (such as forests) as retreats, where people in the community travel to worship. Natural habitat protection has resulted from the sacredness of natural habitats.[41]

5.2.5 *Technological Factors*

Mechanization and other commercial technologies used in industrial land systems to manufacture products for big urban populations have a negative influence on biodiversity and land use. In the MENA region, preindustrial colonial plantations may have opened the way for industrial land systems by introducing land use regimes that were largely focused on fulfilling the needs of urban populations through increasingly globalized mechanical networks.[42] The expansion of industrial land systems often necessitates land conversion, especially in peri-urban areas. Greenfields, once natural landscapes, are converted into industrial zones, contributing to the loss of valuable ecosystems.[43] This process results in reduced biodiversity and the disruption of local food chains and ecological services.

In some cases, mechanization and commercial technologies have driven agricultural intensification. This involves the conversion of natural landscapes into high-yield agricultural fields, often through practices such as monocropping. These agricultural systems are efficient for food production but can deplete soil nutrients,

37 Van Der Veen (n 37) 781.

38 M. Devkota, Y. Singh, Y. A. Yigezu, I. Bashour, R. Mussadek, and R. Mrabet, "Conservation Agriculture in the Drylands of the Middle East and North Africa (MENA) Region: Past Trend, Current Opportunities, Challenges and Future Outlook" in Donald L. Sparks (ed), *Advances in Agronomy* (Elsevier 2022) 253–305.

39 Ibid.

40 United Nations, Department of Economic and Social Affairs, "World Population Prospects" Population Division (UN DESA 2022) https://population.un.org/wpp/ accessed January 27, 2024.

41 Gezahegn Woldemariam et al., "Spatial Modeling of Soil Erosion Risk and Its Implication for Conservation Planning: The Case of the Gobele Watershed, East Hararghe Zone, Ethiopia" (2018) 7 *Land* 1, 25.

42 L. Charfeddine and Z. Mrabet, "The Impact of Economic Development and Social-Political Factors on Ecological Footprint: A Panel Data Analysis for 15 MENA Countries" (2017) 76 *Renewable and Sustainable Energy Reviews* 138.

43 Ibid.

increase pesticide and herbicide use, and lead to the loss of natural vegetation, negatively impacting biodiversity. A growing amount of physical infrastructure, such as railroads, highways, apartment complexes, factories, is being constructed in the MENA region by urban populations that are also influencing landscapes.[44] Demands for land use in support of recreation, and a variety of other land uses, have expanded as a result of urbanized lifeways, leading to an increase in what are known as multifunctional landscapes, or landscapes maintained for multiple functions.[45] Mechanization has facilitated the production of goods and services, contributing to urbanization and the expansion of urban areas. Urban sprawl often encroaches upon nearby natural areas, leading to the conversion of green spaces into built environments. This process fragments ecosystems and exacerbates the loss of biodiversity in urbanized regions. The availability of new technologies and the ease with which they can be applied to the land significantly affect land use and biodiversity. Mountainous locations, for instance, are difficult to mechanize, which limits the kinds of land use changes that might occur there.[46] The likelihood of some type of land use change depends on how quickly and easily land managers adopt new technologies. In a larger sense, the knowledge resources that land managers have access to or possess (e.g. traditional knowledge) have a significant impact on land use decisions.

5.2.6 *Political/Institutional Factors*

These aspects refer to a number of legislative, administrative, and operational initiatives on broad urban land use concerns and procedures that enable urban development objectives. This results in the formulation of the overall spatial framework of cities, including land use and land cover. Policies for urban and land use policies are a broad category of government initiatives that aim to affect how people use land and regulate who owns it.[47]

Numerous factors work against the effective implementation of biodiversity policies in the MENA region. However, the scarcity of accurate information about the state of biodiversity continues to be a major problem.[48] There are different types of policy tools that influence resource utilization and land use. Legislation, executive rules and regulations, financial instruments, public projects and programs, environmental policy, and demography and health policy are only a few examples. The Convention

44 Marina Alberti et al., "The Complexity of Urban Eco-Evolutionary Dynamics" (2020) 70 *BioScience* 9, 772.

45 Stewart Maginnis, William Jackson, and Nigel Dudley, *Conservation Landscapes: Whose Landscapes? Whose Trade-Offs? Getting Biodiversity Projects to Work* (Columbia University Press 2004).

46 Helen Briassoulis, "Combating Land Degradation and Desertification: The Land-Use Planning Quandary" (2019) 8 *Land* 2, 27.

47 Zaaboul (n 16).

48 Andrew Allan et al., "Driving Forces behind Land Use and Land Cover Change: A Systematic and Bibliometric Review" (2022) 11 *Land* 8, 1222.

on Biological Diversity (CBD) mandates that its member states provide regular reports on the state of biodiversity in their nations and carry out conservation measures and policies to preserve healthy populations of species under their control.[49]

The lack of multisectoral resource planning has been a major problem in the MENA region.[50] Negative externalities may result from the interaction of one sector policy adversely influencing the outcome in another sector when sector planning is disjointed. Weak land tenure and ineffective resource management,[51] particularly in communally managed regions such as grasslands and dry forests, are major factors that contribute to landscape alteration. Through traditional agreements and procedures, such as the coordination of the harvesting of forest and rangeland goods and the enactment of laws to prohibit malpractice, these areas have historically benefited from robust governance. These institutions are frequently deteriorating because of newly emerging state capabilities that challenge traditional authority but fall short of offering a workable substitute.

Another important factor is the operation of real estate agencies, private businesses, and developers who contribute to the long-term growth of the city through land market, financing, investment, design, and construction of large-scale developments and infrastructure.[52] These initiatives have significantly changed the spatial organization of cities by promoting urban renewal, infrastructure development, and industrial growth. The secondary aspect of regulations is a further important factor such as centralized norms imposed through official plans and/or directly by governmental entities. Effective regulation aspects in the development of urban areas, for instance, include municipal ordinances that apply various types of land acquisition and property impact taxes, land use ordinances, and ordinances governing urban planning.[53]

Additionally, armed conflicts, political instability, and violent crises in the region have led to significant and widespread migration within these nations as well as within and outside of the region.[54] The frequency of armed conflicts in the region remains one of the important triggers of the alteration of landscapes and habitats. Since the fall of the Ottoman Empire in 1922, the Middle East has been a flashpoint for practically constant political and military instability, especially in the region encompassing Israel, Palestine, and Yemen.[55] Political crises

49 The Convention on Biological Diversity of June 5, 1992 (1760 U.N.T.S. 69).

50 Olawuyi (n 3).

51 Ali Akbar Barati, Hossein Azadi, and Jürgen Scheffran, "Agricultural Land Fragmentation in Iran: Application of Game Theory" (2021) 100 *Land Use Policy* 105049.

52 Ahmed K. Nassar, G. Alan Blackburn, and J. Duncan Whyatt, "Developing the Desert: The Pace and Process of Urban Growth in Dubai" (2014) 45 *Computers, Environment and Urban Systems* 50.

53 Alice Colsaet, Yann Laurans, and Harold Levrel, "What Drives Land Take and Urban Land Expansion? A Systematic Review" (2018) 79 *Land Use Policy* 339.

54 Hadi Beygi Heidarlou, Abbas Banj Shafiei, Mahdi Erfanian, Amin Tayyebi, and Ahmad Alijanpour, "Armed Conflict and Land-Use Changes: Insights from Iraq–Iran War in Zagros Forests" (2020) 118 *Forest Policy and Economics* 102246.

55 Beatriz DeQuero-Navarro et al., "From Conflict to Cooperation: A Macromarketing View of Sustainable and Inclusive Development in Lebanon and the Middle East" (2020) 66 *Environmental Management* 2, 232.

exacerbate the loss of biodiversity and the modification of land cover.[56] Conflict has various effects on how land cover is converted. First, the tragedy of the commons compels each disputing party to exploit available resources before the competing side does the same. Further, increasing settlements speed up the process of changing the land's cover, which reduces ecosystem scale and causes biodiversity to decline.

It is apparent that the needs of the almost eight billion people living in today's increasingly affluent and globalized society must now be met through land usage, with billions more predicted in the ensuing decades. The current decline in biodiversity as represented in the foregoing is the replacement of indigenous and traditional low-intensity land use practices – which have supported biodiversity for millennia – with biologically homogeneous and large-scale industrial landscapes. However, exploiting landscapes to concurrently meet numerous wants is not a panacea and will always include trade-offs and compromises between conflicting objectives, interests, and views, particularly between intensive agriculture and biodiversity. Without addressing these concerns, competing needs may result in undesirable consequences, such as the destruction of landscapes and the replication of structural inequality and social inequities in the design and management of landscapes. To steer these regions toward better land and biodiversity conservation, it will take everything they have learned over the previous 12,000 years, including their profound cultural links to the land, nature, and one another. Concerted efforts toward greater sustainability are now taking place throughout the region in protecting landscapes. Key legal barriers to change, as well as priority actions to address them, are explored in Section 5.3.

5.3 LANDSCAPE ALTERATIONS AND BIODIVERSITY LOSS IN THE MENA REGION: SURVEY OF LEGAL AND INSTITUTIONAL BARRIERS

Existing legislation in the MENA region has significant shortcomings that undermine efforts to address landscape modification and biodiversity loss. These gaps are frequently the result of fragmented or weak legislative frameworks that fail to appropriately address rising biodiversity challenges.

5.3.1 *Lack of Comprehensive Unified Regional Policy Framework on Landscape Alterations*

To address the issues of landscape alterations across the region, comprehensive regional policy on land use and management is required. Many of the MENA region's current environmental regulations are deficient in terms of providing

[56] Heidarlou et al. (n 55).

comprehensive regional safeguards for vital habitats that support diverse and rare flora and fauna. The Arab Strategy for Housing and Sustainable Urban Development 2030 aims to provide a framework for joint Arab action for sustainable urban development while also addressing landscape alteration caused by the rapid and unplanned urbanization in the Arab region.[57] Despite the rise of regional efforts such as this strategy, which highlight the need for land management and collaborative strategies aimed at conserving biodiversity, ecologically sensitive places remain susceptible to landscape changes such as urbanization, agriculture, and infrastructure development, which result in habitat degradation and biodiversity loss.[58] While the strategy recognizes the importance of sustainable land use, it may need to incorporate stronger guidelines to address the prevention of extensive landscape alteration, especially in ecologically sensitive areas. Furthermore, the strategy does not provide comprehensive guidance on how to integrate landscape values into urban planning and design processes. This deficiency affects the consideration of unique landscape qualities when planning development activities.

Recognizing the interplay between climate change, landscape alteration, and biodiversity loss, several MENA countries are integrating ecosystem restoration into their climate adaptation strategies. The United Arab Emirates' Greening the Desert initiative focuses on restoring arid landscapes and protecting biodiversity through afforestation and habitat restoration.[59] Some MENA countries are also developing or enhancing legal frameworks to regulate land use more sustainably. These strategies, which encompasses forest landscape restoration, sustainable land management, and ecosystem approaches with a focus on land use planning, are gaining implementation in areas spanning Morocco, Tunisia, and the mountainous terrains of Oman and Yemen. Morocco, for instance, has implemented land use planning and zoning regulations to control urban sprawl and promote sustainable land management, thereby reducing the impacts of landscape alteration.[60] These endeavors are evident in the nationally determined contributions (NDC) reports, illustrating the region's resolute commitment to combat the challenges to landscape and biodiversity preservation. In 75 percent of these countries, NDCs emphasize the significance of agriculture, while 56 percent incorporate afforestation. Furthermore, 69 percent of the reports outline clear targets and actions for mitigation, with 25 percent focusing on the crucial domain of land management. An additional 13 percent prioritize the management of grazing lands.[61] In the same vein, Qatar has a structured goal for biodiversity

57 Olawuyi (n 21).

58 Ibid.

59 M. Alam and I. A. N. Azalie, "Greening the Desert: Sustainability Challenges and Environmental Initiatives in the GCC States" in A. Alshawi and S. Alshawi (eds), *Social Change in the Gulf Region: Multidisciplinary Perspectives* (Springer Nature 2023) 493–510.

60 F. Ziadat, E. De Pauw, F. Nachtergaele, and T. Fetsi, "A Land Resources Planning Toolbox to Promote Sustainable Land Management" (2021) 10 *Sustainable Agriculture Research* 73.

61 FAO, *Near East and North Africa Regional Overview of Food Insecurity 2016* (FAO 2016).

conversation to protect and sustainably manage the region's unique ecosystems and encourage regional cooperation on biodiversity conservation.

Nonetheless, while these initiatives are commendable, challenges persist. Individual countries struggle to address this global challenge effectively without a united regional legal framework. The MENA region's diverse political, economic, and environmental contexts can sometimes hinder the alignment of common goals among nations. This lack of regional collaboration impedes efforts to create and implement collective strategies for adapting to changing conditions and maintaining ecosystems sensitive to climate impacts and threats to biodiversity. The extensive reorganization required to accomplish integrated environmental management in the MENA countries would necessitate institutional and regulatory reforms, long-term investment, effective governance, regional cooperation for coordinated efforts, and the participation of all stakeholders.[62]

5.3.2 *Weak Enforcement Mechanisms*

All MENA countries have legislation that identifies the need for mandatory environmental impact assessments prior to the commencement of a project, as a tool to spot and prevent landscape alteration and habitat destruction.[63] Other examples of legal frameworks and sanctions for environmental crimes include Egypt's Environment Law No. 4 of 1994, which governs the preservation and protection of natural resources, biodiversity, and landscapes and imposes fines and jail time for degradation or destruction.[64] The goal of Jordan's Environmental Protection Law No. 6 of 2017 is to protect the environment and all of its elements, such as ecosystems and biodiversity.[65] Principles and procedures for environmental management and protection, including biodiversity conservation, are established under Morocco's Law on Environmental Assessment No. 49-17 of 2020.[66] The Saudi Arabia Royal Decree No. M/165 of 2020 set forth sanctions for various environmental infractions,[67] and Saudi Arabia's Basic Law of Governance No. A/90 of

62 Mohamed Zahour, "Food Security in Morocco: Risk Factors and Governance" in *Emerging Challenges to Food Production and Security in Asia, Middle East, and Africa* (Springer International Publishing 2021).

63 Olawuyi (n 3).

64 Republic of Egypt, "Law No. 4 of 1994 on Environment" FAOLEX Database (February 3, 1994) www.fao.org/faolex/results/details/en/c/LEX-FAOC004984/ accessed January 27, 2024.

65 Hashemite Kingdom of Jordan, "Environmental Protection Law No. 6 of 2017" FAOLEX Database (March 19, 2017) www.fao.org/faolex/results/details/en/c/LEX-FAOC173241 accessed January 27, 2024.

66 Law on Environmental Assessment No. 49-17, in UNECE, "Morocco Environmental Performance Reviews: Second Review" ECE/CEP/191 (Geneva 2022) xxv and xxvi https://unece.org/sites/default/files/2023-01/ECE_CEP_191_E.pdf accessed January 27, 2024.

67 Kingdom of Saudi Arabia, "Saudi Arabia Royal Decree No. M/165 of 2020 issuing the Environment Law" (July 10, 2020) www.fao.org/faolex/results/details/en/c/LEX-FAOC201014 accessed January 27, 2024.

1992 underlines the state's obligation to protect the environment and its natural resources.[68]

However, even when environmental regulations are in place, their application and impact are hampered by ineffective enforcement measures.[69] The majority of the momentum has been around defining goals and targets without necessarily connecting them to the rules and laws required to achieve them. Implementation is similarly vital and, if not proactively enforced, can allow ecologically degrading actions to continue without major consequences or adequate fines, allowing individuals and companies to engage in them with little fear of consequences. This may result in widespread noncompliance, which would worsen landscape changes and biodiversity loss. Although many of them have sound legislation in place to safeguard biodiversity, policy enforcement in the MENA region appears lax given that ongoing land use changes are jeopardizing the existence of many plant and animal species that depend on these habitats.[70] Addressing issues with regional landscape changes requires strengthening enforcement mechanisms for environmental law and policy in the MENA area. In addition, the severity of the punishments for environmental legislation violations may not be commensurate with them in some of the MENA countries.[71] The legal and administrative punishments in the Forest Law and the Land Hunting Law, for example, are too light and insufficient. Weak deterrents might encourage illicit activities such as poaching, illegal logging, and habitat destruction, resulting in greater landscape changes and biodiversity loss.[72]

5.3.3 *Fragmented Policy Framework at All Levels*

The MENA region is made up of several countries, each with its own legal system and regulations. This fragmented approach leads to variations in environmental rules, making it difficult to coordinate regional efforts and solve cross-border challenges such as transboundary wildlife protection or shared ecosystem management.[73] The MENA area is distinguished by numerous legal systems that make it difficult to coordinate efforts to address landscape changes and biodiversity loss. Inconsistent policies and regulations leave gaps in the system that can be exploited by individuals looking

68 Kingdom of Saudi Arabia, "Basic Law of Governance No. A/90 of 1992" (February 4, 1992) www.fao.org/faolex/results/details/en/c/LEX-FAOC127539/ accessed January 27, 2024.

69 Ibid., also Olawuyi (n 3).

70 L. Mansour et al., "Mainstreaming the Water-Energy-Food Security Nexus into Policies and Institutions in the MENA Region: National Guidelines on Mainstreaming the Water Energy-Food (WEF) Security Nexus into Policies and Institutions in Egypt and Jordan" (2017) GIZ Report.

71 Devkota et al. (n 40).

72 Abdulaziz S. Alatawi, "Conservation Action in Saudi Arabia: Challenges and Opportunities" (2022) 29 *Saudi Journal of Biological Sciences* 5, 3466.

73 Rafaelle Bertini and Abdallah Zouache, "Agricultural Land Issues in the Middle East and North Africa" (2021) 80 *American Journal of Economics and Sociology* 2, 549.

to benefit from environmentally destructive activities. Furthermore, transboundary conservation initiatives are hampered by a lack of established norms and international cooperation.[74] Addressing fragmentation at the domestic level is essential for effectively tackling the challenges related to landscape alteration and biodiversity conservation in MENA countries. This practical issue arises when different entities with similar mandates undertake parallel initiatives without effective coordination.[75] Resources and expertise may be spread thinly across these duplicated efforts, reducing their overall impact on preserving landscapes and biodiversity. Fragmentation at the domestic level often translates into limited coordination among relevant stakeholders, hampering the development and implementation of holistic conservation strategies. Furthermore, the presence of multiple institutions and agencies responsible for conservation efforts within a single country can result in role duplication, confusion, inefficiency, and even corruption in land management services.[76] This existence of competing and conflicting priorities raises intricate questions regarding the feasibility of developing and executing integrated solutions across various sectors.[77]

5.3.4 *Inadequate Policies on Integration of Traditional Knowledge*

Local communities with strong conservation strategies and abilities are essential to the protection of biodiversity. The preservation of biodiversity and the management of sustainable landscapes can both benefit greatly from the use of local communities' traditional knowledge and practices.[78] The marginalization of indigenous and local populations in conservation efforts may result from the inadequacy of current laws to integrate or recognize the importance of such knowledge. So, maximizing conservation efforts could be significantly enhanced by understanding local customs and traditions. But the spread of globalization poses a serious danger to indigenous and local knowledge of managing natural resources. For instance, one of the goals of the Intergovernmental Platform on Biodiversity and Ecosystem Services is to guarantee that the finest indigenous and local knowledge is included into national or international

74 R. Diab, "Land Legislation in the Middle East and the Need for Modernization Serving the Needs of Lebanon and other Middle Eastern Countries" (Webinar Towards a Post Graduate Program in Land Governance, Beirut, 2020) 34–39.

75 UNECE, "Reconciling Resource Uses in Transboundary Basins: Assessment of the Water-Food-Energy-Ecosystems Nexus" (UNECE 2015) https://unece.org/DAM/env/water/publications/WAT_46_Nexus/ece_mp.wat_46_eng.pdf accessed January 27, 2024.

76 A. Corsi and H. Selod, "Legal, Institutional, and Governance Challenges Facing Land Use in MENA Countries" in H. Selod, S. V. Lall, and N. Lozano-Gracia (eds), *Land Matters: Can Better Governance and Management of Scarcity Prevent a Looming Crisis in the Middle East and North Africa?* (World Bank 2023).

77 Damilola S. Olawuyi, "Sustainable Development and the Water–Energy–Food Nexus: Legal Challenges and Emerging Solutions" (2020) 103 *Environmental Science & Policy* 1.

78 I. S. Selemani, "Indigenous Knowledge and Rangelands' Biodiversity Conservation in Tanzania: Success and Failure" (2020) 29 *Biodiversity and Conservation* 14, 3863.

frameworks for biodiversity conservation.[79] Strengthening landscape preservation in the MENA region depends on filling these legal gaps. To support efficient landscape management and biodiversity conservation, policymakers should prioritize updating and harmonizing environmental laws, improving enforcement mechanisms, encouraging public participation, and incorporating traditional knowledge. Regional cooperation and collaboration can also aid in addressing international issues and advancing a common strategy for environmental conservation in the MENA area.

5.3.5 *Absence of Explicit Policy Mechanisms to Promote Educational Awareness*

Public education and awareness of land management and environmental protection is essential in order to promote conservation practices at local levels.[80] Despite the urgent environmental issues of landscape change and biodiversity destruction in the MENA area, there remains a substantial gap in promoting enhanced awareness.[81] This crucial gap is caused by the lack of explicit provisions and robust mechanisms to raise public knowledge about the negative threats that contribute to these concerns. It is critical to raise knowledge about the factors that have contributed to the problem of landscape change and biodiversity loss. The importance of incorporating environmental education into school curricula at all levels is more often overlooked by regulatory frameworks in the MENA area. These variables may contribute to a low degree of environmental awareness, interest, involvement, and support. The necessity for enhanced public knowledge and participation has received substantial attention. It has been discussed among local scientists in the region and has been cited in national papers on biological diversity law and policy in the region. As a result, it is critical to adopt clear measures and robust policies to raise public awareness of landscape alteration and biodiversity erosion in the MENA area as part of a comprehensive approach to addressing the region's environmental concerns.

Section 5.4 discusses innovative approaches to addressing gaps in integrated land alteration prevention and management in the MENA region.

5.4 ADVANCING LANDSCAPE AND BIODIVERSITY CONSERVATION IN THE MENA REGION: LEGAL AND INSTITUTIONAL RECOMMENDATIONS

In the diverse landscapes of the MENA region, the need for effective landscape and biodiversity conservation is paramount. A unified legal framework, streamlined

79 UNESCO (2019) "Linking Indigenous and Scientific Knowledge to Counter Biodiversity Erosion" https://en.unesco.org/news/linking-indigenous-and-scientific-knowledge-counter-biodiversity-erosion accessed September 10, 2024.

80 Hilary Bell, "Tackling the Legally Disruptive Problem of Climate Change with Disruptive Legal Education" in Damilola S. Olawuyi (ed), *Climate Change Law and Policy in the MENA Region* (Routledge 2022) 251–265.

81 Alatawi (n 68).

governance, and robust enforcement mechanisms are fundamental to preserving these natural treasures. Some recommendations are hereby provided based on the foregoing. These recommendations aim to enhance the legal and institutional framework for landscape and biodiversity conservation in the region and to ensure the long-term preservation of the region's unique natural landscapes and diverse ecosystems.

5.4.1 *Comprehensive Regional Policy Framework*

Establishing a comprehensive regional policy framework for landscape change and policy integration can enhance regional knowledge sharing and coordination on landscape and biodiversity conservation in the MENA region. The creation of frameworks by national and regional governments to support integrated planning across functional territories are critical in this regard. Better integration and coordination of policies are essential if a wider range of policy tools are to be used to drive landscape management, as is suggested in this study. The region may not be able to successfully influence landscape management through the coordination of a larger range of policies without more effective coordination tactics. This might include frequent regional gatherings where industry experts and policy officials debate common concerns and potential solutions. This framework should combine sustainable land management approaches while taking into account the political, social, and economic concerns outlined and described earlier in this chapter.

5.4.2 *Establish Strategic Action Plans for Environmental Education and Communication*

In this context, the development of national strategies and action plans for environmental education and communication plays an important role as a catalyst for raising awareness about landscape transformation and biodiversity preservation. Governments can actively stimulate the adoption of dynamic educational techniques that resonate with contemporary culture by integrating innovative policy measures. This implies incentivizing the development of interactive learning systems in order to keep educational outreach engaging and impactful. Policy instruments can incentivize collaborative partnerships among governmental agencies, nongovernmental organizations, and private firms, creating a broader and more effective reach. Furthermore, incorporating environmental modules into the formal educational curriculum through legislative requirements can ensure a long-term and systemic approach to cultivating ecological consciousness. Countries across the MENA region may leverage the potential of education to achieve revolutionary change in order to protect landscapes and biodiversity for future generations by carefully incorporating innovative policy measures into national policies.

Furthermore, the use of citizen science should be encouraged as a mechanism to bridge in the gaps in biodiversity knowledge, such as landscape preservation, distribution, and biodiversity conservation. Planning conservation initiatives requires comprehensive and reliable biodiversity data. Citizen science involves engaging the public, including local communities and volunteers, in scientific research and data collection efforts. By involving citizens in data collection, observation, and reporting, this approach can help bridge knowledge gaps and generate valuable information.

5.4.3 *Strengthening Enforcement Mechanisms*

The goals set forth in each policy can only be achieved when it is effectively and coherently implemented. Despite this, inefficient policy and strategy execution remains a major obstacle. More policies and strategies need to be developed or existing ones need to be modified. This is crucial for ensuring that laws governing landscape modification and biodiversity preservation are followed effectively. One strategy entails the creation of severe fines and penalties for noncompliance, which serve as a deterrent against actions that endanger the environment. Businesses and individuals should adopt more responsible practices by putting in place a tiered system of punishments that are proportionate to how serious the offense was. The ability of regulatory bodies to monitor and respond to violations can also be improved by giving them more power and resources through policy reforms. Legal frameworks could encourage collaborative agreements between MENA countries, allowing for information sharing and cross-border enforcement actions. Furthermore, through regulatory mandates, emerging technology such as satellite photography and remote sensing can be integrated into enforcement methods, boosting monitoring capacities. Finally, including protections for informants in legal frameworks might encourage people to expose infractions without fear of retaliation, resulting in a more alert enforcement environment. By combining these policy and legal instruments, the MENA region can create a strong enforcement ecosystem that protects landscapes and biodiversity for the benefit of society and the environment as a whole.

5.4.4 *Regional Governance and Cooperation in the MENA for Landscape and Biodiversity*

To address the problems faced by the varied legal systems and policies across the MENA area, a coordinated effort is required to build an integrated and coherent policy framework for landscape and biodiversity preservation. The existing fragmented approach results in discrepancies in environmental regulations, preventing regional activities from being coordinated and cross-border concerns from being effectively resolved. The establishment of a dedicated MENA Environmental Cooperation Council, backed by strong policies, would be a critical solution. Through this they can facilitate policy alignment and establish common standards that bridge the gaps between different countries' legal frameworks. By mandating information exchange, regulations can encourage a culture of collaboration, allowing nations to share successful techniques and collaboratively handle shared difficulties. Furthermore, the implementation of cooperative research endeavors and capacity-building projects, supported by policy commitments, would enable nations to compete on a level playing field, regardless of their development status. The incorporation of regular regional conferences, guided by policies, would showcase progress and innovations, thus fostering mutual inspiration and competition. In this way, strategic policy integration can yield a unified approach to landscape and biodiversity preservation, transcending legal disparities and promoting a harmonious environmental agenda throughout the MENA region.

5.4.5 *Incorporation of Traditional Knowledge into Decision-Making Processes*

Enacting legislation that recognizes the value of traditional knowledge and its contribution to sustainable practices can be a starting point. Legal frameworks should require the assimilation of traditional knowledge into decision-making processes, ensuring its inclusion alongside scientific findings. To protect indigenous communities' intellectual property rights, legislative procedures can be put in place to ensure that traditional knowledge is used with informed permission and equitable benefit-sharing. Creating channels for intergenerational knowledge transmission, such as through legal requirements for mentorship programs or cultural heritage projects, can aid in the preservation and perpetuation of traditional learning. Furthermore, legislations that fosters collaboration between governmental agencies and indigenous groups in the construction of landscape and biodiversity management plans could necessitate the incorporation of traditional knowledge. Legal frameworks can help to encourage collaborative research projects, co-management agreements, and participatory consultations, thereby confirming the importance of traditional knowledge in directing conservation efforts. It is also critical to put in place legal measures to avoid the misuse of traditional knowledge, such as through biopiracy. This could include legislative provisions requiring fair and equitable benefit-sharing when commercial interests arise from the use of indigenous knowledge.

5.4.6 *Improve Education, Awareness, and Cooperation on Biodiversity and Landscape Conservation*

In addition to the aforementioned recommendations addressing the identified legal and institutional barriers, there is a need to improve education and awareness on biodiversity and landscape conservation. First, there is a need to leverage citizen science as a mechanism to bridge in the gaps in biodiversity knowledge, such as landscape preservation, distribution, and biodiversity conservation. Planning conservation initiatives require comprehensive and reliable biodiversity data. Additionally, these programs encourage participants to engage in active environmental responsibility and stewardship.

Second, intensifying collaboration among environmental historians, geographers, land and conservation scientists could make significant strides toward improving societal understanding of past land use patterns and their ecological effects. Neglecting these considerations can lead to erroneous and unfair outcomes when using landscapes to balance out conflicting demands, particularly between intensive agriculture and nature preservation.

Third, to accelerate training and capacity development, increased resource allocation for funding landscape and biodiversity initiatives is essential. MENA countries should increase and dedicate public funds to supporting and enforcing national biodiversity conservation laws and policies, as well as other landscape and biodiversity conservation measures. Furthermore, regional and international cooperation on capacity development and education is required to improve the conservation of species and ecosystems that cross international borders.

5.4.7 *Enhancing Landscape Monitoring for Sustainable Landscape and Biodiversity Management*

To ensure sustainable landscape use and biodiversity preservation in the MENA region, enhancing landscape monitoring is crucial. There is a need to utilize standardized performance indicators, collaboratively refined, to accurately reflect conservation objectives. An integrated monitoring framework should be established across relevant institutions, harmonizing methods and sharing findings for a unified approach. Leveraging modern technologies is also imperative for real-time monitoring, such as remote sensing through satellite imagery and drones, enabling proactive responses to threats. Capacity building is vital via training programs that empower personnel to interpret data effectively, and involving local communities in data collection fosters engagement and broadens monitoring efforts. Furthermore, implementing an adaptive management system informed by monitoring data, allowing the swift adaptation to emerging challenges in land use alterations, is essential. As an example, the impact of infrastructure construction must be strictly monitored. We may anticipate an expansion of infrastructure in the region; however, before beginning such infrastructure initiatives, it is vital to evaluate the impact of infrastructure on biodiversity. For many species, for instance, restricted border areas are frequently their last remaining habitats. Therefore, to ensure that there is enough area left to support such biodiversity, road construction and other infrastructure development should be curtailed in these areas. There must also be transparency in data collection and reporting which ensures accountability and supports informed decision-making for sustainable landscape use. By implementing this interconnected strategy, the MENA region can establish a robust monitoring system that empowers decision-makers, conservators, and communities to actively preserve landscapes and biodiversity.

5.5 CONCLUSION

The rapid alteration of landscapes, due to urbanization, climate change impacts, construction, and economic activities, is a significant threat to biodiversity in the MENA region. Commercialization and capitalism as well as globalization have also eroded entrenched cultural land management practices and knowledge systems, leading to the present situation where indigenous knowledge on environmental preservation and biodiversity is gradually fading. There is a need to preserve the cultural practices of land and biodiversity conservation in the MENA region.

This chapter provided insight on the factors of landscape alterations and biodiversity loss in the MENA region. As the global population increases, meeting the demands of an increasingly affluent and interconnected world necessitates reconciling competing land uses. The shift from traditional, biodiversity-friendly practices to large-scale industrial landscapes has led to alarming biodiversity decline. However, optimizing land for multiple purposes is complex and inherently involves trade-offs between conflicting objectives, interests, and values, particularly between intensive agriculture and conservation. Failing to address these tensions risks exacerbating landscape degradation, entrenching social inequalities, and perpetuating structural injustices in land design and management.

Effective conservation demands a holistic approach, incorporating the traditional knowledge, cultural heritage, and social cohesion that define this region. The results indicate that natural, socio-economic, cultural, and technological factors have directly influenced the structure of landscape in the MENA region. Concerted efforts toward greater sustainability are now taking place throughout the region in protecting their landscapes. Priority actions that include, but are not limited to, establishing a comprehensive unified regional policy framework, strengthening enforcement mechanisms, reducing the impact of infrastructure construction, and enhancing landscape monitoring mechanisms are urgently required.

6

Protecting Land Rights in Biodiversity and Nature-Based Solutions

Ghita Chehbouni

6.1 INTRODUCTION

This chapter explores the complex connections between biodiversity management, land rights, and the successful application of nature-based solutions (NBS) for nature conservation in the Middle East and North Africa (MENA) region. It examines legal challenges and barriers to the application of NBS in the MENA region and innovative approaches to addressing such barriers.

The pursuit of biodiversity conservation through NBS has emerged as a promising pathway to address ecological challenges. NBS are efforts to address environmental problems such a climate change, biodiversity loss, and pollution through ecosystem restoration programs. According to the International Union for the Conservation of Nature (IUCN), "nature-based solutions are actions to protect, sustainably manage, and restore natural and modified ecosystems that address societal challenges effectively and adaptively, simultaneously benefiting people and nature."[1] For example, a common problem is the flooding in coastal areas that occurs as a result of storm surges and coastal erosion. This challenge, traditionally tackled with man-made (gray) infrastructure such as sea walls or dikes, can also be addressed by actions that take advantage of ecosystem services such as tree planting.[2] The term NBS was initially introduced in 2008 by the World Bank,[3] and the concept emerged as a response to the quest for innovative approaches to manage natural systems in a manner that can harmonize the advantages for both the environment and society. In essence, by collaborating with nature instead of opposing it, human communities can create and apply strategies to foster a robust, resource-efficient, and environmentally

[1] IUCN, "About Nature-Based Solutions" www.iucn.org/our-work/nature-based-solutions accessed February 7, 2024.

[2] World Bank, "What You Need to Know about Nature-Based Solutions to Climate Change" (May 19, 2022) www.worldbank.org/en/news/feature/2022/05/19/what-you-need-to-know-about-nature-based-solutions-to-climate-change accessed February 7, 2024.

[3] World Bank, "Biodiversity, Climate Change and Adaptation: Nature-Based Solutions from the World Bank Portfolio" (The International Bank for Reconstruction and Development (IBRD) 2008).

friendly economy.[4] In 2015, the European Commission officially articulated the first definition of NBS as "actions that simultaneously address environmental, social, and economic challenges by maximizing the benefits provided by nature and are inspired by, supported by, or mimic natural processes."[5] The most recent report from the European Commission on NBS also underscores that the concept of NBS represents a novel approach to addressing socio-ecological adaptation and resilience. It places equal emphasis on the social, environmental, and economic dimensions of these solutions, which encompass a spectrum of strategies, ranging from reforestation and habitat restoration to sustainable agriculture and green infrastructure development. NBS, rooted in harnessing natural processes, offer a harmonious pathway toward sustainable development.

However, despite their potential benefits for restoring biodiversity, NBS efforts have also been increasingly linked to allegations of "green grabbing," a situation whereby conservation efforts inadvertently lead to the appropriation of land and resources from local communities.[6] For instance, in the Maghreb region, where pristine coastal habitats and arid landscapes hold immense ecological value, efforts to establish protected areas and promote ecotourism have at times resulted in the displacement of indigenous populations.[7] The case of the Amazigh communities in Morocco's Souss-Massa National Park exemplifies the intricate dynamics at play.[8] While the establishment of the park aimed to preserve the region's unique biodiversity, it led to the involuntary displacement of traditional communities who had coexisted with the environment for generations.

The foregoing example shows how conservation strategies based on NBS which seek to restore ecosystems and safeguard natural resources may inadvertently led to the appropriation of land and resources from local communities, resulting in social and environmental injustices.[9] This paradox underscores the need to align biodiversity and nature conservation objectives with human rights and social equity.[10] The drivers of green grabbing, including neoliberal conservation paradigms, the commodification of nature, and the tendency to place profit above people, all accentuate

4 Science for Environment Policy, "The Solution Is in Nature" brief produced for the European Commission DG Environment Science Communication Unit, UWE Bristol (2021) 24 *Future Brief* 4.

5 Barbara Sowińska-Świerkosz and Joan García, "What Are Nature-Based Solutions (NBS)? Setting Core Ideas for Concept Clarification" (2022) 2 *Nature-Based Solutions* 2–4.

6 Fairhead James, Leach Melissa, and Scoones Ian, "Green Grabbing: A New Appropriation of Nature?" (2012) 39 *Journal of Peasant Studies* 2, 237.

7 Annabelle Houdret, "The Water Connection: Irrigation, Water Grabbing and Politics in Southern Morocco" (German Development Institute 2012).

8 Julius Arnegger, *Protected Areas, the Tourist Bubble and Regional Economic Development: Two Case Studies from Mexico and Morocco* (Würzburg University Press 2014) 80–102.

9 Damilola Olawuyi, *The Human Rights Based Approach to Carbon Finance* (Cambridge University Press 2016) 1–25.

10 O. Adeola Francis, "Environmental Injustice and Human Rights Abuse: The States, MNCs, and Repression of Minority Groups in the World System" (2001) 8 *Human Ecology Review* 39.

the potential for adverse human rights consequences.[11] Local communities, often marginalized and dependent on these ecosystems, bear the brunt of these outcomes, experiencing displacement and loss of livelihoods. Such forced displacements and the associated disruption of cultural ties and traditional ways of life raise concerns about the adverse social impacts of green grabbing. Such instances underscore the importance of integrating a human rights-based approach that considers the rights and needs of local communities in biodiversity and nature conservation programs.[12]

Drawing lessons from Morocco, this chapter discusses the need for a human rights-based approach (HRBA) to nature conservation and biodiversity, especially the application of NBS, to avoid adverse human rights impacts on lands, livelihoods, and peoples, especially indigenous communities. Focusing on the intricate dynamics, challenges, and potential solutions, this chapter sheds light on the paradox where well-intentioned conservation endeavors inadvertently lead to the appropriation of land and resources from local communities. Drawing on relevant literature and case studies, it provides a comprehensive analysis of the underlying drivers, impacts, and recommendations to address the unintended consequences of green grabbing in the context of NBS.

The chapter is organized into four distinct sections, each serving a unique purpose. After this introduction, Section 6.2 delves into the HRBA to NBS, offering insights into how human rights principles can underpin NBS programs to address adverse impacts on forests, peoples, and local communities. Section 6.3 examines legal and institutional barriers to implementing a rights-based approach to conservation within the MENA region, drawing valuable lessons from the Moroccan experience. Finally, Sections 6.4 and 6.5 present a set of recommendations aimed at guiding the practical implementation of NBS, offering actionable insights for effective conservation efforts. This structured approach allows for a comprehensive exploration of the subject matter, from its fundamental concepts to the real-world challenges and solutions.

6.2 LAND RIGHTS, BIODIVERSITY, AND NATURE-BASED SOLUTIONS

Land rights are intertwined with biodiversity conservation as they govern the use and management of, and access to, natural resources. The emphasis on biodiversity and land conservation and management has gained paramount importance on the global stage, particularly within the context of sustainable development. Academic research and international agreements have both highlighted the critical role that biodiversity

11 Fairhead James, Leach Melissa, and Scoones Ian, "Green Grabbing: A New Appropriation of Nature?" (2012) 39 *Journal of Peasant Studies* 2, 240. See also C. E. Wieckardt, S. Koot, and N. Karimasari, "Environmentality, Green Grabbing, and Neoliberal Conservation: The Ambiguous Role of Ecotourism in the Green Life Privatised Nature Reserve, Sumatra, Indonesia" (2022) 30 *Journal of Sustainable Tourism* 11, 2614.

12 Olawuyi (n 9).

plays in maintaining ecosystem resilience and supporting human well-being. As underscored by the United Nations Environment Assembly (UNEA), biodiversity constitutes the intricate web of life, encompassing ecosystems, species, and genetic diversity. Empirical studies have demonstrated the far-reaching impacts of biodiversity loss on ecosystem stability, ecosystem services, and human societies.[13] The Intergovernmental Science-Policy Platform on Biodiversity and Ecosystem Services, a significant multistakeholder initiative, has provided comprehensive assessments of the state of global biodiversity, raising awareness about the urgent need for action.[14] In tandem with academic insights, international agreements such as the Convention on Biological Diversity (CBD) and the United Nations Framework Convention on Climate Change (UNFCCC) have emphasized the interconnectedness of biodiversity, climate change, and sustainable development.[15] By capitalizing on the inherent resilience of ecosystems, NBS address environmental challenges while yielding co-benefits such as climate adaptation, water security, and improved livelihoods. UNEA underscores the transformative potential of NBS in shaping policies, guiding investments, and fostering international collaboration. The assembly's resolutions and initiatives echo the need to mainstream these solutions in national and global strategies. By enhancing ecosystem services, NBS pave the way for resilient communities, enhanced food security, and improved quality of life.

NBS, rooted in ecological processes, offer promising avenues to tackle environmental challenges. In the realm of climate policies, there has been a growing emphasis on NBS in approximately forty nationally determined contributions (NDCs), representing the commitments made by states under the Paris Agreement.[16] NBS are increasingly seen as pragmatic options with the potential for swift implementation and the capacity to yield multiple co-benefits for both climate and biodiversity. These benefits extend to mitigation actions, such as reducing greenhouse gas emissions through initiatives such as reforestation, as well as adaptation strategies such as enhancing resilience to climate impacts through measures such as coral reef restoration. Nevertheless, it is crucial to pay special attention to how the integration of ecosystems into climate initiatives may either support or potentially harm biodiversity

[13] Damilola Olawuyi and Olaitan Olusegun, "Achieving the United Nations Sustainable Development Goals on Biological Diversity in Nigeria: Current Issues and Future Directions" (2018) 7 *Global Journal of Comparative Law* 1, 37.

[14] Intergovernmental Science-Policy Platform on Biodiversity and Ecosystem Service, "Global Assessment Report on Biodiversity and Ecosystem Services" (May 14, 2019) https://zenodo.org/records/6417333 accessed February 7, 2024.

[15] Secretariat of the Convention on Biological Diversity, "Interlinkages between Biological Diversity and Climate Change: Advice on the Integration of Biodiversity Considerations into the Implementation of the United Nations Framework Convention on Climate Change (UNFCCC) and Its Kyoto Protocol" ad hoc Technical Expert Group on Biological Diversity and Climate Change www.cbd.int/doc/publications/cbd-ts-10.pdf accessed February 7, 2024.

[16] Y. Laurans, R. Ruat, and P. Barthélemy, "Comment les États entendent 'compter sur la nature' pour leurs stratégies climat" (Institute for Sustainable Development and International Relations 2016) 5 Issue Brief 16, 4.

as NDCs are put into practice. By capitalizing on the inherent resilience of ecosystems, NBS address environmental challenges while yielding co-benefits such as climate adaptation, water security, and improved livelihoods.[17] Crucially, the integration of NBS dovetails seamlessly with the conservation of biodiversity. By safeguarding habitats, promoting sustainable land use, and restoring ecosystems, these solutions fortify the intricate tapestry of life on earth. UNEA's advocacy for NBS amplifies their role as catalysts for sustainable development, echoing the imperative to transition toward inclusive and ecologically responsible pathways.

NBS, as endorsed by UNEA and supported by academic research, emerge as a pivotal approach to address these challenges and support sustainable development. These solutions encompass a spectrum of strategies rooted in harnessing natural processes to achieve societal goals while conserving biodiversity. Academic studies have highlighted the multifaceted benefits of NBS, ranging from carbon sequestration and disaster risk reduction to enhanced biodiversity conservation. The CBD's Aichi Biodiversity Targets and the Paris Agreement under the UNFCCC also underscore the synergies between biodiversity conservation, climate action, and sustainable development. The integration of NBS into national policies and international frameworks aligns with UNEA's vision of a world where human progress is intricately intertwined with the preservation of biodiversity. UNEA underscores the transformative potential of NBS in shaping policies, guiding investments, and fostering international collaboration. The assembly's resolutions and initiatives echo the need to mainstream these solutions in national and global strategies. By enhancing ecosystem services, NBS pave the way for resilient communities, enhanced food security, and improved quality of life.[18]

However, while NBS present many promises, it is critically important to ensure that such approaches safeguard and strengthen the rights of indigenous peoples and local communities in the use and governance of natural resources. Overlooking the human dimensions of conservation risks marginalizing local communities and exacerbating inequities.[19] The 2020 adoption of the IUCN Global Standard for NBS is significant, given its explicit criteria and indicators pertaining to the inclusion and rights of indigenous peoples and local communities.[20] Without compliance

[17] Paul L. G. Vlek, Asia Khamzina, and Lulseged Tamene, "Land Degradation and the Sustainable Development Goals: Threats and Potential Remedies" (2017) http://ciat-library.ciat.cgiar.org/Articulos_Ciat/biblioteca/LAND_DEGRADATION_AND_THE_SDGs-THREATS_AND_POTENTIAL_REMEDIES.pdf accessed February 7, 2024.

[18] United Nations General Assembly, "Global Health and Foreign Policy" Resolution adopted by the General Assembly on December 18, 2013, A/RES68/98 (February 7, 2014) https://documents.un.org/doc/undoc/gen/n13/445/33/pdf/n1344533.pdf?token=EoDg1dyEikB1XMkTho&fe=true accessed February 7, 2024.

[19] Ibid.

[20] IUCN, *Global Standard for Nature-Based Solutions: A User-Friendly Framework for the Verification, Design and Scaling up of NBS* (IUCN 2020). https://portals.iucn.org/library/sites/library/files/documents/2020-020-En.pdf accessed February 7, 2024.

with these criteria, an initiative cannot be formally recognized as an NBS activity. However, it is essential to note that the mere adoption of the IUCN Global Standard does not guarantee the integration of rights within NBS practices. Simply adopting the standard does not automatically translate into its effective implementation. There is a potential risk that the standard might be disregarded in other international agreements or diluted as stakeholders hastily label various activities as NBS.[21] Therefore, it is imperative to actively promote and ensure the practical adoption of the NBS standard by governments and other stakeholders. True commitment to upholding the principles of the standard, as well as implementing human rights safeguards to address adverse impacts of NBS programs on fundamental human rights, is vital to ensure that NBS initiatives genuinely encompass the inclusion and rights of indigenous communities and local populations.[22]

An HRBA offers a transformative lens to reconcile biodiversity conservation and land rights, promoting sustainable outcomes for both.[23] The intersection of land rights, biodiversity conservation, and an HRBA to NBS is an important and complex topic. This approach emphasizes the rights and well-being of local communities and indigenous peoples while striving to achieve conservation goals. This approach acknowledges that indigenous peoples and local communities often have a deep connection to and dependency on their land and resources. It emphasizes their rights to participation, prior informed consent, and benefit-sharing in conservation initiatives.[24] Secure land tenure and resource rights can empower local communities to engage in sustainable land management and conservation practices. Acknowledging and respecting indigenous knowledge, involving communities in decision-making processes, and ensuring equitable benefit-sharing are pivotal steps to mitigate the unintended consequences of green grabbing.

This approach aligns with the principles of the United Nations Declaration on the Rights of Indigenous Peoples (UNDRIP),[25] which emphasizes the imperative to harmonize biodiversity conservation with human rights and social justice through an HRBA. UNDRIP, adopted by the United Nations General Assembly in 2007, serves as a cornerstone for recognizing the rights and contributions of indigenous

[21] Ibid.

[22] Mikkel Funder and Marie Ladekjær Gravesen, "How to Support a Rights-Based Approach to Nature-Based Solutions: Recommendations for Danish Development Cooperation" (Danish institute for International Studies, February 2022). www.diis.dk/en/research/how-to-support-a-rights-based-approach-to-nature-based-solutions accessed February 7, 2024.

[23] Damilola Olawuyi, "Advancing Climate Justice in International Law: An Evaluation of the United Nations Human Rights Based Approach" (2015) 11 *Florida A&M Law Review* 1, 103 https://commons.law.famu.edu/cgi/viewcontent.cgi?referer=&httpsredir=1&article=1145&context=famulawreview accessed February 7, 2024.

[24] David Boyd, *The Environmental Rights Revolution: A Global Study of Constitutions, Human Rights, and the Environment* (UBC Press 2011).

[25] United Nations General Assembly, *United Nations Declaration on the Rights of Indigenous Peoples* (Office of the High Commissioner for Human Rights 2007) www.ohchr.org/en/indigenous-peoples/un-declaration-rights-indigenous-peoples accessed September 15, 2024.

peoples across the globe, particularly in the context of environmental and biodiversity conservation.[26] The HRBA places emphasis on addressing and mitigating human rights impacts of NBS by integrating five interconnected human rights norms and principles into decision-making, namely: participation and inclusion; access to information; nondiscrimination and equality; empowerment and accountability; and legality and access to justice (the PANEL Principles).[27] As Olawuyi notes, by implementing the PANEL principles in the design, approval, finance, and implementation of projects, policymakers could have better opportunities to anticipate and consider the overall impacts of a project on the public and then take steps to mitigate them.[28] The HRBA emphasizes the need to ensure that projects or policies intended to advance environmental protection and development do not result in adverse human rights consequences.[29] By recognizing the intricate interplay between biodiversity conservation, human rights, and green grabbing, policymakers and practitioners can work toward inclusive solutions that prioritize community rights, equitable benefit-sharing, and collaborative governance. Such a rights-based approach to biodiversity and ecosystem management would address inequalities in conservation efforts, thereby fostering harmonious coexistence between NBS and the preservation of human rights, local livelihoods, and cultural heritage.[30]

In the MENA region, the intersection of land rights, biodiversity conservation, and NBS presents a complex landscape influenced by cultural, legal, and environmental factors. The region's diverse ecosystems, from the Mediterranean coasts to arid deserts, are critical for both biodiversity preservation and local livelihoods. However, rapid urbanization, agricultural expansion, and resource extraction have often encroached upon indigenous and local communities' land rights, leading to conflicts between development and conservation goals. The MENA region's complex legal and institutional frameworks further complicate the situation.[31] For instance, in Morocco, the shift toward recognizing indigenous Amazigh

26 Ibid.

27 Olawuyi (n 23). See also United Nations, "The Human Rights Based Approach to Development Cooperation towards a Common Understanding among UN Agencies" (2003) https://unsdg.un.org/resources/human-rights-based-approach-development-cooperation-towards-common-understanding-among-un accessed February 7, 2024.

28 Olawuyi (n 23).

29 United Nations Human Rights Based Approach (HRBA) Portal, "The Human Rights Based Approach to Development Cooperation: Towards a Common Understanding among UN Agencies" (2003) https://hrbaportal.org/the-human-rights-based-approach-to-development-cooperation-towards-a-common-understanding-among-un-agencies/ accessed February 7, 2024.

30 UNEP, *Adopting a Human Rights-based Approach to Ecosystem-Based Adaptation: A Contribution to Sustainable Development* (UNEP 2022); also Mikkel Funder and Marie Ladekjaer Gravesen, "How to Support a Rights-Based Approach to Nature-Based Solutions: Recommendations for Danish Development Cooperation" (Danish Institute for Development Studies, February 23, 2022).

31 Saad Ahmad, Eleni Karampi, Lucy Ridout, and Kotono Takeshita, *Anti-Discrimination Laws in Middle East and North Africa: Egypt, Iran, Türkiye, and Tunisia* (Minority Rights 2024) https://minorityrights.org/resources/anti-discrimination-laws-in-middle-east-and-north-africa-egypt-iran-turkiye-and-tunisia/ accessed September 15, 2024.

communities' land tenure rights has set a precedent for aligning biodiversity conservation with human rights.[32] The recognition of these communities' traditional knowledge and their role in sustainable resource management is pivotal for successful NBS. Addressing such intricacies requires a holistic approach that integrates local perspectives, respects indigenous rights, and harnesses NBS to promote both biodiversity conservation and community well-being. By adopting inclusive policies that involve local communities in decision-making, MENA countries can create a harmonious coexistence between land rights, biodiversity, and NBS that embodies the principles of sustainability and social equity.

6.3 LEGAL AND INSTITUTIONAL BARRIERS TO IMPLEMENTING A RIGHTS-BASED APPROACH TO CONSERVATION IN THE MENA REGION: LESSONS FROM MOROCCO

This section examines the opportunities and challenges to implementing an HRBA to NBS in the MENA region. The legal and institutional framework plays a pivotal role in protecting land rights and addressing the specter of green grabbing within the realm of designing and implementing NBS for biodiversity and nature conservation. Crafting a robust legal framework involves enacting policies that prioritize the recognition and protection of local communities' land tenure rights. This entails acknowledging their traditional knowledge, cultural ties, and historical use of land. In addition, integrating mechanisms for obtaining free, prior, and informed consent from affected communities before initiating conservation projects is essential to ensure their meaningful participation and prevent involuntary displacement.[33]

6.3.1 *Legal Challenges Associated with the Human Rights-Based Approach: Lessons from Morocco*

The intricate legal and institutional barriers to implementing a rights-based approach to conservation in the MENA region are exemplified by Morocco's experiences. Morocco's legal amendments, including constitutional changes recognizing indigenous rights, have played a pivotal role in overcoming barriers to conservation. For instance, though not without criticisms, the recognition of Amazigh communities' customary land tenure rights empowers them to contribute to conservation efforts

[32] S. Gagliardi, "Indigenous Peoples' Rights in Morocco: Subaltern Narratives by Amazigh Women" (2019) 23 *International Journal of Human Rights* 1–2, 281; Bernadette Montanari and Sylvia I. Bergh, "Why Women's Traditional Knowledge Matters in the Production Processes of Natural Product Development: The Case of the Green Morocco Plan" (2019) 77 *Women's Studies International Forum*, 102275.

[33] UNEP (n 30); see also Olawuyi (n 9).

while preserving their cultural heritage.[34] This recognition underscores the potential for integrating indigenous perspectives into broader conservation strategies.[35]

Institutionally, establishing oversight bodies responsible for monitoring and evaluating the social and environmental impacts of NBS can mitigate the risk of green grabbing.[36] Collaborative governance structures that include representatives from local communities, civil society, and governmental bodies can facilitate transparent decision-making processes. By fostering inclusive engagement, respecting land rights, and embedding legal safeguards within institutional mechanisms, the potential for green grabbing can be significantly reduced, enabling NBS to achieve their intended conservation objectives while safeguarding the rights and well-being of those directly affected by these initiatives.[37]

Morocco's journey toward recognizing and safeguarding indigenous and local community rights offers invaluable insights. The nation's efforts in implementing sustainable environmental practices and conservation initiatives have yielded significant accomplishments. In 2016, Morocco was among the early signatories of the Paris Agreement, showcasing its commitment to addressing climate change.[38] Morocco has formulated its NDC with ambitious objectives aimed at substantial carbon emissions reduction.[39] This is despite the fact that the country is responsible for only a small share of the global problem of climate change, at 0.18 percent of global greenhouse gas emissions.[40] Notably, Morocco is one of only two global economies (along with Gambia) whose target is within the 1.5°C threshold.[41] In practical terms, this signifies that the kingdom is committed to achieving a net-zero-emission economy by around 2050.[42]

34 Article 5 of Morocco's 2011 constitution states that "Tamazight constitutes an official language of the State, being common patrimony of all Moroccans without exception." *Maroc: Constitution* (July 29, 2011) www.refworld.org/legal/legislation/natlegbod/2011/fr/17605 accessed February 08, 2024.

35 Minority Rights Group International, "Submission to the United Nations Universal Periodic Review of Morocco" (November 2022) https://minorityrights.org/app/uploads/2024/01/upr41-mrg-morocco-full.pdf accessed February 08, 2024.

36 UNEP (n 30); see also Olawuyi (n 9).

37 UNEP (n 30); see also Olawuyi (n 9).

38 Kingdom of Morocco, "Nationally Determined Contribution" (2021) https://unfccc.int/sites/default/files/NDC/2022-06/Moroccan%20updated%20NDC%202021%20_Fr.pdf accessed February 7, 2024.

39 Ibid.

40 International Monetary Fund: Middle East and Central Asia Dept, "Morocco: Request for an Arrangement under the Resilience and Sustainability Facility-Press Release; Staff Report; Supplement; Staff Statement; and Statement by the Executive Director for Morocco" (IMF Staff Country Reports 2023) (354), A00, Box 1 www.elibrary.imf.org/view/journals/002/2023/354/article-A001-en.xml#RA001bx01 accessed February 7, 2024.

41 The 2014 Intergovernmental Panel on Climate Change AR5 serves the scientific basis for the 2015 Paris Agreement. It sets the 1850–1900 period as a proxy for the pre-industrial period. To date, the planet has warmed 1.2°C above pre-industrial levels. C. F. Schleussner et al., "Science and Policy Characteristics of the Paris Agreement Temperature Goal" (2016) 6 *Nature Climate Change* 7, 827.

42 This is in order to minimize the worst climate impacts, and avoid irreversible damage to our societies, economies, and the environment. Kingdom of Morocco (n 38).

Morocco's legal framework for environmental rights is primarily composed of the Constitution, international agreements, and national laws and regulations.[43] The Constitution of Morocco, amended in 2011, recognizes the right to a healthy environment as a fundamental human right, setting the foundation for environmental protection and sustainable development.[44] Additionally, Morocco has ratified several international conventions, such as the Paris Agreement and the Convention on Biological Diversity, contributing to the legal framework supporting environmental rights within the country. Morocco's Green Generation Strategy 2020–2030 places human rights and the welfare of farmers at the heart of agricultural development and biodiversity management.[45] Furthermore, in Morocco, a range of environmental institutions diligently oversees and enacts policies, regulations, and conservation measures. These include the Ministry of Energy, Mines, and Environment, which spearheads the development and execution of initiatives concerning environmental protection, sustainable development, and energy management.[46] The High Commissioner for Water, Forests, and Combating Desertification is instrumental in managing forests and water resources and combating desertification while preserving biodiversity. The National Office for Electricity and Drinking Water plays a pivotal role in the supply of clean drinking water and electricity, emphasizing environmentally conscious energy production. Furthermore, the Agency for the Development of Renewable Energy and Energy Efficiency focuses on advancing renewable energy and enhancing energy efficiency. Alongside these key bodies, the Regional Environmental Directorates operate at the local level, implementing environmental regulations and policies. Together, these entities have a mandate to collaboratively advance biodiversity conservation, water resource management, climate change mitigation, sustainable energy initiatives, and the overall goal of promoting environmental sustainability throughout Morocco.

During the years 2001–2018, Morocco's environmental development has shown significant improvement, especially in the infrastructure aspect. Morocco invested 64.2 billion Moroccan dirhams between 1995 and 2017 to improve access to water in rural areas (97 percent) and urban areas (100 percent) and sanitation throughout the country.[47] Morocco spent US$33.8 million for the period of 2014–2015 to widen and extend electricity access in the country. This could explain the increase in the proportion of the rural population with access to electricity from 97.8 percent in 2016

43 See a list of Morocco's legislation, *Country Profile: Morocco*, FAOLEX www.fao.org/faolex/country-profiles/general-profile/en/?iso3=MAR accessed February 7, 2024.

44 *Maroc: Constitution* (n 34).

45 Kingdom of Morocco, "Green Generation Strategy 2020–2030" www.maroc.ma/en/content/generation-green-2020-2030 accessed February 7, 2024.

46 See Chapter 4.

47 National Office of Electricity and Drinking Water, "L'Electricité au Service du Développement" www.one.org.ma/FR/pdf/Brochure%20institutionnelle%202019%20ONEE%20BE%20version%20fran%C3%A7aise.pdf accessed February 7, 2024.

to 99.78 percent in 2020.[48] The country's commitment to renewable energy can be demonstrated through the projects that have been set up, such as the solar station Nour with a total investment of US$9 billion, which will help provide 52 percent of the kingdom's energy needs by 2030. Moreover, Morocco has implemented a set of programs to integrate sustainability into port management through the adoption of International Convention for the Prevention of Pollution from Ships with an investment of 200 million Moroccan dirhams. Morocco has strengthened its legal framework to protect fishery resources in an effective manner and has banned the use of gillnets. To preserve the national environment from desertification and wildfires, the national strategy Morocco Forests 2020–2030 is targeting the protection of the national forests. However, Morocco is still struggling with the extinction of some endangered species of wild fauna and flora. Hence, the government has strengthened its legal arsenal (Law No. 29-05) and adopted the international convention concerning the trade of endangered species. Moreover, within the framework of international cooperation, financing mobilized amounts of nearly US$200 billion between 1980 and 2020.[49]

Despite the progress, however, a lack of clear and explicit mention of land and indigenous rights in environmental legislation remains a key challenge to a rights-based approach.[50] Legal frameworks need to evolve to explicitly acknowledge the rights of these communities to their ancestral lands and resources. The constitutional amendments in Morocco, which recognized indigenous rights, exemplify the significance of such legal reforms. Institutionally, empowering local communities through participatory approaches is essential. Morocco's progress in engaging with indigenous Amazigh communities serves as a model for meaningful community participation in conservation decision-making. Additionally, the shift toward decentralized governance in Morocco's regionalization initiatives signifies the potential for enhancing local autonomy and ensuring that conservation strategies align with community priorities. By adapting and applying these lessons, the MENA region can foster a rights-based conservation paradigm that not only protects its rich biodiversity but also upholds the rights and well-being of indigenous and local communities, paving the way for sustainable and equitable conservation outcomes.

The pursuit of an HRBA to NBS in Morocco encounters several significant legal challenges. While NBS initiatives are inherently rooted in the environmental purposes to achieve sustainability and addressing climate change, they must be

48 Ministry of Energy Transition and Sustainable Development, "Stratégie Nationale de L'Efficacité Energétique à L'horizon 2030" (2022) www.mem.gov.ma/Lists/Lst_rapports/Attachments/33/Strat%C3%A9gue%20Nationale%20de%20l'Efficacit%C3%A9%20%C3%A9nerg%C3%A9tique%20%C3%A0%20l'horizon%202030.pdf accessed February 7, 2024.

49 Ibid.

50 Minority Rights Group International (n 35). See also International Land Coalition, "New Moroccan Land Laws Imperil Amazigh People" (August 9, 2019), available at https://emena.landcoalition.org/es/newsroom/new-moroccan-land-laws-imperils-amazigh-people/ accessed February 7, 2024.

implemented in a way that respects and upholds human rights, such as the right to a healthy environment, access to clean water, and protection of indigenous people's land rights. First, the lack of clear recognition of land and resource rights for indigenous communities and local populations poses a substantial challenge.[51] Without explicit legal protection, conflicts and disputes over land use and resource access could undermine NBS efforts. Additionally, the absence of human rights language within Morocco's environmental and biodiversity legislation complicates the alignment of NBS projects with international human rights standards.[52] Morocco's constitutional amendments have played a pivotal role in advancing biodiversity conservation by recognizing and prioritizing the rights of indigenous communities and local populations. The 2011 constitutional reforms marked a watershed moment in this regard, as they acknowledged the cultural and historical ties of indigenous Amazigh communities to their ancestral lands and resources.[53]

Morocco's constitutional amendments have played a pivotal role in advancing biodiversity conservation by recognizing and prioritizing the rights of indigenous communities and local populations. This discrepancy can lead to ambiguity in addressing human rights violations. The need for institutional coordination between entities that are responsible for human rights and environmental protection highlights the complexity of harmonizing conservation objectives within the rights of local communities. The 2011 constitutional reforms marked a watershed moment in this regard, as they acknowledged the cultural and historical ties of indigenous Amazigh communities to their ancestral lands and resources. For instance, the inclusion of Article 5 in the Moroccan Constitution explicitly recognized Amazigh as an official language and celebrated the diverse cultural heritage of the nation.[54] The recognition of Amazigh communities' traditional land tenure rights has empowered them to contribute to conservation efforts in the Souss-Massa National Park.[55] This recognition ensures the inclusion of indigenous perspectives in conservation planning and demonstrates the significance of legal reforms in promoting equitable conservation.

These amendments underscored the importance of environmental protection and sustainable development, enshrining the state's responsibility to safeguard

[51] IUCN, "A Rights-Based Path for People and Planet: Realising Human Rights in the Post-2020 Global Biodiversity Framework" (2022) www.iucn.org/story/202212/rights-based-path-people-and-planet-realising-human-rights-post-2020-global accessed February 7, 2024.

[52] IUCN, "Towards the Implementation of Nature-Based Solutions in Climate Policies in Morocco and Tunisia" (July 6, 2018) www.iucn.org/news/mediterranean/201807/towards-implementation-nature-based-solutions-climate-policies-morocco-and-tunisia accessed February 7, 2024.

[53] Article 5 of Morocco's 2011 constitution states that "Tamazight constitutes an official language of the State, being common patrimony of all Moroccans without exception."

[54] The state works for the protection and for the development of the Arabic language, as well as the promotion of its use. Likewise, Tamazight (Berber/Amazigh) constitutes an official language of the state, being a common patrimony of all Moroccans without exception.

[55] Julius Arnegger, *Protected Areas, the Tourist Bubble and Regional Economic Development: Two Case Studies from Mexico and Morocco* (Würzburg University Press 2014) 80–102.

natural resources and preserve ecological balance for future generations. The recognition of indigenous rights and the commitment to environmental preservation within the constitutional framework have provided a solid foundation for biodiversity conservation efforts in Morocco, demonstrating the potential of legal reforms to align conservation objectives with respect for local cultures and traditions.[56] In analyzing the narratives of Amazigh cultural groups and movements, it is crucial to differentiate between the movements' agendas and demands to the state on one hand and the needs and concerns of the overall Amazigh population, and specifically women, on the other. Different strategies and priorities seem at play in the Amazigh movement's demands for group rights.[57]

Furthermore, the absence of constitutional recognition pertaining to ancestral lands, group or indigenous rights, and the acknowledgment of diverse ethnicities is a significant lacuna in the legal framework.[58] This deficiency not only overlooks the historical and cultural significance of these elements but also fails to provide the necessary safeguards for the rights and identities of indigenous communities. This omission can lead to a range of socio-political challenges, including land disputes, cultural erosion, and the marginalization of minority groups. Therefore, it is imperative that the legal system evolves to encompass these vital aspects, ensuring a more inclusive and equitable society. This approach was confirmed by the 2014 census, which contained no ethnicity-based questions but merely questions on mother tongue and daily spoken languages. In addition to this, it is unconstitutional to form linguistic- and ethnic-based political parties or to bring harm to the permanent characteristics of the kingdom.[59]

Closely related to lack of clear recognition of HRBA in environmental legislation are institutional gaps that limit the coordination between environment, biodiversity, and human rights institutions.[60] Human rights are fundamentally linked to environmental conservation, yet the absence of cohesive collaboration between relevant institutions complicates the effective integration of these crucial aspects into policies and practices. Insufficient coordination often leads to disjointed efforts, resulting in a fragmented approach toward ensuring both environmental protection and the preservation of human rights. Yet in Morocco, as is the case in many MENA countries, environmental and human rights programs are within the purview of different institutions and agencies with diverse programs and objectives.[61] Lack of clear integration of their respective programs and mandate, and the limited sharing

56 Minority Rights Group International (n 35).

57 Silvia Gagliardi, "Indigenous Peoples' Rights in Morocco: Subaltern Narratives by Amazigh Women" (2019) 23 *The International Journal of Human Rights* 1–2, 281.

58 See Damilola Olawuyi, *Environmental Law in Arab States* (Oxford University Press 2022).

59 Gagliardi (n 57).

60 Damilola Olawuyi, "Sustainable Development and the Water–Energy–Food Nexus: Legal Challenges and Emerging Solutions" (2020) 103 *Journal of Environmental Science & Policy* 1.

61 Minority Rights Group International (n 35).

of information and best practices, constrain the integration required to mainstream and adopt the HRBA in the design and implementation of NBS programs.

As NBS takes root across the region as a tool for halting biodiversity loss, there is a need for clear and comprehensive rights-based instruments that integrates land rights and the protection of indigenous communities in NBS programs. Section 6.4 discusses a step-by-step approach for implementing an HRBA to NBS.

6.4 MINDING THE GAPS: RECOMMENDATIONS

Advancing a human rights-based approach to NBS demands a multidimensional framework that harmonizes ethical, legal, and environmental considerations. Here are some key recommendations to ensure an HRBA to NBS in Morocco and across the MENA region.

First is the need for clear and comprehensive national strategies and legislation on NBS as a tool for promoting biodiversity and nature conservation. Without a clear regulatory framework on NBS, its implementation may remain ad hoc and incoherent. In addition to recognizing a rights-based approach in national biodiversity strategies and action plans, a clear regulatory framework on NBS will provide an opportunity for MENA countries to mandate the need for human rights due diligence in the design and implementation of NBS to detect and address adverse human rights impacts that may arise.[62] Failure to clearly mandate biodiversity actors to track the human rights impacts of programs such as NBS, especially on at-risk groups such as indigenous peoples, local communities, peasants, and rural women, exacerbates land grabs and a lack of clear integration of human rights considerations in implementation. As Boyd and Keene note, "such laws should include substantial penalties for noncompliance, and should require that all businesses and their subsidiaries: conduct pre-investment due diligence on the potential human rights and environmental risks associated with their contemplated operations and supply chains."[63] In addition to mandating human rights due diligence before the approval of NBS schemes, there is also a need to continue to monitor the implementation of such programs such that initiatives that do not satisfy human rights and environmental standards commensurate with both national and international law could be promptly detected and stopped.[64] Urgent drafting and enactment of supporting legislation, integration of laws, adequate resource allocation, and enhanced community involvement through awareness campaigns and participation in decision-making processes are crucial recommendations for

[62] David Boyd and Stephanie Keene, "Human Rights-Based Approaches to Conserving Biodiversity: Equitable, Effective and Imperative" Policy Brief 1 (August 2021) www.ohchr.org/sites/default/files/Documents/Issues/Environment/SREnvironment/policy-briefing-1-summary.pdf accessed February 7, 2024.

[63] Ibid.

[64] Ibid. See also Olawuyi (n 9).

addressing these challenges and advancing an HRBA to nature conservation and biodiversity programs.

Equally important is the need to foster institutional coordination between human rights and environmental institutions. The siloed nature of these institutions impedes the development of comprehensive strategies that can effectively balance environmental sustainability with the safeguarding of human rights. Establishing stronger institutional coordination and collaboration mechanisms is imperative to harmonize efforts, ensuring that environmental conservation aligns with the principles of human rights and vice versa, fostering a more holistic and effective approach to sustainable development. Collaborative governance involves partnerships between government entities, local communities, and other stakeholders in decision-making processes. In Morocco, collaborative models such as co-management have proven pivotal in surmounting institutional barriers. The co-management of Argan forests in the Souss-Massa region exemplifies how local communities, governmental bodies, and nongovernmental organizations could collaboratively manage these ecosystems. This approach fosters a sense of ownership among local communities, enabling them to actively participate in conservation strategies.[65] Collaborative governance empowers communities to be active partners rather than passive beneficiaries.[66] The High Atlas Foundation's Agdal Restoration Project stands as a testament to this approach, where local communities contribute their traditional knowledge to restore Agdal systems.[67] This collective decision-making process reinforces cultural ties to the land, promoting both conservation and socio-economic development.[68] Morocco's progress and challenges in implementing collaborative governance models offer valuable lessons to the broader MENA region. By promoting community engagement, recognizing customary land tenure systems, and ensuring equitable benefit-sharing, MENA countries can address legal and institutional barriers while fostering conservation rooted in local knowledge and values.[69]

6.5 CONCLUSION

The alignment of academic research and international agreements with UNEA's emphasis on biodiversity conservation and NBS underscores the global recognition of biodiversity's vital role. As academic insights inform international agreements and

65 Arnegger (n 55).

66 UNEP (n 30), see also Olawuyi (n 9).

67 Laurent Auclair et al., "Patrimony for Resilience: Evidence from the Forest Agdal in the Moroccan High Atlas Mountains" (2011) 16 *Ecology and Society* 4. See also Kira Walker, "A Model for Land Management, Morocco's Agdals Are at Risk of Disappearing" (*New Lines Magazine*, November 15, 2023) https://newlinesmag.com/reportage/a-model-for-land-management-moroccos-agdals-are-at-risk-of-disappearing/ accessed February 08, 2024.

68 Walker (n 67).

69 M. Meziani, "Beyond Participation: Can Collaborative Management Enable Adaptive Co-management in Morocco?" (2004) 56 *World Development* 11.

policy decisions, and as UNEA champions these strategies, a united effort emerges to secure a sustainable future where biodiversity flourishes alongside human development. NBS presents innovative pathways to address pressing environmental challenges, but their efficacy hinges on the acknowledgment of land rights. The intricate link between land rights and conservation underscores the necessity of equitable solutions that uphold the rights of indigenous and local communities while pursuing biodiversity protection and sustainable development.

An HRBA is imperative to safeguard land rights within NBS. Instruments such as the UNDRIP emphasize the importance of free, prior, and informed consent in development projects that impact indigenous lands. Integrating these principles ensures equitable decision-making and recognizes the cultural significance of land for communities. Morocco's experiences underscore the significance of collaborative governance in transcending legal and institutional barriers to conservation. By engaging communities, acknowledging indigenous rights, and promoting inclusive decision-making, MENA countries can pave the way for harmonious conservation efforts that uphold human rights, cultural heritage, and biodiversity.

7

Gender-Responsive Implementation of Biodiversity and Nature Conservation Treaties

Adenike Adebukola Akinsemolu

7.1 INTRODUCTION

This chapter explores gender dimensions of biodiversity and nature conservation. It discusses the need for gender-responsive implementation of biodiversity and nature conservation treaties, the gaps in gender-responsive implementation of conservation initiatives in the Middle East and North Africa (MENA) region, and innovative approaches for addressing such gaps.

Climate change is driving a worrying decline in biodiversity through environmental changes that disturb and threaten species and their natural habitats.[1] As temperatures rise, rainfall patterns change, and water levels rise in the oceans, the planet is gradually losing its biodiversity as more plant and animal species face a heightened risk of extinction. Further, marine, freshwater, and terrestrial ecosystems are changing as diseases increase, plants and animals die, and diverse species lose their sources of food. The prevailing threats to biodiversity are projected to continue growing.[2] Some of the countries in the MENA region that are highly vulnerable to the climate-induced loss of marine biodiversity include Libya, Oman, Iraq, and Syria.[3] On land, drought is driving rapid biodiversity loss in the MENA region. The region is the driest part of the world, only having a mere 2 percent of the world's renewable water resources according to the International Water Management Institute.[4] Extended periods of drought in the region accelerate biodiversity loss as animals and plants that lack the ability to cope with extreme temperatures and lack of water can no longer survive.[5]

1 Damilola S. Olawuyi, *Climate Change Law and Policy in the Middle East and North Africa Region* (Routledge 2022) 1–15.

2 Ibid.

3 Razieh Namdar, Ezatollah Karami, and Marzieh Keshavarz, "Climate Change and Vulnerability: The Case of MENA Countries" (2021) 10 *International Journal of Geo-Information* 11, 794 www.mdpi.com/2220-9964/10/11/794 accessed September 23, 2023.

4 International Water Management Institute, "Planning for Drought in MENA" (2022) www.iwmi.cgiar.org/2022/08/planning-for-drought-in-mena/ accessed September 23, 2023.

5 Ibid., 3.

To halt the gradual loss of biodiversity due to climate change, resource overexploitation, and other causes, the MENA region is looking to coordinated interventions to save its natural environment from further degradation, protect ecosystems, and promote nature-based solutions. MENA countries are signatories to the wide range of biodiversity and nature conservation treaties adopted globally to fight against climate change through nature conservation and biodiversity restoration interventions.[6] Despite progress made in biodiversity and nature conservation across the region, a lack of clear and comprehensive gender mainstreaming in biodiversity and nature conservation efforts remain a key problem and a barrier to sustainable progress.[7] The Convention on Biological Diversity (CBD) acknowledges the importance of integrating women's knowledge of biodiversity and its conservation in biodiversity programs.[8] Yet the ability of women to access the land, finance, technologies, and programs needed to take part in and influence decision-making on biodiversity conservation and education, including to become biodiversity entrepreneurs, remain limited across the MENA region.[9] The MENA region is often cited in studies as the region where women are more vulnerable to the disproportionate impacts of climate change and biodiversity loss but are less likely to play key roles in addressing such impacts due their underrepresentation in formal political structures.[10] Lack of gender balance in the leadership or management of biodiversity programs may limit the full consideration of the intersectionality of the effects of climate change, such as the loss of biodiversity, and gender.[11] To speed up the implementation of nature and biodiversity treaties, draw from the knowledge and contribution of all members of society, unlock more of their benefits to nature and biodiversity, and ensure the equitable distribution of the benefits of biodiversity and nature, there is a need to address extant gender gaps in the design and implementation of biodiversity programs in the MENA region.[12]

6 Olawuyi (n 1).

7 Sally Abi Khalil, "If Women Don't Lead, We'll Lose the Battle Against Climate Crisis" (Reliefweb 2022) https://reliefweb.int/report/world/if-women-dont-lead-well-lose-battle-against-climate-crisis accessed September 23, 2023.

8 Convention on Biological Diversity, "Addressing Gender Issues and Actions in Biodiversity Objectives" (2020) www.cbd.int/gender/doc/cbd-towards2020-gender_integration-en.pdf accessed September 23, 2023.

9 Jamal El-Ouahi and Vincent Larivière, "On the Lack of Women Researchers in the Middle East and North Africa" (2023) 128 *Scientometrics* 1 https://link.springer.com/article/10.1007/s11192-023-04768-5 accessed February 13, 2024.

10 IISD, "Climate Response for Drylands Must Include Women" (June 17, 2023) https://sdg.iisd.org/commentary/guest-articles/climate-response-for-drylands-must-include-women/ accessed February 13, 2024; see also Rolla Khadduri et al., "MENA Regional Overview: Gender and Equality" https://manniondaniels.com/wp-content/uploads/2022/12/MENA-overview-Gender-and-Equality.pdf accessed February 13, 2024.

11 El-Ouahi and Larivière (n 9).

12 Damilola S. Olawuyi, *Environmental Law in Arab States* (Oxford University Press 2022) 6.

This chapter explores the gender dimensions of biodiversity and nature conservation and uses two approaches to gender-responsive implementation to demonstrate how they can be harnessed to promote the gender-responsive implementation of conservation initiatives in the MENA region. The chapter is divided into five sections. After this introduction, Section 7.2 explores the gender dimensions of biodiversity and nature conversation, highlighting the linkages between gender and biodiversity to infer the elements of a gender-responsive approach to biodiversity and nature conservation. Section 7.3 explores some of the international laws that recognize the linkages between gender and biodiversity, including the resolutions of the conventions that bind the countries in the MENA region in their commitment to protecting nature and biodiversity. Section 7.3 also explores the gender responsiveness of the implementation approaches of nature and biodiversity programs in the MENA region and identifies some gaps in the involvement of women in driving nature and biodiversity conservation efforts in the region. Section 7.4 outlines some recommendations to make the implementation of nature and biodiversity conservation programs in the MENA region more gender inclusive. Section 7.5 is the concluding section.

7.2 GENDER DIMENSIONS OF BIODIVERSITY AND NATURE CONSERVATION

Gender responsiveness focuses on addressing the root causes of gender-based marginalization and exclusion in the design and implementation of biodiversity programs. In many societies, due to prevailing structures of inequality in access to education, financing, land, and formal political and decision-making structures, women are often underrepresented in the formulation and implementation of nature conservation and biodiversity programs.[13] The drivers of systemic gender inequality and their implications of biodiversity and nature conservation are examined in this section.

7.2.1 *Gender-Based Differences in the Value of Biodiversity and Nature Conservation Knowledge*

Many societies operate under a system of privilege, which controls its members' access to the sources of power.[14] These sources of power include education and information, economic participation, the ownership of resources, and position on

[13] Khadduri et al. (n 10). See also Damilola S. Olawuyi, "Gender, Indigeneity and the Search for Environmental Justice in Post-colonial Africa" in Carmen Gonzalez, Sara Seck, and Sumudu Attapatu (eds), *Cambridge Handbook of Environment Justice and Sustainable Development* (Cambridge University Press 2021).

[14] Megan Jones and Jennifer Solomon, "Challenges and Supports for Women Conservation Leaders" (2019) 1 *Conservation Science and Practice* 6, 36 https://conbio.onlinelibrary.wiley.com/doi/pdf/10.1111/csp2.36 accessed September 23, 2023.

the social hierarchy. Inequalities in access to the sources of power usually lead to limited access to power as well. Therefore, inadequate access to education and economic opportunities in many countries and societies often translates to limited access to resources, which in turn leads to a lower social status.[15] In the MENA region, this relationship between education, economic participation, resources, and power often leads to a cycle of disempowerment for women, who reach lower levels of education compared to their male counterparts.[16] Since 2013, there has been sustained progress across the region in terms of significant investments in the education of women, which has closed the gender parity gap in education and healthcare, with Tunisia, Morocco, Qatar, Saudi Arabia, Oman, and Algeria leading in gender parity in education in the MENA region.[17] However, progress made in narrowing the gender gap is yet to fully address barriers to active participation in formal and political decision-making structures, especially as it relates to the environment. For example, in 2023, women made up just 10 percent of environmental ministers in the MENA region.[18] Further, women's increased educational attainment has not addressed their disempowerment since their economic participation has remained the same.[19] With their limited economic participation, women are unable to accumulate the resources that their male counterparts combine with education and knowledge to use as leverage for leadership, decision-making, and participation in nature and biodiversity conservation programs.[20]

Discernibly, the reliance on education, economic participation, and resource ownership as sources of power may disproportionately shut out women from leading and contributing to the biodiversity conservation programs devised by nature and conservation treaties. This is despite women's knowledge of the environment and nature conservation being invaluable and their concern for the environment being a great source of insight into sustainability.[21] Women have access to first-hand information and knowledge regarding the effects of climate change on biodiversity

15 Olawuyi (n 12).

16 El-Ouahi and Larivière (n 9)

17 "In education and health, the MENA countries have closed over 96 percent of the gender gap." See Paul Salem, "Middle East Futures will Pivot on Women" (Middle East Institute 2023) www.mei.edu/publications/middle-east-futures-will-pivot-women#:~:text=In%20education%20and%20health%2C%20the,only%20been%20closed%20by%2015%25 accessed February 13, 2024.

18 See IISD, "Climate Response for Drylands Must Include Women" (June 17, 2023) https://sdg.iisd.org/commentary/guest-articles/climate-response-for-drylands-must-include-women/ accessed February 13, 2024.

19 Ragui Asaad et al., "Explaining the MENA Paradox: Rising Educational Attainment, Yet Stagnant Female Labor Force Participation" (2020) 43 *Demographic Research* 817 www.ncbi.nlm.nih.gov/pmc/articles/PMC8345317/ accessed September 23, 2023.

20 Ibid.

21 Endalcachew Bayeh, "The Role of Empowering Women and Achieving Gender Equality to the Sustainable Development of Ethiopia" (2016) 2 *Pacific Science Review B: Humanities and Social Sciences* 1, 37 www.sciencedirect.com/science/article/pii/S2405883116300508 accessed September 23, 2023.

and could be the key to the development of effective interventions. The socially ascribed roles of women in the MENA region include cooking, cleaning, household maintenance, shopping, and taking care of children.[22] Taking on these roles in their households exposes women to the effects of climate change daily. For instance, they are aware of changes in water quality, which is a key pillar of biodiversity as it is crucial for the survival of plant and animal species.[23] Similarly, women in the region observe changes in vegetation while women along the coastal areas in the region learn of changes in marine diversity since they shop and cook for their families. Despite having all this information on biodiversity, which would make their contributions to nature and biodiversity conservation programs invaluable, little value is placed on their knowledge, leading to their exclusion as both sources of information and recipients of knowledge and training on environmental awareness.[24]

7.2.2 *Gender-Based Differences in Roles Relevant to Biodiversity and Nature Conservation*

Women are perfectly placed to play an integral role in relation to biodiversity and nature conservation in two ways. First, in many countries, women are the key decision-makers in their households' food consumption. Consequently, they can play the primary role of driving green consumption to protect biodiversity.[25] For instance, the MENA region has recorded a gradual shift from its traditional diet, which mainly comprised grains, vegetables, and fruits, to a less diverse and more Westernized diet consisting of animal proteins, refined fats and sugars, and processed foods.[26] Besides contributing to a prevalence of diet-related noncommunicable diseases in the region, the change in diet has contributed to the loss of biodiversity. Women can drive a transition back to the indigenous diet, prompting

22 Oxfam, "Counting on Women's Work without Counting Women's Work" (2019) https://oxfamilibrary.openrepository.com/bitstream/handle/10546/620811/rr-counting-womens-work-unpaid-care-mena-region-030619-en.pdf;jsessionid=9719A18B8AC7179026098 48F28B9E0C5?sequence=1 accessed September 23, 2023.

23 Alice Newton et al., "Editorial: Ecosystem Services, Biodiversity, and Water Quality in Transitional Ecosystems" (2023) 11 *Frontiers in Ecology and Evolution* www.frontiersin.org/articles/10.3389/fevo.2023.1136750/full accessed September 23, 2023.

24 Xia Ling and Yanhong Liu, "The Coordination of Environmental Protection and Female Discrimination based on the Concept of Affirmative Action" (2023) 4 *International Journal of Environmental Research and Public Health* 20, 3419 www.ncbi.nlm.nih.gov/pmc/articles/PMC9963526/ accessed September 23, 2023.

25 Women For Biodiversity, "Building Resilience and Weaving Gender Responsive Approaches to Biodiversity Governance" report of a training workshop www.women4biodiversity.org/cnx-workshop-report-english/ accessed February 13, 2024. See also Atlantic Council, "Cultivating Change: Women As Catalysts for Agricultural Transformation in the MENA Region" (September 29, 2023) www.atlanticcouncil.org/blogs/menasource/n7-agriculture-middle-east-women/ accessed February 13, 2024.

26 Rachel Bahn, Sibelle Labban, and Nahla Hwalla, "Impacts of Shifting to Healthier Food Consumption Patterns on Environmental Sustainability in MENA Countries" (2018) 14 *Sustainability Science* 14 https://link.springer.com/article/10.1007/s11625-018-0600-3 accessed September 23, 2023.

agricultural activities in the region to revert to indigenous crops, which will improve biodiversity by restoring healthy soil microbiomes and bringing back animals and plants that were in symbiotic relationships with indigenous crops.[27] This role strategically places women in the best position to implement some of the recommendations of nature conservation and biodiversity treaties while promoting the health of their communities. Second, women in the MENA region take on the primary caregiving roles when raising their children.[28] In their role as their children's main source of influence, women have the opportunity to improve current and future generations' environmental awareness and turn ecological consumption into a universal habitual behavior.[29]

Despite being in a position to drive sustainability through conscious consumption and by raising the next generation to conserve nature, obstacles remain for the full integration of women in nature conservation and the preservation of biodiversity.[30] Relegating women to passive roles in nature conservation neglects women's valuable contributions while preventing them from participating in future conservation efforts by upholding the social norms that prevent them from playing active roles in the initiatives. This locks them in a cycle of exclusion and limited access to opportunities to change the status quo.

7.2.3 *Gender-Based Differences in Priorities Relevant to Biodiversity and Nature Conservation*

Women's disproportional access to economic opportunities, land resources, and formal decision-making structures in the MENA region weakens the full integration of the perspectives and priorities of women in biodiversity and nature conservation programs.[31] First, fewer women at the decision-making table often means that the knowledge women acquire in their role as homemakers is not fully reflected in deliberations and decision-making. The teams that design and implement the recommendations of biodiversity and nature conservation treaties remain largely male-led and male-dominated.[32] For instance, only 30 percent of the 10,000 experts who advise the members of the body that advises the parties to the treaties on species and nature

[27] Ana Deaconu, Geneviene Mercille, and Malek Batal, "Promoting Traditional Foods for Human and Environmental Health: Lessons from Agroecology and Indigenous Communities in Ecuador" (2021) 1 *BMC Nutrition* https://bmcnutr.biomedcentral.com/articles/10.1186/s40795-020-00395-y accessed September 23, 2023.

[28] Noora Lari and Noor Al-Emadi, "Measuring Parental Involvement in Dual-Earner Qatari Families" (2022) 31 *Journal of Child and Family Studies* 2997 https://link.springer.com/article/10.1007/s10826-021-02183-z accessed September 23, 2023.

[29] Ibid., 15.

[30] Khadduri et al. (n 10).

[31] Ibid.

[32] Ibid.

conservation are women.[33] The male domination trickles down to the teams that break down the interventions at national and local levels. Therefore, women, their needs, and the knowledge they can contribute to the conservation of nature and biodiversity are undervalued, making them a low priority in the inception, implementation, and outcomes of nature and biodiversity preservation programs. For example, while many biodiversity interventions focus on formal and centralized approaches led by regulatory institutions, the importance of soft interventions such as homegrown forest restoration, tree planting, nature-based solutions, and climate-smart dietary changes may be excluded. Second, community norms around women's participation in public affairs often limit women's bargaining power regarding their inclusion in biodiversity conservation programs and even less authority in contributing their knowledge to conversations on the preservation of biodiversity.[34] This problem is not exclusive to women in the MENA region. In fact, less than half of the global female population has influence over nature conservation priorities compared to 65 percent of men.[35] The prevailing lopsidedness in representation raises the need to dismantle drivers of gender-based disparity and inequality in the design and implementation of biodiversity and nature conservation programs in order to ensure that both formal and informal knowledge are fully maximized in biodiversity efforts.

7.2.4 *Gender-Based Differences in Access, Use, and Control of Resources*

The implementation of the recommendations of biodiversity and natural resource conservation initiatives is a resource-intensive endeavor. At the very least, it requires access to or ownership of land, access to natural resources, and access to financial resources. Historically, women in many MENA societies have been tasked with the management and conservation of resources in their households, which often tilts access to financial resources and resource allocation in favor of men.[36] In the MENA region, women's access to resources is often restricted by their limited economic participation.[37] Further, the position of women in the social hierarchy

[33] Razan Mubarak, "Why Women Have an Essential Role in Biodiversity Conservation" (Climate Champions 2021) https://climatechampions.unfccc.int/why-women-have-an-essential-role-in-biodiversity-conservation/?gclid=CjwKCAjwmbqoBhAgEiwACIjzEOFKUNpy4HrAIWdOJxSPiWff3itEqyptpgNbhNlepHHVJ6a2LmqrXRoCQ7MQAvD_BwE accessed August 23, 2023.

[34] R. Schuster et al., "Measuring Community Norms Around Women's Empowerment in the West Bank: Opportunities and Challenges of a Novel Approach Using Cultural Consensus" (2019) 9 *SSM-Population Health*, 100489 www.sciencedirect.com/science/article/pii/S2352827318302568 accessed September 23, 2023.

[35] Robyn James, "Breaking the Bias: How to Deliver Gender Equity in Conservation" (*Nature* 2023) www.nature.com/articles/d41586-023-00779-7#:~:text=Women%20benefit%20from%20more%20women,for%20cultural%20change%20as%20well accessed September 23, 2023.

[36] Rolla Khadduri et al. (n 10). Also Payal Mago and Isha Gunwal, "Role of Women in Environment Conservation" (2019) *SSRN Electronic Journal* https://papers.ssrn.com/sol3/papers.cfm?abstract_id=3581051 accessed August 23, 2023.

[37] Ibid., 10.

discussed earlier and their lack of legal and social protections limit women's ownership of resources further. As such, women can use these resources but their access to them is limited. In some North African countries, for instance, no more than 20 percent of land is registered in the names of women.[38] Even when women succeed in having land registered in their name, their access is controlled by their spouses or male relatives. Therefore, when the owners of land and other natural resources are called upon to make decisions on biodiversity and nature conservation, women are left out. Their exclusion extends to the ownership of communal resources, culminating in their exclusion from the implementation of conservation efforts at the community level. Women's limited access to household and communal resources stems from gender roles, which have historically confined women to unpaid domestic labor. Although more women are attaining higher levels of education and some are working outside the home, the gap in ownership and access to resources is still significant since women only make up less than 20 percent of landowners.[39] Their limited ownership of resources is responsible for women's limited involvement in implementing biodiversity and nature conservation interventions.

Finally, there are obvious gender differences in participation, decision-making, and access to the benefits of biodiversity and nature conservation. The foregoing gender dynamics of biodiversity culminate in the disproportionate participation of women in all levels of conservation. Limited economic participation shuts women out of influencing policy and making decisions related to leadership in the design and implementation of conservation programs. Similarly, their relegation to passive roles prevents their active participation in decision-making, which prevents their needs from being prioritized. Consequently, they fail to benefit from conservation efforts as much as their male counterparts.

7.3 A GENDER-RESPONSIVE APPROACH TO BIODIVERSITY: SCOPE AND CONTENT

A gender-responsive approach should guarantee women's participation in the conservation of nature and biodiversity to enrich conservation efforts with their knowledge, ensure that the programs accommodate the needs of all members of society, and promote the equitable sharing of the benefits of the programs.

[38] K. Deininger, T. Hilhorst, and V. Songwe, "Identifying and Addressing Land Governance Constraints to Support Intensification and Land Market Operation: Evidence from 10 African Countries" (2014) 48 *Food policy* 76 www.sciencedirect.com/science/article/pii/S0306919214000438 accessed August 23, 2023.

[39] T. Halonen, "Securing Women's Land Rights for Increased Gender Equality, Food Security and Economic Empowerment" (United Nations 2023) www.un.org/en/un-chronicle/securing-women%E2%80%99s-land-rights-increased-gender-equality-food-security-and-economic#:~:text=Its%20Gender%20Action%20Plan%20acknowledges,desertification%2C%20land%20degradation%20and%20drought accessed September 23, 2023.

Two approaches can promote the gender-responsive implementation of biodiversity and nature conservation treaties.

7.3.1 *The Synergistic Approach*

A synergistic approach to gender-responsive implementation in relation to the conservation of nature and biodiversity refers to the identification and development of important linkages between gender equality and biodiversity. In the MENA region, these critical links include women's right to access, use, and have control over natural resources, contribute to the implementation of programs that target biodiversity goals, and address the problems that women face in their roles and contributions to the implementation of the different conventions and treaties.[40] Under the approach, synergies between efforts to promote gender equality and the implementation of the treaties would be established. Ideally, the synergies would be established at all levels of implementation, starting with the gender constitution of the advisors to the parties to the treaties down to the implementation of specific programs at the local level. However, more realistic entry points include affirmative action when constituting local implementation committees, eliminating barriers to access to information, consulting both genders when breaking down the interventions proposed by the treaties into local programs, and promoting equality in sharing the benefits accruing from the initiatives. The synergistic approach would improve nature and biodiversity conservation in the MENA region by harnessing women's knowledge, mobilizing skills, and influence in household decisions to promote the conservation of biodiversity.

7.3.2 *Gender Transformative Approach*

Comparatively, the gender transformative approach promotes the gender-responsive implementation of the resolutions of the treaties through the three dimensions of equity, namely recognition, procedure, and distribution.[41] In this context, recognition refers to the acknowledgment and respect for all parties, their values, and the knowledge they hold in relation to biodiversity and nature conservation. Since women are highly knowledgeable about nature and biodiversity conservation, their involvement in the implementation of the ratified interventions is invaluable. For instance, women in Morocco have demonstrated the value of their knowledge on biodiversity through large-scale projects that produce food for their communities

40 UN Women, "Towards a Gender-Responsive Implementation of the Convention on Biological Diversity" (2018) www.cbd.int/doc/c/34b8/2445/f3c7ee9df40a841577c51638/cop-14-inf-21-en .pdf accessed September 23, 2023.

41 F. Booker, "Gender and Biodiversity Conservation – Progress and Future Directions" (International Institute for Environment and Development 2018) www.iied.org/gender-biodiversity-conservation-progress-future-directions accessed September 23, 2023.

while preserving biodiversity in their country.[42] The women are growing plants that are indigenous to their country, such as cumin, quinoa, and cactus to produce food in cooperatives that empower them financially and increase their economic participation while restoring the soil microbiome and protecting indigenous plant and animal species. Procedure refers to the involvement of every person who is affected by the degradation of nature and loss of biodiversity in decisions relating to the implementation of interventions. Their involvement in decision-making requires unlimited access to information and knowledge. With women playing a more prominent role in conservation programs, joint decision-making will yield better outcomes that address the needs of both genders. Third, distribution refers to the equitable participation in the benefits or negative impacts of the biodiversity and nature conservation interventions. Consequently, both men and women will benefit equally from the implementation of the resolutions of the treaties.

7.3.3 *Recognition of the Linkages between Gender and Biodiversity in Nature Conservation and Biodiversity Treaties*

7.3.3.1 Convention on Biological Diversity

The CBD's primary purpose was to establish a global regime to regulate access to the genetic resources used for scientific research. Essentially, the CBD was created and ratified to preserve genetic diversity, which is the foundation of species and ecosystem diversity, by allowing every country with the means to advance knowledge of genetics to do so. Therefore, its secondary purpose was to ensure the fair distribution of the benefits of the research conducted using genetic resources. Some of these benefits include innovations that protect biodiversity such as the use of genome-based approaches to promote conservation.[43] The 195 countries that ratified the CBD renewed their commitment to the protection and preservation of biodiversity in 2010 by adopting the Nagoya Protocol to advance fairness and equity in the distribution of the benefits arising from the utilization of genetic resources. The CBD recognizes several gender gaps in the implementation of its resolutions. These gaps include the limited visibility of women's relationship with biodiversity and their ecosystems, the little value attached to their knowledge on biodiversity, their needs and priorities, and their limited capacities to contribute to biodiversity goals, which diminish as climate

[42] Bernadette Montanari and Sylvia Bergh, "Why Women's Traditional Knowledge Matters in the Production Processes of Natural Product Development: The Case of the Green Morocco Plan" (2019) 77 *Women's Studies International Forum* www.sciencedirect.com/science/article/pii/S0277539518303704 accessed September 23, 2023.

[43] Kathrin Theissinger et al., "How Genomics Can Help Biodiversity Conservation" (2023) 39 *Trends in Genetics* 7, 545 https://pubmed.ncbi.nlm.nih.gov/36801111/#:~:text=The%20availability%20of%20public%20genomic,for%20scientifically%20informed%20management%20decisions accessed September 23, 2023.

change exacerbates their vulnerabilities.[44] To ensure the full implementation of the CBD, all parties in the MENA region must put in place gender-responsive biodiversity programs that address these and other gender-related gaps.

7.3.3.2 The Kunming-Montreal Global Biodiversity Framework

In December 2022, the parties to the CBD adopted the Kunming-Montreal Global Biodiversity Framework (GBF) as a response to the dangerous deterioration of nature and the resulting threat to over a million species. The parties to the CBD deemed the framework a necessary intervention to stop and reverse nature loss to protect the billions of people globally whose lives are impacted by climate change. The GBF has provisions for promoting equality in the global efforts to stop biodiversity loss and restore fast-declining ecosystems. Notably, it has a unique provision that requires its parties to recognize the contributions of local communities and indigenous people.[45] The provision was adopted following the realization that often, the knowledge and potential contribution of indigenous people and local communities to biodiversity protection and nature conservation efforts are ignored while the two groups shoulder the negative effects of conservation programs.[46] Further, the framework recognizes that local, national, and regional circumstances vary. Consequently, it has a provision allowing its parties to design their own approaches to nature conservation and implement their own solutions to biodiversity loss and protection. However, members are required to ensure that all nature conservation programs and activities to stop or reverse biodiversity loss target the framework's four universal goals.

In addition to its resolution to involve all members of the communities in its member countries in the implementation of its resolutions, the GBF isolates gender inclusivity in promoting biodiversity as one of its targets. Target 23 of the GBF resolves to foster gender equality in its implementation by providing equal opportunities and empowering women's capacity to contribute to the preservation of biodiversity by acknowledging their right to own land and natural resources, welcoming their participation in decision-making and encouraging their leadership.[47]

[44] Convention on Biological Diversity, "Addressing Gender Issues and Actions in Biodiversity Objectives" www.cbd.int/gender/doc/cbd-towards2020-gender_integration-en.pdf accessed February 13, 2024.

[45] Conference of the Parties to the Convention on Biological Diversity, "Kunming-Montreal Global Biodiversity Framework" (2022) www.cbd.int/gbf/#:~:text=The%20Kunming%2DMontreal%20Global%20Biodiversity,year%20consultation%20and%20negotiation%20process accessed September 24, 2023.

[46] R. Montgomery, "Positioning Human Heritage at the Center of Conservation Practice" (2020) 5 *Conservation Biology* 5, 1122 https://pubmed.ncbi.nlm.nih.gov/32045032/ accessed September 24, 2023.

[47] Convention on Biological Diversity, "Cop15: Final Text of Kunming-Montreal Global Biodiversity Framework" (2022) www.cbd.int/article/cop15-final-text-kunming-montreal-gbf-221222#:~:text=Ensure%20gender%20equality%20in%20the,natural%20resources%20and%20their%20full%2C accessed September 23, 2023.

7.3.3.3 Convention on International Trade in Endangered Species of Wild Fauna and Flora

The Convention of International Trade in Endangered Species of Wild Fauna and Flora (CITES) was ratified to protect wild animal and plant species from extinction. It was established following growing concern over the extinction of then prominent animal and plant species. When CITES was formed in the 1960s, the trade in animal and plant species was ongoing but the threat of extinction was not as imminent as it is today. Nevertheless, the member countries had the foresight to impose restrictions on the trade. CITES was founded on the recognition of the need to protect habitats and biodiversity following the discovery of the ripple effects of the exploitation of animals and plants. The overexploitation of some animal and plant species depletes their population leading to habitat loss which, in turn, leads to the loss of more plant and animal species.[48] By binding themselves to the rules established in CITES, the 184 parties to the convention recognized the role of species in the ecosystem and hoped to stop the cycle of biodiversity loss and promote sustainability. The members affirm their dedication to maintaining balance in natural ecosystems and protecting biodiversity through the protection of more species through joint efforts to monitor and protect endangered plant and animal species and regular conferences to develop new strategies to prevent further loss of biodiversity.

CITES acknowledges gaps in gender and its role in the implementation of its resolutions by recognizing that women's interaction with the international trade in wild plants and animals is overlooked and their role in the sustainable use and conservation of biodiversity undermined.[49] Consequently, they remain marginalized in making decisions related to the protection of engendered species and biodiversity, accessing and sharing in the benefits of the restoration of biodiversity, and enjoying the benefits of the international trade of wild species.[50] With these acknowledgments only documented as part of CITES's Gender Action Plan in 2022, their impact is yet to have a significant impact in the implementation of the previous resolutions of the parties to the convention.

7.3.3.4 Convention on the Conservation of Migratory Species of Wild Animals

The Convention on the Conservation of Migratory Species of Wild Animals (CMS) is a global framework for the sustainable exploitation and conservation

48 CITES, "Convention on International Trade in Endangered Species of Wild Fauna and Flora" (2023) https://cites.org/eng/disc/text.php accessed September 23, 2023.

49 Convention on International Trade in Endangered Species of Wild Faina and Flora, "Action Plan on Gender Related Matters" (2022) https://cites.org/sites/default/files/documents/E-CoP19-Com-II-03.pdf accessed September 23, 2023.

50 Ibid.

of migratory animals. It also champions the preservation of the animals' habitats through coordinated efforts with the member countries whose jurisdictions lie along the migratory routes of the targeted animals. CMS relies on memoranda of understanding that can be adapted by specific regions or neighboring countries based on their conservation needs. In addition to its parties, CMS brings on other organizations, particularly nongovernmental organizations and corporate partners, to advance its conservation agenda. Since its ratification, CMS has habitually adopted resolutions that acknowledge, stop, and attempt to reverse biodiversity loss by identifying and adopting strategies to address threats to migratory species and their habitats. It focuses on species-specific solutions such as working with select member countries to reduce unsustainable fisheries that threaten migratory chondrichthyan species, the use of visualization tools to map the flight paths of migratory birds and track the birds to protect them from illegal harvesting, and the use of artificial light to guide migratory land animals across their migratory paths.[51]

These, and other, biodiversity and nature conservation treaties recommend solutions based on the aspects of nature degradation and biodiversity loss they target. The Stockholm Convention recommends the universal prohibition of the production, use, and trade of persistent organic pollutants (POPs), the safe disposal of existing stockpiles of the chemicals, and the adoption of environmentally friendly alternatives. The Stockholm Convention further recommends that its members embark on public education to sensitize their citizens about the dangers of the chemicals.[52] Some of the recommendations can only be enforced at a national level but anyone is invited and encouraged to participate in other solutions, including campaigns against the use of POPs, participation in public education, and the use of alternative chemicals. Similarly, the recommendations of CMS include legal and administrative actions that can only be completed by the governments of member countries and activities that require the involvement of local communities. For instance, one of the recommendations of CMS is the reduced use of wild meat as a source of food. The recommendation requires legislation to save affected wild animals and the ecosystems that depend on the animals' existence but the effectiveness of such laws requires the participation of local communities. Most of the treaty's recommendations have a similar structure. These include efforts to protect marine biodiversity by restricting fishing and the preservation of the habitats of migratory animals.[53]

[51] Convention on the Conservation of Migratory Species of Wild Animals, "Progress Report on Relevant Activities Undertaken within the Framework of the Convention on the Conservation of Migratory Species of Wild Animals (CMS) for the United Nations Open-Ended Informal Consultative Process on Oceans and the Law of the Sea" (2020) www.un.org/depts/los//general_assembly/contributions_2020/CMS.pdf accessed September 23, 2023.

[52] Ibid., 7.

[53] Ibid., 6.

The actionable recommendations of the Kunming-Montreal Global Biodiversity Framework are more community-centered and inclusive compared to those of the other treaties. This is understandable, since the framework is the most current of all five. The recommendations include the participation of local communities in conservation initiatives, a provision for the recognition of different value systems and the appropriate adjustment of interventions, and a whole-of-society approach to the preservation of biodiversity.[54] Finally, CITES and the CBD make recommendations that focus more on policy and regulation but have provisions for the involvement of citizens and local communities in the protection of nature and access to genetic resources and the benefits of genetic research. Notably, the CBD makes a provision for knowledge sharing, allowing local and indigenous communities to contribute to the pool of genetic knowledge, learn from the genetic resources the convention protects, and gain from the fair benefit-sharing of knowledge derived from genetic resources. Similarly, CITES champions the involvement of residents of member countries in the conservation of wild plant and animal species whose exploitation threatens biodiversity and sustainability.[55]

7.4 GENDER-RESPONSIVE IMPLEMENTATION OF NATURE AND BIODIVERSITY PROGRAMS: LIMITATIONS AND WAYS FORWARD IN THE MENA REGION

Nature conservation and biodiversity conservation treaties have increasingly embraced gender awareness and equity and are working toward entrenching the gender-responsive implementation of their resolutions. However, several legal and institutional gaps remain in fully integrating the gender-responsive implementation of nature and biodiversity programs in the MENA region.

While MENA countries have prioritized gender equality in education, health, and environment programs, the lack of specific national strategies or guidelines on integrating gender in biodiversity programs continues to leave stakeholders without guidance on the specific requirements and steps to achieve gender responsiveness in biodiversity programs. For instance, the national strategy for the conservation of biodiversity in Saudi Arabia does not make a single mention of gender, nor does it elaborate upon the roles of stakeholders to integrate gender considerations in the design and implementation of biodiversity and nature conservation programs.[56] Similarly, in several countries across the region, comprehensive environmental laws and guidelines on sustainability and biodiversity strategy and action

[54] Ibid., 1.

[55] Richard Niesenbaum, "The Integration of Conservation, Biodiversity, and Sustainability" (2019) 11 *Sustainability* 17, 4676 www.mdpi.com/2071-1050/11/17/4676 accessed September 24, 2023.

[56] National Commission for Wildlife Conservation and Development, "The National Strategy for Conservation of Biodiversity in the Kingdom of Saudi Arabia" (2005) www.cbd.int/doc/world/sa/sa-nbsap-01-en.pdf accessed September 24, 2023.

plans have been enacted but none of them mention gender or integrate gender mainstreaming.[57] In Morocco, for instance, progress toward gender equality has regressed despite efforts to integrate gender into environmental and biodiversity action plans.[58] The lack of gender language in the legislation limits the inclusion of women in their implementation of the treaties that rely on national policies, strategies, and action plans. The lack of gender language in the legislation may also indirectly affirm the social hierarchies and power relations that are responsible for women's limited involvement in nature and biodiversity conservation in the MENA region.[59]

The lack of gender mainstreaming in biodiversity conservation action plans and the lack of gender and human rights language in environmental and biodiversity legislation culminate in limited resources and capacity for women to participate in the conservation of nature and biodiversity. This worsens the existing gender-based inequalities in ownership and access to resources in the MENA region, further alienating women in the inception and implementation of action plans for the conservation of biodiversity.

7.4.1 *Recommendations for Action*

The foregoing limitations raise the need for proactive and innovative ways of promoting the gender-responsive implementation of biodiversity and nature conservation treaties.

First is the need for MENA countries to integrate gender mainstreaming with their conservation policies or establish separate policies to enforce the participation of women in the conservation of biodiversity. The policies can include gender quotas for the committees tasked with the implementation of the national action plans derived from the resolutions of nature and biodiversity conservation treaties and requirements that women should be involved in all stages of biodiversity programs, from inception through implementation to evaluation of outcomes. They can achieve this by requiring the collection of gender-sensitive data before the inception of the programs, adhering to gender quotas in all personnel involved in the programs, considering the needs of all genders when setting project objectives, and allocating the benefits of the programs equitably. Further, policies can require that

57 Reem Al-Hababi, "The Evolvement of Qatar's Environmental Sustainability Policy: The Strategies, Regulations, and Institutions" (2022) 9 *Gulf Studies: Sustainable Qatar* 17 https://link.springer.com/chapter/10.1007/978-981-19-7398-7_2#:~:text=Perhaps%20the%20most%20significant%20law,habitats%20and%20preserve%20endangered%20species accessed September 24, 2023.

58 United Nations, "Environmental Performance Reviews: Morocco" (2022) https://unece.org/sites/default/files/2023-01/ECE_CEP_191_E.pdf accessed September 24, 2023.

59 United Nations Economic Commission for Europe, "Toolbox: How to Mainstream Gender in Environmental Policy" (2021) https://unece.org/sites/default/files/2021-03/toolbox-gender-mainstreaming-environment.pdf accessed September 24, 2023.

all environmental and biodiversity laws and regulations be assessed with a gender lens to ensure that they make provisions for the involvement of women.

Second, environmental and biodiversity legislation across the MENA region should adopt gender and human rights language to guarantee the participation of all genders in the conservation of gender and biodiversity. The use of gender-sensitive language ensures that both men and women feel included and addressed by the legislation.[60] Governments across the MENA region can use gender language to increase the participation of all genders in biodiversity conservation efforts by avoiding exclusionary language such as manpower and spokesman, mentioning both men and women in relation to action plans, and referring to both genders as being on the same level. The legislation can be enhanced further through design and visual elements that portray men and women participating in biodiversity conservation programs.

Third, in addition to entrenching gender mainstreaming in legislation and incorporating gender language to ensure the participation of all in nature and biodiversity conservation, countries in the MENA region can allocate funds to the empowerment of women. This can include establishing scholarships for women in higher education, particularly in STEM (science, technology, engineering, and mathematics) subjects, to increase the number of women with specialized education and knowledge on biodiversity conservation, who can head or contribute to national environment and biodiversity programs. Some countries in the region such as Qatar are making significant investments in women's education in STEM and other fields.[61] More funding can be allocated to increasing the economic participation of women in the region. Combined, their education and economic participation can promote the further participation of women in nature and biodiversity conservation.

Fourth, women are highly underrepresented in formal political structures and decision-making roles related to conservation. When they are included in conservation committees that are tasked with the implementation of biodiversity and conservation treaties, it is usually in administrative roles.[62] This creates the illusion of gender inclusivity, but in reality the status quo is upheld and women remain on the sidelines in decision-making despite research showing that involving them yields better outcomes for nature conservation. For instance, the inclusion of women on the executive committees of forest conservation programs in Nepal led to the reduced exploitation of forest resources, promoting biodiversity conservation in the region.[63] The national committees driving the implementation of the resolutions

60 Ibid., 49.

61 Ibid., 9.

62 Ibid., 17.

63 Marinella Leone, "Women As Decision Makers in Community Forest Management: Evidence from Nepal" (2019) 138 *Journal of Development Economics* 180 www.sciencedirect.com/science/article/abs/pii/S0304387818304929 accessed September 24, 2023.

of nature and biodiversity treaties can involve women in decision-making for better outcomes in several ways.

MENA countries should establish policies that require gender-inclusive communal involvement in the implementation of other resolutions at the community level. The Kunming-Montreal Global Biodiversity Framework has made a few strides toward gender-inclusive implementation of its interventions by acknowledging that gender equality is necessary for their successful implementation. The countries can build on the acknowledgment of the need for gender inclusion by setting a minimum gender distribution of the members of individual intervention implementation committees. Putting women on the committees will introduce new perspectives on the implementation of different interventions and guarantee women's enthusiastic participation. Essentially, involving both men and women in decision-making roles will transform the implementation of biodiversity and conservation treaties in the MENA region into a communal affair. Furthermore, MENA countries could require the contributions of women at all stages of the implementation of their biodiversity and nature conservation interventions. As the most recent treaty, the Kunming-Montreal Global Biodiversity Framework has adopted a great approach to guarantee the involvement of local and indigenous communities in the implementation of its interventions. All treaties could adopt a similar approach by acknowledging the crucial role women play in conservation as the custodians of natural resources and require the documentation of their contributions to the implementation of interventions within their communities. Requiring implementation committees to listen to and document women's contributions and suggestions will ensure that their knowledge is used in decision-making and their needs are considered.

Fifth, the involvement of women in decision-making both directly and through their contribution to the knowledge pool that influences decisions is a good but superficial start to promoting the gender-responsive implementation of the resolutions and recommendations of biodiversity and nature conservation treaties. A lasting solution would involve addressing the problems that cause the limited involvement of women in nature conservation. One of these problems is women's limited access to and control of resources. Traditionally, social norms in the MENA region boxed women into the roles of wives and mothers, limiting their ability to earn an income outside of the two roles.[64] The ripple effect of these gender roles in the region is evident in women's limited ownership of resources such as land, access to natural resources that serve as sources of income such as oceans, and access to tools of social mobility such as education. While biodiversity regulations and legislation cannot reverse centuries of tradition, they can adopt gender mainstreaming in the implementation of interventions that target community resources. Through the gradual

[64] Austin Phiri et al., "A Review of Gender Inclusivity in Agriculture and Natural Resources Management under the Changing Climate in Sub-Saharan Africa" (2022) 1 *Cogent Social Sciences* 8, 2024674 www.tandfonline.com/doi/full/10.1080/23311886.2021.2024674 accessed September 24, 2023.

adoption of gender mainstreaming, biodiversity laws can establish a new culture of communal ownership and responsibility for natural resources. Moving forward, the responsibility of implementing the treaties and driving the protection of the natural environment would fall on all members of the community regardless of their gender.

Sixth, the education and the distribution of information on conservation, including the existence, purpose, and recommendations of the treaties, are not universal. Women, particularly in rural areas, interact with their natural environment more than the men in their communities. They are the first people in their communities to experience climate change and are the conduits and custodians of knowledge of their environment. However, most of the information they hold is informal and drawn from the experiences and lessons of the women who came before them. Comparatively, the knowledge and education that drives the biodiversity and nature conservation treaties is primarily formal and based on scientific research. These types of education and knowledge are not perceived to have the same value. As such, the knowledge that women have accumulated is devalued and disregarded while formal knowledge is valued highly. Policies that integrate respect for this knowledge combined with the scientific knowledge acquired by the women who benefit from the budgetary allocations to women's education and empowerment would be game changers in the gender mainstreaming of the implementation of the treaties.

Gender mainstreaming will promote the gender-responsive implementation of the treaties by securing women's place in biodiversity programs without resorting to affirmative action. The implementation of the treaties would be driven by both scientific knowledge and the indigenous knowledge held by women. The efforts of one group of women in Lebanon confirm that women can improve conservation efforts if allowed to share their knowledge of nature with their communities. The women in the group exchange knowledge, learn from each other, and use their knowledge to preserve natural resources and restore biodiversity.[65] As the knowledge that women hold enriches the implementation process, women will have access to formal knowledge as well. The impacts of women's increased access to education and information will manifest in more than their involvement in the design and implementation of the recommendations of the treaties. Since limited education is one of the factors that are responsible for gender differences in access to economic resources, exposure to more education and knowledge will increase women's access to economic opportunities, giving them access to and control of resources.[66]

Finally, women are underrepresented in leadership roles in the committees driving the implementation of biodiversity and nature conservation treaties. The lack of gender balance in leadership robs the implementation process of the benefits of their

65 D. Obeidat, "How Women Are Leading Nature Conservation in Lebanon" (*Bird Life International* 2020) www.birdlife.org/news/2020/03/08/how-women-are-leading-nature-conservation-in-lebanon/#:~:text=For%20these%20incredible%20women%2C%20this,off%20a%20full%2Dblown%20 initiative accessed September 24, 2023.

66 Ibid., 25.

inclusion, which include improved outcomes of the projects.[67] The national councils driving the implementation of nature and biodiversity conservation treaties can harness the benefits of the increased empowerment of women and their increased specialization in the sciences to increase women's leadership in conservation efforts. With more women in leadership roles in nature and biodiversity conservation programs, countries in the MENA region could redefine their leadership structures to base leadership on knowledge, values, needs, and priorities and abandon traditional structures, which are based on rights and access to resources and decision-making power. Under the new leadership structures, implementation committees would be constituted to include representatives of both genders to ensure that the needs of the entire community are prioritized and the knowledge of all members utilized. Consequently, both men and women would have equal chances at leadership, decision-making, and benefit-sharing.

7.5 CONCLUSION

To coherently prevent, halt, and reverse the prevailing degradation of nature and loss of biodiversity and their effects on nature, international law recognizes the need for broad-based inclusivity and gender mainstreaming. While every member of the population is feeling the effects of rapid biodiversity loss, women in the MENA region are particularly vulnerable. Their vulnerability stems from systemic barriers that limit the abilities of women to effectively participate in formal decision-making, access economic opportunities, exercise control over land, property, and natural resources, and take decisions on relocation in case of extreme vulnerabilities. Without dismantling such barriers, the abilities of women to take part in and influence decision-making on biodiversity and nature conservation may remain limited.

A starting point is for MENA countries to implement clear and comprehensive policies on mainstreaming gender considerations in biodiversity programs at domestic and regional levels. MENA countries can promote a gender-responsive implementation of biodiversity and nature conservation programs by ensuring the involvement of women in decision-making relating to nature conservation and biodiversity, paving the way for them to share leadership roles in the programs and eliminating barriers in their access to resources, knowledge, and the benefits of the programs.

[67] Ibid., 13.

8

Pandemics, Biodiversity Conservation, and the Limits of the One Health Framework in the MENA Region

Devyani Tewari, Irehobhude O. Iyioha, and Chidimma Ewelukwa-Ike

8.1 INTRODUCTION

This chapter examines the nature, scope, and applicability of the One Health approach as a framework for advancing integrated public health and biodiversity management in the Middle East and North Africa (MENA) region. It unpacks legal and institutional barriers that may limit the effective implementation of the One Health framework in the MENA region and proposes legal innovations for addressing such gaps.

The One Health approach has gained importance in recent years,[1] especially in the wake of the COVID-19 outbreak. The One Health approach is a holistic approach that recognizes the interdependence of human, animal, and environmental health and the nexus between the health of ecosystems and the species that inhabit them, including humans.[2] The One Health approach is more pertinent at the present time because "the unsustainable exploitation of animal resources" has been recognized as a predominant cause of the rise in pandemics and zoonotic diseases in regions where they were previously nonexistent.[3] Zoonotic diseases are defined as contagious diseases that are transmitted "from animals to humans, such as human immune deficiency virus (HIV and AIDS), Middle East respiratory syndrome, Zika, *Nipah encephalitis*, severe acute respiratory syndrome, Ebola Virus Disease (EVD), avian and birds influenza, and COVID-19."[4] Therefore, these global problems have raised the relevance of the One Health approach as a holistic health and biodiversity management framework to prevent the recurrence and spread of devastating diseases across the world. Public health scholars have lent

1 Centers for Disease Control and Prevention, "One Health Basics" www.cdc.gov/onehealth/basics/index.html accessed July 15, 2023.
2 Ibid.
3 Damilola S. Olawuyi, *Environmental Law in Arab States* (Oxford University Press 2022) 249.
4 Ibid.; UNEP, *UNEP Frontiers 2016 Report: Emerging Issues of Environmental Concern* (United Nations Environment Programme 2016) 18–28; Intergovernmental Science-Policy Platform on Biodiversity and Ecosystem Service (IPBES), *Workshop Report on Biodiversity and Pandemics of the Intergovernmental Platform on Biodiversity and Ecosystem Services* (IPBES Secretariat 2020) 2–5.

support to this argument by observing that as the entire global population combats a pandemic, the transition from solely "health" to the more comprehensive concept of "One Health" is essential for achieving better public health outcomes.[5] Scholars suggest that the One Health approach should guide the formulation of biodiversity laws and policies in order to promote coherence and a connected approach to safeguarding animal and human health.[6]

However, complexities arise in the application of the One Health approach within the context of a global public health disease outbreak, especially in a culturally rich, as well as economically and politically distinctive, area such as the MENA region. Besides these qualities, a key distinctive feature in this region is the history of conflicts and civil unrest.[7] Although responses of states to the pandemic in the MENA region have generally been uneven, the responses of countries such as Iraq, Libya, Syria, and Yemen have been significantly impacted by insurgencies and civil wars.[8] Furthermore, some of these countries have exceedingly limited public health infrastructure – itself worsened by war and civil unrest – that has resulted in an increase in the number of lives lost due to the pandemic.[9] Notably, social, cultural, economic, religious, and political factors have traditionally constituted impediments to the transplantation of legal norms from one region of the world to another and to the domestic implementation of international legal norms.[10]

Ostensibly incessant conflicts and the resultant socio-economic destabilization in the MENA region – as most evidently exemplified by the Israeli–Hamas war[11] – bring to the fore the nature of the contextual challenges in the region that we must confront in any analysis of the promises and limits of the One Health approach. Only a month into the war, the World Health Organization (WHO) stated that thirty-nine health facilities in Gaza had already been damaged.[12] Hospitals were also compelled to close or reduce services due to the reduction of electricity and fuel supplies.[13] This and similar conflicts have far-reaching ramifications for public health and biodiversity.

[5] Pooja Jorwal, Swati Bharadwaj, and Pankaj Jorwal, "One Health Approach and COVID-19: A Perspective" (2020) 9 *Journal of Family Medicine and Primary Care* 12, 5888.

[6] Ibid.; Centers for Disease Control and Prevention (n 1).

[7] Mohammed Karamouzian and Navid Madani, "COVID-19 Response in the Middle East and North Africa: Challenges and Paths Forward" (2020) 8 *Lancet Glob. Health* 7, E886.

[8] Ibid.

[9] Ibid. See also: Robert Kubinec, "COVID-19 Responses in the Middle East and North Africa in Global Perspective" (Project on Middle East Political Science) https://pomeps.org/covid-19-responses-in-the-middle-east-and-north-africa-in-global-perspective accessed July 13, 2023.

[10] Irehobhude O. Iyioha, "Substantive Effectiveness, Women's Health and the Limits of International Human Rights Law" in Anna Kirkland and Marie-Andree Jacobs (eds), *Research Handbook on Socio-Legal Studies of Medicine and Health* (Edward Elgar 2020) 222.

[11] "Intense Bombings' by Israeli Forces around Gaza Hospitals amid Blackout" (Al Jazeera, November 5, 2023) www.aljazeera.com/news/2023/11/5/intense-bombings-by-israeli-forces-around-gaza-hospitals-amid-blackout accessed November 6, 2023.

[12] Ibid.

[13] Ibid.

Given the paucity of literature on the application of the One Health approach in the MENA region, we ask whether and how such an approach works or might work given the diversity of human experience in various regions of the world and the distinctiveness of experiences in the MENA region. This inquiry necessitates an assessment of the factors or conditions for the successful implementation of the One Health approach in the region, and therefore is a fitting subject for analysis through impact or effectiveness analysis – an area of law that offers conceptual tools for studying the effectiveness of laws, policies, and programs. Specifically, this chapter asks: How effective is the One Health approach in relation to the advancement of public health services and biodiversity conservation in the MENA region? What are the limits of the One Health approach in light of the unique historical, social, economic, and political factors that may limit the effective implementation of the One Health approach in the MENA region? These questions are of significant relevance owing to the growing importance of the One Health approach globally, as well as the limited academic discourse on the effectiveness of policy proposals, such as the One Health approach.[14] Additionally, as discussed later, the One Health approach has been guided by the colonial knowledges of scientific, health, and ecological disciplines.

These questions are explored in this chapter through the theoretical lens of substantive legal effectiveness (SLE) – an analytical framework within the field of impact studies – which offers a three-dimensional framework for analyzing law's failings and successes.[15] The social, economic, and political contexts of many countries in the MENA region make the promises and limits of the One Health approach in the region a fitting subject for analysis through the theoretical lens of impact and effectiveness analysis.[16]

Through analyses of law, policy, and programmatic objectives, as well as internal and external limitations to the functioning of given laws, policy frameworks, and programs, SLE offers a curated outline of how law's failure to reflect the diverse identities, needs, and social contexts of the target population – especially those who are already socially, economically, ethnically, and/or historically marginalized – affects law, policy, and program effectiveness.[17] In advancing conceptual and analytical tools to predict under what conditions given laws are most effective, SLE offers a distinctive approach to assess the promises and limits of the One Health approach. Additionally, we draw on scholarship in the field of decolonization of knowledges regarding public health-related issues to posit

[14] C. Machalaba et al., "Applying a One Health Approach in Global Health and Medicine: Enhancing Involvement of Medical Schools and Global Health Centers" (2021) 87 *Annals of Global Health* 1.

[15] See Irehobhude O. Iyioha, "Law, Normative Limits and Women's Health: Towards a Jurisprudence of Substantive Effectiveness" in Irehobhude O. Iyioha (ed), *Women's Health and the Limit of the Law: Domestic and International Perspectives* (Routledge 2020), recipient of the Canadian Association of Law Teachers (CALT) Award for a paper that makes a significant contribution to legal literature.

[16] Ibid. See also Iyioha (n 10).

[17] Ibid.

recommendations to enhance the effectiveness of the One Health approach with respect to the MENA region.

This chapter is organized in five sections. After this introduction, Section 8.2, provides an overview of the One Health approach. Section 8.3 examines the limits of the applicability of the One Health approach in the MENA region through the lens of SLE by providing insights into the contextual backdrop of MENA countries. Section 8.4 offers recommendations on strengthening the effectiveness of the One Health approach toward enabling its possible effective application in the MENA region. Section 8.5 is the concluding section.

8.2 THE ONE HEALTH APPROACH: NATURE, SCOPE, AND IMPLICATIONS FOR BIODIVERSITY PROTECTION

The WHO and Convention on Biological Diversity study titled *Connecting Global Priorities: Biodiversity and Human Health – A State of Knowledge Review*, published in 2015, suggested One Health as a comprehensive framework for unified endeavors, while also linking it to other related approaches, such as EcoHealth.[18] The One Health approach to public health infection management views public health as interconnected with the health of animals and the environment that humans and animals share.[19] The WHO defines the One Health approach as "an integrated, unifying approach to balance and optimize the health of the people, animals and the environment."[20] As interactions between humans and animals increase, so does the likelihood of the spread of zoonotic diseases, vector-borne diseases, and tropical diseases.[21]

The One Health approach has gained prominence in the United States, as well as internationally, as an effective and integrated way to combat diseases "at the human-animal-environment interface."[22] To fulfill its objectives of monitoring and fighting threats to public health and to study the manner in which diseases spread among individuals, animals, and the environment, the American Centers for Disease Control and Prevention employs a One Health approach.[23] An effective employment of the One Health approach involves the cooperation, collaboration, and coordination of experts in human health (such as medical personnel, including public health practitioners and epidemiologists), animal health (such as veterinarians and agricultural workers), environmental health (including

18 Hans Keune et al., "One Health and Biodiversity" in Ingrid Visseren-Hamakers and Marcel T. J. Kok (eds), *Transforming Biodiversity Governance* (Cambridge University Press 2022) 98.

19 Centers for Disease Control and Prevention (n 1).

20 World Health Organization, "One Health" (World Health Organization, September 21, 2017) www.who.int/features/qa/one-health/en/ accessed September 15, 2023.

21 Centers for Disease Control and Prevention (n 1).

22 Ibid.

23 Ibid.

ecologists and wildlife experts), and other related areas (e.g. lawmakers and law enforcement).[24] In brief, a One Health approach entails the design and implementation of nexus and integrated programs, policies, legislation, and research in which multiple sectors communicate and work together to achieve better health outcomes.[25]

The One Health approach consists of four components: the geographical component, the ecological component, the human activities component, and the food-agricultural component.[26] The geographical component examines how a combination of the globalized trade in animal and animal products and global warming has increased the spread of infectious vector-borne diseases such as Rift Valley fever in Saudi Arabia and Yemen – countries where these diseases did not previously exist.[27] In such a scenario, when countries around the world are more interconnected than they have ever been, the world requires the establishment of productive systematic "international systems on animals and animal products traceability" grounded on "real-time data exchange among trade partners."[28] This would enable countries to take necessary and effective actions to "prevent the introduction of foreign pathogens" in their territories.[29] The ecological component examines the part played by wildlife and, more generally, environmental factors in the introduction and perpetuation of infections.[30] The human activities component emphasizes the elementary significance of the unification of "veterinary and human medicine into a 'one medicine' strategy" and, more generally, the need to adopt a multidisciplinary approach.[31] Lastly, the food-agricultural component underscores the fundamental necessity for a holistic view toward the entire "production chain, following a 'farm to fork' approach."[32]

Although the One Health framework purportedly aims to protect human as well as animal and environmental health, these objectives can sometimes come into conflict. Horwitz et al., and Roiko et al., summarize the intricate nature of environment–human health relationships with particular regard to the paradoxical nature of the "health imperative," which may be oppositional to the "environmentalist's paradox."[33] What this means is that where, from an environmental perspective, one

[24] Ibid.

[25] World Health Organization (n 20).

[26] Paolo Calistri, S. Iannetti, Maria Luisa Danzetta, V. Narcisi, F. Cito, Daria Di Sabatino, R. Bruno, F. Sauro, M. Atzeni, Andrea Carvelli, and Armando Giovannini, "The Components of 'One World–One Health' Approach" (2013) 60 *Transboundary and Emerging Diseases* 4, 5.

[27] Ibid., 6.

[28] Ibid.

[29] Ibid.

[30] Ibid., 5.

[31] Ibid.

[32] Ibid.

[33] Keune et al. (n 18) 99; Pierre Horwitz, C. Max Finlayson, and Philip Weinstein, *Ramsar Technical Report* No. 6: *Healthy Wetlands, Healthy People: A Review of Wetlands and Human Health Interactions* (Secretariat of the Ramsar Convention on Wetlands and the World Health Organization 2012); Anne

would imagine a clear linkage between environmental and human health, the environmentalist's paradox demonstrates that environmental degradation, as for example through the use of DDT in malaria prevention, can benefit human health "in the short-term."[34] The opposing narrative from the human health vantage point is that a healthy or healthier environment – one free from DDT's toxic impact – can then cause diseases affecting human health through the festering of the female anopheles mosquito, which transmits malaria to humans.[35]

Nevertheless, in their evaluation of the benefits of the One Health approach, Queenan et al. have argued that there is enough evidence to claim that the One Health approach is beneficial to the health of humans as well as ecosystems and biodiversity.[36] In their view, this is because the Sustainable Development Goals (SDGs) are interlinked and have health rooted within them.[37] They argue that an attempt to realize the SDGs through "the currently defined and segregated health systems (and their often linear approach to solving health challenges)," while overlooking the interconnectedness of human "health, ecosystems services and biodiversity," will only augment "the antagonistic tensions between SDGs," thereby adversely impacting progress.[38] Their suggestion for achieving the One Health 2030 Agenda is based upon the acknowledgment of human beings as a constituent of an ecosystem upon which humans rely and within which human beings are obliged to support, rather than weaken, the services that they and other constituents depend upon.[39]

However, criticism of the One Health approach, especially in its application to the Global South, persists. Two different studies by Morand and Lajaunie and Lainé and Morand emphasize that "ethical reflection" in the realm of human health and biodiversity would require scrutinizing relevant scientific fields – that is, "biology, ecology, evolution, human medicine, animal medicine, political science, environmental studies, anthropology and law, their epistemology and, for some, deep roots in the colonial sciences based on a paternalistic perspective," and as governed by Western perspectives "on reality."[40] As a result, numerous

Roiko et al., "Managing the Public Health Paradox: Benefits and Risks Associated with Waterway Use" in I. R. Tibbetts et al. (eds), *Moreton Bay Quandamooka and Catchment: Past, Present, and Future* (The Moreton Bay Foundation 2019).

34 Ibid.

35 Ibid.

36 Kevin Queenan et al., "Roadmap to a One Health Agenda 2030" (2017) 12 *CAB Reviews* 1, 12.

37 Ibid.

38 Ibid.

39 Ibid.

40 Keune et al. (n 18) 103; Serge Morand and Claire Lajaunie, "Linking Biodiversity with Health and Well-being: Consequences of Scientific Pluralism for Ethics, Values and Responsibilities" (2019) 11 *Asian Bioethics Review* 2, 153; Nicolas Lainé and Serge Morand, "Linking Humans, their Animals, and the Environment Again: A Decolonized and More-than-Human Approach to 'One Health'" (2020) 27 *Parasite* 55, 1.

"ethical responses" to public health disasters have been suggested, such as "One Bioethics," "One Health Ethics," "Global Health Ethics," and, more recently, "Planetary Health Ethics," with as yet no agreement among bioethicists.[41] Recognition of scientific pluralism seems necessary for interdisciplinarity, with the need to acknowledge "the values and practices" of all scientific realms.[42]

In today's globalized epidemiological environment,[43] distinguished by the emergence and spread of diseases between humans and animals and the swift decline of biodiversity, social sciences research demonstrates that there is no singular "one size fits all" solution to the threats to public health and the environment.[44] Although public health scholars studying middle-income and low-income countries have applauded the goal and relevance of the One Health approach, they have observed that its application in these countries is fraught with complexities.[45] This is because, unlike developed countries, middle-income and low-income countries lack the economic resources and institutional capacity in areas of public health and epidemiology.[46] Further, these countries are beset with various socio-political-economic challenges which act as barriers to the applicability of the One Health approach.[47] Public health scholars have observed that a lack of governmental funding for public health purposes and reliance on donor funding remain the greatest challenges to the applicability of the One Health approach in these countries.[48]

These debates call into question whether the One Health approach offers a singular solution to addressing the threats. Thus, questions about the limits and possibilities of the One Health approach, given the distinct socio-economic, historical, and political factors highlighted earlier that may limit the effective implementation of the One Health approach in the MENA region, are valid as well as timely. Section 8.3 explores these concerns through the overarching theoretical framework of SLE, while drawing on the theoretical contributions of researchers in the movement on decolonization of knowledges on ecological and public health-related issues. In order to set the contextual basis for the relevance of an effectiveness analysis through SLE, we begin the discussion with a review of the social, economic, political, and historical influences that shape public health systems in the MENA region.

41 Ibid.
42 Keune et al. (n 18) 103.
43 Serge Morand, *La prochaine peste: Une histoire globale des maladies infectieuses* (Fayard 2016).
44 Lainé and Morand (n 40) 8.
45 Peninah M. Munyua et al., "Successes and Challenges of the One Health Approach in Kenya Over the Last Decade" (2019) 19 *BMC Public Health* 3, 1; Nachiket Mor, "Organising for One Health in a Developing Country" (2023) 17 *One Health* 1.
46 Munyua et al. (n 45) 2; Mor (n 45) 7.
47 Mor (n 45) 7.
48 Munyua et al. (n 45) 7; Ibid., 7.

8.3 APPLICATION OF THE ONE HEALTH APPROACH IN THE MENA REGION: LEGAL BARRIERS AND LIMITATIONS

8.3.1 *Context of the MENA Region: The Social, Economic, Political, and Historical Factors that Shape Public Health Systems*

The One Health approach, as we have observed in the foregoing, faces significant implementation challenges due, among other things, to limited economic and institutional capacities in jurisdictions where resources are limited. The Arab countries of the MENA region are frequently viewed as one "homogeneous union" because of their linguistic and religious similarities.[49] However, they vary in many respects, including in their public policy provisions, health policies, and institutional capacities.[50] While the affluent Gulf monarchies have the capacity to provide outstanding medical facilities, less prosperous nations offer less than adequate public healthcare facilities.[51] About "20 hospital beds exist" per 10,000 inhabitants in Arab countries, whereas the European Union has fifty-two hospital beds per 10,000 individuals.[52] At the beginning of the pandemic, Tunisia reportedly provided "a maximum of 200 intensive care beds in public hospitals," while merely "550 respirators were available in Morocco."[53]

The availability of personal protective equipment and testing kits has remained scarce in several MENA countries, if not wholly inaccessible for impoverished populations.[54] In countries with a large number of "internally displaced persons, refugees or otherwise undocumented persons," health provisions are not comprehensive or specific enough to include them all – a shortfall which becomes especially hazardous during a public health disaster, such as a pandemic.[55] Countries in the region include the prosperous "Gulf monarchies, where blue-collar migrant workers" – whose population easily outnumbers the local population – have very little access to healthcare services.[56] A unifying factor of the MENA region is the meager budgetary

[49] Zeina Hobaika, Lena-Maria Möller, and Jan Claudius Völkel, "Introduction: The MENA Region and COVID-19 – Concept and Content" in Zeina Hobaika, Lena-Maria Möller, and Jan Claudius Völkel (eds), *The MENA Region and COVID-19: Impact, Implications and Prospects* (Routledge 2022) 1.

[50] Ibid.

[51] Ibid.

[52] Ibid.; Hasan Falah Hasan, "Legal and Health Response to COVID-19 in the Arab Countries" (2021) 14 *Risk Management and Healthcare Policy* 1141, 1151.

[53] Hobaika et al. (n 49); George Joffé, "COVID-19 and North Africa" (2020) 25 *Journal of North African Studies* 4, 515, 517.

[54] Hobaika et al. (n 49) 1–2.

[55] Ibid., 2; Sarah Wehbe, Sasha A. Fahme, Anthony Rizk, Ghina R. Mumtaz, Jocelyn DeJong, and Abla M. Sibai, "COVID-19 in the Middle East and North Africa Region: An Urgent Call for Reliable, Disaggregated and Openly Shared Data" (2021) 6 *BMJ Global Health* 1, 3.

[56] Hobaika et al. (n 49) 2; Yara M. Asi, "Migrant Workers' Health and COVID-19 in GCC Countries" (Arab Center, July 7, 2020) www.arabcenterdc.org/policy_analyses/migrant-workers-health-and-covid-19-in-gcc-countries/ accessed November 3, 2023.

health expenditure of the Arab countries, which is only half that of "the global average in 2017."[57] Therefore, it is not surprising to see MENA countries perform "only moderately to badly in the 2016 Healthcare Access and Quality Index," which assesses health care quality and access in 195 countries."[58]

These data provide critical insights into questions of capacity, resilience, and readiness regarding the ability of countries in the region to implement the One Health approach. In setting out the factors that shape legal effectiveness, SLE – as discussed in Section 8.3.2 – invites a consideration of factors that are internal and external to law and its workings, such as the objectives of a law or policy framework and the framing of its legal provisions, as well as social, economic, political, historical, and moral considerations that shape the framing of laws and ultimately influence its reception and effective implementation. As we further explain in Section 8.3.2, the social, economic, political, and historical factors discussed in the foregoing constitute significant barriers to the design, structural cohesiveness, and implementation of legal frameworks and/or policies in the One Health approach for many parts of the MENA region.

For example, the prevalence of significant disease burdens, resources shortages, and limited institutional capacities, and the human costs from these burdens, can (and often do) shift state attention from biodiversity conservation and innovative solutions to the ostensibly more pressing problem of survival. In this context, where burdens are unevenly distributed and a healthcare system faces significant challenges, SLE posits a misalignment of legislative or policy intent or objectives and the structural requirements for its success. Take, for example, experiences during the pandemic where it was a luxury to see a doctor;[59] this state of affairs resulted in significant disadvantages for vulnerable segments of the population, especially refugees, internally displaced persons, women, children, persons with disabilities, and persons from underprivileged sections of society in the MENA region. These disadvantages were significantly worsened by pre-existing inequalities that conditioned what resources these populations could access or the contributions they could make to alleviate conditions during the pandemic.

Furthermore, COVID-19 accentuated women's vulnerability in a unique manner: It increased their unpaid labor, as well as incidences of abuse and violence, and law enforcement agencies in the MENA region were not responsive to the drastic increase in domestic violence and killings of girls and women.[60] With the rate of

57 Hobaika et al. (n 49) 2; Hasan (n 52) 1152.

58 Hobaika et al. (n 49) 2; Rafael Lozano, "Measuring Performance on the Healthcare Access and Quality Index for 195 Countries and Territories and Selected Subnational Locations: A Systematic Analysis from the Global Burden of Disease Study 2016" (2018) 391 *The Lancet* 2236.

59 Hobaika et al. (n 49) 4.

60 Lina Abou-Habib, "Unequal Gender Relations and the Subordination of Women in the MENA Region: What the Covid-19 Pandemic Has Taught Us" in *Dossier: An Unexpected Party Crasher – Rethinking Euro–Mediterranean Relations in Corona Times, 25 Years after the Barcelona Process* (IEMed Mediterranean Yearbook 2020) 161.

women's political-economic participation in the MENA region being one of the lowest in the world and the MENA region being infamous for severely patriarchal laws that control girls' and women's autonomy,[61] a legitimate question that arises is whether the One Health approach – which requires mainstreaming in a manner attentive to pre-existing inequalities, the mobilization of broad-based efforts that respect women's contribution to knowledge creation, and broad interdisciplinary collaborative efforts – can thrive in the region.

It is against this background that we consider two questions central to this chapter: What are the limits to the applicability of the One Health approach in the MENA region? And what types of laws and policies can effectively address the needs of vulnerable groups in the MENA region given its challenges?

8.3.2 *Examining the Limits of the One Health Framework through the Lens of SLE*

The SLE theory offers a three-pronged analysis of the interconnected conditions for a law, policy, or program's effectiveness, involving the alignment of: (1) *structural/organizational cohesiveness* and *clarity of objectives*; (2) *internal elements* relating, among other things, to the social facts embodied in law, clarity of language, nonambiguity in choice of diction and proper interpretation, and the need for attention to the identities, needs, and social contexts of legal subjects; and (3) *external elements* of moral, factual, and scientific correctness.[62] According to the theory of SLE, law has a "twofold character," the first being an *internal* character which reflects law's content and internal workings, and the second being an *external* character which depicts the moral underpinnings of law.[63] The internal character of law – or law's *internal elements*, which comprises law's content – necessarily includes the language of law or legal diction, the interpretations of legislative language, and social facts that are embodied in law. Indeed, law's content is primarily constituted by the *social norms* of the specific region to which it applies.[64] This content is informed by prevailing sociocultural, political, and related values that shape the lawmaking process.[65] According to this theory, law's internal character influences "law's effectiveness" due, broadly and primarily, to the nature, framing, and interpretation of the content of a given law (denoted as *internal limits*), while its external character – as defined by moral, factual, and scientific correctness – influences its effectiveness through public "perceptions about the correctness" of law's content (described as *external limits*).[66]

61 Ibid., 162.
62 Iyioha (n 10) 61.
63 Ibid.
64 Ibid.
65 Ibid.
66 Ibid., 61–62.

Thus, the second character of law – the *external element*, which captures law's enduring alignment with shared or perceived moral values – posits that laws that are presumed "to be morally, factually or scientifically and contextually correct and cohesive" are most likely to achieve compliance and hence be effective.[67] Hence, SLE suggests that laws are most effective – as may be measured by a high level of compliance – when their internal character or internal design reflects the law's external character or external morality.[68] Toward this goal and as a reflection of law's aspiration to justice, the contents of an effective law ought to reflect "the *diverse identities*" of the specific population "and their normative perceptions" – qualities that ensure their contextual cohesiveness.[69] Further, law's aspiration toward fulfilling a society's perceptions of justice necessitates that it reflects "the *diverse needs*" of the specific population.[70] This condition for legal effectiveness requires that laws are attentive to local conditions, realities, and challenges, and to the possibilities of compliance or noncompliance.

Applying SLE theory to the One Health approach, we focus on the misalignment between societal needs, cultural identities, and socio-political context on the one hand and the expectations of the One Health approach on the other. Through these principles, we identify three core barriers which limit the application of the One Health approach to the MENA region.

8.3.2.1 Legal and Institutional Barriers

STRUCTURAL DEFICITS AND THE INTERNAL LIMITS OF LAW The foregoing discussion of SLE has identified three primary pathways for conceptualizing law's limits and effectiveness: *structural/organizational cohesiveness* and *clarity of objectives*; *internal elements*; and *external elements*.[71] Structural deficits may arise from the framing of particular legal frameworks, policies, or programs, or from institutionalized processes. Structural or organizational cohesiveness requires, among others, that a system of laws, policies, or programs must, in design, be attentive to other bodies of laws, policies, and programs with the capacity to impact on the effectiveness of the former. This may require institutional collaboration, cross-sectoral coordination, and multiministerial planning.

The One Health approach presents unique structural challenges when set against a jurisdictional context lacking the resources, capacity, and political will for broad institutional planning. The successful implementation of the One Health approach would require institutional coordination between health and environment ministries and institutions to address how policies and practices in one sector, for example

67 Ibid., 62.
68 Ibid.
69 Ibid., 27, 62.
70 Ibid.
71 Iyioha (n 10) 61.

the health sector, may negatively impact policies and practices in the environment sector, and vice versa. Beyond the impact of existing inequalities and challenges in many parts of the region, as outlined in the introductory discussion of social, political, economic, and historical barriers, the implementation of the One Health approach faces a lack of appropriate lateral and multilateral coordination necessary for its successful implementation in the region.

Similarly, the second principle of SLE posits, among other things, that a law or policy may face internal limits due to factors such as legislative gaps, ambiguity in legislative provisions, and interpretational challenges. The One Health approach in the MENA region reflects the tenets of this principle. The One Health approach confronts barriers relating to a lack of clear recognition of its framework in existing legal instruments, as well as a lack of clear recognition of biodiversity in health legislation. This lack of reference in extant legislative or policy frameworks creates legislative gaps that give rise to implementational and, ultimately, interpretational problems. For example, the lack of stipulation in extant legislative or policy mandates might suggest a lack of institutional support for implementation. Further, and most importantly, the referential gap raises questions about law and policy legitimacy and relevance – both of which diminish the importance of the One Health approach and what could be achieved through it in the region.

INTERNAL AND EXTERNAL LIMITS OF LAW: THE IMPORTANCE OF LOCAL CONTEXTS As already noted, SLE's *internal elements* of law highlight the importance of synergies between the social facts embodied in law and the identities, needs, and social contexts of legal subjects if a given law or policy is to compel or motivate behavioral changes. Social facts as embodied in law reflect legislative goals or objectives, or the aspirations of policymakers.[72] They may capture or challenge the norms, values, and moralities of legal subjects.[73] Thus, legislative language and the ways it is used to convey extant values or introduce new norms is not in itself neutral. In embodying particular visions and goals, it attracts responses that can significantly impact receptivity and compliance.[74]

Similarly, SLE's *external element* of law – which hypothesizes that laws that reflect the moralities, values, and contexts of legal subjects are most likely to take root and be effective – draws attention to the importance of popular acceptance and compliance with laws to law's effectiveness.[75] While acceptance and compliance are conditioned on a range of factors that include, but are not limited to, personal values, moralities, and entrenched practices, the foregoing social, economic, political, and historical

[72] Iyioha (n 10).

[73] See generally Irehobhude O. Iyioha, "Beyond the Act: Public Health, Human Rights, and the Impact of Laws on Violence against Women in the African Region" in R. N. Nwabueze (ed), *Modern Essays on Nigerian and Comparative Law* (Cambridge Scholars 2019).

[74] Iyioha (n 10).

[75] Ibid., 62.

realities in the MENA region present established, entrenched, and therefore predictive barriers to the successful implementation of the One Health approach.

Building on these principles, we argue that key shortcomings of the One Health approach in the MENA region reflect challenges grounded in the internal and external limits of law. These include a lack of recognition of the social contexts of the Global South, especially its history, politics, economic and cultural contexts, and continuous struggle – in some jurisdictional regions – to de-entangle itself from the vestiges of colonization. The culture of the region, for example, dictates different sets of values, visions, and practices, especially with regard to biodiversity conservation, from those of the Global North. Take, for example, the case of the animal rights movement in the West. While a keen interest in the protection and preservation of animal and plant life are key pockets of biodiversity conservation in the Global North, and while organizations such as People for the Ethical Treatment of Animals that advocate for animal lives have gained audiences in the western hemisphere, especially in North America, discourses about animal rights are yet to find a footing – whether cultural or economic – in the MENA region, where meat consumption is part of a staple diet and fuels economies.

This misalignment between cultural and economic practices, as well as dietary preference in the region and broader expectations of a One Health approach that necessarily prioritizes practices that nurture and protect the human–animal interface, points to a lack of contextual cohesiveness of the One Health approach in the MENA region.[76] This disparity between (regional) *context* and (legislative/policy/programmatic) *purpose* – as enunciated by SLE – can severely limit the application of the One Health approach to the region and, ultimately, its effectiveness.

Beyond the case of socio-cultural context as defined by values, norms, and religious or dietary practices, the MENA region is characterized in parts by an interplay of several, sometimes conflicting, political and economic factors that have brought a number of problems in their wake. These include: poor public health infrastructure, weakened biodiversity, war, refugee crises, income inequalities within and between countries, high income inequities within the richer MENA countries, a high rate of gender-based violence, and an exacerbation of public health crises based on the aforementioned factors, as was the case with the 2020 pandemic, which impacted disadvantaged groups more than any other segment of the population. These far-reaching impacts do not create effective conditions for the practice of norms that underlie a One Health approach. Where survival in all its forms – political, cultural, and economic – are priorities, as it is in some countries in the region, there is expected to be a prioritization of pressing societal and population needs. These factors reflect a misalignment between the needs of legal subjects and the proposed policy – factors that have been demonstrated to impact law and policy effectiveness.

[76] Ibid.

8.3.2.2 Knowledge Barriers: Coloniality and the One Health Approach

SLE posits the need for greater attention to the subjects of a law, policy, or program, along with its objectives and how it is structured. In the application of a One Health approach in the MENA region, it would therefore be important to consider whether the tenets of the One Health approach would find a receptive audience in the region; how popular perceptions about the approach might impact on compliance; whether the conditions at play in the region are such that would allow the objectives of the One Health approach to be met; and whether the conceptual offerings of the One Health approach align with what can reasonably be realized in light of the targeted audience. Along these lines, it is necessary to consider existing knowledge systems and conservation practices in the region and how the introduction of new approaches, such as the One Health approach – even when well conceived – may be regarded as destabilizing or unnecessary in light of the perceived effectiveness of traditional practices and knowledge systems.

Indeed, a One Health approach that aspires to unite a divided world around its vision and prescriptions needs an integration of its elements with local knowledges of different communities in the different MENA countries. Researchers involved in the movement of decolonization of knowledge in relation to ecological[77] and health-related issues[78] have suggested the incorporation of local knowledges and needs in the existing body of ecological and health-related knowledges.[79] Thus, it is necessary to conduct "case-based contextual studies in close collaboration" with local communities in MENA countries in order to incorporate their knowledge of their environment into the existing legal, public health, ecological, and scientific frameworks.[80] Each MENA country is unique, with its diverse populations having their own different set of needs, viewpoints, and knowledges; therefore, working and collaborating directly with local populations is extremely important.

These case studies with local communities will inevitably result in questioning the meaning of "knowledge and the dominant relations behind it."[81] This will have far-reaching implications for the global scientific community, starting with the imperative to engage in dialogue and consider various viewpoints and knowledge systems in local communities in the Global South,[82] specifically the MENA region. This decolonization of health and ecological knowledge will advance the

[77] Lainé and Morand (n 40) 8; Ferdinand Malcom, *Une écologie décoloniale: penser l'"écologie depuis le monde caribéen* (Le Seuil 2019).

[78] Lainé and Morand (n 40) 8; Eugene T. Richardson, "On the Coloniality of Global Public Health" (2019) 6 *MAT* 4, 101.

[79] Lainé and Morand (n 40) 8.

[80] Ibid.

[81] Ibid.

[82] Ibid.

applicability of the One Health approach in the MENA region. Section 8.4 offers concrete recommendations to strengthen the effectiveness of the One Health approach with respect to the MENA region.

8.4 ADVANCING THE ONE HEALTH APPROACH FOR BIODIVERSITY AND NATURE CONSERVATION IN THE MENA REGION: RECOMMENDATIONS

8.4.1 *The One Health Approach for Biodiversity and Nature Conservation in the MENA Region: A Holistic Approach*

In outlining the interconnectedness of the health of humans, ecosystem, and animals,[83] the One Health approach offers a distinctive, interdisciplinary vision for achieving biodiversity conservation. Otu and others have stressed the need to prioritize the One Health approach, noting that urbanization, armed conflict, and deforestation in African countries exacerbates the risk of zoonotic infections.[84] The MENA region is vulnerable to zoonotic threats,[85] and the COVID-19 pandemic exposed the threat posed by zoonotic diseases to the health of the continent.[86] There is an increase in the frequency of emerging and re-emerging infectious disease epidemics.[87] It is therefore necessary to explore recommendations for effectively advancing the One Health approach in the MENA region.

Despite the benefits that the One Health approach promises, there are several limitations and challenges, as outlined earlier, that have affected the advancement and practical application of the One Health approach in the MENA region. According to Gibbs, adoption of the "One World-One Health" concept – which affirms the linkages between human, animal, and environment health – will help in solving the health challenges of the twenty-first century.[88] However, there is more to be done to ensure the effectiveness of the One Health approach in the MENA region. Alkaldi et al. have observed that in Palestine, major interrelated sectors, such as health, environment, and agricultural sectors, are fragmented and lack

83 Mishal S. Khan et al., "The Growth and Strategic Functioning of One Health Networks: A Systemic Analysis" (2018) 2 *Lancet Planet: Health*, e264.

84 Akaninyene Asuquo Otu et al., "Africa Needs to Prioritize One Health Approaches that Focus on the Environment, Animal Health and Human Health" (2021) 27 *Nature Medicine* 5, 1.

85 Hoda K. Hassan, "One Health Should Be the New Nexus of Global Health in the Middle East and North Africa Region" (IHP, March 3, 2022) www.internationalhealthpolicies.org/featured-article/one-health-should-be-the-new-nexus-of-global-health-in-the-middle-east-and-north-africa-region/ accessed October 21, 2023.

86 Ibid.

87 Ibid.

88 E. Paul J. Gibbs and Tara C. Anderson, "One World-One Health and the Global Challenge of Epidemic Diseases of Viral Aetiology" (2009) 45 *Veterinaria Italiana* 1, 35.

coordination.[89] This fragmentation exacerbated the impact of the COVID-19 pandemic on unstable states in the region, for example Gaza, and exacerbated and exposed the fragility of Gaza's health system.[90]

Further, there is a need for concerted efforts to ensure the effectiveness of the One Health approach in the MENA region. The theory of SLE, which we have used to contextualize the problems of the One Health approach when applied in the MENA region, is again useful in setting out recommendations for ensuring the effectiveness of the One Health approach in the region.

8.4.2 *Advancing the One Health Approach: Through the Lens of SLE Theory*

In the foregoing, we have categorized the challenges facing the One Health approach in the MENA region through SLE's conceptualizations of law's internal and external limits. We have outlined various social, economic, political, and historical factors that have affected the application of the One Health approach in the region.[91] As discussed, political uprisings, protests, and armed conflict have impacted several countries in the MENA region over the years.[92] Colonization and civil unrests have also been identified as challenges that have impeded multisectoral cooperation and monitoring to enhance a One Health approach to health.[93] Further, we have noted that the absence of structured collaboration and coordination across sectors and institutions can lead to policy incoherence,[94] which compounds the advancement and effectiveness of the One Health approach in the region.

SLE is relevant in proffering recommendations for the advancement of the One Health approach in the MENA region because the disconnect between the One Health approach and the distinctive identities, needs, and contexts – broadly defined – in the MENA region (all factors that have been shown to be crucial for legal, policy, and program effectiveness) has significant consequences for the practical implementation of the approach in the region. Further, questions about the nature of its conceptual prescriptions, structure of relevant initiatives to effectuate

89 Mohammed Al Khaldi et al., "Social Determinants of Health in Fragile and Conflict Settings: The Case of the Gaza Strip, Palestine" in Ismail Laher (ed), *Handbook of Healthcare in the Arab World* (Springer 2020).

90 Ibid.

91 Laith Al-Eitan, Suhaib Sendyani and Malek Alnemri, "Applications of the One Health concept: Current status in the Middle East" (2023) 5 *ournal of Biosafety and Biosecurity* 21.

92 Kedar Mate et al., "Review of Health Systems of the Middle East and North Africa Region" in Stella R. Quah (ed), *International Encyclopedia of Public Health* (Elsevier 2017) 347, 356.

93 Ibid.

94 Samer Abuzerr, Kate Zinszer, and Abraham Assan, "Implementing Challenges of an Integrated One Health Surveillance System in Humanitarian Settings: A Qualitative Study in Palestine" (2021) 9 *SAGE Open Medicine* 1.

the One Health approach, and its overriding objectives – factors that SLE posits are critical for effectiveness – remain unaddressed.

Overcoming the increasingly complex health and security challenges facing the MENA region requires a focus on developing effective health systems, especially effective public health and disaster response systems. To effectively advance a biodiversity approach in the MENA region, we make the following recommendations.

8.4.2.1 Decolonizing the One Health Approach

Decolonization entails recognizing and addressing the historical and ongoing impacts of colonization on health systems, policies, and practices.[95] To ensure the effectiveness of the One Health approach in the MENA region, it is important to recognize and consider cultural sensitivities, local knowledge, and the diverse interests and needs of different countries within the region.[96] Involving local communities in the design, implementation, and incorporation of local knowledge and needs in the existing body of ecological and health-related knowledge[97] and in the evaluation of One Health initiatives, ensures relevance and sustainability.[98] Decolonizing the One Health approach also involves acknowledging and valuing the diverse knowledge systems and practices that exist within the region and addressing the power imbalances within the One Health approach.[99] This includes challenging the dominance of Western institutions and experts in shaping the agenda and priorities of One Health initiatives in the region.[100] Further, decolonizing the One Health approach in the MENA region involves recognizing and addressing the historical and ongoing impacts of colonization on health and the environment.

Incorporating decolonial perspectives into the One Health approach in the MENA region makes it possible to create more inclusive and relevant strategies for addressing limitations and challenges to the effectiveness of the One Health approach in the region.[101] Local communities often have a deep connection to their natural surroundings and possess valuable traditional knowledge that can contribute to biodiversity conservation efforts. As such, achieving effective implementation of the One Health approach in the region necessitates recognizing the rights, knowledge, and cultural practices of local communities and respecting their traditional

[95] Seye Abimbola and Madhukar Pai, "Will Global Health Survive Its Decolonisation?" (2020) 396 *The Lancet* 1627.
[96] Susan B. Rifkin, "Lessons from Community Participation in Health Programmes" (2014) 9 *Health Policy Plan* 3, 177.
[97] Lainé and Morand (n 40) 8.
[98] Rifkin (n 96).
[99] Abimola and Pai (n 95) 1628.
[100] Ibid.
[101] Rifkin (n 96).

ecological knowledge, as these hold valuable insights into sustainable resource management and biodiversity conservation.[102]

Local communities ought to be involved in decision-making processes and the design and implementation of biodiversity conservation initiatives and efforts.[103] To achieve effectiveness, it is important to ensure equitable access to natural resources for local communities and address issues of resource exploitation and overuse. Decolonizing the One Health approach and obtaining the support of local communities are essential for achieving an effective One Health approach and realizing sustainable biodiversity conservation in the MENA region.

8.4.2.2 Intersectoral Collaboration

The WHO Constitution in 1946 envisioned a comprehensive view of health in its definition of health as a state of complete physical, mental, and social well-being and not merely the absence of disease and infirmity.[104] Collaboration is important for achieving the goals of the One Health approach.[105] To ensure its effective deployment in all regions, especially the MENA region, which is the focus of this chapter, there is a need for interdisciplinary collaboration among various sectors,[106] including the health, agriculture, environment, and wildlife conservation sectors. Effective legal mechanisms can ensure that intersectoral collaboration is legally mandated and operationalized, and strong governance across all One Health sectors in North Africa with interministerial, interdisciplinary, and multisectoral collaborations can significantly advance the One Health approach in the region.[107] Encouraging collaboration between diverse disciplines, including human and veterinary medicine, ecology, anthropology, and social sciences, can lead to a more holistic understanding of health issues.[108] Collaboration entails a clear concept and shared vision for One Health's future. Dialogue and interdisciplinary engagements are necessary steps toward achieving this.

8.4.2.3 Education and Capacity Building

Creating awareness about the One Health approach is important to ensure a proactive and effective application of the approach across the MENA region.[109] The

[102] Ibid.
[103] Ibid.
[104] Constitution of the World Health Organization 2006.
[105] Keune et al. (n 18).
[106] Anaïs Léger et al., "A One Health Evaluation of the University of Copenhagen Research Centre for Control of Antibiotic Resistance" (2018) 5 *Frontiers in Veterinary Science* 1.
[107] Otu et al. (n 84).
[108] Peter Rabinowitz, Matthew Scotch and Lisa Conti, "Human and animal sentinels for shared health risks" (2009) 45 *Veterinaria Italiana* 1, 1.
[109] Otu et al. (n 84).

introduction of the One Health concept in primary, secondary, and tertiary education will raise awareness and create a natural understanding of systems and their interlinked nature.[110] To progressively realize their goal of advancing citizens' right to health, MENA countries should invest in training programs for relevant stakeholders, including policymakers, health practitioners, ecologists, veterinarians, lawyers, judges, enforcement agencies, and other relevant stakeholders. These programs should focus on enhancing knowledge and understanding of One Health principles, legal frameworks, and enforcement mechanisms.

8.4.2.4 Strategic Humanitarian Response to the One Health Approach

To ensure the effectiveness of the One Health approach in the MENA region, One Health guidelines and strategic plans need to be implemented,[111] especially in war-prone countries of the MENA region. Disasters and humanitarian crisis exacerbate infectious diseases[112] and disrupt conservation efforts; they also hinder the implementation of effective biodiversity conservation strategies. Armed conflicts in the MENA region will most likely divert attention and resources away from environmental and education programs to focus on humanitarian responses. The focus on immediate humanitarian needs often overshadows long-term conservation efforts, as governments and institutions are preoccupied with addressing immediate security and humanitarian concerns. To ensure the effectiveness of the One Health approach, there is a need to integrate the One Health approach in peace building and post-conflict reconstruction.

8.5 CONCLUSION

The One Health approach provides a platform for collaboration to detect, prevent, and respond to zoonotic diseases. In this, the One Health approach offers a multidisciplinary approach to health.[113] All organisms live within an ecosystem or environment, and changes in the environment play a role in animal-mediated diseases.[114] The emergence of zoonotic diseases confirms the interconnectedness of the environment, humans, and animals. Thus, the One Health approach is an important strategy for the reduction of major global public health threats, such as novel zoonotic diseases and microbial resistance,[115] as well as for the general improvement of human health.[116]

[110] Keune et al. (n 18).
[111] Otu et al. (n 84).
[112] Hassan (n 85).
[113] Al-Eitan et al. (n 91).
[114] Ibid., 26.
[115] Ibid., 29.
[116] Ibid.

We have applied the theory of SLE as a useful framework for articulating the limits and challenges of the One Health approach in the MENA region and for outlining possible solutions to these challenges. The SLE theory affirms the challenges that arise when law does not reflect the diverse identities, needs, and contexts of all subject to law, especially those who are already socially, economically, ethnically, and/or historically marginalized, and posits that these, along with other structural and external factors are important criteria for evaluating law's effectiveness.[117]

There are entrenched limits to law's ability to deliver on its mandate.[118] Often, many of the limits to law's effectiveness are equally at play in programs and policy frameworks. Law regulates a vast scope of socio-cultural, political, and economic behavior in society and acts upon virtually all areas of endeavor.[119] Thus, as a key instrument for regulation, control, and reform,[120] law can influence behavior in significant ways, and perceptions about the character of law play an important role in fostering compliance with or rejection of law's prescriptions.

The application of an impact and effectiveness-based analysis, such as SLE, to explore the promises and limits of the One Health approach enables a broader assessment of the barriers to its implementation in the MENA region – one that extends beyond a traditional, positivist analysis of law and the conditions for its successful implementation. Through SLE, we have identified a set of challenges that map onto SLE's principled approaches to the study of law's limits: These are structural, internal, and external limits. Through each of these concepts, we have explored the ways in which (1) the lack of institutional coordination (structural limits), (2) legislative gaps and referential gaps in policies, and policy provisions that are decontextualized from the needs, identity, and social context of the relevant population (internal limits), and (3) the disparities between legislative or policy objectives and the values, norms, and/or moralities of legal subjects in relevant communities constitute barriers to the successful realization of the One Health approach in the MENA region.

The One Health approach represents a strategy that has the potential to unite societies toward the fulfillment of important goals, even as its particular tenets have the propensity to attract diverse perspectives, especially in the MENA region – a region with a distinctive cultural identity. It is our hope that the One Health approach is developed and deployed with sensitivity to the unique character and distinctive qualities of the MENA region and, importantly, with attention to the importance of alignment between the objectives, structure, and prescriptions of a law, policy, or program and the needs, identities, and social contexts of those who must live with the new norms.

117 Iyioha (n 10) 61–62.
118 Ibid., 20.
119 Ibid., 61–62.
120 Ibid., 17.

9

Access and Benefit-Sharing in the MENA Region

Elena I. Athwal

9.1 INTRODUCTION

This chapter examines the legal and institutional framework on access and benefit-sharing (ABS) in the Middle East and North Africa (MENA) region. It explores the drivers and dimensions of ABS risks in the MENA region, gaps in existing legal frameworks on ABS in the region, and innovative approaches for addressing such gaps.

The MENA region is rich in diverse species of plant and animal genetic resources.[1] Drought resistant medicinal plants such as *amaranth* are found in large quantities in several MENA countries.[2] Other medicinal species, for example, *Silybum marianum*, *Artemisia herba alba*, or *Ricinus communis* are used extensively across the region and are widely accepted as the foundation of European herbal medicine.[3] In Iraq's Sulaymaniyah province alone, the medicinal use of several plant species, such as *Adiantum capillus-veneris*, *Borago officinalis*, *Thymus vulgaris*, and *Ziziphus jujuba* are well documented as regional herbal remedies.[4] The wide variety of

[1] Damilola Olawuyi, *Environmental Law in Arab States* (Oxford University Press 2022) 245–274.

[2] Anuradha et al., "Genetic Resources and Breeding Approaches for Improvement of Amaranth (Amaranthus spp.) and Quinoa (Chenopodium quinoa)" (2023) 10 *Frontiers in Nutrition* https://doi.org/10.3389/fnut.2023.1129723.

[3] H. Azaizeh, S. Fulder, K. Khalil, and O. Said, "Ethnobotanical Knowledge of Local Arab Practitioners in the Middle Eastern Region" (2003) 74 *Fitoterapia* 98 https://doi.org/10.1016/S0367-326X(02)00285-X accessed October 1, 2023.

[4] H. M. Ahmed, "Ethnopharmacobotanical Study on the Medicinal Plants Used by Herbalists in Sulaymaniyah Province, Kurdistan, Iraq" (2016) 12 *Journal of Ethnobiology and Ethnomedicine* 8 https://doi.org/10.1186/s13002-016-0081-3 accessed October 1, 2023. For an excellent and comprehensive table of medicinal species from across the MENA region in Iran, Iraq, Egypt, Sudan, and Turkey, see A. S. Dehyab, M. F. A. Bakar, M. K. Al Omar, and S. F. Sabran, "A Review of Medicinal Plant of Middle East and North Africa (MENA) Region as Source in Tuberculosis Drug Discovery" (2020) 27 *Saudi Journal of Biological Sciences* 2457, Table 1 https://doi.org/10.1016/j.sjbs.2020.07.007 accessed October 1, 2023. For a comprehensive survey of medicinal herbs in the Gulf, including Qatar, Oman, Saudi Arabia, and Yemen, see: A. M. Abu-Odeh and W. H. Talib, "Middle East Medicinal Plants in the Treatment of Diabetes: A Review" (2021) 26 *Molecules* 742 https://doi.org/10.3390/molecules26030742 accessed October 1, 2023.

species may be surprising to some; although the MENA region is perceived to be covered in desert, the region is actually very rich in biodiversity, with abundant and unique fauna and flora, both in its terrestrial and marine environments.

However, the MENA region faces a host of issues such as the loss of biodiversity, water scarcity, the lack of arable land, air and water pollution, climate change, and the endangerment of rare plants and animal species.[5] Furthermore, with years of political instability and armed conflict that have affected the MENA region over the last few decades, a rapidly growing population, and sprawling urban growth, the ability of the region to withstand and respond to environmental shocks will need to be bolstered.[6] More specifically, there is a need for comprehensive regulation on ABS to protect, conserve, and ensure the sustainable management and use of the diverse genetic resources found in the MENA region. The Aichi targets outlined for the United Nations Decade on Biodiversity 2011–2020, the Convention on Biological Diversity (CBD), and the Sustainable Development Goals (SDGs) all recognize the need to address legal barriers to equitable and responsible ABS.

ABS is a principle aimed at ensuring the equitable sharing of benefits arising out of the utilization of genetic resources and associated traditional knowledge.[7] This concept is particularly significant in the context of biodiversity conservation and sustainable use of natural resources. The main objectives of ABS are to prevent biopiracy (unauthorized and uncompensated commercial use of biological resources), encourage conservation, and support the sustainable development of communities that conserve and maintain these resources.[8]

Despite the growing recognition of the importance of ABS in the MENA region, an examination of the legal and institutional barriers that limit access to the rich genetic resources in the region is yet to receive exhaustive examination in the literature. This chapter fills this gap. This chapter contains five sections, this introduction being the first. After briefly discussing the importance of genetic resources and the need for ABS within the context of limitations of the MENA region, Section 9.2 examines the international legal framework and procedures on equitable ABS, discussing the five primary legal requirements of ABS under the treaties.[9] Section 9.3 examines the status of implementation in the MENA region to determine the extent

5 I. Abumoghli, "Environmental Outlook for the West Asia Region" in H. Pouran and H. Hakimian (eds), *Environmental Challenges in the MENA Region: The Long Road from Conflict to Cooperation* (Gingko 2019) 10–30; M. K. Tolba and N. W. Saab (eds), *Arab Environment: Future Challenges: 2008 Report of the Arab Forum for Environment and Development* (AFED 2008).

6 Olawuyi (n 1) 4.

7 Convention on Biological Diversity Secretariat, "Access and Benefit-Sharing: Uses of Genetic Resources in Traditional Knowledge" The Bonn Guidelines National Implementation (Secretariat of the Convention on Biological Diversity 2010) www.cbd.int/abs/infokit/brochure-en.pdf accessed November 1, 2023.

8 Ibid.

9 Convention on Biological Diversity, "Aichi Biodiversity Targets" www.cbd.int/sp/targets/ accessed September 30, 2023.

to which MENA countries meet the elements outlined in Section 9.2, focusing on the latest trends and developments in specific case studies. Section 9.4 then provides recommendations on how to address each of the legal and institutional problems. Section 9.5 is the concluding section.

9.2 INTERNATIONAL LEGAL FRAMEWORK AND PROCEDURES ON EQUITABLE ABS

Derived from diverse sources such as plants, animals, and micro-organisms, genetic resources have a broad spectrum of applications, from basic scientific research to commercial ventures. Various entities, such as research bodies, universities, and corporations spanning pharmaceuticals to cosmetics, harness these genetic resources. This global access to genetic resources for a range of purposes not only propels economic growth but also underscores the inherent value of biodiversity and the essence of ecosystem services.[10]

9.2.1 *Historical Evolution and Essence of Benefit-Sharing*

Benefit-sharing[11] focuses on a partnership-centric approach to distributing economic, socio-cultural, and environmental advantages associated with biological resources.[12] Rooted in human rights law, the idea has evolved with a special emphasis on sustainable development, tying it to core principles such as equity, solidarity, development assistance, and sovereignty over natural resources. Historically, the principle of Permanent Sovereignty over Natural Resources (PSNR) encapsulated the early manifestations of benefit-sharing.[13] The 1962 United Nations General Assembly Resolution on PSNR underscored the judicious management of resources, conservation, and prevention of wasteful exploitation. Subsequent global debates, such as the New International Economic Order, brought the concept of benefit-sharing to the fore in the context of sustainable development.[14]

[10] Ibid. (nos 44, 46, and 47). See also: Centre of Excellence for Biodiversity Law (CEBLAW).

[11] Using the definition found in Morgera, who conceptualizes benefit sharing as "the concerted and dialogic process aimed at building partnerships in identifying and allocating economic, socio-cultural and environmental benefits among state and non-state actors, with an emphasis on the vulnerable." See E. Morgera, "The Need for an International Legal Concept of Fair and Equitable Benefit-Sharing" (2016) 27 *European Journal of International Law* 2, 353.

[12] J. Cabrera, J. Medaglia, and F. Perron-Welch, "Rules and Practices of International Law on Benefit-Sharing for Sustainable Development" in Volker Mauerhofer, Daniela Rupo, and Lara Tarquinio (eds), *Sustainability and Law: General and Specific Aspects* (Springer 2020).

[13] N. J. Schrijver, "Natural Resources, Permanent Sovereignty Over" in R. Wolfrum (ed), *Max Planck Encyclopedia of Public International Law* (Oxford University Press 2012).

[14] United Nations General Assembly (UNGA), "Declaration on the Establishment of a New International Economic Order" (May 1, 1974) UNGA Res 3201 (S-VI).

9.2.2 *Specific Instruments and Protocols*

A plurality of international instruments aim to protect and advance equitable ABS. First, the UN SDGs act as a coherent and inclusive framework for coordinated economic, social, and environmental initiatives to promote the inclusive, harmonized, and equitable implementation of sustainable development goals across all spheres. Similarly, UN declarations, resolutions, and other mechanisms on ABS, although nonbinding, provide supportive international, regional, and local networks in which collective efforts can be framed and mutually implemented. Second, clear and comprehensive targets, such as the Aichi Targets, provide a set of goals against which nations can innovate national action plans and strategies specific to their local and regional biodiversity and social fabric. Lastly, the Post-2020 Framework takes the Agenda for Sustainable Development forward to 2030 and 2050 with new, mandated transparency, enforcement, and accountability mechanisms.

Third, and most important, are legally binding treaties, such as the CBD,[15] with its Cartagena[16] and Nagoya[17] Protocols, the Convention on International Trade in Endangered Species of Wild Fauna and Flora,[18] the Convention on Migratory Species (CMS),[19] and the Ramsar Convention on Wetlands (Ramsar),[20] the Biodiversity Indicators Partnership,[21] the Protect Planet Initiative (Protect Planet),[22] which provide international legal frameworks on biodiversity and nature conservation, including ABS. The Nagoya Protocol on Access and Benefit Sharing of Genetic Resources (Nagoya Protocol),[23] in particular, is an essential component of the Global Biodiversity Framework, providing a mechanism to ensure the fair and equitable sharing of benefits arising from the utilization of genetic resources.

15 United Nations Convention on Biological Diversity (1992) www.cbd.int/doc/legal/cbd-en.pdf accessed September 30, 2023.

16 Convention on Biological Diversity, "The Cartagena Protocol on Biosafety" https://bch.cbd.int/protocol accessed September 30, 2023.

17 Convention on Biological Diversity, "The Nagoya Protocol on Access to Genetic Resources and the Fair and Equitable Sharing of Benefits Arising from Their Utilization (ABS) to the Convention on Biological Diversity" www.cbd.int/abs/ accessed September 30, 2023 (hereafter Nagoya Protocol).

18 Convention on International Trade in Endangered Species of Wild Fauna and Flora (CITES) https://cites.org/eng accessed September 30, 2023.

19 United Nations, Convention on Migratory Species (CMS), also known as the "Bonn Convention" (2020). www.cms.int/en/legalinstrument/cms accessed September 30, 2023.

20 Ramsar Convention on Wetlands (Ramsar) (1971) www.ramsar.org/ accessed September 30, 2023.

21 Biodiversity Indicators Partnership (2006) www.bipindicators.net accessed September 30, 2023.

22 United Nations Environment Programme World Conservation Monitoring Centre (UNEP-WCMC) "Protected Planet" (2000) www.unep-wcmc.org/en/protected-planet accessed September 30, 2023; see also Protected Planet www.protectedplanet.net/en accessed September 30, 2023; and the International Union for Conservation of Nature (IUCN) www.iucn.org/ accessed September 30, 2023.

23 Adopted on October 29, 2010 and enforced on October 12, 2014. Convention on Biological Diversity, "The Nagoya Protocol on Access to Genetic Resources and the Fair and Equitable Sharing of Benefits Arising from Their Utilization (ABS) to the Convention on Biological Diversity" www.cbd.int/abs/ accessed September 30, 2023.

Its purpose is to solidify a clear legal pathway for one of the CBD's three goals: the equitable sharing of benefits from the utilization of genetic resources.[24] Initially, genetic resources were universally accessed, based on the "common heritage of mankind" principle.[25] This unrestricted access saw a shift with the advent of intellectual property rights and proprietary claims on genetic resource derivatives. In 1992, the CBD framed a legal structure, acknowledging countries' sovereignty over these resources; this framework mandated that access to these resources would be determined by national laws, with potential provisions for benefit-sharing.[26] However, unauthorized access continued, urging the international community to create sharper regulations, leading to the Nagoya Protocol's inception during the 7th Conference of the Parties to the CBD in 2004.[27]

The Nagoya Protocol is fundamentally anchored in three tenets: access, benefit-sharing, and compliance, collectively termed the "ABC of ABS." The dialogue surrounding the Nagoya Protocol saw developing countries emphasizing benefit-sharing and stringent compliance, while their developed counterparts prioritized uniform access. The debate also revolved around the governance of ABS, with developed nations advocating for private agreements and developing nations leaning toward biopiracy prevention.[28]

9.2.2.1 Nagoya Protocol Analysis

The Nagoya Protocol's essence lies in its mandate that any value, be it commercial or otherwise, derived from the use of genetic resources – like organisms or DNA – by one nation from another, ought to be shared with the country of origin. For instance, if pharmaceutical enterprises extract products from natural origins or indigenous knowledge from local communities in developing countries, the Protocol stipulates equitable compensation or benefit-sharing from these resources.[29]

[24] Convention on Biological Diversity, "About the Nagoya Protocol" www.cbd.int/abs/about/default.shtml/ accessed September 30, 2023.

[25] Chelsea Bowling, Elizabeth Pierson, and Stephanie Ratté, "The Common Concern of Humankind: A Potential Framework for a New International Legally Binding Instrument on the Conservation and Sustainable Use of Marine Biological Diversity in the High Seas" (United Nations 2016) www.un.org/depts/los/biodiversity/prepcom_files/BowlingPiersonandRatte_Common_Concern.pdf accessed September 17, 2023.

[26] Convention on Biological Diversity, "The Nagoya Protocol on Access to Genetic Resources and the Fair and Equitable Sharing of Benefits Arising from Their Utilization (ABS) to the Convention on Biological Diversity" www.cbd.int/abs/ accessed September 17, 2023.

[27] Secretariat of the Convention on Biological Diversity, "Nagoya Protocol on Access to Genetic Resources and the Fair and Equitable Sharing of Benefits Arising from Their Utilization to the Convention on Biological Diversity: Text and Annex" (United Nations Environmental Programme 2011) www.cbd.int accessed September 17, 2023.

[28] Ibid.

[29] Ibid.

The Nagoya Protocol, in its current form, seems to lean favorably toward the users, predominantly biotech companies in developed nations, granting them broad access rights. In contrast, the providers, largely developing nations, navigate tighter controls. The Nagoya Protocol also curtails some of the CBD's more liberal clauses.[30] It is essential to ensure that the value of the Nagoya Protocol is assessed for developing countries: in particular, there must be a high degree of scrutiny over the provisions, observing their development during negotiations. Second, it is imperative to compare the Nagoya Protocol's stipulations within the original scope of the CBD. Third, the value must be ascertained to determine if the provisions align with the aspirations and apprehensions of developing countries. Lastly, it is crucial to strategize ways for developing countries to leverage the Nagoya Protocol's adaptability for their advantage.[31]

9.2.2.2 Key Legal Requirements of ABS under the Nagoya Protocol

Before accessing genetic resources, users must obtain prior informed consent (PIC) from the providing country. This ensures that countries have a say in how their resources are utilized and under what conditions. Second, it is important to agree upon the Mutually Agreed Terms (MAT). These are contractual agreements that determine the terms of use of genetic resources and the nature of benefits to be shared. They ensure that both provider and user parties are on the same page regarding expectations and obligations. Third, benefit-sharing assumes that the contracting parties must take legislative measures to ensure that benefits arising from the utilization of genetic resources are shared in a fair and equitable manner. This can be in the form of monetary or nonmonetary benefits. Fourth, the Nagoya Protocol recognizes the role of traditional knowledge, in particular that of indigenous and local communities (ILCs) in conserving biodiversity. When accessing genetic resources associated with traditional knowledge, users must obtain PIC or approval and involvement from the concerned ILCs. Lastly, countries must ensure that genetic resources utilized within their jurisdiction have been accessed in line with the PIC and that MAT have been established, as required by another contracting party, to ensure compliance with the Nagoya Protocol.[32]

The Nagoya Protocol, with its core ABS principles, serves as a model for nations in establishing their domestic frameworks. By emphasizing mutual agreements, transparency, and benefit-sharing, it seeks to foster a global environment wherein genetic resources are no longer just the subjects of conservation but also the sources of equitable development.

[30] Ibid.
[31] Ibid.
[32] Ibid.

9.2.3 *Aichi Targets*

In order to support the implementation of the CBD at the national level, the Strategic Plan of the CBD Secretariat came up with twenty ambitious, yet achievable, targets collectively known as the Aichi Targets.[33] Nations were called upon to

> review, and as appropriate, update and revise their National Biodiversity Strategies and Action Plans (NBSAPs) in line with the Strategic Plan for Biodiversity 2011–2020; develop national targets, using the Strategic Plan and its Aichi Biodiversity Targets as a flexible framework, and integrate these national targets into the updated NBSAPs; take into account national priorities and capacities with a view of also contributing to the collective efforts to reach the global Aichi Biodiversity Targets; adopt the updated NBSAPs as a policy instrument; use the updated NBSAPs for the integration of biodiversity into national development, accounting and planning processes; and monitor and review implementation of the NBSAPs and national targets, using indicators.[34]

In this manner, the CBD Secretariat aims to achieve its vision by 2050, in which "biodiversity is valued, conserved, restored and wisely used, maintaining ecosystem services, sustaining a healthy planet and delivering benefits essential for all people."[35] However, concerns among Global South countries relating to the limited economic benefits from bioprospecting projects could hinder the Aichi targets' implementation.[36]

9.2.4 *Post-2020 Global Biodiversity Framework*

Although the CBD strove to ensure that the Aichi Targets were ambitious, yet achievable, the need for an extended international global biodiversity framework arose in 2020, when a stocktaking of the 2011–2020 Strategic Plan of the CBD goals[37] revealed that none of the Aichi Targets had been entirely achieved by 2020.[38] Hence, in order to define targets and pathways for the conservation and sustainable use of

33 Convention on Biological Diversity, "Strategic Plan for Biodiversity 2011–2020 and the Aichi Targets: Living in Harmony with Nature" www.cbd.int/doc/strategic-plan/2011-2020/Aichi-Targets-EN.pdf accessed September 30, 2023.

34 Ibid.

35 Ibid.

36 J. Cabrera Medaglia, "Access and Benefit-Sharing: North–South Challenges in Implementing the Convention on Biological Diversity and Its Nagoya Protocol" in S. Alam, S. Attapatu, C. G. Gonzales, and J. Razzaque (eds), *International Environmental Law and the Global South* (Cambridge University Press 2015) 192–213.

37 Malte Timpte, Elisabeth Marquard, and Cornelia Paulsch, "Analysis of the Strategic Plan 2011–2020 of the Convention on Biological Biodiversity (CBD) and First Discussions of Resulting Recommendations for a Post-2020 CBD Framework" (Institute for Biodiversity – Network [IBN], October 2018) www.cbd.int/doc/strategic-plan/Post2020/postsbi/ibn.pdf accessed September 30, 2023.

38 Secretariat of the Convention on Biological Diversity (2020) *Global Biodiversity Outlook 5*. www.cbd.int/gbo/gbo5/publication/gbo-5-en.pdf accessed September 30, 2023.

biodiversity for the next decade and beyond, the CBD Secretariat, on July 12, 2021, released the first official draft of a new Post-2020 Global Biodiversity Framework to guide actions worldwide through 2030 to preserve and protect nature and its essential services to people.[39] Then, on December 19, 2022, at the Conference of the Parties (COP) 15 in Montreal, Canada, the landmark Kunming-Montreal Global Biodiversity Framework (GBF) agreement was realized, providing for the protection of 30 percent of land area and 30 percent of marine environments under protection by 2030.[40] This is a significant improvement on the current 17 percent of land and 8 percent of marine areas being safeguarded as of February 2023.

The GBF was not intended to be used only under the CBD and associated protocols but also under other biodiversity-related conventions, the Rio Conventions, other multilateral environmental agreements, other international processes and instruments, and the broader international community.[41] The criteria have also been put forward in the so-called SMART concept of targets which the CBD defines as specific, measurable, ambitious, realistic, and time-bound.[42]

Subsequent decisions coming out of COP15 were the proposed interim budget for the program of work of the CBD, including the Cartagena Protocol and the Nagoya Protocol, and mechanisms for planning, monitoring, reporting and review, resource mobilization, capacity building and development, technical and scientific cooperation, and digital sequence information on genetic resources.[43] The GBF includes four goals and twenty-three targets to be achieved by 2030, with four long-term goals for 2050 related to the 2050 Vision for Biodiversity, listed under three main categories: reducing threats to biodiversity, meeting people's needs through sustainable use and benefit-sharing, and tools and solutions for implementation and mainstreaming.[44] Yet another significance of the Post-2020 Framework is that it mandates that transnational companies and financial institutions monitor, assess, and transparently disclose risks and impacts on biodiversity through their operations,

39 United Nations Environment Programme (UNEP), "1st Draft of the Post-2020 Global Biodiversity Framework" (July 12, 2021) www.unep.org/resources/publication/1st-draft-post-2020-global-biodiversity-framework accessed September 30, 2023.

40 United Nations Environment Programme (UNEP), "COP15 Ends with Landmark Biodiversity Agreement" (December 20, 2022) www.unep.org/news-and-stories/story/cop15-ends-landmark-biodiversity-agreement accessed September 30, 2023.

41 Convention on Biological Diversity, "First Draft of the Post-2020 Global Biodiversity Framework" CBD/WG2020/3/3 (July 5, 2021) 2 www.cbd.int/doc/c/abb5/591f/2e46096d3f0330b08ce87a45/wg2020-03-03-en.pdf accessed September 30, 2023.

42 Convention on Biological Diversity, "The Post-2020 Biodiversity Framework: Targets, Indicators and Measurability Implications at Global and National Level" CBD/SBSTTA/23/INF/3 and CBD/SBSTTA/23/2/Add.4 (November 13, 2019) 6 www.cbd.int/doc/c/0590/6ddd/ab6b9375338ff831dcf5541d/sbstta-23-inf-03-en.pdf accessed September 30, 2023.

43 Convention on Biological Diversity, "COP 15 Decisions" www.cbd.int/meetings/COP-15 accessed September 30, 2023.

44 Convention on Biological Diversity, "Final Text of Kunming-Montreal Global Biodiversity Framework" (December 22, 2022) https://prod.drupal.www.infra.cbd.int/sites/default/files/2022-12/221222-CBD-PressRelease-COP15-Final.pdf accessed September 30, 2023.

portfolios, and supply and value chains.[45] This enforcement mechanism was seen as critical to the ability to achieve the objectives of the CBD.

In summary, a plurality of global partnerships exist which form the backbone of efforts to enhance ABS and safeguard biodiversity. First, the SDGs act as a coherent and inclusive framework for coordinated economic, social, and environmental initiatives to promote the inclusive, harmonized, and equitable implementation of sustainable development goals across all spheres. Second, legally binding conventions and treaties, such as the CBD, with its Cartagena and Nagoya Protocols, Convention on International Trade in Endangered Species of Wild Fauna and Flora, CMS, and Ramsar, provide mechanisms which allow for the enforcement of mutually agreed upon rules and regulations in international law. Third, partnerships, initiatives, declarations, resolutions, and other mechanisms, although nonbinding, provide supportive international, regional, and local networks in which collective efforts can be framed and mutually implemented. Fourth, clear and comprehensive targets, such as the Aichi Targets, provide a set of goals against which nations can innovate national action plans and strategies specific to their local and regional biodiversity and social fabric. Lastly, the Post-2020 Framework takes the agenda forward to 2030 and 2050 with new, mandated transparency, enforcement, and accountability mechanisms.

9.3 STATUS OF THE IMPLEMENTATION OF REGIONAL EFFORTS ON ABS

In the context of ABS, there is a discernible global trend toward the development and strengthening of legislative frameworks. Countries around the world are increasingly recognizing the imperative of formulating comprehensive and robust laws and policies to govern access to genetic resources and ensure equitable sharing of benefits derived from their utilization. Similarly, the MENA region is steadily fostering a commitment to biodiversity conservation, aligning its strategies and actions with the goals of the Nagoya Protocol. However, the integration and navigation of multifaceted biodiversity legislations and protocols remain a challenging venture, highlighting a crucial need for more refined and region-specific strategies in order to bridge existing gaps and fortify the implementation of conservation initiatives.

9.3.1 *Lack of Clear and Comprehensive Biodiversity Laws Including ABS and Digital Sequencing*

While there is a growing awareness on biodiversity and nature conservation across the MENA region, clear and comprehensive regulatory frameworks on ABS will

45 Ibid.

need to be elaborated across the region. For example, in Qatar, Kuwait,[46] and the United Arab Emirates (UAE),[47] the growing commitment to ABS is observed through national reports and the implementation of various legislative and administrative measures designed to uphold the principles of the Protocol. Various laws and legislative frameworks have been enacted to regulate and control biodiversity and endorse conservation measures, resonating with the ethos of the Nagoya Protocol.[48] These countries have manifested their committed stance toward biodiversity conservation and the principles of the Nagoya Protocol.

Despite the progress and efforts, however, challenges such as a significant lack of awareness on ABS, lack of statistical data on ABS,[49] and compliance concerns linger,[50] highlighting a continuing need for advancing awareness, fine-tuning legal frameworks, and fortifying implementation measures.[51]

Similarly, despite the growing global consensus and global shift toward the recognition and inclusion of digital sequence information (DSI) in ABS frameworks,

46 See Convention on Biological Diversity, Access and Benefit-Sharing Clearing-House, "Interim National Reports on the Implementation of the Nagoya Protocol" ABSCH-NR-QA-239041-2 (last updated: December 25, 2017) https://absch.cbd.int/en/database/ABSCH-NR-QA-239041-2 accessed September 11, 2024 (hereafter ABS Clearing House Report: Qatar); Convention on Biological Diversity, Access and Benefit Sharing Clearing House, "Interim National Report on the Implementation of the Nagoya Protocol" ABSCH-NR-KW-238942-1 (last updated: December 3, 2017) https://absch.cbd.int/en/database/NR/ABSCH-NR-KW-238942-1 accessed September 17, 2023.

47 Convention on Biological Diversity (CBD), Access and Benefit-Sharing Clearing-House (ABSCH), "Interim National Reports on the Implementation of the Nagoya Protocol (NR)" (United Arab Emirates) https://absch.cbd.int/en/database/ABSCH-NR-AE-259627-1 accessed September 11, 2024 (hereafter ABS Clearing House Report: UAE); United Arab Emirates, Ministry of Climate Change and Environment, "UAE Issues Federal Decrees Supporting Convention on Biological Diversity Protocols" (September 24, 2014) www.moccae.gov.ae/en/media-center/news/24/9/2014/uae-issues-federal-decrees-supporting-convention-on-biological-diversity-protocols.aspx#page=1 accessed September 17, 2023 (hereafter the "UAE MoCCAE decrees on protocols").

48 See for example Qatar's Draft Law on International Trading in all Kinds of Endangered Species and Their Products. In Qatar, substantial national initiatives such as the Katara Biodiversity Genomes Programme and the "Qatar Genetic Resources and Benefit-Sharing Interim National Report 2017" (Qatar GRBS Report), illustrate extensive efforts in promoting genomic biodiversity studies, prioritizing the preservation of significant species, and implementing comprehensive strategies for the fair and equitable sharing of benefits derived from genetic resources. The collaborations with local and international entities, such as the United Nations Environment Programme (UNEP), and the alignment with Qatar National Vision 2030, underscore the nation's commitment to fostering environmental sustainability and addressing the challenges in biodiversity laws and ABS awareness. The UAE has several biodiversity laws: Federal Decree No. (77) of 2014 (Cartagena Protocol), Federal Decree No. (75) of 2014 (Nagoya–Kuala Lumpur Supplementary Protocol), and Federal Decree No. (76) of 2014 (Nagoya Protocol); however, there are numerous procedural delays and complexities in providing evidence of PIC and establishing MAT. Nevertheless, the UAE's Federal Law No. 8 of 2021 emphasizes accessing genetic resources and promotes equitable sharing. Kuwait recently ratified the Nagoya Protocol, and has designated a national focal point as per Article 13 of the Nagoya Protocol, but has not yet established a comprehensive ABS framework. Kuwait acknowledges an urgent need for trained national capacity to apply ABS legislation.

49 Ibid.

50 Ibid.

51 Nagoya Protocol (n 17); ABS Clearing House Report: Qatar (n 46).

progress on DSI remain slow across the region.[52] The evolution of new technologies that enable the development of products based solely on digital molecular information, known as DSI, has raised hot and controversial debates on the regulation of ABS resulting from such digital utilization.[53] Countries worldwide are realizing the pivotal role DSI plays in both commercial and noncommercial spheres and are thus adapting their legal and regulatory frameworks accordingly.[54] In light of this, MENA countries might benefit from addressing DSI in their ABS frameworks, both in terms of access to DSI and benefit-sharing obligations arising from its use. Addressing DSI comprehensively can help streamline national efforts and potentially fortify the realization of biodiversity goals, aligning with international trends and ensuring robustness in the region's biodiversity conservation strategies.

As the global conversation pivots toward the significance of DSI in the realm of ABS, the MENA region stands at an opportune juncture to integrate DSI considerations into its regional strategy. A cohesive regional approach addressing DSI can foster unified standards for access, utilization, and benefit-sharing of genetic sequence data, thereby promoting both the conservation and sustainable use of the region's rich biodiversity.[55] By proactively incorporating DSI provisions into regional ABS strategy, MENA countries can position themselves at the forefront of ABS negotiations, benefiting from international collaborations and research, and reducing disparities in the treatment of DSI across the region.[56]

9.3.2 *The Need for a Regional Strategy on ABS*

The countries in the MENA region have collaborated with institutions such as the Secretariat of the CBD and the UNEP to develop ABS strategies aligning with the objectives of the Nagoya Protocol.[57] The CBD and UNEP often provide technical support, guidance, and resources to assist nations in crafting their ABS frameworks

[52] M. Bagley, E. Karger, M. Ruiz Muller, F. Perron-Welch, and S. Thambisetty et al., "Fact-Finding Study on How Domestic Measures Address Benefit-Sharing Arising from Commercial and Non-commercial Use of Digital Sequence Information on Genetic Resources and Address the Use of Digital Sequence Information on Genetic Resources for Research and Development" CBD/DSI/AHTEG/2020/1/5 (January 20, 2020).

[53] Convention on Biological Diversity, "Digital Sequence Information on Genetic Resources" CBD/COP/DEC/15/9 (December 19, 2022) www.cbd.int/doc/decisions/cop-15/cop-15-dec-09-en.pdf accessed January 27, 2024; see also Convention on Biological Diversity, "Digital Sequence Information on Genetic Resources: What Has Been Done on Digital Sequence Information on Genetic Resources" (December 12, 2023) www.cbd.int/dsi-gr/whatdone.shtml accessed January 27, 2024.

[54] Ibid.

[55] Bagley et al. (n 52).

[56] Ibid.

[57] Qatar News Agency, "MME Signs Agreement with UNEP to Establish Biodiversity Database in Qatar" (September 13, 2021) www.qna.org.qa/en/News-Area/News/2021-09/13/0049-mme-signs-agreement-with-unep-to-establish-biodiversity-database-in-qatar accessed September 17, 2023.

and in enhancing the capacities of relevant stakeholders.[58] These international entities play a crucial role in fostering dialogue, sharing best practices, and enabling cooperation among countries in the region to address common challenges related to ABS and biodiversity conservation. Engagement usually involves capacity-building workshops and consultations focused on enhancing the understanding of ABS principles and developing national ABS frameworks.[59] However, there remains the marked absence of a cohesive regional strategy on ABS.

There is a need for a clear and comprehensive regional strategy on ABS by regional bodies such as the League of Arab States (LAS), Gulf Cooperation Council (GCC), and the Organization for Islamic Cooperation. Such a consolidated regional approach is what would be required to move forward in a robust manner. In addition to the broader international agreements outlined in Section 9.2.2, countries in the MENA region participate in various regional organizations pertaining to environmental protection such as the GCC Standardization Organization,[60] and partnerships, such as between UNEP and the GCC, in projects for greater transparency and accessibility of data on the environment,[61] or even associations such as the Arab Forum for Environment and Development (AFED).[62] Nevertheless, there has not been widespread or prominent documentation of regional organizations in the MENA region collaboratively working on Nagoya Protocol's ABS mechanisms in a significant manner. While several countries in the region have shown interest in the Nagoya Protocol and have taken steps individually, cohesive regional efforts or initiatives spearheaded by organizations such as the GCC, LAS, or the Organization of Islamic Cooperation (OIC) have not been distinctly highlighted in publicly available records.

A regional approach would indeed provide many significant benefits through the various institutions. First, with respect to the GCC, the collective could initiate and facilitate cross-border collaborations on biotechnology research among member countries. For instance, joint research programs on plant genetic resources can be established to promote the conservation and sustainable use of biodiversity. The GCC could also work toward developing unified guidelines and protocols for ABS to ensure harmonized practices among member states. This could include common procedures for obtaining PIC and establishing MAT.

58 United Nations "Convention on Biological Diversity" (1992) www.cbd.int/doc/legal/cbd-en.pdf accessed November 1, 2023.

59 Ibid.

60 GCC Standardization Organization (GSO) www.gso.org.sa/en/ accessed November 1, 2023.

61 Cooperation Council for the Arab States of the Gulf, Secretary General, "Air Quality and Monitoring and Data Management Guidebook for the States of the Gulf Cooperation Council" (UNEP West Asia Office and Secretariat General of the Gulf Cooperation Council, March 2022) https://issuu.com/zoienvironment/docs/air-quality-monitoring_en accessed November 1, 2023.

62 Arab Forum for Environment and Development (AFED) www.afedonline.org/en/home accessed November 1, 2023.

Second, the LAS could organize regional workshops and training sessions to enhance the understanding of ABS principles among member countries. This could focus on building legal expertise and raising awareness about the Nagoya Protocol. The LAS could also spearhead the creation of a regional database for genetic resources, aiding in the tracking and sharing of benefits derived from their utilization.

Third, the OIC could establish a fund to support research and development projects that align with ABS principles. This fund could also facilitate technical assistance to member countries in the MENA region for developing their national ABS frameworks. The OIC could also play a role in ensuring that traditional knowledge associated with genetic resources is acknowledged and protected, promoting benefit-sharing with ILCs.

Fourthly, the Mediterranean Action Plan (MAP), under UNEP, could promote initiatives aimed at the conservation of biodiversity in the Mediterranean region, ensuring that ABS principles are integrated into broader environmental protection efforts. The MAP can serve as a platform for dialogues among Mediterranean countries to discuss challenges and best practices related to ABS implementation.

Lastly, the Arab Maghreb Union (UMA),[63] for example, could lead efforts to develop regional conservation strategies that incorporate ABS principles, focusing on the preservation of genetic resources in the Maghreb region. The UMA could also facilitate collaborative projects among member states to explore and utilize genetic resources, ensuring fair and equitable benefit-sharing.

By actively involving regional bodies in the creation and implementation of ABS strategies, the MENA region can ensure a more cohesive and collaborative approach to biodiversity conservation and sustainable utilization of genetic resources.

9.3.3 *Lack of Institutional Coordination between Environmental Institutions*

Exploring further, the lack of institutional coordination between environmental institutions becomes evident in the context of implementing the Nagoya Protocol. The necessity for harmonized coordination between various environmental entities is exemplified by the challenges faced by the nations of the region, highlighting the imperative need for streamlined cooperation to enhance the effectiveness of ABS implementation.

Specific examples demonstrating the issues in institutional coordination are the irregularities in sharing data with the ABS Clearing-House and challenges associated with documenting practices and indigenous knowledge tied to genetic resources, as outlined under Article 14.2 of the Nagoya Protocol.[64] These issues may

63 Arab Maghreb Union (UMA) https://maghrebarabe.org/fr/ accessed November 1, 2023.
64 Nagoya Protocol (n 17).

indicate some lack of coordination between the various institutions involved in implementing ABS legislation and strategies.

The emergence of DSI further complicates the institutional coordination landscape. The handling, sharing, and monitoring of genetic sequence data involve technical nuances that require specialized knowledge and capabilities.[65] Establishing clear lines of responsibility and communication between institutions becomes paramount, particularly when considering the potential commercial and noncommercial implications of DSI.[66] Institutions within the MENA region may need to bolster their technical capacities and foster interinstitutional collaborations to adeptly navigate the challenges and benefits presented by DSI in the broader context of ABS.[67]

For example, from the information provided in the Interim National Report, updated in 2022, it appears that one of Qatar's greatest challenges could be associated with a marked absence of specific staff designated to administer functions directly related to the implementation of the Nagoya Protocol, as indicated in Item 63 of the ABSCH report, where it is mentioned that Qatar does not have specific staff for this purpose.[68] This lack of designated staff could possibly hinder effective the institutional coordination and execution of the Nagoya Protocol's provisions. Moreover, considering the responses in Items 61 and 62,[69] the absence of established mechanisms for budgetary allocations of funds and lack of financial resources made available for the purposes of implementing the Nagoya Protocol might also signify challenges in implementing transboundary cooperation as outlined in Article 11.1.[70] Without budgetary allocation and specific financial resources, the cooperation needed to manage genetic resources found in the territories of more than one party may be impacted. It may be significant to note that there is no additional information provided about any difficulties or challenges encountered for becoming a party to the Nagoya Protocol, as mentioned in Item 60.[71]

However, the presence of clear and specific challenges in institutional coordination and financial allocations might be hampering Qatar's ability to fully and robustly implement the Nagoya Protocol, making them critical areas of focus in advancing compliance with international agreements on biodiversity and ABS.

The UAE, under the Ministry of Climate Change and Environment, has distinctly demarcated roles and outlined mechanisms for benefit-sharing. Additionally, the challenges faced by the UAE in implementing the Nagoya Protocol can be consolidated into themes of institutional coordination, transboundary cooperation, capacity building, awareness-raising, and resource allocation. For instance, the

65 Bagley et al. (n 52).
66 Ibid.
67 Ibid.
68 ABS Clearing House Report: Qatar (n 46).
69 Ibid.
70 Nagoya Protocol (n 17).
71 ABS Clearing House Report: Qatar (n 46).

UAE has established roles and mechanisms for benefit-sharing, with checkpoints at the Federal Authority for Identity and Citizenship, Customs and Port Security,[72] and collaborations with research centers. Despite this, there are irregularities in sharing data with the ABS Clearing-House,[73] pointing to potential gaps in institutional coordination.[74] Transboundary cooperation[75] is emphasized in Article 11 of the Nagoya Protocol,[76] but the specific mechanisms the UAE employs in this regard are not detailed. Furthermore, while the UAE has enacted laws such as Federal Law No. 8 of 2021,[77] to govern access to genetic resources, the specifics of transboundary cooperation mechanisms are unclear.[78] Capacity-building and awareness-raising measures are in place,[79] but continuous efforts may be necessary for effective implementation of the Nagoya Protocol.[80] Financially, the UAE relies on internal budgetary allocations without external support, potentially limiting resource availability. Lastly, the human resource constraint is evident as fewer than five staff members[81] were assigned for administering functions related to the Nagoya Protocol as of 2022.[82] These themes underscore the need for the UAE to strengthen various facets of its approach to fully realize the objectives of the Nagoya Protocol.

In conclusion, the primary challenges in implementing the Nagoya Protocol in the region seem to revolve around institutional coordination, transboundary cooperation, capacity building, awareness-raising, financial, and human resource aspects.

9.3.4 *Resource Gaps*

The critical resource gaps found in analyzing the reports from the case studies revolve around limited awareness and understanding of ABS protocols, inadequate information-sharing mechanisms, and insufficiencies in enforcement and compliance measures, which collectively impact the equitable sharing of benefits derived from genetic resources and impede international collaboration and transparency in biodiversity conservation.

The first critical gap is the lack of awareness and understanding of ABS protocols and procedures.[83] This deficiency likely hinders the implementation and compliance of ABS regulations and can lead to potential international conflicts and loss

72 Government of the United Arab Emirates, Federal Authority for Identity, Citizenship, Customs and Port Security https://icp.gov.ae/en/ accessed October 1, 2023.
73 See ABS Clearing House Report: UAE (n 47).
74 Ibid.
75 Ibid.
76 Nagoya Protocol (n 17).
77 United Arab Emirates, "Legislations" (n 48).
78 ABS Clearing House Report: UAE (n 47).
79 Ibid.
80 Ibid.
81 See section 63 of the report.
82 Ibid.
83 ABS Clearing House Report: Qatar (n 46).

of biodiversity. Raising awareness and fostering understanding of ABS protocols is fundamental to promoting responsible access to and utilization of genetic resources, thereby contributing to the conservation and sustainable use of biodiversity.

Second, the evident gap in information-sharing mechanisms is rather acute.[84] The unavailability of information to the ABS Clearing-House and the absence of provisions encouraging users and providers to share information on the implementation of ABS measures can jeopardize international cooperation and transparency. Improving information sharing is crucial for aligning with Article 14.2 of the Nagoya Protocol and fostering a collaborative environment that advances the mutual benefits and equitable sharing of genetic resources.[85]

The consideration of DSI in ABS transactions may affect resource gaps. Addressing DSI necessitates bolstered information-sharing mechanisms to effectively handle, monitor, and share genetic sequence data.[86] As the global discourse shifts toward DSI integration into ABS frameworks, MENA countries should anticipate its intricacies and challenges.[87]

Lastly, the apparent inadequacy in the enforcement of ABS compliance and the lack of cooperative measures in dealing with cases of alleged violations of ABS measures indicate a significant gap in compliance and enforcement.[88] Without robust enforcement mechanisms and international cooperation to address noncompliance, the objectives of the Nagoya Protocol may remain unrealized. Strengthening enforcement mechanisms and enhancing international collaboration are essential for addressing violations effectively and ensuring the fair and equitable sharing of benefits arising from genetic resources.

9.3.5 *Capacity Gaps in the MENA Region*

Capacity gaps in the MENA region are evident in several key areas of the implementation of the Nagoya Protocol, hindering the holistic adoption and execution of its principles related to the fair and equitable sharing of benefits arising from the utilization of genetic resources. These gaps manifest as limitations in engaging with indigenous and/or local communities, ambiguities in the adoption and application of model legal clauses and best practices, deficits in awareness and institutional support, unassessed effectiveness of legal frameworks, and potential constraints in resource allocation and international cooperation.[89]

84 Ibid.
85 Nagoya Protocol (n 17).
86 Bagley et al. (n 52).
87 Ibid.
88 ABS Clearing House Report: Qatar (n 46).
89 See the Convention on Biological Diversity, Access and Benefit-Sharing Clearing House, for the countries in the region.

Incorporating DSI, which can underscore capacity gaps, into ABS frameworks in the region demands a deep understanding of genetic sequence data and its implications for benefit-sharing. The emergent nature of DSI necessitates specialized training and updated policy frameworks. Particularly, managing DSI from publicly accessible databases introduces challenges affecting benefit-sharing, emphasizing the need for the MENA region to enhance capacities in this area.[90]

Qatar has shown its commitment to the Nagoya Protocol, emphasizing transboundary cooperation and the significance of genetic resources for environmental stability.[91] However, several capacity gaps have emerged in the implementation process. The first is community engagement. Qatar faces some limitations in engaging at the local level during the Nagoya Protocol's implementation, as per Article 11. Second, while Qatar promotes model clauses, conduct codes, and best practices according to Articles 19 and 20,[92] the extent of their adoption within the country remains unclear. Third, there is a notable deficit in awareness and capacity building for the Nagoya Protocol's objectives, underscored by the absence of dedicated staff for its administration and no clear strategy for awareness-raising.[93] Lastly, the absence of specified budgetary allocations for the Nagoya Protocol's enactment points to significant financial capacity gaps.

In comparison with other countries in the region, the UAE has implemented legislative measures such as Federal Law No. 8 of 2021,[94] although the enforcement or effectiveness in real-world scenarios remains to be seen. Second, while the UAE has made efforts to raise awareness, the impact of these efforts and the status of funds for capacity building remain somewhat unclear. Both Qatar and the UAE face challenges in fully implementing the Nagoya Protocol, stemming from gaps in community engagement, adherence to standards, awareness and capacity building, and financial and institutional limitations. These challenges underscore the need for a thorough evaluation and refinement of strategies for effective implementation of the Nagoya Protocol.

9.4 NAVIGATING THE ABS LANDSCAPE IN THE MENA REGION: RECOMMENDATIONS AND A PATH FORWARD

In addressing the challenges and gaps within the biodiversity and ABS frameworks, this section delves into several pivotal areas. First, it underscores the paramount need for clear and comprehensive laws governing biodiversity and ABS. Second, it then transitions to the importance of introducing regional biodiversity action plans paired with a cohesive ABS strategy. Subsequent subsections focus on bolstering

90 Bagley et al. (n 52).
91 ABS Clearing House Report: Qatar (n 46).
92 Nagoya Protocol (n 17).
93 ABS Clearing House Report: Qatar (n 46).
94 United Arab Emirates, "Legislations" (n 48).

institutional coordination among environmental entities, ensuring adequate budgetary allocations to nurture ABS and biodiversity initiatives, and finally the pivotal role of universities in enhancing ABS capacity development through targeted academic courses.

9.4.1 *Enact Clear and Comprehensive Laws Governing Biodiversity and ABS*

The ABS landscape in the MENA region underscores a critical urgency: the establishment of clear and comprehensive laws on biodiversity and ABS. Kuwait's recent ratification of the Nagoya Protocol reveals the initial stages of its alignment with the protocol's mandates.[95] However, the absence of comprehensive frameworks in countries such as Saudi Arabia, Oman, Bahrain, and Yemen underscores the importance of establishing or enhancing their respective biodiversity and ABS legislative blueprints.[96] Addressing the evident gaps in the ABS framework, various countries have exhibited the significance of charting lucid, actionable pathways. For example, countries without defined strategic blueprints need to construct and regularly update their NBSAPs. This emphasis on policy clarity and periodic revision, aligned with standards such as the Nagoya Protocol, not only addresses changing biodiversity conditions but also ensures that nations remain compliant with evolving international standards. This evolution should ideally culminate in a cohesive ABS strategy, encompassing every facet from institutional coordination to public awareness.

9.4.2 *Adopt Regional Biodiversity Action Plans and ABS Strategy*

While in many domains there has been tremendous progress, the MENA region continues to face challenges with the overall ABS framework. A clear, actionable pathway is crucial for these nations to enhance ABS mechanisms, and one of the first steps is revisiting their NBSAPs. Countries without a strategic roadmap must develop NBSAPs, incorporating ABS goals in line with the Nagoya Protocol. Those with NBSAPs need regular updates to keep up with evolving biodiversity conditions and international standards. For instance, Qatar, known for its consistent alignment with global standards such as the Aichi Biodiversity Targets, needs a rejuvenation of its Biodiversity Strategies established in 2004.[97] The UAE is another example, showcasing dedication through its Comprehensive Biodiversity Strategy (2014–2021)[98] and aligning with the broader objectives of the CBD.

95 See list of Interim Reports (n 92).

96 Ibid.

97 State of Qatar, "National Biodiversity Strategy and Action Plan of 2004" (October 1, 2004) FAOLEX No LEX-FAOC181049 www.informea.org accessed October 1, 2023.

98 UAE Biodiversity Strategy (n 58).

Yet a regional approach can be beneficial for the MENA nations, especially given the shared challenges and ecological similarities. While countries such as Qatar and the UAE have shown advancements in ABS mechanisms, there remains a need for a coordinated regional strategy. This is particularly salient for countries such as Saudi Arabia, Oman, Bahrain, and Yemen, which may benefit from regional insights and shared resources. A united regional initiative might provide mutual support, shared expertise, and collaborative projects that propel the entire region forward in biodiversity conservation and ABS alignment.

9.4.3 *Accelerate Institutional Coordination between Environment Institutions*

Central to enhancing the ABS framework is strengthening institutional frameworks and coordination. Countries should establish centralized ABS authorities or dedicated bodies for overseeing ABS processes. Enhanced inter-agency collaboration is paramount, ensuring a harmonized implementation of ABS mechanisms. This involves promoting communication, especially between bodies responsible for biodiversity conservation, research, trade, and indigenous rights. For instance, Qatar's alignment with Aichi Biodiversity Targets and various legislative measures underpins its commitment to fostering coordination between various national and international standards. The importance of this institutional collaboration is also evident in the UAE, with its federal decrees aligning with the CBD protocols and its active partnerships with universities, research centers, and international stakeholders, emphasizing the significance of collective and coordinated efforts.

Centralized coordination is crucial for the success of ABS processes. While countries such as Qatar and the UAE have made strides in fostering coordination, there is a need for enhanced collaboration across the region. Sharing best practices, pooling resources, and joint capacity-building initiatives can provide a solid foundation for these countries, especially those at the foundational stages of ABS implementation.

9.4.4 *Budgetary Allocations to Advance ABS and Biodiversity Programs*

Enhancing transparency and stakeholder engagement is pivotal. Establishing ABS information portals will offer centralized access to ABS regulations and data, fostering transparency. Periodic multistakeholder dialogues, involving governmental entities, businesses, and researchers, can be a platform to address ABS challenges and brainstorm solutions. Qatar, with its strong legislative framework and nineteen ratified biodiversity-related agreements, exemplifies robust budgetary allocation. Additionally, tangible conservation projects, such as mangrove planting and artificial coral reefs, underscore Qatar's commitment. The UAE's draft law initiative, targeting conservation and the sustainable use of plant genetic resources, further accentuates the importance of clear budgetary commitments.

However, securing dedicated funds for ABS and biodiversity projects is pivotal. Countries such as Qatar and the UAE have showcased budgetary commitments, but a unified regional financial strategy can amplify efforts. While some countries in the MENA region, such as Yemen and Oman, might face economic constraints, a collaborative approach involving wealthier nations can ensure that all members have access to the resources needed for ABS and biodiversity initiatives.

9.4.5 *Increased Capacity Development on ABS through University Courses*

Awareness and education are essential for a robust ABS framework. Countries should integrate ABS principles into educational curricula. This will instill respect and understanding for genetic resources in future generations. Public awareness campaigns, leveraging media and community outreach, can highlight the importance of ABS. Qatar, in particular, seeks to elevate biodiversity consciousness and promote grassroots-level conservation initiatives. Additionally, the rights of ILCs must be legally recognized, making them integral to ABS negotiations. Capacity building through workshops will enable ILCs to effectively partake in ABS discussions. The UAE's collaborations with educational institutions reflect the significance of capacity-building efforts in biodiversity conservation.

Effective and harmonious implementation of ABS mechanisms in the MENA region hinges upon robust institutional coordination. Countries, as showcased by Qatar's alignment with international biodiversity standards and the UAE's collaborative approaches, underscore the necessity for centralized authorities and interagency cooperation. By fostering these interconnections, nations not only streamline ABS processes but also ensure that biodiversity conservation efforts align seamlessly with international protocols and best practices. Such coordinated endeavors pave the way for a sustainable and equitable future in the realm of biodiversity conservation in the region.

9.5 CONCLUSION

In conclusion, the nexus between biodiversity and human civilizations is particularly evident in the varied landscapes of the MENA region. This intertwining relationship requires a meticulous approach to ABS, ensuring not just protection but the equitable distribution of the dividends derived from genetic resources. The region, despite many commendable advancements, faces challenges that can be addressed through internal introspection and global alignment. First, tapping into its own reservoir of traditional wisdom, heritage, and expertise to design ABS mechanisms that truly mirror the region's unique ecological and socio-cultural backdrop. Second, aligning these systems with international standards, making the region an active and influential participant in global discussions on conservation, research, and trade. With these dual approaches, the MENA region is poised to transition from mere custodians of their vast genetic wealth to leaders who demonstrate the combination of conservation and sustainable progress. By placing equitable utilization and holistic development at the heart of their ABS strategies, MENA countries can navigate the multifaceted challenges of the twenty-first century.

A unified approach, encapsulating the revision of National Biodiversity Action Plans, strengthening bioethics, and galvanizing stakeholder collaboration, can pave the way forward. Drawing on the experiences of Qatar and the UAE, it is evident that a regionally adapted, collaborative approach can truly unlock the potential of MENA countries. By championing biodiversity conservation and ensuring equitable benefits, the MENA region can ensure that its invaluable genetic resources are a lasting legacy, thus ushering in a new era when the region emerges as a model of sustainable and inclusive progress in the ever-evolving twenty-first century.

10

Biodiversity Entrepreneurship in the MENA Region

Josephine Ilesanmi

10.1 INTRODUCTION

This chapter discusses the increasing significance of biodiversity entrepreneurship for advancing nature conservation and biodiversity in the MENA region. It examines the roles of sustainability-focused, nature-based small and medium eco-enterprises (NB-SMEEs), which, although are not substitutes for other conservation strategies, are important contributors toward the halting and reversal of biodiversity loss.[1] The chapter evaluates legal and institutional barriers to the promotion and scale-up of NB-SMEEs in the MENA region and dynamic legal innovations for addressing those barriers.

There is increased worldwide interest in homegrown, sustainability-focused NB-SMEEs, run by eco-entrepreneurs (also known as ecopreneurs), and ecological citizens that develop the sustainable, pro-biodiversity business models needed to halt or reverse the loss of nature.[2] NB-SMEEs are therefore pro-biodiversity business models and enterprises that aim to halt and reverse biodiversity loss through a sustainable co-benefit approach.[3] The Kunming-Montreal Global Biodiversity Framework (GBF) specifically calls on countries to "increase the application of ecosystem-based approaches to address biodiversity loss."[4] Specifically, targets 14, 16, 19 of the GBF call for several stages of implementation. First, at the level of governance, the targets call for the all-sector integration of biodiversity values through policy reform, regulations, and strategic planning and development. Second, at the grassroots level,

1 D. Lobo, P. Reich and A. Ardichvili, "Conservation Entrepreneurship: A New Frontier in Conservation Science" (2023) 282 *Biological Conservation* 110078.

2 L. Ossowska, D. Janiszewska, and G. Kwiatkowski, "The Entrepreneurship Ecosystem of Food Festivals – A Vendors' Approach" (2022) 15 *Sustainability* 2, 906, 15020906.

3 International Finance Corporation, *Biodiversity Finance Reference Guide* (2023) 2 www.ifc.org/content/dam/ifc/doc/mgrt/biodiversity-finance-reference-guide.pdf accessed January 12, 2024.

4 Kunming Declaration, "Declaration from the High-Level Segment of the UN Biodiversity Conference 2020," under the theme: "Ecological Civilization: Building a Shared Future for All Life on Earth" (Part 1) 4, para 10 www.cbd.int/doc/c/df35/4b94/5e86e1ee09bc8c7d4b35aaf0/kunmingdeclaration-en.pdf accessed January 14, 2024.

the targets suggest a focus on localism and citizen empowerment. Third, with the aim of engaging diverse actors, the targets call for the education of and promotion of local and indigenous communities with the capacity to recognize and capture sustainable value from natural resources, such as through incentives and supported nature-based business models, which would halt, restore, and conserve nature and biodiversity, contributing to 2030 and 2050 Sustainable Development Goal targets.[5] The GBF calls on all governmental and nongovernmental actors to participate, contribute, and advocate for the mobilization of supportive polices, laws, and financial channels that can accelerate the establishment and formalization of these nature-based business models.

Nature-based solutions have been defined by the United Nations as "actions to protect, conserve, restore, sustainably use and manage natural or modified terrestrial, freshwater, coastal and marine ecosystems which address social, economic and environmental challenges effectively and adaptively, while simultaneously providing human well-being, ecosystem services, resilience and biodiversity benefits."[6] As discussed in Chapter 6, ecosystem-based approaches and nature-based solutions such as "reducing deforestation and other land use change and degradation; restoring degraded lands and ecosystems; and enhancing soil management in agricultural and range lands" are crucial for halting biodiversity loss.[7] In this regard, the 2018 Sharm el Sheikh Declaration on Investing in Biodiversity for People and Planet specifically contains commitments by states to "mobilize actions to reduce nature-based risks and leverage nature-based solutions, resources and other natural innovations and technologies, to further achieve the objectives of the Convention on Biological Diversity."[8] The declaration also recognizes the need to "create financial

5 Convention on Biological Diversity, "The Biodiversity Plan for Life on Earth: Introductory Sections of GBF" Kunming-Montreal Global Biodiversity Framework (Section B: Purpose, No 4) www.cbd.int/gbf/introduction/ accessed January 14, 2024; and International Finance Corporation, "Biodiversity Finance Reference Guide" (May 2023) www.ifc.org/content/dam/ifc/doc/mgrt/biodiversity-finance-reference-guide.pdf accessed January 14, 2024.

6 United Nations Environment Assembly, "Nature-Based Solutions for Supporting Sustainable Development" (March 7, 2022) UNEP/EA.5/Res.5: https://wedocs.unep.org/bitstream/handle/20.500.11822/39864/NATURE-BASED%20SOLUTIONS%20FOR%20SUPPORTING%20SUSTAINABLE%20DEVELOPMENT.%20English.pdf?sequence=1&isAllowed=y accessed January 14, 2024; see also European Investment Bank, "Investing in Nature-Based Solutions: State-of-Play and Way Forward for Public and Private Financial Measures in Europe" (2023) 2 www.eib.org/attachments/lucalli/20230095_investing_in_nature_based_solutions_en.pdf accessed January 14, 2024, which defines nature-based solutions as "solutions that are inspired and supported by nature, which are cost-effective, simultaneously provide environmental, social and economic benefits and help build resilience."

7 European Investment Bank (n 6). See also Convention on Biological Diversity, "Sharm el Sheikh Declaration on Investing in Biodiversity for People and Planet" (November 16, 2018) 3 www.cbd.int/doc/c/b88b/15fd/ce60b9f3cccb30be25a7c42a/sharmelsheikh-declaration-egypt-en.pdf accessed January 14, 2024.

8 Convention on Biological Diversity, "Sharm el Sheikh Declaration on Investing in Biodiversity for People and Planet" (November 16, 2018) 2 www.cbd.int/doc/c/b88b/15fd/ce60b9f3cccb30be25a7c42a/sharmelsheikh-declaration-egypt-en.pdf accessed January 14, 2024.

and nonfinancial incentives aimed at mainstreaming biodiversity in development sectors, consistent with international obligations."[9] These instruments show the growing recognition of the need for states and business enterprises to develop and promote nature-based solutions and investments that can accelerate biodiversity conservation and protection.

By investing in goods, services, and projects that advance biodiversity, business enterprises can be at the forefront of leveraging nature conservation to advance sustainable economic growth. According to the *Biodiversity Finance Reference Guide*, opportunities created from these nature-based enterprises are projected to have an estimated value of US$10.1 trillion, yearly, and 395 million job opportunities by 2030,[10] promoting sustainability, economic diversification, and local empowerment. The growing recognition of the social, economic, and environmental benefits of investing in nature-based solutions are leading to increased rise in NB-SMEEs, that is business models primary focused on implementing nature-based solutions, technologies, goods, services, and projects that advance the conservation, restoration, and promotion of biological diversity in a sustainable manner.[11] This includes through the implementation of conservation, restoration, and nature-based solutions, or support for them through financing or insurance.[12]

Drawing on international instruments, MENA countries have attempted to craft the law and policy frameworks required for promoting NB-SMEEs to ensure sustainability and co-benefits.[13] However, as demonstrated in this chapter, overgeneralized policies, weak legal frameworks, and fragmented institutional structure have created barriers and an unfavorable entrepreneurial context for the rapid growth of NB-SMEEs.[14] Legal, financial, and regulatory barriers that hinder the innovation, establishment, and operationalization of nature-based eco-ventures in the MENA region must be carefully addressed. While several studies have examined the importance of eco-entrepreneurship as a tool for halting biodiversity loss, an in-depth examination of the legal and policy barriers that hinder the growth of NB-SMEEs has remained absent. This chapter fills a gap in this regard. It examines the strategic transformations of biodiversity law and policy that are required to promote

9 Ibid.

10 International Finance Corporation (n 3) 1, 2–5.

11 P. Pereira, C. Yin, and T. Hua, "Nature-Based Solutions, Ecosystem Services, Disservices, and Impacts on Well-Being in Urban Environments" (2023) 33 *Current Opinion in Environmental Science & Health* 100465.

12 European Investment Bank, *Resilience and Renewal in Europe* www.eib.org/en/publications/20220211-investment-report-2022 accessed January 12, 2024.

13 Damilola Olawuyi, *Environmental Law in Arab States* (Oxford University Press 2022) 245–272.

14 V. Litskas et al., "Innovation in Water Education Programs in the Eastern Mediterranean to Enhance Security and Socio-Economic Development under Climate Change" (2023) 8 *Euro-Mediterranean Journal for Environmental Integration* 243; M. Mabrouk, "Assessing the Effectiveness of Nature-Based Solutions-Strengthened Urban Planning Mechanisms in Forming Flood-Resilient Cities" (2023) 344 *Journal of Environmental Management* 118260; J. Rodenbiker, "Green Silk Roads, Partner State Development, and Environmental Governance: Belt and Road Infrastructure on the Sino-East African Frontier" (2022) 55 *Critical Asian Studies* 2, 169.

these pro-biodiversity NB-SMEEs across the region. After developing a profile of law and governance barriers facing NB-SMEEs in the region, it proposes dynamic legal solutions for addressing such barriers.

The chapter is organized in five sections. After this introduction, Section 10.2 unpacks the nature, scope, and elements of biodiversity entrepreneurship and its importance for the development priorities of MENA countries. Section 10.3 examines law and governance barriers to NB-SMEEs across the region. Section 10.4 offers recommendations on the dynamic legal innovations required to address those challenges. Section 10.5 is the concluding section.

10.2 NATURE, SCOPE, AND ELEMENTS OF BIODIVERSITY ENTREPRENEURSHIP

Biodiversity entrepreneurship encompasses the natural environment, societal value creation, and entrepreneurship theory.[15] The environment, ecosystem, and biophysical elements support and sustain all life in interstice and diverse ways.[16] Nature and biodiversity provide food, shelter, nonrenewable and renewable energy, clean air, and water; regulate biophysical systems that maintain water, soil, and air quality; and generate services and resources.[17] In addition to its environmental and ecosystems value, biodiversity is critical to economic growth.[18] A country's economic wealth and viability is tied to a healthy and resilient ecosystem and biodiversity.[19] For example, two-thirds of crop production in agribusiness rely on animal pollination while half of global gross domestic product is generated directly from renewable and nonrenewable natural resources, such as wood and natural stones used for construction and infrastructure development, which is valued at US$44 trillion.[20] Given the strategic importance of preserving and conserving biodiversity, it is essential to mainstream pro-biodiversity programs into all key sectors and development planning.

Biodiversity loss is a global emergency.[21] Over 37,000 species are on the verge of extinction.[22] Anthropogenic activities are causing the rate of extinction to

[15] D. C. Magnaye, "Climate Smart Agriculture Edu-tourism: A Strategy to Sustain Grassroots Pro-biodiversity Entrepreneurship in the Philippines" in U. Stankov et al. (eds), *Cultural Sustainable Tourism. Advances in Science, Technology & Innovation* (Springer 2019) 203–218.

[16] R. E. Bitoun, G. David, and R. Devillers, "Strategic Use of Ecosystem Services and Co-benefits for Sustainable Development Goals" (2023) 31 *Sustainable Development* 3, 1296.

[17] E. D. Kooijman et al., "Innovating with Nature: From Nature-Based Solutions to Nature-Based Enterprises" (2021) 13 *Sustainability* 3, 1263.

[18] International Finance Corporation (n 3) 1–5.

[19] P. Dasgupta and S. Levin, "Economic Factors Underlying Biodiversity Loss" (2023) 378 *Philosophical Transactions of the Royal Society B: Biological Sciences* 1881.

[20] International Finance Corporation (n 3) iii–v.

[21] C. Rodríguez-Garavito and D. R. Boyd, "A Rights Turn in Biodiversity Litigation?" (2023) 12 *Transnational Environmental Law* 3, 498.

[22] M. J. Evans et al., "Reintroduction Biology and the IUCN Red List: The Dominance of Species of Least Concern in the Peer-Reviewed Literature" (2022) 38 *Global Ecology and Conservation* e02242.

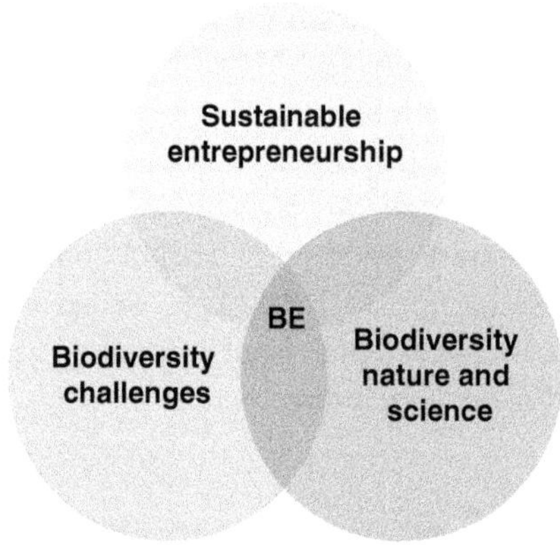

FIGURE 10.1 Biodiversity entrepreneurship
Source: Author.

be 100 times faster than what might otherwise be a natural pace.[23] There is an urgent need to halt and reverse biodiversity loss through innovative investment approaches that leverage biodiversity conservation as a tool for sustainable economic development. For example, the incorporation of low-impact development tools, such as vegetative swale, permeable pavements, infiltration trenches, green roofs, bioretention cells, and rain gardens, in urban-planning phases in Egypt showed a significant reduction in volume of runoff flood water by 73.7 percent.[24] More projects such as the 2019 Falaj restoration, implemented at Wadi Shees, and the 2021 Al Bithnah Environmental Conservation and Rehabilitation project, are needed.[25]

As demonstrated in Figure 10.1, biodiversity entrepreneurship has emerged as a framework for promoting the development and implementation of business models and solutions aimed primarily at conserving the natural environment and halting biodiversity loss.[26] Its primary aim is to leverage entrepreneurship, namely the start-up or running of business enterprises, that is focused on developing ecological value.[27] Biodiversity entrepreneurship is an effective vehicle through which to

[23] P. Hunter, "Genetics against Extinction: New Conservation Strategies Consider Genetic Diversity and Habitat Loss" (2023) 24 *Science and Society* 7, 202357521.

[24] A. Young, B. Bhattacharya, and C. Zevenbergen, "A Rainfall Threshold-Based Approach to Early Warnings in Urban Data-Scarce Regions: A Case Study of Pluvial Flooding in Alexandria, Egypt" (2021) 14 *Journal of Flood Risk Management* 2, e12702.

[25] Emirates Nature-WWF, *Annual Report: A Conservation Diary* (2022) 19, 23 www.emiratesnaturewwf.ae/sites/default/files/doc-2022-05/Emirates%20Nature-WWF%202021%20Annual%20Report%20ENG.pdf accessed January 12, 2024.

[26] Joshua Bishop (ed), *The Economics of Ecosystems and Biodiversity* (Routledge 2018) 1–15.

[27] M. Stefano, "Towards an Ecological Economic Theory of Innovation" http://dx.doi.org/10.2139/ssrn.4394539 accessed January 12, 2024.

generate pro-biodiversity solutions and management strategies.[28] Biodiversity entrepreneurship marries the key concepts of entrepreneurship (entrepreneur, entrepreneurial opportunity, entrepreneurship context, and entrepreneurship outcome)[29] and the sustainability triple bottom line (social, economic, and environmental value),[30] while integrating the nature and science of biodiversity (spatial diversity, element of time, interconnectedness, dynamic value, and stakeholder interaction),[31] to develop innovative business models that halt and reverse biodiversity.

Hence, biodiversity entrepreneurship is put forward as the process of entrepreneurs recognizing, exploiting, and generating entrepreneurial opportunities to create sustainable entrepreneurial outcomes via ecological solutions focused on halting and reversing biodiversity loss. This has led to the shift from traditional, centralized monopoly business models toward decentralized, disruptive, localized, community-led business modes captured by citizens.

10.2.1 *Framework for Pro-biodiversity Business Model Innovation*

As demonstrated in Figure 10.2, which draws extensively from Lobo's framework for conservation entrepreneurship,[32] biodiversity entrepreneurship and business model innovations can be framed as having six core elements:

1. *Spatial diversity*: In assessing entrepreneurial opportunities, considerations of a wide range of biogeographical characteristics must be included to design the right business models that are able to capture the right opportunities and provide sustainable value.
2. *Element of time*: The entrepreneurial opportunities will vary with the season, will naturally fluctuate according to the level of species diversity, and must be considered in business model design.
3. *Interconnectedness*: Ecopreneurs and NB-SMEE owners must consider the biophysical impact of enterprise (entrepreneurial outcome) in order to prevent nature disservice and bioperverse effects.[33]
4. *Dynamic value*: Sustainable business model innovations interact with the entrepreneurial ecosystem (entrepreneurial context), which in turn act as

[28] S. Herbert, P. Bradley, and M. Everard, "Exploring the Prioritisation of Biodiversity amongst Small- to Medium-Sized Enterprise Leaders with Strong Bigger-than-Self Value Orientation" (2023) 32 *Business Strategy and the Environment* 8, 5633.

[29] Lobo et al. (n 1) 110078.

[30] A. T. Rosário, R. J. Raimundo, and S. P. Cruz, "Sustainable Entrepreneurship: A Literature Review" (2021) 14 *Sustainability* 9, 5556 14095556.

[31] M. McBrien, M. Zimonyi, and D. Astley, "Climate Disclosure Standards Board (CDSB)" (2021) *World Scientific Encyclopedia of Climate Change* 29.

[32] Lobo et al. (n 1).

[33] E. D. Kooijman et al. "Innovating with Nature: From Nature-Based Solutions to Nature-Based Enterprises" (2021) 13 *Sustainability* 3, 1263.

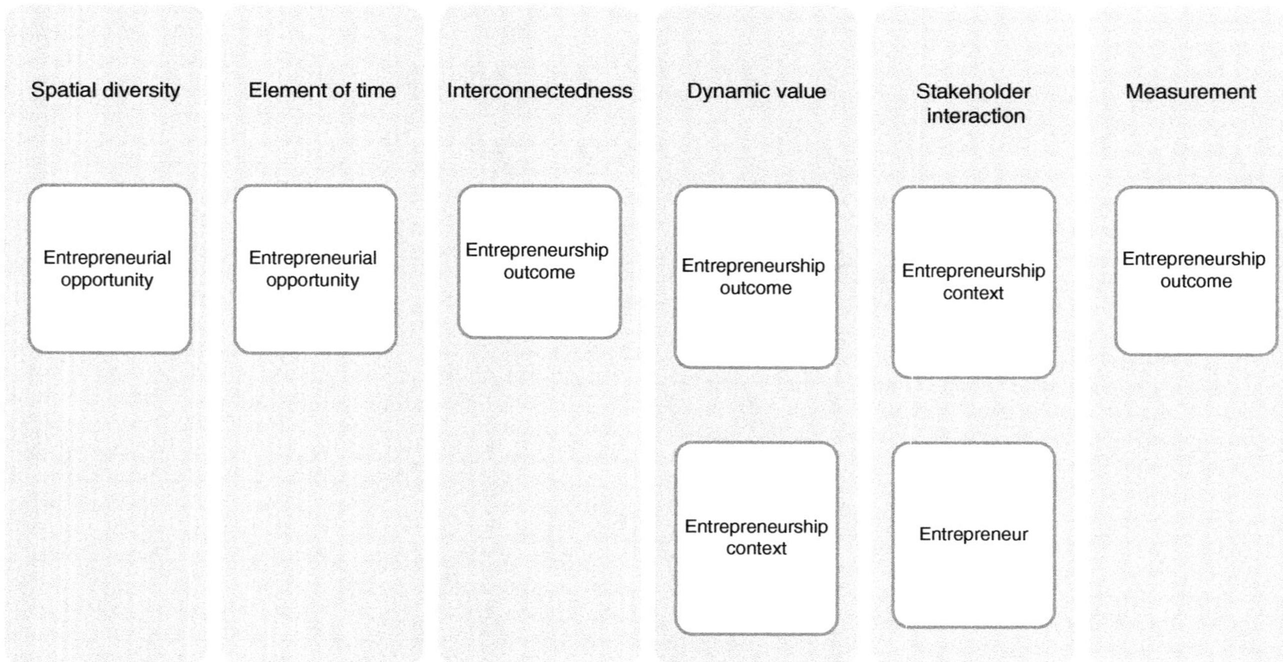

FIGURE 10.2 Elements of biodiversity entrepreneurship and business model innovations
Source: Author.

either the promoters of or the barriers to capture sustainable value at various diversity scales (entrepreneurial outcome).

5. *Stakeholder interaction*: Entrepreneurs, actors, governing bodies, and community members influence the entrepreneurial context. Multistakeholder collaboration is therefore required to effectively maximize biodiversity financing and address legal and regulatory frameworks that act as barriers or promoters of nature-based business models.
6. *Measurement*: This captures the requirement for homogenous, consistent, comparable, and clear typology in metrics, assessment, and the information collation process,[34] to measure, accurately capture, and present value to investors, financial institutions, and stakeholders.

The six elements emphasize the strategic investment in biodiversity and nature-based programs that can offer environmental, social, and economic co-benefits. Small and medium-sized enterprises (SMEs) are increasingly identified as effective incubators for rapidly generating such nature-based sustainable business model innovations that halt and reverse biodiversity loss.[35] SMEs are the backbone of global economy and account for 80–90 percent of total business in the MENA region,[36] as they are resilient and responsive to societal needs.[37] NB-SMEEs provide nature-based solutions that generate relative or absolute restoration and reversal of biodiversity loss, while bringing both social benefits that are noneconomic and economic value to eco-entrepreneurs and society.[38] These nature-based solutions include forest conservation efforts, ecotourism, green spaces, blue-green infrastructure, and nature-based innovation and projects that mitigate against floods, regulate atmospheric temperatures, and contribute to the health and well-being of urban citizens,[39] and are operated via local and civil participation. Furthermore, NB-SMEEs are categorized based on direct value contribution (entrepreneurial outcome) such as: green buildings, sustainable framing, water treatment and management, conservation, restoration, and the creation and the management of biodiversity. NB-SMEEs can contribute indirect entrepreneurial outcomes such as biodiversity assessment techniques, smart technologies for biodiversity monitoring,

34 Taskforce on Nature-Related Financial Disclosures, "Recommendations of the Taskforce on Nature-Related Financial Disclosures" (2023) 3 https://tnfd.global/wp-content/uploads/2023/08/Recommendations_of_the_Taskforce_on_Nature-related_Financial_Disclosures_September_2023.pdf accessed January 12, 2024.

35 Herbert et al. (n 28) 3440.

36 Wael El-Deouki Bedda, "Entrepreneurial Marketing for the International Growth of Niche SMEs: An Explanatory Study in the MENA Region" PhD Thesis (Cardiff Metropolitan University 2022) 12.

37 J. DiBella et al., "Exploring the Potential of SMEs to Build Individual, Organizational, and Community Resilience through Sustainability-Oriented Business Practices" (2022) 32 *Business Strategy and the Environment* 1, 721 https://doi.org/10.1002/bse.3171 accessed January 14, 2023.

38 Lobo et al. (n 1).

39 Ibid.

green financial services, advisory services, and research, innovation, and education.[40] The benefits of NB-SMEEs include increased biodiversity, pollution mitigation, and ecosystem resilience to environmental hazards, as well as greater food security and human health and well-being.

The success of these NB-SMEEs is either enabled or constrained by interactions within the entrepreneurial context.[41] These include societal pressures, norms, regulations, and policies which influence consumption patterns, market structure, and purchase behavior. Currently, NB-SMEEs are growing at a slow pace in the MENA region due to legal and policy barriers in the entrepreneurial context that limit the innovation, establishment, and operationalization of these NB-SMEEs.[42] These barriers hinder the research, innovation, and legalization of NB-SMEEs via a lack of clear implementation guidelines for ecological citizens and ecopreneurs, limited financial channels, lack of social capital and access to land, low capacity to capture and clearly define value, and low market demand for nature-based management solutions.[43] Section 10.3 discusses the role of law and governance in addressing such barriers to NB-SMEEs in the MENA region.

10.3 LEGAL AND INSTITUTIONAL BARRIERS TO BIODIVERSITY ENTREPRENEURSHIP IN THE MENA REGION

International instruments such as the Convention on Biological Diversity (CBD) and the GBF encourage states to integrate nature-related solutions into legal instruments, sectoral policies, and public development projects and planning to address biodiversity loss.[44] This includes addressing law and governance gaps that hinder the development and management of NB-SMEEs in a manner that promotes citizen-led efforts to halt biodiversity loss.[45]

Drawing from international treaties, MENA countries have attempted to craft the law and policy frameworks required for governing and implementing nature-related solutions and ecosystem management strategies to ensure sustainability and co-benefits.[46] However, overgeneralized policies, weak legal frameworks, and

[40] S. McQuaid et al., "Innovating with Nature: Factors Influencing the Success of Nature-Based Enterprises" (2020) 13 *Sustainability* 22, 12488.

[41] R. Zaidi et al., "Do Entrepreneurship Ecosystem and Managerial Skill Contribute to Startup Development?" (2023) 12 *South Asian Journal of Business Studies* 1, 25.

[42] M. J. Collier et al., "An Integrated Process for Planning, Delivery, and Stewardship of Urban Nature-Based Solutions: The Connecting Nature Framework" (2023) 3 *Nature-Based Solutions* 100060.

[43] E. D. Kooijman et al., "Innovating with Nature: From Nature-Based Solutions to Nature-Based Enterprises" (2021) 13 *Sustainability* 3, 1263.

[44] CBD, "Preparation for the Post-2020 Biodiversity Framework" www.cbd.int/conferences/post2020 accessed January 12, 2024.

[45] See CBD, "Expert Input to the Post-2020 Global Biodiversity Framework: Transformative Actions on All Drivers of Biodiversity Loss Are Urgently Required to Achieve the Global Goals by 2050" www.cbd.int/doc/c/5735/c241/efeeac8d7685af2f38d75e4e/sbstta-24-inf-31-en.pdf accessed January 12, 2024.

[46] Olawuyi (n 13) 245–272.

fragmented institutional structures in the MENA region have created barriers and an unfavorable entrepreneurial context for the rapid growth of NB-SMEEs.[47] Some of the salient legal, regulatory, and financial barriers to NB-SMEES across the region are now discussed.

10.3.1 *Lack of Coordinated Implementation of National Biodiversity Strategies*

Although several MENA countries have developed National Biodiversity Strategies, institutional barriers that prevent the coherent and holistic implementation of such strategies, including the development of specific strategies that support and facilitate NB-SMEEs, remains a key gap.[48] For example, the Convention on the Conservation of Wildlife and Their Natural Habitats in the Countries of the Gulf Co-operation Council (the GCC Wildlife Convention), Articles 6 and 7, calls for the establishment of governing committees and secretariats focused on monitoring of wildlife and natural habitat.[49] Similarly, the Arab League Educational, Cultural and Scientific Organization (ALESCO) encourages Arab states to collaborate and generate frameworks that provide education and training for community members in protection and conservation practices of nature-based cultural heritage.[50] Also, the Arab Declaration on Environment and Development and Future Prospects calls on Arab states to establish initiatives, polices, and legislation that promote the preservation of natural heritage and the integration of environmental awareness into educational syllabi.[51] These instruments emphasize the need for multistakeholder engagement and coordination in the design and implementation of biodiversity policies and programs, including Nature Based Strategies.

Yet across the region, evidence of the establishment of intragovernmental risk management bodies to implement Nature Based Strategies are slow to emerge. Given the wide range of institutions that are responsible for approving and implementing biodiversity entrepreneurship programs, especially finance, environment, commerce, technology, and infrastructure agencies and institutions, the sectoral

[47] V. D. Litskas et al., "Innovation in Water Education Programs in the Eastern Mediterranean to Enhance Security and Socio-economic Development under Climate Change" (2023) 8 *Euro-Mediterranean Journal for Environmental Integration* 253; Mabrouk et al. (n 10).

[48] J. S. Singh, "The Biodiversity Crisis: A Multifaceted Review" (2002) 82 *Current Science* 6, 638–647.

[49] Olawuyi (n 13) 245–272; see also: Cooperation Council for the Arab States of the Gulf, "Convention on the Conservation of Wildlife and Their Natural Habitats in the Countries of the Gulf Co-operation Council," Articles 6 and 7 www.gcc-sg.org/en-us/CognitiveSources/DigitalLibrary/Lists/DigitalLibrary/Forests%20pastures%20and%20wildlife/1274593978.pdf accessed January 14, 2024.

[50] Ibid.

[51] Ibid.; see also United Nations Digital Library, "Arab Declaration on Environment and Development and Future Prospects" (1991) https://digitallibrary.un.org/record/1292205?ln=es accessed January 14, 2024.

implementation of Nature Based Strategies and lack of coordination among the wide range of regulatory institutions remains a key hindrance.[52] A lack of coordination among regulatory institutions has led to vulnerabilities in the infrastructure and technologies required for the implementation of innovative nature-based business models.[53] Governance fragmentation reduces the collaborative capacity and access to financial support required for start-up NB-SMEEs.[54] Furthermore, the lack of harmonized institutional structures and implementation strategies to simplify incorporation requirements and reduce bureaucracy and lengthy procedures creates inefficiency, overlapping responsibilities, and an inability to translate regulations to the local level.[55] Additionally, the lack of specific committees specialized in providing and enforcing standards and principles for implementing NB-SMEE strategies, as well as the lack of effective coordination between related and connected agencies that facilitate approvals of nature-based SMEE projects, hinders coherent implementation.

Furthermore, a lack of specific institutions, organizations, and committees that mainstream NB-SMEEs within national governance remains a key problem.[56] While NB-SMEEs are gaining increased recognition and awareness across the region, the establishment of focal agencies that will spearhead nature-based entrepreneurship and investments remains slow. Institutional harmonization and the creation of strategic governing committees are required to integrate and enforce nature-based implementation regulatory standards, steward financial resources, establish polices that promote collaborations, and broaden financial channels that facilitate the innovation, capacity building, establishment, growth, and upscaling of NB-SMEEs.[57]

10.3.2 *Unclear Legal Framework for Nature-Based Enterprises*

A significant barrier to the growth of NB-SMEEs is the lack of clear and specific mention of biodiversity-focused eco-entrepreneurship and NB-SMEEs in national

52 I. Abumoghli and A. Goncalves, "Environmental Challenges in the MENA Region" https://wedocs.unep.org/bitstream/handle/20.500.11822/31645/EC_MENA.pdf?sequence=1&isAllowed=y accessed January 12, 2024.

53 R. Namdar, E. Karami, and Keshavarz M., "Climate Change and Vulnerability: The Case of MENA Countries" (2021) 10 *ISPRS International Journal of Geo-Information* 11, 794.

54 P. Laderach et al., "Strengthening Climate Security in the Middle East and North Africa Region" position paper (CGIAR FOCUS Climate Security 2022/3).

55 R. Mrabet et al., "Policy Review: Up-scaling (Co)-benefits, Opportunities, and Alternatives: Policy Review Document and Institutional Feasibility Analysis Report" (REACT4MED Consortium 2022) 1–10.

56 On the need for mainstreaming NBS in national governance, see: UNEP, "Compendium of Contributions on Nature-Based Solutions" https://wedocs.unep.org/bitstream/handle/20.500.11822/29988/Compendium_NBS.pdf accessed January 12, 2024.

57 Ibid.

biodiversity legislation and strategies.[58] Article IX of the African Convention on the Conservation of Nature and Natural Resource, which applies to MENA countries in the Maghreb region, encourages states to integrate conservation practices and programs in regional and urban planning. Article XII calls for legislation that protects and prevents the loss of nature-based cultural heritage, animals, and plants. Article XVII calls for legislation integrated into the intellectual and traditional property and land ownership rights of community members that promote autonomy in conservation and promotion of biological diversity practices. Also, the Arab Declaration to the World Summit on Sustainable Development encourage parties to integrate sustainable management innovations that promote biodiversity and ecosystem conservation while capturing economic value from rich religious and cultural heritage. Yet there is a lack of clear regulatory frameworks and laws that integrate NB-SMEEs into the financial sector, as well as the development and implementation of government projects. Additionally, context-based polices that clearly capture and generate pro-biodiversity projects and increase market demand for nature-based technologies and solutions are generally lacking.[59]

To make NB-SMEEs attractive to social entrepreneurs, there is a need for tailored strategies and legislation that address barriers to the development and formalization of such ventures. For example, Ecuador has specifically implemented the PROAmazonia project to "enable economic transformation by supporting local entrepreneurial efforts to sustainably develop non-timber forest products, thus increasing the economic value of the forests, while maintaining ecosystem function and diversifying income sources for local communities."[60] The project enables social entrepreneurs to access the financing, business registration, resources, and tools needed for them to undertake forest conservation projects. There is a need for MENA countries to specifically design and implement such legal intervention programs and efforts. The lack of tailored legislation and policies that integrate NB-SMEEs into conservation, investment, and financial planning exposes nature-based entrepreneurs to broadly framed business laws and procedures that may not have been designed with environmental conservation in mind. This results in delays and the slow uptake of NB-SMEEs.[61]

Second, ensuring compliance with environmental impact assessment laws can open up opportunities for NB-SMEEs to emerge. For example, the GCC Wildlife

58 J. S. Singh, "The Biodiversity Crisis: A Multifaceted Review" (2002) 82 *Current Science* 6, 647; M. Hachaichi and T. Baouni, "Downscaling the Planetary Boundaries (PBS) Framework to City Scale-Level: De-risking MENA Region's Environment Future" (2020) 5 *Environmental and Sustainability Indicators* 100023.

59 Mabrouk et al. (n 10).

60 See UNEP, "Compendium of Contributions on Nature-Based Solutions" https://wedocs.unep.org/bitstream/handle/20.500.11822/29988/Compendium_NBS.pdf accessed January 12, 2024.

61 M. Hachaichi and T. Baouni, "Downscaling the Planetary Boundaries (PBS) Framework to City Scale-level: De-risking MENA Region's Environment Future" (2020) 5 *Environmental and Sustainability Indicators* 100023.

Convention Article 1(3) calls for clear regulations and legislations for environmental impact assessment (EIA) pre-project approval requirements to quantify impact on biodiversity.[62] Similarly, Article 1(3) also calls for GCC countries to enact legislation making environmental assessments compulsory. The Kuwait Regional Convention on Protection of Marine Environment and Protocols require associated parties to draw from international law to develop marine pollution prevention measures.[63] Virtually all MENA countries have also enacted legislation that mandate EIAs, including the examination of biodiversity impacts, prior to the approval of key development projects.[64] However, gaps in the enforcement of such mandatory EIA standards, especially the tendency of large-scale and politically sensitive projects to evade EIAs, often reduce biodiversity considerations in some projects. Similarly, generalized EIAs without a clear focus on biological diversity and other tangible and intangible conservation needs have been highlighted as gaps in the MENA region.[65] Enforcing EIA standards will automatically increase the need for biodiversity solutions and accelerate the demand for goods and services offered by NB-SMEEs. For example, laws that require the mapping of natural heritage via a remote sensing survey allow the quantifying, characterizing, and raising of awareness of the unique biological diversity for specific regions, as well as specific opportunities of sustainable value creation. Similarly, most marine protected areas in the MENA region have focused more on natural heritage in appraisals and management plans with little emphasis on cultural heritage.[66] This significantly impacts ecotourism business models and limits the governance and support required to establish and grow ecotourism business models. These limitations can engineer the reputational damage of ecological citizens and result in negative impacts on end-users. Ensuring the comprehensive implementation of EIA programs, such as the integration of cultural heritage in marine protection areas, can significantly support and accelerate NB-SMEE growth and upscaling.[67]

10.3.3 *Unclear Legal Framework on Joint Governance and Partnerships*

ALESCO encourages Arab states to collaborate through joint and strategic partnerships with community members and heritage institutions, among others, to integrate social perspectives and develop management strategies that sustainably maximize social value.[68] Yet the lack of comprehensive stakeholder engagement in

62 Olawuyi (n 13) 245–272.
63 Ibid.
64 Ibid.
65 Mabrouk et al (n 10).
66 C. Breen et al., "Integrating Cultural and Natural Heritage Approaches to Marine Protected Areas in the MENA Region" (2021) 132 *Marine Policy* 104676.
67 Ibid.
68 Olawuyi (n 13) 269–260.

the design and implementation of biodiversity and nature conservation programs remains a key challenge in the MENA region.

Across the region, public participation in environmental decision-making is often structured in formal institutions such as the Shura Council.[69] While important, such a top-down decision-making approach limits the potential of countries to harness partnerships with nonstate actors such as stakeholders, entrepreneurs, indigenous communities, landowners, and government institutions toward halting and reversing biodiversity loss. The lack of clear and comprehensive laws to define the roles and responsibilities of state and nonstate actors often limits public–private partnerships and the shared governance of biodiversity programs.[70]

There is a need for more partnerships for the financing, planning, and implementation of nature-based projects. For example, the World Wide Fund for Nature collaboration with local and global experts to assess the United Arab Emirates' (UAE) coastal ecosystem and value the natural capital functions by identifying the locations of ecological corridors, evaluating the ecological knowledge, and analyzing the scientific data, which in turn can be used to develop contextual nature-based solutions and intervention strategies for the conservation, restoration, and innovation of NB-SMEEs.[71]

Substantive collaborations with universities and institutions that promote research and development regarding nature-based innovation and eco-entrepreneurship will also need to be accelerated across the MENA region.[72] The objective of transitioning to a knowledge economy through environmental education, research, and capacity building has been identified in national visions and is a priority in several countries in the region.[73] While environmental education and entrepreneurship programs are increasing, the need for biodiversity-focused collaborations with higher education institutions remains prevalent. An effective ecosystem management strategy incorporates both scientific and societal-based evidence approaches in identifying and creating pro-biodiversity strategies and conservation practices.[74] ALESCO encourages collaboration and joint action in the area of conservation and protection through organized training and frameworks that promote strategic partnerships and joint actions, and the Arab Declaration to the World Summit on

69 Ibid.

70 B. Macura, L. Secco and A. Pullin, "What Evidence Exists on the Impact of Governance Type on the Conservation Effectiveness of Forest Protected Areas? Knowledge Base and Evidence Gaps" (2015) 4 *Environmental Evidence* 24; also A. Elmahdi et al., "Urban Flash Floods Mitigations: Enhancing the Link between Water, Sanitation and Energy Services in Urban Settings in the MENA Region" (2020) 4 *Advancements in Civil Engineering & Technology* 2.

71 Emirates nature-WWF (n 25) 17–18.

72 A. Orrnert, *Drivers and Barriers to Environmental Engagement in the MENA Region* (Institute of Development Studies 2020) 1–5.

73 See for example, Government of Qatar, *Qatar National Vision 2030* (General Secretariat for Development Planning [GSDP] 2008).

74 Mabrouk et al. (n 10).

Sustainable Development encourages collaborative efforts toward biological diversity and ecosystem conservation and to develop sustainable management practices with co-benefit values.[75] These instruments underpin the need for regulatory institutions across the MENA region to promote shared programs aimed at accelerating biodiversity-focused entrepreneurship and NB-SMEE business models.[76]

10.4 MINDING THE GAPS: RECOMMENDATIONS

Accelerating nature-based solutions for biodiversity across the region will require clear and comprehensive legal frameworks and strategies to promote the active development of citizen-led NB-SMEE business models. To advance NB-SMEE business models, all MENA countries need to reform legal frameworks that impede or slow down their implementation. This includes the need to develop national accountability strategies that develop into local and community innovation, assessments, and reporting. The MENA region can draw on international frameworks, especially the GBF, to inform policy reforms in finance and governance institutions to transform national policy and legal and institutional frameworks. This will broaden financial channels by promoting: green financing, incentives, and subsidies; reporting standards; and enterprise requirements to disclose nature-related dependencies, opportunities, risks, and impacts as an eligibility requirement to assess green investors, green loans, incentives, and subsidies. For example, the Priceless Planet Coalition created an initiative for funding management projects to restore forest ecosystems and mangrove habitants in the UAE and hence legitimate the grounds to solicit financial resources from banks and other partners.[77] By adopting the Avoid, Reduce, Restore and Regenerate, Transform framework, the MENA region can develop policies that support NB-SMEEs with minimal to no impact to biodiversity, and pro-biodiversity business models that directly or indirectly reduce, restore, and regenerate ecological productivity and biophysical and ecosystem functions and services.[78] For example, transformative policies that encourage human resource development, auditing and accountancy, education programs, information technology, and a flexible and favorable legal framework (e.g. incentives, tax breaks, exemption from antitrust laws, low-credit interest, access to information, infrastructure, and land)[79] can engineer a favorable entrepreneurial context that supports the rapid establishment and growth of NB-SMEEs in the MENA region.

The GBF calls for a decentralized governance approach toward community-based, citizen-led management strategies to tackle biodiversity loss. Implementation

75 Olawuyi (n 62) 245–272.
76 Mabrouk et al. (n 10).
77 Emirates nature-WWF (n 25) 45–46.
78 Taskforce on Nature-Related Financial Disclosures (n 34).
79 E. Ribasauskiene et al., “Evaluating Public Policy Support for Agricultural Cooperatives” (2019) 11 *Sustainability* 14, 3769.

will require holistic and transformative legal and policy frameworks developed by the MENA region that places citizens at the center of pro-biodiversity governance. The GBF supports implementation strategies with indicators such as openness, transparency, and legitimacy, as well as strategies which address gaps in social learning regarding the nature of ecosystems and biodiversity, and which focus on disparities in policy frameworks by eliminating the dominance by few power players in policy design. Furthermore, the GBF supports the integration of ecosystem services and valuation, of perceptions and knowledge of community and indigenous society, and of social and religious values into these implementation strategies.[80] The transformative governance of biodiversity promotes the knowledge and skill empowerment of citizens to develop nature-based sustainable business innovations, access and source for multiple financial channels, and successfully implement pro-biodiversity business models. It integrates pro-biodiversity polices and ecosystem management projects with helpful institutional structures, financial incentives, and support programs that engineer a supportive entrepreneurial context by simplifying the incorporation, registration, and legitimacy of NB-SMEEs in the MENA region. It also facilitates the significant contribution of biodiversity entrepreneurship in achieving both national and international biodiversity targets. For example, the Urban Governance Atlas is an online database of 250 policy instruments aimed at financing and deploying nature-based solutions that halt and reverse biodiversity loss.[81] This licensed platform aims to design inclusive and coherent strategies, green space planning, and ecological restoration projects through a bottom-up, community-led approach. Both government and nongovernmental agencies in MENA nations should utilize such information platforms to design policy instruments that promote citizen-led nature-based solutions, projects, technologies, and social instruments. For example, the Community of Latin American and Caribbean states cooperatives instrument is based on agreements to jointly engage in pro-biodiversity and nature-based activities. The MENA nations can collaborate at a local level to form agreement-based eco-cooperatives of the MENA region.[82]

To advance NB-SMEEs in the MENA region, legal and institutional decluttering is required. There is a need for harmonizing and eliminating the overlap of governing institutions to promote a smooth process regarding eligibility, requirements, and licensing procedures for implementing nature-based start-ups. Unclear regulations and administrative delays must be addressed by narrowing down requirements and the registration time frame as well as incentivizing registration and licensing

[80] I. J. Visseren-Hamakers et al., "Transformative Governance of Biodiversity: Insights for Sustainable Development" (2021) 53 *Current Opinion in Environmental Sustainability* 20.

[81] McKenna Davis, "Nature-Based Solutions in European Policy: A Framework for Enhancing Local Action" (Ecologic Institute: Science and Policy for a Sustainable World, October 5, 2023) www.ecologic.eu/sites/default/files/presentation/2023/Davis-23-EU-Policy-Framework-ERRIN-workshop.pdf accessed January 12, 2024.

[82] Ibid.

processes. This will boost trust in citizens to incorporate nature-based ventures and projects. For example, the concept of an Interinstitutional Gap (IIG) framework is proposed to address institutional gaps and mismatch in a socio-ecological context by assessing interactions and the impacts of constitutional choices and operational outcomes.[83] Furthermore, nature-based government initiatives and projects require specialized institutions and organizations focused on the governing, enforcing, and streamlining of regulations and laws to facilitate approvals and implementation standards for projects and ecosystem management strategies. These institutions will provide a "one-stop shop" for information on how to access financial support, education, skill and incentives, and partnerships for ecopreneurs to help with navigating challenges and optimizing success possibilities in the journey of nature-based entrepreneurship. The institutions also stand as an information pod for investors for a better understanding of methodologies, procedures, and ecological value assessment for informed and confident decision-making. The MENA nations can develop an IIG framework implemented by an assigned organization or government body to address institutional gaps, without which biodiversity and sustainable natural resource management cannot be attained.[84]

The lack of government interest must be addressed to match the urgency to halt and reverse biodiversity loss. Governments and policymakers must design policy frameworks that prioritize the fast-tracking of incorporation and licensing processes for nature-based enterprises. For example, training and programs aimed at empowering and accelerating processes from start-up to establishment must be prioritized in policy design to centralize and maximize social capital toward mitigating biodiversity loss. To maximize social capital, reforms in laws, procedures, rules, and regulations are required to broaden the eligibility and opportunities for public participation in nature-based projects. For example, eliminating eligibility rules limited to nationals, locals, or certain educational qualifications alone can unlock a broad range of public participation and promote inclusivity and democracy in governance, which are indicators of transformative governance favorable to pro-biodiversity innovations. The incorporation and prioritization of nature-based concepts and solutions in EU policy instruments and financial instruments that promote the financing, deployment, and market integration of nature-based solutions can be emulated by governing bodies in the MENA region. For example, the EU Green Infrastructure Strategy (2013) addresses biodiversity; L'Instrument financier pour l'environnement (2018) provides targeted financial support; the Blue Growth Strategy (2012) addresses marine ecosystem; the Forest Strategy (2013) targets forestry; and the Urban Agenda (2016) targets agriculture.[85] In the MENA region, developing

[83] H. Tuihedur Rahman et al., "A Framework for Analyzing Institutional Gaps in Natural Resource Governance" (2017) 11 *International Journal of the Commons* 2, 823.

[84] Ibid.

[85] M. Davis et al., *Nature-Based Solutions in European and National Policy Frameworks* (European Commission 2018) 50.

a framework that integrates and prioritizes nature-based business solutions and concepts in all policy instruments in a consistent, thematic, and synchronized fashion will foster the rapid deployment of NB-SMEEs across the MENA region. For example, creating a thematic nature-based framework – such as marine, terrestrial, agriculture, tourism, biodiversity, adaptation, environmental assessment, or cultural heritage – with assigned policy instruments can encompass the entirety of halting and reversing biodiversity loss while boosting pro-biodiversity business models.

The MENA region lacks substantial innovative partnerships from both national and international organizations. Laws encouraging public–private partnerships must be comprehensive and clear. They must create a supportive environment with multiple supportive incentives such as financial channels, access to research and innovation, technology, training, education, and international collaborations that promote the establishment and growth of NB-SMEEs. Laws which provide clear and comprehensive nature value assessments guidelines, and which clarify the role of government in incentive provisions, implementation standards, and regulatory approvals, will boost the confidence of private investors. For example, partnerships with educational institutions to generate clear scientific-based nature value assessments would help investors to predict returns on investment from nature-based projects, while also promoting the tax and financial incentives from the financial institutions needed to boost project resources and sustainable competitiveness. As already mentioned, the example of the EU intergovernmental Urban Agenda is an initiative that promotes thematic partnerships with EU institutions, governments, cities, and partners to broaden financial channels, build knowledge, and streamline regulations to incentivize nature-based solutions and the sustainable use of natural resources.[86]

Creating a supportive entrepreneurial context for NB-SMEEs will require engineering a favorable market structure for nature-based value proposition in the MENA region. Comprehensive laws that generate government conservation and green-planning projects will secure a favorable market for nature-based technologies, solutions, and enterprises. For instance, laws that promote the integration of artificial ecosystems through green urban planning will provide a steady demand for nature-based technologies and eco-ventures, which allow for the financial growth and asset development required for investment. The Australian Commonwealth Nature Repair Market Bill 2023 creates a favorable framework via biodiversity certificates that are tradable, provides transparent and clear pro-biodiversity entrepreneurial outcomes, and promotes investment in pro-biodiversity projects by companies, Australian landholders, and individuals.[87]

[86] Urban Agenda for the European Union, "Sustainable Use of Land and Nature-Based Solutions Partnership" https://ec.europa.eu/futurium/en/system/files/ged/leaflet_sulnbs_en.pdf accessed January 12, 2024.

[87] S. Daly et al., "Federal Government Introduces New Biodiversity Credit Market Legislation" https://jws.com.au/insights/articles/2023-articles/federal-government-introduces-new-biodiversity accessed January 12, 2024.

Lastly, communities, citizens, and indigenous members of society can engineer a favorable entrepreneurial context by establishing local associations and self-help groups that create community awareness.[88] For example, the Arcandina Foundation promotes awareness of biodiversity in the Ecuadorian community through television shows, while the Inland Shore Wieringermeer Project combines action from ecopreneurs, the indigenous community, and society members to produce ecosystem services and generate new markets.[89] These associations are knowledge hubs that assist in providing information to biodiversity entrepreneurs on the available investment and financial opportunities, intellectual property protection contract designing, and compliance with human rights and environmental, social, and governance requirements, among other things.[90] According to the Taskforce on Nature-Related Financial Disclosures, 80 percent of the world's biodiversity is governed by indigenous community members, and therefore traditional nature-based knowledge provided by community and indigenous members is invaluable and provides a fundamental contribution toward pro-biodiversity management strategies.[91]

10.5 CONCLUSION

Calls for sustainable innovative management strategies to halt and reverse biodiversity loss will require the transformative governance of biodiversity in order to realize the full potential of nature-based enterprises. These nature-based business models require an entrepreneurial context that favors innovation and the successful introduction and integration into market economies and governance institutions. Biodiversity entrepreneurship provides both the incubator and the engine for generating nature-based, pro-biodiversity business models. NB-SMEEs are not a replacement for other conservation practices but they do offer the supplementary solutions needed to steadily halt and reverse biodiversity loss.

However, the lack of a supportive legal, regulatory, and financial entrepreneurial context that promotes these citizen-led NB-SMEEs continues to inhibit biodiversity entrepreneurship across the MENA region. Legal, regulatory, and financial factors are considered the most significant external barriers to the awareness, establishment, and growth of NB-SMEEs and the attainment of the GBF targets of 2030 and 2050 in the MENA region. MENA countries should therefore develop supportive polices, laws, and economic instruments that remove barriers to the market development of nature-based solutions. To facilitate the growth, establishment, and upscaling of NB-SMEEs, MENA countries would need to transition toward transformative

88 J. Singh, "The Biodiversity Crisis: A Multifaceted Review" (2002) 82 *Current Science* 6, 638.

89 Lobo et al. (n 1).

90 S. McQuaid, "Innovating with Nature: Factors Influencing the Success of Nature-Based Enterprises" (2021) 13 *Sustainability* 22, 12488.

91 Taskforce on Nature-related Financial Disclosures (n 34).

governance initiatives that streamline the process for commercializing nature-based solutions and innovations.

Institutional and policy fragmentations that produce generalized polices and regulatory standards that complicate private sector participation in biodiversity initiatives must be dismantled. Given the barriers that such fragmentations pose to the rapid growth of NB-SMEEs, there is a need to promote greater institutional coordination and interoperability between different government agencies and institutions that have roles to play across the business development and entrepreneurial value chain.

Lastly, strategic multistakeholder partnerships between educational institutions, training programs, and think tanks are also key to advancing capacity and knowledge sharing on biodiversity entrepreneurship. Knowledge exchange could enable NB-SMEEs by generating nature-based innovations and technologies that are context-specific, boost investors awareness and understanding, and equip interested stakeholders with the tools needed to increase local participation and the registration of NB-SMEEs.

11

Advancing Nature and Biodiversity Financing in the MENA Region

The Role of Islamic Financing

Tasniem Ahmed Elyass Hussain and Damilola S. Olawuyi

11.1 INTRODUCTION

This chapter evaluates the potential role of Islamic finance as a tool to bridge the gap in current biodiversity financing in the Middle East and North Africa (MENA) region. It examines the legal and institutional challenges to Islamic biodiversity financing in the MENA region and proffers recommendations on how to address them.

Nature and biodiversity conservation has been identified as a key priority in several countries of the MENA region.[1] For example, Article 33 of the Permanent Constitution for the State of Qatar states: "The State shall conserve the environment and its natural balance for the comprehensive and sustainable use of its resources for all generations."[2] Qatar's National Vision 2030 rests on four key pillars, the fourth of which is to "manage the environment such that there is harmony between economic growth, social development and environmental protection."[3] Biodiversity conservation is considered vital, especially in the face of its fast-paced development and industrialization and in light of challenges such as increasing groundwater salinity, degrading soil quality, air pollution, climate change, rising sea levels, and biodiversity and species under threat.[4] In addition to its intrinsic value to nature and other nonhuman elements in the environment, biological resources play a critical role in advancing human society and its economic progress.[5] While there is growing

[1] Damilola Olawuyi, *Environmental Law in Arab States* (Oxford University Press 2022) 245–274.

[2] The State of Qatar, "The Permanent Constitution of the State of Qatar" (2004).

[3] Government of Qatar, *General Secretariat for Development Planning, Qatar National Vision 2030* (General Secretariat for Development Planning 2008) (hereafter Government of Qatar, Qatar National Vision 2030).

[4] Qatar Ministry of Environment, "Qatar National Biodiversity Strategy and Action Plan 2015–2025" (2014).

[5] M. T. Ladan, *Natural Resources and Environmental Law and Policies for Sustainable Development in Nigeria* (Ahmadu Bello University Press 2014) 64–68.

recognition that biodiversity is a valuable global asset for current and future generations, the reality is that the threat to species and ecosystems has never been greater.[6]

Generally, while virtually all MENA countries and stakeholders agree on the compelling need to integrate biodiversity considerations into all aspects of development planning, a lot more will need to be done to mobilize the required finances to implement such targeted biodiversity programs. The Kunming-Montreal Global Biodiversity Framework (GBF) identified that there is currently a finance gap of US$700 billion per year to be met in order to achieve biodiversity protection by 2030.[7] Similarly, a recent United Nations Environment Programme (UNEP) study noted that global investment in nature needs to increase fourfold by 2050, equating to a cumulative total investment of up to US$8.1 trillion and a future annual investment rate of US$536 billion. Forest-based solutions alone would amount to US$203 billion a year.[8] The UNEP report also stated that private finance directed to nature-based solutions must be scaled up, and companies and financial institutions must also be part of the solution by sharing the risk and committing to increase finance and investment in nature-based solutions.[9] In addition to the cost of restoring degraded ecosystems, financing is needed to provide necessary technologies, equipment, capacity development, and patrol vehicles in order to monitor compliance and deter illegal loggers and poachers. As countries seek to recover from the economic impacts of COVID-19, it is important to prioritize financial, institutional, and technological support for conservation agencies, as well as research institutions, to sustain conservation monitoring and enforcement programs.[10]

The MENA region, like other regions of the world, needs to bridge the gap in the availability of financing for nature conservation and biodiversity programs, and Islamic finance has already begun to yield results in this field. Islamic finance promotes the financing of investment activities and projects in accordance with the tenets and procedures of Shari'a law.[11] Islamic biodiversity financing therefore refers to the financing of biodiversity and nature conservation programs using Islamic financial instruments such as *sukuk* (Islamic bond). One distinguishing feature of Islamic finance, as compared to conventional financing methods, is that parties agree to abide by Qur'anic injunctions and prophetic practice in structuring the

6 Olawuyi (n 1) 245–274.

7 United Nations Environment Programme, "Kunming-Montreal Global Biodiversity Framework" www.unep.org/resources/kunming-montreal-global-biodiversity-framework accessed January 31, 2024.

8 United Nations Environment Programme, "State of Finance for Nature 2021" (2021) 6 www.unep.org/resources/state-finance-nature-2021 accessed January 31, 2024.

9 Ibid., 5.

10 Damilola Olawuyi and Elena Athwal, "Halting Biodiversity Loss and Protecting Nature: The Important Role of International Environmental Law" https://dailytrust.com/halting-biodiversity-loss-and-protecting-nature-the-important-role-of-international-environmental-law/ accessed January 31, 2024.

11 Dalal Aassouli, "Mobilizing and Leveraging Islamic Climate Finance in the MENA Region: The Potential Role of National Green Participative Banks" in D. Olawuyi (ed), *Climate Change Law and Policy in the MENA Region* (Routledge 2022).

transaction. For example, the Qur'an and Hadith prohibit the levying of interest (*riba*). Therefore, in selecting Islamic financing, parties choose to exclude *riba*.[12]

The size of the Islamic finance industry is projected to grow to US$3 trillion by the year 2030, with further growth expected in the following decade.[13] Yet the Islamic financing sector is still a niche industry, accounting for only 0.6 percent of global wealth.[14] In 2022, the Qatar Financial Centre developed a Sustainable Sukuk and Bonds Framework, the first in the Gulf Cooperation Council (GCC) region in line with Qatar's National Vision 2030 and Qatar Central Bank's strategic goal of "Developing Financial Markets and Fostering Financial Innovation."[15] Though outside of the MENA region, Malaysia also provides positive examples regarding the growth of Islamic finance in key sectors, including environmental conservation programs. In 2017, Malaysia issued the world's first sustainable and responsible investments (SRI) *sukuk*. Malaysia's Quantum Solar Park issued the largest solar project linked to green *sukuk*, which eventually powered over 90,000 homes, created over 3,000 jobs, and reduced emissions by 193,000 tons of carbon per year. Indonesia soon followed suit, issuing the first sovereign green *sukuk*, amounting to US$1.25 billion and extending its reach beyond Shari'ah investors, with 29 percent new green investors.[16] In 2017, Islamic Development Bank climate finance was estimated to be worth US$644 million.[17] According to the Islamic Finance Development Report 2022, the global Islamic finance industry outperformed pre-COVID levels with a total asset rise of 17 percent, reaching US$4 trillion.[18] These examples showcase environmental, social, and governance (ESG) aspects while demonstrating the

[12] Ibid. For example, Accounting and Auditing Organization for Islamic Financial Institutions (AAOIFI) Standard No. 17 on investment *sukuk* states that "[t]he prospectus must not include any statement to the effect that the issuer of the certificate accepts the liability to compensate the owner of the certificate up to the nominal value of the certificate in situations other than torts or negligence nor that he guarantees a fixed percentage of profit" Shari'ah Standards ss. 17, at 5/1/8/7 (AAOIFI 2015) (Investment Sukuk).

[13] The Global Islamic Finance Report 2018 https://ded.ae/DED_Files/StudiesAndResearch/SGIE-Report-2018-19_Eng_1540649428.pdf accessed October 31, 2023.

[14] ADB and IsDB Joint Report, "Unlocking Islamic Climate Finance in Joint ADB and IsDB Countries" (November 2022) https://events.development.asia/materials/20221109/unlocking-islamic-climate-finance-joint-adb-and-isdb-countries accessed January 31, 2024.

[15] Qatar Financial Centre Media Release, "Qatar Financial Centre: The First in GCC to Introduce a Sustainable Framework for Sukuk and Bonds" (March 16, 2022) www.qfc.qa/en/media-centre/news/list/qatar-financial-centre-the-first-in-gcc-to-introduce-a-sustainable-framework-for-sukuk-and-bonds accessed January 31, 2024.

[16] Securities Commission Malaysia and World Bank Group, "Islamic Green Finance: Development, Ecosystem and Prospects Report, based on the Conference on Harnessing Islamic Finance for a Green Future, Held from 14 to May 15, 2018 in Kuala Lumpur" (March 2019).

[17] AfDB (African Development Bank), ADB (Asian Development Bank), EBRD (European Bank for Reconstruction and Development), EIB (European Investment Bank), IDBG (Inter-American Development Bank Group), IsDB (Islamic Development Bank), and WBG (World Bank Group) (2018), "2017 Joint Report on Multilateral Development Banks' Climate Finance."

[18] ICD and Refinitiv, "ICD-Refinitiv Islamic Finance Development Report 2022" (2022) 6 https://icd-ps.org/uploads/files/ICD%20Refinitiv%20ifdi-report-20221669878247_1582.pdf accessed January 31, 2024.

growth of Islamic finance in sustainable development. There is still room to grow, in terms of greening capital markets through *sukuk* issuances, greening social finance using *zakat*, *takaful*, and *awqaf* for climate and biodiversity programs, and as project financing for green infrastructure. According to the United Nations Development Programme (UNDP), *zakat* alone can mobilize between US$200 billion and US$1 trillion annually for the Sustainable Development Goal (SDG) agenda.[19]

Despite the growing awareness on the potential of Islamic finance as a faith-based approach to financing biodiversity projects and programs, there is a need to address legal and governance challenges that may stifle its wide application. Islamic financing requires regulatory frameworks and national pro-green financing strategies, which including standard-setting procedures and reporting, transparency, and awareness that can attract a diverse and robust investor pool. This chapter examines the role that Islamic financing can play in bridging the financing gap in biodiversity and nature conservation programs. It examines the legal framework to advance Islamic biodiversity financing in the MENA region.

The chapter proceeds in six sections. After this introductory section, Section 11.2 discusses the nature and scope of Islamic biodiversity financing. Section 11.3 makes the case for Islamic biodiversity financing. Section 11.4 analyses the legal and institutional barriers to Islamic biodiversity financing in the MENA region. Section 11.5 discusses the recommendations for addressing these barriers. Section 11.6 is the concluding section.

11.2 NATURE AND SCOPE OF ISLAMIC BIODIVERSITY FINANCING

The rise of faith-based approaches to environmental protection continues to underscore the importance of integrating Islamic principles in the design, financing, and implementation of nature conversation and biodiversity programs.[20] For example, though not legally binding, the Islamic Declaration on Climate Change of 2015 calls on Muslims worldwide to tackle "the root causes of climate change, environmental degradation and the loss of biodiversity."[21] It called upon Muslims to work to preserve the environment using Islamic principles such as *khalifa* (caretaker), with human beings as vicegerents of God on earth, responsible for all beings and the environment, and entrusted with nature to benefit society while safeguarding it from overconsumption;[22] *al-mizan* (balance) requires the equilibrium and balance

[19] AfDB et al. (n 17).

[20] Olawuyi (n 1).

[21] United Nations Climate Change, "Islamic Declaration on Global Climate Change" (2015) https://unfccc.int/news/islamic-declaration-on-climate-change accessed January 31, 2024.

[22] A. Al-Roubaie and A. M. Sarea, "Green Investment and Sustainable Development: The Case of Islamic Finance" (2019) 9 *Journal of Islamic Business and Management (JIBM)* 1, 14 https://doi.org/10.26501/jibm/2019.0901-002 accessed January 31, 2024. See also S. V. R. Nasr, "Islamic Economics: Novel Perspectives" (1989) 25 *Middle Eastern Studies* 516.

of the ecosystem,[23] highlighting the importance of respecting the environment and considering the impact of our economic activities on the environment. These Islamic values are reflected in and form the foundation of Islamic finance, which advocates leveraging Islamic tenets and financial instruments to advance the green economy.[24] The link between the conservation of land and water to belief systems has been prevalent in the MENA region historically; for example, the *hima* system, from the Arabic word "hima" meaning "a protected place" or "protected area," is a traditional system which protected areas of land to promote the sustainable use of resources that has been practiced for more than 1,400 years in the Arabian Peninsula, predating Islam, and eventually evolving to signify a reserved pasture or a piece of land set aside seasonally to allow regeneration.[25] This link is prevalent in most mainstream religions and localized belief systems.[26] It is, therefore, important to keep in mind when considering biodiversity conservation efforts and financing.[27]

The environmental philosophy of Islam relates human beings to their relationship with nature as well as God. The concepts of *khilafah* and *amānah* (custodianship and trust) derived from the Quran and Sunnah emphasize the human role as a mere steward or trustee of the earth and not a proprietor or disposer that can use the environment as it wishes,[28] making it a fundamental duty of humanity to protect and preserve nature.[29] Shari'ah then provides the practical framework within which society can fulfill the role of trustee.[30] Farook identifies several other concepts, including *adl* and *i'tidal* (justice and moderation), akin to equilibrium, requiring moderation and balance in emphasizing natural resources and preventing their undue exploitation, with accountability and belief in the day of judgment as motivators.[31] According to Ammar, Islam emphasizes respect (*ihtiram*) for nature and the use of natural resources in accordance with the trust accorded by God, requiring humans to adhere to five moral obligations, such that nature and its natural resources are: (1) used in a balanced, nonexcessive manner; (2) treated with

23 T. Al-Mubarak and B. Goud, *Environmental Impact in Islamic Finance* (RFI Foundation 2018) 1–70.

24 S. Franzoni and A. A. Allali, "Principles of Islamic Finance and Principles of Corporate Social Responsibility: What Convergence?" (2018) 10 *Sustainability (Switzerland)* 3, 1–11 https://doi.org/10.3390/su10030637 accessed February 6, 2024.

25 Odeh Al-Jayyousi, "Hima as a Model for Natural Resource Management in West Asia and North Africa" (UCN, August 11, 2010). www.iucn.org/about/work/programmes/forest/?5853/Hima-as-a-model-for-natural-resourcemanagement-in-WANA accessed February 6, 2024.

26 Liza Higgins-Zogib et al., "Beyond Belief: Linking Faiths and Protected Areas to Support Biodiversity Conservation" in Sue Stolton and Nigel Dudley (eds), *Arguments for Protected Areas: Multiple Benefits for Conservation and Use* (Earthscan 2010) 145–158.

27 Lekha Laxman et al., "The Islamic Approach to Conserving Biodiversity for Global Sustainability: An Exploration" (2014) 8 *Advances in Environmental Biology* 3, 748.

28 Quran, Surah Al-Baqarah: 30; Surah Sad: 26; Surah Al An'am: 165.

29 Olawuyi (n 1) 16. See also, Quran, Surah As Shams: 7–8; Muhammad Muinul Islam, "Towards Green Earth: An Islamic Perspective" (October–December 2004) 26 *Asian Affairs* 4, 44.

30 T. K. Farook, "Ecology in Islamic Perspective" (2012) XLVI Radiance Views Weekly 28.

31 Ibid.; Laxman et al. (n 27).

kindness (*ihsan*); (3) protected from damage and abuse; (4) shared to ensure equal access and opportunity without discrimination and corruption; and (5) subject to conservation efforts such as laws covering the conservation of forests, water bodies, and animals including Shari'ah relating to the conservation of land, such as protected zones (*haram*) and the reserves (*hima*).[32]

Islamic law also includes many universal guiding principles pertaining to protecting the environment, including the inviolability of human life, protecting animals and plants, saving land, water, and air, and protecting the balance of nature and biodiversity.[33]

11.2.1 *Principles of Islamic Finance*

To understand the Islamic moral economy system, it is important to examine two key concepts: *khilafah* (vicegerency) and *maqasid al Shari'ah* (the objectives of Islamic law).[34] The concept of *khilafah*, as mentioned earlier, is similarly foundational to the Islamic financial system. Human beings, as vicegerents on earth, have the responsibility (*amana*) to inhabit and build a civilization for the good of all humanity and the environment.[35] This intergenerational responsibility requires good governance to manage resources justly and sustainably and implies the engagement, willingness, capacity, and effort to do so.[36] This definition is in line with the World Commission on Environment and Development's definition of sustainable development that meets the needs of the present without compromising the ability of future generations to meet their own needs.[37]

Maqasid al Shari'ah (objectives of Shari'ah) refers to the divine intentions and moral concepts that Islamic law is based on, such as justice, human dignity, free will, and social cooperation.[38] The objectives of Shari'ah, according to Imam Al-Ghazali, are to promote the well-being of all humans, which lies in safeguarding their *din* (faith), *nafs* (human self/life), *'aql* (reason/intellect), *nasl* (posterity), and *mal* (wealth). Anything that ensures the safeguarding of these five serves the public interest and is deemed *maslaha* (good), while anything negatively impacting them is deemed *mafsadah* (prejudice).[39] Contemporary scholars have integrated

32 Nawal H. Ammar, "Islam, Population and the Environment: A Textual and Juristic View" in Harold G. Coward (ed), *Population, Consumption, and the Environment: Religious and Secular Responses* (NYU Press 1995) 123–136, and 131–132.
33 S. Sikandar Shah Haneef, "Principles of Environmental Law in Islam" (2002) 17 *Arab Law Quarterly* 3, 241.
34 Aassouli (n 11).
35 Haneef (n 33).
36 Aassouli (n 11).
37 Ibid.
38 Ibid.
39 A. Abozaid and A. W. Dusuki, "The Challenges of Realising Maqasid al-Shari'ah in Islamic Banking and Finance" (2007) *IIUM International Conference in Islamic Banking*, 7–8 http://iaif.ir/images/khareji/articles/other/60.pdf accessed February 6, 2024.

new objectives linked to contemporary global issues such as human life and dignity, and environmental preservation, which includes the protection of the environment against damage, pollution, and excessive use of its natural resources.[40]

In addition to striving to achieve the objectives of Shari'ah in all its activities, Islamic finance should not involve elements contrary to Shari'ah principles. According to Hanif, there are four basic principles of Islamic finance: (1) the business or project must be *halal* (permitted), precluding businesses and any income generated from prohibited businesses related to alcohol, pork, prostitution, and gambling; (2) the prohibition of *riba* (interest) in the financial agreement, as stated in the Quran and Sunnah;[41] (3) the prevention of *gharar* (uncertainty) when conducting a trade (*gharar* refers to an undetermined liability, uncertain item of payment, and ambiguous transfer of goods and services of parties involved in a transaction); nd (4) the prohibition of *myser* (gambling), unlawful wealth acquisition, or a means of obtaining wealth easily by chance, through seizing other's rights or otherwise.[42]

Islamic finance also strives to ensure that transactions are linked to real economic activities or transactions and that Islamic financial instruments emphasize risk sharing and equal profit-and-loss sharing through different means of financing, including profit-and-loss sharing partnerships (*mudarabah*), profit-and-loss sharing joint ventures (*musharakah*), and Shari'ah-compliant lending instruments (*sukuk*).[43] Risk sharing aligns with Islamic finance principles of shared responsibility and facilitates equitable distribution of gains and losses, promoting ethical financial practices.

11.3 THE CASE FOR ISLAMIC BIODIVERSITY FINANCING

The *New Nature Economy* report states that over half the world's gross domestic product depends on nature, and its ongoing loss is a systemic risk for the global economy,[44] a risk that the private sector is beginning to recognize. The impetus to advance nature conservation, both as part of responsible investment and corporate social and environmental responsibility and as a driver for sustainable prosperity, is resulting in increased investment in biodiversity. The International Finance Corporation has developed an indicative list of "investment projects, activities, and components that help protect, maintain, or enhance biodiversity and ecosystem services, as well as promote the sustainable management of natural

[40] Aassouli (n 11).

[41] Quran, Surah Ar Rum: 39, Surah An Nisa: 130, Surah Al Baqarah: 275–281.

[42] M. Hanif, "Economic Substance or Legal Form: An Evaluation of Islamic Finance Practice" (2016) 9 *International Journal of Islamic and Middle Eastern Finance and Management* 2, 295.

[43] See Nabil Saleh, "Definition and Formation of Contract under Islamic and Arab Laws" (1990) 5 *Arabic Law Quarterly* 101.

[44] United Nations Environment Programme (UNEP), "State of Financing for Nature: Report" (2021) 10 www.unep.org/resources/state-finance-nature-2021 accessed February 6, 2024.

resources."[45] Biodiversity financing and investment is therefore a rapidly growing subset of green financing which aims to increase the financing of projects aimed at halting biodiversity loss and promoting nature conservation.[46] Businesses, financial institutions, and investors are becoming increasingly aware of the how environmental damage worsens local and community resistance to investment, and they also see that biodiversity loss and environmental damage have negative material impacts on supply chains, capital flows, and employee productivity.[47] Additionally, financial institutions are exposed to reputational and transition risks when financing companies with major negative impacts on biodiversity.[48] This growing realization has seen the rise of nature-based financing and investments in many parts of the world.[49]

Despite this growth, investment in nature-based solutions lags when compared to investment in climate financing. For example, private investment accounts for 56 percent of annual capital flows of US$579 billion into climate investments, as returns to investments in renewable energy investment and energy efficiency are understood by and attractive to commercial banks, investment banks, and institutional investors.[50] However, private finance accounts for only 14 percent of nature-based solutions, US$18 billion out of US$115 billion a year, spanning capital mobilized through sustainable agricultural and forestry supply chains, private equity investments, biodiversity offsets financed by private sectors, philanthropic capital, private finance leveraged by multilateral organizations, and forest and other land use-related carbon markets.[51] Banks and investors are deterred from investment in nature-based solutions as they often lack sufficiently predictable and long-term revenue streams due to the high transaction and structuring costs that reflect their current immaturity and small scale.[52] Risk assessment techniques are mostly backward-looking and can be replaced by forward-looking, scenario-based analyses to better capture the risks associated with climate, biodiversity, and ecosystem service losses, which would help them accurately appraise risk and support high-quality investment decisions.[53] The UNEP suggests financial instruments to derisk investment, including support for result-based financing schemes such as green or

45 International Finance Corporation, Biodiversity Finance Reference Guide (2022) www.ifc.org/en/insights-reports/2022/biodiversity-finance-reference-guide accessed February 6, 2024.

46 Ibid. See also Recommendations of the Taskforce on Nature-Related Financial Disclosures (September 2023) https://tnfd.global/wp-content/uploads/2023/08/Recommendations_of_the_Taskforce_on_Nature-related_Financial_Disclosures_September_2023.pdf?v=1695118661 accessed February 6, 2024.

47 UN Global Compact, UNCTAD, UNEP FI, and UN PRI, "Private Sector Investment and Sustainable Development" (2015) www.unglobalcompact.org/library/1181 accessed February 6, 2024.

48 UNEP (n 44).

49 Ibid.

50 Ibid., 41.

51 Ibid.

52 Ibid.

53 Ibid., 37.

conservation bonds supplied by national and international development finance institutions to support green investments.[54] Islamic financing instruments can fill this gap and encourage more investment.

11.3.1 *Viability of Islamic Financing of Nature and Biodiversity*

The Islamic finance market grew globally by between 10 percent and 15 percent annually from 2000 to 2012, attracting Muslim and non-Muslim countries.[55] Shari'ah-compliant assets rose by more than 160 percent between 2009 and 2011, and in 2016, the industry held about US$1.6 trillion in banking assets concentrated in the GCC countries.[56] The Islamic Finance Development Report 2022 showed that the global Islamic finance industry demonstrated resilience and growth, outperforming pre-COVID levels with a total asset rise of 17 percent reaching US$4.0 trillion, expanding the industry's influence and size. The largest sector, Islamic banking, accounting for 70 percent of the Islamic finance industry grew by 17 percent to US$2.8 trillion, partially due to continued high demand for Islamic banking, especially from noncore Islamic finance jurisdictions, signaling the growth of new markets and the plateauing of the sector in the more mature jurisdictions.[57]

The Islamic Finance Development Indicator (IFDI) provides Islamic finance stakeholders such as governments and financial institutions with a detailed analysis of key factors driving the development and growth of the Islamic financial industry worldwide. As of 2021, the GCC sits at the top IFDI scores by region, followed by Southeast Asia, South Asia, and other MENA countries. Saudi Arabia ranks 2nd, Bahrain 4th, Kuwait 5th, the United Arab Emirates (UAE) 6th, Oman 7th, Qatar 9th, Jordan 13th, and Sudan 14th out of the 136 countries assessed.[58] The GCC and MENA regions come in first and second place when analyzing Islamic Finance Assets by Region at US$1,617 billion and US$1,300 billion, respectively.[59] Similarly, Islamic Banking Assets amount to US$1,188 billion and US$1,100 billion, respectively.[60] The reverse is true for Takaful Assets, the smallest of the Islamic finance industry, accounting for just 2 percent of total global Islamic finance assets, with other MENA countries coming in first at US$30,080 billion followed by GCC countries at US$23,597 billion.[61]

54 Ibid., 34.
55 Ibid.
56 Margherita Calderone et al., "Investing in Financial Inclusion for Climate Resilience and Adaptation: The Role of Islamic Financial Services" Briefing Note for UN Climate Summit 2019 by ODI and Islamic Relief Worldwide (IRW) (May 2019) 4.
57 ICD and Refinitiv (n 18) 6.
58 Ibid., 11–13.
59 Ibid., 25.
60 Ibid., 31.
61 Ibid., 37.

A major contributing factor to its rise and growth is its foundation in equity-based principles, namely: (1) risk sharing and profit-and-loss sharing between the provider and beneficiary of capital, making suppliers of funds investors instead of debtors; (2) asset-based transactions which link financing directly with underlying assets and "real" sector activity; (3) prohibition of interest and speculative behavior which discourages hoarding and prohibits extreme uncertainty, risk, and gambling; and (4) sanctity of contracts and preservation of property rights.[62]

The philosophies of sharing risk and linking finance to the real economy limit the amount of debt created as it cannot exceed the value of the physical asset. Barring derivative instruments for speculation would make the system comparatively resilient and stable.[63] This is evidenced by Calderone et al., quoting Beck et al., when they state that this makes Islamic banks better capitalized, have higher asset quality, and be less likely to disintermediate during crises and, hence, enjoy better stock performance during the recent financial crisis.[64] Islamic finance promotes transactions that are based on profit-and-loss sharing, which contributes to macroeconomic and financial stability.[65]

Not only is Islamic finance, with assets currently at US$2.5 trillion and expected to reach US$3.8 trillion in 2022, well placed to create instruments that drive capital toward the SDGs,[66] but also that it is a stable, less risky industry that is resilient, making it a good alternative for investors.

Regarding sustainability, MENA countries adopted sustainability guidelines through ESG disclosure, SRI, or green *sukuk*, further aligning Islamic finance with global sustainability trends. Saudi Arabia's stock exchange launched ESG disclosure guidelines in October 2021. Oman's Capital Market Authority announced it was developing *sukuk* regulations that cover SRI, including social (*waqf*), sustainable, and green *sukuk*, in July 2021. Kuwait also amended their regulations in February 2022 to introduce new types of bonds, including green and sustainable *sukuk*.[67] This shows the promising growth and development of the Islamic finance industry in the MENA region that can be galvanized to support biodiversity, with the use of Islamic financial instruments helping fill in the financial gaps needed for countries in the MENA region to advance green and sustainability projects, especially through the use of green *sukuk*.

In 2018, Indonesia successfully issued the world's first sovereign green *sukuk* worth US$1.25 billion as part of its initiative to combat climate change.[68] It raised US$2

62 Munawar Iqbal and Philip Molyneux, *Thirty Years of Islamic Banking: History, Performance and Prospects* (Palgrave 2005).
63 Aassouli (n 11).
64 Calderone et al. (n 56).
65 Aassouli (n 11) 12.
66 ICD and Refinitiv (n 18).
67 Ibid., 62–63.
68 D. Siswantoro and H. V. Surya, "Indonesian Green Sukuk (Islamic Bond) of Climate Change: A Revisited Analysis" (2021) 716 *IOP Conference Series: Earth and Environmental Science* 1 https://iopscience.iop.org/article/10.1088/1755-1315/716/1/012044 accessed February 6, 2024.

billion in private investments and financed twenty-three public green and sustainable projects.[69] Since then, research has been conducted on how green *sukuk* could serve as financing to combat climate change issues.[70] Green *sukuk* has been promoted as one of the Islamic financial instruments to fulfill the sustainability gaps in achieving the SDGs,[71] as a financing tool for green projects in the wind energy sector in Italy,[72] for financing sustainable waste management projects in Indonesia,[73] as the tool to fill the financing gap for green projects to mitigate climate change and achieve SDGs in sub-Saharan Africa,[74] and to be considered along with cash *waqf* to help finance afforestation programs by Organization of Islamic Cooperation countries.[75]

Sukuk is the second-largest asset sector in the global Islamic finance industry, growing by 14 percent to US$713 billion in *sukuk* outstanding. The issuance of ESG *sukuk* has reached a new high of US$5.3 billion, led by Saudi Arabia, and continued growth is expected with the mainstreaming of ESG investments and the strong GCC demand to use *sukuk* to help fund green and sustainability transition projects. *Sukuk* issuance in Saudi Arabia grew by 31 percent, from US$38 billion in 2020 to US$49.9 billion in 2021. Malaysia, a more mature *sukuk* market, grew by 11 percent over the same period.[76]

Other studies also support other tools, such as the role of *zakat* in supporting green economic growth in Malaysia.[77] Redistributive systems such as *zakat* (obligatory donations), *sadaqah* (voluntary donations or charity), and *waqf* (endowments on property made to religious, educational, or charitable causes) are all viable tools for Islamic social financing for environmental protection. The UNDP and the Islamic

[69] Greget Kala Buana and Muhammad Didi Hardiana, "Islamic Finance's Answer to SDGs and Climate Change" (July 3, 2019) www.undp.org/blog/islamic-finances-answer-sdgs-and-climate-change accessed February 6, 2024.

[70] Al-Roubaie and Sarea (n 22).

[71] T. Khan, "Reforming Islamic Finance for Achieving Sustainable Development Goals" (2019) 32 *Journal of King Abdulaziz University, Islamic Economics* 1, 3 https://marz.kau.edu.sa/Files/320/Researches/72810_45967.pdf accessed February 6, 2024.

[72] D. Campisi, S. Gitto, and D. Morea, "Shari'ah-Compliant Finance: A Possible Novel Paradigm for Green Economy Investments in Italy" (2018) 10 *Sustainability (Switzerland)* 11, 1 https://doi.org/10.3390/su10113915 accessed February 6, 2024.

[73] H. F. Hariyani and H. Kusuma, "Green Sukuk-Based Project on Sustainable Waste Management in Indonesia" (2020) 12 *Al-Iqtishad: Jurnal Ilmu Ekonomi Syariah* 2, 165 https://doi.org/10.15408/aiq.v12i2.15129 accessed February 6, 2024.

[74] Aassouli (n 11).

[75] S. I. Abdullahi, "Financing Afforestation in the Organization of Islamic Cooperation Countries: What Role for Islamic Economics and Finance?" (2020) 32 *JKAU: Islamic Econ* 2, 161 www.researchgate.net/publication/339791255_Financing_Afforestation_in_the_Organization_of_Islamic_Cooperation_Countries_What_Role_for_Islamic_Economics_and_Finance accessed February 6, 2024.

[76] ICD and Refinitiv (n 18) 6, 46.

[77] N. A. Hamid, R. Muda, M. M. Alam, N. Omar, and F. A. A. Nadzri, "Contribution of Islamic Social Capital on Green Economic Growth in Malaysia" (2019) 9 *International Journal of Business and Management Science* 2, 239.

Development Bank (IsDB) estimated that *zakat* alone could help mobilize US$200 billion to US$1 trillion annually for the SDG agenda.[78] The Organisation for Economic Co-operation and Development cites estimates of *awqaf* assets between US$410 billion and US$3 trillion, with an estimated return of US$150 billion annually.[79] These can potentially be used to finance SDGs and CBD and GBF targets.

Article 20 of the CBD committed developed countries to provide new and additional financial resources to meet the costs of implementing measures that fulfill their obligations to the convention.[80] Although higher levels of resources do not always guarantee higher levels of conservation or sustainable use of biodiversity, research shows that, on average, more resources allocated to biodiversity activities are associated with reduced biodiversity loss.[81]

Financial inclusion strategies can ensure that low-income earners, individual producers, women's collectives, and small and medium-sized enterprises (SMEs), especially those active in arid and semi-arid lands, can access and use formal financial services. Expanding financial inclusion is often seen as a philanthropic activity rather than a business enterprise; for example, in the context of Islamic microfinance, there is a tendency to view *zakat* as the only appropriate source of funding, but charity is not necessarily the best model for developing larger and more reliable commercially motivated streams of funding.[82] These include Islamic microfinance solutions such as *qard hassan* (interest-free loans), *ijara* (leasing), and *takaful* (mutual guaranteed insurance), cooperative models such as mutual insurance based on a group of participants donating funds into a pool that members can then use in the event of specified unfavorable circumstances and expand investment opportunities and reach. The IsDB recognized this and called on experts in Islamic finance to develop new semi-formal Islamic microfinance products for entrepreneurs and SMEs.[83]

Countries in the MENA region can look to Indonesia as an example of how complementary different forms of Islamic finance can be, where *zakat*, Islamic microfinance, and *waqf* can uplift people from poverty. At the same time, *sukuk* can unlock investment to promote inclusive and sustainable economic growth.[84]

78 UNDP and Baznas, "Unlocking the Potential of Zakat and Other Forms of Islamic Finance to Achieve the SDGs in Indonesia" (2018) www.undp.org/indonesia/publications/unlocking-potential-zakat-and-other-forms-islamic-finance-achieve-sdgs-indonesia accessed February 6, 2024.

79 Organisation for Economic Co-operation and Development (OECD), "How Islamic Finance Can Help Achieve the Sustainable Development Goals" (OECD 2020) OECD Development Cooperation Policy Papers, 30.

80 Article 20. Financial Resources, Convention on Biological Diversity www.cbd.int/convention/articles/?a=cbd-20 accessed February 6, 2024.

81 Convention on Biological Diversity, "Estimation of Resources Needed for Implementing the Post-2020 Global Biodiversity Framework" preliminary second report of the Panel of Experts on Resource Mobilization, Subsidiary Body on Implementation (June 18, 2020) CBD/SBI/3/5/Add.2 www.cbd.int/doc/c/c3f7/163d/b1f2c13650603784 2cebc521/sbi-03-05-add2-en.pdf accessed February 6, 2024.

82 Calderone et al. (n.56).

83 Ibid.

84 Buana and Hardiana (n 69).

11.4 LEGAL AND INSTITUTIONAL BARRIERS TO ISLAMIC BIODIVERSITY FINANCING IN THE MENA REGION

Although Islamic finance is one of the fastest-growing emerging global financial markets, it has yet to reach its true potential. In Muslim-majority countries, financial inclusion rates, such as the proportion of the population having borrowed from a bank, are approximately 24 percent below that of non-Muslim countries.[85] Across the MENA region, many disadvantaged Muslims have limited or no access to formal financial systems, either conventional or Islamic. Countries in the MENA region also underperform in access to SME lending relative to countries with similar gross domestic product.[86] Thus, despite the growing awareness of the potential of an Islamic finance approach to financing environmental projects and biodiversity programs specifically, several legal and governance challenges hinder its application in the MENA region.

The section outlines the key legal and institutional barriers to applying Islamic biodiversity financing in the MENA region.

11.4.1 *Lack of Standardized Green Islamic Finance Legislation and Policies*

One of the most significant barriers to the widescale adoption of Islamic green finance is the absence of clear and standardized legal frameworks and policies that tackle the unique nature and risks of the Islamic finance industry.[87] Islamic banks face unique risks that challenge their legal and regulatory frameworks. The industry has two key standard-setters: the Accounting and Auditing Organization for Islamic Financial Institutions (AAOIFI) for Shari'ah accounting and auditing standards and the Islamic Financial Services Board (IFSB) for regulatory and supervisory standards.[88]

The application of these standards, however, is not uniform across countries. A recent International Monetary Fund survey shows that, to date, standards set

85 D. Karlan, A. Osman, and N. Shammout, "To Borrow or Not to Borrow: Religious Norms and the Elasticity of Demand for Credit" Working Paper (February 2017) Poverty Action Lab www.povertyactionlab.org/sites/default/files/research-paper/4267_To-Borrow-or-Not-to-Borrow_Osman-et.al_.Feb%202017pdf.pdf accessed February 6, 2024.

86 D. Pearce, "Financial Inclusion in the Middle East and North Africa: Analysis and Roadmap Recommendations" (World Bank 2010) Financial Flagship www.findevgateway.org/library/financial-inclusion-middle-east-and-north-africa-analysis-and-roadmap-recommendations accessed February 6 , 2024.

87 See Aassouli (n 11).

88 International Monetary Fund, "Islamic Finance: Opportunities, Challenges, and Policy Options" (April 2015) IMF Staff Discussion Note SDN 15/05, 17.

by the AAOIFI and the IFSB are applied in only a limited number of countries. Of the twenty-nine countries surveyed, eight apply AAOIFI accounting standards and six apply IFSB standards regarding risk management. The lack of consistent application of AAOIFI and IFSB standards, especially in countries where Islamic banks are active, risks undermining transparency and creates scope for "regulatory arbitrage." Increased regulatory clarity in banking laws and regulations and enhanced dialogue between Islamic standard-setters and national regulators are needed.[89]

There is also a wide range of approaches regarding the regulatory framework for Islamic banking. Saudi Arabia and the United Arab Emirates indicated that a single integrated regulatory framework applied to all banks, with no reference to Islamic banking or Islamic banks; Jordan and Qatar noted that a single integrated regulatory framework applied to all banks, with references identifying provisions applying only to Islamic banking; Bahrain, Iraq, and Kuwait pointed out that there were two separate independent regulatory frameworks, one for Islamic banking and another for conventional banking; and Lebanon and Syria indicated the existence of a mixed approach, with a similar regulatory framework adopted for areas that apply to Islamic and conventional banks but separate guidelines and regulations issued for areas that are specific to Islamic banking.[90]

Cross-border operations have expanded without regulatory harmonization, and these developments indicate a need for increased regulatory clarity and harmonization, closer cooperation between Islamic and conventional financial standard-setters, and further enhancement of tools for adequate supervision.[91] Regulators also do not always have the capacity or willingness to ensure Shari'ah compliance, undermining the consistency of approaches within and across borders. Greater harmonization should be sought across and within countries, including through better implementation of existing standards for Shari'ah governance and possibly by establishing central boards at the national level.[92]

For Islamic green financing to be successful, robust, standardized, and comprehensive, environmental laws and policies need to be in place. Given the growth rate of Islamic financing in the MENA region and its increasing importance, governments need to provide supportive legal and regulatory frameworks to accelerate the recognition, financing, and implementation of Islamic green financing. Fast-tracking the adoption of robust environmental standards, climate change legislation, and renewable energy policies could open up green investment, which will not only achieve environmental objectives but could also stimulate social and economic co-benefits and progress.

89 Ibid.
90 Ibid., 18.
91 Ibid., 6.
92 Ibid.

11.4.2 *Gaps in the Shari'ah Governance Framework and Challenges in Implementation*

Despite efforts to set Islamic finance standards, in many countries, the industry is governed by a regulatory and supervisory framework developed for conventional finance that does not fully consider the unique nature of Islamic finance.[93] The industry also operates in an environment where legal and tax rules, financial infrastructure, and access to financial safety nets are either absent or, if available, do not adequately consider the unique characteristics of Islamic finance.[94]

There is also a lack of a clear and detailed contractual framework that allocates risks.[95] Given that the application of Islamic financing for green and SDG-linked projects is still in the early stages of development, clear and detailed information on how risks, returns, and responsibilities will be allocated are yet to emerge comprehensively, which could deter investors.

The issuance of *sukuk*, for example, in many countries takes place without a comprehensive strategy to develop the domestic market. Richardson, in his comparative study of responsible *sukuk*, including green *sukuk*, showed some of the challenges faced, such as those experienced by the UAE in promoting green *sukuk* due to a lack of practical actions, internal sustainability programs, and legal and guidance frameworks.[96] National authorities should develop the necessary infrastructure, enhance clarity over investors' rights, and provide a benchmark for the private sector.[97]

Insufficient guidelines on standard operating procedures and templates, and unclear Shari'ah audit requirements, among other things, also raise concerns about the consistency and effectiveness of the Shari'ah governance process across Islamic financial institutions (IFIs), as it leaves room for interpretation and variation in the implementation of Shari'ah compliance measures, leading to discrepancies and challenges in ensuring uniform processes and standards of compliance within the industry, promoting adherence to best practices, and ensuring that IFIs are well equipped to meet Shari'ah governance requirements effectively.

Calderone et al. list several other challenges, especially when expanding Islamic financial services. They include a lack of regulatory clarity, outdated credit assessment techniques, lack of systemic market analysis, the absence of risk-based client identification and eligibility criteria, weak customer protection, low investment in developing financial skills and capabilities, and efforts in building trust in product authenticity.[98]

[93] Ibid., 8.

[94] Ibid.

[95] E. Richardson, "The UAE and Responsible Finance: Can Responsible Finance *Sukūk* Help the UAE in Fulfilling Its Sustainability Ambitions?" (2020) 34 *Arab Law Quarterly* 4, 313 https://doi.org/10.1163/15730255-BJA10013 accessed February 6, 2024.

[96] Ibid.

[97] IMF (n 88) 7.

[98] Calderone et al. (n 56).

AAOIFI issues standards on the Shari'ah Governance of Islamic Finance Institutions regarding responsibility, transparency, and adherence to Shari'ah standards. These are essential for building public trust in the integrity and sanctity of IFIs' business practices.[99] However, studies have shown gaps in Shari'ah governance frameworks and challenges regarding their implementation.

Transparency and accountability mechanisms also need to be tightened. A survey by Hasan found that among IFIs, only 23 percent in the GCC properly examined the Shari'ah Board's performance and contribution to Shari'ah compliance issues. This highlights a deficiency in governance practice, as regular evaluation of Shari'ah Board members' performance is essential to maintain competence and prevent conflicts of interest.[100] Independence is another major factor. Farook and Farooq concluded that appointing scholars by management or shareholders of Islamic banks and financial institutions and their remuneration by the same entities raises concerns about conflicts of interest.[101]

Studies which have evaluated the socially responsible performance of IFIs also highlighted the concern of IFIs with being only focused on Shari'ah compliance rather than being proactive in becoming socially responsible and impactful.[102] This has translated into lagging behind global ESG initiatives by not becoming signatories to principles such as the Equator Principles, UN Principles for Responsible Investment, and the Global Reporting Initiative.[103] Furthermore, they are lagging behind SRI practices in their corporate social reporting policies. Many financial institutions returned weak reporting scores; however, Oman, Bahrain, and Kuwait are generally making good strides for the GCC and MENA regions.[104]

11.4.3 *Capacity Gaps*

A lack of capacity and competency is one of the biggest issues. Although research by Hassan et al. conducted in Saudi Arabia demonstrated that respondent's knowledge and application of the Shari'ah Governance Framework's goals was strong,[105] this is

[99] A. Hassan, M. Sadiq Sohail, and M. M. R. Munshi, "Shariʿah Governance and Agency: Dynamics of Islamic Banking Operations in the Kingdom of Saudi Arabia" (2022) 14 *ISRA International Journal of Islamic Finance* 1, 89.

[100] Z. Hasan, "A Survey on Shari'ah Governance Practices in Malaysia, GCC Countries and the UK" (2011) 4 *International Journal of Islamic and Middle Eastern Finance and Management* 1, 30.

[101] S. Z. Farook and M. O. Farooq, "Shariah Governance, Expertise and Profession: Educational Challenges in Islamic Finance" (2013) 5 *ISRA International Journal of Islamic Finance* 1, 137.

[102] S. Sairally, "Evaluating the Corporate Social Performance of Islamic Financial Institutions: An Empirical Study" (2013) 6 *International Journal of Islamic and Middle Eastern Finance and Management* 3, 238.

[103] S. Sairally, "Integrating Environmental, Social and Governance (ESG) Factors in Islamic Finance: Towards the Realisation of Maqāṣid Al-Sharīʿah" (2015) 7 *ISRA International Journal of Islamic Finance* 2, 145, 151.

[104] ICD and Refinitiv (n 18) 7.

[105] Hassan et al. (n 99).

not the case for other MENA states. A study in Oman showed that the Central Bank of Oman was more lenient in appointing Shari'ah Supervisory Board members due to a limited number of experts.[106]

To successfully navigate the entire project chain of an Islamic green-financed project requires skill and sophistication. To promote Islamic green financing, it is vital to strengthen the capacity of IFIs in core areas of green technology, SDGs, and environmental law. It can be improved in many countries through tailored capacity development programs. Financial institutions can also improve their internal capacity by employing environmental lawyers and practitioners trained to assess legal risks across the entire value chain of environmental and biodiversity projects.[107]

11.4.4 *Shari'ah Compliance Concerns*

The absence of a clear operational framework for all financial intermediaries in the early days of Islamic finance was deeply challenging. While developing models, Islamic finance experts adopted the "replication approach," integrating Shari'ah elements into conventional financial products and eliminating non-compliant aspects.[108] Although this approach facilitated the industry's growth, it now faces criticism for not fully embodying Islamic finance's true spirit and objectives.[109]

The director of the Durham Centre for Islamic Economics and Finance highlighted the growing concerns with norms in the Islamic finance industry moving closer to conventional finance. He states that pursuing perceived benefits using *maslahah* (public interest) has led to a convergence of Islamic finance with mainstream, conventional banking practices resulting in questions regarding the essence versus the form of Islamic finance.[110]

Maslahah has been employed in controversial practices such as organized *tawarruq* (financing option involving purchasing items on credit and selling to a third party for cash), as it is believed that stakeholders, including Muslims, are not only looking for Shari'ah compliance but also pricing parity and would shift to conventional finance if they did not have access to products that offer competitive

[106] Abdulrahman Alnofli and Engku Rabiah Adawiah Engku Ali, "Perceptions on Shariah Governance Framework of Islamic Banking in Oman: Issues and Challenges" (2019) 3 *International Journal of Fiqh and Usul Al-Fiqh Studies* 2, 106.

[107] Aassouli (n 11).

[108] Hanif (n 42).

[109] M. Laldin and H. Furqani, "Innovation versus Replication: Some Notes on the Approaches in Defining *Shari'ah* Compliance in Islamic Finance" (2016) 54 *Al-Jami'ah: Journal of Islamic Studies* 2, 249 https://doi.org/10.14421/ajis.2016.542.249-272 accessed February 6, 2024.

[110] Islamic Economic Talk by Professor Dr Mehmet Asutay (August 30, 2019) https://fem.usim.edu.my/sharing-session-by-professor-mehmet-asutay/ accessed February 6, 2024.

pricing compared to conventional alternatives.[111] Some concerns around *tawarruq* lead to an industry heavily reliant on debt-based financing contracts rather than equity-based financing through real economic activities and risk sharing among parties involved.[112] *Tawarruq* currently holds a dominant position in the Islamic finance market in Malaysia despite being banned by scholars from the GCC due to its resemblance to interest-based loans.

Rosly echoed these sentiments, stating that this convergence raises concerns about whether the industry has maintained its distinctiveness in substance or merely in appearance, especially considering instruments such as *tawarruq*, which have started to resemble interest-bearing loans, blurring the lines between Islamic and conventional banking.[113] Kamali also asserts that due to numerous transformations and the industry's increasing resemblance to conventional products, Islamic finance is facing a significant challenge in terms of losing its stakeholders' credibility and confidence. This erosion of confidence may result from the industry's deviation from its original values, spirit, and objectives.[114]

Hence, it becomes imperative to critically assess the extent of similarities between Islamic finance and its conventional counterpart. While Islamic finance initially aimed to not only fulfill economic needs but also provide a moral and ethical alternative to conventional finance, the evolving landscape and practices within the industry warrant careful consideration and reflection on its alignment with these founding principles.

11.5 UNLOCKING THE FULL POTENTIAL OF ISLAMIC BIODIVERSITY FINANCING: RECOMMENDATIONS

Achieving the goal of advancing nature and biodiversity in the MENA region through Islamic financing requires the commitment of governments across the MENA region to address the legal and regulatory gaps and limitations noted in this chapter through a good governance approach to Islamic green financing. This entails comprehensively mainstreaming Islamic law principles into environmental legislation, policies, programs, budgets, and funds. It also recognizes the importance of incentivizing financial institutions and private sector investors to increase their participation in Shari'ah-compliant financing for biodiversity.[115]

111 R. Haneef, "Is the Ban on 'Organised *Tawarruq*' the Tip of the Iceberg?" (International Shari'ah Research Academy for Islamic Finance 2009) research paper No 2/2009 https://ifikr.isra.my/library/pub/162 accessed February 6, 2024.

112 Abozaid and Dusuki (n 39).

113 S. A. Rosly, "Islamic Finance Practices: Danger of Convergence" (*Wahed: Global Halal Investing Journal* January 30, 2019) https://inceif.edu.my/kmimpact/2019/03/05/islamic-finance-practices-danger-of-convergence/ accessed February 6, 2024.

114 M. H. Kamali, "Ethics and Finance: Perspective of the *Shari'ah* and Its Higher Objectives (Maqasid)" (2012) 3 *Islam and Civilization Renewal* 4 https://icrjournal.org/index.php/icr/article/view/508 accessed February 6, 2024.

115 Aassouli (n 11).

First, national authorities in MENA countries need to accelerate the standardization of Islamic financial law through clear legislation that clarifies and addresses legal contentions and ambiguities. Comprehensive standards and frameworks should be produced in collaboration with regulatory bodies and the government to formulate robust Shari'ah governance regulations, promoting the stability and growth of the Islamic finance industry. These should include standard operating procedures and streamlined reporting and governance processes to facilitate consistency and expedite regulatory assessments, as well as audits and reporting and impact monitoring and assessment tools that will enhance accountability, the credibility of green *sukuk* issuances, and stakeholder protection. Long-term investors prefer legal, tax, and regulatory clarity and well-established market infrastructures.[116] Impact assessment, measurement, and transparency increase investors' confidence about the sustainability impact of the instruments they invest in. Developing environmental and social impact indicators can increase the transparency of green *sukuk* and, therefore, attract a broader base of ethical investors.

Establishing a "coalition of the willing" for Islamic financial services, which promotes the links between the biodiversity arena and the Islamic finance sector in key policy and industry forums, would bring together "conventional" climate and disaster risk financing players and donors with Islamic finance actors to facilitate knowledge exchange and learning. For example, insights gained from successful green bond projects could inform decision-makers developing green *sukuk*. This initiative should also raise awareness and promote research to identify best practices that adhere to Shari'ah principles and knowledge management and sharing.[117]

Second, the knowledge gap and lack of qualified human resources should be addressed through continuous training programs to enhance competency, foster awareness, and contribute to a shift in the institutions' overall mindset from Shari'ah committee members, boards, and management teams to lawyers and civil servants. Efforts should be made to the enhance market awareness of both customers and IFIs about Shari'ah compliance and Islamic financial tools. Awareness campaigns and educational initiatives can play a pivotal role in achieving this objective, as well as promoting sustainable behavior and societal accountability by engaging investors, financial institutions, public institutions, and civil society on sustainable development issues.[118]

Third, given that Islamic green financing is newly developing across MENA countries, regional interaction and knowledge sharing between countries with experience and practice can promote expertise on how Islamic green financing can best preserve biodiversity. GCC countries who have taken the lead with green *sukuk* can share their experience with North African countries who have just begun exploring

[116] Ibid.
[117] Calderone et al. (n 56).
[118] Aassouli (n 11).

them.[119] Policymakers can focus on three main objectives: maintaining financial stability, meeting nature and biodiversity finance needs, and promoting Islamic financing through cooperation and knowledge sharing within the MENA network, and also with other Islamic countries such as Malaysia and Indonesia, which are leading in the field. Rather than replicating conventional financial products, a regional knowledge-sharing platform could help tackle the common challenges and identify the best approaches in designing and implementing green *sukuk* and other Shari'ah-compliant financing initiatives.[120]

11.6 CONCLUSION

Biological resources play a critical role in advancing human society and its economic progress, and biodiversity conservation is vital. The reality is that the threat to species and ecosystems has never been greater, especially in the MENA region, and this drastic decline puts into perspective the importance of achieving targets and finding the means to finance them. The MENA region can bridge this financing gap by maximizing the full value of Islamic finance.

Rooted in the principles of *khilafah* and *maqasid al Shari'ah*, Islamic values and biodiversity goals are aligned in intergenerationally protecting our nature and biodiversity. Islamic finance promotes wealth redistribution, and social equality promotes stable and resilient investment opportunities that include profit-and-loss and risk sharing, making it not only a viable approach to financing biodiversity but one that can attract private investment due to its low-risk nature.

This shows promising growth and development of the Islamic finance industry in the MENA region that can be galvanized to support biodiversity with the use of Islamic financial instruments such as green *sukuk*, *zakat*, *waqf*, and *takaful* to advance green and sustainability projects, with room for development in terms of financial inclusion strategies that can ensure that low-income earners, individual producers, women's collectives, and SMEs also have access to financial services.

To achieve the goal of advancing nature and biodiversity in the MENA region through Islamic financing, commitments from governments across the MENA region are needed to address the legal and regulatory gaps and limitations through a good governance approach to Islamic green financing. National authorities in MENA countries need to accelerate the standardization of Islamic financial law through clear legislation, comprehensive standards, and frameworks that allow for the promotion, stability, and growth of the Islamic finance industry. Knowledge-sharing initiatives, especially regional ones, should promote research, expertise, and best practices on how Islamic green financing can best preserve biodiversity. Efforts should be made to enhance market awareness of both customers and IFIs about

[119] Ibid.
[120] Ibid.

Shari'ah compliance and Islamic financial tools, promoting sustainable behavior and societal accountability and increasing investor confidence.

Islamic financing provides viable opportunities for countries in the MENA region to attract investment from the private sector to fill the financing gap to fund efforts to halt the erosion of biodiversity in the MENA region. As Islamic finance becomes more prevalent, and laws become more standardized and harmonized, this could lead to real sustainable change and protection of one of the most vulnerable natural environments.

12

Toward Securing the Preservation of Wetlands and Environmental Water Share

Hamun Wetlands Case Study

Mohsen Abdollahi

12.1 INTRODUCTION

This chapter examines the need for a nexus and ecosystem approach to the management of wetlands in the context of water share agreements. It examines the nature, scope, and content of the ecosystem approach, barriers to their effective implementation, and innovative legal approaches to promote such strategies.

Wetlands are home to several flora and fauna that make up biodiversity in a country or region.[1] International law therefore emphasizes the need for the preservation of wetlands in order to preserve and conserve biodiversity.[2] According to the Convention on Wetlands of International Importance especially as Waterfowl Habitat (Ramsar Convention),[3] a wetland is "simply an area that holds water either temporarily or permanently. Wetlands include wadis, oases, swamps, marshes, fens, bogs, and mires."[4]

The MENA region is home to 223 wetland ecosystems, in which more than 100 "Wetlands of International Importance" are in Arab region.[5] Iran also is home to twenty-five Wetlands of International Importance,[6] of which the Hamun wetlands are among this list. In this region, in addition to serving a breadth of other functions such as sediment regulation, pollutant filtration, and nutrient cycling, wetlands are natural buffers against droughts, as they store, purify, and replenish water, providing year-round access for domestic and agricultural use.[7]

1 Damilola Olawuyi, *Environmental Law in Arab States* (Oxford University Press 2022) 256–260.
2 Ibid.
3 Convention on Wetlands of International Importance especially as Waterfowl Habitat (adopted February 2, 1971, entered into force December 21, 1975) 996 UNTS 245 (Ramsar Convention).
4 Olawuyi (n 1) 256–260.
5 Ibid., 256–257.
6 See: Hamun-e-Puzak, South End, and Hamun-e-Saberi and Hamun-e-Helmand, The Secretariat of the Convention on Wetlands (Ramsar, Iran 1971), "The List of Wetlands of International Importance" (May 9, 2023) 27 www.ramsar.org/sites/default/files/documents/library/sitelist.pdf accessed February 9, 2024.
7 Hannah Marcus, "Ecosystem-Based Adaptation: An Unseized Opportunity to Combat Water Insecurity in the Middle East" Medium (Planetary Health Alliance, October 14, 2021)

According to the Ramsar Convention, wetlands constitute a resource of great economic, cultural, scientific, and recreational value and the contracting states are committed to the "wise use of wetlands in their territory." Despite the importance of wetlands to biodiversity, they are disappearing three times faster than forests due to climate change, plastic pollution, construction and infrastructure development, the impacts of changing rainfall patterns, and drought, among other environmental factors.[8]

Having in mind the environmental changes and the growing number of environmental norms, the question is how the contracting parties of the existing water management agreements could coherently comply with these agreements and implement their obligations relating to biodiversity and nature conservation under international environmental law in general and conventional and customary law governing international water courses in particular. While Article 5 of the Ramsar Convention has generally obliged contracting parties to consult with each other on implementing obligations arising from the convention in international wetlands, it does not include any rule on the duty of riparian wetland states to allocate the required water share for securing the preservation of wetlands.

The Ramsar Convention is not the only instrument in this regard. The majority of water management agreements adopted prior to emerging international environmental norms regarding the protection of watercourse environment did not take into account the environmental considerations. The Afghan–Iranian Helmand River Water Treaty of 1973 is another salient example in this regard. While the Helmand River is the main source of Hamun internationally registered wetlands, the treaty does not refer to environmental water requirements of them. This raises questions on how to ensure the integrated management of wetlands and water resources in an ecosystems and nexus manner that addresses cross-cutting risks to biodiversity.

The "ecosystem approach," which has been initiated by the 1992 Biodiversity Convention and consolidated by the 1997 Convention on the Law of Non-navigational Uses of International Watercourses, obliges states to protect and preserve the marine environment of international watercourses by "taking into account generally accepted international rules and standards." This chapter examines how the implementation of an ecosystems approach to wetland management can advance biodiversity and nature conservation.

This chapter is divided into five sections. After this introduction, Section 12.2 examines international legal obligation of wetland states. The interplay between international legal regimes of wetlands preservation and watercourses utilization is also discussed. It also deals with the emergence of the ecosystem approach as a

https://phalliance.medium.com/ecosystem-based-adaptation-an-unseized-opportunity-to-combat-water-insecurity-in-the-middle-east-7375e0018687 accessed February 9, 2024.

8 United Nations Environment Programme (UNEP), "'Wetlands and Biodiversity' Is the Theme for World Wetlands Day 2020" (January 30, 2020) www.unep.org/news-and-stories/story/wetlands-and-biodiversity-theme-world-wetlands-day-2020 accessed February 9, 2024.

response to the need to protect international watercourses. Section 12.3 examines legal barriers to the effective implementation of the ecosystem approach, drawing specific lessons from the Hamun wetlands and Hirmand River. Section 12.4 provides recommendations on how to advance nexus and ecosystems approaches in the management of wetlands and watercourses. Section 12.5 is the concluding section.

12.2 WETLANDS AND BIODIVERSITY: INTERNATIONAL LEGAL FRAMEWORK

Wetlands are vital for humans, for other ecosystems, and for our climate, providing essential ecosystem services such as water regulation, including flood control and water purification.[9] Wetland biodiversity matters for our health, our food supply, tourism, and jobs.[10] Therefore, the obligation for countries to protect and conserve the ecosystem of international watercourses and wetlands is a central part of international law. In fact, wetlands protection is the contact point of several legal regimes, including wetland protection, biodiversity preservation, and international water law. The principle of sustainable lakes management, which recognizes the complementarity of water and biodiversity management, is the core aim of these regimes. In this regard, in 2022, the UN Environment Assembly "[r]equests all Member States and members of specialized agencies, and invites relevant international organizations, where applicable, to … protect, conserve, restore and ensure the sustainable use of lakes, including aspects such as water quality, erosion, sedimentation and aquatic biodiversity, through integrated management at all levels, as set out in targets 6.5 and 6.6 of the Sustainable Development Goals."[11] It calls on countries to "support the advancement of sustainable lake management at all levels, in coordination with relevant conventions, as appropriate, including the Convention on Wetlands of International Importance."[12]

This resolution builds on previous international legal instruments, such as the Ramsar Convention, which aim to halt the worldwide loss of all wetlands and to conserve them, through sustainable use and management. The Ramsar Convention was signed in Ramsar, Iran on February 2, 1971.[13] According to the Ramsar Convention, wetlands are of great economic, cultural, scientific, and recreational value and the contracting states[14] are committed to the "wise use of

9 Olawuyi (n 1).
10 Ibid.
11 United Nations Environment Programme (UNEP), "Resolution Adopted by the United Nations Environment Assembly on March 2, 2022 5/4. Sustainable Lake Management" (March 7, 2022) UNEP/EA.5/Res.4, 1(a) https://wedocs.unep.org/bitstream/handle/20.500.11822/39749/K2200671%20-%20UNEP-EA.5-Res.4%20-%20ADVANCE-.pdf?sequence=1&isAllowed=y accessed February 9, 2024.
12 Ibid., para 2(a).
13 Ramsar Convention (n 3).
14 Ibid., Preamble, para 3.

wetlands in their territory."[15] In the case of international wetlands, "the Contracting Parties shall *consult* with each other about implementing obligations arising from this Convention especially in the case of a wetland extending over the territories of more than one Contracting Party or where a water system is shared by Contracting Parties." Despite this general and customary obligation of consultation,[16] among the riparian states there is no reference to the environmental water requirements for these wetlands. It seems that the standard of "wise use of wetlands," has been considered as an adequate guide in this regard.

The Scientific and Technical Review Panel of the Ramsar Convention has published a series of handbooks for the "wise use of wetlands." According to the first one, "wise use of wetlands is the maintenance of their ecological character, achieved through the implementation of ecosystem approaches, within the context of sustainable development."[17] Further, Handbook 10 of this convention provides extensive guidance and recommendations for managing and allocating water resources.[18] In this line, according to the United Nations Economic Commission for Europe's handbook on water allocation in a transboundary context, "understanding water availability for different needs, uses and functions, in different seasons and climate and in development scenarios, is a key requirement for sustainable and equitable water allocation,"[19] and "[i]n modern water allocation arrangements, environmental needs are assessed and an environmental reserve is recommended to be set aside before allocating water to other uses."[20] This handbook also emphasizes the concept of sufficient minimum flow for prevention over abstraction during low-flow periods.[21]

Any allocation of water resources in international wetlands cannot be done without reference to the related rules and principles of international water law.[22] The 1992 Helsinki Convention on the Protection and Use of Transboundary Watercourses

[15] Ibid., Article 3(1): "The Contracting Parties shall formulate and implement their planning so as to promote the conservation of the wetlands included in the List, and as far as possible the wise use of wetlands in their territory."

[16] Construction of a Road in Costa Rica along the San Juan River (*Nicaragua v Costa Rica*) [2015] ICJ Rep 104.

[17] Ramsar Convention Secretariat, "Wise Use of Wetlands: A Conceptual Framework for the Wise Use of Wetlands" Ramsar handbooks for the wise use of wetlands, Vol. 1 (2007) 22 www.gwp.org/globalassets/global/toolbox/references/wise-use-of-wetlands-ramsar-2007.pdf accessed August 15, 2023.

[18] Ramsar Convention Secretariat, "Water Allocation and Management: Guidelines for the Allocation and Management of Water for Maintaining the Ecological Functions of Wetlands" Ramsar handbooks for the wise use of wetlands, Handbook 10 (4th ed., 2010) www.ramsar.org/sites/default/files/documents/pdf/lib/hbk4-10.pdf accessed August 15, 2023.

[19] UNECE, *Handbook on Water Allocation in a Transboundary Context* (United Nations 2021) ECE/MP.WAT/64, 18 https://unece.org/sites/default/files/2022-12/ECE_MP.WAT_64_Handbook%20on%20water%20allocation%20in%20a%20the%20transboundary%20context.pdf accessed February 9, 2024.

[20] Ibid., 41.

[21] Ibid., 42.

[22] Ibid., 24.

and International Lakes (Helsinki Convention),[23] and the 1997 Convention on the Law of the Non-navigational Uses of International Watercourses (Watercourses Convention),[24] are the most relevant instruments in this regard. Furthermore, the Helsinki Convention promotes sustainable use of transboundary waters. While it was originally adopted as a regional treaty in 1992,[25] it became open to ratification by any country in 2016.[26] The Helsinki Convention entered into force on February 6, 2013 and has forty-seven member states.[27] State parties to the Helsinki Convention, inter alia, "shall, take all appropriate measures … (c) To ensure that transboundary waters are used in a reasonable and equitable way, taking into particular account their transboundary character, in the case of activities which cause or are likely to cause transboundary impact."[28] In addition, they are committed to the exchange of information,[29] bilateral and multilateral cooperation,[30] and consultation on the issues covered by the provisions of this convention.[31]

In comparison with the Helsinki Convention, the Watercourses Convention is a global legal framework that establishes basic standards and rules for cooperation between watercourse states on the use, management, and protection of international watercourses. It provides that "the most fundamental obligations contained in the Convention do indeed reflect customary norms."[32] According to Article 5(1) of this convention: "Watercourse States shall in their respective territories utilize an international watercourse in an equitable and reasonable manner." According to paragraph 2 of Article 5, to be equitable and reasonable, the use must also be consistent with adequate protection of the watercourse from pollution and other forms of degradation.[33] Moreover, the "utilization of an international watercourse in an equitable and reasonable manner within the meaning of Article 5 requires

23 Helsinki Convention on the Protection and Use of Transboundary Watercourses and International Lakes (adopted March 17, 1992, entered into force October 6, 1996) (Helsinki Convention, also Water Convention) https://treaties.un.org/Pages/ViewDetails.aspx?src=IND&mtdsg_no=XXVII-5&chapter=27&clang=_en accessed August 15, 2023.

24 United Nations Convention on the Law of the Non-navigational Uses of International Watercourses (May 21, 1997) 36 ILM 700 (Watercourses Convention).

25 Ibid. See Articles 23, 25.

26 See Amendments to Articles 25 and 26 of the Convention on the Protection and Use of Transboundary Watercourses and International Lakes, Madrid (adopted November 28, 2003, entered into force February 6, 2013) ECE/MP.WAT/14; C.N.639.2012 https://treaties.un.org/Pages/ViewDetails.aspx?src=TREATY&mtdsg_no=XXVII-5-b&chapter=27&clang=_en accessed August 15, 2023.

27 Helsinki Convention (n 23).

28 Ibid., Article 2 (2) (c).

29 Ibid., Article 6.

30 Ibid., Article 9.

31 Ibid., Article 10.

32 Stephen McCaffrey, "The UN Convention on the Law of the Non-navigational Uses of International Watercourses: Prospects and Pitfalls" in M. A. Salman and Laurence Boisson de Chazournes (eds), *International Watercourses: Enhancing Cooperation and Managing Conflict*, Technical Paper No 414 (World Bank 1998) 26.

33 Ibid., 19.

taking into account all relevant factors and circumstances, including (a) Geographic, hydrographic, hydrological, climatic, ecological and other factors of a natural character."[34]

In addition to Article 5, watercourse states are obliged to "protect and preserve the ecosystems of international watercourses,"[35] and shall take all necessary measures to "protect and preserve the marine environment, including estuaries, taking into account generally accepted international rules and standards."[36] By using the term of "ecosystems of international watercourses," the Watercourses Convention fostered the initiation of "ecosystem approach," which seeks to integrate and mainstream other environmental considerations in the allocation and management of international wetlands.

12.2.1 *The Emergence of an Ecosystem Approach: A Response to the Need for the Protection of International Watercourses*

As earlier mentioned, the duty to "protect and preserve the ecosystems of international watercourses" is an independent obligation of riparian states. In other words, watercourse states are obliged not only "to utilize an international watercourse in an equitable and reasonable manner but to exercise due diligence to protect and preserve watercourse ecosystems."[37]

The ecosystems approach has principally emerged under the auspices of the 1992 Convention on Biological Diversity (CBD).[38] Article 2 of the CBD provides that "[e]cosystem means a dynamic complex of plant, animal, and micro-organism communities and their nonliving environment interacting as a functional unit." Therefore, an "ecosystem approach" requires consideration of the whole system rather than individual components.[39] It aims to advance the integrated management of land, water, and other aspects of the ecosystem in a manner that advances wetland preservation as well as biodiversity.[40]

In accordance with Article 1 of the CBD, the conservation of ecosystems is one of its three main objectives and Article 8(f) obliges state parties to "rehabilitate and restore degraded ecosystems." Some of the provisions of the CBD may be regarded

34 Watercourse Convention (n 24), Article 6(1).

35 Ibid., Article 20.

36 Ibid., Article 23.

37 McCaffrey (n 32) 19.

38 Owen McIntyre, "The Protection of Freshwater Ecosystems Revisited: Towards a Common Understanding of the 'Ecosystems Approach' to the Protection of Transboundary Water Resources" (2014) 23 *RECIEL* 1, 90.

39 Owen McIntyre, "The Emergence of an 'Ecosystem Approach' to the Protection of International Watercourses under International Law" (2004) 13 *RECIEL* 1, 1.

40 See Convention on Biological Diversity, "Ecosystem Approach" www.cbd.int/ecosystem#:~:text=The%20ecosystem%20approach%20is%20a,use%20in%20an%20equitable%20way accessed October 19, 2023.

relevant in the protection of international watercourses too. These include the duty to cooperate "through international organizations for conservation and sustainable use of biological diversity,"[41] the identification of "processes and categories of activities which have or are likely to have significant adverse impacts on the conservation and sustainable use of biological diversity, and monitor their effects through sampling and other techniques,"[42] impact assessment and minimizing adverse impacts,[43] and an exchange of information.[44] As elaborated under the CBD regime, it "prioritizes conservation with a view to ensuring ecosystem functioning and resilience. It conditions sustainable use to the taking into account of the limits of ecosystem functioning and promotes connectivity."[45]

To advance the ecosystem approach, the fifth meeting of state parties adopted a set of principles to guide the practical implementation of the ecosystem approach,[46] and the United Nations Economic Commission for Europe (UNECE) adopted the 1993 Guidelines on the Ecosystem Approach in Water Management.[47] Article 20 of the Watercourses Convention should be read along these lines as well. Also, the general obligation to "protect and preserve the ecosystems of international watercourses" should be read with respect to the principle of equitable and reasonable utilization set out in Article 5 of the Watercourses Convention. According to the International Law Commission commentary on Article 20, "[t]he obligation to 'protect' the ecosystems of international watercourses is a specific application of the requirement contained in Article 5 that watercourse States are to use and develop an international watercourse in a manner that is consistent with adequate protection thereof."[48]

A similar obligation has been adopted under Article 23, which provides that "Watercourse States shall … take all measures with respect to an international watercourse that are necessary to protect and preserve the marine environment, including estuaries, taking into account generally accepted international rules and standards." While the article emphasizes on the "marine environment," the obligation set forth in Article 23 is not, however, to protect the marine environment,

41 Convention on Biological Diversity, Article 5.

42 Ibid., Article 7(c).

43 Ibid., Article 14 (a).

44 Ibid., Article 17.

45 E. Morgera, "The Ecosystem Approach and the Precautionary Principle" in M. Faure (ed), *Elgar Encyclopedia of Environmental Law* (Edward Elgar 2017) 70–80.

46 See Convention on Biological Diversity Decision V/6, Ecosystem Approach, UN Doc UNEP/CBD/COP/5/23 (June 22, 2000).

47 UN Doc ECE/ENVWA/31 (1993) https://unece.org/DAM/env/water/publications/documents/Library/Old_documents_found_library/ECE_ENVWA_31_eng.pdf accessed August 16, 2023.

48 International Law Commission, "Commentaries on the Draft Articles on the Law of the Non-navigational Uses of International Watercourses and Commentaries Thereto and Resolution on Transboundary Confined Groundwater" (1994) II Yearbook of the International Law Commission, part 2, 119.

per se, but to take measures "with respect to an international watercourse" that are necessary to protect the environment.[49]

In the years after the adoption of the Watercourses Convention, many international conventions and instruments,[50] creating regimes for the utilization of watercourses, have moved beyond the traditional doctrines of the utilization of international watercourses. As McIntyre has argued, the ecosystem-oriented approach has become a normative one that should be taken into account in any regime of utilization and protection of international watercourses.[51] He notes that "[i]t is possible to discern, from the recent practice of States and international organizations in relation to shared water resources, a shift in emphasis from a purely territorial and resource utilization focus, to a more ecosystem-oriented approach."[52] In his recent article he concluded: "As the so-called 'ecosystems approach' receives ever wider and more emphatic support among the international community, any remaining doubts regarding its normative status in international water resources law must inevitably recede."[53]

While the required measures for implementation of the "ecosystems approach" are not much developed,[54] this approach should be regarded as a response to the need for the protection of international watercourses. The reality is that when the continued existence of an international watercourse ecosystem is under threat, there would not be a clear view for the sustainable utilization of such a watercourse, thus the environmental protection of the ecosystem itself is an inevitable obligation.

The Colorado River, and the resulting deterioration of the ecosystem of the Colorado Delta,[55] is a dramatic example in this regard.[56] Due to the overallocation of the waters of the Colorado, freshwater flows into the delta have been reduced by nearly 75 percent during the course of the twentieth century, resulting in a concomitant reduction of delta wetlands to about 5 percent of their original extent.[57] The delta's current ecological condition is characterized by dried mudflats, vegetation loss, and species endangerment. Stakeholders now advocate the addition of a minute to the 1944 Treaty between the USA and Mexico governing allocation of the waters of the river,[58] which would expressly dedicate water to delta conservation.[59]

49 Ibid., 124.
50 McIntyre (n 39) 1.
51 Ibid., 2.
52 Ibid.
53 McIntyre (n 38) 95.
54 Ibid.
55 Reprinted in McIntyre (n 39) 4.
56 The Hamoun international wetlands and international Hirmand watercourse are also discussed in Section 12.3.
57 D. F. Luecke et al., "A Delta Once More: Restoring Riparian and Wetland Habitat in the Colorado Delta" (1999) *Environmental Defense Fund* 4, www.edf.org/sites/default/files/425_delta.pdf accessed September 13, 2024.
58 Treaty Respecting the Utilization of Waters of the Colorado and Tijuana Rivers and of the Rio Grande (February 3, 1944), printed in 3 UNTS 314, 56.
59 See, generally, R. E. Verner, "Short Term Solutions, Interim Surplus Guidelines, and the Future of the Colorado River Delta" (2003) 14 *CJIELP* 2, 241.

12.2.2 *The Legal Status of Ecosystem Obligations*

There are divergent views regarding the legal status of ecosystem obligations. While commentators such as Fuentes,[60] and Brunée and Toope,[61] are reluctant to recognize these obligations as customary, it would appear that the International Law Commission has taken a different approach by declaring that "[t]here is ample precedent for the obligation contained in Article 20 in the practice of States and the work of international organizations," before proceeding to list a wide range of relevant authorities.[62] McCaffrey and McIntyre have reached the same conclusion.[63] McCaffrey, after referring to three principles expressed in the convention (i.e. equitable and reasonable utilization, not to cause significant harm, and to notify potentially affected riparian states of the planned measures on an international watercourse), concluded that "other provisions of the Convention, such as some of those relating to the environment, are closely related to, or even flow from these principles. To the extent that these provisions are based on the fundamental principles, they too might be said to reflect custom."[64]

The ecosystem approach creates an obligation of conduct,[65] which encompasses an obligation of due diligence.[66] As the International Law Commission commentary cited: "As with the obligation to 'protect' ecosystems under Article 20, the obligation to prevent pollution 'that may cause significant harm' includes the duty to exercise due diligence to prevent the threat of such harm."[67] Thus it cannot be read as an absolute or an obligation of result.[68] The most significant procedural due diligence requirements include early interstate notification and consultation, and where necessary negotiation, in respect of potentially harmful planned projects or uses of international watercourses. Each can only meaningfully be performed in conjunction with an environmental impact assessment (EIA) which includes the transboundary effects of the project in question.[69]

[60] X. Fuentes, "Sustainable Development and the Equitable Utilization of International Watercourse" (1998) 69 *BYIL* 171.
[61] Jutta Brunnée and Stephen J. Toope, "Environmental Security and Freshwater Resources: A Case for International Ecosystem Law" (1994) 41 *YIEL* 5, 70–71.
[62] International Law Commission (n 48) 283.
[63] McIntyre (n 38) 95.
[64] McCaffrey (n 32) 27.
[65] An 'obligation of conduct' is an obligation to make an honest endeavour, notwithstanding the outcome.
[66] Ibid., 21. See also International Law Commission (n 48) 122.
[67] Ibid., International Law Commission (n 48) 122.
[68] "Obligations of result" refer to the requirement where a party is bound to achieve a specific result. For the distinction between obligation of conduct and obligation of result in international law see: Rüdiger Wolfrum, "Obligation of Result Versus Obligation of Conduct: Some Thoughts About the Implementation of International Obligations" in Mahnoush H. Arsanjani, Jacob Cogan, Robert Sloane, and Siegfried Wiessner (eds) *Looking to the Future: Essays on International Law in Honor of W. Michael Reisman* (Brill/Nijhoff 2010) 363–383.
[69] Owen McIntyre, "Environmental Protection and the Ecosystem Approach" (2018) *Research Handbook on International Water Law*, 136.

Notwithstanding the clear status of ecosystem obligation in current international environmental law, "the precise implications of an obligation to protect the ecosystems of international watercourses are not altogether clear."[70] The retroactive effect of the ecosystem approach can result in implementation challenges. By recognizing the normative and customary status of the ecosystem approach, watercourse states are under a duty to protect the ecosystems of international watercourses.[71] This includes the obligation to take into account all environmental considerations, including the survival of the ecosystems of international watercourses, in any ongoing and future agreements on the management or allocation of water resources. In this regard, the Economic Commission for Europe's handbook on water allocation in a transboundary context declares that, "in modern water allocation arrangements environmental needs are assessed and an environmental reserve is recommended to be set aside before allocating water to other uses."[72] However, the retroactive application of a new normative approach to previous customary water shares and contractual management of international watercourses is problematic.

Article 23 of the Watercourses Convention obliges watercourse states to take all measures that are necessary to protect and preserve the marine environment of international watercourse, "taking into account generally accepted international rules and standards." If the phrase "generally accepted international rules and standards" is seen as a dynamic criterion, the major parts of the problem will be solved. The International Law Commission commentary provides that "[t]he phrase refers both to rules of general international law and to those derived from international agreements, as well as to standards adopted by states and international organizations pursuant to those agreements."[73] As a result, one cannot consider the "rules of general international law" as a static one.

In the Gabcikovo-Nagymaros Project case (*Hungary v Slovakia*),[74] the International Court of Justice (ICJ) had an opportunity to deal with this problem when "Hungary argued that subsequently imposed requirements of international law in relation to the protection of the environment precluded performance of the Treaty,"[75] and "Slovakia argued, in reply, that none of the intervening developments in environmental law gave rise to norms of jus cogens that would override the Treaty."[76] The ICJ held that

> [n]either of the Parties contended that new peremptory norms of environmental law had emerged since the conclusion of the 1977 Treaty, … the Court wishes to point out that *newly developed norms of environmental law are relevant for the*

[70] McCaffrey, *The Law of International Watercourses* (2nd ed., Oxford University Press 2007) 458.
[71] McIntyre (n 38) 95.
[72] UNECE (n 19) 41.
[73] International Law Commission (n 48) 125.
[74] Gabcikovo-Nagymaros Project case (*Hungary v Slovakia*) [1997] ICJ Rep.
[75] Ibid., para 97.
[76] Ibid.

> *implementation of the Treaty and that the parties* could, by agreement, incorporate them through the application of Articles 15, 19 and 20 of the Treaty. These articles … require the parties, … to take new environmental norms into consideration when agreeing upon the means to be specified in the Joint Contractual Plan.[77]
>
> The awareness of the vulnerability of the environment and the recognition that environmental risks have to be assessed on a continuous basis have become much stronger in the years since the Treaty's conclusion. These new concerns have enhanced the relevance of Articles 15, 19, and 20.[78]

A careful reading of Article 19 of the 1977 treaty shows that, like Article 23 of the 1997 Watercourses Convention, this article is exposed to divergent interpretations. On the other hand, the ICJ, by recalling its opinion that "the environment is not an abstraction but represents the living space, the quality of life and the very health of human beings, including generations unborn,"[79] and the necessity of assessment of "environmental risks on a continuous basis," has considered the phrase "environmental norm" to be a dynamic standard.[80] The court has concluded that "new norms have to be taken into consideration, and such new standards given proper weight, not only when States contemplate new activities but also when continuing with activities begun in the past. This need to reconcile economic development with protection of the environment is aptly expressed in the concept of sustainable development."[81]

In parallel with the ICJ, the Permanent Court of Arbitration has unequivocally found that:

> It is established that principles of international environmental law must be taken into account even when (unlike the present case) interpreting treaties concluded before the development of that body of law. The Iron Rhine Tribunal applied concepts of customary international environmental law to treaties dating back to the mid-nineteenth century, when principles of environmental protection were rarely if ever considered in international agreements and did not form any part of customary international law. Similarly, the International Court of Justice in Gabcíkovo-Nagymaros ruled that, whenever necessary for the application of a treaty, "new norms have to be taken into consideration, and […] new standards given proper weight." It is therefore incumbent upon this Court to interpret and apply this 1960 Treaty in light of the customary international principles for the protection of the environment in force today.[82]

77 Ibid., para 112, emphasis added.
78 id.
79 Advisory Opinion on the Legality of the Threat or Use of Nuclear Weapons [1996] ICJ Rep para 29.
80 [1997] ICJ Rep (n 74) para 112.
81 Ibid., para 141.
82 Arbitration regarding the Indus Waters Kishenganga (*Pakistan v India*) (2013) XXXI, RIAA 452.

Therefore, it can be concluded that while the ecosystem approach is a new customarily emerged normative standard in the regime of the utilization of international watercourses, it should be taken into account in the interpretation and application of both the previous and recent water management agreements. The importance of this finding is shown in Section 12.3, where the critical situation of the Hamun international wetlands makes it necessary to revise the Hirmand River agreement for allocating environmental water share. In Section 12.3 the legal and institutional challenges of the ecosystem approach are discussed.

12.3 LEGAL AND INSTITUTIONAL CHALLENGES OF THE ECOSYSTEM APPROACH: LESSONS FROM THE HAMUN INTERNATIONAL WETLAND CASE STUDY

The challenges of the ecosystem approaches may be discussed from different points of views. Drawing lessons from the Hamun international wetland, this section focuses on the legal and institutional challenges to the implementation of the ecosystems approach in practice.

12.3.1 *The Hamun International Wetlands*

As the third largest lake in Iran,[83] the Hamun wetlands consist of three separate lakes that join to form one large wetland when completely under water.[84] Hamun-Hirmand is in the south/southwestern part, Hamun-e-Sabereen is the northwestern part, and Hamun-e-Pouzakare is located in the northeastern part of the Sistan Plain.[85] The Sistan Basin lies on the Iran–Afghanistan border. Melted snow from the Hindu Kush Mountains of Afghanistan nourishes this dry basin. The Helmand River carries the snowmelt across the Margo Desert and into the Sistan Basin, where the water pools into Lake Hamun.[86]

[83] Middle East Images, "Climate Crisis in Hamun Lake" https://meimages.com/projects/hamun-lake/ accessed February 10, 2024.

[84] European Commission, "Hamoun Is Our Breath – Restoring Wetlands to Save Livelihoods' European Commission International Partnerships" https://international-partnerships.ec.europa.eu/news-and-events/stories/hamoun-our-breath-restoring-wetlands-save-livelihoods_en accessed August 6, 2023.

[85] Iran submitted Hamoun Lake as a Natural Heritage site. See UNESCO World Heritage Convention, "Hamoun Lake" (Date of Submission: February 5, 2008) Ref No: 5276 https://whc.unesco.org/en/tentativelists/5276/ accessed August 1, 2023.

[86] US Department of the Interior, DOI Inspector General, United States Geological Survey (USGS), "Science for Changing World, Lake Hamoun, Iran and Afghanistan" Earth Resources Observation and Science (EROS) Center – Earthshots https://eros.usgs.gov/media-gallery/earthshot/lake-hamoun-iran-and-afghanistan accessed August 11, 2023.

Hamun has been registered as the first Iranian wetland in the List of Wetlands of International Importance of the Ramsar Convention.[87] Due to the natural importance of Hamun Lake, Iran has proceeded to register it in the list of United Nations Educational, Scientific and Cultural Organization World Heritage sites (Natural Site) as well.[88] Hamun is a spring season lake. In seasons of high precipitation, the area of lake is about 5,700 km^2. Approximately 3,800 km^2 of its area lies within Iranian territory and the rest is located in Afghanistan. The lake has great habitats and an abundant variety of flora and fauna. A considerable number of peregrine birds migrate here from distant places. It has been a place of residence since 4000 BC, nomads have been lived here for long time, and the place enjoys a great variety of scenic beauty.[89]

Hamun is located in an extremely arid area which is known for its dust storms and droughts. Therefore, notwithstanding the annual short rainfall in the region, over 90 percent of the total flow to the lake is provided by transboundary Hirmand/ Helmand River.[90] Further, climate change and the unsustainable management of natural resources, including damming by Iran and Afghanistan, have exacerbated the situation in the region such that, over the past twenty years, Hamun has completely dried up. Only in rare years, with an increase in rainfall, have small sections of the lake reappeared.[91] The Helmand River, at approximately 1,300 km in length, is the longest river in Afghanistan. Originating from the Koh-e Bābā heights of the Hindu Kush Mountain range (about 40 km west of Kabul), draining the entire southwestern portion of Afghanistan (approximately 100,000 square miles), the river moves southwest toward the Iranian border, passing through the provinces of Wardak, Oruz-gān, Helmand, and Nimruz. South of Zaranj, the river flows northward, forming the Afghanistan– Iran border for 55 km before emptying into the Hamun lakes.[92]

The Helmand median annual water output is 2.200 million cubic meters and, although its course runs mainly through Afghanistan, its most irrigable banks lie in Iran. "The Sistan provinces in both countries depend on the Helmand almost as much as Egypt does on the Nile."[93]

87 Ramsar Convention Secretariat (n 6) 25–26. According to Article 2(4) of the Convention: "Each Contracting Party shall designate at least one wetland to be included in the List when signing this Convention or when depositing its instrument of ratification or accession, as provided in Article 9."

88 UNESCO World Heritage Convention (n 85).

89 Ibid.

90 Mahdi Akbari et al., "Desiccation of the Transboundary Hamun Lakes between Iran and Afghanistan in Response to Hydro-climatic Droughts and Anthropogenic Activities" (2022) 48 *JGLR* 878.

91 Middle East Images (n 83).

92 Encyclopedia Iranica, "Helmand River i. Geography" www.iranicaonline.org/articles/helmand-river-i accessed August 14, 2023.

93 Ibid.

12.3.2 *The Legal Challenge of the Application of an Ecosystem Approach*

12.3.2.1 The Retroactive Application of the Ecosystem Approach: The Necessity of Integration

As discussed in Section 12.2, the retroactive application of the ecosystem approach to the previous international obligations is a normative challenge. Efforts to apply the ecosystems approach to the legal regime of Hirmand River have revealed the implementation challenges in a practical context. The Hirmand case study shows that the retroactive application of the ecosystem approach cannot effectively protect ecosystems, especially endangered wetlands.

Setting aside of the long history of Iran–Afghanistan dispute over the Hirmand River,[94] the conclusion of the Afghan–Iranian Helman-River Water Treaty in March 13, 1973 is a turning point in this regard. Article II of the treaty allocates about 0.82 km^3 water flow from Hirmand River as the water right of Iran. The article provides that Afghanistan shall deliver Iran an average of 22 m^3/s plus 4 m^3/s (for "goodwill and brotherly relations"),[95] providing a basis for monthly allocation of the Hirmand River flow to Iran. Monthly flow deliveries are based on "normal water year" (Article II), which is defined as a year with total flows upstream of Kajaki Dam being more than 5.661 km^3 between October 1 and the following September 30 (Article I). Therefore, this treaty is flexible in dry years; for example, water deliveries are adjusted proportionally to deviations from predefined normal years (Article IV). Also, Afghanistan must supply water of a quality that can be treated, if necessary, for irrigation and domestic uses (Article VI).[96]

While the Iranian Department of Environment has estimated that, for the ecological restoration of the lakes, 7.67 km^3 environmental flow is needed annually,[97] the 1973 treaty does not anticipate any environmental water share for the Hamun wetlands. Due to the date of the conclusion of the treaty (almost fifty years ago), it does not appear to be coordinated with the ecosystem. In fact, the wording of the Article II is limitative: "The total amount of water from the Helmand River to be delivered by Afghanistan to Iran in a normal water year, is limited to an average flow of twenty-two cubic meters per second." Consequently, Iran utilizes all treaty-allocated water for potable and agricultural uses.[98] Iran reserves its water share

[94] See A. Amini, S. Z. Ghoreishi, and H. Mianabadi, "Understanding 1973 the Helmand Treaty by Invoking Rules of Interpretation According to Vienna Convention 1969" (2021) 11 *JWIM* 2, 249 (in Persian). For the English abstract of the Article, see https://jwim.ut.ac.ir/article_82737.html?lang=en accessed February 10, 2024.

[95] For example, 22 cubic meters per second/4 cubic meters per second.

[96] See also Akbari et al. (n 90) 877.

[97] Iran Department of Environment (DOE) "Determining the Environmental Flow Needs of Hamoun Wetlands" (2014) reprinted in Akbari et al. (n 90) 877.

[98] Akbari et al. (n 90) 877.

in four reservoirs named the Chah Nimeh Reservoirs (CNRs): CNR1 (Cap: 0.220 km^3), CNR2 (Cap: 0.090 km^3), CNR3 (Cap: 0.320 km^3), and the last and largest reservoir, the CNR4 (Cap: 0.810 km^3).[99] First, three reservoirs were constructed in 1983, and the last one was commissioned in 2008.[100] The main purposes of CNRs in Iran are to meet the agricultural (0.4 km^3/yr), domestic (0.11 km^3/yr), and industrial (0.03 km^3/yr) demands of the Sistan region based on the current status of the basin, totaling 0.54 km^3/yr.[101]

The limitative wording of the treaty is not limited to Article II; the last paragraph of Article V strictly specifies that "Iran shall make no claim to the water of Helmand River in excess of the amounts specified in this Treaty, even if additional amount of water may be available in the Helmand Lower Delta and may be put to a beneficial use by Iran." While it seems that the treaty has barred Iran from any claim to the water in excess of the amounts specified in this treaty, the text can be construed to befit an environmental approach. In fact, Iran has been banned from the water in excess of the amounts its water share for itself (for more potable, agricultural, and industrial uses), there is nothing stopping Iran from claiming the water for *internationally* protected wetlands. The Hamun wetlands is saturated with overflow of the river during spring when the CNRs are full and the rest of the overflow is conveyed to the lakes.[102] In addition to climate change and the reduction of precipitation during the past decade, blocking Iran's water share and damming the Hirmand River have exacerbated the situation, leading to the complete evaporation of the lakes.

In fact, the construction of the Kamal Khan Dam (March 2021) on the lower Helmand River in Afghanistan's Nimroz province has severely affected Iran's share of water from the Helmand River, not to mention the amount that flows into Sistan Baluchistan. According to the 1973 treaty, Helmand's water has to be measured and allocated between Iran and Afghanistan at the Kamal Khan Dam. Removing water from the river system upstream, from the historical point of measurement at Kamal Khan Dam, has complicated the water problem even more.[103]

The implementation of the ecosystem approach to previous legal instruments such as the Helmand River Treaty faces the normative challenge of stability and legal certainty. It has been argued that the implementation of this approach "is the apparent conflict between the adaptivity required by the approach and the

[99] Ibid., 878.

[100] Absaran Consulting Company, "Chah Nimeha Water Resources Planning Report: Studies of the Second Phase of Water Supply in Sistan Plain" (2015) (in Farsi), reprinted in: Akbari et al. (n 90) 878–879.

[101] Iran DOE (n 97).

[102] Akbari et al. (n 90) 886.

[103] Fatemeh Aman, "Water Dispute Escalating between Iran and Afghanistan" (2016) South Asia Center, Atlantic Council 6 www.atlanticcouncil.org/wp-content/uploads/2016/09/Water_Dispute_Escalating_between_Iran_and_Afghanistan_web_0830.pdf accessed July 4, 2023.

traditional virtues of law, such as stability and legal certainty."[104] However, as argued by Langlet and Rayfuse, this perceived tension between stability and flexibility is not always inevitable. While legal certainty sometimes acts as a hindrance to adaptivity, it also serves as a framework for driving environmental adaptive change.[105] This is what the ICJ found in the Gabcikovo-Nagymaros Case in 1997. In this case, the ICJ found that

> newly developed norms of environmental law are relevant for the implementation of the Treaty and that the parties could, by agreement, incorporate them through the application of Articles 15, 19 and 20 of the Treaty. These articles do not contain specific obligations of performance but require the parties, in carrying out their obligations to ensure that the quality of water in the Danube is not impaired and that nature is protected, to take new environmental norms into consideration when agreeing upon the means to be specified in the Joint Contractual Plan.
>
> By inserting these evolving provisions in the Treaty, the parties recognized the potential necessity to adapt the Project. Consequently, the Treaty is not static and is open to adapt to emerging norms of international law. By means of Articles 15 and 19, "new environmental norms can be incorporated in the Joint Contractual Plan."[106]

Contrary to the 1977 agreement between the parties of the Gabcikovo-Nagymaros Case, the Afghan–Iranian 1973 Helmund-River Water Treaty is a static instrument.[107] It neither considers the environmental norms nor allows Iran to claim more water share than its contractual right, even if "additional amounts of water be available in the Helmand Lower delta."[108] Therefore, there is no choice but to amend the treaty by taking into account the new environmental norms governing the management of international watercourses, including ecosystem protection obligations, since watercourse states have continuous obligations in this regard under customary international law.

As a matter of fact, Afghanistan, even before building the Kamal Khan Dam, did not respect its obligations under 1973 treaty. By opening the dam, as had been anticipated by Iran, the situation became even worse. Nowadays, Afghanistan is choosing not to deliver the water share of Iran under the 1973 treaty but to reserve the overflow of the river water behind the dam. A recent study shows that "[u]pstream regulations are the main cause of inflow delivery reduction to the lakes. The construction of

[104] Nicolas de Sadeleer, *Environmental Principles: From Political Slogans to Legal Rules* (Oxford University Press 2002) 235.

[105] David Langlet and Rosemary Rayfuse, "Challenges in Implementing the Ecosystem Approach: Lessons Learned" in David Langlet and Rosemary Rayfuse (eds), *The Ecosystem Approach in Ocean Planning and Governance: Perspectives from Europe and beyond* (Brill/Nijhoff 2018) 449–450.

[106] [1997] ICJ Rep (n 74) para 112.

[107] Afghan-Iranian Helmand River Water Treaty (Helmand March 13, 1973) https://faolex.fao.org/docs/pdf/bi174405.pdf accessed February 10, 2024.

[108] Ibid., Article V.

Chah Nimeh Reservoir 4 (capacity of 0.81 km^3 for domestic and agricultural use in a socio-economically disadvantaged region of Iran) and Kamal Khan Dam (capacity 0.05 km^3) has aggravated the situation."[109] The study ends by recommending that riparian countries revisit "the 1973 treaty … to share the Hirmand River inflow considering the environmental right of the lakes."[110]

Current tension between Iran and the Taliban regime happened when the former Iranian president warned the Taliban "to take the issue of [Helmand] water and Iran's share of water seriously." The Taliban hit back with their spokesperson Zabihullah Mujahid, stating that Iranian officials should present their request "using appropriate words."[111] While declaring its commitment to the 1973 treaty, the reality is that the Taliban, concordant with former governments of Afghanistan, has not complied with its obligations under the treaty and has denied the Iranian water share for several years. Surprisingly, the Taliban, in response, claimed the lack of enough water is due to drought,[112] and at same time did not cooperate with the Iranian commissioner for measuring water flow. Whereas the Taliban claim "there is no water in the Kamal Khan dam, and if the water from the Kajaki dam is released, it will not reach there,"[113] its obligation under the treaty is an independent obligation. For the purpose of allocating Iran's water share from the Hirmand flow, the flow of water shall be measured "at the hydrometric station at Dehrawud on the Helmand River upstream from the entrance to Kajaki Reservoir,"[114] either in a "normal water year" or "in year when due to climate factors the amount of flow is less than that of a normal water year."[115] The treaty has variant regulations for different climates in either normal or abnormal water years. Therefore, Afghanistan could not collect all water flow of the river at downstream of the Dehrawud hydrometric station, and at the same time claim that "[i]f we release … [water] to Iran, then it will travel hundreds of kilometers in the dry river of Helmand and reach Iran as currently, there is no water in the Kamal Khan dam, and if the water from the Kajaki dam is released, it will not reach there."[116]

109 Akbari et al. (n 90) 889.

110 Ibid. See also Mahdi Akbari and Ali Torabi Haghighi, "Satellite-Based Agricultural Water Consumption Assessment in the Ungauged and Transboundary Helmand Basin between Iran and Afghanistan" (2022) 13 *Remote Sensing Letters* 12, 1244.

111 Holly Dagres, "Iran and Afghanistan Are Feuding Over the Helmand River: The Water Wars Have No End in Sight" (July 7, 2023) www.atlanticcouncil.org/blogs/iransource/iran-afghanistan-taliban-water-helmand/ accessed August 16, 2023.

112 "[R]ecent years have seen a terrible drought in Afghanistan and the region. As a result, the water table has dropped, several of our provinces, including the Helmand River, are experiencing drought, and there is a lack of water." see Statement of Islamic Emirate regarding recent remarks of Iranian President, No 428 (May 19, 2023) Islamic Emirate of Afghanistan www.alemarahenglish.af/statement-of-islamic-emirate-regarding-recent-remarks-of-iranian-president/ accessed August 16, 2023.

113 Ibid.

114 Article 1(b).

115 Article 4.

116 Statement of Islamic Emirate Afghanistan No 428 (May 19, 2023) (n 112).

Whatever the result of the claims of the parties, the ecosystem of the Hamun wetland is under threat. As a result, it is necessary that the ecosystem approach is officially integrated in the legal regimes for the protection of wetlands and international watercourses and that the institutions of the aforementioned regimes interact with each other regarding the effective protection of endangered ecosystems. The latter issue is discussed in the Section 12.4.

12.3.2.2 Lack of Institutional Coordination between Water and Biodiversity Institutions

The Hirmand case study reveals another challenge of the application of ecosystem approach in the management of Hamun wetlands: a lack of institutional coordination between water and biodiversity institutions.

As a matter of law, the Hirmand Treaty has some arrangements and mechanisms for the implementation of its provisions. According to Article 8: "Each party shall appoint a Commissioner and a Deputy Commissioner from among its nationals who shall represent their respective countries in the implementation of this Treaty." The Complementary Protocol 1 of the treaty specifies the scope of authorities, duties, and responsibilities of the commissioners. However, the Afghan party does not cooperate in this regard. In such a situation, an environmental convention's treaty bodies may play a constructive role. As mentioned earlier,[117] the Hamun wetlands have been registered as the first Iranian wetland in the List of Wetlands of International Importance of the Ramsar Convention from one side, and both riparian states, Iran an Afghanistan, are parties of the CBD from the other side.[118] Both conventions seek the same goal: the protection of the wetlands. Therefore, the coordination between the secretariates of these conventions could foster their efforts of protection in urgent case like the Hamun wetlands.

It should be noted that the Ramsar Convention collaborates with other conventions which focus on biodiversity issues, including the CBD through the Biodiversity Liaison Group,[119] established in 2002,[120] and the Memorandum of Co-operation has been signed between the secretariates of the conventions in 2005.[121] However, these

[117] See Ramsar Convention Secretariat (n 6).

[118] Ibid.

[119] Convention on Biological Diversity, "Liaison Group of Biodiversity-related Conventions" (January 20, 2022) www.cbd.int/blg/ accessed October 10, 2023.

[120] Ramsar Convention Secretariat, "Partnerships with other Conventions" www.ramsar.org/about/partnerships/partnerships-other-conventions accessed October 11, 2023. See also "Partnerships" (4th ed., Ramsar Handbook 10) www.ramsar.org/sites/default/files/documents/pdf/lib/hbk4-05.pdf accessed October 11, 2023.

[121] Memorandum of Co-operation between the Convention on Wetlands (Ramsar, Iran 1971) and the Convention on Biological Diversity (adopted May 10, 2005) (Liaison Group) www.cbd.int/doc/agreements/agmt-ramsar-2005-05-10-moc-web-en.pdf accessed October 11, 2023.

developments are not sufficient and there needs to be a joint mechanism for joint implementation of the conventions.

12.3.2.3 The Necessity of Integration of Local Communities and Private Sector

The local communities are the main beneficiaries of the ecosystem's resources; therefore, their awareness and participation are crucial for the conservation of biodiversity of any ecosystem and protection of wetlands.[122] It is interesting to note that neither the Ramsar or Watercourses Convention paid attention to such participation, whereas the local communities are traditionally interested in the management of the wetlands and watercourses. By contrast, the CBD explicitly recognizes "the desirability of sharing equitably benefits arising from the use of traditional knowledge, innovations and practices relevant to the conservation of biological diversity and the sustainable use of its components."[123] Therefore, state parties

> shall, as far as possible and as appropriate: respect, preserve and maintain knowledge, innovations and practices of indigenous and local communities embodying traditional lifestyles relevant for the conservation and sustainable use of biological diversity and promote their wider application with the approval and involvement of the holders of such knowledge, innovations and practices and encourage the equitable sharing of the benefits arising from the utilization of such knowledge, innovations and practices.[124]

Like local communities, the private sector has long been identified as an important partner of international organizations in their achievement of development goals.[125] While the CBD has obliged its member states to "[e]ncourage cooperation between its governmental authorities and its private sector in developing methods for sustainable use of biological resources,"[126] or "take legislative, administrative or policy measures, as appropriate, with the aim that the private sector facilitates access

122 Such awareness and participation are necessary since "official conservation policies that severely limit human use of natural resources for the sake of biodiversity conservation, such as strict protected areas, too often have harmful effects on livelihoods and the well-being of human populations living in or around these areas," Isabel Ruiz-Mallén, Antonio De la Peña, Maria Elena Méndez-Lopez, and Luciana Porter-Bolland, "Local Participation in Community Conservation: Methodological Contributions" in Luciana Porter-Bolland, Isabel Ruiz-Mallén, Claudia Camacho- Benavides, and Susannah R McCandles (eds), *Community Action for Conservation Mexican Experiences* (Springer 2013) 117.

123 Convention on Biological Diversity, Preamble.

124 Ibid., Article 8(j).

125 United Nations Conference on Trade and Development (UNCTAD), "Private Sector Engagement in Biodiversity-Related Conventions: Special Focus on the Sector of Natural Ingredients for the Cosmetics and Food Industries" (May 11, 2007) https://unctad.org/meeting/private-sector-engagement-biodiversity-related-conventions-special-focus-sector-natural accessed October 12, 2023.

126 Convention on Biological Diversity, Article 10(e).

to, joint development and transfer of technology,"[127] the Ramsar and Watercourses Conventions are silent in this regard. The CBD Conference of Parties (COP) has singled out the private sector as an important player in the conservation, sustainable use of biodiversity, and the equitable sharing of benefits that are derived from this resource.[128]

By finding the importance of the involvement of the local communities and private sector for the preservation of wetlands it is clear that any application of the CBD-based ecosystem approach to the management of international wetlands should involve these partners. In today's globalized world, global governance requires that local communities and the private sector, including multinational enterprises, are involved in any development and management projects.

In sum, local communities are at the heart of any wetlands development and management project and the private sector has access to the financial resources and the latest knowledge and technologies which are necessary for the effective protection of wetlands. Therefore, the application of the ecosystem approach, without the involvement of local communities and the private sector, would be insufficient.

12.4 ADVANCING THE ECOSYSTEMS APPROACH TO BIODIVERSITY MANAGEMENT: RECOMMENDATIONS

The ecosystem approach is a new way of dealing with the parts of the environment which include international wetlands and watercourses. The emergence of this approach was inevitable as a consequence of the rise of environmental awareness since the 1970s, when the majority of international agreements for the management of international wetlands and watercourses had been concluded. Therefore, paying attention to the following recommendation is necessary for the effective protection of wetlands through the application of an ecosystem approach.

12.4.1 *Need for Official Incorporation of the Ecosystem Approach*

The application of an ecosystem approach to international agreements should be analyzed on a case by case basis.[129] Notwithstanding the experience of other legal

[127] Ibid., Article 16(4).

[128] Ibid. See decision VIII/17.

[129] Duncan E.J. Currie, "Ecosystem-Based Management in Multilateral Environmental Agreements: Progress towards Adopting the Ecosystem Approach in the International Management of Living Marine Resources" (2007) *WWF International Global Species Programme*, 6–8 https://wwfeu.awsassets.panda.org/downloads/wwf_ecosystem_paper_final_wlogo.pdf accessed August 16, 2023. Also, see: "The Ecosystem Approach: Its Mandate and Implementation" (August 28, 2007) Deep Sea Conservation Coalition www.sprfmo.int/assets/Meetings/Meetings-before-2013/International-Consultations-2006-to-2009/IntCons-4-2007-Noumea-New-Caledonia/5ad27dd026/SP-04-Inf-3-DSCC-ecosystem-approach-brief.pdf accessed August 16, 2023.

disciplines, such as the CDB,[130] the precise implications of this approach, to protect the ecosystems of international watercourses, are not altogether clear enough.[131] While some academic work has been done in this regard,[132] further normative steps, even through soft law instruments, would be required in order to clarify the implication of this approach. Such steps have already been taken by the adopting the "principles of the ecosystem approach,"[133] under the framework of the CBD, by the CBD/COP) at its 5th meeting. Parties, and other government and international organizations, have been called upon to apply the ecosystem approach by giving consideration to these principles.[134] A similar normative endeavor is recommended under the Ramsar and Watercourses Conventions.

12.4.1.1 Need for Institutional Coordination between Water and Biodiversity Institutions

This chapter showed that three separate legal regimes regarding wetlands, biodiversity, and watercourses have the same goal, which is the preservation and conservation of ecosystems. The ecosystem approach is the contact point between three conventions: the Ramsar Convention (1971), the CBD (1992), and the Watercourses Convention (1997). It can improve the capacity of the secretariats of these conventions for the effective protection of wetlands. This could not be achieved except through close coordination between these conventions. It should be noted that cooperation between the Ramsar Convention and the CBD has already been commenced and the Biodiversity Liaison Group established in this regard.[135] This initiation is a good first step, which should develop through the adoption of a special procedure for joint action in urgent cases such as the desiccating Hamun wetlands. By such joint action, any member state of these conventions could bring international community attention to the environmental crisis in the one internationally registered wetland.

130 See R. D. Smith and E. Maltby, "Using the Ecosystem Approach to Implement the Convention on Biological Diversity: Key Issues and Case Studies" (2003) IUCN https://portals.iucn.org/library/sites/library/files/documents/cem-002.pdf accessed August 16, 2023.

131 McCaffrey (n 70) 458.

132 Ruby Moynihan, "An Ecosystem Approach in International Law Concerning Transboundary Freshwater Ecosystems" in *Transboundary Freshwater Ecosystems in International Law: The Role and Impact of the UNECE Environmental Regime* (Cambridge University Press 2021) 152–201. See also Ruby Moynihan Magsig, "An Ecosystem Approach in International Environmental Law Relevant to Transboundary Freshwater Ecosystems" (2022) 6 *Chinese Journal of Environmental Law* 125.

133 Convention on Biological Diversity, "The Ecosystem Approach and Adaptive Management" (2000) CBD Decision V/6: The Ecosystem Approach, COP 5 of the CBD www.cbd.int/doc/meetings/esa/ecosys-01/other/ecosys-01-dec-cop-05-06-en.pdf accessed August 16, 2023.

134 Ibid., 2.

135 See Liaison Group (n 119).

12.4.1.2 Need for the Integration of Local Communities and the Private Sector in Development and Management Plans

As mentioned in Section 12.3.2.3, the role of local communities and the private sector in development and management plans are significant. The Ramsar and Watercourses Conventions have ignored the capacities of these relevant sectors of local and international societies. As discussed earlier, the integration of these sectors in the management of wetlands is essential for the effective preservation of wetlands. Therefore, as a principle it is recommended that the ecosystem approach should involve all relevant sectors of society including local communities and private sector.[136] By such an integration, from one side, all forms of relevant information, including scientific and indigenous and local knowledge, innovations, and practices will be considered; and scientific and technological development will be absorbed into the management and development plans of wetlands in the other hands. Further, the integration of the private sector into the management and development plans of the wetlands also encourages this sector to invest in and finance those plans.

12.5 CONCLUSION

The legal regime of every aspect of the environment, including international wetlands and watercourses, cannot be addressed in isolation. Accordingly, while the customary "ecosystem approach" has rapidly emerged after the conclusion of the Ramsar Convention and many water management agreements, its obligations should be taken into account in terms of the interpretation and application of those instruments. Judicial decisions and doctrines support this finding. However, the precise implications of this approach to protect the ecosystems of international watercourses are not altogether clear; thus, further normative steps, even through soft instruments, for clarifying the implication of this approach are required. To this end, the adoption of "principles" that are similar to what has been adopted under the framework of the CBD is recommended.[137] Also, the effective application of an ecosystem approach requires that local communities and the private sector should be integrated in development and management plans, and institutional coordination between water and biodiversity institutions should increase. This coordination should be overseen by the adoption of a special procedure for joint action in urgent cases such as the desiccating Hamun wetlands.

The case study in this chapter shows the need for normative and institutional development. The treaty governing the transboundary Hirmand River between Iran

[136] See Principle 12 of the principles of the ecosystem approach that states: "The ecosystem approach should involve all relevant sectors of society and scientific disciplines." CBD Decision V/6: The Ecosystem Approach, COP 5 of the CBD (n 133).

[137] Ibid.

and Afghanistan is the sole water resource of the Hamun international wetlands and prevents Iran from claiming any additional water over that which is allocated. Afghanistan denies any environmental water share for the desiccating lakes, and Iran intends to use all of its water share for growing potable and agricultural uses. The result stifles the last chance of restoring one of the first internationally registered wetlands under the Ramsar Convention. It is therefore imperative for Iran and Afghanistan to amend the treaty in order to allocate an appropriate environmental water share to the Hamun wetlands.

13

Biodiversity and Marine Protected Areas

An Analysis of the Fishing-Oriented MPA Legal Framework in Morocco

Samira Idllalène and Hicham Masski

13.1 INTRODUCTION

This chapter examines the importance of marine protected areas (MPAs) as tools for the management of fish and other marine species. Drawing lessons from the MPA legal framework in Morocco, it analyses the legal gaps and barriers in the management of fishing-oriented MPAs (MPA-Fs) and proposes recommendations on how to strengthen the management of MPAs to advance biodiversity and the protection of the marine and ocean ecosystem.

The Moroccan coastal zone is a major transition area between tropical ecosystems in the south and temperate ones in the north, and between the Atlantic and the Mediterranean. The particularly high productivity of the northwest Atlantic upwelling systems has, from the beginning of the industrialization of fishing vessels (mid-twentieth century), attracted distant fleets.[1] Since the 1980s and the establishment of its Exclusive Economic Zone, Morocco has developed a thriving fishing sector that has become one of the most productive in Africa and the 17th in the world.[2] On the land side, the coastal zone is populated by nearly 9.5 million inhabitants.[3] Since 2000, it has contributed close to 82 percent of national industrial production, 54 percent of tourism, and 71 percent of banking activity.[4] The trend toward littoralization reaches more than 55 percent.[5] Economically coveted, Moroccan coastal areas are home to a wide variety of contrasting ecosystems with diverse habitats that have been under intense pressure for several decades.[6] For example, all bottom species stocks assessed

[1] Kifani Souad, Masski Hicham, and Faraj Abdelmalek, "The Need of an Ecosystem Approach to Fisheries: The Moroccan Upwelling-related Resources Case" (2008) 94 *Fisheries Research* 1, 36, 42.

[2] Food and Agriculture Organization, *The State of World Fisheries and Aquaculture 2022* (FAO 2022).

[3] Haut Commissariat au Plan (HCP), 2010 www.hcp.ma/Les-Comptes-nationaux-provisoires-de-2010_a635.html accessed February 11, 2024.

[4] Ibid.

[5] Ibid.

[6] Kifani Souad et al. (n 1).

in the 2000s are in a state of overexploitation,[7] and this situation persists for the latest published assessments.[8] This situation enhances the vulnerability of marine populations and their hosting ecosystems to natural or anthropogenic pressures.

To address threats to biodiversity, in 2010 Morocco enacted Law 22-07 relating to protected areas.[9] The aim of the law is to classify and conserve specific areas by setting up a network of protected areas covering all natural ecosystems across the country. These ecosystems include wetlands, forests, archaeological sites, and sites with faunal or floristic landscape value. Law 22-07 is in line with the Convention on Biological Diversity (CBD) ratified by Morocco in 1995.[10] According to Article 2 of the CBD, a protected area means "a geographically defined area, which is designated or regulated and managed to achieve specific conservation objectives." MPAs contribute to biodiversity conservation and can help in both mitigation and adaptation to the impacts of climate change.[11] Law 22-07 includes MPAs in the general definition of protected areas. The typology of protected areas under the law is based on the classification made by the Master Plan for Protected Areas (PDAP),[12] established in 1996 by the Moroccan Department of Water and Forests.[13] The PDAP identifies and classifies Sites of Biological and Ecological Interest (SIBE) according to their degree of degradation and the protective measures to which they must be subject by priority. However, since 2010 no MPA has been created on the basis of Law 22-07 on protected areas.[14] In fact, the regulations which make it possible to classify the identified SIBEs into protected areas have never been adopted. Yet new MPAs for

7 Food and Agriculture Organization, *The State of World Fisheries and Aquaculture 2008* (FAO 2008).

8 Institut National de Recherche Halieutique (INRH), "Observatoire Halieutique" https://observatoire-halieutique.ma accessed February 11, 2024.

9 Law No. 22-07 relating to Protected Areas, promulgated by the Dahir No 1-10-123 of July 16, 2010. Official Bulletin No. 5866 (August 19, 2010) 1581.

10 Kingdom of Morocco, National Biodiversity Strategy and Action Plan, Vol. 3 www.cbd.int/countries/?country=ma accessed February 11, 2024. See also: United Nations Environment Programme (UNEP) and the European Union Plan of Action for the Mediterranean, "Le cadre juridique des Aires Marines Protégées au Maroc: Fiches synthétiques" in P. Emmanouilidou et al. (eds), *SPA/RAC* (Projet MedMPA Network 2019).

11 C. M. Roberts et al., "Marine Reserves Can Mitigate and Promote Adaptation to Climate Change" (2017) 114 *Proceedings of the National Academy of Sciences* 24, 6167, 6175.

12 Kingdom of Morocco, "Sustainable Development in Morocco: Achievements and Perspectives, from Rio to Rio +20" Plan Directeur sur les Aires Protégées (Ministry of Energy, Mines, Water and Environment, Department of Environment, June 2012) 39 https://sustainabledevelopment.un.org/content/documents/1010file.pdf accessed February 11, 2024.

13 Samira Idllalène and Hicham Masski, "Les aires marines protégées: nouvel outil de gouvernance côtière ? Le cas du Maroc" in Marie Bonnin et al. (eds), *Aires Marines Protégées Ouest Africaines, défis scientifiques et enjeux sociétaux* (IRD 2015).

14 However, the existing national parks with a marine part were reversed in the legal regime of Law 22-07 in February 2022. See for example, Arrêté du ministre de l'agriculture, de la pêche maritime, du développement rural et des eaux et forêts No 457-22 du 12 rejeb 1443 (14 février 2022) portant classification du Parc national d'Al Hoceima. No 7080 – 5 ramadan 1443 (7 avril 2022). On the same date, two additional national parks with coastal areas (Souss Massa and Khnifiss) were similarly reclassified under the provisions of Law 22-07.

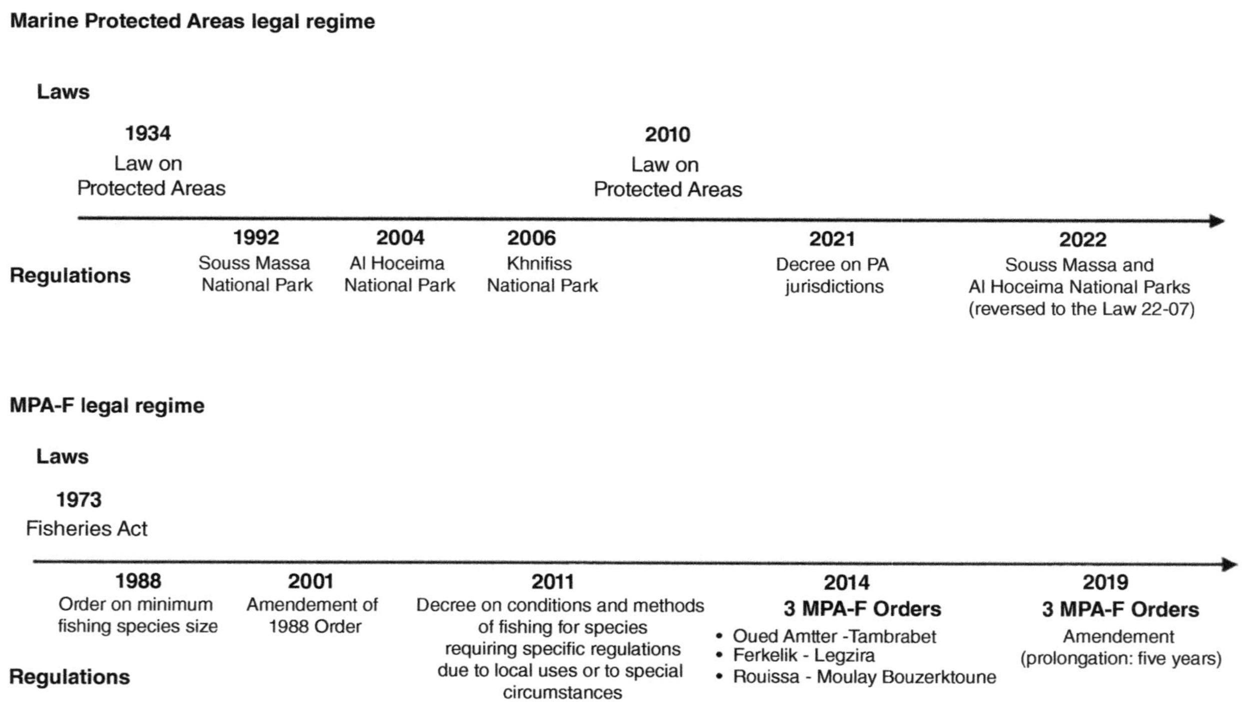

FIGURE 13.1 Concurrent evolution of separate legal regimes for MPAs and MPA-Fs
Source: Authors.

fisheries were de facto created in the framework of the Fisheries Act of 1973 (see Figure 13.1).[15] However, the legal status of these MPAs is disconnected from Law 22-07 on protected areas and can even contradict the protected areas legal regime.

Originally, MPA-Fs were developed in the form of a fisheries management plan within a circumscribed area, with open or closed areas to fishing, regulation of fishing gear, commercial size of certain species, and fishing effort, among other things (Table 13.1).

TABLE 13.1 *Main provisions of the ministerial decisions creating the MPAs for fisheries*

Legal techniques	Explanation
Zoning	The three ministerial decisions (MDs) on MPA-Fs establish three types of zoning: – A defined fishing area where the conditions and technical procedures for fishing the fish species listed in Article 1 are determined. – A no-take zone with a list of prohibited species and either annual or five-year time restrictions. For example, from September 1 to March 1 it is prohibited to fish certain species among the list of species in Article 2 of MD No. 336–314 of (February 3, 2014) ("Al Boran" MPA). The three decisions list the geographic coordinates of each area.
Regulated species	– The three MDs establish lists of species in Article 1 that are affected by the restrictions of these decisions. The names of the species are quoted in French and in Latin. Some of these species are subject, in the no-take areas, to seasonal restrictions on an annual basis or for a period of five years. – All three MDs refer to MD No. 1154–1188 on the minimum legal market size of fish species.
Fishing gear	– The three MDs provide a list of prohibited fishing gear for the species listed in Article 1. They specify that gear-related prohibitions must be listed on the fishing license. Among the fishing gear, the MDs refer to those that are prohibited by the general legislation and regulations in force. – In addition to the fishing gear for which the prohibition is general in the area covered by the MDs, these texts add other types of prohibited fishing gear for which the prohibition is annual. It lists for each type of fishing gear and the dates during which they are prohibited. – One of these MDs (the Al Boran MPA decision) added another fishing instrument to this list, namely the bottom trawl (Article 8). – The Massa MPA restrictions exclude all kinds of fishing nets and the smallest hooks (hook opening less than 6 mm), while the other two MPAs ban or reduce drastically the use of most problematic gear.

(*continued*)

15 Dahir promulgating Law No 1-73-255 of 27 Chaoual 1393 (November 23, 1973) forming Regulations on Maritime Fisheries, Official Bulletin No 3187.

TABLE 13.1 *(continued)*

Legal techniques	Explanation
Fishing vessels	– All three MDs adopt the same rules regarding vessel tonnage restrictions in MPA-Fs which shall not exceed 2 tonnage units. However, this limit has been revised in the amended texts of these MDs published in 2021. In fact, according to these modifying texts, the tonnage of the vessels has been increased to 3 tonnage units.
Other obligations	– The three MDs require the masters of the vessels and the fishing skippers, who have a fishing license for species mentioned in Article 1 in the fishing area defined in Article 2, to comply with the 2011 decree with regard to keeping a fishing logbook and declaring their catches.

Source: Compiled by author.

Three MPA-Fs were created as part of the Millennium Challenge Corporation (MCC)-funded project to assist small-scale fisheries.[16] Ten years after the establishment of the MPA-Fs project, the legal regime underpinning MPA-Fs remains unclear. At the outset, these so-called MPA-Fs have a different legal regime from the classic protected areas legal regime. Indeed, these MPAs are established outside the Law on Protected Areas which was in force at the time of their creation (Figure 13.1).[17]

This chapter examines how such legal barriers and gaps to MPA-F management in Morocco can be coherently addressed to advance biodiversity and for the conservation of fisheries resources and marine ecosystems. The chapter is organized into five sections. After this introduction, Section 13.2 explains the contribution of MPAs to biodiversity and fisheries conservation under international and regional laws. Section 13.3 examines the legal frameworks on MPAs in Morocco, with a focus on the main provisions of Law 22-07 on protected areas, and examines why MPA-Fs have not been integrated into the existing legal framework relating to MPAs, and especially what the consequences are or could be in terms of the place of these MPAs in environmental law, as well as their real effectiveness. Section 13.4 offers recommendations on how to better strengthen the management of MPAs to advance biodiversity and the protection of the marine ecosystems. Section 13.5 is the concluding section.

16 This project is part of the agreement "Compact" (2008–2013) between the Moroccan government and the Millennium Challenge Corporation (MCC). Morocco and the MCC signed in August 2007 a compact agreement of US$697.5 million (in force September 15, 2008), aiming to modernize industrial sectors and target areas in which the country had competitive advantages such as fisheries (five projects in all). The Small-Scale Fisheries Project is one on them and it is designed to modernize fishing practices. See Millennium Challenge Corporation (MCC), *Closed Compact Report: Morocco Compact* (signed: August 31, 2007; entry into force: September 15, 2008; compact end date: September 15, 2013) www.mcc.gov/resources/doc/closed-compact-report-morocco/ accessed February 11, 2024.

17 Law No 22-07 (n 9) 1582.

13.2 THE CONTRIBUTIONS OF MPAS TO BIODIVERSITY AND FISHERIES CONSERVATION

Since the second COP to the CBD in 1995, there has been a growing emphasis on the necessity to conserve marine biodiversity. The Jakarta Mandate on Conservation and sustainable use of marine and coastal biological diversity is an illustration of this interest.[18] In 2004, at the COP to the CBD, there was consensus that "marine and coastal protected areas are vital tools and methods in the preservation and responsible utilization of marine and coastal biodiversity."[19] At COP10 in Nagoya, parties adopted a revised and updated Strategic Plan for Biodiversity, including the Aichi Biodiversity Targets, for the 2011–2020 period.[20] It encompasses five strategic goals. One of these goals aims "[t]o improve the status of biodiversity by safeguarding ecosystems, species and genetic diversity." In fact, parties agreed to postpone the deadline for achieving the objective of conserving 10 percent of their marine and coastal regions within protected areas to 2020 (Aichi Target 11).[21] In addition to this quantitative target, five supplementary qualitative targets relating to MPAs were included. They encompass the following elements: ecological representativeness, effective management, connectivity, integration into the surrounding landscapes and seascapes, and embracing areas of particular importance for biodiversity and ecosystem services.[22] These principles were recently affirmed in the Kunming-Montreal Global Biodiversity Framework as adopted at COP15 in 2022.[23]

The significance of MPAs for biodiversity preservation is also emphasized by numerous other international legal agreements, both on a global and regional scale. As an example, in the Mediterranean region the Protocol concerning Specially Protected

[18] The Jakarta Mandate work program was adopted in 1998 at the COP meeting in Bratislava. It encompasses five components: (1) integrated marine and coastal area management (IMCAM); (2) marine and coastal living resources (MCLR); (3) marine and coastal protected areas (MCPAs); (4) mariculture; (5) alien species and genotypes. See: Convention on Biological Diversity, "Marine and Coastal Biodiversity" (January 25, 2024) www.cbd.int/marine/ accessed February 11, 2024.

[19] Convention on Biological Diversity, "Decision Adopted by the Conference of the Parties to the Convention on Biological Diversity at Its Seventh Meeting VII/5" marine and coastal biological diversity (April 13, 2004) UNEP/CBD/COP/DEC/VII/5 Review of the programme of work on marine and coastal biodiversity www.cbd.int/doc/decisions/cop-07/cop-07-dec-05-en.pdf accessed February 11, 2024.

[20] Convention on Biological Diversity, "Strategic Plan for Biodiversity 2011–2020, Including Aichi Biodiversity Targets" (January 21, 2020) www.cbd.int/sp/ accessed February 11, 2024.

[21] See: UNEP/CBD/COP/10/27. Siân E. Rees et al., "Defining the Qualitative Elements of Aichi Biodiversity Target 11, with Regard to the Marine and Coastal Environment in Order to Strengthen Global Efforts for Marine Biodiversity Conservation Outlined in the United Nations Sustainable Development Goal 14" (2018) 93 *Marine Policy* 250.

[22] Ibid.

[23] See Convention on Biological Diversity, "Decision Adopted by the Conference of the Parties to the Convention on Biological Diversity: The Kunming-Montreal Global Biodiversity Framework" (December 19, 2022) CBD/COP/DEC/15/4 www.cbd.int/doc/decisions/cop-15/cop-15-dec-04-en.pdf accessed February 11, 2024.

Areas and Biological Diversity (SPA/BD) was adopted within the framework of the Barcelona Convention on the Protection of the Marine Environment and Coastal Zone of the Mediterranean (1995).[24] This protocol's objective is to establish a network of specially designated marine areas with the goal of conserving natural habitats that are at risk, as well as habitats crucial for the survival of endangered species.[25] The list of Specially Protected Areas of Mediterranean Importance (SPAMI) was established by the parties with a view to promoting cooperation in the management and conservation of natural areas and the protection of threatened species and their habitats. The SPA/BD Protocol provides the criteria for the choice of protected marine and coastal areas likely to be included on the SPAMI list. For an area to qualify for inclusion in the SPAMI list, it should among other conditions possess a regional value (uniqueness, naturalness, natural and cultural representativeness, diversity, and presence of habitats of crucial importance) and it should have distinctive significance for scientific exploration in the natural sciences and serve as a valuable resource for environmental education or awareness initiatives (Article 8.2 SPA/BD Protocol, Annex 1).[26] Besides, areas eligible for inclusion in the SPAMI list should have a legal status guaranteeing their effective long-term protection (SPA/BD Protocol, Annex 1, C).

Similarly, there is an injunction to create MPAs in the Abidjan Convention for Cooperation in the Protection and Development of the Marine and Coastal Environment of the West and Central Africa Region (March 23, 1981).[27] Article 11 on Specially Protected Areas states: "The Contracting Parties shall, individually or jointly [...] take all appropriate measures to protect and preserve rare or fragile ecosystems as well as the habitat of depleted, threatened or endangered species and other marine life." The article specifies that parties have to establish protected areas and "prohibit or control any activity likely to have adverse effects on the species, ecosystems or biological processes in such areas."

At the global level, the Convention on Wetlands of International Importance especially as Waterfowl Habitat (Ramsar Convention) is an international treaty aimed at the conservation of wetlands around the world.[28] The criteria for the classification of wetlands in the Ramsar List of Wetlands of International Importance are quite similar to those for MPAs under the CBD (representativeness, rarity, and uniqueness) and are important for conserving biodiversity. In fact, Ramsar sites often overlap with other MPAs of different legal status. Among these statutes we find the United Nations

24 Specially Protected Areas Regional Activity Centre (SPA/RAC 2020) www.rac-spa.org/spami accessed February 11, 2024.

25 Ibid.

26 Ibid.

27 United Nations Environment Programme, "West and Central Africa: The Abidjan Convention" www.unep.org/explore-topics/oceans-seas/what-we-do/working-regional-seas/regional-seas-programmes/west-and accessed February 11, 2024.

28 Convention on Wetlands of International Importance especially as Waterfowl Habitat (adopted February 2, 1971, entered into force December 21, 1975) 996 UNTS 245 (Ramsar Convention).

Educational, Scientific and Cultural Organization (UNESCO) biosphere reserves.[29] These are sites (terrestrial, marine, and coastal) that promote solutions reconciling the conservation of biodiversity with its sustainable use. Designated by states under the intergovernmental Man and the Biosphere Program, established by UNESCO in 1970, they have two main objectives.[30] The first is to develop the necessary foundations for the sustainable use and preservation of the biosphere. The second is to improve the relationships between human beings and their environment. Biosphere reserves have three main functions: conservation of biological diversity, cultural and economic development (socio-culturally and environmentally sustainable), and logistical support (for research and education).[31] While they do not have a binding legal status, biosphere reserves are developing rapidly, including at a transboundary level, as is the case with the Intercontinental Biosphere Reserve of the Mediterranean, which extends from Morocco to Spain and encompasses marine areas.[32]

MPAs are also recognized under other international treaties on nature conservation, such as the Convention on the Conservation of Migratory Species of Wild Animals (Bonn Convention, 1979) and the UNESCO Convention on the Protection of the Underwater Cultural Heritage (2001), as well as through specific international treaties on preventing marine pollution, such as the International Convention for the Prevention of Pollution from Ships (1973–1978).[33]

Despite the increased recognition of MPAs, there is scientific debate about whether to consider the measures put in place to manage fishery resources as part of MPAs.[34] Expanding MPAs to include these measures could indeed help achieve the 10 percent target more quickly. Over time, it appears that there has been a convergence between these two approaches.[35] In fact, the categories of protected areas established by the International Union for Conservation of Nature (IUCN), which are globally recognized, allow for the inclusion of protected areas within the

29 UNESCO, "Man and the Biosphere (MAB) Programme: What Are Biosphere Reserves?" www.unesco.org/en/mab/wnbr/about accessed February 11, 2024.

30 Ibid.

31 Ibid.

32 UNESCO, "Intercontinental Biosphere Reserve of the Mediterranean, Morocco/Andalucía, Spain" https://en.unesco.org/biosphere/wnbr/mediterranean accessed February 11, 2024.

33 UNEP-MAP-RAC/SPA, "International Legal Instruments Applied to the Conservation of Marine Biodiversity in the Mediterranean Region and Actors Responsible for Their Implementation and Enforcement" (RAC/SPA Tunis and European Commission 2010) www.cbd.int/doc/meetings/mar/ebsaws-2014-03/other/ebsaws-2014-03-submission-rac-spa-9-en.pdf accessed February 11, 2024.

34 Jean-Yves Weigel et al., "Marine Protected Areas and Fisheries: Bridging the Divide" (2014) 24 *Aquatic Conservation: Marine and Freshwater Ecosystems* S2. See also Tundi Agardy et al., "Dangerous Targets? Unresolved Issues and Ideological Clashes around Marine Protected Areas" (2003) 13 *Aquatic Conservation: Marine and Freshwater Ecosystems* 4, 353, 367. Also: Michael Kriegl et al., "Marine Protected Areas: At the Crossroads of Nature Conservation and Fisheries Management" (2021) 8 *Frontiers in Marine Science* 676264.

35 Jake Rice et al., "The Role of MPAs in Reconciling Fisheries Management with Conservation of Biological Diversity" (2012) 69 *Ocean and Coastal Management* 217, 230.

objective of the sustainable use of resources (Category VI).[36] This category covers natural areas which "are managed to protected their biodiversity in such a way as to provide as sustainable flow of products and services for the community."[37] This inclusion is contingent upon certain conditions. Specifically, four conditions must be fulfilled: (1) The area must align with the general definition of a protected area; (2) at least two-thirds of the area should be maintained and intended to remain in its natural state; (3) large commercial plantations are not allowed; and (4) a management authority must be established.[38] The key point is that the area must be managed so that the long-term protection and maintenance of its biodiversity is assured. Consequently, it could provide an appropriate framework for incorporating measures to protect fisheries resources, especially taking into account that the nature of fisheries management is changing to a more sustainable paradigm through the ecosystem approach to fisheries.[39]

Currently, only 2.7 percent of the ocean is under a high level of protection. This limited level of ocean conservation is primarily attributed to conflicts with fishing and other activities that involve the extraction of resources.[40] The MPA Atlas indicates that there are only a limited number of MPAs in Morocco. Yet Morocco has ratified the conventions mentioned earlier and has enacted a specific law for protected areas that is applicable to MPAs. At the same time, the country has created MPA-Fs. The lack of MPAs in Morocco can be explained by several factors, among which is the fact that MPAs do not have a clear and dedicated legal regime.

13.3 LEGAL FRAMEWORKS ON MPA-FS IN MOROCCO

MPAs are regulated by the general provisions of Law 22-07 on protected areas. The legal framework set for MPAs in international law, including regional instruments that Morocco is a party to, are applicable. In fact, as an example, the national park of Al Hoceima in the Mediterranean was classified as a SPAMI under the Protocol on Marine Protected Areas and Biodiversity in the Mediterranean. The maritime part of this national park was therefore extended adequately (19,600 ha).[41] The

36 Craig L. Shafer, "Arguments for and against IUCN Protected Area Management Category VI with a Review of State Versus Community Governance" (2020) 53 *Journal for Nature Conservation* 125, 697.

37 EUROPARC and IUCN, "Guidelines for Protected Area Management Categories – Interpretation an Application of the Protected Area Management Categories in Europe" (EUROPARC and WCPA, Grafenau Germany, 2000) 13.

38 Ibid.

39 Serge M. Garcia, *The Ecosystem Approach to Fisheries: Issues, Terminology, Principles, Institutional Foundations, Implementation and Outlook* (FAO 2003).

40 Enric Sala et al., "Protecting the Global Ocean for Biodiversity, Food and Climate" (2021) 592 *Nature* 7854, 397, 402.

41 Najoua Ghouat et al., "Environmental Governance Deficiency of Protected Areas in Morocco, Case of Al Hoceima National Park" (2021) 20 *Environmental Engineering and Management Journal (EEMJ)* 11.

regulation that created this national park was also amended in order to be in agreement with Law 22-07 of 2010.[42] Besides, several regulations enacted by the Ministry of Fisheries establish no-take reserves in some specific areas.[43] Furthermore, the Fisheries Act has also provisions (Article 16) that were used for setting MPA-Fs.[44] In application to this article, three regulations create MPA-Fs in Morocco. Nevertheless, the regulations already mentioned lack a specific definition for these MPAs. As noted earlier, even the appellation "MPAs" does not exist in these legal texts. One regulation (a Ministerial Decision (MD) or Order) creates an MPA in the Mediterranean coast and two in the Atlantic coast of Morocco.[45] As shown in Figure 13.2, these legal texts are the following:

- Decision of the Minister of Agriculture and Maritime Fisheries No 337-314 of February 3, 2014, regulating the fishing of certain fish species in the maritime area located in the Atlantic between Ferkelik and Legzira, also called the "Massa" MPA.[46]
- Decision of the Minister of Agriculture and Maritime Fisheries No 335-314 of February 3, 2014, regulating the fishing of certain fish species in the maritime area located in the Atlantic between Rouse and Moulay Bouzerktoune, also called the "Mogador" MPA.[47]

42 The National Park of Al Hoceima in the Moroccan Mediterranean Coast was created in 2004 by a decree for the application of the 1934 Law on National Parks. In 2022, the Ministerial Order by the Ministry of Agriculture, Fisheries, Rural Development, Water and Forests gave the Al Hoceima National Park the legal status of a National Park under Law No 22-07 on Protected Areas. This order somewhat regularized the legal status of the park by placing it under the new regime established in 2010. However, the Order was released on February 2022. See: BO No 7080 – 5 ramadan 1443 (April 7, 2022). Two other national parks with a maritime area (Souss Massa and Khnifiss on the Atlantic coast) were also reclassified within regulations published in the same official bulletin.

43 For example, the regulations relating to the temporary ban on fishing for monk seals, other marine mammals, and certain other marine species. These regulations are continually renewed. Arrêté No 660-19 du 6 rejeb 1440 (13 mars 2019) prorogeant la durée de validité de l'"arrêté No 2806-09 du 10 novembre 2009 relatif à l'interdiction temporaire de pêche des phoques-moines et autres mammifères marins ainsi que de certaines autres espèces marines www.fao.org/faolex/results/details/fr/c/LEX-FAOC092473/ accessed February 11, 2024.

44 It states: "Maritime fisheries not provided for in this Dahir or those that require different regulations due to local customs or specific circumstances shall be regulated by Decree. The same applies to nets intended for the capture of small fish species, such as mullets, eels, anchovies, etc., as well as for traps, fish weirs, longlines, … and other various fishing gear" (translation).

45 According to Moroccan law, the decisions of the ministers (except those provided by the prime minister) are called "arrêtés." In this chapter, we use the appellation Decision(s) or Orders for "arrêtés."

46 Decision of the Minister of Agriculture and Maritime Fisheries No 337-14, 3 Rabii II 1435 (February 3, 2014) regulating the fishing of certain fish species in the maritime area located in the Atlantic between Ferkelik and Legzira, BO No 6326, 23 Rabbi I 1436 (January 15, 2015) 603. The appellation "Massa" MPA comes from the Fisheries Department. This is also the case for the names given to the other MPAs ("Mogador" and "Al Boran").

47 Decision of the Minister of Agriculture and Maritime Fisheries No. 335-14, 3 Rabii II 1435 (February 3, 2014) regulating the fishing of certain fish species in the maritime area located in the Atlantic between Rouissa and Moulay Bouzerktoune, BO no 6326 (January 15, 2015) 599.

- Decision of the Minister of Agriculture and Maritime Fisheries No. 336-314 of February 3, 2014, regulating the fishing of certain fish species in the maritime area located in the Mediterranean between Oued Amtter and Tambrabet, also called the "Al Boran" MPA.[48]

The three MDs were published in the same official bulletin.[49] Each of them states in their preamble that the selection of the locations and the species intended for protection were determined after discussions with the Maritime Fisheries Chambers and their federation. Additionally, they considered the recommendations provided by the National Institute for Research on Maritime Fisheries.[50]

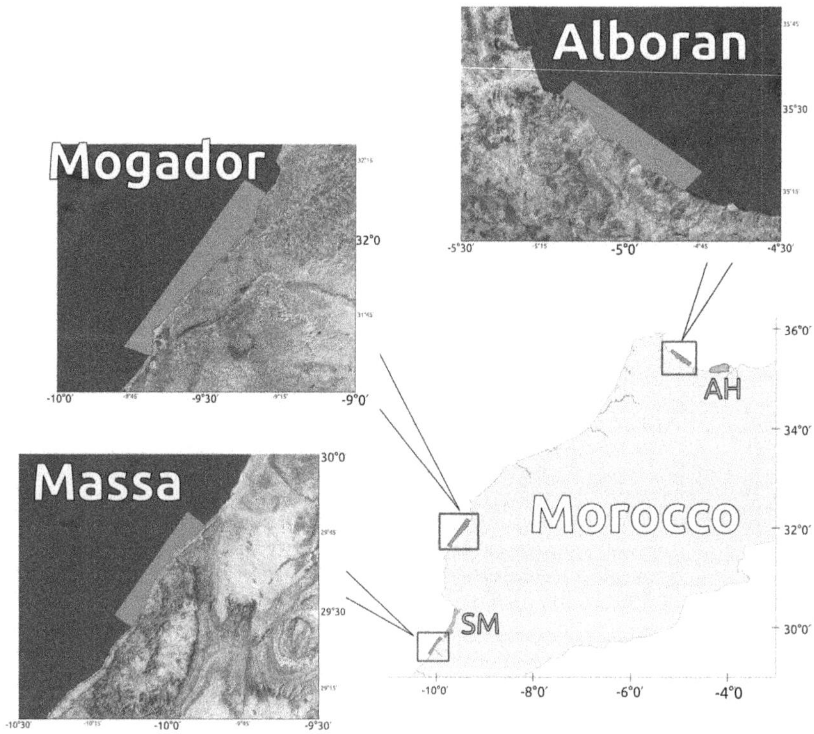

FIGURE 13.2 MPA-F locations

[48] Decision of the Minister of Agriculture and Maritime Fisheries No. 336-14, 3 Rabii II 1435 (February 3, 2014) regulating the fishing of certain fish species in the maritime area located in the Mediterranean between Oued Amtter and Tambrabet, BO no 6322, 9 Rabbi I 1436 (January 1, 2015) 126.

[49] Decision of the Minister of Agriculture and Maritime Fisheries, Official Bulletin No 6326 of January 15, 2015, 599.

[50] INRH (Institut national de recherches halieutiques) is the main scientific institution in charge of providing scientific advice to the fisheries sector. INRH is part of the Ministry of Maritime Fisheries (n 8) www.inrh.ma accessed February 11, 2024.

The three MDs' provisions echo a decree published in 2011, relating to setting the conditions and methods of fishing for species requiring specific regulations due to local uses or special circumstances.[51] This decree itself applies the provisions of the law regulating maritime fisheries.[52] In fact, Article 16 of this law states that: "The maritime fisheries not provided for in the present Dahir or those which must be regulated differently because of local customs or particular circumstances shall be regulated by decree. The same shall apply to nets intended for the capture of small fish: morettes, eels, anchovies, etc.; to traps, pots, longlines, nets and other various fishing gears."[53]

Table 13.1 summarizes the main provisions of these decisions through their five main components: zoning, regulated species, fishing vessels, fishing gears, and other obligations.

On the one hand these Orders are based on Decree No 2-10-164 of April 11, 2011 (the "2011 Decree"). On the other hand, several provisions refer to other MDs that complete them. Indeed, the restrictions on the size of the species are the same in general Fisheries Regulations.[54] Thus, the size of species that can be caught is the same inside and outside the MPAs. These decisions have all been amended in order to extend their duration, as some of their provisions were due to expire five years after their publication in the official bulletin.[55] The amending texts were published in the same Official Bulletin of February 6, 2020.[56] In sum, these MDs do not mention the Law on Protected Areas but are based on the law on fisheries. Therefore, it is not clear if they can actually be considered as protected areas.

[51] Décret No 2-10-164 du 7 Joumada I 1432 (11 avril 2011) fixant les conditions et modalités de pêche des espèces de poissons nécessitant une réglementation particulière en raison des usages locaux ou de circonstances particulières, BO No 5940 – Joumada II 1432 (5 mai 2011).

[52] Dahir promulgating the law No. 1-73-255 of 27 Chaoual 1393 (November 23, 1973) forming Regulations on Maritime Fisheries, Official Bulletin No. 3187, as amended and supplemented.

[53] Translation added.

[54] For example: Order of the Minister of Agriculture and Maritime Fisheries No. 4195-14 of Safar 2, 1436 (November 25, 2014) regulating the fishing of certain species of hake; Order of the Minister of Agriculture and Maritime Fisheries No. 4198-14 of Safar 2, 1436 (November 25, 2014) regulating the fishing of certain species of shrimp; Order of the Minister of Agriculture and Maritime Fisheries No. 4201-14 of Safar 2, 1436 (November 25, 2014) regulating the fishing of large crustaceans.

[55] Except for the MPA on the Atlantic called "Massa" between Ferkelik and Legzira. In fact, the ministerial decision, creating this MPA the five year restriction is not mentioned.

[56] Official Bulletin No 6854 of February 6, 2020 (11 joumada II 1441) 260. These texts are the following: Decision of the Minister of Agriculture, Maritime Fisheries, Rural Development, Water and Forests No. 4065-19 of 23 Rabii II 1441 (December 20, 2019) amending the Decision of the Minister of Agriculture and Maritime Fisheries No. 335-14 of 3 Rabii II 1435 (February 3, 2014) regulating the fishing of certain fish species in the maritime zone located in the Atlantic between Rouissa and Moulay Bouzerktoune; Decision of the Minister of Agriculture, Maritime Fisheries, Rural Development, Water and Forests No. 4067-19 of 23 Rabii II 1441 (December 20, 2019) amending the Decision of the Minister of Agriculture and Maritime Fisheries No. 337-14 of 3 Rabii II 1435 (February 3, 2014) regulating the fishing of certain fish species in the maritime zone located in the Atlantic between Ferkelik and Legzira; Decision of the Minister of Agriculture, Maritime Fisheries, Rural Development, Water and Forests No. 4066-19 of 23 Rabii II 1441 (December 20, 2019) amending and supplementing the Decision the Minister of Agriculture and Maritime Fisheries No. 336-14 of 3 Rabii II 1435 (February 3, 2014) regulating the fishing of certain fish species in the maritime area located in the Mediterranean between Oued Amtter and Tamrabet.

13.3.1 *Protected Areas Legal Regime*

Protected areas in Morocco were governed by a law dating from 1934, which served to establish the existing national parks.[57] The PDAP of 1996 aimed to establish an inventory of potential sites for the creation of protected areas. These SIBEs are classified in this plan in categories according to the priority of their subsequent classification as protected areas by law. This law was passed in 2010 (Law 22-07).[58]

First, the law provides a definition of protected areas. This definition includes both terrestrial and marine areas. The law establishes five categories of protected areas based on the IUCN categories.[59] Law 22-07 repeals the National Parks Act of 1934. As a result, the existing national parks should be placed in one of the new categories established by the new law (Article 40).[60] The same is true for SIBES, which by virtue of their classification in one of these categories will become legally binding protected areas.

In what follows, we first briefly introduce the main provisions of Law 22-07 by explaining the definition and categories of protected areas and then the process and conditions of their management.

13.3.1.1 Definition and Legal Categories of the Protected Areas

Law 22-07 reforms completely the existing legal framework applicable to protected areas. This reform focuses in particular on the following three main aspects: a broader definition of protected areas and their objectives; creation of new categories of protected areas; and stronger involvement of the population and local communities in the creation and management of protected areas. The law defines protected areas as "any geographically delimited, duly recognized, specially developed and managed land and/or marine area for the purpose of ensuring the protection, maintenance and enhancement of biological diversity, the conservation of natural and cultural heritage, its enhancement, its rehabilitation for sustainable development and the prevention of its degradation" (Article 1).[61]

The law makes distinctions among various types of protected areas, varying in their compatibility with sustaining human activities. These protected areas, which

[57] Dahir of September 11, 1934 on the creation of national parks, Official Bulletin of October 25, 1934, 1074.

[58] Law No 22-07 relating to Protected Areas, promulgated by Dahir n1-10-123 of July 16, 2010. BO No 5866 of August 19, 2010, 1582.

[59] Dudley Nigel (eds), *Guidelines for Applying Protected Area Management Categories* (IUCN 2008). See also, Day Jon, Dudley Nigel, Hockings Marc et al., *Guidelines for Applying the IUCN Protected Area Management Categories to Marine Protected Areas* (IUCN 2012).

[60] This was done recently by Orders of the Minister of Agriculture, Maritime Fisheries, Rural Development, and Water and Forests published in the Official Bulletin No 7080 of April 7, 2022.

[61] Dahir No 1-10-123 of 3 Chaabane 1431 (July 16, 2010) promulgating the Law No 22-07 relating to Protected Areas, BO No 5866 of 8 Ramadan 1431 (August 19, 2010) 1581.

can be terrestrial or marine or both, are: the national park, the natural park, the biological reserve, the natural reserve, and the natural site.

The *national park* is a natural area, terrestrial and/or marine, whose purpose is to protect biological diversity, landscape, and cultural values and/or geological formations of special interest and to offer the public opportunities to visit, for cultural, scientific, educational, recreational, and tourist purposes, while respecting the natural environment and the traditions of the local populations.

The *natural park* is distinguished by its aim to protect and enhance the natural heritage while ensuring the maintenance of its ecological functions and the sustainable use of their natural resources.

Biological reserves can only be located on a public domain and have a very strong remit to preserve biological diversity. Their aim is the maintenance of natural species, vegetal or animal, as well as their habitat, in view of their conservation and their preservation.

Natural reserves are established for the purposes of conservation and maintaining the good condition of sedentary or migratory fauna, flora, soil, water, fossils and geological formations, and geomorphological sites of particular interest that should be preserved or rehabilitated. They are used for scientific research and environmental education purposes only.

The *natural site* is dedicated to the protection of one or more natural elements that deserve to be protected because of their rarity, their representativeness, their aesthetic qualities, or their landscape, historical, scientific, cultural, or legendary importance, whose conservation or preservation is of general interest.

The law presents a new method of nature conservation for all these protected areas.

13.3.1.2 Methods of Creation and Management of Protected Areas According to the Law on Protected Areas

According to Law 22-07, protected areas can aim, in addition to the conservation of the natural and cultural heritage, to further scientific research and can contribute to economic and social sustainable development. It also envisions the establishment of a zoning system that distinguishes between areas with different protection regimes, taking into account the development objectives, the constraints arising from the nature of the area, and the constraints justified by the needs of the people living there (Article 3).

Law 22-07 grants the initiative to create protected areas to the administration and to local communities (Article 9). The project for the creation of a protected area is preceded by a three-month public survey. The purpose of this survey is to allow the public to become aware of the project and to formulate its opinions and observations (Article 11). The project for the creation of the protected area must include a presentation of the project as well as a graphic document indicating the zoning, the buffer zone, if any, as well as the boundaries of the protected area (Article 12). It must also present the main orientations for the protection, enhancement, and sustainable development of the protected area's resources as well as a draft regulation setting out the rules for the use of the protected area. The protected area must have a development and management plan, the draft of which is established at the initiative of the competent administration, in consultation with the local communities and the populations concerned (Article 19). The management plan includes specific measures and restrictions to ensure the conservation of the protected area.

Law 22-07 provides that the competent administration may concede the management of the protected area to any legal person of public or private law (Article 25). Legal restrictions on ownership and use rights within the boundaries of the protected areas result upon its creation. In this regard, a compensation procedure is provided (Article 16). Other restrictions and prohibitions regarding a series of activities "likely to harm the natural environment, the conservation of fauna and flora, or to alter the character and elements of the ecosystem of the protected area" are included in the law. Hunting and fishing are among these activities as well as the introduction of animal or plant species (Article 18).

From this, it can be understood that the legal framework for MPAs can be established according to Law 22-07. Therefore, it is legitimate to question the place of MPA-Fs within this framework. As we saw in Section 13.3, the legal framework for MPA-Fs was established outside the Law on Protected Areas (Law 07-22). How then does this framework claim to govern protected areas when it has no connection to the basic law? Can MPA-Fs established outside Law 07-22 be considered as genuine MPAs? This is what we address in the following Section 13.3.2.

13.3.2 *In Search of the Legal Status of MPA-Fs: Legal Barriers and Challenges*

How can we situate the MPA-Fs within the legal and institutional framework applicable to the protection of biodiversity in Morocco? As we have seen, three MDs (or Orders given by the Ministry of Fisheries) deal with the legal regime of these MPA-Fs. However, these MDs do not specify anywhere that they relate to MPAs. In fact, these Orders are referring to "maritime areas" in the Atlantic or Mediterranean where the regulation of fishing for certain species seems relevant due to specific circumstances and particular usages (as stated in the 2011 Decree to which these MDs are referring). So, are these areas truly meeting the criteria of being MPAs? Before addressing these questions, it is important to examine why MPA-Fs were not established under Law 22-07.

13.3.2.1 Why are MPA-Fs Not Established under Law 22-07 on Protected Areas?

MPA-Fs were created in 2014. Law 22-07 on protected areas was enacted in 2010 (Figure 13.1). It would have been logical for the new MPA-Fs to be established under the current law governing protected areas. Yet the government chose to establish the

MPA-Fs under the Fisheries Act. We can explain this choice as being due to several political factors.

First of all, we need to keep in mind that the MPA-Fs were created in the framework of the MCC Small Fisheries Project. The main purpose of this project is to strengthen fishing capacities and to regulate fishing activity.[62] Second, the Fisheries Department was the primary interlocutor in this project. This department handles management tasks and was not responsible for protected areas. Third, the negotiation process was complex and it was difficult to find a suitable category under Law 22-07 that could correspond to MPA-Fs.

13.3.2.2 MPA-Fs are Created under the Small-Scale Fisheries Project Supervised by the Ministry of Fisheries

The diagnosis report preceding the establishment of MPA-Fs highlights that the selection of the appropriate legal framework for their creation was a complex and challenging process. This required several negotiation meetings and the establishment of several scenarios for the integration of these MPAs into the Moroccan legal and institutional system.

The MPA-Fs project was carried out within the framework of the Small-Scale Fishing MCC project, (Small-Scale Fisheries Project) as part of its second component called Fish Landing Sites and Port Facilities Activity.[63] This project falls under the jurisdiction of the Department of Fisheries.[64] Yet the management of protected areas in Morocco was previously (and still is) carried out by the Department for Water and Forests (HCEFLCD),[65] which can be described as a "historical" manager in this field. Therefore, including these new MPAs in one of the categories of Law 22-07 means that HCEFLCD would have had a role in their creation and management. In addition, the lack of regulations to implement Law 22-07, which would at least designate the protected areas management entities, has made the situation challenging.[66]

13.3.2.3 The Sluggish Progression in Enacting Regulations under Law 22-07

One of the arguments advanced during the consultation phase regarding the legal status of MPA-Fs pertains to the slow process of establishing protected areas under Law

[62] See n 16.
[63] Ibid.
[64] See n 3.
[65] The High Commission for Water and Forests and the Fight against Desertification (HCEFLCD), now transformed into an agency: Agence nationale des eaux et forêts www.eauxetforets.gov.ma/SitePages/Index.aspx accessed February 11, 2024.
[66] The Decree of 2021 has now settled the situation since it clarifies the attribution of each ministry as to the management of protected areas. Thus, MPAs would be under the responsibility of the Department of Fisheries, while MPAs with a terrestrial part would come under the competence of both this department and the Department of Forests. Recently the Fisheries Ministry has been expanded to include the Department of Forests. The new name of this Ministry therefore is the Ministry of Agriculture, Maritime Fisheries, Rural Development and Water and Forests.

22-07. It should be recalled that the MPA-Fs project was adopted only a few months before the closing of the Small-Scale Fisheries Project of the Compact between Morocco and the MCC (2008–2013). It was therefore necessary to act quickly.[67]

In fact, in order to establish an MPA under Law 22-07, it would have been necessary to undertake first a public survey of three months, establish and publish the management plan in the official bulletin, and undertake specific measures within the Department of Forests to manage and conserve the protected areas' resources. The sluggish progress in implementing regulations to Law 22-07 remains an ongoing challenge. To date, no particular regulations categorizing the designated SIBEs into one of the protected area categories have been approved. But even assuming that MPA-Fs could be created under Law 22-07, it was necessary to find the category of protected area that best suited them.

It is important to delve into the legal structure of these new MPA-Fs in order to answer to the following question: Are these areas truly meeting the criteria of being MPAs?

13.3.2.4 Should MPA-Fs Be Considered as MPAs?

Upon reviewing the MDs that establish the MPA-Fs, one can observe that they are more oriented toward fisheries management tools rather than marine conservation legal instruments. In fact, these MDs are outside the scope of the protected areas legal regime as established under Law 22-07. Moreover, these regulations are not effective.

13.3.2.5 MPA-F Regulations Are Fisheries Management Legal Tools

In fact, the legal techniques selected in the three MDs creating the new MPA-Fs are the same as the classical techniques used for fisheries management under the Fisheries Act. For example, zoning, which forms the central component of these MDs, is a practice that has been employed by the Fisheries Department in its regulations for a considerable time (Table 13.1).[68]

Two observations can be made in this regard. First, in terms of the legal technique used (zoning, fish size restrictions, etc.), these MDs add almost nothing to the texts that are not labeled "MPAs." Second, as for their content, the contribution of these

[67] Millennium Challenge Corporation, "Final Evaluation Brief: Modernizing the Small-Scale Fisheries Value Chain in Morocco. Fishers Report Improved Conditions, but the Project Did Not Increase Revenues" (November 2022) www.mcc.gov/resources/doc/evalbrief-112822-mar-fisheries accessed February 11, 2024.

[68] For example, the Decision of the Minister of Agriculture and Maritime Fisheries No 4198-14 (November 25, 2014) regulating the fishing of certain species of shrimp. Arrêté du ministre de l'agriculture et de la pêche maritime No 4198-14 du 2 safar 1436 (25 novembre 2014) règlementant la pêche de certaines espèces de crevettes, BO No 6322, rabii I 1436 (1er janvier 2015), p. 136. For more examples, see n 57.

texts lies in the fact that they add a layer in terms of seasons and duration of the prohibition and restriction rules. Basically, they are part of these regulations. In sum, their added value to fisheries regulation is more quantitative rather than qualitative.

In fact, from a strict legal viewpoint, and taking the example of the three so-called MPA-Fs, it could be argued that all the MDs based on the 2011 decree are also establishing MPA-Fs.[69] Indeed, the difference between these MDs and the three MDs creating the MPA-Fs is the fact that the three MDs are applicable to several species whereas the other MDs target a single species or at least one category of species. Apart from this, the two categories of texts (i.e. the so-called MPA-F MDs on the one hand, and the other MD targeting unique species on the other hand) contain the same types of provisions, namely: zoning, prohibition of certain types of fishing gear, restrictions on the tonnage of vessels authorized to fish, restrictions on the size of species, and an obligation to land the catches. For example, the restrictions about nets and hooks (hook opening less than 6 mm) are primarily intended to protect the smallest fish and reduce bycatch. However, these restrictions are almost the same everywhere, even outside the MPA.[70]

If a comprehensive examination of the regulations of MPA-Fs and other fishing regulations established under the 2011 decree demonstrates that the legal regulations of MPA-Fs lack substantial progress compared to the existing fishing regulations, it would be beneficial to evaluate whether these texts provide any additional advantages compared to the legislation governing protected areas.

In contrast to Law 22-07, the regulations of MPA-Fs do not include the fundamental conditions commonly found in legislation governing protected areas.[71] Consequently, MPA-Fs can be viewed as legal anomalies.

13.3.2.6 MPA-Fs Operate Outside the Scope of Foundational Protected Area Law

MPA-F regulations make no mention of the fact that they are MPAs. The name "MPA-Fs" comes mainly from the communication around the MCC Small-Scale Fisheries Project made by the Department of Fisheries and by the MCC itself. The legal texts establishing these "MPAs" come under the legislation of marine fisheries and not of protected areas. On the other hand, by analyzing their content and, in a preliminary way, their implementation, one realizes that these "MPAs," instituted far from the legislation on protected areas, may have little or no real added value in advancing biodiversity conservation.

69 Ibid. This is the case for example for Order of the Minister of Agriculture and Maritime Fisheries No. 4198-14 of Safar 2, 1436 (November 25, 2014) regulating the fishing of certain species of shrimp. See footnote 57 above.

70 See Section 13.1.

71 Lausche Barbara, "Guidelines for Protected Areas Legislation" (2011) 81 *IUCN Environmental Policy and Law Paper*.

In fact, as mentioned earlier, Law 22-07 is the legal framework for establishing protected areas according to a specific procedure and conditions. These conditions are notably: the public consulting before the creation of the MPA, and the management plan and committee. Regarding the first aspect, it is true that the creation of the MPA-Fs was preceded by a process of consultation with the fisheries community. Indeed, during the implementation phase of the national strategy for MPA-Fs, a "selection stage" involved the utilization of a structured multicriteria approach to pinpoint pilot sites. This process included consultation with stakeholders and scientists. Prior to the establishment of the MPA-Fs, surveys were conducted in 2012 in the selected areas involving the local fisheries' administration and fishermen. Thematic focus groups were conducted in each of the three selected areas and a scientific fisheries survey was conducted in the Mediterranean.[72] The results were used for the preparation of the MPA-F management plans.[73]

As for the management plans, they were intended to be used as guides for the MPA users and managers. They identified the Fisheries Department as the authority responsible for the application of the management plan and included the creation of a national consultative committee, a scientific committee, and a local management committee.[74] The management plans give the geographic limits of the MPA-Fs and those of the no-take areas identified inside the limits of the MPA-Fs, and then detail all the management rules.[75] These plans also included sections detailing: (1) the financial sources for the administration of the MPA-Fs, (2) the capacity building of the managers, (3) the equipment dedicated to the surveillance, and (4) surveillance and enforcing regulations. These management plans, which had a validity of five years after the MPA-Fs Declaration (2015), have neither been published nor been used for the management of the MPA-Fs.

Therefore, on-the-ground MPA-Fs are still largely unknown to the fishermen. In fact, about half of the ports' staff, as well as fishermen at project sites near MPA-Fs, and several government agency employees had no knowledge of the status of MPA-Fs.[76] This point was raised in the evaluation report of the Small-Scale Fisheries Project, which provides interesting details on the implementation (or rather the lack of implementation) of the MDs creating the MPA-Fs.[77] In this sense, the report indicates that the majority of personnel and fishermen who were cognizant of the regulations (such as the bans on harvesting specific species within the "MPAs" or the

72 Masski Hicham, "Investigation of a Subtidal Fish Community in a South-Western Mediterranean Settlement Area of Morocco" (2015) 31 *Journal of Applied Ichthyology* 1, 208, 210.

73 One of the authors, Masski Hicham, was part of the whole project as a fisheries ecologist and was one of the two key experts during the "selection stage."

74 Tarik Dahou et al., "Savoirs experts vs savoirs territoriaux" (2023) 14 *Développement durable et territoires* 1 http://journals.openedition.org/developpementdurable/22421 accessed February 11, 2024.

75 Ibid.

76 Abbie Turiansky et al., *Morocco Fisheries Evaluation Final Report* (Mathematica 2021) 61.

77 Ibid.

restrictions on certain fishing equipment) understood that these regulations were either not being enforced or that fishermen were not adhering to them.[78]

As for the government stakeholders, even if they were aware of the status of the MPAs, they "gave mixed reports; some stated that the regulations were in place and others believed that the MPA sites had not yet been activated."[79] The report underlines the problem of the enforcement of these MPAs, particularly in the absence of basic conditions constituting the MPAs, such as the monitoring committee. Yet governance is a key factor in protected area effectiveness as it is widely demonstrated.[80] It is also provided for in Law 22-07.[81] Nevertheless, the MPAs are not instituted in the framework of this law. The Maritime Fisheries Act does not mention a management committee for MPAs, nor does it mention MPAs anywhere. As we have seen, this law, which served as a basis for the three MDs creating MPA-Fs, only deals with the regulation of fisheries, including in terms of their rational management. Its Article 16, about particular circumstances justifying the adoption of specific fisheries management measures, is not sufficient as a legislative framework for MPAs. The lack of a management committee and of a published management plan for the MPA-Fs can explain their noneffectiveness.

13.3.2.7 The Legal Restrictions in the MPA-Fs Are Not Effective as Tools for Fisheries Conservation

MPA-Fs regulations refer to a Ministerial Order of 1988 determining the minimum allowable catch size.[82] The problem with this Ministerial Order is that it fails to safeguard juvenile individuals of most bottom fish species until they reach sexual maturity. Among the twenty-seven species or groups of species (e.g. *Pagrus sp.*) covered by the 1988 Order, twenty-three species have a minimum catch size allowance based on their length at first maturity, and ten species have a length at first maturity that is at least 1.5 times greater than the allowed catch size.

Another frequently employed regulatory measure involves temporarily prohibiting the use of specific fishing equipment or the harvesting of certain species, known as fishing time closure. The goal of these methods is to protect sensitive ecological periods in the fish life cycle, especially adult spawners and spawning habitats. The prohibition of almost all fishing nets during the coldest months (December to February) offers a real advantage to the success of the spawning

[78] Ibid.

[79] Ibid.

[80] Dearden Philip et al., "Trends in Global Protected Area Governance 1992–2002" (2005) 36 *Environmental Management*, 89, 100.

[81] See Section 13.2.

[82] Arrêté du ministre des pêches maritimes et de la marine marchande No 1154-88 du 20 safari 1409 (3 octobre 1988), fixant la taille marchande minimale des espèces pêchées dans les eaux maritimes marocaines as amended in 2001 (Bulletin officiel, No 3962, 5 octobre 1988, 326).

process for temperate and subtropical species, which are the most abundant in Moroccan waters. Nonetheless, the use of the beach seine in the Alboran MPA-F, allowed from May to January, is extremely destructive for newborn fish for which the settlement period begins in March, and they are heavily harvested by the beach seine during spring and summer.[83]

Regarding the no-take area within the MPA-Fs, it is inadequate to achieve the commonly accepted objective for MPAs. It is crucial to remember here that protected areas Category VI were accepted by the IUCN as a protected area under specific conditions. One of these conditions is that two-thirds of the area should be maintained and intended to remain in its natural state.[84]

The intrinsic gaps in the regulations of MPA-Fs contradict the fundamental elements of protected areas. Besides, these regulations were undermined by new, contradictory regulations.

13.3.2.8 Lack of Legal Coherence in the Management of MPA-Fs

MPA-Fs' legal rules were undermined by the trawling regulations. In fact, alongside the establishment of permanent no-take zones in the Mogador and Alboran MPAs, the exclusion of all trawling activities inside the MPAs with a reinforced control was a clear benefit to habitat protection. This was especially true for the Alboran MPA, where trawling activities were known to be a real threat to shallow (up to 10 m depth) marine areas. This benefit was partially lost when an issued Order (No 4202-4214, November 25, 2014) reduced the exclusion area for trawlers to 1.5 nautical miles while the MPA extended to 3 nautical miles.[85] Along the Atlantic coast, the benefit offered by the MPAs when compared to adjacent areas was drastically reduced when the Vessel Monitoring System launched by Fisheries Department in September 2013 began to produce tangible results.[86] During the subsequent two years, the reenforcement and effectiveness of the control reduced the violations to the trawl ban inside 3 nautical miles from the coastline.

Based on the preceding analysis, it becomes evident that MPA-Fs lack the enforcement and efficacy typically associated with protected areas. Their adoption

83 Hicham Masski, "Investigation of a Subtidal Fish Community in a South-Western Mediterranean Settlement Area of Morocco" (2015) 31 *Journal of Applied Ichthyology* 1, 208, 210.

84 EUROPARC and IUCN, Guidelines for Protected Area Management Categories – Interpretation and Application of the Protected Area Management Categories in Europe (EUROPARC and WCPA, Grafenau Germany, 2000) 13. See Section 13.2.

85 Order of the Minister of Agriculture and Maritime Fisheries No 4202-14 of Safar 2, 1436 (November 25, 2014) setting the minimum distances from which the use of dragging nets is authorized in the Mediterranean. Official Bulletin No 6322 (January 1, 2015) 139.

86 Imad El Khalkhali and Houda Yejjou, "Evaluation d'usage du VMS (vessel monitoring system) dans le secteur de la pêche maritime au Maroc" (2017) 21 *International Journal of Innovation and Applied Studies* 2, 209.

was tailored specifically to fisheries, potentially biasing their intended purpose. Their assimilation into the legal and institutional framework has not yielded any tangible impact on the ground. On the contrary, MPA-Fs not only represent a legal anomaly but also contradict other specific regulations. Consequently, it is crucial to contemplate methods for enhancing and reinforcing their initial objectives, which they have failed to accomplish.

13.4 STRENGTHENING THE MANAGEMENT OF MPA-FS TO ADVANCE MARINE BIODIVERSITY CONSERVATION AND SUSTAINABLE USE: RECOMMENDATIONS

Given the inefficacy of the MPA-Fs, one potential solution could involve their incorporation into the Protected Areas Act No 22 to grant them authentic enforceability. To achieve this, it is vital to evaluate the suitable category for their integration within the protected areas. Once the category is determined, it is crucial to adhere to the established process for creating protected areas as outlined in Law 22-07. Indeed, the adoption of the new MPA-Fs needs to be recommenced and reassessed. Additionally, the establishment of their management committee and the revision and publication of their management plan in the official bulletin are imperative steps.

13.4.1 *The Necessary Integration of MPA-Fs into the Protected Areas Act (Law 22-07)*

An analysis of the categories established by Law 22-07 reveals that the most suitable category for MPA-Fs would be the natural park category or the national park category. In fact, the other categories (biological reserve, natural reserve, natural site) are more specifically focused on the conservation of the biodiversity, while MPA-Fs as mentioned focus on the sustainable use.

MPA-Fs could correspond to the category of natural park, which is the second category of protected areas created by the law under Article 5. Indeed, as mentioned earlier, the natural park could encompass ecosystems representing a particular interest "which it is advisable to protect and develop, while ensuring the maintenance of its ecological functions and the sustainable use of their natural resources." This definition recalls the definition of the IUCN Category VI discussed earlier.[87] In fact, this category also has social and economic objectives in addition to conservation. It is the most widely used protected areas category, especially in developing countries.[88] Indeed, it includes almost 40 percent of all protected areas worldwide (terrestrial

[87] See Section 13.2.

[88] Craig L. Shafer, "Arguments for and against IUCN Protected Area Management Category VI with a Review of State versus Community Governance" (2020) 53 *Journal for Nature Conservation* 125697.

and marine).[89] This possibility was indeed discussed during the negotiation process of MPA-Fs. We have previously analyzed that MPA-Fs do not entirely fulfill the conditions required to incorporate Category VI into the IUCN categories.[90]

MPA-Fs could also correspond to the category of national park as it is defined by Law 22-07, as mentioned earlier, as a natural area, terrestrial and/or marine, whose purpose is "to protect biological diversity […] and to offer the public opportunities to visit, for cultural, scientific, educational, recreational and tourist purposes, while respecting the natural environment and the traditions of the local populations." While this definition does not expressly mention fishing as an activity allowed in the national park, we could make an analogy with tourism, which is tolerated to a certain extent in the national park. The integration of MPA-Fs in one of these categories will necessitate the amendment of the MDs establishing them. These decisions should adopt a clear definition of attributions and responsibilities in MPA-Fs.

13.4.2 *The Need for a Clear Definition of Attributions and Responsibilities in MPA-Fs*

The amendment of the MPA-F regulations would be facilitated by the adoption of the new decree of 2021 for the application of Law 22-07.[91] Indeed, under this decree, MPAs would be managed by the Department of Maritime Fisheries, while MPAs would be partially managed by this department and by the Department of Water and Forests. This distribution of competences could facilitate the creation of future MPAs and the implementation of Law 22-07. Therefore, these existing fishing-oriented MPAs could be transitioned into the new protected area framework, ensuring their proper designation as genuine protected areas. Nevertheless, the amendment of the legal status of the MPA-Fs would require a comprehensive review of their legal provisions to better align them with the purpose of sustainable use. In this regard, it is crucial to take into account the scientific advice and the aforementioned IUCN conditions to create this kind of MPA.

Once reverted to the legal status of protected areas under Law 22-07, the MPA-Fs should encompass effective measures to ensure their management according to the objectives of the CBD. First, the new regulations should clearly identify the administrations and entities in charge of the management of each MPA-F and clarify their missions. While the decree of 2021 clarifies who is in charge of MPAs, it does not detail the missions of each department according to the different categories of MPAs. The fact that these two departments are now merged into one ministry does not

89 Ibid., 2.

90 See Section 13.3.

91 Decree No. 2-18-242 (April 27, 2021) taken for the application of certain provisions of Law No 22-07 relating to Protected Areas, Official Bulletin No 7062 of February 3, 2022, 75.

suffice to resolve the issue of attributions responsibilities, which is crucial for the efficient management of the MPAs.[92] Second, it is important that the management plan of the MPA-F is made public and has a binding effect.

13.4.3 *The Need for Robust and Binding Management Plans*

As mentioned earlier, the initial management plan elaborated for the MPA-Fs was never published in the official bulletin. This lack has resulted in rendering the MDs establishing the MPA-Fs legally nonbinding.

Moreover, from a procedural standpoint, the management plan should adhere to the stipulations outlined in the Law on Protected Areas, as discussed in Section 13.3. In this regard, it should be presented for input and feedback from fishermen and other relevant stakeholders. Furthermore, the initial management plan should be updated in order to take into account the current ecological and economic situation of the area covered by it. Indeed, the management plan should correspond to the needs of each protected area. In this regard, it should focus more on conservation. In fact, the protection of habitats and of the most important ecophases in the life cycle of species, especially spawning and juvenile aggregations, are among the essential objectives to be achieved by an MPA.[93] Allowing as many fish as possible to reach maturity by protecting juveniles is essential for the renewal of adult cohorts. The adoption of the length at first maturity as the minimum allowable catch size is essential for the reconstruction of fish communities.[94] Hence, the use of fishing gear with a high impact on small juveniles, such as the beach seine, should be prohibited. Furthermore, the presence of large and older individuals is important to increase the resilience of fish communities.[95] It is then important to protect a significant proportion of adult individuals, and not just during the mating season. Two of the MPA-Fs have no-take areas, but these are too small to be effective in the protection of large individuals (less than 2.5 percent of the MPA area). The size of the no-take areas needs to be increased to provide refuge for the largest individuals. The physical disturbance from trawling and dredging is recognized as a major threat to marine biodiversity and must be significantly reduced or eliminated.[96] Trawling

92 Since the recent government reorganization, the Ministry of Fisheries and Agriculture has been amalgamated with the Ministry of Forests and Water and is now referred to as the Ministry of Agriculture, Fisheries, Rural Development, Water, and Forests.

93 Kirsten Grorud-Colvert et al., "The MPA Guide: a Framework to Achieve Global Goals for the Ocean" (2021) 373 *Science* 6560.

94 Rainer Froese, "Keep it Simple: Three Indicators to Deal with Overfishing" (2004) 5 *Fish and Fisheries* 1, 86, 91.

95 Charles Birkeland and Paul K. Dayton, "The Importance in Fishery Management of Leaving the Big Ones" (2005) 20 *Trends in Ecology and Evolution* 7, 356, 358.

96 Simon F. Thrush and Paul K. Dayton, "Disturbance to Marine Benthic Habitats by Trawling and Dredging: Implications for Marine Biodiversity" (2002) 33 *Annual Review of Ecology and Systematics* 1, 449, 473; Michel J. Kaiser, "Recent Advances in Understanding the Environmental Footprint of

is explicitly banned in all three MPA-Fs but needs to be effectively enforced, especially in the Alboran MPA-F, through greater control and enforcement to prevent trawler incursions, which are still reported by local artisanal fishermen. The use of small artisanal dredges is allowed in the Alboran MPA-F, where it is stated that this gear will only be used on sandy and muddy seabeds. This fishery produces thousands of tons of shellfish every year, so its impact on the seabed may not be negligible. The impact of this gear on the seabed and benthic communities needs to be assessed in order to minimize it.

Enhancing the management of MPA-Fs is crucial to achieving their primary objective and aligning them more closely with the legal framework of protected areas, including the CBD. This can notably occur through clarifying the responsibilities of stakeholders in the MPA-Fs and adopting a robust, enforceable management plan that is widely recognized and published in the official bulletin. Consequently, the current management approaches outlined in the three MDs establishing the MPA-Fs should be reassessed, and these legal texts should be amended accordingly.

13.5 CONCLUSION

Established in the framework of the Fisheries Act of 1973, MPA-Fs were created by three Ministerial Orders in 2014 in the margin of the existing Law on Protected Areas of 2010 (Law 22-07). This dual legal treatment results in confusion regarding their legal status. Additionally, the legal mechanisms employed for their regulation are largely ineffective. While they could potentially be classified under the IUCN Category VI of MPAs, MPA-Fs do not adhere to the fundamental conditions necessary to be recognized as genuine protected areas. In fact, the no-take areas within these MPAs, for example, are not as significant as they should be according to the standard criteria for MPAs. Moreover, the legal documents establishing these MPA-Fs apply the general regulations on fisheries management that are applicable outside the boundaries of the MPAs. Furthermore, these Ministerial Orders are not consistent with other conflicting general texts that permit trawling within the MPA-Fs, for example.

It is essential to conduct an evaluation of these MPA-Fs, alongside a comprehensive revision of the legal documents that established them. This revision should encompass both substantive and formal aspects. In fact, several management rules provided in the three Ministerial Orders establishing the MPA-Fs need to be amended and/or reinforced. Furthermore, as these legal texts are adopted within the framework of the Fisheries Act (Article 16), they are inherently temporary. The most recent revision of their duration was undertaken in 2019. Consequently, another

Trawling on the Seabed" (2019) 97 *Canadian Journal of Zoology* 9, 755, 762. Jan Geert Hiddink et al., "Selection of Indicators for Assessing and Managing the Impacts of Bottom Trawling on Seabed Habitats" (2020) 57 *Journal of Applied Ecology* 7, 1199, 1209.

review is supposed to be conducted in 2024 likely for an additional five-year period. The problem with these revisions is that they are not made upon a reassessment of the MPA-Fs. The first official assessment of these MPA-Fs was done by the MCC itself in the framework of a global assessment of the MCC project.[97] In fact, the MCC assessed whether enhancing conditions for small-scale fishers and promoting the sustainable utilization of fishing resources had led to an overall enhancement in the economic efficiency and productivity of Morocco's Small-Scale Fisheries System.[98] The evaluation study was based on fisher surveys, administrative data on fish sales, infrastructure assessments, key-informant interviews, and focus groups.[99]

An important step forward is an assessment of the biodiversity within and outside the MPA-Fs, which is essential for evaluating their sustainability. This assessment will undoubtedly facilitate their reclassification as authentic MPAs under Law 22-07. The merger of the Ministry of Fisheries with the Department of Forests and Water, along with the adoption of a decree to define the stakeholders for MPAs, notably partial MPAs, has the potential to bring about a shift in the governance of MPA-Fs.

97 Turiansky et al. (n 76).

98 Mathematica, "Evaluation of the Morocco Small Scale Fisheries Project 2018–2022" www.mathematica.org/projects/evaluation-of-the-morocco-small-scale-fisheries-project≥ accessed February 11, 2024.

99 Ibid.

14

World Heritage Protection and Biodiversity in the MENA Region

Robert Home

14.1 INTRODUCTION

In 1972, the United Nations Educational, Scientific and Cultural Organization (UNESCO) held its World Heritage Convention (WHC) in Paris. The fifty-year anniversary of that event was celebrated in November 2022, at a conference in Delphi (Greece).[1] The first site to be "inscribed" as a World Heritage (WH) site was a biodiversity site (the Galapagos Islands, inscribed in 1978), soon followed in 1980 by another – Socotra (Yemen) in the Middle East and North Africa (MENA) region.[2] The year 2022 also marked another fiftieth anniversary celebration in Stockholm, of the 1972 Conference on the Human Environment, with the theme of "a healthy planet for the prosperity of all – our responsibility, our opportunity."[3] This showed how biodiversity and sustainable development have grown as global concerns facing the urgent need for climate change action. Considering that many of the WH sites are also key biodiversity areas (KBAs) that are critical to the survival of several rare species of flora and fauna, an integrated and nexus governance approach is required to address the synergies, as well as common and multiscale threats to both WH and biodiversity.[4]

This chapter aims to explore issues facing WH sites, especially relating to biodiversity in the MENA region. It discusses the challenges to the effective conservation and protection of heritage sites in the region and the need for a holistic approach to conservation and biodiversity. It draws upon data and publications of the WHC and the limited academic literature on biodiversity issues in WH. It examines the

[1] WHC, *Future of World Heritage in Challenging Times: Enhancing Resilience and Sustainability* (WHC 2022).

[2] UNESCO, "World Heritage List" https://whc.unesco.org/en/list/&order=year accessed January 28, 2024.

[3] UNEP, "Stockholm+50: A Healthy Planet for the Prosperity of All – Our Responsibility, Our Opportunity: Guidance Note for Stakeholder Consultation" https://wedocs.unep.org/20.500.11822/37858 accessed January 28, 2024.

[4] The Key Biodiversity Area Partnership, "About Key Biodiversity Areas" www.keybiodiversityareas.org/about-kbas accessed 12 January, 2024.

shift in WHC priorities toward a more balanced WH list and its actions to identify endangered properties and even delete some from the list. This reinforces the responsibilities of state parties (SPs) who have signed the convention (most of the UN membership) to give legal protection to sites and strengthen site management and regulatory controls.

The chapter demonstrates that greater attention is now being given to biodiversity and ecosystem elements in a changing policy environment about climate action, while recognizing that existing biodiversity protection often overlaps with WH protection. The chapter also aims to offer an educational resource on WH for environmental law programs and students. After this introduction, Section 14.2 discusses the evolution of WH ideas and institutions in the past fifty years. Section 14.3 examines the biodiversity challenges facing WH in the MENA region, Section 14.4 unpacks legal and regulatory challenges facing a holistic approach to conservation and biodiversity in the MENA region. Section 14.5 offers conclusions and recommendations on advancing biodiversity WH protection for the MENA region.

14.2 UNESCO WORLD HERITAGE FIFTY YEARS ON: ISSUES OF BIODIVERSITY AND SUSTAINABLE DEVELOPMENT

UNESCO was founded in 1946 in a time of global recovery after the Second World War, and the idea of WH followed from the need to repair monuments and cultural heritage.[5] The WHC, and its Intergovernmental Committee for the Protection of the Cultural and Natural Heritage of Outstanding Universal Value (OUV), manage the process for "inscribing" or listing WH sites, which are classified as either cultural or natural, or a mixture of both. Of the ten criteria defining OUV, the first six refer to cultural heritage and the last four to natural heritage. Natural WH sites are often chosen for their scenic beauty but may also be iconic for biodiversity and conservation, while biodiversity issues can be important for all WH sites.

WH listings reveal much about the changing geopolitics and power relationships of the world and UNESCO (see Table 14.1).[6] A Eurocentric bias is shown by the fact that Europe and North America (classed as a single region in WHC statistics) have nearly half of the WH sites, and some individual SPs have large numbers of them, headed by Italy (58), China (56), and Germany (51). Since 1994 the WHC's global strategy has sought to develop a more representative, balanced, and credible WH list, with new frameworks for identifying the prized OUV requirement.[7] Both

[5] UNESCO, "Sharing Humanity" www.unesco.org/en/sharing-humanity accessed November 23, 2023.

[6] R. Harrison (ed), *Understanding the Politics of Heritage* (Manchester University Press 2009).

[7] ICOMOS, "The World Heritage List: Filling the Gaps – an Action Plan for the Future. An Analysis by ICOMOS" (February 2004) www.google.com/url?sa=t&rct=j&q=&esrc=s&source=web&cd=&ved=2ahUKEwiOqu_5voCEAxVVC3kGHbk8CxcQFnoECBsQAQ&url=https%3A%2F%2Fwhc.unesco.org%2Fdocument%2F102409&usg=AOvVaw13rUQppRl2mOs4UuTI7LfG&opi=89978449 accessed January 28, 2024. See also S. Labadi, "A Review of the Global Strategy for a Balanced,

TABLE 14.1 *Distribution of WH sites by region and type*

Zone/region	Cultural	Natural	Mixed	Total	Percentage	State parties with inscribed properties
Africa	54	39	5	98	8.5	35
Arab states	80	5	3	88	7.6	18
Asia and Pacific	195	70	12	277	24.0	36
Europe and North America	468	66	11	545	47.2	50
Latin America and Caribbean	100	38	8	146	12.7	28
Total	897	218	39	1,154	100	167

Source: Compiled by author from WHC statistics, 2021.

cultural and natural WH sites have biodiversity aspects, and experts have recognized their importance for the good management of both.[8]

WH sites have high visibility for promoting tourism and conservation protection.[9] Most foreign direct investment into them comes from international tour operators, hotel chains, and airlines, and in providing transport infrastructure and creating local jobs, but often without much other benefit to local people. Domestic and international tourism make WH a major vehicle of cultural exchange, with filming and fashion photography in particular contributing to the OUV of a WH site. The SPs to the WHC are well aware of the benefits for tourism and wider cultural influence, but WH sites come at a price to the SP, which is responsible for protecting and managing them with legislation and appropriate resources. Many WH cultural sites are deteriorating from the impacts of tourism, while natural sites are especially vulnerable to damage to their biodiversity. In 1999, the International Cultural Tourism Charter sought to improve management and reduce the adverse impacts of mass tourism,[10] through the tourism industry working together with the conservation and local community. While the COVID-19 pandemic reduced tourist numbers and closed some sites, it may have eased pressure on some ecosystems but also caused significant revenue loss, and damaging and illegal activities grow when there are fewer staff to prevent them.

Representative and Credible World Heritage List 1994–2004" (2005) 7 *Conservation and Management of Archaeological Sites* 2, 89 www.tandfonline.com/doi/abs/10.1179/135050305793137477 accessed January 28, 2024.

8 A. Persic and G. Martin, "Links between Biological and Cultural Diversity: Report of International Workshop" UNESCO SC/EES/AP/5865/40 (2008).

9 R. Buckley, "Tourism and Natural World Heritage: A Complicated Relationship" (2017) 57 *Journal of Travel Research* 5.

10 International Council on Monuments and Sites (ICOMOS), "International Cultural Tourism Charter: Managing Tourism at Places of Heritage Significance" ICOMOS at the 12th General Assembly in Mexico (October 1999) www.icomos.org/en/newsletters-archives/179-articles-en-francais/ressources/charters-and-standards/162-international-cultural-tourism-charter accessed January 28, 2024.

The institutions and conservation concepts for WH have evolved significantly over the past fifty years. The official advisors to the WHC in the cultural category are the International Centre for the Study of the Preservation and Restoration of Cultural Property[11] and the International Council on Monuments and Sites.[12] The latter, founded in 1965, comprises some 110 national committees, 28 international scientific committees, and some 10,000 experts. For natural WH sites and biodiversity, the official WHC advisor is the International Union for Conservation of Nature (IUCN),[13] founded in 1948, with a membership of over 1,400 governmental and nongovernmental organizations, and drawing upon the services of some 16,000 experts.

The institutional landscape around biodiversity and conservation has developed further since the WHC in 1972, with more international actors created, notably the United Nations Environment Programme (UNEP)[14] and the Convention on Biological Diversity (CBD),[15] which entered into force in 1993. The WHC is now one of eight key international biodiversity-related conventions, but it is unique among them because its remit is both natural and cultural heritage. The IUCN produces "red lists" of threatened species and ecosystems, and recognizes many site categories beyond WH, with its World Commission on Protected Areas but one among its various agencies. The Global Biodiversity Framework now assesses the conservation prospects of WH sites as a test for the broader success of conservation worldwide.[16] Natural WH sites encompass most major ecosystems, and within the cultural category cities contain historic urban landscapes and green space that embody a long and intimate relationship between people, culture, and their natural environment, often reflecting land use methods that enhance biological diversity.

The WHC became part of a more complex global governance reality when in 2015 the UN General Assembly adopted its Sustainable Development Agenda to the year 2030, identifying seventeen Sustainable Development Goals (SDGs) and seen as a "critical juncture" in the global policy agenda.[17] Global wealth inequalities, political conflicts, an accelerating climate crisis, and the COVID-19 pandemic have all combined to reduce resources, change relationships, and bring in new actors. A more decentred political theory of the nation state has emerged, which

[11] International Centre for the Study of the Preservation and Restoration of Cultural Property (ICCROM) www.iccrom.org accessed January 28, 2024.

[12] International Council on Monuments and Sites (ICOMOS) www.icomos.org/en accessed January 28, 2024.

[13] International Union for Conservation of Nature (IUCN) www.iucn.org accessed January 28, 2024.

[14] United Nations Environment Programme (UNEP) www.unep.org accessed January 28, 2024.

[15] Convention on Biological Diversity (CBD) www.cbd.int accessed January 28, 2024.

[16] International Union for Conservation of Nature (IUCN), "World Heritage: A Unique Contribution to Biodiversity Conservation," CLT/WHC/NHU/2023/BRO/14, 10.58337/LSRE8424 9 (2023).

[17] A. Sorensen, "Taking Critical Junctures Seriously: Theory and Method for Causal Analysis of Rapid Institutional Change" (2022) 28 *Planning Perspectives* 5, 929 https://doi.org/10.1080/02665433.2022.2137840 accessed January 28, 2024.

sees the state less as sovereign and monolithic and rather as a creation of contingent actions of different groups and individuals, diverse beliefs about public authority, and contending (and perhaps unstable) cultural traditions and practices.[18] These changed attitudes have an effect upon how WH is seen and protected.

WH appears in the Sustainable Development Agenda under SDG 11 (sustainable cities), target 11.4: "Strengthen efforts to protect and safeguard the world's cultural and natural heritage."[19] Biodiversity affects both the natural and cultural categories of WH sites. Natural WH sites make up less than 1 percent of the earth's surface but more than a fifth of mapped global species richness, and a fifth of cultural WH sites are located in KBAs threatened by global climate change. The IUCN, in 2021, found that the deterioration of WH site conditions was of "significant concern" in 30 percent of natural sites and critical for a further 7 percent.[20]

Target 11.4 of SDG 11 is only one of the many targets that have been set for the SDGs, but WH is also relevant to other elements of the Sustainable Development Agenda, which include SDG 13 (climate change), SDG 14 (life below water), SDG 15 (life on land), and SDG 17 (partnerships for goals). The WHC warned that climate change was a significant threat to its properties nearly twenty years ago, and the Paris Agreement (2015) on climate change saw WH sites as key focal points for building clean and resilient futures, fulfilling a role as climate change observatories.[21] SDG 14 marks out marine and coastal ecosystems in WH sites as playing a crucial role in climate regulation, storing as they do an estimated 15 percent of the world's blue carbon assets.[22] SDG 15's mission is to "protect, restore and promote sustainable use of terrestrial ecosystems, sustainably manage forests, combat desertification, and halt and reverse land degradation and halt biodiversity loss" – all of which relate to WH sites.

Furthermore, the WHC is one of eight key international biodiversity-related conventions, being unique in dealing with both natural and cultural heritage, which contribute to conserving ecosystem integrity and biodiversity. While making up less than 1 percent of the earth's surface, they harbor over a fifth of mapped global species richness, and a fifth of cultural WH sites are located in KBAs. These supposedly highly protected sites are, however, not immune from the threat of global climate change and pressures from human activities, so SPs are now being encouraged to integrate WH into National Biodiversity Strategies.[23]

18 M. Bevir and R. A. W. Rhodes, *The State as Cultural Practice* (Oxford University Press 2010).

19 Xinyuan Wang et al., "A Preliminary Study on Target 11.4 for UN Sustainable Development Goals" (2018) 6 *International Journal of Geoheritage and Parks* 2, 18.

20 IUCN, "World Heritage Outlook 3" (2020) www.iucn.org/resources/publication/iucn-world-heritage-outlook-3 accessed November 26, 2023.

21 UNESCO World Heritage Convention, *Climate Change and World Heritage* (UNESCO 2007).

22 UNESCO, *Marine World Heritage: Custodians of the Globe's Blue Carbon Assets* (UNESCO 2020).

23 World Heritage: A Unique Contribution to Biodiversity Conservation (IUCN 2023) CLT/WHC/NHU/2023/BRO/14, 10.58337/LSRE8424.

Biodiversity appears as the last of the ten criteria (x) for WH site selection, which was defined as containing "the most important and significant natural habitats for in-situ conservation of biological diversity, including those containing threatened species of outstanding universal value from the point of view of science or conservation."[24] In the present century, climate change and human population growth have raised the importance of biodiversity issues, and more sites are joining the tentative list under criterion (x), while climate change continues to degrade the OUV, integrity, and authenticity of many WH sites. State tourism and development strategies and site visitor management plans often fail to take account of climate change impacts, while site managers may lack financial resources and expertise.[25] Aspects of biodiversity and WH in the specific challenging circumstances of the MENA region are discussed in Section 14.3.

14.3 BIODIVERSITY AND WH IN THE MENA REGION

The MENA region is usually considered to cover twenty or twenty-one countries but there is no generally agreed definition. The WHC places it within its "Arab states" region, which is divided into three distinct subregions: the Gulf (Bahrain, Kuwait, Oman, Qatar, Saudi Arabia, United Arab Emirates, and Yemen), the Maghreb (Algeria, Libya, Mauritania, Morocco, and Tunisia), and the Middle East (Egypt, Iraq, Jordan, Lebanon, Palestine, Sudan, and Syria).[26] This chapter also includes a discussion of examples from Iran, Gaza, the West Bank, and Jerusalem. The hugely varied MENA region has country populations ranging from Egypt, with some 100 million people, to Djibouti, with fewer than a million. The largest country by land area is Algeria at 381,740 km^2 (mostly desert); the smallest is the Gaza Strip at 360 km^2 and a population density of over 5,000 people per km^2, contrasted by Mauritania (mostly desert) with fewer than four. The region has one of the world's most rapidly expanding populations, which are increasingly found in urban areas and may be displaced by conflict and climate change. Lebanon has the highest net international emigration at forty emigrants per 1,000 population, with many more people leaving than entering. MENA's Gulf states are among the richest countries

[24] UNESCO World Heritage Convention, "The Criteria for Selection" https://whc.unesco.org/en/criteria accessed November 25, 2023.

[25] A. Markham et al., *World Heritage and Tourism in a Changing Climate* (UNEP 2016); H. G. Brauch, "Policy Responses to Climate Change in the Mediterranean and MENA Region during the Anthropocene" in J. Scheffran et al. (eds), *Climate Change, Human Security and Violent Conflict* (Springer 2012) 719–794; D. Broom, "How the Middle East Is Suffering on the Front Lines of Climate Change" (World Economic Forum 2020) www.weforum.org/agenda/ accessed September 15, 2024; K. Waha et al., "Climate Change in the MENA Region and Their Implications for Vulnerable Population Groups" (2017) 17 *Regional Environmental Change* 6, 1623.

[26] UNESCO World Heritage Convention (WHC), "Arab States: States Parties" https://whc.unesco.org/en/statesparties/?searchStates=&id=&region=4 accessed January 28, 2024.

in the world, while other countries in the region are fragile or failing states with extreme levels of poverty and unemployment.[27]

The WHC has eighty-two sites in its Arab States region. Of these, the vast majority (seventy-four) are in the cultural category, including some of the oldest continuously occupied towns in the world, and the physical legacies of Carthaginian, Greco-Roman, Judaeo-Christian, and Islamic civilizations. The natural or mixed sites are much fewer in number (currently five natural and three mixed), and substantially less than the global mix (9 percent compared to 18 percent). The region is ecologically rich and varied, yet only has five WH sites under the relevant qualifying criterion of significant natural habitats and ecosystems, and these tend to be physically remote and cover large areas, requiring careful management. For example, millions of migratory birds pass through the region each year, and the Ramsar Convention on "wetlands of international importance especially as waterfowl habitat" is named after the MENA Iranian city on the Caspian Sea that in 1971 hosted the event.[28] The region now has dozens of the world's 2,000 Ramsar sites, with the Banc d'Arguin WH site (Mauritania) an important stopover on the East Atlantic Flyway migration route.

Over the years the Middle East has involved UNESCO in much political controversy and conflict that has altered its membership and affected its WH sites, particularly related to the geopolitics of oil and the contested status of Israel/Palestine. For example, two years after the first WHC was held in Paris, the United States of America, in 1974, suspended its payments in protest at UNESCO's opposition to the state of Israel and recognition of the Palestinian Liberation Organization. The USA left entirely in 1983, rejoined to win international support when it was preparing to invade Iraq in 2003, only to leave again in 2017, partly over Israel but also because the Trump administration refused to pay its contributions. (In 2023 the Biden administration committed to rejoining.[29]) The UK followed the USA by leaving in 1983 but rejoined in 1997 after a change of government. Israel, which had been an early and active UNESCO member and had multiple WH sites, left in 2017, reluctantly following the USA.[30] The Oslo Accords gave Palestine UN observer status in 2011, making it eligible for WH sites (it now has three inscribed). The Old Jerusalem WH site, disputed between Israel and Jordan, is still not assigned to any state, with its permanent status remaining unresolved in international law.[31]

27 World Bank data. See World Bank, "Middle East and North Africa (MENA): Overview" www.worldbank.org/en/region/mena/overview accessed January 28, 2024.

28 Ramsar Convention, "Wetlands of International Importance Especially as Waterfowl Habitat" (February 2, 1971) www.ramsar.org/sites/default/files/documents/library/scan_certified_e.pdf accessed January 28, 2024.

29 UN News, "United States Commits to Rejoin UNESCO" (June 12, 2023) https://news.un.org/en/story/2023/06/1137577 accessed January 28, 2024.

30 Jerusalem Post, "Goodbye UNESCO" (January 2, 2019) www.jpost.com/opinion/goodbye-unesco-576180#google_vignette accessed January 28, 2024.

31 Oslo Accords, UN Security Council Resolutions 242 and 338 (1993).

Regional instability has been damaging to MENA's WH sites, many of which the WHC lists as endangered.[32] The destruction of sites and assets important for cultural identity can be an explicit goal of modern asymmetrical warfare. One example is the occupation by the Islamic State of Iraq and Syria (ISIS) of the Palmyra WH site (Syria), which resulted in the destruction of many of its structures and the public execution of its antiquities director in a symbolic rejection of non-Islamic cultural values.[33]

A less extreme WH dispute, between Bahrain and Qatar over some islands in the Persian/Arabian Gulf, was adjudicated in the International Court of Justice in 2001,[34] which granted some to Bahrain and others to Qatar. Qatar had built a fort at Zubarah in 1939 to defend against Bahrain and contentiously in 2013 secured it as its first inscribed WH site, described as the best-preserved example of an eighteenth/nineteenth-century trading and pearl town in the Gulf region.[35] This did not prevent Bahrain's head of state, during the diplomatic crisis of 2017–2021 between Qatar and its neighbors, publicly condemning what he called the Qataris' illegal aggression against Zubarah some eighty years before.

The impact of these conflicts is such that the region now has many WH sites listed as endangered by the WHC, increasing from eight in 2010 to twenty-two in 2021 (although three were reinstated over the same period). All of Syria's WH properties have been added since the outbreak of the Syrian civil war in 2013.[36] The WHC defines danger broadly, including accelerated deterioration, impacts of development projects upon water levels, changes in land use or ownership, abandonment and armed conflict, serious natural calamities (such as fires, earthquakes, landslides, volcanic eruptions, floods, and tsunamis), and vulnerability to looting and other predations.[37]

Oman has the unenviable distinction of having the first and only site in the MENA region to be removed entirely from the WH inscribed list. Only two other WH sites, both in Europe and in the cultural category, have been delisted by the WHC because it found new development projects compromised OUV: the Elbe Valley in Germany

32 L. Meskell (ed), *Archaeology under Fire: Nationalism, Politics and Heritage in the Eastern Mediterranean and Middle East* (Routledge 1998).

33 S. Al Kuntar and S. Zucker, "Palmyra: The Modern Destruction of An Ancient City" (Smarthistory, January 5, 2018).

34 *Qatar v Bahrain*, Maritime Delimitation and Territorial Questions between Qatar and Bahrain, Merits, Judgment, I.C.J. Reports 2001, 40 www.icj-cij.org/sites/default/files/case-related/87/087-20010316-JUD-01-00-EN.pdf accessed January 28, 2024.

35 Tobias Richter and Hanne Nymann (eds), *Qatar Islamic Archaeology and Heritage Project: End of Season Report – Stage 2, Season 1, 2009–2010* (University of Copenhagen and Qatar Museums Authority 2011) 1–369.

36 UNESCO World Heritage Convention, List of World Heritage in Danger https://whc.unesco.org/en/danger/ accessed January 28, 2024.

37 Article 11(4) of WHC (Paris 1972).

and Liverpool in the UK.[38] Oman's natural WH site, the Arabian Oryx Sanctuary, covered nearly three million hectares of Oman's desert and had been inscribed in 1994 as a natural WH site to preserve the rare oryx, extinct in the wild since 1972, but with a free-ranging herd reintroduced in 1982. The reintroduction failed, and WH status was revoked partly because of predation of the wildlife, but primarily because the government opened most of the site to oil prospecting; the Arabian oryx population on the site had fallen from 450 in 1996 to sixty-five in 2007, when it was delisted. The future of the endangered oryx was, however, helped when Saudi Arabia got WH status in 2022 for "Uruq Bani Ma'arid," one of the planet's most spectacular desert landscapes in the so-called empty quarter.[39] This new listing supported the reintroduction of the oryx and partly compensated for the situation in Oman.

The MENA region's Gulf states, rich in fossil fuels and among the wealthiest in the world, have recently emerged rather belatedly as champions of environment, heritage, and biodiversity. Since 2006 Oman has obtained six WH listings (but losing one as discussed earlier), Bahrain three, the United Arab Emirates one (Abu Dhabi's Al Ain Oasis),[40] and Qatar one (Zubarah).[41] Saudi Arabia got its first WH listings in 2008 for three sites and went on to add five more between 2014 and 2023. The latest additions (2023) to the WH list include eight in the MENA region, going some way to creating a more balanced and representative global distribution.

The WHC maintains a list of "tentative" WH sites that are not yet inscribed but which SPs consider suitable, after due consultation and participation with stakeholders. Such is the enthusiasm by SPs for proposing WH sites that there are currently more on the tentative list than have already been inscribed: Iran, for example, has sixty-one on its tentative list, over twice as many as its twenty-seven inscribed sites. Tentative nominations are required to precede by at least one year before

38 UNESCO World Heritage Convention News, "Oman's Arabian Oryx Sanctuary: First Site Ever to Be Deleted from UNESCO's World Heritage List" (June 28, 2007) https://whc.unesco.org/en/news/362#:~:text=The%20World%20Heritage%20Committee%20deleted,which%20was%20inscribed%20in%201994 accessed January 28, 2024; "Dresden Is Deleted from UNESCO's World Heritage List" UNESCO World Heritage Convention News, 33rd WHC, Seville, Spain (June 22–30, 2009) https://whc.unesco.org/en/news/522#:~:text=The%20World%20Heritage%20Committee%20decided,outstanding%20universal%20value%20as%20inscribed.%22 accessed January 28, 2024; "World Heritage Committee Deletes Liverpool – Maritime Mercantile City from UNESCO's World Heritage List" (July 21, 2021) www.unesco.org/en/articles/world-heritage-committee-deletes-liverpool-maritime-mercantile-city-unescos-world-heritage-list?TSPD_101_R0=080713870fab2000d9ef4152177af75169877456987a91f7d0e1cd8edfcd6bd5b5ad3a81158c962a08cd97cdb9143000af7e6e4d77348302da3c52659db59df535140fdfddb19a49161c03d258b223f3a0c4574295bde989a2660b8279b4c567#:~:text=The%20World%20Heritage%20Committee%2C%20holding,universal%20value%20of%20the%20property accessed January 28, 2024.

39 UNESCO World Heritage Convention, "Uruq Bani Ma'arid" https://whc.unesco.org/en/list/1699/ accessed January 28, 2024.

40 UNESCO World Heritage Convention, "Cultural Sites of Al Ain (Hafit, Hili, Bidaa Bint Saud and Oases Areas)" https://whc.unesco.org/en/list/1343/ accessed January 28, 2024.

41 UNESCO World Heritage Convention, "Al Zubarah Archaeological Site" https://whc.unesco.org/en/list/1402 accessed January 28, 2024.

TABLE 14.2 *Natural/mixed WH sites in the MENA region*

Country (year inscribed)	Site	Brief description
Egypt (2005)	Wadi Al-Hitan	Western Desert fossil remains of the emergence of the whale as an ocean-going mammal
Iran (2006)	Lut Desert, or Dasht-e-Lut	Arid subtropical area, spectacular sand ridges from wind erosion, stony deserts and dune fields
Iran (2019)	Hyrcanian Forest	Deciduous broad-leaved forests some 850 km along the Caspian Sea coast
Iraq (2016) Mixed	Ahwar Refuge of Biodiversity and Landscape of Mesopotamian Cities	One of world's largest inland delta systems, in a hot and arid environment, with remains of Sumerian cities
Jordan (2005) Mixed	Wadi Rum	Inhabited by many human cultures since prehistoric times
Jordan (2007)	Dana Biosphere Reserve	Four biogeographical zones with great biodiversity, endangered species, and rock formations
Mauritania (1989)	Banc d'Arguin	Nesting and migratory birds, sand dunes, shallow coastal waters
Saudi Arabia (2022)	'Uruq Bani Mu'arid	"Empty Quarter" diverse fauna and flora in extreme desert
Tunisia (1980)	Ichkuel	Biodiversity with many endemic species
Yemen (1980)	Socotra Archipelago	Unique biodiversity, endemic species

Source: Compiled by author from natural/mixed sites on the World Heritage List.[42]

formal submission, and SPs are expected to review and resubmit their tentative listings at least every ten years. Since most of the tentative sites listed globally are over ten years old (some dating from the 1990s), many more decades will be needed for them to upgrade or convert to inscribed status. With funding constraints, the impact of the COVID-19 pandemic, and WHC concerns about poor management arrangements on inscribed sites, SPs might do better to improve their existing WH site management before seeking to add more. Table 14.2 shows existing inscribed MENA WH sites in the natural and mixed category.

14.4 LEGAL, REGULATORY, AND POLICY ISSUES ON WH AND BIODIVERSITY IN THE MENA REGION

Article 29 of the 1972 convention requires SPs to submit periodic reports on the state of conservation of their sites, and the WHC's Arab states region (comprising most of MENA) was reviewed after its third cycle of periodic reporting (2018–2021) at the

[42] UNESCO World Heritage Convention, "World Heritage Sites" https://whc.unesco.org/en/list/?search=&id_search_region=4&order=region&components=1 accessed January 28, 2024.

44th WHC session held in Fuzhou (China) in 2021. This was a substantial document providing valuable evidence on current issues in the region, and this section examines them in descending order from international to national and local levels of law and governance.[43] WHC decisions may not have the force of international law, but SPs as signatories have undertaken to uphold the convention, which gives the WHC significant powers and sanctions through its procedures of WH inscription and its tentative and endangered lists. The third-cycle action plan framework for the region identified three strategic objectives going forward: a more representative and balanced WH list; better protection, conservation, and management of WH, particularly for endangered sites; and better integration of sustainable development policies in WH management.

14.4.1 *WH Processes for Inscription, Tentative Lists, and Endangered Sites*

SPs propose sites as WH sites to the WHC, which announces each year new sites for inscription. The numbers of new sites peaked at sixty-one in the millennium year of 2000 but have since fallen to an annual average of about twenty-two. The WHC's control over inscription gives it considerable power over sites coming forward, and the associated procedures can be lengthy and costly, but that has not discouraged SPs from seeking more WH listings. The third-cycle review for the region found that its SPs saw the highest benefits of WH status as strengthened protection and conservation, better conservation practices, enhanced honor and prestige, and increased tourism and site presentation, while they attached less importance to associated economic and social development.

The WHC aspires to a balanced, representative, and credible list, with in theory no limits on the number of WH sites and no quotas for SPs to reach. The costs of the listing process can put poorer and smaller countries at a disadvantage, making obtaining and sustaining funding an important issue. The primary criterion for inscription is OUV, with additional criteria of authenticity (the ability of a property to convey its significance over time) and integrity (sustaining that significance over time).[44] The MENA region added eight new sites in 2023, a significant increase that reflected in particular a greater interest from the oil-rich Gulf states.

The extreme inequalities between and within MENA states may impede future WH sites from coming forward. WHC expectations for WH sites have grown over

[43] Report on the results of the Third Cycle of the Periodic Reporting exercise in the Arab States, WHC 44th session, Fuzhou (China) July 2021.

[44] J. Jokilehto, "Considerations on Authenticity and Integrity in World Heritage Context" (2006) 2 *City & Time* 16; H. Stovel, "Effective Use of Authenticity and Integrity As World Heritage Qualifying Conditions" (2007) 2 *City & Time* 3, 3; UNESCO Paris 2018. See also: UNESCO World Heritage Convention, "World Heritage Policy Compendium" https://whc.unesco.org/en/compendium/ accessed January 28, 2024.

the years, as governed by its Operational Guidelines.[45] When first issued in 1977 they comprised thirty-one paragraphs but had expanded dramatically to 290 by 2021, imposing additional commitments and responsibilities, alongside associated guidance on such matters as tourism and visitor management. WHC requirements can delay inscription, as the example of Oman's *Aflaj* cultural WH site shows.[46] It took two years from the initial report in 2007 before inscription in 2009, because the WHC required new laws to protect the property, a management plan with community involvement, local management systems, and the formation of an interdisciplinary management committee. Eventually the Oman government was able to satisfy the WHC requirements for sustainable management, supporting the physical restoration of the *Aflaj* and associated structures.[47]

The SPs in the region prepare "tentative lists" of sites that may convert into listing applications, which the WHC publicizes through its website. Tentative lists can generate dialogue and cooperation, among SPs and various communities and stakeholders, but the third-cycle report found in the region poor engagement with nongovernmental organizations (NGOs), local industries, local authorities, and landowners. It identified a need to better consider WH requirements and criteria, to address the issues of sites being impacted by conflict or losing potential OUV, and to integrate a sustainable development perspective. SPs are also expected to compile heritage inventories/registers which can be used to identify suitable sites for the tentative list, and to broaden stakeholder involvement in heritage. With funding constraints and other adverse factors, some SPs should improve existing site management before seeking to add more. Cultural and natural heritage are now expected to be a strategic element in national sustainable development policies and strategies in areas such as involving indigenous peoples and local communities, and ensuring growth, employment, and investment in tourism.

The WHC has identified some fourteen negative factors that can affect the OUV of WH properties and holds the ultimate sanction of removing a site from the list after a period on the WHC public endangered list, a requirement of Article 11(4) of the convention.[48] Among the dangers affecting the region are conflict, influx of refugees, serious decline in populations of valuable species, development pressures and mining activities, impact of dam projects upon water tables and supply, increasing salinity, decline of migrating bird populations, illegal grazing, and poaching.

45 UNESCO World Heritage Convention, "The Operational Guidelines for the Implementation of the World Heritage Convention" https://whc.unesco.org/en/guidelines/ accessed January 28, 2024.

46 UNESCO World Heritage Convention, "State of Conservation: Aflaj Irrigation Systems of Oman" https://whc.unesco.org/en/soc/?action=list&id_site=1207 accessed January 28, 2024.

47 UNESCO World Heritage Committee, "Final Decisions of the 33rd Session of the World Heritage Committee" WHC-09/33 COM/20 (2009).

48 UNESCO, "Convention Concerning the Protection of the World Cultural and Natural Heritage, adopted by the General Conference at Its 17th Session, Paris" (November 16, 1972) Article 11(4) https://whc.unesco.org/archive/convention-en.pdf accessed January 28, 2024.

Endangered status for a WH site is perceived nationally not only as a dishonor but also damaging for tourism revenues. In 2023, of fifty-six entries on the global endangered list, the MENA region had over a third (twenty-one), a significant proportion mostly reflecting the impact of conflicts such as the Syrian civil war.[49]

The 2030 Sustainable Development Agenda gives high importance to protecting biological and cultural diversity and ecosystems, and biodiversity protection involves multiple international conventions as well as WH. Protected wetlands, for instance, overlap wholly or partially with over 150 Ramsar sites globally, and marine and coastal ecosystems in WH sites cover over 2 million km^2, with a crucial role in climate regulation, for instance storing 15 percent of the world's blue carbon assets in seagrasses and tidal marshes.[50]

14.4.2 *National Legislation, Policy, and Funding*

Each SP is responsible for protecting and managing its WH sites through national legislation such as heritage monument protection and nature conservation. The adequacy of such legal protections depends upon the resources and capacity of SPs and their particular legal histories and traditions. In the MENA region these vary widely, which is a consequence of successive legal systems over centuries, including Roman and Byzantine rule under the Justinian legal code, Islamic and Ottoman law, and more recently colonial interventions by European powers (particularly Britain and France but also Spain, Italy, and Portugal).[51] National legal systems are further complicated by the survival of subnational legal traditions within different communities – ethnic, tribal, and religious.[52] WH statutory protection relies upon SP capacity and political will to undertake law reforms where needed.

The WHC third-cycle review of the region noted various new heritage laws or amendments to existing but found several SPs with only partially adequate legal protection for natural heritage in particular. SPs identified deficiencies in legal frameworks to include a need for updated definitions of terms and concepts, the role and capacity of the judiciary, impacts of conflict and security matters, decentralization, and coordination among stakeholders. All of the natural WH properties in the region were recommended for better and more stable funding. The third-cycle review also identified that effective cooperation between different levels of government was sometimes lacking for identifying, protecting, and presenting WH.

49 UNESCO, "List of World Heritage Sites in Danger" https://whc.unesco.org/en/danger/ accessed January 28, 2024; see also IUCN, IUCN-ROWA Programme 2020–2025 www.iucn.org/sites/default/files/2022-07/situation_analysis_0.pdf accessed January 28, 2024.

50 UNESCO, "UNESCO Marine World Heritage: Custodians of the Globe's Blue Carbon Assets" (2020).

51 H. Patrick Glenn, *Legal Traditions of the World* (5th ed., Oxford University Press 2014).

52 Boaventura de Souza Santos and Maria Paula Meneses, *Knowledge Born in Struggles: Constructing Epistemologies of the South* (Akal Madrid 2020).

Reforms to land laws, for example, can have a significant impact upon WH sites and are currently being promoted for the region by the World Bank, UN Habitat's Global Land Tools Network, and other international agencies. Under this initiative two Arab Land Conferences were held in Abu Dhabi in 2018 and Egypt in 2021, with hundreds of registrations and much exchange of valuable knowledge, and a World Bank research study on "land matters" was published in 2023, which encouraged more regional cooperation and improved land governance.[53]

14.4.3 *Local Management*

Local management systems are the front line for protecting and conserving WH sites and need resources and capacity building. Management failings may be affected, not only by political disruptions and conflicts but also by inadequate resources and staffing. One of the requirements of listing, sometimes lacking in the region, is defining WH site boundaries and often also a geographical buffer zone around the property, especially where the site has sensitive ecosystems needing careful management. The planning and management of land use should protect and police the site against unwanted interventions from developers and incoming populations, who are often refugees displaced by environmental and other factors. When the UK's port city of Liverpool was delisted in 2021, at the same WHC session when the third-cycle review was presented, the WHC judged that local planning decisions to allow development for a football stadium and a mixed-use development had caused "serious deterioration and irreversible loss" to its OUV.[54] A key local management issue is how to manage tourism, especially increased tourist visitor numbers: In MENA annually hundreds of thousands visit the main sites, although falling to only hundreds in those less visited. Tourist overload can damage a site's OUV and the biodiversity that is supposed to be protected. Sites nominated for inscription may not satisfy tests of their OUV, and there has been some criticism about whether WH status is worth the trouble.[55]

The third-cycle report review recommended making capacity development a priority for the region. For more than half of the region's WH properties, available human resources only partially met the management needs, while funding for projects usually came from external funds and most SPs lacked a national capacity-building strategy for WH site staff. Unsurprisingly the conflict-affected countries were most likely to suffer from inadequate budgets for both cultural and natural heritage conservation.

One ground for optimism is the increased availability of geospatial technologies and better connectivity with academic networks. For example, stakeholders are

[53] A. Corsi and S. Harris, *Land Matters: Can Better Governance and Management of Scarcity Prevent a Looming Crisis in the Middle East and North Africa?* (World Bank 2023).

[54] WHC Committee Decision: 44 COM 7A.34, 44th session (2021).

[55] W. Ndoro, "World Heritage Sites in Africa: What Are the Benefits of Nomination and Inscription?" in W. Logan (ed), *A Companion to Heritage Studies* (John Wiley 2015).

applying geospatial technology for WH management, generating 3D "digital twins" (as was done for Palmyra's monuments destroyed by ISIS), LIDAR surveys of WH sites, and mapping to prepare against future threats, both natural and man-made. With the apparently insatiable demand for WH tourism, so-called digital nomads using new technologies are becoming a new kind of tourist with less direct impact upon the biodiversity that needs protection because they may not visit in person.[56]

14.4.4 *Education, Participation, and Public Awareness*

While not governed under legislation, the third-cycle regional review found that participation of local communities was often poor and needed mechanisms to promote the effective participation of different stakeholders. A more decentralized state could allow local people and social capital to contribute more. The review also found that education, information, and awareness-raising was better among researchers, the tourism industry, national/international tourists, and NGOs than among local authorities, communities, and landowners. Youth, children, women, and indigenous peoples showed less awareness and understanding of the topic, and heritage could have a stronger function in the life of communities through the use of WH resources to use heritage and biodiversity to improve local economic and living conditions. Local authorities at the subnational level are the most directly involved agencies but the local agents responsible for cultural heritage may themselves have limited understanding of basic principles or knowledge of the relevant history, creating a need for specialist training. SDG 4 (education) includes Target 4.7 to link education to other SDGs and promote sustainable development within a lifelong learning framework.[57]

14.4.5 *Intangible Cultural Heritage and Climate Change Issues*

The 2003 Convention for the Safeguarding of Intangible Cultural Property added a new dimension to WH,[58] recognizing that cultural activities are vehicles of identity, values, and meaning, and the third-cycle report identified WH properties in the region with associated inscribed intangible practices/traditions. Changes in traditional ways of life and knowledge systems are having a negative impact on WH properties, for example the erosion of ancestral fishing methods by unsustainable fishing techniques and the abandonment of traditions and long-established skills, changing traditional uses of building materials.

[56] K Vagena, "Digital Nomads and Tourism Industry" (2021) *Academia Letters*, Article 765.

[57] United Nations Department of Economic and Social Affairs (UN DESA), "Goal 4: Ensure Inclusive and Equitable Quality Education and Promote Lifelong Learning Opportunities for All" https://sdgs.un.org/goals/goal4 accessed January 28, 2024.

[58] UNESCO Intangible Cultural Heritage, "Text of the Convention for the Safeguarding of the Intangible Cultural Heritage" https://ich.unesco.org/en/convention accessed January 28, 2024.

Climate action is increasingly seen as requiring not only new knowledge but also the rediscovery and revival of old ones, which have been neglected in the fast-moving "modernization" that is now seen as contributing to global warming and climate change. One intangible cultural heritage listing with relevance for WH properties in the MENA region was made in 2020 for Japan: "Traditional skills, techniques and knowledge for the conservation and transmission of wooden architecture."[59] The MENA region has long experience designing for a hot and dry climate, but much of that traditional knowledge has been neglected or forgotten and often relegated to an academic subdiscipline of "vernacular architecture."[60] Those concerned with sustainable architecture are now seeking ways to learn from old building methods and alternative building materials. UNESCO's World Heritage Earthen Architecture Programme (2007–2017) has boosted interest in both traditional and new forms of it and identified 150 WH properties built with this ancient technology.[61]

Among the ancient MENA traditions for adapting buildings to extreme climate conditions are the so-called wind catchers (in Iran known as *bâdgir*): tall, chimney-like structures that capture cool prevailing winds and redirect them downwards into buildings.[62] In 2017 the WHC inscribed as a WH site the Iranian city of Yazd, nicknamed the "City of windcatchers," and also the country's windmills (or *Asbads*). Another MENA tradition relevant to climate change is the *qanat* (known across the region under different names). Thousands of kilometers of such systems exist to move water underground from an aquifer or well at higher attitudes to supply settlements and irrigation without the need for pumping and losing little to evaporation.[63] The WH sites of Oman's system (known as *aflaj*) and the "garden city" of Al Ain (Abu Dhabi) were inscribed in 2006 and 2011, respectively.[64] A revival of such systems through community engagement can be promoted through WH and intangible cultural heritage, although much needs to be done.

14.5 CONCLUSIONS AND RECOMMENDATIONS

From the preceding sections some concluding recommendations can be offered on biodiversity and WH in the MENA region. The WHC's third-cycle action plan

59 W. Weber and Y. Simos (eds), *Lessons from Vernacular Architecture* (Routledge 2013).

60 B. Rudofsky, *Architecture without Architects: A Short Introduction to Non-pedigreed Architecture* (MOMA 1964).

61 UNESCO World Heritage Convention, "Report on the World Heritage Thematic Programmes" WHC/16/40.COM/5D 2016.

62 O. Saadatian et al., "Review of Windcatcher Technologies" (2012) 16 *Renewable and Sustainable Energy Reviews* 3, 1477; P. Sangdeh and N. Nasrollahi, "Windcatchers and Their Applications in Contemporary Architecture" (2022) 3 *Energy and Built Environment* 1, 56.

63 N. Fuzhan et al., "Qanat Water Supply Systems: A Revisit of Sustainability Perspectives" (2015) 13 *Environmental System Research* 4.

64 A. K. Al Dhaheri and Aflaj Al Ain, *From the Past to the Present* (Abu Dhabi Government 2021).

framework for the region in 2021 identified three strategic objectives: a representative and balanced WH list; better protection, conservation, and management of WH, particularly for endangered sites; and better integration of sustainable development policies in WH management.

To discuss these in turn, after fifty years of WH listing since the originating convention in 1972, the emphasis upon cultural rather than natural categories has shifted toward issues of sustainability and biodiversity, especially since the international CBD. Aiming toward a more representative and balanced WH list, new WH inscriptions in the MENA region between 2010 and 2018 have included several of biodiversity significance: the Sanganeb Marine National Park and Dungonab Bay/Mukkawar Island Marine National Park (Sudan, natural, 2016); the Ahwar of southern Iraq (refuge of biodiversity and the relict landscape of Mesopotamian cities, mixed, 2016); the Al-Ahsa Oasis (Saudi Arabia, cultural, 2018); and most recently 'Uruq Bani Mu'arid (Saudi Arabia, natural, 2023).[65]

The action plan's second strategic objective – better protection, conservation, and management of WH – has many challenges, especially maintaining the OUV of WH sites. The third-cycle report found that this was often compromised by challenges of climate change, extreme weather events, and conflict. Heavy rains and flooding have an impact on earthen structures, with ensuing growth of vegetation on external facades causing cracks and fissures. Other threats include falling water tables, overfishing reducing marine life, land conversion by growing human populations, overgrazing, wild plant collection, and commercial hunting. Boundary delineation of some WH properties and their buffer zones has been found inadequate to maintain their OUV.

The third-cycle report also found that visitor management and tourism strategies sometimes did not effectively maintain the OUV, with insufficient cooperation between the tourism industry and WH site management. Capacity building is needed in sustainable tourism for WH sites. improving the management of biodiversity and better public awareness. All these actions depend upon more resources and sometimes better legislation and policing. Better public awareness of heritage and biodiversity issues requires formal and informal education and the participation of hitherto overlooked or excluded groups such as local indigenous and nomadic communities. Teaching and training materials for integrating living heritage into nonformal education can bring it closer to local communities, with WH still often little known by local communities, landowners, and young and indigenous peoples.

The third and last strategic objective of the third-cycle WHC action plan for the region is better integration of sustainable development policies in WH management. The UN Sustainable Development Agenda includes many SDGs relevant to biodiversity – 11, 13, 14, and 15, and also 17 ("Partnerships for the Goals"). There are many different kinds of partnerships that can help biodiversity protection

[65] UNESCO, "List of World Heritage Sites" https://whc.unesco.org/en/list/ accessed January 12, 2024.

of world heritage. Multidisciplinary research is breaking down the traditional paradigms of academic and professional knowledge, and the contribution of local indigenous or traditional knowledge, especially for natural heritage, biodiversity, and climate action, is now becoming better recognized. Wider participation and inclusive partnerships are bringing together researchers, politicians, professionals, local communities, and educators to develop new approaches to sustainable development. Technological advances in academic publishing are creating a wider reach for open-access online research, and improved communication technology offers many opportunities for the generation, management, and transfer of knowledge. The 2020s are identified as the "decade of action" for the Sustainable Development Agenda, and WH and biodiversity are important vehicles for that action.

PART III

Lessons Learned and Future Directions

15

Integrating Biodiversity into Environmental Impact Assessments

Lessons from the EIA Process in the Tigris and Euphrates Basin

Rozhgar A. Mahmood, Qaraman M. Hasan, and Damilola S. Olawuyi

15.1 INTRODUCTION

This chapter examines the important role of environmental impact assessments (EIAs) as tools for biodiversity and nature conservation in the Middle East and North Africa (MENA) region. Drawing on lessons from three major projects, concerns have been heightened about their biodiversity risks to the Tigris and Euphrates river basin, namely the Güneydoğu Anadolu Projesi (GAP) project in Turkey,[1] the Tropical Water Projects in Iran,[2] and drainage projects in Iraq.[3] The chapter discusses how project developers and planners can maximize the full value of EIAs to better anticipate and manage such biodiversity risks.

In practice, an EIA can be used to identify and minimize potential significant harm caused by water resource projects and industrial developments in relation to water quantity and quality measures. Conducting a transboundary EIA for water projects across borders is therefore a recognized procedural obligation of international customary law.[4] EIAs provide a framework for project planners and regulators to effectively anticipate and prevent transboundary harm associated with large-scale dams and other water projects. As discussed in Chapter 3, failure to address the adverse

[1] Republic of Turkey, Ministry of Industry and Technology, "Southeastern Anatolia Project" www.gap.gov.tr/en/what-s-gap-page-1.html accessed January 29, 2024.

[2] Tehran Times, "Rouhani Opens Tropical Water Project in Kermanshah" (May 3, 2019) www.tehrantimes.com/news/435382/Rouhani-opens-tropical-water-project-in-Kermanshah accessed January 30, 2024.

[3] C. J. Richardson and N. A. Hussain, "Restoring the Garden of Eden: An Ecological Assessment of the Marshes of Iraq" (2006) 56 *BioScience* 477.

[4] The EIA is the process of identifying, predicting, evaluating, and managing the biophysical, social, health, and other relevant impacts of development proposals prior of taking any major decision and commitments. The EIA process includes consideration of all significant impacts, namely direct, indirect, and cumulative impacts. See: B. Sadler et al., *Environmental and Social Impact Assessment for Large Scale Dams* (World Commission on Dams Secretariat 2000).

impact of development projects on water security could worsen biodiversity loss and the extinction of plants and animals that depend on wetlands and other natural habitats. Understanding the relationship between the EIA and protecting biodiversity, and when it becomes significant, is therefore determinative in defining the impacts one assesses when conducting EIAs.

Across the MENA region, all infrastructure development projects are legally required to undergo some form of EIA to receive governmental approval or regulatory permit.[5] However, as demonstrated in this chapter, the terms and scope of an EIA are largely open to interpretation. This ambiguity is compounded by uncertainty in reconciling the damage which could result from projects and the legal concept of harm to diversity, which proponents must guard against. Concerns have been raised relating to the reduction of water levels in the Tigris and Euphrates rivers as a result of large-scale dam projects undertaken since 1950, permanent changes to the wetland ecology of the region, and a lack of widespread engagement from stakeholders impacted by such projects, all of which raise the need for a more comprehensive implementation of EIA norms in the MENA region.[6] Furthermore, the implementation of EIA processes will need to be better monitored across the MENA region before and after the approvals of development activities, in order to ensure that approved activities are being implemented in accordance with approved environmental quality standards and technologies.[7] This is not exceptional, even in new mega-projects such as the Grand Ethiopian Renaissance Dam, which may cause floods in the Nile Delta in both Egypt and Sudan,[8] or in the GAP in Turkey, which has led to biodiversity loss, as discussed in Section 15.3.

While several studies have examined the importance of EIAs as an important anticipatory tool for halting biodiversity loss, the challenges hindering its effective implementation to address biodiversity risks in the MENA region has yet to be exhaustively analyzed. This chapter fills a gap in this regard. It draws salient lessons from how the lack of comprehensive EIAs in water projects on the Tigris and Euphrates river basin has had diverse and adverse consequences on the environment and biodiversity of the basin. It discusses how the EIA could be enhanced in current and future developments in the basin by improving legal frameworks at the national level, increasing institutional capability, and integrating technological advancement into the fabric of EIAs.

5 Damilola Olawuyi, *Environmental Law in Arab States* (Oxford University Press 2022) 115–118.

6 Ibid. See also Katalyn A. Voss, James S. Famiglietti, MinHui Lo, Caroline de Linage, Matthew Rodell, and Sean C. Swenson, "Groundwater Depletion in the Middle East from GRACE with Implications for Transboundary Water Management in the Tigris–Euphrates–Western Iran Region" (2013) 49 *Water Resources Research* 904.

7 Olawuyi (n 5) 115–119.

8 Mohamed Mostafa Mohamed and Samy Ismail Elmahdy, "Remote Sensing of the Grand Ethiopian Renaissance Dam: A Hazard and Environmental Impacts Assessment" (2017) 8 *Geomatics, Natural Hazards and Risk* 2, 1225.

The chapter proceeds in five sections, this introduction being the first. Section 15.2 maps the interdependent relationship between EIAs and biodiversity protection, drawing from key international law instruments, including the Convention on Biological Diversity (CBD), the Convention on Environmental Impact Assessment in a Transboundary Context (Espoo) and International Court of Justice (ICJ) cases. This section demonstrates how the legal scope of the EIA is changing, based on a gradual evolution in international environmental law (IEL), particularly pertaining to biodiversity, to embrace a more comprehensive vision of biodiversity protection. Despite this positive change, biodiversity protection is still not sufficient in many countries in the MENA region. Section 15.3 examines the negative impacts of ignoring EIAs in the case of dams and projects on the Tigris and Euphrates river basins. The lack of a comprehensive EIA process has contributed to the considerable loss of biodiversity, as well as cultural and heritage values, in the wetlands south of Iraq. Section 15.4 discusses how gaps such as the lack of clear recognition of biodiversity in EIA legislation, inadequate stakeholder engagement, weak integration of human rights standards in assessments and planning processes, the lack of institutional coordination between water and environmental institutions, and resource and capacity constraints all weaken the EIA process for these projects. To address these gaps in EIA implementation in current development projects and other future development projects across the MENA region, Section 15.5 discusses the need for human rights impact assessments as part of a comprehensive planning process. Section 15.6 is the concluding section.

15.2 THE EIA AS A TOOL FOR BIODIVERSITY PROTECTION AND NATURE CONSERVATION

The need for EIAs arose out of growing global environmental awareness in the 1950s and 1960s, and the recognition that industrial and other development projects were producing undesirable consequences on the environment.[9] In 1989, the United Nations Environment Program (UNEP) called for the necessity of concluding an international agreement on biological diversity. Work began by a specialized team in 1989 to prepare the agreement. This team continued its work and was called the Intergovernmental Negotiating Committee. It announced its adoption of the text of the international agreement in 1989, at the Nairobi Conference, and it was later concluded.[10] The agreement was announced to be open for signature at the Earth Summit in Rio de Janeiro on June 1992, and it entered into force on December 1993. One hundred ninety-three parties joined it. The goal of the agreement was "[p]romoting practices that lead to a sustainable future."[11]

9 Ibid.

10 C. Y. Keong, *Global Environmental Sustainability Case Studies and Analysis of the United Nations' Journey toward Sustainable Development* (Elsevier, 2021) 63–202.

11 Convention on Biological Diversity, 1760 UNTS 79, 31 ILM 818 (1992) (Date of Adoption, May 22, 1992; Place of Adoption, Rio de Janeiro).

In its preamble, the convention expressed its awareness of the fundamental value of biological diversity and ecological values, expressed its concern about the serious discrepancy in biological diversity due to human activities, and stressed at the same time that the basic condition for the conservation of biological diversity is the maintenance of ecosystems and habitats. The general objectives of the agreement, as stated in Article (1), is to ensure the conservation of biological diversity, the sustainable use of its components, and the fair and equitable sharing of the benefits arising out of the utilization of genetic resources.[12]

For worldwide biodiversity, the most significant overall initiative is the CBD from 1992; the arrangement and the convention period put the focus on what biodiversity is, what it means to mankind, and what the globe will resemble for our children if we fail in safeguarding biodiversity at all its levels.[13] Here, the importance of the EIA is raised as a critical tool for the careful decision-making for the sustainable management of our resources, for considering best practices for protecting biodiversity in the long term, and for the care for the wider range of biodiversity beyond national borders. Article 14 of the CBD requires parties to mandate EIAs for their proposed projects that are likely to have significant adverse effects on biological diversity with a view to avoiding or minimizing such effects and, where appropriate, allow for public participation in such procedures.[14] It also requires parties to introduce appropriate arrangements to ensure that the environmental consequences of programs, activities, and policies that are likely to have significant adverse impacts on biological diversity are duly taken into account.

Conducting a transparent EIA in accordance with the CBD is a preeminent issue for international rivers or transboundary rivers because water projects and changing water flows from upper-stream countries to downstream countries will have an impact on the biodiversity of river basins. The CBD confirmed countries have permanent sovereignty over natural resources inside their boundaries, but they are responsible for not causing damage to the environment beyond their territories.[15] This is known as the do-no-harm principle in the IEL, which directly relates to the EIA and protecting biodiversity.

15.2.1 *The Do-No-Harm Principle and the EIA: Protecting Biodiversity*

The do-no-harm principle – avoiding or minimizing environmental harm – has been expressed differently, but the meaning is the same. We use do-no-harm as the abbreviation for all the earlier terms. It is considered one of the most significant

[12] Ibid.

[13] L. S. Anderson, C. E. Davies, and D. Moss, "The UN Convention on Biological Diversity" (1997) 5.

[14] Convention on Biological Diversity (June 5, 1992) 1760 UNTS 79, 143; 31 ILM 818 (1992), Article 14.

[15] Ibid., Article 3.

principles for the international IEL.[16] It is one of the four essential principles of IEL with regard to the management of transboundary rivers.[17] According to the do-no-harm principle, states in transboundary river basins have a right to utilize the rivers. Still, they have a responsibility not to damage the environment of other states. It is usually linked to an equitable and reasonable allocation of transboundary rivers.[18] However, the overallocation of the rivers, in many cases, leads to damage to the environment of other states and biodiversity loss.

The do-no-harm principle has had a strong position since the twentieth century and at the early stages of the evolution of the IEL. The Madrid Declaration in 1911 insisted that changing the course of water, which leads to harm or putting waste into the water, is forbidden, as mentioned in Article 2.[19] In the *Corfu channel* case, the ICJ mentioned that states are responsible for damages to other states due to activities inside their territory.[20] Thus, the do-no-harm principle developed in customary international law until the UN Convention on the Law of the Non-navigational Uses of International Watercourses (Watercourses Convention) was formally recognized in 1997. Article 7 of the Watercourses Convention mentions that states are responsible for taking all necessary measures to avoid damage to other states during all stages of utilizing international watercourses.[21]

According to the Watercourses Convention, the EIA is one of the most significant measures and tools for avoiding harm to other states. Article 12 of the Watercourses Convention clearly identified the EIA as a precautionary measure to prevent harm to transboundary rivers as the article refers to notifying other states and sharing information prior to planning projects, "including the results of any environmental impact assessment, in order to enable the notified States to evaluate the possible effects of the planned measures."[22] This means states should conduct the EIA at the early stages of planning and designing projects, then share the results of the EIA with riparians to avoid harm, or take precautions, which is an effective method for communication and communication.

Similar requirements were raised in the Convention on the Protection and Use of Transboundary Watercourses and International Lakes (Water Convention), but with

16 Owen McIntyre, "The Current State of Development of the No Significant Harm Principle: How Far Have We Come?" (2020) 20 *International Environmental Agreements: Politics, Law and Economics* 601.

17 Stephen C. McCaffrey, Christina Leb, and Riley T. Denoon, *Research Handbook on International Water Law* (Edward Elgar Publishing 2019) 83.

18 Charles Harper, Charles L. Harper, and Monica Snowden, *Environment and Society: Human Perspectives on Environmental Issues* (Routledge 2017) 52–53.

19 Madrid Declaration of the Institute for International Law on International Regulations regarding the Use of International Watercourses for Purposes Other than Navigation (1911).

20 Corfu Channel Case (*United Kingdom v Albania*) (Merits and Judgment) (1949) ICJ Rep 22.

21 United Nations Convention on the Law of the Non-navigational Uses of International Watercourses (May 21, 1997) 36 ILM 700 (International Watercourses Convention).

22 Ibid.

fewer details and in weaker language compared to the Watercourses Convention in 1977. The Water Convention encourages parties to apply the EIA "as far as possible" to reduce the negative impacts on other states.[23] However, the CBD more comprehensively linked the do-no-harm principle and the EIA to protect biodiversity beyond the national border. In addition to the provisions of Article 14 of the CBD, which introduces the EIA as a requirement for all projects that may have a negative impact on biodiversity, public engagement is also recommended in the EIA process.[24]

As well as these important conventions, the Convention on Environmental Impact Assessment in a Transboundary Context (Espoo Convention) provided sufficient details regarding the procedure and practice of an EIA to achieve a better level of sustainable management of our natural resources. The Espoo Convention's Article 1(vi) defined the EIA as a "means a national procedure for evaluating the likely impact of a proposed activity on the environment."[25] Under the Espoo Convention, parties are responsible for undertaking the EIA "prior to a decision to authorize or undertake a proposed activity."[26] This national procedure is a critical precautionary step for avoiding harm at the national and transboundary levels and protecting biodiversity. It would also result in the proper implementation of the do-no-harm principle. However, as Section 15.3 demonstrates, the lack of comprehensive implementation of the EIA process remains a key challenge in the MENA region. This is despite the fact that the countries of the MENA region are part of several regional environmental conventions that bind them to apply the EIA in designing their projects.

15.3 MEGA-PROJECTS WITHOUT COMPREHENSIVE EIAS ON THE TIGRIS AND EUPHRATES RIVERS

Despite the clear recognition of the importance of EIAs in regional and national instruments in the MENA region, the tendency of several development projects, especially large-scale dam projects with adverse impacts on biodiversity, to bypass the EIA process remains a key challenge.[27] This is evident in the Tigris and Euphrates basins. Turkey, Iran, Syria, and Iraq are the main riparian countries within the basin. Each of them continually works to guarantee that they have access to the

[23] United Nations Economic Commission for Europe (UNECE), Convention on the Protection and Use of Transboundary Watercourses and International Lakes, 1992, UN Doc ECE/MP.WAT/41 (UNECE Water Convention).

[24] Convention on Biological Diversity, Article 14.

[25] UNECE, Convention on Environmental Impact Assessment in a Transboundary Context (Espoo Convention) (adopted February 1991, entered into force September 10, 1997) 1989 UNTS 309.

[26] Ibid., Article 2(3).

[27] Olawuyi (n 5) 124–125. See also Economic and Social Commission for Western Asia (ESCWA), "A Study on the Evaluation of Environmental Impact Assessment in Selected ESCWA Countries" (July 17, 2001) E/ ESCWA/ENR/2001/8;.

necessary water supplies to suit their household, agricultural, and industrial needs.[28] In the absence of inclusive agreements and collaboration for the equitable sharing of water resources, riparian countries took unilateral steps and implemented projects that caused the reduction of the water quality of the entire basin and worsened its local and agricultural benefits with an adverse impact on biodiversity.[29]

As dam construction permits exert control over large amounts of water, the riparian state can dictate flows and water availability in downstream countries. In the last fifty years, upstream countries on the Tigris and Euphrates have competed and built major dams on the two rivers and their tributaries without including EIAs and local people in the decision-making process.[30] Empirical studies have demonstrated that Turkey's and Iran's water projects have significantly reduced water quality and quantity in Iraq at surface and groundwater levels.[31] These projects are exacerbating climate change consequences for the two rivers.[32]

The main issue in the basin is that all countries, but mainly the upstream states, have constructed many dams, and large-scale irrigation and hydropower projects, without proper consultation and communication with each other.[33] These dams have been built without an assessment of their impact on the environment. Most significant is Turkey's extensive damming of the Euphrates, which has caused a drastic reduction of the water quality as a result of the decrease in the amount of water entering downstream territories. The water reduction due to these mega-dams contributed to biodiversity loss in Iraq; many species, including ferruginous duck, are under real threat.[34]

In addition, decision-makers in the GAP project failed to apply international standards in constructing these dams and managing them. They largely ignored the EIA, resulting in the destruction of the cultural heritage of the Kurdish people, and the disregard for their cultural and environmental values. The GAP's external credit companies claimed that they undertook the EIA but never shared it with the public.[35] Another crucial issue is that neither Turkey nor Iran have signed or ratified

28 Nadhir Al-Ansari, "Hydro Geopolitics of the Tigris and Euphrates" in *Recent Researches in Earth and Environmental Sciences: 2nd International Conference on Advanced Science and Engineering 2019 (ICOASE2019) Zakho-Duhok, Kurdistan Region – Iraq* (Springer International Publishing 2019) 53.

29 Ibid., 60.

30 Katalyn A. Voss et al., "Groundwater Depletion in the Middle East from GRACE with Implications for Transboundary Water Management in the Tigris-Euphrates-Western Iran Region" (2013) 49 *Water Resources Research* 904.

31 Ibid.

32 Nadhir Al-Ansari et al., "Water Quality within the Tigris and Euphrates Catchments" (2018) 8 *Journal of Earth Sciences and Geotechnical Engineering* 95.

33 Aysegül Kibaroglu, "State-of-the-Art Review of Transboundary Water Governance in the Euphrates–Tigris River Basin" (2019) 35 *International Journal of Water Resources Development* 4, 9.

34 A. A. Al-Zubaidi, "The Importance of Geodiversity on the Animal Diversity in Huwaiza Marsh and the Adjacent Areas, Southeastern Iraq" (2017) 14 *Bulletin of the Iraq Natural History Museum* 235.

35 Itzchak E. Kornfeld, *Mega-Dams and Indigenous Human Rights* (Edward Elgar 2020) 126–127.

the Watercourses Convention.[36] This significant convention obliges states to share transboundary rivers equitably and avoid environmental damage to other states. The negative impacts of these dams are considerable on the lower part of the Tigris and Euphrates river basins or the marshlands and wetlands in the south of Iraq. The marshland is considered the birthplace of human civilization, with great environmental, cultural, and biodiversity values for Iraq and the world.[37]

15.3.1 *GAP: Development Projects or Destruction of Natural and Cultural Values*

In the 1970s, Turkey started the damming project GAP, which was announced in the 1980s as a program to intensify the irrigation and hydroelectric capabilities of Turkey's southeastern region. This project consists of a total of twenty-two dams (with a capacity of around 120 billion cubic meters). It contains nineteen hydroelectric electricity-generating stations across the Tigris–Euphrates basin, which were expected to be completed by 2010 but which has been extended to the end of this decade, approximately 73 percent of which have been finished, and several irrigation projects.[38]

Mesopotamia, the land between the two rivers, was known as the most ancient productive farming area in the history of humanity. The Tigris and Euphrates played a major role in creating and developing the Sumerian, Babylonian, and Assyrian civilizations.[39] The GAP project grants Turkey the hegemony to monopolize the water of the Tigris and Euphrates rivers. This hegemony has already had an impact on

36 United Nations Convention on the Law of the Non-navigational Uses of International Watercourses (May 21, 1997) 36 ILM 700 (International Watercourses Convention), also Qaraman Hasan, *A Trans-national Analysis of Equitable Utilisation and Minimisation of Environmental Harm under Environmental Laws at International, Federal and National Levels* (University of Waikato 2023) 222–223.

37 The marshlands of Iraq and the Relict Landscape of the Mesopotamian Cities is a mixed serial heritage property located in the southern region of the Republic of Iraq. The nominated property comprises seven components, four of which are natural with associated cultural value whereas the three other components are cultural. The natural components include the Huwaizah and the central, east, and west Hammar Marshes, while the cultural components comprise the archaeological cities of Uruk and Ur together with the Tell Eridu archaeological site. Republic of Iraq, "The Ahwar of Southern Iraq: Refuge of Biodiversity and the Relict Landscape of the Mesopotamian Cities" document prepared by the National Committee for the Environmental and Cultural Management of the Ahwar and their World Heritage Nomination (January 2014) 3.

38 GAP-RDA (Southeastern Anatolia Project – Regional Development Administration), "History of GAP" (October 24, 2022) www.gap.gov.tr/en/ accessed January 31, 2024. The construction of dams and irrigation tunnels was originally set to be completed by 2010, but this has now been delayed by several years, due to the funding problems that are directly related to Turkey's dispute with Syria and Iraq over the rights to water resource, the World Bank has refused to provide loans because Turkey refused to comply with the international standards for such projects. See Joost Jongerden, "Dams and Politics in Turkey: Utilizing Water, Developing Conflict" (2010) 17 *Middle East Policy* 139.

39 Mohammed Al-Najim, "Impact of Tigris and Euphirates Water Crisis on the Environmental Catastrophe of Iraqi Marshlands" (2005) 34–38 Iraqi Geological Journal 96.

agricultural production in the area and the livelihoods of millions of people who depend on it, whether for agriculture or as a primary source for everyday use for drinking and household needs.[40] The completed GAP projects have already made life difficult in the downstream countries, and if the damming continues according to the current trend, the adverse effects of diversity loss in the region will be grave.

Since the beginning of the GAP in 1989, the water salinity of the Euphrates has started to increase rapidly, which is predicted to increase drastically as the GAP approaches full development.[41] This constant decrease in the water quality in the downstream basins will make Iraq unable to reclaim its previous rich agricultural soils effectively.[42] Additionally, it would halt the naturally occurring discharge of salt and other contaminants from the Euphrates–Tigris system, whose soils are generally heavy and have drainage issues, making them unsuitable for agricultural use.[43] The daily functioning of the power plant will produce water surges downstream of the dam, which will harm the ecology below.

The downstream countries' human and animal health will be further complicated by these variables, which will severely degrade the river environment and make it difficult for many species to survive.[44] The Tigris basin is renowned for its vast biological diversity, despite the fact that many parts of it have never been subjected to biological surveys. Mesopotamia is also the birthplace of numerous plants and agriculture.[45] Its extensive, intact river environment, which is home to numerous endangered animal and plant species, a significant portion of the Tigris, and its tributaries will be impacted by the upstream GAP. Agriculture, fisheries, and aquaculture have all experienced significant decreases as a result of declining river flows and deteriorating water quality in the basin.[46]

15.3.2 *The Tropical Water Project in Iran*

Iranian development projects on the tributaries of the Tigris have negatively impacted the water quality and quantity of these tributaries since several of them rise in Iran, and as far as Shat Al-Arab is concerned, Iran and Iraq are the two primary riparian

40 Ibid.

41 Laith Al-Oubedi and Dicle Tuba Kilic, *Challenge C: Ecosystem Tigris-Euphrates River Ecosystem: A Status Report* (Mesopotamian Water Forum 2019), 13.

42 According to the 2009 FAO report, there are approximately 6.5–7 million hectares of agricultural land in the Tigris–Euphrates basin that is being irrigated; the majority is Iraqi farmland, which covers about one-fifth of the country, and which is almost entirely dependent on irrigation from the Tigris and Euphrates Rivers. Only in the northeastern plains and mountain valleys is there rain-fed farming. Food and Agricultural Organization of the United Nations (FAO), *Irrigation in the Middle East Region in Figurs-Aquastat Survey 2008* (FAO 2009).

43 Al-Najim (n 39) 96.

44 Ibid.

45 Ibid.

46 Frederick Lorenz and Edward Erickson, *The Euphrates Triangle: Security Implications of the Southeast Anatolia Project* (National Defense University Press 1999) 47.

nations. Iran currently diverts the Tigris River's tributaries through the Tropical Water Project, which is made up of numerous dams and tunnels, before crossing the boundaries of Iraq.[47] According to a Food and Agriculture Organization assessment, Iran began construction of a sizable dam on the Tigris' tributaries in 2004.[48]

The construction of the Daryan dam on the Sirwan River and the Sardasht dam on the Lesser Zab River, both of which flow into the Kurdistan region of Iraq, are the two most recent examples of aggressive dam building along the tributaries of the Tigris River in western Iran. In Khuzestan province, on the Iraqi border farther south, Iran constructed a massive embankment dam, essentially dividing the Hawiza Marshes.[49] Major portions of these wetlands have been completely parched on the Iranian side as a result of the dam construction along the rivers flowing to the Hawiza Marshes, resulting in the dust.[50]

Similar to Turkey, Iran, as an upstream country, has started dam building without assessing its impact on the environment and has failed to apply international standards in constructing these dams and managing them by ignoring the EIA. Here, the negative impacts on Iraq are considerable on the marshlands that are home to rich biodiversity, most of which has been lost due to the drying up of the marshes.

15.3.3 *Previous Iraqi Regimes and Drying up the Marshes*

As well as the negative impacts on dams and water projects in the upstream countries, the previous Iraqi regime deliberately dried up large areas of the marshes in the south of Iraq.[51] The marshlands of Iraq were considered one of the largest wetlands in the Middle East, and one of the ten most important environmental areas on earth, according to UNESCO.[52] The Ahwar supports several criteria related to biodiversity which qualify them to be wetlands of high global importance.[53] These marshes are fed by the branches of the Tigris and Euphrates rivers, in addition to rainfed waters during the winter season and its consequent flooding period.

A portion of the Iran–Iraq boundary passes across the wetlands, and both countries built causeways and drained marshy sections during the 1980s war to improve

[47] Dana Muhammad Faraj, Kawa Z. Abdulrahman, and Nadhir A. Al-Ansari, "The Impact of the Tropical Water Project on the Operation of Darbandikhan Dam" (2022) 36 *Journal of King Saud University-Engineering Sciences* 6, 385.

[48] FAO (n 42).

[49] Kamal Chomani and Tune Bijee, *The Impact of the Daryan Dam on the Kurdistan Region of Iraq* (Save the Tigris and Iraqi Marshes Campaign 2016.

[50] Ercan Ayboga, "Policy and Impacts of Dams in the Euphrates and Tigris Basin" paper for the Mesopotamia Water Forum (2019) Sulaymaniyah, Kurdistan Region of Iraq, 2.

[51] Andrew Lawler, *Reviving Iraq's Wetlands* (American Association for the Advancement of Science 2005).

[52] Al-Najim (n 39) 95.

[53] This recognition was initiated by the inclusion of the Huwaizah Marshes on the Ramsar List in 2006, under five criteria out of nine adopted for the agreement.

access to the front. The Iraqi government began draining the remaining marshes following the first Gulf War and the Shiite Muslim revolt in the south, both of which were unsuccessful, to replace the marsh culture of fishing and rice farming with dry agriculture in order to eliminate the potential of rebellion.[54] To accomplish this goal, the central government began implementing five significant drainage projects to prevent water from the Tigris and Euphrates rivers from reaching the marshes. The region had been heavily polluted by poison gas and army ammunition. As a result, less than 10 percent of the marshes received water supplies by 2000 compared to two-thirds in 1993. Thus, most marsh dwellers were forced to leave their homes, and certain species and flora were gone.[55] The government at the time conducted numerous agricultural projects in the marshlands' dried-out parts to alter the ecology.

Many villages and the plants and animals that lived there were burned when the project was finished. The water was poisoned to kill off all the fish and other aquatic life. The people's primary source of food and money, the rice fields, were also damaged. Due to this operation, 500,000 marshland residents moved to other Iraqi cities or sought asylum in other nations. As a result, the marshes have turned saline and are unusable for farming due to frequent sandstorms.[56] After the fall of the Saddam regime in 2003, the Iraqi government, with the help of other countries and international organizations, started restoring and rehabilitating the Iraqi marshes.[57] The Ahwar of southern Iraq are located in an arid climate; these wetlands are home to a variety of biologically significant ecosystems, including those that support vulnerable species with major conservation and research value. It is one of the most significant freshwater ecosystems in the world.[58]

Because they are major wetlands for the area and the world and our only remaining connection to the ancient Mesopotamian civilizations of the Sumerians, Babylonians, and Assyrians, the destruction of the Mesopotamian marshlands is one of the biggest humanitarian and environmental challenges facing Iraq.[59] It requires both an immediate and long-term planning response in order to restore the marshlands sustainably.[60] It should be regarded as the top environmental priority in Iraq, requiring a management strategy and significant assistance from international donor nations, international organizations, and nongovernmental organizations (NGOs).

54 Lawler (n 51).

55 Sam Kubba, *The Iraqi Marshlands and the Marsh Arabs: The Ma'dan, Their Culture and the Environment* (Trans Pacific Press 2011).

56 Ibid.

57 Nadhir Al-Ansari, "Management of Water Resources in Iraq: Perspectives and Prognoses" (2013) 5 *Engineering* 8, 667.

58 Ibid.

59 Ibid.

60 Abdul Hameed M. Jawad Al Obaidy, "The Challenges of Water Sustainability in Iraq" (2013) 31 *Engineering and Technical Journal* 828.

15.3.4 *The Negative Impacts of Dam Building on a Downstream Country (Iraq)*

Dam building and operation have serious negative effects on the environment and society. In Syria and Iraq, people began to settle along the middle and downstream lengths of the Euphrates and Tigris around 6,000 years ago, which prompted the development of irrigation systems there. The two rivers originate in upper Mesopotamia, where there is abundant precipitation, then flow into central and lower Mesopotamia, where there is little precipitation and insufficient moisture for agriculture.[61] The Tigris and Euphrates rivers and their tributaries provide almost all of the water needed for domestic, industrial, and agricultural purposes.

Access to water in Iraq is significantly impacted by river diversions or flow decreases brought on by dam construction in Turkey and Iran.[62] People in Iraq and northeastern Syria suffer as a result of the GAP's construction, as back-water irrigation is directed into the main channel in its upstream reaches, resulting in a decrease in water quantity and quality.[63] As a result of damming, numerous archaeological sites have already been inundated, but the number of primarily threatened archaeological sites is still unknown because of insufficient assessments of the river valley.[64]

Another issue Iraq is dealing with is salinity. The upstream nations in the Euphrates and Tigris basin are seen to be the main contributors to Iraq's declining water quality by damming and implementing irrigation projects, which slowly raise the water's salinity while reducing its flow.[65] Farmers and fishermen have been adversely affected by salinity, particularly in southern Iraq, where many fish species cannot live due to the salinization of the water.[66] As a result of the farm and agricultural land reduction, intensive dust storms have taken place, climatic changes have been noticed, and higher temperatures are to be expected, and as a consequence regional environmental effects will appear.[67]

61 Qaraman Hasan, Sarkawt Ghazi Salar, Durgeshree Raman, Sam Campbell, and Ibrahim Qasim Palani, "When the Law Is Unclear: Challenges and Opportunities for Data and Information Exchange in the Tigris–Euphrates and Indus River Basins" (2023) 8 *Water Policy* 25, 780.

62 Nadhir Al-Ansari and Sven Knutsson, "Toward Prudent Management of Water Resources in Iraq" (2011) 1 *Journal of Advanced Science and Engineering Research* 63.

63 Ibid.

64 Mesopotamia has a universally great cultural heritage and human history dating back 12,000 years when in the upper regions the first human settlements were established. Around 4000–3500 BC the first big civilizations were founded by the Sumerians.

65 The FAO delegate in Iraq reported that the flow of the country's major rivers had decreased by about 40 percent. The "drop in water delivered downstream from dams constructed in the riparian state, Türkiye," according to the FAO, was cited as a contributing factor in the decreased flow. FAO Representation in Iraq, Drought Situation in Iraq, Submitted to the UN SC661 Committee (May 28, 2000).

66 Al-Ansari et al. (n 31) 103.

67 V. Sissakian, N. Al-Ansari, and S. Knutsson, "Sand and Dust Storm Events in Iraq" (2013) 5 *Journal of Natural Science* 10, 1084.

As well as surface water, groundwater suffers from serious issues. It is expected that groundwater levels will drop further due to the reduction of infiltrated water from the rivers. This will have tremendous effects on the electricity supply and will have severe consequences on irrigation and industrial projects.[68] Further, it is likely that the electricity demands will be covered by the use of oil-heated power plants, thus increasing the emission of greenhouse gases such as carbon dioxide.[69]

In addition, desertification is a major environmental and development problem in Iraq, which is caused by damming due to the decline of water flow of the Tigris and Euphrates rivers, the repeated frequency of drought, water quality degradation, and increasing soil salinity. As desertification leads to lower levels of organisms, it contributes to significant biodiversity loss compared to productive land. Large parts of Iraq have become deserts while it used to be productive farmland. Officials claim that in the last three decades, Iraq has lost most of its agricultural land, which has turned to desert.[70] The increase of desert areas caused frequent sand or dust storms, so the dusty days escalated from twenty-four days in the year between 1950 and 1990 to 200–220 days in a year in 2008–2009. This situation will deteriorate with the reduction of vegetation and palm trees due to the decrease of the Euphrates annual flow as a result of dam construction by Turkey.[71]

Furthermore, the annual individual share of freshwater is another substantial environmental challenge. Iraqi officials and researchers claim that for a decade between 2009 and 2018, the individual share of fresh water has decreased dramatically, mainly due to the dam building by Turkey.[72] The drying of wetlands is another negative impact of dam construction by the upstream countries; due to filling the dams of the GAP, some of the Iraqi marshlands have lost about 55 percent of their area since the construction of the GAP.[73]

In recent years, the Tigris and Euphrates rivers' flow has taken on a significant amount of importance. In order to prevent further tensions in the Middle East, the growing demands for water by riparian nations would likely result in significant

68 For instance, research has shown that due to the WTP construction, about 48.4 percent of the power generation capacity of the Darbandikhan dam will be lost and the water surface elevation in the reservoir would be significantly affected. See Dana Mohammed Faraj et al., "The Impact of the Tropical Water Project on the Operation of Darbandikhan Dam" (2022)36 *Journal of King Saud University - Engineering Sciences* 6, 385.

69 Al Ansari and Knutsson (n 62).

70 Republic of Iraq, Ministry of Environment, "Sixth National Report to the Convention on Biodiversity" www.undp.org/iraq/publications/sixth-national-report-convention-biodiversity accessed January 31, 2024.

71 Al Ansari and Knutsson (n 62) 62.

72 Republic of Iraq, "Environmental Statistics for Iraq 2021" (Agricultural Indicators) A report by the Central Statical Organizations (CSO) (2022) https://cosit.gov.iq/ar/env-stat/envi-stat (in Arabic) accessed January 31, 2024.

73 H. Salmabadi and M. Saeedi, "A Real Fluctuations Monitoring of Al-Azim/Al-Havizeh Wetland during the 1986–2017 Period Using Time-Series Landsat Data" The Second International Conference on Strategic Ideas for Architecture Urbanism Geography and Environment (2018) Mashhad Iran.

disputes in the near future so there is a need for more global attention.[74] These ecosystem services will continue to break down if the basin maintains its current pattern of poor management and in the absence of comprehensive agreements on resource sharing, which will result in enormous biodiversity losses to the region's economies and to the livelihoods of the citizenry living within the basin.[75]

15.4 INTEGRATING BIODIVERSITY INTO EIA: LEGAL GAPS AND RESPONSES

Although the majority of the papers and reports that are released by the United Nations water, environment, and agricultural organizations focus on the effects of drought, which is related to global climate change as a primary cause behind the catastrophic environmental problems and biodiversity loss in Iraq, it is not a coincidence that since the 1970s, the drought level has increased dramatically in Iraq, even without significant changes in the temperature and precipitation in the country. Overall, the upstream and downstream countries of the Euphrates and Tigris basins ignored and did not apply the EIA prior to building mega-dams on the two rivers, which is the main reason for the detrimental impact of water flow reduction and biodiversity loss. Many signs of biodiversity loss have been already observed in the basin, including loss of vegetation cover and agro-diversity, wildlife displacement, and ecological connectivity.[76] Long-standing environmental problems in the MENA region generally include (1) water shortage and quality, (2) land degradation and desertification, (3) coastline deterioration, and (4) urban and industrial pollution, which only vary in extent and severity between countries.[77]

15.4.1 *Legal Gaps: Legislation that was Never Fully Implemented*

Weak regulatory and enforcement frameworks exacerbate these issues, which have a significant negative economic impact and environmental harm. In accordance with some of these nations' existing environmental legislation, such as Article 2872 of the Republic of Turkey's Environmental Law of 1983, the EIA should be considered before any mega-dam development.[78] However, the law does not provide a clear guide for actually implementing the EIA and how the EIA process should be enacted and executed outside Turkey. Additionally, according to the Environmental Protection and Enhancement Law of 1974, which designates the Department of

[74] Al-Najm (n 39) 99.

[75] Al-Oubedi and Kilic (n 41) 13.

[76] Nasrat Adamo, Nadhir Al-Ansari, and Varoujan Sissakian, "How Dams Can Affect Freshwater Issues in the Euphrates–Tigris Basins" (2020) 10 *Journal of Earth Sciences and Geotechnical Engineering* 43.

[77] Karma el-Fadel Muatasem El-Fadel, "Comparative Assessment of the EIA in the MENA Countries Challenges and Prospects" (2004) 24 *Environmental Impact Assessment Review* 553.

[78] Environment Law, Law No. 2872 of 1983, published in: 18132 Official Gazette of the Republic of Türkiye (August 11, 2008).

Environment as the regulatory authority overseeing EIA, specific EIA requirements and procedures are established in Iran.[79] This law states that any action that could have a significant adverse effect on the environment may only be approved after an EIA has revealed its effects. It will look into the proposed measure's geophysical, social, and cultural repercussions as well as its effects on flora, fauna, and habitats; transboundary effects are not included.

An analysis of domestic law reveals that the Euphrates–Tigris riparian states, particularly Turkey and Iran, used EIA as a local regulatory tool without considering the diverse effects outside their borders. Nevertheless, only Syrian law expressly requires the consideration of transboundary consequences. Article 14 of Decree 225/2008 addresses potential transboundary effects.[80] The extent to which the proposed policy's transboundary effects must be considered by the competent authorities when determining whether or not it is environmentally acceptable and is still up for debate. How much the Syrian government takes into account transboundary implications while making decisions is unknown.

Federal Law 27/2009 is the main piece of environmental protection legislation in Iraq. Prior to the adoption of measures that are likely to have a major impact on the environment, an EIA must be undertaken, according to Article 10 of the legislation.[81] However, it does not mandate that transboundary effects be considered. Furthermore, Federal Law 27/2009's provisions are still quite ambiguous, and federal legislators have not yet approved any follow-up regulations that would clarify EIA obligations or procedures and it does not provide sufficient detail on the various steps and issues involved in conducting the EIA process. Also, there is a lack of legal provision for strategic environmental assessment.

Furthermore, the countries bordering the Euphrates–Tigris river system are not signatories to any international agreements that would oblige them to carry out transboundary EIAs before deciding on a course of action that might have a significant impact on the Euphrates–Tigris river system. Additionally, regional agreements only cover particular geographic regions.

Overall, the bulk of developing countries' failure to implement the EIA process successfully is attributed to a lack of competent implementation or political will, which is the primary cause of the EIA process failing in the MENA region, as it is in the majority of developing nations where there is still a wide gap between what is really done in practice and what is perceived to be true about EIAs despite significant improvements in law and policy. Although this is insufficient on its own to make the system functional, the fact that there are numerous regulations and an

79 Environmental Protection and Enhancement Law of 1974, published in: 8592 Official Gazette (April 6, 1974).

80 Decree No. 225 of 2008 on Executive Procedures for Environmental Impact Assessment in the Syrian Arab Republic (Decree 225/2008).

81 Law for the Improvement and Protection of the Environment, Federal Law No. 27 of 2009, published in: 4142 Official Gazette of the Republic of Iraq (January 25, 2010).

administrative framework may be considered one asset of the EIA system in Iraq and the MENA region. There are a number of defects and problems with the EIA system in the MENA region that are typically commensurate with flaws in many developing nations.

Wide-ranging challenges are encountered when implementing EIA in the MENA region. First is the lack of meaningful public involvement at all levels of the EIA process as well as ongoing environmental ignorance. Developers make an effort to avoid public input. For instance, the GAP case reports have found that those still resident in the reservoir area and those already displaced by conflict do not appear to have been consulted about the dam.[82] The same concerns have been raised about theTropical Water Project (TWP) WTP dam construction in Iran.[83]

A second key challenge to implementing the EIA process effectively is the unavailability and inaccuracy of data defining environmental baseline conditions. Thus, decisions about effect evaluation are based more on personal judgment than on scientific research and prediction. As in the GAP dam construction reports found, due to security concerns in the area, it is doubtful that a comprehensive assessment of historic, cultural, or spiritual sites could occur in any of the reservoir regions.[84]

Third is the lack of a national policy culture that encourages EIA implementation and application and acknowledges the dedication, administrative infrastructure, and methodological resources at the necessary levels.[85] A lack of clear and comprehensive national strategies on evaluating biodiversity risks in mega-projects often result in inconsistency in evaluating biodiversity risks in EIA reports which could have an impact on programs, plans, and policies.[86] Furthermore, in practice, the EIA screening and scoping are typically focused on the possible effects of a single proposed project, ignoring the cumulative environmental effects of multiple projects in the same area on biodiversity and nature conservation.[87] There is a need for clear and comprehensive guidelines on the nature and extent of specific biodiversity-related scoping and screening that should be done to identify, address, and prevent biodiversity and nature risks in mega-projects.

Fourth is the inadequacy of regulatory fines and sanctions relating to EIA infractions in the MENA region generally. For example, the lack of clear and comprehensive EIAs in the case of dam construction of the Euphrates–Tigris basin are mostly

82 Maggie Ronayane, *The Cultural and Environmental Impacts of Large Dams in Southeast Türkiye, Fact Finding Mission Report* (University of Ireland and Kurdish Human Rights Association February 2005) 5.

83 Fatemeh Khosravi, Urmila Jha-Thakur, and Thomas B Fischer, "The Role of the Environmental Assessment EA in the Iranian Water Management" (Environmental Assessment and Management Research Centre, School of Environmental Science, University of Liverpool 2018) 9.

84 Ronayane (n 82) 38.

85 Ibid. Also Olawuyi (n 5).

86 Ibid.

87 Khosravi et al. (n 83) 10.

caused by a lack of harsh enough sanctions for noncompliance with EIA legislation and policies. Such inadequacy or nonenforcement of regulatory sanctions are often tied to political pressure, with research indicating the potential for governments in some countries to prioritize economic development over the environment.[88]

15.5 ENHANCING BIODIVERSITY THROUGH COMPREHENSIVE EIAS

Dam construction under the GAP Plan, Tropical Water Project in Iran, and other projects in both Iraq and Syria should not be continued without undertaking EIAs to avoid further environmental issues and biodiversity loss. If they continue, they would cause political turmoil and misery for millions with considerable biodiversity loss in Syria and Iraq. Baghdad now has little influence over its neighbors in the region and scant resources to repair its deteriorating water systems in the post-ISIS environment due to years of turmoil and internal conflict. A comprehensive plan to address the nation's environmental issues has not been developed due to weak IEL in the region. Currently, the Ministry of Water Resources is battling to reconcile the conflicting demands for water for irrigation, drinking, industry, and hydroelectricity while some of the nation's hydrological infrastructure is still damaged by fighting or militant activity.

However, biodiversity protection in the ancient basin should not be less prioritized among riparians and proper implementation of all stages of the EIA is the first and crucial step to achieving most of the environmental goals in the region. It is suggested that these nations get through the challenges they are facing when using EIA because a successful and efficient implementation of the tool could be the answer for the Euphrates and Tigris basin countries.

To maximize the full value of EIA as a tool for advancing biodiversity and nature conservation, there is a need for comprehensive legislation that mandates the transparent conduct of EIAs prior to the approval or commencement of any mega-project with a potential impact on biodiversity. All development plans, programs, initiatives, and projects must be based on comprehensive EIAs that address all potential environmental and social risks, including risks to water bodies. EIA legislation, like other environmental regulations, should be precise about how enforcement is to take place and should be unambiguous about what constitutes effective penalties.

Second and related to this is the need for a national policy environment that encourages the use of EIAs and acknowledges the commitment, administrative and methodological infrastructure, and resources at the necessary levels. Such policies would elaborate the need for effective public engagement during the EIA process, as any EIA process is unlikely to be successful without productive engagement with potentially affected stakeholders. In addition to conducting targeted vulnerability assessments to determine potential risks to marginalized and at-risk groups such as

[88] Khosravi et al. (n 83) 13.

women, youth, and indigenous groups, there is also a need to ensure that all pertinent points of view are taken into account throughout. The scoping and review phases of the EIA process need effective engagement with regulatory agencies, stakeholders, and the general public. Furthermore, NGOs, academic institutions, and organizations that are impacted must be adequately consulted and enabled to participate in EIA processes.

Third, after the necessary scoping on biodiversity risks, consideration of mitigation measures should be given to each impact individually and collectively. For example, in instances of heightened risks of biodiversity loss in marginalized communities and areas, there is a need for tailored programs to address such adverse impacts. Additionally, mitigation must take into account the role of technologies to gather data on biodiversity risks and to monitor the implementation of mitigation measures.[89] Digital technologies, "such as Environmental Systems Research Institute (ESRI) StoryMaps, purpose-built web-solutions and bespoke-built websites,"[90] can also ensure that EIA reports are produced and disseminated in a manner that is accessible to the general public, through the use of local languages and reporting approaches that aid public awareness and knowledge.

Fourth is the need for improving capacity building on the design and implementation of EIA programs. As awareness on environmental law increases across the MENA region, there is a need to ensure tailored education programs on biodiversity conservation and management with a focus on environmental planning through EIAs.[91] Critical to promoting awareness on EIAs is the need for MENA universities to ensure the teaching of environmental law-related courses as core courses in bachelors, masters, juris doctor and doctoral research programs. Furthermore, there is a need for executive certificates and courses on EIA design and implementation in order to promote practical knowledge and best practices on EIA reporting, EIA data collection and dissemination using digital technologies, and avoiding social exclusions in the design and implementation of EIAs. Such certificate programs can enhance continuous professional development and in-house training, thereby increasing the number of EIA professionals, as well as on promoting environmental awareness needed to avoid biodiversity risks in mega-projects.

15.6 CONCLUSION

Despite prevailing ambiguities and uncertainties in the legal enforcement mechanisms, EIAs remain important tools for averting and addressing biodiversity risks relating to mega-projects, especially infrastructure developments such as the GAP

89 Laurel Northmore and Malcolm D. Hudson, "Digital Environmental Impact Assessment: An Exploration of Emerging Digital Approaches for Non-Technical Reports" (2022) 92 *Environmental Impact Assessment Review* 106689.

90 Ibid.

91 See Chapter 17.

project in Turkey, the Tropical Water Project in Iran, and drainage projects in Iraq that have adverse impacts on the biodiversity of river basins. The transboundary environmental issues raised by these projects have the potential to destabilize an already tense region further. Compliance with the requirements of international biodiversity law and policy with regard to EIAs and environmental planning can serve as a foundation for discussions, and policymakers should be aware of the ground rules well before the crisis develops further. An international agreement is urgently needed to handle the issue of distributing the Tigris and Euphrates rivers' water supplies among the riparian nations fairly and equitably to avoid other interconnected environmental issues such as biodiversity loss.

Additionally, none of the riverine nations, especially the upstream hegemons, should be permitted to continue freely constructing huge dams and using the water from the two rivers without EIAs and in defiance of earlier IEL. No riparian state along the Euphrates–Tigris has publicly stated their stance on the need for a transboundary EIA. All riparian states should hold bilateral and multilateral negotiations on dam activities and integrating an EIA. When new projects are being planned or implemented, international development and financing entities helping with water infrastructure projects in the Euphrates–Tigris basin should ensure that environmental and impact evaluations are undertaken prior to the commencement of such infrastructure development activities.

16

Multistakeholder Participation in Biodiversity and Nature Conservation in the MENA Region

Funmilola Ayotunde

16.1 INTRODUCTION

This chapter analyzes the importance of involving diverse stakeholders in biodiversity management in the Middle East and North Africa (MENA) region and proposes the multistakeholder participation (MSP) approach as an integrated framework for achieving productive and sustainable stakeholder engagement in biodiversity and nature conservation. While the literature has extensively highlighted the benefits of involving a broad range of stakeholders in environmental decision-making, minimal attention has been devoted to the opportunities and challenges of applying multistakeholder approaches to biodiversity and nature conservation efforts in the MENA region. Applying the MSP as a normative tool, this chapter prescribes legal and institutional framework considerations for ensuring the valuable contributions of multiple participants and community-based programs in biodiversity and nature conservation in the MENA region.

The MENA region is one of the world's most endowed in natural and biological resources.[1] However, the region's hot and arid climatic conditions, including desertification, drought, land and ecosystem degradation, and loss of biodiversity, pose complex challenges for nature conservation.[2] Water scarcity and climate change impacts aggravate the rapid loss of the region's rich biodiversity.[3] With the declining biodiversity and deteriorating socio-economic conditions of vulnerable groups in the MENA region, especially local communities, the urgent need for cohesive and concerted strategies for biodiversity and nature conservation readily comes to bear.

Although there have been recent legislative and policy developments in MENA countries and at the regional level to halt biodiversity loss, there is a pressing need

[1] See Chapter 1. See also International Monetary Fund, *Regional Economic Outlook: Middle East and Central Asia – Mounting Challenges, Decisive Times* (IMF 2022) Statistical Appendix.

[2] See Chapter 1.

[3] Mina Devkota et al., "Conservation Agriculture in the Drylands of the Middle East and North Africa [MENA] Region: Past Trend, Current Opportunities, Challenges and Future Outlook" (2022) 172 *Advances in Agronomy* 253.

to provide more opportunities for community-based participation and the broad-based engagement of diverse stakeholders to contribute to environmental policy development and the pragmatic realization of action plans. Such important stakeholders include civil society, academia, nongovernmental organizations, and other members of the public, especially noncitizens.[4] Public participation in developing and implementing nature-based solutions to biodiversity challenges brings about numerous benefits: access to diverse perspectives and local knowledge; improving public support and a sense of ownership and responsibility regarding conservation initiatives; opportunities for public education of the importance of biodiversity and citizen's roles in conservation efforts; and enhanced compliance with conservation regulations. The public can contribute significantly to the long-term sustainability of the ecosystem and the success of conservation plans due to their vested interest in the success of the initiatives they collectively developed and executed.

Environmental management programs will also need to carefully respond to the needs of often marginalized groups such as women, children, low-income individuals and families, and those residing in coastal areas.[5] Often situated in coastal or rural regions, local communities are highly vulnerable to environmental shocks. They are especially susceptible to the impacts of biodiversity loss because of their heavy and direct reliance on biodiversity-dependent ecosystem services. Hence, the declining biodiversity affects their access to basic needs, fresh water, and food, causing a decrease in agricultural production and means of sustenance. Therefore, this chapter focuses on local communities as vulnerable groups bearing enormous and disproportionate burdens of biodiversity loss and groups with unique knowledge that could help reverse declining biodiversity.

Community-based conservation programs recognize the interconnection between nature and culture and seek to incorporate community traditions, values, knowledge, and socio-economic development into environmental conservation.[6] Such programs require the active participation of local institutions and give community members and institutions control over aspects of conservation plans that directly impact them. Community participation in biodiversity programs is essential to promote community environmental stewardship, long-term commitment to sustainable use of biodiversity components, and equitable sharing of conservation responsibilities, costs, and benefits.[7] Community-based conservation programs protect local communities' rights and encourage partnerships between local communities and private and public agencies to preserve the ecosystem. They lead to social, economic, and ecological development, incentivize biodiversity and nature preservation, and lead to a healthier ecosystem.

4 Damilola Olawuyi, *Environmental Law in Arab States* (Oxford University Press 2022) 105–108.

5 Ibid.

6 Nafeesa Esmail, "What's on the Horizon for Community-Based Conservation? Emerging Threats and Opportunities" (2023) 38 *Trends in Ecology & Evolution* 666.

7 Ibid.

Considering the widely acknowledged significance of community-based nature conservation, this chapter highlights the centrality of local communities in environmental regulation and the efficient implementation of nature conservation schemes. This chapter consists of five sections. Following this introduction, Section 16.2 provides the contextual overview and basis for the MSP approach to biodiversity and nature conservation. Section 16.3 analyzes the factors for effective and beneficial multiparty collaboration. Despite the identified benefits of MSP in environmental management, Section 16.4 discusses potential barriers to the proposed inclusive approach – in light of MENA countries' subsisting top-down conservation regulatory systems and practices. Section 16.5 recommends strategies for addressing or circumventing the obstacles, and Section 16.6 provides a conclusion.

16.2 THE MULTISTAKEHOLDER APPROACH TO BIODIVERSITY AND NATURE CONSERVATION

The MSP approach to biodiversity and nature conservation involves the collaboration and engagement of diverse stakeholders in planning and executing conservation policies.[8] It is an inclusive strategy that seeks to garner diverse perspectives and contributions of people and institutions with stakes in a project or initiatives to achieve more comprehensive and sustainable outcomes. This approach is increasingly proposed by the UN, encouraging all its entities and states to promote dialogue between those with stakes in a given issue or decision.[9] The multistakeholder strategy is an offshoot of the human rights-based approach (HRBA) to development, a UN-led normative framework that situates recognition and respect for human rights at the core of every decision-making process.[10] The HRBA promotes human empowerment through rights awareness, access to remedies and institutional promotion, and protection of human rights. The human rights-based approach is underpinned by five principles: universality, indivisibility, equality and nondiscrimination,

[8] Other interrelated concepts include multistakeholder engagement, multistakeholder dialogue, and multistakeholder partnership. Although these concepts have some variations, they are sometimes used interchangeably.

[9] UN DESA, International Decade for Action, Water for Life (2015) UN-Water Annual International Zaragoza Conference www.un.org/waterforlifedecade/waterandsustainabledevelopment2015/multistakeholder_dialogue_17_01_2015.shtml accessed August 29, 2023.

[10] After the Secretary-General of the UN called for the mainstreaming of human rights into all the works of the UN in 1997, various UN organizations met in 2003 to develop a Common Understanding on the Human Rights-Based Approach in response to the considerable changes in the international development community at that time. United Nations Office of the Human Rights High Commissioner, Statement by Mr. Kofi Annan, Secretary-General of the United Nations to the Opening of the Fifty-Fourth Session of the Commission on Human Rights (March 16, 1998) SG/SM/98/53; United Nations Sustainable Development Group, "The Human Rights Based Approach to Development Cooperation towards a Common Understanding Among UN Agencies" (2003) https://unsdg.un.org/resources/human-rights-based-approach-development-cooperation-towards-common-understanding-among-un accessed August 25, 2023.

participation, and accountability.[11] Stakeholder participation in decision-making and project execution is one of the cardinal standards for mainstreaming human rights standards into public governance.

The MSP approach involves various stakeholders or interest groups in decision-making. The meaningful participation of social actors, such as local communities and vulnerable groups, is fundamental to attaining development goals,[12] hence the interrelationship between effective participation and development. In a broader sense, participation and human empowerment are foundational to the human rights approach to nature conservation. In this context, participation goes beyond an instrument for obtaining public acceptance of a policy; participation is a right that must be respected.[13] The key objective of stakeholder engagement is to enhance trust among different actors, share information and institutional knowledge, and generate solutions and relevant best practices.[14] For biodiversity and nature protection initiatives, the MSP approach can help catalyze more acceptable decisions and greater sustainability of the outcomes, and minimize technical, environmental, social, and financial risks.[15] The MSP framework is a shift from top-down strategies where government agencies, extractive corporations, and investors, far removed from the daily realities of local communities and the majority of the public, formulate policies and execute projects.

The engagement of diverse stakeholders in tackling complex environmental challenges and nature conservation has gained popularity in the literature,[16] and found

11 Ibid.

12 As Amina Mohammed, Deputy Secretary-General of the UN observes, to achieve the 2030 Agenda for Sustainable Development and the seventeen Sustainable Development Goals (SDGs) and commitment to leave no one behind, "we need to ensure that we provide a voice and platforms for the meaningful participation and engagement of the most marginalized, vulnerable and excluded communities and individuals." Amina Mohammed, "Participation, Consultation and Engagement: Critical Elements for an Effective Implementation of the 2030 Agenda" (2018) 2 *UN 2030 Agenda* 55.

13 The idea of participation has its theoretical root in the participatory development theory of international law. Many other theories can be brought to bear on participation; these include, multistakeholder theory (promotes the active involvement of different stakeholders in decision making), liberal democracy (promotes the principles that protect the rights of individuals as protected by law), civic republicanism (underscores the interconnection of individual freedom and civic participation for the common good), and deliberative democracy (which is a form of democracy in which deliberation is central to decision making). Participatory development theory, however, is remarkably important to the environmental and natural resource management discourse. George Pring and Susan Noé, "The Emerging International Law of Public Participation Affecting Global Mining, Energy, and Resources Development" in Donald Zillman, Alastair Lucas, and George Pring (eds), *Human Rights in Natural Resource Development: Public Participation in the Sustainable Development of Mining and Energy Resources* (Oxford University Press 2002) 13.

14 Karin Bäckstrand, "Multi-stakeholder Partnerships for Sustainable Development: Rethinking Legitimacy, Accountability and Effectiveness" (2006) 16 *European Environment* 290.

15 UNEP, Promoting Dialogue, Dams and Development Projects (Information Sheet No 4, DU/CP/3010-01-17/Rev, 2007).

16 See for example, Tasos Hovardas, "Social Sustainability as Social Learning: Insights from Multi-stakeholder Environmental Governance" (2021) 13 *Sustainability* 7744; Anne-Birgitte Albrectsen, *Why*

expression in international law.[17] The Convention on Access to Information, Public Participation in Decision-Making and Access to Justice in Environmental Matters (Aarhus Convention)[18] and its Protocol on Pollutant Release and Transfer Registers (PRTRs)[19] provide the legal basis for procedural environmental rights. The preamble of the Aarhus Convention underscores the importance of access to information and public participation in decision-making, which includes improvements in the quality and execution of decisions, enhanced public awareness, providing avenues for the public to articulate their concerns, and the creation of opportunities for public authorities to address the public's anxieties.[20] The Aarhus Convention obliges state parties to provide a mechanism for public participation and access to information in environmental decision-making.[21]

Particularly, the UN Convention on Biological Diversity (CBD) aims to promote "the conservation of biological diversity, the sustainable use of its components and the fair and equitable sharing of the benefits arising out of the utilization of genetic resources."[22] With the overarching aim of fostering actions to protect and sustainably use biodiversity for current and future generations, the CBD encourages state parties to extensively utilize local communities' cultural practices and expertise applicable to biodiversity protection and sustainability.[23] State parties are also obliged to implement environmental impact assessment procedures and, where appropriate, give the public the opportunity to participate.[24] The first protocol to the CBD, the Cartagena Protocol on Biosafety to the Convention on Biological Diversity (Cartagena Protocol), requires state parties to promote and ensure public

Collaboration Will Be Key to Achieving the Sustainable Development Goals (World Economic Forum 2017); Giuseppe Ioppolo et al., "Sustainable Local Development and Environmental Governance: A Strategic Planning Experience" (2016) 8 *Sustainability* 180.

17 The legal basis for public participation is grounded in various international, regional, and national instruments. Notably, international human rights law recognizes the right of everyone to take part in public affairs that impact their interests. The Universal Declaration of Human Rights affirms everyone's right to participate, directly or through their democratically elected representatives, in the governance of their state. Article 21, United Nations General Assembly, Universal Declaration of Human Rights (December 10, 1948, 217 A [III]). Article 25 of the International Covenant on Civil and Political Rights states that "every citizen shall have the right and opportunity to take part in the conduct of public affairs, directly or through freely chosen representatives," International Covenant on Civil and Political Rights (December 16, 1966, Treaty Series, Vol. 999 at 171).

18 Convention on Access to Information, Public Participation in Decision-Making and Access to Justice in Environmental Matters (June 25, 1998, Treaty Series, Vol. 2161 at 447) (Aarhus Convention).

19 United Nations General Assembly, Protocol on Pollutant Release and Transfer Registers to the Convention on Access to Information, Public Participation in Decision-Making and Access to Justice in Environmental Matters (October 8, 2009, Treaty Series, Vol. 2626 at 119) (PRTRs).

20 Aarhus Convention (n 18) Preamble.

21 Aarhus Convention (n 18), Articles 6–8.

22 Article 1 of the Convention on Biological Diversity, United Nations, December 29, 1993, Treaty Series, Vol. 1760 at 79.

23 Ibid., Article 8(j).

24 Ibid., Article 14(1).

awareness and involvement in safely transporting, using, and handling living modified organisms relating to biodiversity conservation and sustainable use.[25]

Other international instruments that promote the rights to participation and access to information in environmental matters include the UN Framework Convention on Climate Change (UNFCCC),[26] the Stockholm Convention on Persistent Organic Pollutants (SCPOP),[27] and the UN Convention to Combat Desertification in those Countries Experiencing Serious Drought and/or Desertification, Particularly in Africa (UNCCD).[28] The United Nations has repeatedly stressed the importance of inclusive participation in environment-related policies.[29] As demonstrated in this chapter, despite the long-standing recognition of the significant role of the public in environmental management and development,[30] environmental laws and policies in the MENA region are yet to fully reflect this ideal.

16.3 ELEMENTS OF EFFECTIVE MULTISTAKEHOLDER PARTICIPATION

Participation is not a one-way information-sharing process but involves all parties influencing the decision-making process through information sharing, deliberations, transparency, and collective decision-making. Due to the diversity of participants with various priorities and aspirations, varying levels of influence, and

[25] Article 23 of the Cartagena Protocol on Biosafety to the Convention on Biological Diversity (adopted January 29, 2000, entered into force September 11, 2003) 2226 UNTS 208.

[26] The UNFCCC states that in order to actualize states' commitments in the convention, states are required to provide access to information concerning climate change and its effects, create opportunities for public involvement in the process of addressing climate change and developing sufficient responses, and promote extensive public participation in the development of public awareness programs concerning climate change. Articles 4(1)(i) and 6(a) of United Nations Framework Convention on Climate Change, May 9, 1992, Treaty Series, Vol. 1771, 107.

[27] The SCPOP underscores the responsibility of state parties to promote and implement measures to provide all available information to the public concerning persistent organic pollutants, to ensure public participation in addressing persistent organic pollutants, to provide opportunities for the public to provide input on the implementation of the convention, and to encourage public awareness about organic pollutants. Article 10(1) of Stockholm Convention on Persistent Organic Pollutants, May 17, 2004, Treaty Series, Vol. 2256 at 119.

[28] The UNCCD "gives new recognition to the essential roles of both village-level and NGO participation in policy planning and implementation." The convention affirms the duty of states to facilitate public participation and promote awareness in the attempt to combat desertification and mitigate the consequences of drought. Article 5 of United Nations Convention to Combat Desertification in those Countries Experiencing Serious Drought and/or Desertification, Particularly in Africa, December 26, 1996, Treaty Series, Vol. 1954 at 3.

[29] For instance, parties to the United Nations Framework Convention on Climate Change commented that climate adaptation actions should be in accordance with a "participatory and fully transparent approach, taking into consideration vulnerable groups, communities and ecosystems." Paragraph 12, UNFCCC, Report of the Conference of the Parties on its Sixteenth Session, held in Cancun from November 29 to December 10, 2010 (FCCC/CP/2010/7/Add.1, March 15, 2011).

[30] For example, see Principles 10, 20–22 of The Rio Declaration on Environment and Development (August 12, 1992) The United Nations Conference on Environment and Development, A/CONF.151/26 [Vol. I].

economic and social disparities, the successful application of the MSP approach in environmental management depends on the level of institutional integration of the fundamental and interdependent components of the approach.

The first issue is stakeholders' access to adequate information. Information is a requisite for stakeholders' informed deliberation, and the quality of stakeholders' participation is defined significantly by their access to accurate information. The UN Human Rights Committee, in the case of *Toktakunov v Kyrgyzstan*, explained that the right to access information is not restricted to journalists or media, but private individuals and public groups can also exercise the right on issues of legitimate public concern.[31] To implement democratic and inclusive frameworks and programs that foster transparency, accountability, and reliability, such as the MSP approach, states must periodically and "proactively make available clear, complete, timely, reliable and relevant public sector data and information that is free of cost, available in an open and nonproprietary machine-readable format, easy to find, understand, use and reuse, and disseminated."[32] The Rio Declaration on Environment and Development: Application and Implementation affirms the importance of access to information for effective public participation in environmental issues.[33] It states that everyone "shall have appropriate access to information concerning the environment that is held by public authorities … and the opportunity to participate in decision-making processes. States shall facilitate and encourage public awareness and participation by making information widely available."[34]

The Aarhus Convention underscores the need to provide the public with prior information before participation.[35] Furthermore, recognizing the interconnection of access to information and public participation, the PRTRs' objective is to enhance the public's access to information in order to expedite public participation in environmental decision-making.[36] Drawing from international law instruments and jurisprudence on environmental rights, providing adequate information to the public is a prerequisite to effective participation in and the actualization of environmental rights. While there might be minimal restrictions to information sharing,

[31] *Toktakunov v Kyrgyzstan* (2011) UN Human Rights Committee, CCPR/C/101/D/1470/2006, para 6.3.

[32] Organization for Economic Co-operation and Development, "Recommendation of the Council on Open Government" (December 14, 2017) C[2017]140-C/M [2017]22 at para 7.

[33] Principle 10, United Nations Economic and Social Council, Rio Declaration on Environment and Development: Application and Implementation (April 1997) 5th session of the Commission on Sustainable Development E/CN.17/1997/8.

[34] Ibid., Article 7.

[35] Aarhus Convention (n 18) Article 7. Judicial precedents also emphasize the principles ingrained in the Aarhus Convention. For related case law on the Aarhus Convention, see the UN compilation. United Nations Economic Commission for Europe, "Case Law Related to the Convention" (2021) https://unece.org/environment-policy/public-participation/tfaj/case-law-related-convention accessed August 15, 2023.

[36] PRTRs (n 21) Article 1.

they can only operate within legal boundaries, but stakeholders must receive adequate and prior notification to make informed decisions.

Prior notification is the first of many steps in MSP. It involves informing the public about a planned project or initiative, for example, the project's environmental considerations, long-term implications, if known, impact on the host/local communities, and involved state agencies. Notification is a single-sided communication process in which the public is informed about a proposed initiative and receives the necessary data. Such notice and materials should be received well before deliberations to give stakeholders ample time to consult with their group members and experts and prepare for deliberations. Prior notice with adequate information prevents conflicts and is the first step in gaining community buy-in.

Second, there must be appropriate representation of identified stakeholders. The MSP approach is a unique democratic model "whose goals reach beyond multiparty representation. They give allocated seats to different groups rather than majority vote, and make room for extensive deliberation, giving voice to weaker or smaller interests."[37] Environmental degradation and biodiversity loss affect everyone and have multijurisdictional implications. However, some groups are overly impacted compared to others due to aggravating conditions such as proximity to extractive projects, living in a coastal region, and living with disabilities. Therefore, while ecological challenges impact every citizen, the MSP approach seeks to acknowledge diverse interests and give those often neglected in decision-making the avenue to contribute to environmental conservation.

To have appropriate representation, individuals and groups with legitimate stakes in environmental issues should be identified without discrimination. Aside from those usually involved in environmental management, such as government departments, those directly impacted and highly vulnerable to environmental challenges, such as local communities, should be represented. Stakeholders must be allowed to choose their representatives without government or external interference. It is not enough to appoint someone with ties to a community or group but far removed from their daily realities. Representatives' knowledge of communities' lived experiences impacts the quality of their inputs during deliberations. Therefore, representatives must be members of and have ongoing connections with the group or community they represent. Elections from various interest groups and communities allows for broad representation and perspectives. For instance, while communal representatives can provide historical and practical insights, scientists can contribute technical and research-based data. It is not enough to have diverse participants; delegates' expertise also matters.

Third, deliberative democracy is another essential component of the MSP approach, which involves making decision-making conditional on stakeholder

37 Jeroen F. Warner, "More Sustainable Participation? Multi-stakeholder Platforms for Integrated Catchment Management" (2006) 22 *International Journal of Water Resources Development* 15, 21.

deliberations. That is, decisions are made subject to voluntary, free, and fair consideration by all parties. Access to information, the weight accorded to participants' decisions, and the possibility of further dialogue and reconsidering issues are preconditions of productive stakeholder deliberations.[38] Deliberative democracy promotes the recognition of and respect for each stakeholder's views, giving equal weight to their opinions because they represent the uniqueness of each stakeholder and the group they represent.[39] Each stakeholder must be considered equal, and their views and values accorded unbiased consideration. Issues raised should be open to discussion and questions, with participants consciously working toward a resolution agreeable to all or a majority. Although not all stakeholders' interests and opinions can be accepted or implemented, they must be duly considered. It may be difficult to achieve equality considering the financial and power imbalance between stakeholders, but institutions should consciously work toward ameliorating such barriers.

Fourth, conflict management mechanisms are essential in the MSP model and could define stakeholders' trust in the process. Due to differing priorities, perspectives, and values, misunderstandings among stakeholders are common. Therefore, to inculcate inclusive practices, institutions must maintain an efficient strategy for mitigating conflicts, mediating differences, problem solving, and helping parties work together regardless of their differences. An effective and unbiased dispute resolution process can help address power imbalance among participants, promote fair deliberations, mitigate knotty and time-consuming fallouts, and facilitate stakeholder collaboration. If poorly managed or unresolved, disputes may stall deliberations or lead to the untimely dissolution of multiparty processes.

Fifth, transparency and accountability are fundamental aspects of the MSP approach. Information concealment, discrimination against some groups, and favoritism in deliberations are hindrances to effective stakeholder collaboration. Onderscheid defines transparency as "being open about points of view, opinions, assumptions and expectations; being open about relevant business interests; supplying all relevant parties with all relevant information."[40] Processes shrouded in secrecy and bigotry cannot thrive as stakeholders will not trust the outcome, thereby defeating the whole essence of the process. Stakeholders are accountable not only to the government but also to one another, and the government is accountable to the public to implement environmental policies and ensure compliance by actors such as extractive corporations and foreign investors. States can foster transparency and

[38] Amy Gutmann and Dennis Thompson, "*Why Deliberative Democracy?*" (Princeton University Press 2004) 4.

[39] See Janette Hartz-Karp and Dora Marinova, "Using Deliberative Democracy for Better Urban Decision-Making through Integrative Thinking" (2020) 5 *Urban Science* 3.

[40] Het Onderscheid, "What Characterizes a Strategic Shareholder Dialogue?" in Rob Van Tulder et al. (eds), *The Strategic Stakeholder Dialogue* (English translation by Lewis Van Leeuwen, Erasmus University Rotterdam and Schuttelaar & Partners 2004) 29.

accountability by creating a channel for communities to submit complaints to the government department responsible for addressing complaints regarding environmental conservation or related issues. Institutions must establish clear policies and guidelines to ensure stakeholders' transparency and accountability, such as participants' responsibility to divulge necessary information, prohibition of backroom politics, and periodic publication of stakeholder deliberation reports.

Lastly, the MSP model is open-ended and requires committed participants who are willing to dedicate time and resources to ensure successful outcomes, including through the long-lasting project-monitoring, evaluation, and reporting phase. This phase requires a planned-out procedure, known to all participants, specifying how they can track and report on the progress of collectively developed plans. To facilitate evidence-based monitoring, evaluation, and reporting in conservation management, a quorum of stakeholders must be empowered to call for follow-up dialogue at reasonable intervals, participate in data collection and assessment, articulate their grievances, and demand accountability from defaulters. This is only feasible if participants can access government officials and representatives of other groups who are responsive to the concerns of others. This level of commitment to MSP is necessary because other factors may come to light after the commencement of a conservation strategy, or new concerns may arise after the conclusion of the initial deliberation phase. More so, accountability is a continuous process and requires the dedication of all stakeholders. Regular and continuous dialogue and feedback between stakeholders will help to address budding conflicts, foster long-term stakeholder contributions, and help evaluate compliance with stated objectives.

Despite the proven benefits of multistakeholder engagement methodologies to ecosystem management, the MSP approach has pockets of weaknesses, but the benefits greatly outweigh the identified limitations. The MSP tends to extend the decision-making time frame due to the involvement of multiple stakeholders and a prolonged deliberation process to accommodate parties' needs and contributions. The time commitment may discourage stakeholders, especially government agencies accustomed to working with few parties and making speedy decisions. Additionally, including diverse parties with varying perspectives and priorities may lead to a clog in the wheel of progress. Regardless, the comprehensive contributions from multiple parties, improved quality and practicality of decisions, and widespread stakeholder buy-in are incentives worth the additional time and effort.

16.4 BARRIERS TO MAINSTREAMING THE MSP APPROACH INTO BIODIVERSITY AND NATURE CONSERVATION IN THE MENA REGION

Integrating MSP into the MENA region's legal and institutional structures has inherent setbacks which may delay its successful implementation, but they do not render it inoperable. Addressing the barriers to effective multistakeholder participation is essential if the region is to maximize the full potential of community-driven conservation as a tool for halting biodiversity loss and promoting nature-based solutions in the region. The gaps discussed in this section are not exhaustive but are paramount and cannot be overlooked in successfully implementing the MSP approach in the MENA region's biodiversity and nature conservation.

16.4.1 *Lack of Comprehensive Recognition of Participation Rights in Regulatory and Policy Instruments*

The lack of comprehensive legal recognition of participation rights in environmental and biodiversity conservation regulations and policies is one of the leading barriers to integrating MSP into biodiversity and nature conservation in the MENA region.[41] Across the region, stakeholder engagement is often in the form of formal representation of the public by representatives in the Shoora Council or parliaments.[42] Several MENA countries do not provide direct opportunities for civil society, nongovernmental organizations (NGOs), academia, and members of the public that may be affected by a project or activity to actively participate in conservation strategy planning or implementation. While significant national regulations and strategies seek to promote the sustainable use and conservation of biodiversity, regulators in the MENA region have yet to unlock spaces for broad participation of the general public as legal decision-makers in conservation programs.

MENA countries have intensified their efforts to combat environmental degradation and biodiversity loss by signing international biodiversity and conservation treaties. All the countries in the MENA region have ratified or acceded to the CBD and its first protocol, the Cartagena Protocol.[43] All but Iran, Iraq, and Libya have ratified the second protocol to the CBD, the Nagoya Protocol.[44] The adoption of international instruments aimed at promoting biodiversity conservation and ecological sustainability by several MENA countries is a step in the right direction. However, a few MENA countries have paid minimal attention to the participatory rights provisions in the instruments. For instance, the Kingdom of Bahrain's National Report to the CBD highlights the country's progress in implementing the National Biodiversity Strategy and Action Plan between 2011 and 2014. One of the identified achievements is the improvement of public participation

41 Olawuyi (n 4).

42 Ibid.

43 United Nations Treaty Collection: Status of Treaties, Convention of Biological Diversity [status as at December 7, 2023] https://treaties.un.org/Pages/ViewDetails.aspx?src=TREATY&mtdsg_no=XXVII-8&chapter=27&clang=_en accessed December 4, 2023; United Nations Treaty Collection: Status of Treaties, Cartagena Protocol on Biosafety to the Convention on Biological Diversity [status as at December 7, 2023].

44 Nagoya Protocol on Access to Genetic Resources and the Fair and Equitable Sharing of Benefits Arising from Their Utilization to the Convention on Biological Diversity entered into force October 12, 2014, 3008 United Nations Treaty Series, 3.

in biodiversity conservation, but there is no indication of public involvement in developing or executing the action plan. The country boasts environmental clubs in schools and the involvement of local NGOs in awareness programs and national biodiversity commemoration day planning.[45] While these efforts are important in raising awareness, there remains a need for the more direct involvement of such key stakeholders in the design and implementation of biodiversity strategies and programs. Similarly, as a party to the CBD, Egypt revised its National Biodiversity Strategy and Action Plan (NBSAP) to align with the CBD Strategic Plan. While Egypt acknowledged that the lack of stakeholder participation impeded the actualization of the action plan in the past and committed to policy implementation through a participatory approach, the country's biodiversity strategic goals did not include plans to involve diverse stakeholders in the action plan implementation.[46] Without clear and comprehensive frameworks to widen MSP in the implementation of the NBSAP, advancing community-driven conservation may remain stifled in the country.

Additionally, national legislative and policy developments have been launched to set the region on track for achieving the United Nations Sustainable Development Goal (SDG) 15 on conservation and the sustainable use of the aquatic and terrestrial ecosystems, reverse environmental degradation, and end biodiversity loss.[47] For instance, the United Arab Emirates (UAE) outlined National Development Priorities and Strategies for achieving the SDGs by 2030.[48] Although the plan recognizes the roles of stakeholders in implementing the SDGs, the identified stakeholders are limited.[49] The SDG 14 and 15 implementation report shows that the UAE initiated action plans to conserve biodiversity, but there is no mention of the public's role in implementing SDG 14. For SDG 15, the report recognizes the importance of public awareness, but there is no avenue for citizens to participate in the conservation initiatives. Instead, the emphasis is on raising public awareness about conservation and illegal wildlife trade through workshops, campaigns, and environment day celebrations.[50] Iran also developed national targets and strategies to achieve the

45 The Kingdom of Bahrain Supreme Council for Environment, "Fifth National Report to the Convention on Biological Diversity" (January 2016) UNEP 38.

46 Arab Republic of Egypt, Ministry of Environment, "Egyptian Biodiversity Strategy and Action Plan, 2015–2030" (January 2016) www.cbd.int/doc/world/eg/eg-nbsap-v2-en.pdf accessed December 3, 2023.

47 United Nations Department of Economic and Social Affairs, Sustainable Development: The 17 Goals https://sdgs.un.org/goals accessed December 2, 2023. Only SDGs 14 and 15 specifically refer to biodiversity, but biodiversity loss has significant impacts on the fulfillment of other goals including access to food and clean water, health and well-being, and gender equality. Malgorzata Blicharska et al., "Biodiversity's Contributions to Sustainable Development" (2019) 2 *Nature Sustainability* 1083.

48 National Committee on Sustainable Development Goals, "UAE and the 2030 Agenda for Sustainable Development: Excellence in Implementation" (2017) https://sustainabledevelopment.un.org/content/documents/20161UAE_SDGs_Report_Full_English.pdf accessed December 2, 2023.

49 The three identified stakeholders are youths, private sector, and academic institutions. Ibid., 31–34.

50 Ibid., 120–124.

SDGs.[51] Although the action plan was reportedly developed with the involvement of multiple stakeholders,[52] only executives and experts from government ministries attended the Department of Environment meetings.[53] Despite including public participation in the strategic goals, the action plans focused on public awareness without delineating procedures for public engagements.

Although many of the biodiversity conservation- and environment-related international instruments have been integrated into MENA countries' domestic laws, the regulations and strategic plans fail to recognize the participatory rights of citizens. The lack of a clear and practical process for public engagement in strategic planning and conservation activities creates a critical gap and hinders the sustainability and effectiveness of conservation strategies. For example, the UAE passed a federal law on biosafety of genetically modified organisms in 2020 to protect local genetic resources and biodiversity,[54] and a federal law on access to genetic resources in 2021, in accordance with the Nagoya Protocol. Qatar's Environment Protection Law and Saudi Arabia's Environmental Law have provisions for nature and biodiversity protection.[55] However, none of these laws specifically refer to the right to participate in decision-making on biodiversity or conservation efforts.

Notably, the domestic regulations reflect the top-down and command-and-control approach, seeking to deter actions causing biodiversity loss or ecological degradation through penalties.[56] National and regional policies and action plans do not sufficiently recognize the role of stakeholders and fail to create avenues for diverse stakeholders to participate in environmental preservation processes. This oversight hampers the inclusivity of biodiversity and nature conservation initiatives in the MENA region and the eventual actualization of the set goals.

16.4.2 *Limited Institutional Coordination among Regulatory Agencies*

Besides the regulatory and policy framework gaps, the lack of clear and functional institutional coordination among institutions with biodiversity, environmental, and human rights mandates is another critical challenge for integrating the MSP

[51] Islamic Republic of Iran, Department of Environment, Deputy for Natural Environment and Biodiversity, Revised National Biodiversity Strategies and Action Plan (NBSAP2) 2016–2030.

[52] Ibid., 22.

[53] Ibid., 31–32.

[54] Biosafety of Genetically Modified Organisms (United Arab Emirates Federal Law No. [9] of 2020) (UAE Biosafety Law).

[55] Article 2 of the Qatar Environmental Protection Law (Resolution No. 4 of 2005 by the Chairperson of the Supreme Council of the Environment and Natural Reserves [SCENR]) (Qatar EPL); Article 5[3] of Kingdom of Saudi Arabia Executive Regulation for the Protected Areas for the Environmental Law (issued by Royal Decree No [m/165], 19/11/1441 Hijri) [Saudi Arabia Environmental Law].

[56] See for example Articles 19–24 of UAE Biosafety Law, Articles 66–75 of Qatar EPL, Article 10 of Saudi Arabia Environmental Law.

framework into the MENA region's conservation efforts. The development of national targets and institutions on biodiversity and nature conservation is indicative of governments' recognition of the region's exacerbating environmental challenges and willingness to tackle these issues. However, it is impracticable for uncoordinated institutions to actualize the region's environmental goals. Biodiversity loss disproportionately impacts those mostly dependent on ecosystem services, including the poor, local communities, and subsistence farmers.[57] Environmental planning and economic developments must consider the impacts of the depreciating biodiversity-dependent ecosystem services on disadvantaged social groups to avoid further marginalizing vulnerable communities or groups. Thus, biodiversity and nature conservation transcend the purview of environmental or agricultural institutions and implicate the protection of socio-economic rights.

While MENA countries have developed national and regional institutions to tackle the declining biodiversity and environmental degradation, there remains a significant disconnect between environmental and human rights agencies. The UAE's Ministry of Climate Change and Environment is the federal agency responsible for environmental planning and development of programs on biosecurity and environmental sustainability.[58] The ministry is required to work with local environmental agencies without any mention of the human rights ministry. The Justice, Safety, and the Law Department's web page is silent on environmental or bioconservation issues.[59] For Qatar, the Ministry of Environment and Climate Change is the "sole and main agency responsible for research, enforcement and implementation for all aspects of environmental protection and biodiversity conservation in the entire country."[60] However, the tendency of ministries and agencies to act in silos remains a key challenge.[61] There remains a clear need to strengthen communication and coordination between environment ministries and other relevant agencies and ministries such as human rights, foreign affairs, energy, and agriculture, given the key roles they play in advancing nexus and integrated implementation of biodiversity and nature-based conservation.

57 Anna-Kaisa Tupala, Suvi Huttunen and Panu Halme, "Social Impacts of Biodiversity Offsetting: A Review" (2022) 267 *Biological Conservation* 10943.

58 United Arab Emirates, "Information and Services: Ministry of Climate Change and Environment" www.moccae.gov.ae/en/about-ministry/about-the-ministry/strategic-goals.aspx accessed December 4, 2023.

59 The Justice, Safety and the Law Department's web page provides a list of services they provide including environmental protection, but the section on environmental protection redirects to the Ministry of Climate Change and Environment page. United Arab Emirates, "Information and Services: Justice, Safety and the Law" https://u.ae/en/information-and-services/justice-safety-and-the-law accessed December 4, 2023.

60 Qatar Ministry of Environment, National Biodiversity Strategy and Action Plan 2015–2025 (2014).

61 Holger Hoff et al., "A Nexus Approach for the MENA Region: From Concept to Knowledge to Action" (2019) 7 *Frontiers in Environmental Science* 48, 1. See also Damilola Olawuyi, "Sustainable Development and the Water–Energy–Food Nexus: Legal Challenges and Emerging Solutions" (2020) 103 *Journal of Environmental Science and Policy* 1.

The Conference of the Parties remarked that the objectives of the CBD cannot be achieved until consideration of biodiversity is integrated across sectors. While the focus has been on sectors directly related to biodiversity, such as forestry and agriculture, there is a need "to mainstream the conservation and sustainable use of biological resources across all sectors of the national economy, the society and the policymaking framework is a complex challenge at the heart of the Convention."[62] Human rights protection is a fundamental aspect of environmental causes, and MENA countries risk exacerbating the poor socio-economic conditions of vulnerable groups and further marginalizing local communities if left out of environmental management and activities.

Conservation programs that exclude the public, especially local communities, may yield minimal conservation results but at the expense of vulnerable groups' rights. Disregarding local institutions, "green grabbing," and community displacements have been linked to conservation programs.[63] These human rights challenges may fester if local communities and other stakeholders are not involved in conservation initiatives. To ensure that stakeholders' rights, especially their participatory rights, are recognized and respected in biodiversity and nature conservation programs, MENA countries need to reevaluate their national biodiversity strategies and action plans and create a comprehensive institutional synchronization between their environmental and human rights agencies.

16.4.3 *Limited Institutional Platforms for Local Communities*

The lack of institutional coordination for environmental conservation issues in local communities is a corollary of the limited recognition of participation rights in environmental regulations and policies. The establishment of organized community platforms for collaboration, information exchange, and the coordination of conservation strategies remains slow across the region.[64] Additionally, the lack of organized structures for intercommunal alliances hinders knowledge sharing, environmental awareness, and widespread support for conservation action plans.[65] To facilitate institutional coordination among local communities, government departments need to create a platform for communal deliberation and the collective implementation of set environmental preservation goals. As discussed earlier, regulators in the MENA region have yet to acknowledge citizens' participation rights in conservation

62 CBD Convention of the Parties Decisions, Contribution from the Conference of the Parties to the Convention on Biological Diversity to the World Summit on Sustainable Development: Annex to The Hague Ministerial Declaration of the Conference of the Parties to the Convention on Biological Diversity (COP6 Decision VI/21) paras 10–11.

63 See Chapter 6. See also Neil Dawson et al., "The Role of Indigenous Peoples and Local Communities in Effective and Equitable Conservation" (2021) 26 *Ecology and Society* 19.

64 Hoff et al. (n 61).

65 Ibid. See also H. Jowkar et al., "The Conservation of Biodiversity in Iran: Threats, Challenges and Hopes" (2016) 49 *Iranian Studies* 6, 1065.

programs. Thus, there is no institutional structure to facilitate local communities' collaboration with civil society organizations, private actors, and other stakeholders.

The actualization of MENA countries' conservation targets relies significantly on their recognition of local communities as stakeholders. Although the CBD encourages states to apply local communities' practices and expertise in biodiversity conservation,[66] failure to create institutionalized platforms for local communities' participation in conservation planning remains a preventable limitation to the integration of MSP across the MENA region. Local communities experience various drawbacks, often worsened by limited engagement and support by national authorities. Due to their unique experiences and rich traditional knowledge, these groups can contribute greatly to sustainable conservation practices. They are at the forefront of reversing biodiversity loss and protecting nature, but their voices may remain unheard without institutional platforms and support.

16.4.4 *Finance and Capacity Gaps*

Limited access to the financing needed to develop and implement biodiversity and nature conservation programs remains a key barrier to eco-entrepreneurship and community-driven nature-based solutions in the region.[67] In 2020, the World Bank, for the second time, reported an upswing in the rate of extreme poverty in the MENA region.[68] A combination of environmental degradation impacts, armed conflicts, and the COVID-19 pandemic has had devastating effects on the region and worsened socio-economic inequalities.[69] The region's biodiversity loss has affected local communities further due to low agricultural production, food and clean water scarcity, and other compounding factors. Local communities rely heavily on biodiversity-dependent ecosystem services, and declining biodiversity affects their access to financing and basic needs.

Socio-economic inequalities are a barrier to the effective mainstreaming of MSP in the MENA region because of power imbalances. Inequities among stakeholders and prejudice in MSP processes can create mistrust and time-wasting gridlocks in deliberations. Furthermore, as discussed in Chapter 17, community-driven conservation efforts in the MENA region remain stifled by a lack of capacity and training support. The abilities of stakeholders to design and implement nature-based solutions and conservation programs can be strengthened through conservation-focused accelerator and environmental education programs that promote eco-entrepreneurship.[70]

[66] Ibid., Article 8(j).
[67] See Chapter 10.
[68] The World Bank, "MENA: Global Action Is Urgently Needed to Reverse Damaging Jumps in Extreme Poverty" press release (October 2020).
[69] Ibid.
[70] See Chapter 10.

16.5 MAINSTREAMING THE MSP APPROACH INTO BIODIVERSITY AND NATURE CONSERVATION IN THE MENA REGION: RECOMMENDATIONS

Holistic and functional legal and institutional frameworks are imperative to mainstreaming MSP, but the limitations discussed in Section 16.4 remain hindrances to the MENA region's biodiversity and nature conservation goals. With the requisite normative and institutional structures, the MSP approach could ensure that local communities' aspirations are heard and that stakeholders have coherent institutional platforms to share their distinctive experiences and contribute knowledge and resources to biodiversity and nature conservation. This section proposes recommendations for circumventing the barriers and strategies for integrating MSP and successfully preserving the region's biodiversity and nature.

16.5.1 *Recognition of Stakeholders' Participation Rights in Biodiversity Conservation Regulations and Plans*

The sustainable and productive involvement of diverse interest groups in environmental conservation hinges on national regulatory standards that recognize those individuals or organizations as stakeholders and create avenues for their participation in decision-making and project implementation. A crucial initial step in MSP processes is the identification of interested parties to engage. Which raises the question, who is a stakeholder?

There are varying, and sometimes contested, conceptualizations and applications of the term "stakeholder."[71] Generally, stakeholders are those actively involved in decision-making and those directly (or highly likely to be) impacted by a project, initiative, or policy. Determination of who a stakeholder is depends on what constitutes a legitimate stake.[72] In relation to environmental management, stakeholders are "individuals and social groups relevant to the effective design and implementation of given objectives, mechanisms, policies and programmes."[73] In biodiversity and nature conservation, stakeholders refer to individuals, groups, and entities that are interested in, affected by, involved in, or can influence conservation outcomes. Considering the varying and extensive implications of nature conservation, stakeholders can span local, national, regional, and international realms. At the national

[71] Samantha Miles, "Stakeholder Theory Classification: A Theoretical and Empirical Evaluation of Definitions" (2015) 142 *Journal of Business Ethics* 437.

[72] Mark S. Reed et al., "Who's in and Why? A Typology of Stakeholder Analysis Methods for Natural Resource Management" (2009) 90 *Journal of Environmental Management* 1933.

[73] United Nations Environmental Programme, Overview of Stakeholder Engagement Frameworks under other Instruments and of Potential Approaches for the International Legally Binding Instrument on Plastic Pollution, including in the Marine Environment (Note by the Secretariat, UNEP/PP/INC.1/12, September 9, 2022) 2.

and regional levels, they include government agencies, civil societies, farmers, businesses, scientists, academics, youth groups, and local communities.[74] Stakeholders include a broader range of social actors. Local communities, as actors disproportionately impacted by biodiversity loss and repositories of traditional conservation knowledge, are stakeholders in biodiversity and nature conservation.

The MENA region stands to benefit from inclusive strategies but requires a commitment to inclusive environmental governance and conservation efforts. The United Nations Development Programme, through case study research in Arab states, highlighted the benefits of community-based conservation practices, including improved food security, community conservation awareness, knowledge of sustainable use of resources, capacity for early warning processes, and local community buy-in and ownership of ecological policies and adaptation plans.[75]

The practical implementation of the MSP approach in MENA's biodiversity and nature conservation will depend on the amendment of existing regulatory frameworks and policies to expunge barriers to stakeholders' involvement and restrictive and discriminatory yardsticks for identifying stakeholders. MENA states' national biodiversity strategies and action plans must be revised to recognize the participation rights of stakeholders, including local communities, acknowledge the essential roles of local communities, and create opportunities for their participation in conservation governance and implementation. National biodiversity conservation laws and other related environmental regulations must align with MSP principles by recognizing environmental stakeholders, including local communities, and their right to participate in conservation planning and activities, and by creating avenues for their involvement in environmental decision-making.

16.5.2 *Institutional Coordination between Human Rights and Environmental Institutions*

The objectives of legal and policy regimes on nature and biodiversity preservation can only materialize through viable and responsive organizational coordination. The CBD proposes national biodiversity strategies and action plans as the primary planning and implementation tool for achieving the convention's objectives.[76] In the same vein, the Subsidiary Body on Implementation of the convention envisages national biodiversity strategies and action plans as implementation tools required to foster the integration of biodiversity "at all relevant levels within political, economic

74 For a conceptual analysis of stakeholders in environmental decision-making, see Neal Haddaway et al., "A Framework for Stakeholder Engagement during Systemic Reviews and Maps in Environmental Management" (2017) 6 *Environmental Evidence* 1.

75 United Nations Development Programme, *Climate Change Adaptation in the Arab States: Best Practices and Lessons Learned* (UNDP 2018).

76 Article 6 of the CBD.

and social sectors."[77] This implies that biodiversity cannot be addressed only by environmental agencies but also by integration into different public sectors with the objective of "taking biodiversity into the core agenda and objectives of their decision-making."[78] Although multiple government institutions are responsible for environmental protection,[79] biodiversity conservation is usually within the precinct of specified environment ministries. For example, the UAE's Ministry of Climate Change and Environment and Qatar's Ministry of Environment and Climate Change are tasked with biodiversity conservation and other environmental matters. Furthermore, these ministries are not required to collaborate with human rights bodies. Even for ministries involved in environmental protection generally, there is often little or no alliance with the justice or human rights system.

This demonstrates a prevalent misconception that human rights protection is mutually exclusive of environmental protection. This gap in environmental laws and policies transcends MENA national and regional spheres. At the international level, the UN Special Rapporteur on Human Rights and the Environment decried the UN Post-2020 Global Biodiversity Framework for making no reference to human rights or requiring human rights due diligence in conservation planning.[80] The ongoing biodiversity crisis requires reconsidering what conservation really means and how conservation plans can be implemented in a rights-based manner. Likewise, the MENA region's biodiversity and nature conservation regimes have a human rights blind spot that must be addressed urgently. Without a robust and sustainable organizational alliance between environmental and human rights institutions, MENA countries risk further infringing the rights of local communities and other vulnerable groups. A human rights-based approach to biodiversity and nature conservation is only possible with a comprehensive and coherent organizational setup to integrate the visions and programs of human rights and environment ministries. In addition to prioritizing human rights in biodiversity and nature conservation regulatory and policy frameworks, MENA countries need organizational restructuring to desegregate human rights and environmental institutions.

77 CBD Subsidiary Body on Implementation, Update on Progress in Revising/Updating and Implementing National Biodiversity Strategies and Action Plans, including National Targets (2018) cbd.int/doc/c/fcae/4aa8/dd3362074b26490c6088oabd/sbi-02-02-add1-en.pdf accessed December 8, 2023.

78 Simo Sarkki et al., "Are National Biodiversity Strategies and Action Plans Appropriate for Building Responsibilities for Mainstreaming Biodiversity across Policy Sectors? The Case of Finland" (2016) 59 *Journal of Environmental Planning and Management* 1377.

79 Riyad Fakhri, Laila Dalaa, and Saad Belkasmi, "Enhancing the Effectiveness of National and Regional Institutions in Addressing Climate Change in the MENA Region" in Damilola Olawuyi (ed), *Climate Change Law and Policy in the Middle East and North Africa Region* (Routledge 2022) 111–112.

80 Office of the United Nations High Commissioner for Human Rights, "Human Rights-Based Approaches to Conserving Biodiversity: Equitable, Effective and Imperative: A Policy Brief from the UN Special Rapporteur on Human Rights and the Environment, David R Boyd and Stephanie Keene" Policy Brief No 1 (August 2021) 3.

16.5.3 *Institutional Platform for Local Communities*

As regulatory frameworks are optimized to protect participation rights, local communities need institutional platforms to participate in conservation programs effectively. The importance of coherent and well-organized institutional frameworks for successful stakeholder inclusion in environmental management cannot be understated. The MSP approach gives local communities the avenue to participate and the corresponding responsibility to commit to conservation deliberations and activities. MENA's diverse local communities lack well-structured institutional platforms to collaborate, disseminate information and interests, and share resources and knowledge as they combat biodiversity loss and nature degradation.

As Axner aptly states, "when you have many groups with different views, resources, and skills applying their intelligence and strength to solve a problem together, the results can be like the work of superheroes."[81] The variety of local communities in MENA countries is not a limitation of the MSP approach but a much-needed intellectual diversity and richness in shared living experiences. By engaging in MSP processes, various communities and groups could learn how to form and maintain associations and develop the dexterity needed to manage group members. However, for efficient coordination and collaboration, local communities need well-structured institutions to synchronize their interests, disseminate information, and work toward their collective goals.

Local communities need an independent public department to enable collaboration with other communities and stakeholders. Respective communities could develop organizations for internal administration but need government support in building and maintaining an extensive intercommunal structure. The government can also support local institutions by providing management, negotiation, organizational development training, and financial resources to establish and run the organizations without government interference. Such well-coordinated institutional structures would ensure the adequate dissemination of information, recognition of every group's interest, community planning, and attainment of collective objectives.

16.5.4 *Enhancing Stakeholders' Capacity*

The compounding impacts of environmental challenges and socio-economic variables often create tremendous burdens and inequalities for local communities. The MENA region's local communities have been significantly impacted by biodiversity decline, and their basic needs might distract them from contributing effectively to biodiversity and nature conservation. To foster community-based conservation

[81] Marya Axner, "Promoting Coordination, Cooperative Agreements, and Collaborative Agreements among Agencies" https://ctb.ku.edu/en/table-of-contents/implement/improving-services/coordination-cooperation-collaboration/main accessed February 11, 2024.

programs, MENA states must meet the capacity needs of communities through fund allocations and technical assistance. Regional organizations, businesses, and civil organizations can also help alleviate the burdens of local communities' participation in MSP conservation processes by providing financial support. Allocated funds and financial aid can cover the cost of developing and executing community-based conservation strategies, consultation with experts, implementing awareness projects, and progressing monitoring and assessment. In addition to financial support, MENA countries can demonstrate a strong commitment to stakeholder engagement in environmental conservation by implementing capacity-building initiatives tailored to the peculiarities of different local communities, including environmental education, cultural knowledge integration, and technological training.

Aside from capacity building for local communities, developing the capacity of other stakeholders, including civil societies, youth groups, women groups, scientists, academics, and private enterprises will improve their awareness, integration of sustainable practices, and ability to set goals and launch and execute biodiversity and nature conservation programs effectively. Various groups' needs will differ, ranging from financial needs to technical support, tools, workshops, and knowledge of biodiversity and nature preservation. Some capacity needs, such as knowledge gaps and management skills, can be met through stakeholder collaboration. This further highlights the need for the MSP approach and institutional platform to facilitate stakeholders' convergence, support, and collaboration. Having different groups with coherent structures represented in biodiversity and nature conservation management will improve the outcomes of the MENA region's biodiversity conservation initiatives.

16.6 CONCLUSION

MENA countries have ratified or acceded to the CBD and other international instruments on biodiversity and nature preservation. There has also been progress across the region in terms of developing national strategies and policies to promote sustainable use and conservation of biodiversity and nature. While the growing pace of regulations, policies, and strategic action plans reflect MENA states' political willingness to tackle biodiversity loss, there remains a pressing need to address gaps in community-driven biodiversity and nature-based solutions. Particularly, the lack of institutionalized frameworks for stakeholder engagement and participation in conservation has not fostered widespread MSP.

Meaningful stakeholder participation is fundamental to developing and achieving extensive compliance with conservation policies. It is therefore important to transform legal and institutional frameworks on biodiversity to accentuate MSP, while providing finance, education, knowledge sharing, and collaborative engagement opportunities for a wide range of actors. As the MENA region grapples with the compounding implications of biodiversity loss and threats to human health and means of sustenance, there is also a pressing need to adopt a human rights approach to conservation and enhance regional policy outcomes. The command-and-control or punitive approach to biodiversity management alone is not a realistic normative foundation for tackling the MENA region's deteriorating biodiversity and the associated challenges.

The MSP approach can foster the involvement and commitment of diverse stakeholders to biodiversity and nature conservation in the MENA region. This approach offers several benefits, including diverse perspectives and expertise, better decisions, enhanced legitimacy and credibility of environmental policies, wider public buy-in and implementation of biodiversity conservation plans and policies, and greater awareness and comprehension of the implications of biodiversity loss and the need for preservation. As environmental conditions change over time, the MSP approach allows for adaptable strategies that can be modified and applied to evolving occurrences. By involving diverse stakeholders, MENA countries can improve public knowledge, acceptability, and compliance with conservation laws and promote the widespread sustainable use of biodiversity components and practices that address citizens' environmental, social, and economic needs.

Social actors play a significant role in shaping the actualization of environmental protection policies, much more than state agencies recognize. To harness the contributions of diverse stakeholders in biodiversity and nature conservation, MENA states need a paradigm shift and profound evaluation and modification of the normative underpinnings of conservation-related laws, policies, and action plans to protect participation rights, form institutional alliances between environmental and human rights institutions, and provide the resources to facilitate effective stakeholder involvement in conservation planning and activities.

17

Strengthening the Implementation of Biodiversity Treaties through Environmental Law Education

Eghosa O. Ekhator

17.1 INTRODUCTION

This chapter argues that reliance on environmental law education can be one of the strategies to improve the implementation of biodiversity treaties in the Middle East and North Africa (MENA) region. Drawing lessons from emerging best practices on environmental law education across the region, this chapter examines the role of environmental law education in advancing biodiversity and nature conservation. It discusses legal and institutional gaps that hinder the profusion of environmental law education in the MENA region and the key reforms necessary to address such gaps.

Biodiversity is vital to humanity and its continued existence cuts across the rights and duties of states and their obligations pursuant to a plethora of international environmental agreements.[1] Notwithstanding the avalanche of international mechanisms promoting biodiversity protection, there has been a massive decrease in biodiversity resources in many parts of the world, including the MENA region.[2] For example, the habitat loss of indigenous species within the MENA region is rising at a striking rate due to natural and human causes.[3] The MENA region has rich and diverse ecosystems which are currently under threat.[4] The 2015 International Union for Conservation of Nature (IUCN) Red List states that thousands of species within the MENA region are under threat, arising from the decline in biodiversity sources.[5] Some of the factors impacting negatively on the biodiversity in MENA include desertification, droughts, climate change, and wildfires.[6]

1 Generally, see Malgosia Fitzmaurice, Meagan S. Wong, and Joseph Crampin, *International Environmental Law: Text, Cases and Materials* (Edward Elgar 2022).

2 There are diverse conceptualizations or understandings of which countries are part of the MENA region. This chapter adopts the categorization enunciated in Chapter 1.

3 Gazliya Nazimudheen, "Things to Know about Habitat Loss in MENA" (EcoMENA, August 24, 2022) www.ecomena.org/habitat-loss-in-mena/ accessed October 15, 2023.

4 Damilola S. Olawuyi, *Environmental Law in Arab States* (Oxford University Press 2022) 248–260.

5 The IUCN Red List of Threatened Species www.iucnredlist.org/ accessed October 15, 2023.

6 Generally, see Rajaa El Kassab, "A Region in Danger! Biodiversity in the Arab Region" (Policy Commons, August 15, 2022) https://policycommons.net/artifacts/2654130/a-region-in-danger-biodiversity/3677034/ accessed October 15, 2023.

Hence, El Kassab argues that the decline or worsening of biodiversity in the region is connected "to human activities that result from government policies as well as lack of awareness of the importance of biodiversity and its role in achieving food security and the protection of natural resources."[7] As a result, some countries in the MENA region are categorized as biodiversity hotspots and have "lost at least 70 percent of its primary native vegetation."[8] For example, Morocco has suffered from worsening droughts and this has had negative impacts on biodiversity in the country.[9] This is said to exemplify the extent of the threats to biodiversity in the MENA region. The situation has been worsened by the negative impacts of climate change, which is "considered one of the key drivers of biodiversity loss – intensified effects on the region's wildlife, plants and other species are expected to increase."[10] Furthermore, notwithstanding its substantial energy resources, the adverse or arid geographical circumstances of the MENA region (e.g. it is one of the driest, most water-stressed, and most food insecure areas in the world) makes it enormously susceptible to several environmental difficulties.[11]

Against this backdrop, halting the rapid loss of biodiversity is of paramount importance to the MENA region. There have been concerted moves by the international community and relevant stakeholders in developing measures or mechanisms to ensure the survival of biodiversity, including by promoting environmental awareness and education.[12] Environmental education is a process or means that enjoins individuals (including students) to explore environmental and allied issues, participate in problem solving, and take action to improve and protect the environment.[13] Environmental education initiatives play a major role in improving environmental awareness in societies. This becomes of utmost importance in societies or countries that are facing the burden of environmental injustices.[14] Higher education institutions in the MENA region "can play lead roles in promoting the SDGs [Sustainable Development Goals] through courses, training, and research programs that expose students to the various legal regimes governing human relationships with the

7 Ibid., 1.

8 Critical Ecosystem Partnership Fund, "Biodiversity Hotspots Defined" www.cepf.net/our-work/biodiversity-hotspots/hotspots-defined accessed October 15, 2023.

9 Kira Walker, "MENA's Biodiversity Shrinking under the Pressure of Climate Change" (Nature Middle East December 13, 2022) www.natureasia.com/en/nmiddleeast/article/10.1038/nmiddleeast.2022.79#:~:text=The%20rich%20biodiversity%20found%20in,and%20animal%20resources%3B%20and%20pollution accessed October 15, 2023.

10 Ibid.

11 Generally, see Olawuyi (n 4).

12 Phillipe Sands and Jacqueline Peel, *Principles of International Environmental Law* (4th ed., Cambridge University Press 2018) 385.

13 Fatima Eshun et al., "A Survey of the Role of Environmental Education in Biodiversity Conservation in the Greater Accra Region of Ghana" (2022) 2 *Conservation* 2, 297, 298.

14 Generally, see Osamuyimen Enabulele and Eghosa O. Ekhator, "Improving Environmental Protection in Nigeria: A Reassessment of the Role of Informal Institutions" (2022) 13 *JSDLP* 1, 162.

environment."[15] As the Association of Environmental Law Lecturers in Middle East and North African Universities (ASSELLMU) notes: "[I]mplementing holistic and comprehensive ELE [Environmental Law Education] courses can enhance evidence-based policy-making, societal awareness, and local empowerment on environmental law and sustainability in the region, specifically on issues related to water, energy and food security, climate change, clean technology entrepreneurship and preservation of cultural heritage."[16]

This chapter argues that awareness and understanding of biodiversity issues should be embedded in the law curriculum via environmental law education within the MENA region. Environmental law education, which is a subset or subcategory of environmental education, "focuses on the study of the core principles of law relating to the protection of the environment."[17] Environmental law education can be integrated or actualized via already existing environmental programs offered by universities or as part of the legal education curriculum in the MENA region. In many parts of the world, scholars and other relevant stakeholders have suggested that awareness of environmental sustainability issues and climate change should be mainstreamed or embedded in the legal curriculum of educational institutions (especially universities), and accordingly the MENA region should not be left out. The environment is an amalgamation of a wide-ranging and rich variety of biodiversity sources and therefore it should be protected.

This chapter examines challenges to environmental law education on biodiversity and nature conservation in the MENA region. It examines how law students and lawyers in the MENA region could be better equipped with the requisite knowledge of the legal framework on biodiversity. The chapter is divided into five sections including the introduction. Section 17.2 discusses the role of environmental education in promoting the utility of treaties on biodiversity. Section 17.3 discusses the evolution of environmental law education in the MENA region and the challenges to biodiversity legal education in the MENA region. Section 17.4 examines how those challenges can be addressed through law and policy responses. Section 17.5 is the concluding section.

17.2 THE ROLE OF ENVIRONMENTAL EDUCATION IN PROMOTING ENVIRONMENTAL AWARENESS IN MENA

Generally, education (whether in formal or informal settings) can provide the tools to enable individuals and societies to tackle the scourge of environmental crisis or degradation.[18] Education can have transformative impacts on how society and

[15] ASSELLMU, Training Manual for the Train-the-Trainers (TTT) Program in Environmental Law for Higher Education Institutions in the MENA Region (August 2021) 21 www.hbku.edu.qa/sites/default/files/train-the-trainers_eng.pdf accessed October 15, 2023.

[16] Ibid.

[17] Ibid., 20.

[18] Generally, see Enabulele and Ekhator (n 14).

individuals treat or act toward their environment. This is evident in the rise of transnational litigation filed by civil society organizations against multinational corporations in different parts of the world. In some of these lawsuits, the knowledge and expertise of individuals (litigants) and organizations have had positive impacts on the business strategy and activities of multinational corporations.[19]

Education is vital for the equitable and sustainable use or consumption of biodiversity sources, and it is "crucial for mainstreaming biodiversity."[20] Thus, within the MENA region context, environmental education can be integral as one of the tools in tackling biodiversity-related negative impacts on society. Environmental education can be traced to the mid-eighteenth century when scholars and educators suggested that students should "study nature, not book."[21] Thus, some scholars have suggested that the early inspiration for environmental education can be traced to the works of philosophers and scholars who wrote on the utility of nature and the environment in the eighteenth century.[22] However, the term "environmental education" is said to have been used first in 1948, and the activities of the various UN international conferences on the environment have given a fillip to the rise of environmental education initiatives at the domestic and international levels.[23] Also, the United Nations Environment Programme (UNEP) and the United Nations Educational, Scientific and Cultural Organization (UNESCO) have also played a massive role in the spread of environmental initiatives in different parts of the world.[24]

At the international level, many instruments promote the use of environmental education and awareness. For example, SDG 4 focuses on "ensuring inclusive and quality education and promote lifelong opportunities for all" by 2030. Also, Target 4.7 of SDG 4 avers that "all learners acquire the knowledge and skills needed to promote sustainable development, including, among others, through education for sustainable development and sustainable lifestyles" by the year 2030.[25] Furthermore, the UNESCO Education for Sustainable Development (ESD) 2030 Framework

19 Generally, see Sufyan Droubi et al., "Transforming Education for the Just Transition" (2023) 100 *Energy Research & Social Science* 202103090.

20 UNESCO, "Education and Awareness" www.unesco.org/en/biodiversity/education accessed September 17, 2023.

21 Generally, see Najib Saab, Adan Badran, and Abdul-Karim Sadik, "Environmental Education for Sustainable Development in Arab Countries' Annual Report of Arab Forum for Environment and Development" (AFED 2019) 1 www.afedonline.org/en/reports/details/environmental-education-for-sustainable-development-in-arab-countries accessed October 15, 2023.

22 See ibid.

23 Generally, see Afe Babalola and Damilola S. Olawuyi, "Advancing Environmental Education for Sustainable Development in Higher Education in Nigeria: Current Challenges and Future Directions" (2021) 13 *Sustainability* 19, 10808.

24 Generally, see Elizabeth M. Mrema and Aphrodite Smagadi, "The United Nations Environment Programme: Promoting Climate Law Education in the Middle East and North Africa" in Damilola S. Olawuyi (ed), *Climate Change Law and Policy in the Middle East and North Africa Region* (Routledge 2022).

25 Also, see Babalola and Olawuyi (n 23).

recognizes ESD as an important core of quality education and an essential facilitator of the seventeen SDGs.[26] Also, Article 6 of the United Nations Framework Convention on Climate Change 1992 acknowledges the utility of environmental education in the plethora of efforts of countries in tackling the climate change crisis. Thus, there are moves at the international and national levels to promote environmental education at different levels of study in various parts of the world.

There are also laws and policies promoting environmental education and awareness within the MENA region. For example, the Sustainable Development Initiative in the Arab Region 2002 encourages all Arab countries to integrate environmental education at all educational levels, "with a view to raising a new generation whose members are aware and conscious of their responsibility for environmental protection."[27] Similarly, Article 7 of Qatar's Environmental Protection Law states that "all authorities responsible of education shall include environmental awareness subjects in all the educational stages."[28] Also, the Qatar National Vision 2030 aims to promote the development of environmentally friendly citizenry that appreciates the preservation or conservation of its natural heritage and its neighbors.[29] Furthermore, the United Arab Emirates has developed its National Environmental Education and Awareness Strategy 2015–2021, whose main aim is to integrate or embed environmental education throughout all education stages.[30] Thus, laws and policies on environmental education are burgeoning within the MENA region. Arguably, this is not fully reflective of the whole region.[31] However, scholars aver that there is a growing consciousness in environmental awareness in the educational systems within the MENA region.[32]

17.2.1 *Evolution of Environmental Law Education*

Environmental law is a fast-growing and distinct legal discipline in the MENA region.[33] Furthermore, environmental law education is emergent in different parts of the world (including the MENA region). Environmental law education is a subset or subcategory of environmental education, and its emphasis is on the study of

[26] UNESCO, "Education for Sustainable Development: Towards Achieving the SDGs (ESD for 2030) and Its Roadmap for Implementation from 2020–2030" https://unesdoc.unesco.org/ark:/48223/pf0000370215.locale=en accessed October 17, 2023.

[27] League of Arab States, "The Sustainable Development Initiative in the Arab Region" www.un.org/esa/sustdev/partnerships/activities_initiate/101202_sd_initiative_arab_region.pdf accessed February 12, 2024.

[28] Law No 30 of 2002 Promulgating the Law of the Environment Protection 30/2002 www.fao.org/faolex/results/details/en/c/LEX-FAOC055012/ accessed February 12, 2024.

[29] Qatar National Development Strategy 2011–2016; General Secretariat for Development Planning: Doha, Qatar, 2011. Also cited in Babalola and Olawuyi (n 23) 13.

[30] United Arab Emirates, National Environmental Education and Awareness Strategy (2021) www.moccae.gov.ae/assets/b4a14e05/national-environmental-education-and-awareness-strategy-2015-2021-en.aspx accessed October 17, 2023.

[31] Generally, see Mrema and Smagadi (n 24).

[32] Generally, see Saab et al. (n 21). However, for contrary views, see Mrema and Smagadi (n 24).

[33] Generally, see Train-the-Trainers (n 15); Saab et al. (n 21).

the fundamental principles of law concerning the protection of the environment.[34] UNEP has also been at the forefront of developing the global or international rule of law and environmental law education in different parts of the world.[35] This has also helped in the promotion and deepening of environmental law education initiatives in several parts of the world. Furthermore, students on environmental law programs or courses are expected to be exposed to a plethora of legal frameworks regulating human interactions with environment. Environmental law is also premised on a plethora of values, strategies, theories, assumptions, and regulatory principles.[36] Environmental law education also accentuates the utility or relevance of practical skills and requirements on how relevant stakeholders, including lawyers, academics, law firms, and businesses, can forestall, avert, and "mitigate environmental lability in their operations, especially through corporate social responsibility, sustainability reporting, green supply chains and procurements, and strategic risk management."[37]

In the context of biodiversity and nature conservation, environmental law education should also expose students and relevant stakeholders to the various national and international legal regimes on biodiversity and nature conservation. Furthermore, environmental law education for biodiversity and nature conservation should also equip relevant stakeholders in society with the necessary tools, knowledge, and practical skills to tackle the scourge of rapid loss of biodiversity and protect nature conservation.

Furthermore, according to the Training Manual for the Train-the-Trainers (TTT) Program in Environmental Law for Higher Education Institutions in the MENA Region, the elements of environmental law education include:

1. Critical thinking taught to students through application of theory, law, and evidence to assess and draw conclusions.
2. Awareness and sensitivity to the challenges facing the environment, including gaps in law and governance structures.
3. Information and knowledge exchange on the local contexts, barriers, and motivations to improve or maintain environmental quality, including ethics, religious, and/ or cultural values.
4. The delivery of pedagogical skills to students to identify and help resolve environmental challenges, and the deployment of legal solutions innovatively.
5. Participation by students in activities that lead to the technical and legal resolution of environmental challenges.
6. Legal vocation training for students through various pedagogical approaches.
7. Development and application of suitable pedagogical approaches, depending on contexts of environmental law education.[38]

34 Train-the-Trainers (n 15) 20.
35 Train-the-Trainers (n 15); Mrema and Smagadi (n 24).
36 Generally, see Stuart Bell et al., *Environmental Law* (9th ed., Oxford University Press 2017).
37 Train-the-Trainers (n 15) 21.
38 Ibid., 21–22.

In different parts of the world, there have been concerted moves to develop environmental law education or environmental law teaching as one of the tools to prepare law students and lawyers with the knowledge and expertise to deal with the myriad environmental crises afflicting different parts of the world. This takes on more prominence against the backdrop of the negative impacts of climate change occurring in different parts of the world. Hence, today's law students and legal practitioners ought to be trained to deal with these issues.[39] Consequently, the overarching academic pedagogical consensus is that teaching on sustainability and environmental-related issues should be integrated into the core or compulsory law curriculum and not just solely located in environmental law programs or modules.[40]

The last twenty years have seen an astronomical increase in environmental law education in different parts of the world.[41] However, in many parts of the world, environmental law education is not compulsory for law students or fully integrated into the legal education curriculum.[42] This is particularly important given the background of the current climate crisis, the impacts of which are particularly felt in the MENA region. Notwithstanding these impacts, scholars have argued there is lack of climate change awareness in the MENA region.[43] For example, Olawuyi argues that:

> Despite the grim reality of climate change, the MENA region remains one of the least prepared regions facing it. Clear and comprehensive legal frameworks on climate change have not been so easily forthcoming in many parts of the region. Furthermore, climate change education is still at an alarming stage of infancy in the region.[44]

Hence, many tertiary or higher education institutions within the MENA region have not integrated climate education into their curricula.[45] Hence, akin to many universities in different parts of the world, climate education is not integrated into the training requirements for law students and legal practitioners.[46] Arguably the MENA region is no different.

According to Fowler and others, environmental law education emerged in the 1970s as a key constituent of the undergraduate law curriculum in various countries in different parts of the world.[47] There has also been a massive rise in the

39 Also, see Kim Bouwer et al., "Climate Change Isn't Optional: Climate Change in the Core Law Curriculum" (2023) 43 *Legal Studies* 2, 240.

40 Generally, see ibid.

41 Generally, see Mrema and Smagadi (n 24).

42 Mrema and Smagadi (n 24); Rob Fowler et al., "From 'Marginality' to 'Mainstream': The Evolution of Teaching and Learning in Environmental Law" in Amanda Kennedy et al. (eds), *Teaching and Learning in Environmental Law: Pedagogy, Methodology and Best Practice* (Edward Elgar, 2021); Bouwer et al. (n 39).

43 Olawuyi (n 4); Mrema and Smagadi (n 24).

44 Olawuyi (n 4) 4.

45 Generally, see Olawuyi (n 4); Mrema and Smagadi (n 24).

46 Generally, see Bouwer et al. (n 39).

47 Fowler et al. (n 42).

development of environmental law at the postgraduate and graduate levels in different countries. However, in some parts of world, environmental law has no place in the legal education curriculum, hence some scholars have argued that environmental law is not part of mainstream legal education and thus only a marginal component.[48] In the UK, environmental law is not a core or compulsory component of the undergraduate legal education curriculum and some scholars have argued that few students take up the study of environmental law for various reasons, including lack of future career prospects in the field.[49] Thus, there is a rapid decline in the number of students studying environmental law in UK universities.[50] However, there have been various suggestions made by relevant stakeholders, including academics and legal associations, on how to improve the study of environmental law and the need for the explicit integration of environmental law into the university legal curriculum in the UK.[51] On the other hand, in the UK and many other parts of the world, law students (and legal academics) are clamoring for the inclusion of environmental law into the university legal education curriculum.[52]

17.2.2 *Environmental Law Education in the MENA Region*

According to Kameri-Mbote, the director of the UNEP Law Division, "environmental law education systems are relatively at a nascent stage especially within the MENA region. Additionally, environmental law has conventionally not been taught as a core legal subject thus leading to fragmented approaches in its teaching."[53] However, the last few years has seen a growing appetite for environmental law education in the MENA region.[54] There has been a massive rise in the number of universities offering environmental protection-related topics in their curriculum in the MENA region. For example, in the 2019 report of the Arab Forum for Environment and Development (AFED) on "Environmental Education for Sustainable Development in Arab Countries," a survey of the fifty-seven highest-ranked universities in the Arab region was conducted.[55] This survey is said to be the foremost wide-ranging review of environmental law components in schools and university curricula in Arab

48 Generally, see Fowler et al. (n 42); Steven Vaughan et al., "Of Density and Decline: Reflections on Environmental Law Teaching in the UK and on the Co-production of Environmental Law Scholarship" in Amanda Kennedy et al. (eds), *Teaching and Learning in Environmental Law: Pedagogy, Methodology and Best Practice* (Edward Elgar 2021).

49 Generally, see Vaughan (n 48).

50 Generally, see ibid.

51 For some of the suggestions, see Bouwer et al. (n 39).

52 Generally, see Bouwer et al. (n 39). Also, see Tolulope N. Ogboru, "Environmental Education: Moving Environmental Law from Marginality to Mainstream" 3 *International Journal of Law and Clinical Legal Education* 83.

53 Train-the-Trainers (TTT) (n 15) 3.

54 Generally, see Mrema and Smagadi (n 24).

55 Saab et al. (n 21).

countries, in view of recognizing the various lacunae and suggesting strategies to improve the role of education in promoting environmental protection and the implementation or enforcement of the SDGs in the region.[56] Some of the findings of the survey include that in the last decade, universities in Arab countries have seen a fast increase in programs or courses connected to the environment and sustainable development.[57] Also, the AFED report found that, in total, fifty-seven universities in the survey offered 221 degree courses or programs relating to environmental issues or topics.[58] However, the majority of the these programs are scientific and technical degrees, which appears to take prominence over law, education, policy, and economics programs.[59]

However, there have been various initiatives that have been developed within the MENA region to assist relevant stakeholders, including environmental law lecturers and scholars, on how to embed environmental awareness and environmental education within their curricula or practices. An example is the Training Manual for the TTT Program in Environmental Law for Higher Education Institutions in the MENA Region, which was jointly organized by the UNEP and ASSELLMU.[60] ASSELLMU has been at the forefront of seeking to mitigate the gaps in the frameworks on environmental legal education within the MENA region.[61] The program also aims to enhance the pedagogy and the delivery of environmental law programs and courses within the MENA region.

Despite the rise in domestic and regional policies, mechanisms, and laws on the environment within the MENA region, it is contended that "environmental law education is still at an alarming stage of infancy in the region, especially when compared to many other regions."[62] Furthermore, in many parts of the MENA region, there have not been deliberate moves to integrate biodiversity awareness into environmental education. For example, there is a need for more specific and tailored workshops and TTT programs on biodiversity in the MENA region to further promote the integration of biodiversity awareness into environmental legal curricula in the various universities and higher education institutions within the MENA region. Biodiversity within the MENA region is currently under serious threat, and this has become a major issue among governments and other relevant stakeholders in the region.[63] In many parts of the world, governments are developing mechanisms and legal frameworks (including ratifying relevant biodiversity treaties) to tackle the biodiversity threats, and the MENA region is not left out. Furthermore, one strategy

56 Ibid., 7.
57 Ibid.
58 Ibid.
59 Ibid., 75.
60 Train-the-Trainers (n 15).
61 Ibid.
62 Ibid., 18.
63 Generally, see Walker (n 9).

is to "ensure that people are conscious of biodiversity conservation is through education."[64] Hence, reliance on environmental law education can be one of the strategies to improve the implementation of biodiversity treaties within the MENA region.

Section 17.3 focuses on the barriers militating against the successful implementation of legal education as a tool to improve the implementation of biodiversity treaties within the MENA region.

17.3 CHALLENGES TO BIODIVERSITY LEGAL EDUCATION AS A STRATEGY FOR ENHANCING THE IMPLEMENTATION OF BIODIVERSITY TREATIES IN THE MENA REGION

There are various challenges affecting the successful integration of explicit biodiversity awareness and training into legal education within the MENA region. Some of these barriers or challenges include the marginality of environmental law in legal education in parts of the MENA region, a shortage of qualified environmental law scholars and lecturers, funding and resource constraints, and political crises.

17.3.1 *Lack of Comprehensive Legislation on Biodiversity and Nature Conservation*

In the MENA region, environmental law has arguably come to prominence and of age, and it is one of the strategies that is being used to tackle environmental challenges in the region. According to Olawuyi, all states in the region have developed primary legislation focused on environmental protection and secondary regulations focusing on various environmental issues such as wildlife, fisheries, biodiversity, and the protection of endangered species.[65] However, many MENA countries lack comprehensive laws relating to biodiversity and nature conservation. For example, according to the information available on the Convention on Biological Diversity (CBD) website, many countries in the MENA region have ratified the CBD, but they are yet to take concrete actions to implement or achieve the 2020 Aichi Biodiversity Targets.[66] Furthermore, regarding Jordan and its international biodiversity commitments, the CBD website states that Jordan's overall "legislative framework is in place but still requires further development."[67] Arguably, this is representative of

[64] Eshun (n 13) 297.

[65] Olawuyi (n 4) 30. On the other hand, scholars including Joseph A. Omojolaibi and Solomon P. Nathaniel, "Assessing the Potency of Environmental Regulation in Maintaining Environmental Sustainability in MENA Countries: An Advanced Panel Data Estimation" (2022) 22 *Journal of Public Affairs* 3, e2526, have argued that environmental laws and regulations do not successfully improve environmental sustainability in the MENA region.

[66] CBD Website, "List of Parties" www.cbd.int/information/parties.shtml accessed October 15, 2023.

[67] CBD Website, "Country Profile: Jordan-Main Details" www.cbd.int/countries/profile/?country=jo accessed October 15, 2023.

countries in the MENA region. Thus, very few countries, including the United Arab Emirates (UAE), have developed explicit legal and institutional frameworks on biodiversity and nature conservation in the MENA region.[68]

17.3.2 *Marginality of Environmental Law Education on Biodiversity in the MENA Region*

A major issue afflicting environmental law education is that it is not part of mainstream legal education in many parts of the world. As Fowler and others aver: "Marginality suggests that a subject sits at the fringes of the discipline of law, is inconsequential, and is seen as a luxury rather than an essential component of a good legal education."[69] This is also exemplified in the marginality of environmental law in the legal education curriculum in the MENA region. Well-respected scholars, and numerous reports and surveys, have confirmed that environmental law education is peripheral and is not mainstreamed in the legal curriculum in the MENA region.[70] Even though environmental education is integrated in the university curriculum in many universities in the MENA region, environmental law education is still lacking in many places. Thus, as alluded to earlier, environmental law is not a core course of study in legal education in many parts of the MENA region. For example, Ahmed Elseidi, one of the leading environmental lawyers in Egypt, suggests: "Unlike the US, Egypt lacks advanced legal education courses that detail environmental rights and justice, hindering citizens from understanding the severity of their country's issues."[71] This exemplifies the current state of environmental law education in some parts of the MENA region. Hence, scholars have alluded to the fact that there are very few higher education institutions with specialist courses (including biodiversity and nature conservation) in the region that promote students' knowledge and capacity regarding environmental law and related issues including sustainable development.[72] Furthermore, the marginal status of environmental law in the MENA region exemplifies or ensures that biodiversity awareness and nature conservation is severely lacking in legal education curricula in the region. This is also accentuated by the near absence of specialist biodiversity law courses in the MENA region.

68 Generally, see United Arab Emirates Ministry of Climate Change and Environment www.moccae.gov.ae/en/knowledge-and-statistics/biodiversity.aspx accessed October 15, 2023.

69 Fowler et al. (n 42) 8.

70 Olawuyi (n 4); Train-the-Trainers (n 15); Saab et al. (n 21).

71 Generally, see Alicia Santiago, "Enviro Law in Egypt: Egypt's Only Public Interest Environmental Lawyer Visits Eugene" (*Eugene Weekly*, June 29, 2023) https://eugeneweekly.com/2023/06/29/enviro-law-in-egypt/#:~:text=Unlike%20the%20U.S.%2C%20Egypt%20lacks,their%20country%27s%20issues%2C%20Elseidi%20says accessed October 15, 2023.

72 Generally, see Olawuyi (n 4) 30.

17.3.3 *Shortage of Biodiversity and Environmental Law Expertise in the MENA Region*

In many parts of the world (especially in MENA countries), there is a shortage of environmental law scholars, especially with expertise and a focus on biodiversity and nature conservation, and this remains a noteworthy barrier to the teaching of the subject in the MENA region.[73] Thus, in MENA countries, there is an acute shortage of legal expertise on biodiversity and nature conservation and a paucity of legal scholarship on biodiversity and nature conservation. Accordingly, this is also a reflection of the current state of environmental law teaching in the MENA region.

Furthermore, the shortage of biodiversity and environmental law expertise has negative impacts on the development of university law courses or programs focused on biodiversity and nature conservation in the region. This in turn impacts negatively on the promotion of biodiversity awareness in MENA countries.

17.3.4 *Resource Constraints*

Some of the major issues impacting the successful implementation of environmental education initiatives in the MENA region are resource constraints or challenges, especially regarding the teaching of environmental education and environmental law. The teaching of environmental law requires access to and availability of materials. The teaching materials or resources (which includes textbooks, journal articles, and course materials) on environmental education and environmental law education are mainly in the English language.[74] In the MENA region, the principal language of teaching is Modern Standard Arabic, and hence some MENA educators regularly "struggle to access the lion's share of available climate law teaching resources, raising the need for more translation of resources, as well as designing learning resources and platforms in Arabic, to provide greater access to learning resources on climate change law to MENA academics and students."[75] Furthermore, some relevant stakeholders at a regional conference in the region have suggested that a major reason for the slow development of environmental law education in the MENA region is the absence of authoritative texts or books focused on environmental law in the region.[76] However, there is a need for more

73 Generally, see Hilary C. Bell, "Tackling the Legally Disruptive Problem of Climate Change with Disruptive Legal Education" in Damilola Olawuyi (ed), *Climate Change Law and Policy in the Middle East and North Africa Region* (Routledge 2021).

74 Also, see ibid.

75 Ibid., 258.

76 Damilola S. Olawuyi, "Conference Highlights Need to Introduce Environmental Law to Higher Education Curricula in the Middle East" (IUCN, November 28, 2018) www.iucn.org/news/world-commission-environmental-law/201811/conference-highlights-need-introduce-environmental-law-higher-education-curricula-middle-east accessed October 15, 2023. However, in recent times there have been specialist books published on the nature and content of environmental law by some

books and resources explicitly focused on biodiversity laws, nature conservation, and biodiversity awareness in the MENA region.

Closely associated with this are financial constraints that limit the implementation of biodiversity education and awareness programs. In many parts of the world, governments are reducing the budgetary funds allocated for funding environmental education initiatives due to the economic and financial reasons among others.[77] For example, the COVID-19 pandemic has had negative impacts on funding of environmental projects in the MENA region.[78] Furthermore, given the economic and income inequalities in the MENA region, some scholars have argued that this makes the MENA region one of the most unequal in the world.[79] For example, some of the wealthiest countries are found in the MENA region, which is also home to some of the poorest countries in the world. This also has negative impacts, including the disparities in the quality of university education in the MENA region and hence some of the universities in the region are unable to retain and attract experts in the environmental law discipline.[80] Many of the existing environmental education initiatives in the MENA region are majorly sponsored by international donors and are thereby unsustainable in the long term.[81]

Additionally, the funding of biodiversity and nature projects, including environmental law education initiatives focusing on biodiversity and allied issues, are expensive.[82] Thus, there is an acute lack of funding for environmental law education initiatives (including educational initiatives focusing on biodiversity and nature conservation awareness) in many MENA countries. Arguably, the lack of funding severely impacts the development of biodiversity and nature conservation awareness initiatives in environmental law education in higher institutions of learning in the MENA region.

17.3.5 *Impacts of Conflict on Environmental Education in the MENA Region*

The MENA region has for many years remained an epicenter of a series of conflicts and wars.[83] The region has been affected by a plethora of recent armed conflict

leading including scholars in the MENA region. See for example, Damilola Olawuyi, *Environmental Law in Arab States* (Oxford University Press 2022); Damilola Olawuyi (ed), *Climate Change Law and Policy in the Middle East and North Africa Region* (Routledge 2021); Samira Idllalène, *Rediscovery and Revival in Islamic Environmental Law* (Cambridge University Press 2021).

77 However, see Max Roser and Esteban Ortiz-Ospina, *Financing Education* (Our World in Data 2016).

78 Generally, see Zainab Lokhandwala, "The Fallout of Covid-19 on Environmental Law in the Middle East and North Africa" (2020) Opinio Juris in Comparatione.

79 Generally, see Bell (n 73).

80 Generally, see ibid.

81 Generally, Saab et al. (n 21).

82 Generally, see World Bank, "Sustainable Land Management and Restoration in the Middle East and North Africa Region: Issues, Challenges, and Recommendations" (2019) https://elibrary.worldbank.org/doi/abs/10.1596/33037 accessed October 15, 2023.

83 Hadi B. Heidarlou et al., "Armed Conflict and Land-Use Changes: Insights from Iraq–Iran War in Zagros Forests" (2020) 118 *Forest Policy and Economics* 102246.

and examples include Yemen, Syria, Iraq, and Libya.[84] Conflict and instability have had negative impacts on education (including environmental education) in parts of the MENA region.[85] This poses tremendous challenges for educators and students who can end up being displaced and unable to access education sites or safely access educational materials, and thus cannot engage in face-to-face education activities.[86] Accordingly, conflict in parts of the MENA region is one of the major barriers impacting negatively on the implementation of environmental law education (including educational measures focused on biodiversity and nature conservation) initiatives and policies in the region. Furthermore, a plethora of relevant stakeholders, including academics, have blamed the lack of biodiversity and nature conservation research in the MENA region on the conflicts, poverty, wars, and economic woes affecting some countries in the region.[87] Thus, governments in the region are prioritizing human needs and fighting poverty rather than developing educational initiatives on biodiversity and nature conservation.[88] For example, in Iran, Jowkar and others suggest that in the last two decades, environmental protection appears not to be a pressing issue for the government because it is finding it difficult to meet the economic expectations of its citizens.[89] Thus, in some parts of the MENA region, environmental education (including biodiversity and nature conservation awareness) has been negatively impacted by socio-political factors.

17.4 STRENGTHENING ENVIRONMENTAL LAW EDUCATION ON BIODIVERSITY IN THE MENA REGION: RECOMMENDATIONS

Environmental law education can be one of the integral tools or strategies in strengthening the implementation of biodiversity treaties in the MENA region. Some of the recommendations analyzed in this section include mitigating the marginality of environmental law education on biodiversity, integrating or embedding biodiversity awareness in environmental law education, capacity building for environmental law academics, improved funding of environmental education initiatives in the MENA region, and biodiversity litigation as tool for the implementation of biodiversity treaties.

84 Beatriz DeQuero-Navarro et al., "From Conflict to Cooperation: A Macromarketing View of Sustainable and Inclusive Development in Lebanon and the Middle East" (2020) 66 *Environmental Management* 2, 232.
85 Generally, see Bell (n 73) and Saab (n 21).
86 Bell (n 73).
87 Walker (n 9).
88 Generally, see Walker (n 9).
89 Houman Jowkar et al., "The Conservation of Biodiversity in Iran: Threats, Challenges and Hopes" (2016) 49 *Iranian Studies* 6, 1065.

17.4.1 *Comprehensive National Policy and Legislation on Biodiversity and Nature Conservation*

It is essential that MENA countries enact comprehensive laws and regulations for biodiversity and nature conservation issues to provide clear framework for the implementation, monitoring, and enforcement of biodiversity and natural conservation and allied issues.[90] Thus, governments in the MENA region need to implement or create "dedicated action plans to halt and reverse the loss of critical habitats and species, enhance water management practices and conserve vital freshwater, and mainstream sustainability and conservation in key social and economic activities."[91] Furthermore, MENA countries can take inspiration from the actions and strategies enshrined in the UAE's framework on biodiversity and nature conservation. For example, the UAE has a comprehensive framework on biodiversity and nature conservation.[92] The UAE has signed, and in some cases ratified, various international treaties and mechanisms focusing on biodiversity and nature conservation, including the CBD, the Convention on the International Trade in Endangered Species of Wild Fauna and Flora, the Nagoya-Kuala Lumpur Supplementary Protocol on Liability and Redress to the Cartagena Protocol on Biosafety, the United Nations Convention to Combat Desertification, and the Ramsar Convention on Wetlands.[93] Furthermore, the UAE has a plethora of action plans on biodiversity and nature conservation, including the National Biodiversity Strategy 2014–2021.[94] Thus, the UAE can be an inspiration to other MENA countries on how to develop a comprehensive legal framework on biodiversity and nature conservation.

17.4.2 *Mitigating the Marginality of Environmental Law Education in the MENA Region*

Generally, it should be noted that although environmental law is not a core component of the legal education curriculum, this does not necessarily mean that such courses will not have students or academics conducting research on it. For example, in North America and parts of Europe, notwithstanding the elective or non-core status of environmental law, it is quite popular and has a firm place in the

[90] Also, see Olawuyi (n 2) 12.

[91] PwC Middle East, "Nature and Biodiversity: Creating a Nature Positive Future" (2023) www.pwc.com/m1/en/publications/nature-biodiversity.html accessed October 15, 2023.

[92] Generally, see the United Arab Emirates Ministry of Climate Change and Environment, "A Guide to Biodiversity Conservation in the UAE" (May 2023).

[93] Ibid. Also, see the Convention on Biological Diversity (CBD) website, "United Arab Emirates – Main Details" www.cbd.int/countries/profile/?country=ae#:~:text=In%20addition%2C%20the%20UAE%20has,by%20%E2%80%9CEmirates%20vision%202021%E2%80%9D accessed October 15, 2023.

[94] United Arab Emirates Ministry of Climate Change and Environment, "Biodiversity" www.moccae.gov.ae/en/knowledge-and-statistics/biodiversity.aspx accessed October 15, 2023.

legal curriculum, with large numbers of students.[95] In several developing countries, notwithstanding the elective status of environmental law in the legal curriculum, environmental lawyers and activists have used their expertise of environmental law as means of engaging in social change.[96] Thus, in the context of MENA countries, environmental law (incorporating biodiversity and nature conservation) should be fully integrated and made a core component of the legal curriculum in the region. This is akin to the move taking place in some developing countries. Therefore, in some developing countries, including Indonesia, the Philippines, India, and China, environmental law is becoming a mandatory or core aspect of the undergraduate legal curriculum.[97] Mainstreaming environmental law is a key strategy that can be used in promoting environmental law education and this will have positive impacts on enhancing environmental awareness including biodiversity and nature conservation awareness in the MENA region. This is arguably in line with the AFED report on environmental education in the MENA region, that there is an urgent need to reinforce topics including environmental law in the legal education curriculum in the MENA region.[98] Thus, this will help bring to the fore the relevance or utility of biodiversity awareness and nature conservation in environmental law education in the MENA region.

17.4.3 *Embedding Biodiversity Awareness in Environmental Law Education in the MENA Region*

Awareness and understanding of biodiversity issues should be embedded in the law curriculum in the MENA region. For example, this can be done via already existing environmental programs offered by universities or as part of the legal education curriculum in the MENA region. Akin to what Bouwer has termed as "climate consciousness" in legal practice,[99] there should be explicit embedding or integration of biodiversity consciousness or awareness into the legal education curriculum in universities or higher education institutions and in legal practice (especially environmental law practice) in the MENA region. According to Preston: "Climate change places a responsibility on lawyers to adopt a climate conscious rather than a climate blind approach in their daily legal practice. A climate conscious approach requires an active awareness of the reality of climate change and how it interacts with daily

95 Generally, see Fowler et al. (n 42).
96 Amanda Kennedy et al. (eds), *Teaching and Learning in Environmental Law: Pedagogy, Methodology and Best Practice* (Edward Elgar 2021).
97 Fowler et al. (n 42) 11.
98 Saab et al. (n 21) 13.
99 Kim Bouwer "Climate Consciousness in Daily Legal Practice" (*Journal of Environmental Law Blog*, May 22, 2015) https://blog.oup.com/2015/05/climate-consciousness-daily-legal-practice/?utm_source=feedblitz&utm_medium=FeedBlitzRss&utm_campaign=oupblog accessed October 15, 2023; Brian Preston, "Climate Conscious Lawyering: Implementing a Climate Conscious Approach in Daily Legal Practice" (2021) 95 *Australian Law Journal* 51.

legal problems."[100] Hence, due to the severe nature of biodiversity threats in the MENA, the legal education curriculum and the training of lawyers should be totally revamped to contain explicit allusions to the utility of international and national legal frameworks on biodiversity, practices, principles, and awareness of biodiversity issues. Arguably, this can play a positive role in the development of legal strategies to help tackle the source of biodiversity threats in the MENA region. Thus, promoting the effectiveness and the implementation of biodiversity treaties in the MENA region will enhance the various measures developed to tackle the sources of the threats to biodiversity.

Furthermore, many laws and policies have been developed in the MENA region for the protection and conservation of biodiversity sources. Thus, law students and lawyers in the MENA region should be supported via environmental law education to understand the implications of these laws and policies and their impacts in the MENA region. Furthermore, students in the MENA region, via biodiversity awareness in environmental law education, will be able to understand that the international conventions on biodiversity are legal mechanisms that create obligations on countries that have ratified the conventions. Thus, countries that have ratified such treaties are expected to adapt their legal frameworks or laws to ensure that all the commitments arising from the international treaties or conventions are met locally.[101] Arguably, awareness or knowledge of the legal implications of biodiversity treaties "provides the student with a standpoint from which to critically assess the behavior of governments, parliaments, authorities, and businesses,"[102] regarding the implementation of biodiversity treaties in the MENA region. Furthermore, by virtue of Article 27 of the Vienna Convention on the Law of Treaties, contracting parties or countries to treaties cannot rely on national laws as reasons or justifications for not respecting their expected obligations or commitments under such treaties. Thus, MENA countries should adhere to the various obligations arising from the plethora of international conventions relating to biodiversity and nature conservation and other allied issues that they have signed and ratified.

Awareness of the legal frameworks on biodiversity is not enough; society (especially lawyers and university law students) in the MENA region should also develop a deep understanding of how biodiversity will be influenced and shaped by society's response to biodiversity threats in the region.[103] This will arguably lead to improving of the skill sets or expertise of lawyers regarding biodiversity awareness or biodiversity-related issues in the MENA region.

Furthermore, according to Hulme, international conventions relating to biodiversity issues or "nature conservation treaties include mandatory obligations to

[100] Preston (n 99) 51.
[101] Generally, see Droubi (n 19).
[102] Droubi (n 19) 7.
[103] Generally, see Bouwer (n 99) for analysis of the utility of a climate consciousness approach from a UK perspective.

conduct conservation training and education."[104] For example, Article 27 (1) of the World Heritage Convention (WHC) 1972 explicitly accentuates the relevance of states engaging in the awareness of natural heritage issues to "strengthen appreciation and respect by their peoples."[105] This arguably serves as a mobilization tool for society to support and value its conservation and natural heritage protection.[106]

This chapter adopts the view of Lavey on the utility of climate change education integration into law school curriculum,[107] and this is also applicable to biodiversity awareness expected from environmental lawyers within the MENA region. Thus, Lavey suggests that effective lawyering premised on knowledge, skills, and understanding regarding the various risks from undulating environmental conditions should underpin legal education.[108]

Furthermore, in the context of biodiversity and nature conservation, effective lawyering should also be underpinned by knowledge and awareness of the biodiversity and nature conservation issues in the MENA region. Hence, legal practitioners in MENA countries should be at the forefront of biodiversity consciousness or awareness in their legal practice in the MENA region. Additionally, UNESCO avers that "[e]ducation is essential for the sustainable and equitable use of biodiversity and its conservation. It is also crucial for mainstreaming biodiversity."[109] Thus, environmental education is essential to actualizing the SDGs (especially SDG 15) in the MENA region.[110] Additionally, leading scholars on environmental law in the MENA region at a conference in 2018 advocated for the explicit integration of environmental law (which also includes biodiversity and nature conservation) in the higher education curricula in the region.[111]

[104] Karen Hulme, "Using International Environmental Law to Enhance Biodiversity and Nature Conservation during armed conflict" (2022) 20 *Journal of International Criminal Justice* 5, 1155, 1173. Also, Hulme states that Article 12 and 13(a) CBD; Article 3(3) Bern Convention; Article 5(e), 22(c), 23, 27–28 WHC; and Article 4(5) Ramsar Convention provide for environmental education in their provisions.

[105] Generally, see Articles 27 and 28 of the WHC which focuses on environmental education. Furthermore, the recognition of education as a strategy to enhance knowledge and awareness about biodiversity is explicitly acknowledged by the CBD.

[106] Generally, see Hulme (n 104).

[107] Warren G. Lavey, "Toolkit for Integrating Climate Change into Ten High-Enrollment Law School Courses" (2019) 49 *Environmental Law* 513.

[108] Ibid., 515–516.

[109] UNESCO, "Biodiversity: Education and Awareness" (December 20, 2022). www.unesco.org/en/biodiversity/education accessed October 15, 2023.

[110] SDG Resources for Educators – Life on Land https://en.unesco.org/themes/education/sdgs/material/15 accessed October 15, 2023. Furthermore, this resource further states that "[b]iodiversity education contributes to integrating protective ecosystem and biodiversity values into national and local planning, development processes, poverty reduction strategies and accounts."

[111] Damilola S. Olawuyi, "Conference Highlights Need to Introduce Environmental Law to Higher Education Curricula in the Middle East" (IUCN, November 28, 2018) www.iucn.org/news/world-commission-environmental-law/201811/conference-highlights-need-introduce-environmental-law-higher-education-curricula-middle-east accessed February 12, 2024.

17.4.4 *Capacity Building of Environmental Law Academics*

Different initiatives have been developed in the MENA region to mitigate the shortage environmental law scholars, improving the skill sets of academics and various stakeholders, including UNEP and ASSELLMU.[112] For example, UNEP in collaboration with various stakeholders have played a crucial role in the expansion of international environmental law and principles and has supported different countries in developing and enhancing capacities or expertise in environmental law.[113] Regarding environmental law education, UNEP has supported various initiatives to develop environmental law education in different parts of the world, including Africa, Asia, and the MENA region.[114] For example, UNEP in collaboration with Professor Olawuyi was instrumental in the creation of the ASSELLMU in 2018. The ASSELLMU is a professional network of environmental law scholars and one of its major objectives is conducting research on the practice and implementation of environmental law in the region.[115] Since its inception, the ASSELLMU has organized several conferences that have served as avenues or platforms for bringing environmental law teachers, practitioners, lawyers, and trainers together to exchange knowledge with each other.[116]

As one of the strategies of improving the skill sets of environmental law scholars and teachers in the region, ASSELLMU has also organized a series of events and developed the teaching of environmental law toolkits. For example, the Training Manual for the TTT Program in Environmental Law for Higher Education Institutions in the MENA Region, which was jointly organized by the UNEP and ASSELLMU.[117] This training program was developed to support academics conducting research or teaching environmental law-related courses or programs in the MENA region. Furthermore, the "overarching objective of this TTT Programme is to enhance the technical capacity for environmental law education in MENA universities through an in-depth exploration of innovative approaches for curriculum design, teaching pedagogies, and student assessment."[118] Thus, the regular occurrence of this and similar capacity-training events will continually improve the skill sets of environmental law scholars and arguably help in mitigating the shortage of environmental law experts in the region. Additionally, specialist training should be organized for environmental law scholars and lawyers to enhance their knowledge and pedagogy relating to biodiversity law and awareness and nature conservation in the MENA region. For example, ASSELLMU,

112 Generally, Mrema and Smagadi (n 24).
113 Mrema and Smagadi (n 24) 30.
114 Generally, see Fowler et al. (n 42).
115 ASSELLMU website, "About Us" https://assellmu.org/about-us/ accessed October 15, 2023.
116 Ibid.
117 Train-the-Trainers (n 15).
118 Ibid.

UNEP, and other relevant stakeholders should explicitly embed the knowledge of biodiversity laws, awareness, and nature conservation issues in their training courses. These training courses should be organized for environmental scholars, lawyers, and policymakers in the MENA region to deepen their knowledge or understanding of biodiversity and nature conservation issues. Furthermore, continuous training of environmental law teachers, researchers, and academics will enhance the delivery of environmental law education programs in universities in the MENA region.

17.4.5 *Improved Funding of Environmental Education Initiatives in the MENA Region*

There is a need for increased funding of the ASSELLMU and other similar environmental education initiatives (including biodiversity and nature conservation) in the MENA region. The funding of environmental education initiatives and environmental programs is said to be on the decline in several states in the MENA region.[119] The number of environmental initiatives is on the rise in the MENA, and this needs increased funding from the government and other relevant stakeholders for these initiatives to be successfully implemented. Hence, the AFED report suggests that financial resources ought to "be raised independently of international donors in order to enhance both the quality and evidence base of environmental topics."[120] Furthermore, richer MENA countries, including Saudi Arabia and the UAE, have an integral role to play by funding environmental education initiatives (including those focused on biodiversity and nature conservation) in other MENA countries.

17.4.6 *Mitigating Impacts of Conflicts on Environmental Education Initiatives*

The movement to online teaching and use of technology could help improve access to environmental education by students during conflicts in the MENA region. Thus, online-learning platforms can serve as lifeline for students in MENA, whose education has been negatively impacted by the conflict.[121] Consequently, this requires reliance on technology and if the computer network is able to cope with the demands and if the students affected by conflict can get online, they can potentially access education.[122] The COVID-19 pandemic has shown the world (especially the education sector) that online-learning platforms can serve as good alternatives to

119 Generally, see Saab et al. (n 21).
120 Ibid., 9.
121 Generally, see Bell (n 73).
122 Bell (n 73) 258.

face-to-face teaching and many schools and universities have fully embraced the technology to enable access to education and its resources, during and even after the COVID-19 pandemic, including in the MENA region.

Furthermore, the reliance on online teaching and use of technology can improve access and create open more opportunities for environmental law education focusing on biodiversity and nature conservation awareness in the region. For example, more people can be trained through online or virtual learning platforms on the utility of biodiversity and nature conservation awareness in the MENA region. Also, various online tools such as videos, e-learning tools, and other educational technology resources can enhance the quality of the learning and teaching of biodiversity and nature conservation issues in the region.[123]

17.4.7 *Biodiversity Litigation as a Tool for the Implementation of Biodiversity Treaties in the MENA Region*

Due to the failings and weaknesses of domestic and international regulatory mechanisms in different parts of the world, the use of litigation is now regularly relied upon by individuals, victims, and other relevant stakeholders in holding governments, multinational corporations, and other entities accountable for their actions in different parts of the world.[124] For example, due to the existing weaknesses in the global climate governance regime, climate litigation has become a popular strategy or mechanism utilized by climate change victims and their representatives in various jurisdictions in both developing and developed countries in holding multinationals and states accountable for climate inaction.[125] Arguably, due to the impact of climate litigation at the national and international levels, some scholars have argued for the development of biodiversity litigation as one strategy that can be relied upon to enhance the implementation of the various biodiversity conventions at the domestic level.[126]

There are different definitions and conceptualizations of biodiversity litigation.[127] However, this chapter adopts the definition by Futhazar et al., and they define

[123] Also, see Bell (n 73) for similar allusions in the context of climate change education in MENA countries.

[124] Rhuks Ako and Eghosa O. Ekhator, "The Civil Society and the Regulation of the Extractive Industry in Nigeria" (2016) 7 *Journal of Sustainable Development Law and Policy* 1, 183.

[125] See, Pedi Obani and Eghosa Ekhator, "Transnational Litigation and Climate Change in Nigeria" in *Symposium: Nigeria and International Law: Past, Present and the Future* (AfronomicsLaw Blog 2021) www.afronomicslaw.org/category/analysis/transnational-litigation-and-climate-change-nigeria accessed October 15, 2023.

[126] Generally, see Guillaume Futhazar, Sandrine Maljean-Dubois, and Jona Razzaque (eds), *Biodiversity Litigation* (Oxford University Press 2022).

[127] Generally, see Clyde & Co website, "Biodiversity litigation: Environment Analysis" (April 12, 2022) www.clydeco.com/en/insights/2022/04/biodiversity-litigation-environment-analysis accessed October 15, 2023.

biodiversity litigation as "any legal dispute at the national, regional or international level that concerns conservation of sustainable use of and access and benefit-sharing to genetic resources, species, ecosystem and their relations."[128]

There is the potential or possibility for biodiversity litigation to hold governments accountable for their international biodiversity commitments within MENA. Successful biodiversity litigation has taken place in other developing countries, including India, Brazil, and Tanzania.[129] However, biodiversity litigation remains largely untested in the MENA region. Environmental biodiversity awareness can improve the knowledge or expertise of litigants and other relevant stakeholders in successfully exploring the potential of biodiversity litigation to seek redress for landscape alteration and habitat degradation resulting from development activities and projects in the MENA region. Reliance on litigation as a legal strategy has achieved some success in transnational human rights litigation instituted against multinational corporations and governments in different parts of the world.[130] Successful litigation can have positive impacts on the regulation of different sectors or industries in countries.[131] Thus, successful biodiversity litigation could strengthen the implementation of biodiversity treaties in the MENA region.[132]

17.5 CONCLUSION

Various international and regional instruments and policies have underscored the importance of environmental education in advancing biodiversity and nature conservation. In the MENA region, there has been an in increase in the number of environmental education initiatives; however, environmental law education (including initiatives on biodiversity and nature conservation) is still at the fringes of the university curriculum in the region.

This chapter has undertaken a critical analysis of the current state of environmental law education in the MENA region. Notwithstanding the marginal status of environmental law education in several countries in the region, it can serve as one of the strategies to strengthen the implementation of the plethora of biodiversity treaties in the region. Several recommendations are made in this chapter on how to improve the status of environmental law education in the region and these measures can be replicated in other developing countries as well. The

[128] Futhazar et al. (n 126) 15.

[129] Boya Jiang, "10 Landmark Cases for Biodiversity" (ClientEarth China, October 11, 2021) www.clientearth.org/latest/documents/10-landmark-cases-for-biodiversity/ accessed October 15, 2023.

[130] Generally, see Ako and Ekhator (n 124).

[131] Ibid.

[132] Also, see Rob Fowler, "The Role of the IUCN Academy of Environmental Law in Promoting the Teaching of Environmental Law" (2017) 8 *IUCNAEL e-Journal* www.iucnael.org/en/academy-journal/previous-issues/86-journal/issue/640-issue-2017 accessed October 15, 2023.

recommendations include mitigating the marginality of environmental law education, embedding biodiversity awareness in environmental law education, the capacity building of environmental law academics, improved funding of environmental education initiatives, mitigating the impacts of conflicts on environmental education initiatives, and the utility of biodiversity litigation. Arguably, the implementation of these recommendations, which are premised on environmental law education in MENA countries, will enhance and localize the implementation of biodiversity treaties in the region.

18

Advancing the Nexus Approach to Biodiversity and Nature Conservation in the MENA Region

Summary and Options for Policymakers

Damilola S. Olawuyi

18.1 INTRODUCTION

This book examines the values, assumptions, and guiding principles that underpin biodiversity and nature conservation law and policy in the MENA region. With case studies from various MENA countries, the book explored the applicable legislation and institutions, as well as emerging innovative and bottom-up approaches for the implementation of biodiversity and nature conservation treaties across the region. This final chapter reviews the salient themes that have been discussed and identifies directions for future action and research.

The MENA region, like many parts of the world, is facing a rapid biodiversity loss emergency.[1] Apart from the threats of extinction of rare plants and animal species needed to sustain a functional ecosystem, MENA countries face increased threats of losing access to rare natural and cultural capital required to support medical innovation, tourism, bio-business and trade, biodiversity entrepreneurship, and economic diversification.[2] Consequently, responding to the current and anticipated social, economic, environmental, and cultural impacts of nature and biodiversity loss is squarely at the forefront of the political and legislative agenda across the region. However, despite the rise in policy formulation on biodiversity and nature conservation, the pace of implementation remains uneven across the region – in terms of having comprehensive laws, policies, training, and harmonized institutions on biodiversity and nature conservation. There is a need for a detailed and up-to-date assessment of emerging regulatory approaches to biodiversity and nature

[1] J. Richardson et al., "Earth beyond Six of Nine Planetary Boundaries" (2023) 9 *Science Advances* 37. See also W. Steffen et al., "Planetary Boundaries: Guiding Human Development on a Changing Planet" (2015) 347 *Science* 736.

[2] See Chapter 1. See also Taskforce on Nature-related Financial Disclosures (TNFD), "Recommendations of the Taskforce on Nature-related Financial Disclosures" (September 2023) stating that nature and biodiversity loss "poses risks for businesses, capital providers, financial systems and economies, and that these risks are increasing in severity and frequency." https://tnfd.global/wp-content/uploads/2023/08/Recommendations_of_the_Taskforce_on_Nature-related_Financial_Disclosures_September_2023.pdf?v=1695118661 accessed January 12, 2024.

conservation across the region to achieve greater clarity, coherence, and integration. This book is an attempt to meet this need.

The eighteen chapters of this book explore the latest developments of biodiversity and nature conservation law and policy across the MENA region, with a focus on the key legal innovations for the sustainable management of the region's rich natural and cultural heritage. The chapters have also explored larger questions on legal and institutional frameworks that can help address broader issues of inadequate protection of land rights in nature-based programs, gender inequality, inadequate stakeholder engagement, lack of transparency, limited access to environmental information, and the inadequate scope of available financing for biodiversity programs. The case studies have also explored innovative legal strategies to address these misalignments and gaps.

This final chapter offers reflections on the case studies. It addresses how lessons from the diverse jurisdictions may inform thinking on how MENA countries can advance existing national strategies and visions on biodiversity and nature conservation through clear and comprehensive legislation. Considering the wide-ranging impacts of biodiversity loss on water, energy, and food security, as well as on cultural heritage, tourism, urban planning, healthcare, human rights, and other key sectors, comprehensive and wide-ranging responses are required. However, as shown in the case studies in this book, sectoral and piecemeal efforts on biodiversity and nature conservation have been prevalent in many MENA countries. This has not fostered a holistic consideration of the interplay and trade-offs between biodiversity and conservation programs and other key sectors and systems, especially the biodiversity, climate, water, energy, and food and health nexus.[3] A failure to situate biodiversity as a fundamental aspect of advancing climate action, ensuring water, energy, and food security, as well as combating pandemics and the spread of diseases, may result in overall ineffectiveness. Therefore, greater effort is required to mainstream biodiversity and nature conservation into all aspects of development planning and decision-making, in order to effectively anticipate and address short- and long-term drivers and impacts of biodiversity loss and enhance benefit-sharing in a holistic manner.

This chapter discusses essential steps for mainstreaming biodiversity and nature conservation into all aspects of governmental decision-making across the MENA region. After this introduction, Section 18.2 discusses legal and institutional reforms that could advance legal preparedness for biodiversity and nature conservation in the region. Section 18.3 is the concluding section.

18.2 MAINSTREAMING BIODIVERSITY PLANS AND STRATEGIES INTO DECISION-MAKING PROCESSES IN THE MENA REGION

There is an urgent need for all MENA countries to establish coherent and holistic governance frameworks that mainstream and advance the cross-sectoral protection

[3] See Chapters 1 and 5–14.

of all aspects of nature and biodiversity, including forests, wildlife, wetlands, fisheries, natural habitats, and protected areas, in development planning.

Biodiversity mainstreaming refers to the process of integrating biodiversity considerations into all aspects of development planning and policymaking.[4] As far back as 2016, the 13th Conference of the Parties (COP) to the Convention on Biological Diversity (CBD) in its Decision XIII/3, called on parties and other stakeholders to "mainstream conservation and sustainable use of biodiversity within and across various sectors, including, agriculture, forestry, fisheries and aquaculture and tourism at all levels and scales" in order to achieve the Aichi Biodiversity Targets.[5] Under this model, biodiversity impacts are carefully considered in an integrated manner to ensure that programs and actions in one sector do not create other adverse impacts in other sectors of the economy. For example, many world heritage sites that play important roles in the tourism sector are also key biodiversity hubs.[6] The process of designing legislation and policies on cultural heritage should therefore include a clear linkage to biodiversity, including tailored frameworks that protect heritage sites from activities that may harm biodiversity. Similarly, given the potential impacts of the food and agriculture sector on land alteration and the degradation of natural habitats, holistic frameworks are required to advance sustainable agricultural practices and technologies to support biodiversity and nature conservation.[7] Likewise, through agroecology – "an approach to agriculture that harnesses biodiversity to build complex, low-impact agricultural systems" – the benefits of biodiversity-focused farming can be harnessed to enhance food security.[8] Mainstreaming biodiversity and nature conservation is therefore essential not only for advancing environmental objectives but also for accelerating social and economic objectives, including food security, trade, economic diversification, and equitable access to land and natural resources, as well as the all-round fulfillment of human rights.

4 Convention on Biological Diversity (CBD), "Mainstreaming Biodiversity in Development Cooperation" (April 26, 2019) www.cbd.int/development/about/mainstreaming.shtml#:~:text=The%20mainstreaming%20of%20biodiversity%20can,or%20governments%20lead%20the%20process accessed January 12, 2024.

5 Convention on Biological Diversity, "Strategic Actions to Enhance the Implementation of the Strategic Plan for Biodiversity 2011–2020 and the Achievement of the Aichi Biodiversity Targets, Including with Respect to Mainstreaming and the Integration of Biodiversity Within and Across Sectors" CBD/COP/DEC/XIII/3 (December 16, 2016) para 2.

6 See Chapter 14. See also UNESCO, "World Heritage and Biodiversity" https://whc.unesco.org/en/biodiversity/#:~:text=Around%2020%25%20of%20UNESCO%20cultural,of%20land%2Duse%20that%20enhance accessed January 12, 2024.

7 See Chapter 5.

8 FoodPrint, "Biodiversity and Agriculture" (published: February 17, 2021; last updated: January 18, 2024) https://foodprint.org/issues/biodiversity-and-agriculture. See also Suchismita Mondal et al. "Harnessing Diversity in Wheat to Enhance Grain Yield, Climate Resilience, Disease and Insect Pest Resistance and Nutrition through Conventional and Modern Breeding Approaches" 7 *Frontiers in Plant Science* (July 6, 2016) www.frontiersin.org/articles/10.3389/fpls.2016.00991/full accessed January 25, 2024.

This section discusses seven important steps that could help stakeholders across different sectors to effectively consider and mainstream biodiversity and nature conservation into all aspects of decision-making.

18.2.1 *The Need for Holistic Law and Policy Responses*

As discussed in Chapter 2, several MENA countries have released their National Biodiversity Strategies and Action Plans (NBSAPs).[9] Some of these NBSAPs address the intersections of biodiversity and nature conservation with all other key sectors, ranging from human rights, to food, water, energy, education, aviation, and healthcare, among other things.[10] They also set out broad plans to integrate biodiversity targets into all aspects of national development policies and reporting. However, despite the release of NBSAPs across the region, clear and comprehensive laws and policies that integrate biodiversity in all key sectors are yet to be fully articulated across key sectors. There remains a clear need for legally binding requirements and targets for stakeholders to mainstream biodiversity and nature conservation, especially nature-based solutions, in all aspects of investment and planning. For example, as discussed in Chapter 8, it is important to integrate a public health perspective into biodiversity planning and policymaking to effectively address the spread of zoonotic diseases such as the COVID-19 pandemic. It is equally important to integrate water management perspectives into biodiversity law and policy to address the impacts of water scarcity and aridity on biodiversity, while also leveraging nature-based solutions to improve water management.[11] Human rights considerations are also important to avoid reactionary responses that may exacerbate land grabs, gender inequity, and other human rights concerns while tackling biodiversity loss.[12] Without an integrated policy response, nature-based programs and projects designed to address biodiversity loss may exacerbate social exclusions, human rights violations, food, water, and energy injustice, environmental impacts, and conflicts in already vulnerable communities.[13]

Therefore, there is an urgent need to strengthen synergies and policy coherence in the design, approval, financing, and implementation of biodiversity and

9 Convention on Biological Diversity, "National Biodiversity Strategies and Action Plans (NBSAPs)" (CBD.int) www.cbd.int/nbsap/ accessed January 15, 2023.

10 See Chapter 2. See also Convention on Biological Diversity, "Actions to Enhance Implementation of the Strategic Plan for Biodiversity 2011–2020" (May 11, 2018) www.cbd.int/sp/actions.shtml accessed January 16, 2023.

11 See Chapter 3. See also Samer Fakhoury and Reem AlHaddadin, "Conservation of Oasis Ecosystems in the MENA Region under Water Stress" (August 2023) www.kas.de/documents/264147/264196/Conservation+of+Oasis+Ecosystems+in+the+MENA+Region+under+Water+Stress.pdf/7b28c843-daac-d33e-8f13-b2fb65224232?version=1.1&t=1692805264626 accessed January 16, 2023.

12 See Chapters 6 and 7.

13 Damilola Olawuyi, "Sustainable Development and the Water–Energy–Food Nexus: Legal Challenges and Emerging Solutions" (2020) 103 *Journal of Environmental Science and Policy* 1.

nature conservation programs and policies across all sectors through an integrative approach. Biodiversity can no longer be addressed from a narrow sector-by-sector lens. Rather, biodiversity must be paramount in policy and decision-making at all levels of government. For example, the CBD's National Reporting Guidelines require countries to provide evidence of "how biodiversity is reflected in poverty reduction strategies and other key cross-cutting policy instruments, and into the various economic sectors."[14] This entails biodiversity proofing all development and investment strategies, plans, and programs to minimize damage to ecosystems while maximizing conservation.[15] Such systematic proofing of polices to address their biodiversity and ecosystems impacts will not only maximize conservation but could also accelerate the widespread implementation of nature-based solutions that advance co-benefits and synergies in climate change mitigation and other sustainability efforts.[16]

18.2.2 *Clear and Comprehensive Legislation on Biodiversity and Nature Conservation*

Second, mainstreaming biodiversity into all aspects of governance and decision-making will require clear regulatory frameworks on biodiversity and nature conservation. As seen from the case studies, one key limitation to halting biodiversity loss across the region is the absence of specific biodiversity legislation in many MENA countries. Some of the legal obligations to protect and conserve biodiversity can be inferred or drawn from general environmental legislation, national visions, and other policy documents. However, such an approach is indeterminate and may not provide an opportunity for a clear and robust understanding of the critical interplay, trade-offs, and synergies that exist in decision-making and planning across the diverse domains impacted by biodiversity loss in the short and long term.

For example, the lack of comprehensive biodiversity legislation often means that several of the obligations relating to biodiversity proofing and the use of market-based mechanisms in biodiversity programs are found in different segregated and compartmentalized pieces of legislation or instruments. Some of these instruments may not specifically refer to important concepts such as biodiversity proofing, biodiversity financing, biodiversity-relevant taxation, biodiversity entrepreneurship, or the use of market-based

[14] CBD (n 5). See also CBD, "Guidelines for the Fifth Annual Report" www.cbd.int/doc/nr/nr-05/NR5-guidelines-en.pdf accessed January 12, 2024.

[15] CBD (n 5), also, for detailed discussion of the concept of biodiversity-proofing, see M. Kettunen, K. Medarova-Bergstrom, M. Rayment, I. Shinner, and G. Tucker, "Common Framework for Biodiversity-Proofing of the EU Budget: Guidance for Cohesion Policy Funds" Report to the European Commission, Institute for European Environmental Policy, London (2014) http://minisites.ieep.eu/assets/1422/cfbp_-_Cohesion_funds.pdf accessed January 25, 2024.

[16] See CBD, "Global Biodiversity Outlook 3: Towards a Strategy for Reducing Biodiversity Loss" www.cbd.int/gbo3/?pub=6667&section=6716 accessed January 12, 2024.

mechanisms to halt biodiversity loss, which may limit their scope of application and implementation.[17] Consequently, while the need for biodiversity and nature conservation is generally clear, the granularity of what it requires in practice remains unclear. This creates interpretation gaps on the legal basis and source of responsibility when it comes to supervising different aspects of national biodiversity actions and strategies. Clear, comprehensive, and specific legislation is critical to effectively mainstream biodiversity and nature conservation into the policy apparatus of governments at all levels.

As the Taskforce on Nature-Related Financial Disclosures recommends, biodiversity governance should emphasize four key actions: avoid, reduce, restore, and regenerate (the AR3T framework).[18] First is the need to *avoid* damage to nature and ecosystems through biodiversity-supportive steps such as conducting environmental impact assessments and strategic assessments to protect biodiversity. Second is the need to *reduce* or minimize likely adverse impacts to biodiversity that cannot be avoided. For example, leveraging biodiversity-smart infrastructure (i.e. buildings, technologies, and systems that reduce biodiversity loss and trade-offs, and enhance conservation) across all key sectors can significantly reduce the risk of biodiversity loss. Third is the need to *restore* and recover species or ecosystems that may have been degraded or diminished. For example, specific efforts to replace endangered species such as the Arabian oryx have resulted in sustained progress over the years resulting in its removal from the list of endangered species in the MENA region.[19] Such efforts should be integrated into biodiversity strategies and policies to ensure that they are sustained. Fourth is the need to *regenerate* or increase the productive capacity of the ecosystem in order to sustain biodiversity. Regenerative practices aim to improve, rehabilitate, and support the natural functioning of the ecosystem.[20] For example, regenerative agriculture has been discussed in studies as a "sustainable land management practice" focused on ecological functions.[21]

A clear legal framework on biodiversity could provide the legal basis and obligations for project planners and stakeholders to integrate the AR3T framework into project development and implementation. For example, biodiversity legislation can mandate the biodiversity-inclusive environmental impact assessment and strategic environmental assessment needed to promptly spot and address adverse impacts of

[17] See Organisation for Economic Co-operation and Development, Scaling up Finance Mechanisms for Biodiversity (2013) chapter 3.

[18] See TNFD (n 2) 97–98.

[19] Ibid. See also Jennifer Bell, "How the Arabian Oryx Was Brought Back from Extinction" (Arab News, January 11, 2019).

[20] TNFD (n 2) 97–98.

[21] See Intergovernmental Panel on Climate Change, "Land Degradation" in P. R. Shukla et al. (eds), *Climate Change and Land: An IPCC Special Report on Climate Change, Desertification, Land Degradation, Sustainable Land Management, Food Security, and Greenhouse Gas Fluxes in Terrestrial Ecosystems* (IPCC nd) www.ipcc.ch/srccl/cite-report/ accessed January 12, 2024. See also P. Newton et al., "What Is Regenerative Agriculture? A Review of Scholar and Practitioner Definitions Based on Processes and Outcomes" (2020) 4 *Frontiers in Sustainable Food Systems* 577723.

projects on biodiversity.[22] Biodiversity legislation can also provide project developers and planners with clarity on the key design standards and measures to comply with at the project design and approval stage. Given the urgency and need to halt biodiversity loss, clear and specific biodiversity legislation could streamline the approval of nature-focused investments and provide incentives for private sector participation, especially in priority biodiversity restoration projects.[23] Biodiversity legislation could also be the basis for clarifying the regulatory models that will underpin integrated response in a country. As Dimitropoulos and Lokhandwala note, there are three major regulatory tools to help transition toward more sustainable development policy choices: command-and-control, market-based approaches, and nudges.[24] MENA countries will need to carefully consider complex socio-economic conditions in their countries and develop a responsive legal framework that provides an effective avenue to accelerate their NBSAPs in a cost-effective manner.

18.2.3 *Frameworks to Enhance Fair and Equitable Access and Benefit-Sharing*

As discussed in Chapter 9, while there is a growing awareness regarding biodiversity and nature conservation across the MENA region, the development of clear and comprehensive regulatory frameworks on access and benefit-sharing (ABS) have been slow across the region. Challenges such as a lack of awareness regarding ABS, a lack of statistical data on ABS, and an inadequate level of compliance with international frameworks on ABS linger across the region, highlighting a continuing need for advancing awareness, fine-tuning legal frameworks, and fortifying implementation measures.

Improving regulatory regimes on biodiversity in general, and ABS in particular, requires a legal, fiscal, and institutional reform agenda aimed at maximizing the full value of ABS across the region. This would be done by developing and implementing comprehensive standards that enhance the access, utilization, and benefit-sharing of genetic sequence data. A starting point is for MENA countries to include clear provisions on ABS in biodiversity legislation to ensure the sustainable use of the region's extensive genetic resources for current and future generations. Aligning such legislation with international standards can enable MENA countries to leverage their comparative advantage as the location of important genetic resources needed globally to advance agriculture, conservation, research, and trade.

Furthermore, it is imperative for regulators and industry associations to collaboratively design model contracts and toolkits that define and conceptualize essential provisions on ABS to be included in research and development (R&D) and technology

22 CBD (n 14). See also Chapter 15.

23 See Chapter 10.

24 G. Dimitropoulos and A. Lokhandwala, "Addressing Climate Change in the MENA Region through Regulatory Design: Instrument Choice Questions" in D. Olawuyi (ed), *Climate Change Law and Policy in the Middle East and North Africa Region* (Routledge 2022) 65–68.

development contracts. Such clarity will enable countries to strike a much-needed balance between ensuring the use of genetic resources for R&D, pharmaceutical, agricultural, and other innovation efforts and preventing abuse and ensuring that benefits resulting from such use are accessed by local communities in a just and equitable manner. Establishing standard contractual provisions relating to data disclosure, reporting, and the allocation of genetic resources and their benefits could clarify expectations and enable all stakeholders to ensure the equitable distribution of the dividends derived from genetic resources. For example, the Swiss Academy of Sciences has developed a template ABS agreement that includes important terms for allocating rights, benefits, and risks with respect to genetic resources in a fair and equitable manner.[25] Similarly, the Chancery Lane Project has developed standard contractual clauses with biodiversity-focused provisions that address a wide range of themes including regenerative farming and soil preservation.[26] Integrating such clauses and provisions in investment contracts, especially land-based investments in agriculture, extractives, and the pharmaceutical and construction sectors, is essential to improving current understanding on just and equitable ABS.

Likewise, lawyers providing counsel on development projects should not only integrate ABS provisions in contracts; they should also advise clients on the importance of managing risks related to the use of genetic resources in local communities in order to avoid disputes and conflicts. Indigenous communities are increasingly insistent on ensuring that their traditional knowledge and genetic resources are used in a fair, inclusive, and just manner in line with international law standards.

18.2.4 *Institutional Coherence and Coordination*

In addition to developing a clear and comprehensive legal framework on biodiversity and nature conservation, establishing the right institutional setup for the practical coordination and cooperation of the diverse stakeholders and institutions will also be essential.[27] While rapid biodiversity loss would affect different sectors, the process of coordinating responses across different agencies and institutions that could be impacted has not been straightforward. Due to the different mandates, priorities, and financial resources between ministries, the attention and focus on mainstreaming biodiversity into their strategies, policies, and programs varies significantly. Consequently, biodiversity and nature conservation programs continue to be implemented and articulated in a largely sectoral and fragmented manner.[28] This

[25] Swiss Academy of Sciences, "Agreement on Access and Benefit Sharing for Non-commercial Research: Sector Specific Approach Containing Model Clauses" (2010) www.cbd.int/abs/doc/model-clauses/noncommresearch-abs-agreement.pdf accessed January 25, 2024.

[26] The Chancery Lane Project, "New Land and Agriculture Clauses" https://chancerylaneproject.org/news/new-land-agriculture-clauses/ accessed August 27, 2023.

[27] See Chapter 4.

[28] See Chapter 16.

makes it complex and difficult to achieve institutional coherence and coordination of efforts across ministries and agencies in the design and implementation of biodiversity policies and responses. Furthermore, the implementation of intersectoral coordination is often stifled by capacity questions. For example, mainstreaming biodiversity into the work of human rights agencies or food ministries would require expanding staff capacity or recruiting experts in biodiversity and environmental science. Similarly, biodiversity-proofing infrastructure development projects by public works authorities could require recruiting staff that can understand, analyze, and implement biodiversity-related legislation and policies. Given that several of these institutions are currently not constituted or designed to analyze and implement biodiversity and nature programs, their ability to effectively analyze and implement different biodiversity-related information and data may be limited by differences in skill sets and expertise.[29] Also, epistemic distinctions and lack of operability by different actors and institutions is fueled by the divergent training, styles, and perspectives of the actors in their respective sectors and fields.[30]

These problems raise the need for greater interoperability and standardization approaches that foster cooperation and minimize duplication among sectors and actors in the design and implementation of climate change projects and programs. As recommended by the CBD, the process of designing NBSAPs is an important starting point for engaging widely with key institutions and stakeholders, including government ministries and departments, business enterprises, civil society, academia, and other key relevant entities that have prominent roles to play in advancing biodiversity and nature conservation programs.[31] Such an early and widespread multistakeholder engagement process is required to secure the commitment of all key institutions and entities. National dialogue should be promoted and aimed at building shared and common understanding on nexus and integrated biodiversity proofing by institutional actors in various sectors. Such dialogue will examine to what extent the mandates of existing institutions are coherent, conflicting, and/or duplicative and also whether there are linked platforms in place to support knowledge and information sharing and intersectoral cooperation on biodiversity and nature conservation. For example, institutions can leverage their respective expertise, facilities, and best practices by engaging with staff and experts across sectors to assist with reviewing and assessing the implication of multisector projects on natural and cultural heritage. Inter-agency linkages and partnerships, through joint initiatives and knowledge sharing, could increase trust and enhance synergistic solutions that encourage coherent responses to identified threats. Furthermore, such dialogue should aim to address barriers to interoperability by promoting the information

29 Ibid.

30 See D. Olawuyi (ed), *Climate Change Law and Policy in the Middle East and North Africa Region* (Routledge 2022) 1–10.

31 CBD (n 4).

sharing and knowledge exchange on biodiversity and nature conservation by all relevant ministries and agencies in open and linked systems, as well as constituting cross-sectoral panels and committees that can provide an informed picture of biodiversity mainstreaming efforts across the country.

18.2.5 *Increased Biodiversity Financing and Investment*

Linked to the question of capacity and institutional coordination is the question of resources. While there is increased awareness on the need for nature-based solutions to halt rapid biodiversity loss across the region, access to financial resources, especially by small and medium eco-enterprises, to advance biodiversity entrepreneurship remains a key challenge.[32] Chapter 11 unpacks the key role of innovative financing approaches, such as Islamic financing, to meet the currently huge financing challenges that face biodiversity-related investments in the MENA region. Legal and governance gaps that stifle the application of Islamic financing, crowdfunding, and other financing tools in different MENA countries must be carefully mapped and addressed in order to support the accelerated development of nature-based solutions and biodiversity projects across the region.

Furthermore, there is a need for increased budgetary allocation and spending on biodiversity programs in the MENA region. Leveraging biodiversity-smart infrastructure across all key sectors will come at a considerable cost.[33] For example, the cost of upgrading existing infrastructure, expanding current institutions, staffing, training, field inspections, project review panels, and program design will require MENA countries to unlock investment from private and public sectors.[34] MENA countries can leverage the significant revenue from extractive industries to drive investment in biodiversity-smart development and nature conservation, especially by accelerating nature-focused innovation. With infrastructure spending in the Gulf region alone projected to reach US$200 billion over the next ten years, MENA countries have expressed the political will to invest income from extractive industries to advance knowledge-based economies.[35] For example, Qatar is developing a Biodiversity Genome Program aimed at enhancing statistical data on genetic resources in the country.[36] This is in addition to the wide range of conservation

[32] See Chapter 10.

[33] Thomas Daum, Frédéric Baudron, Regina Birner, Matin Qaim, and Ingo Grass, "Addressing Agricultural Labour Issues Is Key to Biodiversity-Smart Farming" (2023) 284 *Biological Conservation* 110165.

[34] See Chapter 11.

[35] See D. Olawuyi, "Can MENA Extractive Industries Support the Global Energy Transition? Current Opportunities and Future Directions" (2020) 8 *Extractive Industries and Society Journal* 2, 100685.

[36] QNA, "Katara Unveils Establishment of Biodiversity Genome Program" www.qna.org.qa/en/News-Area/News/2023-09/02/0019-katara-unveils-establishment-of-biodiversity-genome-program accessed January 12, 2024.

projects in the country, such as the lizard biodiversity conservation project, which aim to protect animals that are rapidly becoming endangered such as the Arabian oryx, sand gazelle, ostrich, bustard, and wild rabbit.[37] Saudi Arabia has also launched a number of biodiversity and conversation projects, such as the Red Sea Biodiversity Project, aimed at halting the loss of rare flora and fauna in the Red Sea and across the country, as well as boosting ecotourism.[38] Morocco, Bahrain, Oman, Jordan, and the United Arab Emirates have announced similar biodiversity-related projects, including mountain conservation and payment for ecosystem services (PES) initiatives.[39] If these programs and visions are effectively implemented and sustained, MENA countries could be well placed to achieve biodiversity-smart development, while also achieving socio-economic outcomes such as increased ecotourism, biodiversity entrepreneurship, biodiversity innovation and technology development, and green employment opportunities, including jobs relating to mountain and oasis conservation.[40]

There is a great opportunity for MENA countries to leverage savings from the extractive industries to finance biodiversity programs. For example, MENA countries are home to some of the largest sovereign wealth funds (SWFs) across the world.[41] Such SWF portfolios can provide opportunities for MENA countries to invest in assets and projects worldwide to halt biodiversity loss. For example, the Qatar Investment Authority, Kuwait Investment Authority, the Public Investment Fund of the Kingdom of Saudi Arabia, and the Abu Dhabi Investment Authority are founding members of the One Planet SWF Working Group, which aims to integrate climate change analysis and environmental considerations in investment decisions.[42] Through this commitment, MENA countries aim to allocate SWF investments to finance sustainability initiatives, including nature conservation programs. By integrating biodiversity considerations into the design, financing, and implementation of SWF investments, MENA extractive industries can significantly accelerate the

37 Doha News, "Qatar's Environmental Initiatives: Workshop Unveils Conservation Successes and Commitments" (January 1, 2024) https://dohanews.co/qatars-environmental-initiatives-workshop-unveils-conservation-successes-and-commitments/ accessed January 12, 2024.

38 Mahdyamam, "Saudi Unveils Two Major Biodiversity Development Projects" (June 23, 2021) https://english.madhyamam.com/middle-east/saudi-arabia/saudi-arabia-unveils-two-major-biodiversity-developments-projects-814159 accessed January 12, 2024; see also Abdulaziz S. Alatawi, "Conservation Action in Saudi Arabia: Challenges and Opportunities" (2022) 29 *Saudi Journal of Biological Sciences* 5, 3466.

39 See Chapter 2. See also Damilola Olawuyi, *Environmental Law in Arab States* (Oxford University Press 2022) 245–274; also, Reginald Victor, *Sustainable Mountain Development in the Middle East and North Africa: From Rio 1992 to Rio 2012 and beyond* (FAO, 2012) www.fao.org/3/cc7226en/cc7226en.pdf accessed January 12, 2024.

40 Victor (n 39). See also Fakhoury and AlHaddadin (n 11) 4–5.

41 Olawuyi (n 30).

42 J. Beard, "Eight Asset Managers Unite for One Planet Initiative" (*City Wire*, July 11, 2019) https://citywireselector.com/news/eight-asset-managers-unite-for-one-planet-initiative/a1249346 accessed January 25, 2024.

attainment of the Sustainable Development Goals (SDGs) relating to biodiversity and nature conservation domestically and abroad.[43]

Furthermore, investing in research and innovation can provide MENA countries with the homegrown and state-of-the-art technologies and tools needed to effectively boost nature-based innovations that support biodiversity and conservation efforts. For example, Saudi Arabia's biodiversity research project at the King Abdullah Science and Technology University aims to enhance biodiversity-related innovation and research.[44] MENA countries will need to develop similar sustained research and innovation efforts that can accelerate and support biodiversity-smart development across the region.

18.2.6 *Innovative Pedagogies to Accelerate Biodiversity Education*

Sixth, the rise of biodiversity and nature conservation law and policy across the region raises the need for innovative pedagogies to train and prepare future lawyers and administrators for evidence-based policymaking in this important field. As discussed in Chapter 17, addressing the rapid loss of biodiversity across the region will require innovative and disruptive teaching methods. The author notes that "there is a need for more specific and tailored workshops and TTT programs on biodiversity in the MENA region to further promote the integration of biodiversity awareness into environmental legal curricula in the various universities and higher education institutions within the MENA region." This will require law schools across the region to design tailored courses that provide practical and skill-based learning on biodiversity and nature conservation using a wide range of online and in-class tools. Similarly, in developing biodiversity law and policy courses, it is particularly important to adopt enquiry-based learning methods that will integrate practical skills and knowledge and prepare students to engage in real-world problem solving.[45] For example, biodiversity-related courses should clearly emphasize practical aspects, such as the development and implementation of biodiversity strategies, drafting and negotiating ABS agreements, implementing green building and efficiency standards, and data collection and analysis on biodiversity.

Furthermore, MENA environmental law academics will need to pool their intellectual resources to cooperate in research and capacity development that advance biodiversity and nature conservation. Successful partnerships are necessary to achieve all aspects of sustainable development. This is well recognized by the SDGs; Target 17.9

[43] R. Sharma, "Sovereign Wealth Funds Investment in Sustainable Development Sectors" (UN 2017) www.un.org/esa/ffd/high-level-conference-on-ffd-and-2030-agenda/wpcontent/uploads/sites/4/2017/11/Background-Paper_Sovereign-Wealth-Funds.pdf accessed January 12, 2024.

[44] Mahdyamam (n 38).

[45] See Hilary C. Bell, "Tackling the Legally Disruptive Problem of Climate Change with Disruptive Legal Education" in Damilola S. Olawuyi (ed), *Climate Change Law and Policy in the Middle East and North Africa Region* (Routledge 2021).

encourages countries to enhance international partnerships and support to implement all of the SDGs and develop north–south, south–south, and triangular cooperation.[46]

Target 15.C also encourages countries to "enhance global support for efforts to combat poaching and trafficking of protected species, including by increasing the capacity of local communities to pursue sustainable livelihood opportunities."[47] Similarly, under Target 4.7 countries are to "ensure that all learners acquire the knowledge and skills needed to promote sustainable development, including, among others, through education for sustainable development and sustainable lifestyles."[48] These goals and targets emphasize the need for environmental law academics to continue to develop collaborative research and teaching initiatives that could expand the development of innovative courses on biodiversity and nature conservation law and policy. This type of collaboration was in mind when the Association of Environmental Law Lecturers in Middle East and North African Universities (ASSELLMU) was established in 2018, to serve as a professional network for all MENA environmental law academics.[49] As stated in its Constitution, ASSELLMU aims to provide a forum for the discussion and dissemination of environmental law in the MENA region and to identify and search for MENA solutions to the region's environmental problems. It also aims to "spearhead collaborative and multi-disciplinary projects to foster increased awareness for environmental problems, among students and people in MENA region."[50]

Since its establishment, ASSELLMU has organized a number of conferences and events that aim to enhance knowledge dissemination and information exchange on biodiversity.[51] It is important for international organizations, private sector actors, and governments across the region to provide technical and financial support to sustain such important efforts. ASSELLMU, and similar cooperative networks, will need to work with education stakeholders, such as ministries of education, as well as private and public sector organizations, to identify essential executive courses for the development of professionals working on nature and biodiversity-related projects.

46 United Nations, "Transforming our World: The 2030 Agenda for Sustainable Development" (October 21, 2015) UN Doc A/RES/70/1 https://sdgs.un.org/2030agenda accessed January 12, 2024. See also Sustainable Development Solutions Network (SDSN), "17.9 Enhance International Support for Implementing Effective and Targeted Capacity Building in Developing Countries to Support National Plans to Implement All Sustainable Development Goals, Including through North–South, South–South, and Triangular Cooperation" https://indicators.report/targets/17-9/ accessed January 25, 2024.

47 Ibid.

48 Ibid.

49 See Chapter 2.

50 ASSELLMU, Constitution of the Association of Environmental Law Lecturers in Middle East and North Africa Universities (Adopted in Settat, Morocco in 2019).

51 Salam Al-Zahran, "Conference on: Law on Biodiversity, Nature Conservation, and Cultural Heritage Protection in the Middle East and North African Region" www.kas.de/en/web/rspno/veranstaltungsberichte/detail/-/content/conference-on-law-on-biodiversity-nature-conservation-and-cultural-heritage-protection-in-the-middle accessed January 12, 2024.

Educators can then develop a blend of practical and theoretical courses to provide lifelong learning opportunities for stakeholders tasked with designing and implementing biodiversity and nature conservation programs.

18.2.7 *Need for Biodiversity-Focused Due Diligence*

The rise of biodiversity and nature conservation law and policy in the MENA region increases the need for business enterprises and private actors to anticipate and address biodiversity-related legal risks in their investments and projects. Biodiversity-focused due diligence is the process through which enterprises and public actors investigate the direct and indirect the impacts of their investments and projects on biodiversity in order to avoid legal risks.[52] Legal risks in this context refer to the risk of financial, reputational, or investment loss, legal liability, or dispute settlement costs to a company or institution that may arise from the failure by a business enterprise to mitigate the direct and indirect impacts of biodiversity loss.[53] Direct or indirect contributions to biodiversity loss can result in significant financial, reputational, and disclosure risks for a business enterprise or entity, especially an entity that fails to comply with emerging laws and policies in this area.[54] For example, failure to comply with disclosure requirements relating to the impacts of a business or investment on biodiversity may result in fines and sanctions.[55] On the other hand, the implementation of development projects that adversely impact landscapes, forests, and ecosystems may also trigger lawsuits from impacted communities. For example, investing in NBS and emissions reduction schemes, such as clean development and Reducing Emissions from Deforestation and Forest Degradation projects may result in adverse impacts on human rights, especially through displacements of local communities from their lands and forests, the exclusion of women and youth from decision-making processes, a lack of transparency and accountability, and the inadequacy of judicial remedies for victims.[56] There is a marked increase in the number of cases in different parts of the world that seek to establish the legal and human rights liability of business enterprises for failing to address biodiversity loss.[57]

[52] See Jenni Ramos and Zaneta Sedilekova, "Biodiversity Risk: Legal Implications for Companies and Their Directors" https://commonwealthclimatelaw.org/wp-content/uploads/2022/12/CCLI_Biodiversity_risk_paper_2022.pdf accessed January 12, 2024.

[53] Ibid. See also D. Olawuyi, "Climate Justice and Corporate Responsibility: Taking Human Rights Seriously in Climate Actions and Projects" (2016) 34 *Journal of Energy and Natural Resources Law* 27.

[54] Ramos and Sedilekova (n 50). See also World Economic Forum, "Nature Risk Rising: Why the Crisis Engulfing Nature Matters for Business and the Economy" (January 2020).

[55] See TNFD (n 18).

[56] Damilola Olawuyi, *The Human Rights-Based Approach to Carbon Finance* (Cambridge University Press 2018) 1–25.

[57] See Chapter 1. See for example, *Friends of Nature, Shan Shui Conservation Centre, and Wild China Film v China Hydropower Engineering Consulting Group in China* (2020), in which the Chinese Kunming Intermediate People's Court ordered the suspension of work on the construction of hydropower on the Jiasa River to protect this last major habitat of the endangered green peafowl, which

As more MENA countries adopt biodiversity and nature conservation legislation and policies, similar arguments may be made before the courts. Over time, failure to effectively anticipate and manage biodiversity-related risks could carry significant financial, legal, and reputational risks for business enterprises operating in the MENA region. Such risks may manifest in the form of the disruption, suspension, or closure of projects by supervisory bodies, hefty regulatory fines, and director and shareholder liability, and may impact a company's profitability or ability to maintain a license to operate.[58] Businesses can avoid the increasing backlash associated with biodiversity risks by integrating biodiversity considerations into investment analysis and management processes. Business enterprises in the MENA region, especially those in the extractive and construction sectors, can enhance their capacity to effectively anticipate and manage biodiversity-related risks by participating and engaging with the wide range of voluntary initiatives that aim to support companies to "integrate biodiversity conservation into their internal business practices and operations."[59]

There is also a need to implement comprehensive biodiversity-focused environmental impact assessments that spot and address biodiversity risks prior to commencing development and investment activities.[60] Furthermore, human rights impact assessments and due diligence can enhance the abilities of planners to identify and address the potential adverse impacts of biodiversity programs on human rights, especially the right to a clean, healthy, and sustainable environment, land rights, gender injustice, and inadequate public participation in the implementation of such programs.[61] For example, as discussed in Chapter 4, the loss of forests and other protected areas can trigger several violations of indigenous rights in communities that depend on such resources for their survival, culture, and religion. There is therefore a strong business case, in terms of cost, reputation, and effectiveness, for business enterprises and other actors to integrate biodiversity-focused human rights due diligence in their investment planning and business decision-making, even if the domestic law is silent on such requirements. Adopting sound internal screening processes, as part of corporate due diligence and investment risk management

is the only native peafowl in China. Li Yunqi, "Green Peafowl's Last Habitat vs. 3.7-Billion-Yuan Dam" https://news.cgtn.com/news/2020-03-21/Green-peafowl-s-last-habitat-vs-3-7-billion-yuan-dam-P2bT7sSi5i/index.html accessed January12, 2024.

58 See Guillaume Futhazar et al., *Biodiversity Litigation* (Oxford University Press 2020) 8–10.

59 A good example is the Energy and Biodiversity Initiative which was established to "to develop and promote practices for integrating biodiversity conservation into upstream oil and gas development." IUCN, The Energy and Biodiversity Initiative https://portals.iucn.org/library/efiles/documents/2003-037.pdf accessed January 12, 2024.

60 See Chapter 16.

61 See United Nations Working Group on Business and Human Rights (UN WGBHR), "Corporate Human Rights Due Diligence: Emerging Practices, Challenges and Ways Forward" report to the UN General Assembly, October 2018 (A/73/163). See also UN General Assembly, Resolution A/RES/76/300, "The Human Right to a Clean, Healthy, and Sustainable Environment" (July 28, 2022).

frameworks, could help enterprises to anticipate, mitigate, and address the implications of their investments and projects on biodiversity and ecosystems.

As for the role of lawyers representing companies and investors in transactions and projects, it is important to clarify and emphasize the need for biodiversity and human rights due diligence at early stages of such investments. International bodies and courts insist that business enterprises have a responsibility to address potential and actual adverse human rights impacts across the entire value chain of their operations.[62] As a result, companies, investors, lenders, and insurance underwriters must appropriately investigate, assess, and price biodiversity-related risks that may arise in the transactional context.

As the Taskforce on Nature-Related Financial Disclosures notes, "nature-related risks and opportunities arise from an organisation's dependencies and impacts on nature."[63] Such biodiversity risks may be physical, transition, and disclosures related. Physical risks may flow from activities or investments that adversely impact biodiversity or from the potential loss of earnings resulting from the rapid loss of biodiversity. Physical risks are especially significant for business enterprises that rely on genetic resources from rare and extinction-threatened plants and animals for their activities, such as medicines, pharmaceuticals, and food production.[64] The rapid extinction of such genetic resources may disrupt production activities or may significantly raise transaction costs. On the other hand, transition risks may arise from the increased adoption of biodiversity and nature conservation policies across the MENA region, which may reduce the value or worth of assets or increase compliance costs. For example, ongoing global efforts to halt biodiversity loss may result in new standards that may fundamentally change business structures, limit the availability of funding for land-based investments and projects, raise the cost of debts, capital, and long-dated securities, or ultimately result in stranded assets.[65] These transition risks will need to be carefully considered by lawyers when giving advice, especially given the rapid evolution of biodiversity strategies and policies in the MENA region. Third, as countries adopt biodiversity and nature conservation legislation, business enterprises will have increased obligations to report on biodiversity and nature conservation efforts, as well as the financial impacts of biodiversity-related risks and opportunities on the business and its shareholders.

Legal risks relating to nondisclosure or greenwashing, which may result from misleading or inaccurate biodiversity disclosures, will need to be carefully considered by lawyers when providing advice. Furthermore, the likely impact of biodiversity-related risks and opportunities on the current and future financial position of a

62 UN WGBHR (n61).

63 Taskforce on Nature-related Financial Disclosures (n 18) 33–35.

64 Jenni Ramos and Zaneta Sedilekova (n 50). See also Stefano Giglio, Theresa Kuchler, Johannes Stroebel, and Xuran Zeng, "Biodiversity Risk" (April 2023) www.nber.org/papers/w31137 accessed January 12, 2024.

65 Giglio et al, ibid.

company as reflected in its income statement, cash flow statement, and balance sheet could play significant roles when negotiating asset values.[66] These and other obligations that may arise from emerging biodiversity law and policy must be carefully monitored and considered by lawyers as part of corporate due diligence and contract negotiation processes to prevent legal risks.

18.3 CONCLUSION

The rich and extensive natural capital of the MENA region play pivotal roles in supporting economic, social, and environmental development in key sectors. However, like many other world regions, the MENA region faces a rapid biodiversity loss emergency that requires dynamic legal innovation and response. Furthermore, there is growing evidence that efforts to halt biodiversity loss through nature-based solutions may result in land grabs, the inequitable allocation of benefits arising from genetic resources, displacements, and the inadequate participation of women and youth in decision-making processes. There is therefore an urgent need for nexus and integrated implementation of biodiversity and nature conservation programs to ensure coherence and address inconsistencies.

This book has developed a profile of the multifarious regulatory and institutional gaps that limit the coherent development and application of biodiversity law and policy at national levels. While the manifestations of these challenges may be escalating in some countries, there is a consistent and urgent need for all MENA countries to effectively mainstream biodiversity considerations into all aspects of development planning and decision-making. A starting point will be to develop clear and comprehensive legislation on biodiversity that clarifies the regulatory models and the roles of different agencies and institutions in the implementation of biodiversity and nature conservation programs. There is also a need to address legal and institutional gaps to biodiversity financing and nature-focused entrepreneurship. A supportive governance framework is required to stimulate private sector investment and participation in biodiversity and conservation programs.

Biodiversity mainstreaming should not be seen as a task for governments alone. Business enterprises, investors, lenders, insurance companies, and their lawyers alike all have prominent roles to play in integrating biodiversity considerations into business decision-making processes and planning. As biodiversity and nature conservation legislation and rules emerge, corporate actors can reduce the legal liabilities and risks arising from the direct and indirect impacts of their activities on lands, ecosystems, and cultural heritage by integrating biodiversity and nature considerations into business decision-making processes and planning.

The success, or otherwise, of integrating biodiversity considerations into planning and investment decisions will also depend on available capacity. There is an

[66] Ibid. See TNFD (n 2) 75–80.

urgent need to bridge capacity gaps in the region through increased investment on biodiversity research and education. Higher education institutions have crucial roles to play in developing innovative programs to train and equip stakeholders with the advanced skills needed to integrate biodiversity considerations into their entire operations and value chains. National authorities and industry stakeholders should provide increased support for multistakeholder capacity development programs, such as those spearheaded by UNEP and ASSELLMU, to accelerate the effective implementation of the wide range of international environmental law instruments on nature conservation and biodiversity across the region.

Index

For EU product safety concerns, contact us at Calle de José Abascal, 56–1°,
28003 Madrid, Spain or eugpsr@cambridge.org.

www.ingramcontent.com/pod-product-compliance
Ingram Content Group UK Ltd.
Pitfield, Milton Keynes, MK11 3LW, UK
UKHW050955290926
15470UKWH00006B/1826
* 9 7 8 1 0 0 9 5 1 9 6 7 0 *